D1268284

The Gun Digest® Book of

# Trap & Skeet Shooting

## 5th Edition

**Rick Sapp**

©2009 Krause Publications, Inc., a subsidiary of F+W Media, Inc.

Published by

**Gun Digest® Books**
*An imprint of F+W Media, Inc.*
700 East State Street • Iola, WI 54990-0001
715-445-2214 • 888-457-2873
*www.gundigestbooks.com*

Our toll-free number to place an order or obtain
a free catalog is (800) 258-0929.

All rights reserved. No portion of this publication may be reproduced or transmitted in any form or by any means, electronic or mechanical, including photocopy, recording, or any information storage and retrieval system, without permission in writing from the publisher, except by a reviewer who may quote brief passages in a critical article or review to be printed in a magazine or newspaper, or electronically transmitted on radio, television, or the Internet.

Library of Congress Control Number: 2009923229

ISBN 13-digit: 978-1-44020-388-6
ISBN 10-digit: 1-44020-388-1

Designed by Kara Grundman
Edited by Corrina Peterson

Printed in the United States of America

# ABOUT THE AUTHOR

Rick Sapp was born in Indiana, but grew up in Florida. He attended a military academy before dropping out and enlisting in the army. Eventually completing a degree or two in anthropology, he collapsed into bad company with characters employed by the U.S. Fish & Wildlife Service. They patiently taught him something of hunting, fishing and shooting. Rick has worked for newspapers and magazines; opened and closed his own businesses; and all the while he read, wrote and dreamed. The opportunity to write about the outdoors—the skills and products, the community and, sometimes, the drama—is the culmination of those dreams.

Author Rick Sapp during a light day of shooting near the Rhino Gun Case factory in Williston, Florida.

# TABLE OF CONTENTS

# SAVING THE FAMILY JEWELS

Pulling the trigger of a shotgun is a thrill and perhaps it is a privilege, as well. In the field, something replenishable and edible may die, be harvested – a pheasant, a grouse – while at the range, a clay target may be pulverized.

Shooting is exciting, and shooting a shotgun ought to be a lifetime hobby with a lifetime of exposure to learning opportunities – new shotgun games, new gear, new aspects of the hobby such as loading one's own ammo – friends who share the passion, and opportunities to serve and to teach.

So it is altogether proper to begin a book about something as exciting as blowing things up – in this case, using gunpowder to deadly effect to kill clay pigeons – with a chapter about saving the family jewels…the real jewels, that is, one's vision and hearing.

This is not a chapter about "safety," the most boring pages in any book, the most slept-through session of any hunter education class. Just put me to sleep now.

This is a chapter about looking at pretty girls in bikinis on the beach. This is a chapter about hearing your boyfriend whisper something sweet and exciting in your ear. This is a chapter about hearing the baby monitor in the middle of the night or noticing the child staggering toward the campfire in time to react. This is a chapter about preserving your family jewels, your eyesight and hearing, and it must be the beginning of any shooting odyssey because, over the course of a lifetime, your eyes and ears will offer you the possibility of pleasures that meet or exceed your wildest dreams.

A final reason to begin a trap, skeet and sporting clays book with hearing and vision protection is that by taking care of these health issues – and they are health issues for, barring something catastrophic like a burst eardrum or an exploding barrel, hearing loss especially is subtle, progressive and irreversible – you will become a better shooter.

Stand behind any shooting line and watch people as they pull the trigger, or watch slow motion video. As the shell fires, everyone flinches. Everyone from first time shooters to AAA Trap Masters flinches. Flinching destroys follow-through and interrupts concentration, especially shooting doubles. In its extreme form, flinching can lead to an inability to pull the trigger; a

condition sometimes referred to as target panic.

The difference between the shooter who reacts to a shot so much that it is difficult to get off a follow-up string and the shooter who understands, and accepts, blast and recoil is, of course, experience. Study those folks at the shooting line carefully, though, and you will see that step one in controlling a flinch, in learning proper shooting form, is to protect one's ears and eyes. Thus, our first topic….

## Ears First

### *Measuring Sound*

Humans are counters. We teach numbers to infants and, when we are feeling particularly smart, we teach our animals as well: Esmeralda, the gypsy girl in Victor Hugo's 1831 Hunchback of Notre Dame fascinates fellow Parisians when her goat taps out the month and hour of the day. Today, dogs and parrots star on Animal Planet's popular Pet Star television show responding to trainers' voice commands.

Remarkably, a very inexpensive set of ear plugs provide a high level of protection from the blast of a shotgun. Combine these with a set of ear muffs with noise-interruption circuitry and one has the best hearing protection possible while shooting.

Thus, in dealing with the world, we attempt to quantify what we see and hear. For hearing, for understanding the power or intensity of waves of sound entering our ears, we commonly say something is loud or soft; or, as if it made us more precise, we use a special kind of counting unit called a decibel (dB).

The threshold of hearing is conveniently set at 0 dB and we measure upward from that point:

- 40-60 dB: the shooting instructor (one meter away)
- 80 dB: a spouse shouting to "Shut up!" (two meters away)
- 100 dB: a power lawnmower (one meter away)
- 134 dB: the "threshold of pain"
- 165 dB: a shotgun blast
- 180 dB: a rocket launch

And yet, the decibel measures only a moment in time, and this simple measure of a sound does not tell the entire story. A decibel is a "logarithmic expression" to the base 10, meaning that 100, for instance, is not twice as intense as 50, it's five times as intense.

A single crack of a .22 is not so disturbing, even at 140 dB, but prolonged exposure is entirely different. Riding a motorcycle across the country is an adventure, but a week of unrelenting exposure to 90 dB is over the top. The men who guide your airliner into its terminal docking station wear hearing protection not because the whine of a single jet engine, even an engine in subdued taxi mode, reaches the threshold of pain, but because they bring dozens of airliners to the terminal each day.

The concept of sustained noise became apparent when my 12-year old daughter covered her ears and ran in misery from the bench behind the skeet line. I told her it would be loud and so the first shot, even at a distance of a dozen yards, got her attention. The continual bang of the squad's 12-gauges, however, was overwhelming. As a member of that squad, I had kept the good set of ear muffs and given her the cheap set of disposable, polyurethane foam plugs. Perhaps that was correct, but it was not thoughtful.

### Can You Hear Me Now?

Of course, wearing the better hearing protection on the shooting line was the right thing to do. No one in that squad was getting any younger and none wanted to end up like their dads, leaning forward and turning their "good ear" toward expectant grandchildren standing beside their chair. The men who continually ask you to repeat what you just said; who keep the television's sound volume too loud and fiddle endlessly with the volume control of their hearing aids. These dads came out of World War II or Korea disdaining all things that might make them seem weak and thus have spent

The Pro-Ears Gold Series ear muffs feature dynamic level sound compression with a built in microprocessor so no sound is "clipped." Military Grade circuit boards feature gold connectors and the muffs include auto shut off, low battery indicator and an LED Alert Light. The Gold Series have a noise reduction rating (NRR) of 26.

years shooting and hunting without hearing protection. Now they, and we, are paying the price.

Some gradual hearing loss is natural as one grows older. The delicate bones and membranes of the inner ear lose flexibility, the ability to respond to low dB noises. Heredity is involved, but so is chronic exposure to loud noise and the process is irreversible.

Technically, hearing occurs when sound waves reach the structures inside your ear. There, wave vibrations cause the eardrum to vibrate. Vibrations are amplified by the tiny bones of the middle ear, the hammer, anvil and stirrup; and are then converted into nerve signals that your brain recognizes as sound.

Most hearing loss results from damage to a fluid-filled part of the inner ear called the cochlea. Inside the cochlea, tiny hairs which translate sound vibrations into electrical signals may break or become bent; as a result, their nerve cells degenerate. With nerve cells damaged or missing, electrical signals are not efficiently transmitted to the brain and hearing loss occurs.

### On Looking Good

In the 1982 movie "48 Hours," actor Nick Nolte, playing a hard-nosed detective, tells his wise-cracking criminal sidekick Eddie Murphy, "Class isn't something ya buy. Look at you – you got a $500 suit on, and you're still a low-life."

Eddie Murphy responds, "Yeah, but I look good."

Today we know that looking good is not good enough.

The rules of the ATA, the Amateur Trapshooting Association, for example, are explicit: IV-I-16 – "All persons including competitors, referee/scorers and trap personnel must wear appropriate eye and hearing protection while on the trap field. Failure to comply may result in disqualification."

Shooting without wearing hearing protection is no longer allowed on any supervised range, public or private. Indeed, show up with no protection and you may be (should be) barred from approaching the shooting line. The range may require that you purchase protection; it may even have a bucket of free, disposable plugs for your use.

The definition of "looking good" on a shooting range is now redefined. Instead of the man (or woman) who can stand the pain and still bust clay, it is the shooter with the best possible ear and eye protection.

### More Counting – This Time For Less

Two basic types of hearing protection units are offered commercially: ear plugs, which insert in the ear canal, and ear muffs, which cover the ear. Otherwise, hearing protection may be divided into passive and active. Passive devices protect simply by their presence; active ones employ some electronic supplement.

A 6.8-ounce behind-the-head electronic ear muff may be the answer for those who don't especially enjoy ear muffs ... because muffs are hot or because a fast shotgun mount can sometimes bang the cup. With a NRR 19 rating, this set of Pro-Ears uses four N-size 1.5-volt batteries.

Regardless of which type you prefer to block shooting's extreme dB level, it is important to understand that protective devices are rated with a separate counting system – NRR or noise reduction rating. NRR is supposed to indicate the amount of sound or number of decibels a device will attenuate. An NRR of 25, for example, was supposed to cut perceived noise say from 80 dB to a more manageable 55 dB. NRR was intended to act as a straightforward guide to choose hearing protection. The numbers displayed prominently on packaging, however, often derived from laboratory testing, have not been accurate in real-world situations.

A new NRR system, which will show a range of noise reduction, will soon be in place. The high end of the range will be for those who are fitted perfectly and use the plug or muff conscientiously; the lower end is for those who are more casual about hearing protection. The current ratings will probably fall somewhere in the middle.

In theory, you want a high NRR, #40 being better than #20, but in the real world, protecting your hearing is more complicated. First, everyone's ears, like their fingerprints, are a bit different. Second, you probably should not kill all sound; you want to know when your squad fires and you must hear range commands. You just don't want the blast to deafen you.

The answer to the NRR puzzle is to think of the numbers as a guide and expect that, unless your hearing protection is professionally fitted and used carefully, you will actually receive about two-thirds of the published NRR. (Testing actually shows that range to vary between 5 and 95 percent!)

The cheapest possible product for ear protection is a set of pvc foam earplugs. These are often given away at shooting ranges. The benefit is that they are cheap and effective. Degil (www.degilsafety.com) says its plugs have an NRR rating of 29, the same as the slightly more expensive polyurethane foam plugs.

The benefit of foam plugs is that, while they are disposable, they can also be used for years. They are cheap and effective. They are also easy to crush between the fingertips, insert in anyone's ear and then expand to fit the basic contours of the ear canal.

Degil and others also offer sets of plugs that are not foam and crushable. Often they are a flexible, but resilient plastic and keep their general shape when inserted in the ear. They work in the same manner as foam plugs, using layers or flaps of plastic like baffles to cushion and attenuate sound.

These plugs can be washed with soap and water and, before sharing them, it would be a good idea to do so, allowing them to dry completely before inserting again.

If there is a downside to ear plugs, it is that they are too easy to use. Children, especially, can forget to re-

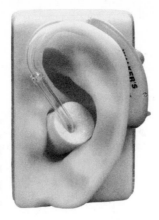

For those who do not care for muffs and find passive systems too thin on noise reduction, a Digital Game Ear from Walker's is a practical alternative.

move them or can push them deep into the ear.

Degil also has a line of passive ear muffs. Here, one size does not fit all preferences or uses, and the NRR ratings vary between 19 and 28. There are styles to wear over caps; styles that hook behind the head for use with hard hats or hook onto a hat bracket; and others fold into a small package. Most styles are adjustable.

Muffs have positive and negative features. Many shooters find earplugs a constant source of irritation. On any crowded range, one observes shooters fiddling with the plugs, constantly adjusting them because they tickle the hairs in the ear or they just don't "feel right." Muffs are easy to pull on and off. No ear wax adheres to them. They are strictly external.

On the other hand, muffs have a hard outer shell. On a hot day, they cause you to sweat uncomfortably. They also slip easily to the side, reducing their effectiveness. For men and women who wear their hair long, muffs present a simple physical problem. And on occasion, you will throw your gun to your shoulder and the hard shell of the muff hits the stock; the surprise can be disconcerting.

Finally, every club or range has one joker who believes it is funny to rap on the outer shell with his fingertip. This, of course, results in a small, but loud and very uncomfortable explosion of sound inside the wearer's ear and a resultant interest in planting the barrel of one's 12-gauge forcefully aside the offender's head.

So what is best, muffs or plugs? Many experienced shooters believe that using the two in combination – inserting earplugs and topping them with a set of muffs – gives the ear the best possible passive protection and increases the effective NRR by 10-15, which is important when in an environment where dBs are routinely above 100.

Twenty or so years ago, however, active hearing protection devices began making their way to shooting ranges. Digital devices are now available to wear in, be-

hind and over the ear. The choice of style is entirely individual because, equipped with noise interruption or compression circuitry, the operation is identical. One pays much more for a custom fit in-the-ear device because they are molded exactly to your ear's configuration, after a local audiologist sends a manufacturer such as SportEAR the molds of your middle ears. In- or around-the-ear styles operate with ¼-v batteries.

Bob Walker's original Game Ear (NRR 29 dB, www.walkersgameear.com) was developed for hunting. It weighs less than ¼-ounce and increases hearing, the company says, up to five times by amplifying high frequency sound with 46 dB of battery power. Even the original design from about 1989 had a safety compression circuit to protect the user from loud sounds, including muzzle blast.

Digital hearing protectors now come with multiple microphones, which are of course very small, and are adjustable for both sound level and frequency. This allows you to talk in a normal tone and to hear range commands while the noise interruption circuitry snaps ON when a gun goes off; you will hear the shot, but the sound will be greatly diminished and that level also is adjustable. The Walker Game Ear IV, for example, has a NRR of 30, and several models are accessorized for cellular telephone and even radio reception.

With a diversity of product styles and prices available now, it is easy – indeed, it is stylish – to protect your hearing. It would be a shame if you did not take this seriously and make the best hearing protection you can afford a part of your shooting wardrobe.

## Now, the Eyes

### Kids Games

As kids, we played mind games. "What's the worst way to die?" we asked one another, or, "If you had to be blind or deaf or couldn't talk, what would you choose?" Perhaps they were only games or perhaps the questioning prepared us for everything we would experience in life. Still, practically everyone believed that blindness would be the worst affliction.

On February 11, 2006, Vice President Dick Cheney shot fellow quail hunter Harry Whittington. Although Whittington was more than 30 yards from and to the rear of Cheney, the shot caught him in the face, neck and chest. Fortunately Cheney was using a 28-gauge gun and Whittington recovered without losing his eyesight, although a pellet lodged near his heart caused a heart attack. Had the vice president been firing a 12-gauge, Whittington might have died and would certainly have been blinded.

So it may surprise you that grown-up games still address questions of health and mortality, though not quite as bluntly. The National Skeet Shooting Associa-

Looking into the sun in a clear sky when you call for a bird is tough enough, but add cold and the glare of a snowy landscape and your visual acuity can be seriously degraded. Manufacturers of shooting glasses offer impact-resistant polycarbonate lenses in a variety of tints to help you acquire a bird. Find the one that is best for your shooting. This Canadian 5-stand shooter has chosen a rose tint.

tion (NSSA) requires "eye protection" for shooters, referees and trap personnel; the National Sporting Clays Association (NSCA) includes spectators. It is the international clay shooting body, FITASC, the Federation Internationale de Tir aux Armes Sportives de Chasse, however, that specifically requires "safety glasses."

But what are safety glasses? What is adequate? And could "adequate" eyewear actually help one become a better shooter? After all, we have argued that adequate ear protection can boost clay scores. Are prescription glasses sufficient? And, though it may offend purists, can one look cool while wearing safety glasses?

## What is "adequate?"

Are "regular eyeglasses" adequate for shooting? Yes and no.

Glasses are not glass. They are usually polycarbonate, a type of plastic. Lightweight. Easily formed and cut for bi- or even trifocals. Exceptionally clear. More resistant to breakage and scratching than glass, polycarbonate can be coated to repel water and dust, enhance contrast, reduce glare and even change shade as light conditions change. Frankly, modern eyeglasses are better than glass.

The problem is that glasses only cover the eye sockets

from direct impact and, because most people put them on and take them off frequently during the day, the frames fit loosely on the face. They can slide down the nose in hot weather, leaving the eyes unprotected. In addition, the polycarbonate lens may stop a ricocheting fragment of clay, but, depending upon the prescription, its thickness may vary and its ability to stop a direct, frontal impact varies.

Your personal eyeglasses may provide a minimal amount of protection, but there are national standards for safety glasses. The American National Standards Institute (ANSI), which supervises the writing of standards and hence, defining "adequate" for all things that may result in injuries (and thus, lawsuits), has a standard for safety glasses.

Its old standard (ANSI Z87.1-1989) seemed a bit comical to those of us outside the legal emporiums. Lenses must be capable of resisting the impact of a one-inch steel ball – or a 44-gram needle if the lenses were plastic – dropped from a height of 50 inches. Lenses needed to withstand the impact of a ¼-inch steel ball traveling 150 fps (feet per second). "The lens," ANSI said, "may neither fracture nor be penetrated." The newest ANSI standard (Z87.1-2003) further discriminates between basic lenses and high impact lenses.

### Deep, Wide And Stylish

To protect the eyes fully, wider and deeper lenses than are normal in daily-wear glasses are immensely superior. There is a boundary though between comfortable, fully protective eyewear and ballistic goggles. While goggles may be the ideal solution, providing practically 100-percent protection and accommodating military specifications for use in hostile environments, their complete enclosure of the eye socket quickly makes them uncomfortable on a summer day or when the wearer is physically active. Many have tiny holes that are supposed to allow them to breathe and thus, with the lens coating, resist fogging, but they often clog with debris and the back strap wrapping tightly around the ears and behind one's head may actually become painful.

If one does not need corrective lenses, the very best solution for shooting eyewear is a pair of glasses from a company that specializes in ballistic eye protection, such as WileyX (www.wileyx.com). Their Talon glasses have deep, wrap-around lenses that meet ANSI high velocity impact standards. Worn comfortably across the bridge of the nose, there is a very small angle through which a pellet or clay particle could damage your eye. Multiple lens colors are available for these polarized eye protectors.

What do colors or coating have to do with eye protection?

Whether a shooter wears ballistic glasses with red or blue tint may not matter for safety, but lens coatings are part of the package, so here is a brief review of popular lens coatings one sees on a shooting range (courtesy of the WileyX lens crafters):

- Light-Adjusting Grey: Darkens or lightens as brightness dictates.
- Smoke: Maximum glare reduction without color distortion.
- Clear: Maximum light transmission for hazy or overcast, dusk/dawn conditions.
- Light Rust: Filters blue, the chief component of glare and haze. Enhances contrast.
- Smoke Green: Maximum glare reduction without distorting color. Great for general use.
- Pale Yellow: The best light enhancing tint. Filters blue; preferred in low light.
- Pale Rose: Improves details, enhances depth perception in low or artificial light.
- Bronze Brown: Increases contrast and enhances ground contours.
- Copper: Great for curbing glare and enhancing color contrast.
- Silver: Z-Oxide mirror over smoke lens. Reduces glare. Excellent on bright days.
- Blue Mirror: Multi-coat, over smoke lenses. Absorb reflections across mirror surface, diminish glare. Ideal in bright conditions.
- Emerald/Amber: An amber tinted lens under a green multi-coat mirror surface. Amplifies color contrast for high visual definition.

In an era of glaring computer screens and too much television, the question of prescription lenses for correctible vision is important. Unless one wears contact lenses topped by glasses with non-correcting ballistic lenses – and many shooters do – it will be worthwhile to make an investment in prescription safety glasses from a company such as WileyX. Prescriptions lenses will cause the glasses to cost twice as much as non-correcting lenses but, if you are careful not to lose or damage them, the glasses will last for many years. As an investment in your health and great shooting, the result will be priceless.

# ACKNOWLEDGEMENTS

It is customary to thank those who have been helpful in developing a volume such as this one. And so we do. The list is quite long. And so I thank you sincerely. It truly would not be possible to turn out a craft volume like this without the very positive support of members of the firearms trade at all levels and turns, from local gun clubs to individual shooters to presidents of multinational corporations, what investigators might call the "products and information chain."

We live in a time when the firearms industry is presented with unexpected challenges and opportunities. The future is certainly foreboding, but the immediate present is unaccountably bright.

Those whose thoughts occupy a certain hemisphere of the brain expect the day is nigh when the world will descend into chaos and anarchy, savagery. Some people actually claim that guns are a root cause of this unaccountable bloodshed, but they are at best historically challenged and at worst political opportunists. Still, we thank this entertaining minority for stimulating our imagination and remind them that, when simple barbarity seized Rwanda in a paroxysm of genocide in 1994, the principal killing instrument was a cheap machete. A few well-placed firearms in the hands of men of courage and imagination could have saved hundreds of thousands of lives.

There are also those who fail to understand that this moment's spectacular sales of firearms and ammunition will not last very long. From a business perspective, our political and social climates are fickle and often subject to unforeseeable whims and currents. The old US president, whom we generally expected to be a friend, actually did little to stimulate retail activity while the new president, about whom we have serious reservations, has, if not "made us rich," certainly swept the shelves clear of old inventory.

Of course, I want to recognize the many that make this book possible. Trap, skeet, sporting clays and the other, less visible shotgun games would not be possible without companies like Brownell's and Weatherby; without retailers like Jay's Sporting Goods or Pickett Weaponry; without ranges and clubs such as Gator Skeet & Trap and the Dallas Gun Club.

This book would most certainly not be possible without you the shooter, however. I have witnessed men having bad days on a range where they would normally bust 100 straight—and not become frustrated, not throw their shotgun like a seven-iron or tennis racket. Women who repeatedly out-shot their husbands—and didn't rub it in. Range officials who dealt with angry shooters with quiet patience. Shooting champions and folks who didn't care about scoring but who love to pull the trigger, and occasionally surprise themselves and astonish their squads.

I would also like to thank a nationally recognized science fiction writer who lives nearby in Florida. Introduced as a fellow writer not long ago, he inquired about my themes and writing passions. When I mentioned this book among others, he sneered, "Oh, a craft writer." The comment stung for a moment. That this well-known individual would scoff at our interests—perhaps they don't shoot the running rabbit on Jupiter—bruised my sense of courtesy until I realized that it was actually a compliment. A craft writer. Of course. And in very good company, too.

*Rick Sapp*

# THE ART OF WINGSHOOTING

Reducing an aerial target to a puff of dust, or a ball of feathers, has been called a combination of art and science. That is about as succinct a definition of wingshooting as I have ever heard. It applies regardless of whether the target is made of pitch and resin, or feathers and bone.

The classic aspects of wingshooting will be addressed in later chapters. As we go along, we will discuss the "tools of the trade:" the newest shotguns, effective loads, proper barrel and stock work, chokes, patterns and the other invaluable aids that play such a large role in wingshooting success.

For now however, the artistic side of wingshooting is worthy of consideration on its own. If you have ever watched a master wingshooter break aerial targets with a consistent combination of fluid grace and blazing speed, I think you will agree that it is true artistry. Nevertheless, it may surprise you to learn that no two shooters execute that artistry in precisely the same way. The reason is that it is extremely rare to be able to shoot directly at a moving target with a stationary gun and hit it. Simply put, one must deliver the shot charge to the place where the target will be when the shot charge arrives. That requires the gun to be moving at the moment the shot is triggered, and most often it will be pointed somewhere other than directly at the target!

In that respect, connecting with an aerial target is no different from an NFL quarterback tossing a deep pass to a sprinting receiver going deep. The quarterback certainly cannot throw the ball directly at the target because it would land far behind. Instead, he must place it at a point where the receiver and the ball expect to meet. The Brett Favres of the world have learned to accomplish that feat without (usually) requiring that their receiver break stride. The journeymen of the game also get the job done, although not quite as impressively and perhaps not in the same manner. The same is true of wingshooting.

## The Basics of Lead

A number of shooting techniques result in the shot charge and target arriving at the same place at the same time. Each requires the shooter to comprehend a slightly different relationship between his muzzle and the target. Nevertheless, even shooters using the same

Author Rick Sapp began his wingshooting career with a Remington 1100 semi-auto and a friend's Springer spaniel named Katy in the pheasant fields of Minnesota and South Dakota. "With a good dog, even a blind man will hit a bird every now and then," Rick says. *(Photo courtesy Don Friberg)*

technique occasionally have different explanations for the relationship they see at the instant they trigger the shot.

Market hunter Fred Kimble is reported to have shot thousands of ducks during the 1800s, but it is said that he could not consistently explain lead—the amount of forward allowance that will put a shot charge effectively on the target—on a flying bird. Still, Kimble is considered by some shotgun historians to have been one of the greatest shots of all time. Kimble said that the most common lead he used on ducks crossing at 40 yards was one bird length. At 60 yards, his lead increased to two bird lengths. That is not much lead! The average mallard measures about 24 inches in length. If the average speed of a flying mallard is about 35 miles per hour and the target range is 40 yards, the lead required would be about 6 ½ feet if the shot charge velocity is 1235 feet per second. Yet, curiously enough, Kimble saw no more than 24 inches of lead.

According to my computer, Kimble could not have killed any ducks. Yet, he is considered to have been one of the finest wingshots who ever lived. How did he do it? This is the point where the individual artistry and ability of a wingshooter surfaces.

There are several shooting techniques useful to put you on a bird. Computer figures can be given for the "sustained lead" method, sometimes called the "maintained lead" by our British friends. As we will see later, this is the only shooting system in which precise leads can be computed and remain close for all shooters. With the leads he said he observed, Kimble could not have used this system. Instead, he had to have used one of the "fast-swing/swing-through" techniques.

The "swing-through" shooter begins with the gun mounted behind the moving target and swings the muzzle through it. He triggers the shot when he reaches a distance in front of the target that his previous experience and subconscious mental computer tells him is correct for lead. Using this technique, the gun is moving faster than the target and there is a delay between thought and action. That microsecond delay involves the body's muscles and the mechanical action of the shotgun. By the time both of these elements are overcome and the primer ignites the shell, the gun has continued to swing past the target and the true lead is actually greater than you perceive. Although Kimble may only have seen two feet of lead on a 40-yard crossing target, his shooting style actually gave him more than that.

You can test the "swing-through" method for yourself. Pound a stake into the ground and back up 30 to 40 yards. Now, swing your shotgun from left to right

**The hallmark of most successful competitors is the ability to focus. This means different things to different people, but it is "compartmentalizing" the brain. Focus on THIS shot. Put the lost bird at the last station completely aside, along with the annoying shooter standing too close to your back and the slightly bent frame of your shooting glasses. Look at – contemplate – one thing: breaking THIS bird.** *(Photo courtesy Winchester)*

There is no greater practice for fields of pheasants than trap or sporting clays. The basics of shooting on the line and in the field are the same. You will, of course, need to put them into practice faster and with more unexpected angles in the rolling hills of South Dakota.

through the stake. Trigger a shot when your eyes tell you the gun muzzle is dead-on the stake. You will not hit it. Your shot will land past the stake in the direction you are swinging.

Repeat this exercise and vary the speed of your swing. You will soon realize that the faster you swing, the farther beyond the stake the shot charge lands.

The quicker your mind perceives the relationship between your muzzle and the target (or "reads the bird picture") and the more consistently you react to it, the more consistent the impact point of the shot charge will be.

This is why no two shooters can be taught in exactly the same manner. A slight difference in swing speed or a minor variation in visual acuity or reflexes will cause shooters using the same "fast-swing/swing-through" technique to steadfastly maintain that they use two completely different amounts of lead on identical targets.

Every individual's basic biomechanics and the way we learn to use our muscles are different, so it is virtually impossible to clone a shooter. Teaching that there is only one correct way to shoot an aerial target denies that individuals are just that, individuals.

To develop into good shooters, each person must first be grounded in the fundamentals. After that, they are free to develop a "personal style." Some shooters are perfectly comfortable with an extremely fast swing on close-range (under 20 yards) targets. They swing so quickly that they will say they see no lead at all; they shoot when the muzzle connects with the bird. Double that distance and some shooters change their shooting style to more of a "sustained lead" or a "pull-away" technique. Why do they abandon the fast swing just because target distance increases? The answer probably is that they are not comfortable trying to quickly perceive the two to three feet of forward allowance they require. They find that, for distant birds, a more controlled shooting technique is not only comfortable, but also effective for them. For other shooters, the reverse might very well be true.

## Stance Is Important

Knowledgeable shooters will attempt to learn as many of the various shooting techniques as they can and then determine which works best for them under varying shooting conditions. One of the fundamentals of any shooting equation, however, is achieving a proper shooting stance.

Your stance provides a platform for your gun and allows you to place the load on the target. That is really all it does, yet this simplification is sometimes overlooked when new shooters are excited about busting birds.

Consider that a rifleman attempting to place a sin-

Where habitat is left standing and farmers are not insistently driven to centerline-to-centerline plowing, farm-country pheasants provide both a challenge for shooters and, in an era of strained budgets, a little extra income for landowners.

**Working with dogs and guns is an art, a thing of beauty that quickly becomes a passion for many sportsmen. When one finds a dog that will point, flush, retrieve and hunts close, expect that years of great hunting lie ahead.**

gle bullet within a five-inch circle at 200 yards from a standing position requires a rigid platform to execute a precise shot. Anything he can do to minimize body movement and sight wobble will be beneficial. Shooting a rifle calls for weight to be evenly distributed, with perhaps a slight emphasis on the rear foot. The shooter's arms holding the gun need to be brought close to the central body mass and the leading hand should be in direct alignment with the body's long axis for best support. The entire objective is to "freeze" the gun long enough to align the sights with the center of the target and trigger the shot.

A shotgunner has very different requirements. The shot must be triggered from a fluidly moving gun and the body must be relaxed enough to swing the gun through a considerable arc. A rifleman who moves his gun more than an inch or so will miss his mark, yet a shotgunner who is for example, taking a high house

station four target in international skeet may need to swing as much as 90 degrees to hit a bird at 20 yards!

Obviously, the stance that works for the rifleman will not work for the shotgunner. Binding themselves into too rigid a stance is one of the biggest mistakes new shooters make.

The shotgunner needs to be able to execute a wide range of movement in both the horizontal and vertical planes. He or she may have to swing quickly on rising, falling or even sharply angled targets. Such fluid movement is best accomplished with greater weight (and hence, balance) on the forward foot. Some shooters prefer a weight distribution in the neighborhood of 60:40 between the front and the back foot; others like even more weight forward. Hips need to be free to pivot and they are what actually drive the body into the shot. Flex in the knees is desirable, but too much may contribute to erratic gun movement.

Many professionals believe that starting young shooters on a lightweight BB or pellet gun is good for introducing them to shooting. After all, there is little shock or recoil; the shooting is inexpensive and close; and except where forbidden by law, the careful parent can teach fundamentals in the back yard.

A rifleman's stance is rigid. A wingshooter's stance must be one of controlled aggression, a coiled spring ready to release upon command.

The stance that works best for a six-foot 200-pound male may not be the best for a shorter or stouter male or for a female shooter. People must establish a stance or body position that lets them do two things: move and swing the gun in a relaxed, controlled manner and yet maintain a stable center of gravity.

The result of "finding their stance" will be a noticeable difference in the way each person assumes the basic position before calling for a target. Nevertheless, the resulting scores may be identical! As I said, you cannot clone shooters.

Sometimes shotgunners alter their stance for different shooting situations. In games shot with a pre-mounted gun (doubles trap, bunker trap and handicap trap), some shooters put a little more flex in their knees and a bit more crouch in their body than when they are shooting from an unmounted position. The reason for changing stance is that these are all rising targets, so increased flex in the knees provides a little more power to drive the gun through the target with a fast-swing technique.

Change to sporting clays, international skeet, 5-stand or other games and a low or even an unmounted gun (now optional in regulated sporting clays matches) works better for many. With a low gun, your upper body assumes a more upright position with slightly straighter knees. The most important aspect of stance in low gun games is that the gun be mounted smoothly and consistently every time. The more flex and body crouch the shooter has, the more their critical shoulder pocket shifts as they move their body to the target. Keeping the body upright and relying on increased hip pivoting achieve a more consistent gun mount.

To become an accomplished wingshooter, you need to understand and practice the fundamentals of stance and gun control. You will need to pay attention to lead on each shooting station on still and windy days. Then, it is simply a matter of seeing a lot of targets flying at different speeds and different angles. If you are conscientious, your mental computer will soon learn to execute the swing and lead and pigeons will begin to break as if you had been shooting all your life.

# CHAPTER 2

# THE OLDEST SHOTGUNNING GAME

The woman with the gun is at least pointing in the right direction, but her stance ensures that she will miss more targets than she hits, even from the 16-yard position. Errors: Vertical stance. Feet together. Left hand too far out on the gun. With a little coaching, she can overcome all of these errors.

Trap shooting has been around for a long time, maybe hundreds of years. An early printed mention was in an English publication called "Sporting Magazine." In 1793, an article stated that trap shooting was already "well established" in England.

Early trap shooters used live pigeons for targets. Birds were held in a box or "trap" until the shooter "called for the bird." An assistant would then pull a string to open the trap's lid.

The first known records of organized trap shooting in the U.S. are probably those contained in the 1831 records of the Sportsman's Club of Cincinnati, Ohio. In 1866, Chas Portlock of Boston, Massachusetts, introduced a glass ball to American target shooters. The balls met with limited success because the levers used to propel them were so inadequately matched to the glass that many balls shattered when they were launched.

Glass ball shooting declined when George Ligowsky invented the first clay pigeon and a machine to throw it effectively in the 1880s. This was significant for shot-gun games because Ligowsky's disc-shaped clay pigeon simulated the flight of a live bird, whereas the glass balls were simply lobbed into the air.

Ligowsky's pigeons were made of clay and baked in an oven. They were apparently quite hard and it took a precise shot to break one. Today's clay targets are made primarily of pitch and are easier to break. The use of live birds gradually fell into disfavor in the 20th century.

## Trap Shooting Today

Today, the Amateur Trapshooting Association (ATA) regulates trap shooting in America. A complete copy of their rules is included in this book.

A trap field consists of a single launcher located in a trap house and partially buried in the ground. Five shooting positions are situated 16 yards behind the trap house and spaced three yards apart. The "16-yard" event, the most common trap game, is shot from these five positions.

From each of the 16-yard positions a lane, marked in

## Classification by Established Average Or Known Ability

| Classification | 16 Yard Singles | Doubles |
|---|---|---|
| SIX CLASSES | | |
| AAA | 98% and over | 96% and over |
| AA | 96.25% and under 98% | 92% and under 96% |
| A | 94.75% and under 96.25% | 89% and under 92% |
| B | 93% and under 94.75% | 86% and under 89% |
| C | 90% and under 93% | 82% and under 86% |
| D | Under 90% | Under 82% |
| FIVE CLASSES | | |
| AA | 97% and over | 93% and over |
| A | 94% and under 97% | 89% and under 93% |
| B | 91% and under 94% | 85% and under 89% |
| C | 88% and under 91 % | 78% and under 85% |
| D | Under 88% | Under 78% |
| FOUR CLASSES | | |
| A | 95% and over | 90% and over |
| B | 92% and under 95% | 85% and under 90% |
| C | 89% and under 92% | 78% and under 85% |
| D | Under 89% | Under 78% |
| THREE CLASSES | | |
| A | 95% and over | 89% and over |
| B | 91% and under 95% | 83% and under 89% |
| C | Under 91% | Under 83% |

## Special Competition Categories for Men and Women*

| Category | Age |
|---|---|
| Sub-Junior | Less than 15 |
| Junior | 15 to less than 18 |
| Veteran | 65 years and older |
| Senior Veteran | 70 years and older |

*Women are identified in ATA rules as "ladies."

yardage increments, leads backward to a point 27 yards behind the trap house. "Handicap trap" is shot from these various yardage markers.

The trap machine launches clay disks at unknown angles for each station. Clays fly within 22 degrees of the right or left of the trap center, which is aligned directly with shooting position three. These oscillating traps have built-in interrupters which break up patterns and prevent the shooter from "reading the trap" or guessing the angle of flight before he or she shoots. Thus, the shooter is never certain where the bird will fly. The only guarantee is that it will be within a defined zone for each of the five stations.

Standard clay targets are used, and they may be any of a number of colors or color patterns. The launcher is calibrated to throw targets at about 41 miles per hour. The pre-set trajectory puts birds between eight and 10 feet above the ground at 10 feet in front of the trap and propels them to a distance between 49 and 51 yards from the trap house.

The two-foot range spread is allowed under ATA rules and compensates for different wind and weather conditions. Most trap ranges set the bird height to about 10 feet under conditions of no wind or a gentle breeze. Should a strong wind blow directly into the trap house, the target trajectory will be set low-

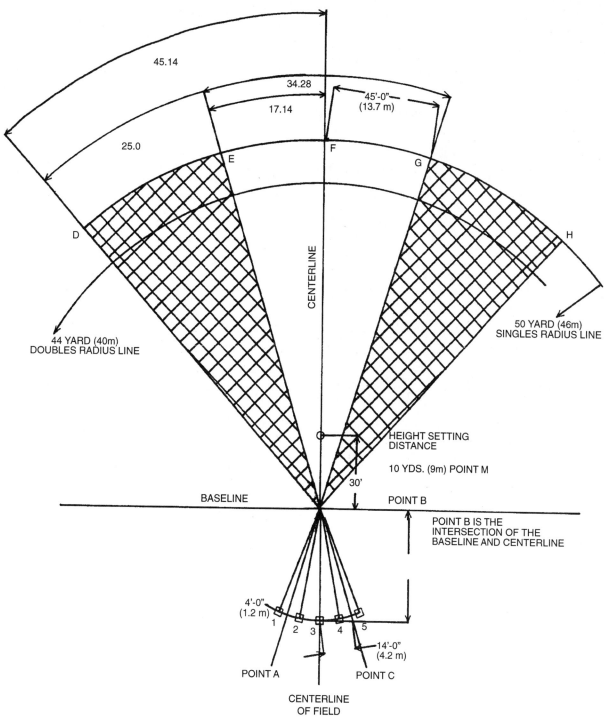

45.14

34.28

45'-0"
(13.7 m)

17.14

25.0

E          F          G

D                                    H

CENTERLINE

50 YARD (46m)
SINGLES RADIUS LINE

44 YARD (40m)
DOUBLES RADIUS LINE

HEIGHT SETTING
DISTANCE

10 YDS. (9m) POINT M

30'

BASELINE                    POINT B

POINT B IS THE
INTERSECTION OF THE
BASELINE AND CENTERLINE

4'-0"
(1.2 m)
1    2  3  4    5

14'-0"
(4.2 m)

POINT A                    POINT C

CENTERLINE
OF FIELD

The "Approach" to a trap field positions the trap house and five stations plus the layout of an approach for handicap shooting. The "Field" shows schematically where the traps will fly within regulation parameters. Newcomers to the game should study this diagram so that they are familiar with the options before they call for their first bird.

er to retard rapid climb of the bird and allow it to travel the minimum 49-yard distance. A head wind can make the target climb rapidly. A tail wind, on the other hand, prevents the target from climbing and under these conditions range personnel usually set the target launch to the full 10-foot height to keep a clay in the

air long enough to make the required 49-yard distance.

Occasionally, wind shift during a match prevents targets from flying within the prescribed height and falling within the required distance. In this case, a competitor is well within his rights to ask the referee to stop the match and reset the machine.

Shotgun sports at Lana'i Pine on the island of Lana'i, Hawaii. The Lana'i course has 14 shooting stations with automated traps, six fully automated competition high towers and single-shooter delay circuitry for individual rounds.

"16-yard" shooting is the most popular trap event. Shooters compete within a class system, based on their previous scores or known ability, to assure that they contend with competitors who have similar skill levels. Previous scores generally require a shooter to have engaged about 300 registered targets, and the percentage of those targets broken will be his or her average. A 16-yard event may have as many as six classes, but if shooter turnout is light, the ATA provides for reducing that number to five, four, or even three classes. (See the accompanying tables for the breakdown.)

ATA rules state that no shotgun with a larger bore than 12-gauge may be used. This allows competitors to shoot any of the smaller gauges, although few do so because the decreased shot charge is too great a handicap for serious competition. If you are shooting for fun, there is nothing wrong with using a smaller gauge, though. Florida's Chris Christian has shot many a round of trap with both the 28-gauge and the 410-bore. "It's fun and frustrating," he says, "but still a lot of fun!"

Formerly, a three-dram, 1 ⅛-ounce 12-gauge load containing premium hard black #7 ½ shot was called a "trap load." The ATA rules are consistent with the 1 ⅛-ounce 12-gauge load of #7 ½ (maximum) shot, and still ban nickel and copper-coated shot, allowing lead, steel, bismuth or "other composite non-toxic shot materials."

Today, with versatile powders, the ATA regulates shells by velocity rather than dram. You cannot shoot registered birds with 12-gauge loads that exceed 1290 fps, 20-gauge loads faster than 1325 fps or 28-gauge loads faster than 1350 fps.

Many shooters today use lighter 12-gauge loads to reduce recoil, reserving the maximum loads for handicap rounds and the second shot in a doubles match.

## Etiquette and Procedures

A single round of trap consists of 25 shots, and a trap squad may contain up to five shooters.

Each shooter will take one of the five positions or stations and the shooter on station one is the first to shoot. Once he has fired, the shooter on station two may then call for a bird and the other shooters call for birds in turn. This rotation is repeated until each shooter has fired five rounds from his station.

At that time, the trap puller/scorer calls "Change," followed by a quick rundown of the number of birds each contestant hit at that station: "Change...1-3, 2-4, 3-5, 4-2, 5-1." This means, "It is time for shooters to move to the next station. The shooter at station number one broke three birds. The shooter on station two broke four birds. Station number three ran it clean (broke all five). Station four only hit two birds and the shooter on station five needs help because he only managed to hit one."

Shooters then move to the next station in a clockwise manner, station one moving to station two and the shooter on number five rotating to station one. When every one has reached their new position, the shooter who originally began the round on station one, the shooter who is now on station two, will again begin. This person is the first shooter at each new station.

Guns may not be loaded until every shooter is on their station and the leadoff shooter has called for his first bird. Knowledgeable shooters load their gun with only one round at a time and only when the shooter two positions ahead of them calls for a bird. When moving between stations, the gun must be unloaded and the action open.

It is common for the scorer to call missed birds as the competitors shoot, shouting the word "Lost" to denote a miss. In order to score a hit, the shooter must only knock a visible piece off the target. This sometimes creates differences of opinion between the scorer and the shooter.

The scorer is invariably right, at least if he is experienced. He is in position to do nothing but watch the

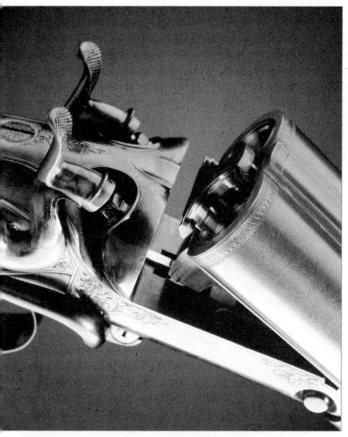

Shooting a drilling—a side-by-side with a rifle barrel underneath—and dressed in the Edwardian style of the early 20th century, members of The Vintagers believe that these days, far too much emphasis is given to a person's score and far too little to the social environment of shooting.

bird as it leaves the house and is unencumbered by the pressures and decisions facing someone with a loaded gun in their hand. Still, scorers are human and they do make occasional mistakes. If a shooter believes the bird broke, it is appropriate to say so. If one or more of his squad mates agrees, a scorer will often change his call.

Trap is fast-paced. In fact, of all the shotgun games, a round of 16-yard trap is usually completed the quickest, in about 12 to 15 minutes.

Trap shooters get used to a quick-paced rhythm and a shooter that is slow or who continually questions the scorer's calls will disrupt it. Such shooters are not viewed in a favorable light by their squadmates.

Courteous trap shooters make every effort to fall into the shooting rhythm of the squad. It is important that, when you take your position, you are ready to shoot. You should have all of the shells and any other accessories you will need in your pockets.

This rhythm is important to many veteran shooters. Often, they will make every effort to shoot on squads composed of others with whom they have shot with in the past and who provide the right rhythm.

Finding and keeping a squad rhythm is not solely for convenience. A herky-jerky squad can disrupt a shooter's concentration and lower his score. Conversely, a smoothly functioning squad that "hits the zone" can elevate a shooter's score. Trap is one of the few shooting games in which the shooters around you, without any conscious effort, can exert a positive or negative influence on your performance.

New trap shooters should be attentive to shooting rhythm. The idea of rhythm on the field is one reason trap shooters have gained a reputation for being somewhat aloof and keeping their opinions to themselves. Whether this is true across-the-board is arguable. However, a trap squad will not usually display the laid-back, gregarious attitude that you often see among skeet or sporting clays shooters. This quality of aloofness should not be considered hostility. It is simply an element of the concentration required to shoot well.

For this same reason, you will not hear much conversation among squad members during a shoot. Unless it is only a fun shoot, squad members will not freely offer advice and shooting pointers while the round is in progress. The best trap squads are focused, businesslike and move quickly. That is the nature of the game. New trap shooters would do well to keep this in mind and emulate it because it will have a positive effect on your score and on your progress as a competitor.

## Shooting Accessories

You need very few accessories to step up to position one on a trap field. Eye protection is extremely important—mandatory, in fact—on any shooting venue and should always be worn. All ranges now require it. Ear protection helps prevent permanent hearing loss and reduces recoil fatigue. Quality hearing protectors go a long way in helping you avoid the development of a flinch. Hearing protection of some sort is now also a requirement.

Shooting vests and shell pouches are convenient. At some point in your shooting career you will want to obtain them. Vests and pouches are not essential for trap, however, because there is not much movement on the field. You have ample time to pick up the box of shells at your feet and haul it to the next station; more than enough time to reach down and grab a shell from it when you are ready to load. If you are saving your empty hulls to reload though, you will need something to put them in and an inexpensive belt pouch works well. Trap is not a complex game. It is fast-paced and great fun.

(For a complete run-down on accessory possibilities, please review the "Accessories" chapter in Section IV.)

# CHAPTER 3

# THE FUNDAMENTALS OF TRAP

This shotgunner's grip may be a little tight and his stance somewhat passive for a long day of busting clay. Still, his ear plugs and eyewear are protective and the hold of the gun against his cheek is positive for a good sight picture.

Shooting trap is not a thinking activity: it is a feeling activity. In the movie Star Wars, the old Jedi knight Obi-Wan Kenobi tutored young Luke Skywalker to "use the force" or to trust his instincts, his "inner eye." At the risk of offending some veteran trapshooters, shooting trap effectively is like "using the force." Targets fly out of the hidden launcher so quickly that there is little time to think, to calculate lead. The best shooters eventually become instinctive.

Trap shooting is deceptively easy. Moving from initial exposure, which can be a frustrating experience, to an ATA "AAA" classification (breaking 98 percent or better in singles and 96 percent or better in doubles) certainly requires a lot of hand-eye coordination, but pointing the gun and pulling the trigger eventually become instinct. Thinking about the shot quickly becomes over-analysis and it can ruin a perfectly good game. Instead, one reacts through a round or, like the old Jedi, learns to trust one's instincts.

In effect, trap is not much different from someone

There is no minimum age required to begin teaching young people to shoot. Whatever the shooting game, a professional introduction opens a lifetime of enjoyment if the youngsters enjoy the day ... and thus it is recommended that a parent not take charge of the instruction!

suddenly tossing a ball at your face. You do not do a lot of thinking about the ball. Your hands automatically come up to intercept it. If you have good reactions and your body is in proper position, you will catch the ball. If not, you may deflect it or, if you really are slow or clumsy, take one in the eye.

That pretty well sums up trap. The only difference between this characterization and actual shots on the field is that, instead of intercepting an incoming baseball with your hands, you are intercepting an outgoing clay target with a shot charge. In both cases, that task is best accomplished if the shooter has assumed the proper body position (or stance) to allow his reflexes to take over.

What follows in this chapter is a systematic plan for getting started in trap. Much of the advice on basic body position and gun handling will also apply to the other clay target games described in this book.

## Proper Gun Hold

We have already mentioned that, unlike a rifle which must be held steady to hit a target, your shotgun must move. If the charge has a chance of intercepting the target, the gun must flow to and through it as the shot is triggered. One of the most frequent causes of missed clay targets at any game is stopping the movement of the gun when the shot is fired. This is "anticipation" and the shot string always flies behind the bird.

Some new shooters induce missing by holding the gun incorrectly. Your shotgun touches your body at four different places: both hands, your cheek and in the shoulder pocket. It must make contact in a consistent manner every time the gun is shouldered or the point of impact of the shot charge will change. In addition, the gun position must be comfortable enough to allow you to move the gun smoothly in any direction, horizontally or vertically. A tightly gripped, locked-in gun mount might be fine for a rifleman, but it is a disaster for a shotgunner.

Grip and stance are basic. However, it is the author's experience that consistent gun mounting is the greatest problem for new shooters, especially those who have rifle-shooting experience. These shooters often incorrectly assume that gun mount and body position should not offer them any freedom of movement. In this assumption, they are simply wrong.

With a shotgun, your leading hand, the one holding the forend of the gun, is more than just a gun support. Think of it like the steering wheel of an automobile, because that is what the leading hand does—it drives the gun in the vertical and horizontal planes. If your hand is improperly positioned on the forend, you will lose some of that control.

Placing your hand too far back toward the receiver offers good biomechanical advantage for moving the gun up and down, but very little for moving it side to side. Too far forward is the reverse difficulty: it reduces your ability to move the gun up and down quickly.

Top shooting coaches recommend that your leading hand should be placed on the forend at a point that allows your elbow to form a 90- to 100-degree angle between your forearm and upper arm. Your leading arm

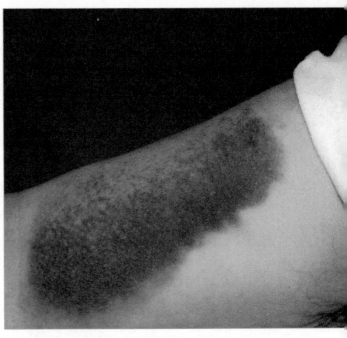

An un-retouched photo of an enormous bruise covering the upper arm after a day of shooting. Such a bruise is painful—though not permanent—and is caused by insufficient attention to proper gun mount and hold.

When introducing non-shooters to a shotgun, it is best to drop down in gauge and even lighten the load so that shock, recoil and blast do not scare them away. In this way, with easy non-pressured instruction, one could gain a lifetime shooting partner.

should then form a 45-degree angle with the side of the gun. This 45-degree angle is the best compromise for both vertical and horizontal movement. A greater angle than 45 degrees inhibits vertical movement, while less restricts horizontal movement. Trap shooters need unrestricted movement in both planes.

Since shooters are built differently, this should simply be considered a starting point from which the shooter can discover his best stance. Nevertheless, many top shooters have found that a slightly different forend hold works best for them.

The arm angle of your trigger hand is another matter. If your elbow is too low, it can reduce the shoulder pocket area into which your gun butt needs to lock. This may cause the gun butt to shift position as it recoils. If your elbow is too high, it will create a large shoulder pocket, but a high arm position strains the muscles of your shoulder and arm. Most shooters find that the best arm position for them lies somewhere between these extremes.

Another variable affecting scores is the position of a shooter's head. Simply put, your head should be erect. When mounting the gun, bring the gun to the face instead of the other way around. Consistent head positioning goes a long way to ensuring that your shot string will fly in the same manner every time you pull the trigger.

## Stance and Weight Distribution

Regardless of build, a shotgunner may constructively think of the body as if it were built like a tank. Everything below the hips is the chassis that provides support; everything above the hips is the turret that pivots to swing the gun. A correct stance allows this to happen.

The feet should be spread a comfortable nine to 15 inches apart. Too wide a stance inhibits upper body movement because it makes the shooter less balanced. Too narrow a stance can decrease a shooter's balance. Weight distribution should favor your leading leg (the left leg for right-handers) with about a 60:40 or even a 65:35 ratio between your front and back leg. Some shooters favor keeping the back leg straight with a bit of flex in the leading knee. Others shoot with both knees slightly bent. Although you will see world class shooters stand in the most unusual positions imaginable, it is advisable to avoid any exaggerated crouch, at least while you are learning.

Those who prefer a more deliberate shooting style often stand relatively upright. Fast and instinctive shooters typically want their knees slightly flexed and they use that stored energy to help drive the upper body and achieve the gun speed needed for this style of shooting.

## Natural Point of Aim

Natural point of aim is the position in which the gun is pointing when a shooter brings his gun to the firing position with no further body movement. When the shot is fired and the gun recoils, it will return to this position.

The concept of a natural point of aim is equally important for riflemen, pistol shooters and shotgunners. Once it is discovered, the shooter has the best natural body position for the selected target and the widest area of body movement available to move to either side of the target.

Finding your natural point of aim for any given target is easy. First, take your normal shooting position and focus on the aiming spot. Now, bring the gun to the firing position and close your eyes. Raise the gun to the recoil position and then lower it back to the original position. Now, open your eyes.

If the gun is back on target, you are at your natural point of aim. Chances are it will be to one side or the other. Correct this by moving your leading foot in the direction you want the gun barrel to move, while shifting your back foot as necessary to maintain your basic stance. Adjustments to natural point of aim are always made with the feet, never with the upper body. Your upper body remains set while the feet are moved to position the gun where you want it to aim. The procedure is the same whether you are shooting a rifle, pistol or shotgun.

Understanding your natural point of aim is critical for a shotgunner because it will determine your swing arc. If your arc is not sufficient to drive through the target, you will lose the bird.

## One Eye or Two?

Human vision operates on the binocular principle. Focused on a single object, your two eyes work in concert to establish depth perception. For most people, one eye—the master eye—will be more dominant and will sharply define the target, while the "off eye" provides the second opinion needed for depth perception. (We will discuss how and why you should determine your master eye in a later chapter.)

Expert shotgun shooters take advantage of the binocular principle and shoot with both eyes open. The master eye looks along the rib while the off eye looks past the barrel, confirming your estimation of depth or distance. With practice, this is easy in skeet and sporting clays. Many shooters, in fact, estimate distance, speed and shot angle without a conscious thought because this is the only real way to track extreme angle targets.

This process is a little tougher for trap shooters because they will naturally sight down the barrel as they wait for the bird. Because targets are primarily mov-

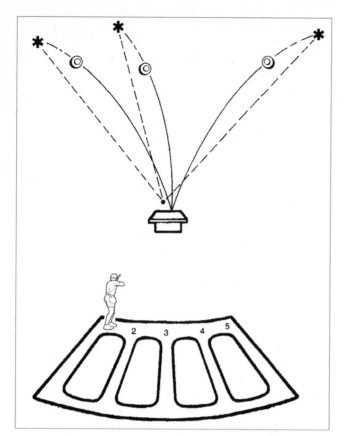

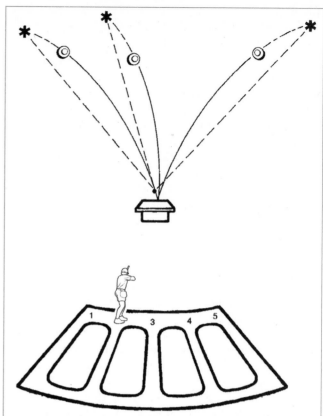

Station One: Target array on station one requires that right-handed shooters fudge their natural point of aim to the left in order to have the swing room required for the extreme left-hand target.

Station Two: Moving one station to the right shrinks the target angles and allows shooters to shift their body position more towards the trap house center.

ing away from the shooter, they can be picked up easily with just one eye. Sometimes your off eye will close as you sight down the shotgun rib on a trap field, even if you have no trouble keeping both eyes open at skeet or sporting clays. Even experienced trap shooters sometimes have to remind themselves consciously to keep both eyes open. This usually happens after they miss two targets in a row!

If you do not shoot trap with both eyes open, you tend to concentrate too much on the rib and bead of the gun and not enough on the target. You are forced to quickly acquire the target as it comes out of the house and determine its exact course. If you do not, the bird gets a long head start and this throws off your timing. With both eyes open, you can maintain the proper rib picture, and quickly acquire the bird.

One of the most important things any shotgunner can do to improve his score shooting any clay target game is to make "both eyes open" a consistent part of the mental checklist he runs through before calling for a bird.

## Muzzle Position

In trap, when you call for a target, you have to start with the gun muzzle in some position. Contrary to the opinions of some experts, there is no single correct position that every shooter should emulate. Actually, there are two techniques that can be effective, "high gun" and "low gun." These terms refer to how high above the trap house a shooter points the gun before the target emerges, not whether the gun butt is on or off the shoulder.

All ATA trap targets emerge from a point near the center of the trap house and on a rising angle. High gun shooters prefer to position the muzzle about four feet above the house and let the bird rise upward and through the barrel. If a shooter is using both eyes, he can pick up the bird quite well with this system, since the off eye will "look through" or past the barrel and will have no problem acquiring the bird. A shooter who uses only one eye will have real problems with a high gun muzzle position.

Most high gun shooters favor high-shooting guns, those that pattern from six to 18 inches above the bead. Combined with a high gun hold and binocular vision, this will let a shooter find the target and break it quickly

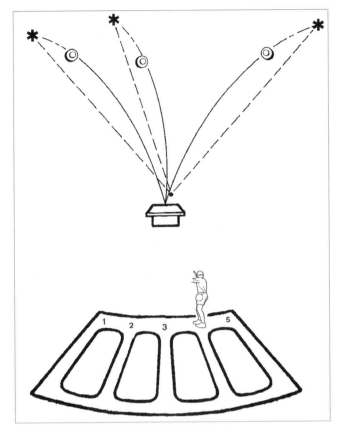

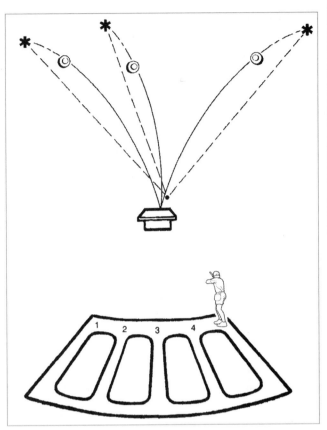

**Station Four:** Right-handed shooters begin to have problems when they reach station four, because of the restricted swing range to their right side. They will have to fudge their natural body position to the right if they intend to hit many extreme right-angled targets.

with a relatively small degree of gun movement. High gun shooters tend to focus their eyes farther from the trap house – about 15 to 17 yards – and break the birds a bit farther onto the field. This is what I call a "deliberate" shooting style, almost rifle shooting with a shotgun.

A high gun hold is probably the most popular technique among veteran shooters. However, it may not be the best way for new shooters to develop their skills. Many coaches believe that new shooters gain skill more quickly if they start with a low gun hold. In this case, the muzzle points at the back edge of the trap house or slightly below it.

There are three reasons why a low gun hold may help a novice shooter develop skills faster.

First, with the gun pointed at the top of the house, the bird will always emerge over the muzzle, with both bird and muzzle within the shooter's vision. For those who cannot shoot with both eyes open, this low hold is one of the few ways they can achieve success in trap. Instant target acquisition combined with a clear muzzle picture makes maintaining a proper sight picture easy.

**Station Five:** This is the toughest station for right-handed shooters. The extreme right-angled target can get away from a shooter if he does not fudge his body position to it. The left-hand targets do not require a lot of swing arc because they appear to the shooter more as straight-aways. Set up for the greater angled target and you will improve your score on this station.

Using the low gun technique, your eyes focus where the bird will first appear. This helps you acquire the bird quickly, which is necessary for a low gun hold to be effective.

Second, a low gun technique requires the shooter to do the most important thing every great shotgunner must learn, swing the gun! The bird will emerge as an orange streak flying past the gun muzzle so a shooter cannot be lazy going after it. The shooter will have to swing quickly to catch it. This awareness builds the shooting speed needed for the shooter to get onto the bird while it is still climbing at high speed and still unaffected by the wind. It is a more consistent target and the shooter does not have to make changes in his sight picture to accommodate environmental extremes. You drill 'em and kill 'em the same way every time. This is the "fast-swing" technique in action. It has one additional benefit: lead is substantially reduced because of the speed of your swing.

The target requiring the greatest lead in trap is the

extreme 22-degree angled shot on stations one and five. Some deliberate shooters say they use anywhere from 18 inches to three feet of lead on these targets and break them at about 35 to 39 yards. Shooting the low gun hold and the fast swing, author Chris Christian says he seriously doubts if he sees a lead greater than two target lengths, about eight inches. "I break those targets at about 30 yards," he says, "where I have a dense, yet optimum pattern from an Improved Cylinder or Light Modified choke with either #8 or #8 ½ loads. On the more gently-angled shots, I shoot at the leading edge of the bird. Lead is not something I spend much time thinking about. I just swing, pull the trigger and smile!"

The final advantage to a low gun hold is that, because of the speed of the swing directly through the bird and the closer break range, you can shoot trap with the low gun technique using a standard field-stocked, flat-shooting gun.

For all of these reasons, the low gun technique is better for a new shooter than the more rigid, deliberate high gun technique. Once a shooter begins with the low gun position and learns the basics, it is not hard to change to a high-shooting gun and the higher hold, should he choose to do so.

## Station Shooting Positions

The last thing a new trap shooter needs to learn is where to put his natural point of aim for each station. This varies depending upon whether the shooter is right- or left-handed, using a deliberate or fast swing, shooting with one or two eyes open, and using a high gun or low gun position. Here are the options by station.

### Station One

The toughest target on this station is the extreme left angle. All shooters have to move their natural point of aim to the left to have the swing-room to hit it. For right-hand shooters this means establishing their natural point of aim near the left corner of the trap house. Lefties may have to go a bit outside the house since they will not have as much swing to the left as a right-hander.

Low gun, fast-swing shooters will then shift the gun back to the rear center of the trap house, just below the edge. Regardless of which angle the target takes, it will come out right over the muzzle. This center-back trap house hold will be the same for a low hold, fast-swing shooter on all five stations.

High gun shooters should place the muzzle at a point above the left-hand corner of the house, although there are some, generally those with Bunker trap experience, who will also use a high-center-back hold for all houses. We will explain why when we get to the chapter on International trap.

### Station Two

At position two, the angles decrease. Move your natural point of aim back toward the center of the house: about two-thirds of the way to center house from the left edge for right-handed shooters, and a little farther left for lefties. High gun shooters position their gun above the house, midway between the center and the left edge.

### Station Three

The angles are even at this center position, and most right-handed shooters tend to take a natural point of aim about six inches right of center house while lefties point about six inches to the left. This gives each some built-in fudge toward their weak swing side. High gun shooters shift the gun about the same distance to the side of center to prevent a straightaway target from hiding under the barrel.

### Station Four

Position four is a mirror image of station two. Right-handed shooters begin fudging their natural point of aim to the right, almost to the edge of the trap house, to accommodate their restricted right-side swing. Lefties remain a bit closer to center trap. The high hold is midway between center and right trap house edge.

### Station Five

This is the mirror image of station one. For right-hand shooters it is one of the toughest shots in trap. It is best to take a natural point of aim about a foot or so past the right edge of the trap house. Lefties should aim close to the edge of the house.

If right-hand shooters do not consider that difficult left-to-right angle and turn their body position with it, they will lose this bird. On station number one, lefties have to do the same thing with the extreme left-angle bird.

## Trap Reading

The last matter that needs addressing is a phenomenon called "reading the trap." Some shooters think they can figure out what target angle is coming next and be ready for it. Experts will tell you that you cannot, at least not often. Anticipating targets is a good way to get caught with your pants down and lose a target. Trying to anticipate target angle is a bad habit and will eventually cause you to shoot lower scores.

Once you have the right body position—those detailed here will serve as starting points—trap becomes an easy game to learn. When the target appears, you simply react. Try not to think. Try not to outsmart the target launch. Just drill the bird in front. What makes trap a challenging game to master is to force the body to make that correct reaction each time a target appears.

# CHAPTER 4

# SHOOTING HANDICAP TRAP

**As you earn your way back from the 16-yard line, the shooting becomes progressively more difficult. Curiously, however, veterans of trap tournaments testify that shooters whose skill has earned them a spot on the 27-yard handicap line are still the ones to beat, even with an 11-yard disadvantage! As they become progressively accustomed to greater distances, good shooters adjust quickly, especially with a little coaching.**

During the early days of trap, all shooters competed on an equal footing. As with any competitive event however, it soon became apparent that all contestants were not created equal. It was not long before the same names began appearing at the top of the leader board, match after match. Since trap has always been more financially-oriented than other clay target games, this was not good for attendance at meets. Why would a shooter with only modest skills or someone whose skills were still growing pay an entry fee when he or she knew they were going to lose it all?

Match organizers realized that if only five or six

shooters had a realistic chance of winning, then five or six was about as big as a match was going to be after all the other shooters figured out who these individuals were. A handicap event was match organizers' way of encouraging more than a half-dozen shooters to show up.

Handicap trap is a singles event shot in the same manner as the standard ATA "16 Yard" match: in the same order, at the same targets and on the same field. The difference is that individual competitors are moved back from the 16-yard front line based on their individual scores and averages. The minimum move is to

Two gunners at a 5-stand event illustrate that there is no one "correct" approach to successfully busting clay. The shooter on the left, shooting a crossing pattern, has an aggressive and stable stance with some weight forward. The shooter on the right, who was in the same squad at the running rabbit station, has a more vertical stance and seems to lean forward at the waist.

19 yards for new lady and new sub-junior (less than 15 years old) shooters or 20 yards for men: the maximum is to 27 yards. Increments are measured in half-yards, but shot in whole yards. Thus, a shooter might be assigned a 23 ½-yard handicap and then shoot from the 23-yard line. The resulting score will compete directly against those shot by all other competitors, no matter what their handicap yardage.

The purpose is to put all shooters on an equal footing by assigning each of them an individual handicap based on their ability. A similar handicapping procedure is followed for golf and other games. Like many handicap systems though, trap's handicapping effort has not always worked perfectly.

In the last few years, it has become apparent that shooters whose skill has earned them a spot on the 27-yard handicap line are still the ones to beat ... even with an 11-yard disadvantage! It is extremely rare, for instance, for a 23-yard shooter to beat a 27-yard shooter, despite the four-yard difference in target distance.

The 27-yard shooters are still superior, their skill and reflexes making them the ones to beat. The 27-yard shooters also win because they understand the critical differences between the game as it is shot from the 16-yard line, and that played from the handicap ranges. There are serious differences, both obvious and subtle.

## Loads and Chokes

The most obvious difference shooting between the 16- and 27-yard positions is of course the distance to the target. A quick 16-yard shooter will break his birds about 30 yards from his shooting position. This is a comfortable range for pattern control. An Improved Cylinder choke is adequate when it is combined with a 1 ⅛-ounce load of #8 ½ shot. That shot size has enough target-breaking power and provides almost as many pellets in the load as a 1 ⅛-ounce #9 skeet load. Because #8 ½ shot fills out an Improved Cylinder pattern very well, it gives the shooter more than enough pattern density and a margin for error, too.

Slower 16-yard shooters often rely on a Light Modified (also called Skeet #2) or Modified choke and the same load with #8 shot. They find this combination works well in the 33- to 37-yard range at which these leisurely shooters usually break their birds.

Start moving shooters back from the 16-yard line however and the game changes. You can forget using #8 ½ shot in any load at any range past 33 to 35 yards; at longer distances, that shot size is not heavy enough to consistently break birds and you will lose some targets that heavier shot pellets would break. Shooting at greater range means you must now choose #8s and tighten your choke to maintain effective pattern density. The down side is that even fast shooters lose some of the margin for error if you are shooting much beyond the 20-yard handicap line. Slower shooters at the same range find they break their targets at about 40 yards, and that requires a denser pattern than a Light Modified or Modified choke will produce. They must increase their choke to decrease the distribution of shot in the pattern.

When you earn your way back to the 27-yard line, breaking birds consistently really gets tough. Quick shooters have a target break point somewhere between 40 and 50 yards, and for leisurely gunners that point is out farther than 50 yards. You still have only 1 ⅛ ounces of shot to do the job even with maximum loads.

The demands on load and choke at this range are severe. For some time, everyone assumed that no 27-yard shooter could break 100 straight targets because the loads would not be up to the task. That did not remain the case for long, as shot quality and wad development rose to the task.

What handicap distance points out however, is that the game requires much more precision the farther one is removed from the comfort of the 16-yard line. Shot size must increase to maintain target-breaking power, but that very increase in size results in a decrease in pattern density over smaller shot. Therefore pattern density must be maintained by using tighter chokes that throw smaller patterns, because the larger the shot size the fewer pellets there are in a given load to make up the pattern. The margin for error goes right into the toilet.

"Any small error at 27 yards is a miss," Florida shooter Lisa Sever says. Lisa earned her 27-yard handicap while she was still in college. "One minute mistake is all it takes to drop out of the top echelon of competition. At the 16-yard line, you can recover and get at least a piece of the bird. Not at the 27-yard line. You must have much more polish in your swing and point."

Shooting from the farther handicap ranges, as Lisa does, requires some serious changes in equipment and mental attitude from that required for 16-yard shooting.

The most notable change is in the firearm used. The majority of top handicap shooters prefer a single-barrel gun with a long sighting radius. This is why we see the graceful 32- and 34-inch-barreled guns so often on the trap line. The longer barrel, yet slightly lighter muzzle weight inherent in such guns (compared to a double gun), provides a more precise aim and greater muzzle control than what can be achieved with the over-and-unders that dominate the doubles game. Many top-quality trap guns are offered as a two-barrel set with both a single barrel and over-and-under barrels fitted to the same receiver.

You can bet that the single-barrel will be choked tighter than a banker's heart. While Modified and Improved Modified chokes are commonly seen on the 16-yard line (with slightly more open chokes being popular in doubles), Full (.035-inch constriction) and even Extra-Full (.040-inch+) are the rule from 27 yards.

Some shooters do quite well with relatively flat-shooting guns, but many top handicap shooters want a high-shooting gun. This allows the shooter to stay under the bird for a more precise target picture than that achieved with a "flat" gun that must be swung up and through the bird to cover it. A higher shooting gun also helps compensate for a shot charge that will be losing velocity and actually be starting to drop in its trajectory as the 40-yard-plus mark is reached.

Shot size normally is confined to #7 ½, although some shooters try to stretch #8 shot in an attempt to maintain a dense pattern. Loads run the gamut from light to full three-dram equivalent, depending on the shooter's preference and confidence level.

Even with the proper equipment, handicap shooters must develop a good mental approach to their handicap. One of the first things they do is beat "the illusion." A target at the 16-yard line appears to be moving fast, so the shooter realizes he must move quickly to catch it. The target seems to leap from the trap and rapidly move out of the shooter's field of view because of his closer proximity. The illusion of speed makes the shooter go after it. Move back the 11-yard difference to the 27-yard line and the picture or the image changes. The shooter's field of view around the field is noticeably much wider. The 27-yard bird emerges into this wider field of view (looking smaller, of course) and it appears to be moving slower! It does not seem to require the immediate "now" movement to catch it. If you buy into "the illusion" that you have time to get onto the bird at 27 yards, you will miss more than you hit.

Even though he is shooting a new Beretta break-open UGB25 XCEL semi-auto 12-gauge, author Rick Sapp has begun his swing through the bird late. He managed to break off a "visible chip," but his chances of vaporizing birds rather than just chipping them diminishes when he is slow to develop his swing and follow-through.

## The Handicap Illusion

This visual illusion, based solely on an 11-yard difference, gives the shooter the impression that he has all the time in the world to get on the target. Actually, because of the narrower arc of swing, there is much less physical gun movement required at the 27-yard line than at the 16-yard mark.

That is the illusion. Although gun movement is certainly reduced, the gun must be moved as quickly—or more quickly—than it would be when shooting from the 16-yard line if the target is to be hit within any reasonable break range.

A slow shooter on the 27-yard line is in for a difficult round. Of course, those who have shot their way back to trap's toughest position are well aware of that, and any tendency toward laggardly shooting behavior would have been put behind them long before.

"You have to get to that 27-yard target just as quickly as you would at 16 yards," Lisa Sever has said. "The appearance of more time is just an illusion, but it fools a lot of newer handicap shooters. For me, one of the keys to handicap shooting is to realize that I do not

have the time that the visual appearance of the target tells me I do, but to also realize that I can't anticipate the target or rush it. I have to make myself wait until I can acquire and read the target before I make my move, then move smoothly and precisely—and without hesitation—to the bird. There is no real change in body or foot position and only the slightest increase in lead on the angled targets. The mental aspect of beating the illusion of more time yet not getting in a big hurry is important in dealing with handicap targets."

The late shooting-great Frank Little offered some additional advice for those who want to become great handicap shooters. Frank's philosophy was that all 16 Yard trap should be considered little more than practice for the 27-yard line. He advocated using the same tight, full choke #7 ½ load at the 16-yard line that you would at the 27-yard line. His reasoning was simple and straightforward: with that choke and load any target that does not become a small puff of black smoke at 16 yards was not pointed well enough to have been hit at 27 yards. If you can hit 16-yard targets with that combination, 27-yard birds will be much easier. That is getting very precise indeed!

## CHAPTER 5

# DEALING WITH DOUBLES

Doubles trap was introduced to the tournament format in about 1911 to spice up the game. It is safe to say it has succeeded quite admirably at that goal.

As the name implies, doubles trap consists of two birds released simultaneously on two separate flight paths: one bird is set to fly at the extreme 22-degree angle to the right while the other is set for the same angle to the left. Since both birds are launched from the same trap, their velocity is slightly less than that of a singles target from the same machine because the added weight of the extra bird robs a couple of feet per second of speed from the throwing arm.

The doubles game is shot from the 16-yard line in a standard five-shooter squad. A full round consists of 25 pairs (50 birds). Shooters fire at five pairs from each station. Thirteen pairs are presented on the first walk through the stations. This is followed by a short break and then the remaining twelve pairs are presented on the next walk-through.

At each station, the shooter loads two shells, firing one shell at each target. The on-the-field official moves the shooters through the five stations, making certain that the proper shooting order is maintained.

Many shooters consider doubles trap the toughest ATA trap game, and it is not quite as popular as singles or handicap trap. One reason it is not extremely popular is that doubles requires shooters to have a gun capable of firing two rounds, and some shooters refuse to put down their expensive single-barrel guns. Another reason, however, is the intimidation factor: many trap shooters have trouble dealing with two targets in the air simultaneously. A lot of that, of course, is mental.

I recently watched a shooter who was a competent skeet and sporting clays gunner step up in a squad of veteran ATA trap shooters for the very first round of doubles trap he had ever fired. This shooter did not even own a trap gun, so he used his sporting clays gun and slipped in Skeet 2 and Improved Modified tubes. Treating the targets just like sporting clays birds, he broke 40 out of 50 the first time he ever shot the game! The trap shooters on the squad, who knew he had never shot the game before, were surprised at how well he picked up this supposedly difficult game. The shooter himself was not surprised. He said he "… didn't think it was all that difficult." He was not intimidated by seeing two targets in the air at the same time because in sporting clays he sees that all the time.

Beretta contract shooter Darby Fennell says that only continuing practice results in high scores, whether one shoots trap, skeet, sporting clays or one of the many variations of those games.

Simultaneous targets are common in skeet and sporting clays. In fact, skeet shooters regularly deal with two targets that are not only traveling slightly faster than doubles trap birds, but also are flying in opposite directions! They find nothing out of the ordinary about seeing two targets at once and do not allow that to intimidate them.

I think some trap shooters who fail to perform as well in doubles as they do in the singles and handicap games have talked themselves into being intimated by seeing two targets in the air. Doubles is not that tough of a game.

Remember that the targets not only fly a bit slower in doubles, but they are locked into one flight path. In sharp contrast to singles trap games, where the bird may take one of a number of different flight paths and the shooter must identify the flight angle very quickly, in doubles the shooter always knows precisely where to look for the birds. The angle will not vary throughout the round. The angle

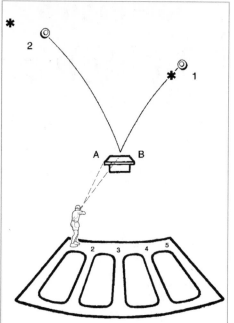

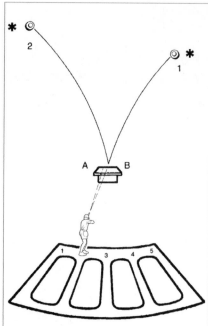

Station One: Line "A" shows proper natural point of aim to left-hand corner of the front of the house for a right-handed shooter (left-handers will want to move further left). Line "B" shows the gun hold moved back to the center of the trap house.

Station Two: Right-handers shift their natural point of aim back to a point half way between the corner and the center of the house.

to the shooter will change as he moves from station to station, but it will always be the same for that station.

This means the shooter can set up for a very quick shot on whichever bird he desires to shoot first and then swing right over for the second. Any shooter who has had experience at skeet doubles will find this familiar.

## Doubles Strategies

Here is a station-by-station look at how some of the best shooters approach this game.

### Station One

The right-hand bird is virtually a straightaway shot while the left-hand bird is an extreme right-to-left quartering shot. The most effective sequence is to set up the initial gun hold dead-on the straightaway. Take it just as fast as possible and then swing quickly over to the outgoing angled target.

The reason for taking the straightaway bird first is simple: it takes less gun movement and as soon as the gun fires the shooter can give all his attention to the tougher, angling bird. If the angling bird is shot first, the shooter is left with a long and possibly falling, straightaway shot that is easy to swing past and miss. In fact, if the straightaway is taken as the second

bird the shooter will actually have to stop his swing and aim deliberately at the bird. That is bad form with a smoothbore. For this reason, veteran doubles shooters recommend that the straightest-flying bird always ought to be shot first.

Right-handed shooters will not find this particularly difficult from station one because they can swing more easily to the left than to the right. If a shooter takes his natural point of aim about six inches to the left of the center of the trap house and then moves the gun back to dead center, he should then have all the body movement the shots require. Left-handed shooters may have to fudge more to the left.

### Station Two

The angle on the left bird is now decreased, while the right-hand bird gains a slight amount of angle to the right. It is no longer a true straightaway. Still, it is the straighter target and should be taken first. It will require shooting at the leading edge of the bird, but the lead is not much for a fast-swinging shooter. Right-handed shooters can position their natural point of aim at the center of the trap house, and most shooters will then have plenty of swing room left for the angled bird. Left-handed shooters may still have to fudge that position a bit to the left of the center of the trap house.

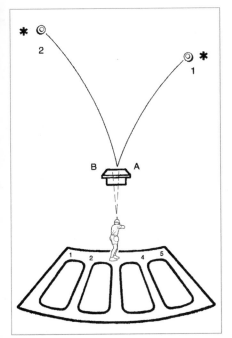

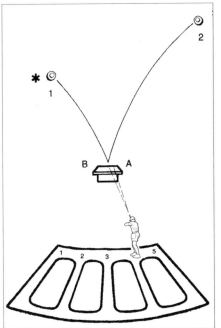

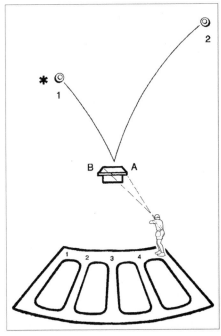

**Station Three:** Equal angle on both targets means the natural point of aim is brought six inches to the right of traphouse center with the gun hold shifted to traphouse center.

**Station Four:** This is the reverse of station two. A right-handed shooter will want a point of aim midway between the house center and right-hand front edge, and a gun hold at traphouse center. The left-hand bird is taken first here.

**Station Five:** This is one of the toughest shots for a right-handed shooter. He will want to take a point of aim to the right-front edge of the house, or maybe even a few feet outside, in order to have the swing room for the right-hand bird.

## Station Three

This is the toughest shot in the doubles game and it intimidates a lot of shooters. Neither bird is more straightaway than the other, and both leave the trap house diverging at a 45-degree angle. Here is where the known course of the target can really pay off.

One of the birds has to be shot first, of course, and many right-handed shooters find they will do better by taking the right-hand bird first, actually fudging their natural point of aim toward it. Their greater left-side swing arc will still give them plenty of time to take the left bird with the second shot. Neither bird will have a great degree of angle to its flight path and little lead is required. Knowing the exact flight path, the shooter can jump his first bird very quickly. Left-handed shooters often do better taking the left bird first.

None of this however is carved in stone. Some shooters find that reversing the above procedure pays off because they do better on long shots that have only a slight quartering angle on them. The shooter must experiment and see what works best for him.

## Station Four

We have now come to the reverse of station two. The left-hand bird becomes the more straightaway and should be taken first. Left-handed shooters can usually set up right on the center of the trap house, but right-handed shooters will likely have to shift their natural point of aim about six inches right of center to have the swing-room needed for the second bird.

## Station Five

This becomes the mirror image of station one, with the left-hand bird being a true straightaway and the right bird flying at an extreme angle. Right-handed shooters often have problems with this station because they fail to shift their natural point of aim far enough to the right to allow them to keep their cheek on the stock for the right-hand bird. I often shift my natural point of aim all the way to the right-hand corner of the trap house just for that reason. You do not need perfect body position on the first bird because it has no flight angle, but the second bird will get away if you run out of swing room. Left-handers often have this same problem on station one.

When a shooter sets up for shots in the above manner, gun movement for all shots becomes consistent. In essence, you square a corner with the gun: straight up on a vertical line for the first bird and straight across (with just a slight upward angle) for the second bird. There is no confusion and, with a little practice, you will find your gun goes to the second bird automatically, just like in skeet doubles.

The faster you can shoot the first target the better off you are, because you will be able to catch the second bird at a consistent spot on its flight path where it is still rising. Having a consistent second target is important because you do not have time to aim. You must swing through the shot and fire quickly, and if you catch the bird at a consistent spot you will have an easy time breaking it consistently.

Shooting the first target quickly is easy in this game because you know exactly where it will appear. Some top shooters who opt for high-shooting guns have refined their initial gun hold on the first target so well that they can break it with almost no gun movement. It becomes much like a skeet low house seven, in that respect.

One problem shooters often have with the first target is that they are thinking about the second one. They try to rush the first bird and often subconsciously start swinging the gun toward the second bird before they trigger the shot on the first. That kind of mistake will lose that first bird every time. One way to avoid this problem is to shoot a practice round of doubles, but only load a shell in the first barrel. Once you realize you cannot possibly get the second bird because there is no shell for it, the natural tendency is to make sure you get the first. Then swing the gun through the second bird and trigger your imaginary shot.

It sounds simple and unorthodox, but the exercise is designed to program your subconscious to make certain you get the first bird. For shooters who consistently have trouble with the first bird, this is a good way to get that on-board computer properly programmed. It does not do any good to hit every second bird if you miss all the first shots; your score is still only 25x50. You get the same score if you hit all the first birds and miss all the second shots. In either case, 25x50 is not a great score. It helps if you can whack both birds in a pair.

Some very good singles shooters often have trouble with the second bird. They fail to realize that the swing they must use to get from the first to the second bird is faster than the same swing they would use to take that bird as a single. If they use the same bird picture, they may well be shooting in front of that bird. A shooter who is consistently missing the second bird should not automatically assume he is behind it. Often, the reverse is actually true.

## Loads and Chokes

Loads and chokes for doubles trap are strictly a matter of personal choice, but it is my experience that many shooters are over-choked for the first bird. Modified is commonly considered to be the best choice for 16 Yard singles, and many shooters select it for their first shot on doubles. However, you have to consider that, because you know exactly where that first bird will be and because you are making a conscious effort to shoot it quickly, you may be taking that target significantly closer to the gun than you would in 16 Yard singles.

When I shoot doubles, I doubt seriously if the first bird gets any farther than 27 yards from the muzzle before I fire. That is almost in the range of a Skeet 1 choke and a load of #9. In fact, I know several shooters who use just that combination for their first shot. My first choice for the first barrel is a 1 1/8-ounce Federal #8 1/2 trap load from an Improved Cylinder choke. There is plenty of target-breaking power in that combination out to about 35 yards and I am not going to let the first target get that far away. The larger pattern, however, will get me some extra birds if I am having a "sloppy" day. If I am shooting one-ounce loads (either #8 1/2 or #8), I tighten down to a Skeet 2 choke, but that is as tight as I will go on the first barrel in doubles.

A Modified choke and #8 shot is much more powerful than one needs for the first target in doubles. The tighter pattern can cost you a slightly mis-pointed bird that a more open pattern would catch.

The second bird is an entirely different story.

The second target will generally be farther out than would be the case in singles. I normally use a Skeet 2 choke for singles with a load of either #8 1/2 or #8, because I am a fast shooter. That is not enough performance for a second bird in doubles, even though I am trying to get there quickly. In doubles, I shift to an Improved Modified choke with a full 1 1/8-ounce three-dram load of #8. For the second bird, most shooters find they need at least one choke tighter than they would in singles.

If you are shooting doubles with a single-barreled repeater having only one choke option, consider a Modified choke with a 1 1/8-ounce #9 Skeet load for the first shot. This load will open up a bit faster than larger shot sizes, giving what amounts to an Improved Cylinder pattern. You will have enough power to break targets to a bit beyond 30 yards. Go with a three-dram 1 1/8-ounce trap load for the second shot. If you reload, consider using softer chilled shot for those #9 to open the pattern for the first shot Then, stick to premium hard shot for the second load.

Doubles trap may be a bit more challenging than other trap games, but in my opinion it is a lot more fun. I have also found it to be excellent practice for sporting clays because you will see many of those kinds of shots on the sporting fields. It is a game well worth playing, especially if you want to learn other games.

# CHAPTER 6

# INTERNATIONAL TRAP

Members of the international competitive shooting community seldom embrace the shooting games that we enjoy in the U.S. They seem to regard the American versions as rigid, somewhat stuffy, and so easy that top shooters can regularly shoot perfect scores. When we look at our trap game and compare it to the international version, even the staunchest patriot has to agree with them.

The result is that competitive shooting events held under the banner of the International Shooting Union or UIT (Union International de Tir, the governing body for international shooting sports) have been modified to increase the level of difficulty and make them far more challenging. That is certainly true for the international version of trap or, as it is sometimes called, "bunker trap" or even "trench trap."

## Trap Machines

The difference in the international and standard U.S. game starts with the machines used to throw the targets. American-style or ATA trap as it will be referred to from this point, uses one clay bird machine that is set to vary the target spread. The machine is placed at ground level and throws targets within a 45-degree arc. The speed of each ATA target is fixed at about 41 mph.

From behind the shooting line, the experienced clay shooter may be puzzled by the layout of international or bunker trap. Just wait until the birds start to fly! Targets fly faster and the angles are more extreme than in American trap. From the front of the bunker, one begins to understand the challenge that international shooters undertake.

Double trap requires a slight change in tactics compared to those used in standard, International trap. Since all targets come out of the trap house at a rising angle, a shooter can use the high gun hold favored by ATA shooters. Unlike in sporting clays, most coaches advise their students to take the trailing bird first and then swing through to the leading target.

International trap uses 15 separate machines, all placed below ground level. Each launcher is adjusted to throw at a specific angle. There are five shooting stations, as in ATA trap, and three machines are allocated for each station. For example, a shooter on station three will take targets only from trap launchers seven, eight and nine. The left-hand trap (the number seven trap) will throw birds at an angle to the right, and the right-hand trap (number nine) throws them to the left. Instead of the maximum ATA angle of 22 degrees from center, the International angle can be as much as 45 degrees for a total arc of 90 degrees. The center trap throws a straightaway bird.

The elevation of the targets is also more varied and can be extreme. ATA targets are fixed to throw at a single elevation, about 30 degrees. International targets may be launched anywhere within a window of 3.0 to 3.5 meters above ground at a point measured 10 meters in front of the trap house. Targets from a trap set to the lowest elevation may travel 70 yards and never rise more than one meter off the ground. The next target thrown may skyrocket almost straight up.

The same variation also exists in target speed. A low target that travels 70 meters may reach a speed of 60 mph and fly directly away from the shooter. That is one of the fastest clay targets that you will ever see. A target thrown at a more vertical angle, one that covers only 60 to 65 meters, will be significantly slower.

The conclusion is that international targets travel farther, faster and at angles twice as extreme as anything seen on a regulation ATA trap field.

Allowed international loads make things more difficult also. The 12-gauge is standard and the maximum allowable shot charge is 24 grams, or about ⅞-ounce. ATA shooters are allowed to use up to 1 ⅛ ounces of shot.

A round of international trap consists of the same 25 targets as ATA, but international shooters get a break here. They are allowed to fire twice at any target and it scores just as dead if it is hit with the first or second shot.

In ATA trap, a shooter fires five rounds per station and rotates to the next station. Not so in the international game. A shooter fires one round and then rotates immediately to the next station. It is a game of constant movement with the shooter making five complete passes down the line. During the course of the round, the shooter receives two targets from the right-hand trap machine, two from the left, and one from the center at each numbered station. Birds are thrown in random order and the shooter does not know what is coming next. Some shooters however, try to remember what has been thrown (much like a blackjack player counting cards). They feel this gives them a slight advantage near the end of the round when they may know (or think they know) what target remains to be thrown from a specific station. Of course, if they make a mistake and are waiting intently for a target that has already been thrown, they are probably going to miss.

Over/unders dominate the international game. Most shooters favor a choke in the .018- to .022-inch constriction range (about Modified) for the first barrel and often use the same #8 ½ shot size favored by international skeet shooters. A fast shooter will generally get onto a target with the first barrel at a range of 25 to 30 yards and #8 ½ pellets have plenty of target-breaking power at that range. Given the increase in pellet count in the load and the more open choke, the gun will throw a wider pattern. The second barrel, however, will be choked down to the Full range (.028- to .032-inch) and stuffed with a #7 ½-size load in the event the shooter misses with the first barrel because the bird must then be broken at a greater range.

## Changes in Technique

The international version of trap is a good bit more challenging than the ATA version, and it requires a change in technique to shoot well. Few people understand the differences (and the changes required) as well as Lloyd Woodhouse, longtime coach of our U.S. Olympic shotgun team.

"The first change an ATA shooter will need to make,"

## International (Bunker) Trap Classification

| Classification | Singles | Doubles |
|---|---|---|
| Master AA | 93.00 percent and up | 90.00 percent and up |
| A | 87.00 – 92.99 percent | 80.00 - 89.99 percent |
| B | 80.00 - 86.99 percent | 70.00 - 79.99 percent |
| C | 73.00 - 79.99 percent | below 73.00 percent |
| D | Below 73.00 percent | Below 60 percent |

Woodhouse notes, "is in his initial gun hold. The ATA version allows you to hold at a higher point over the trap house because those targets will always come up from under the gun. In the international game, you cannot do that, because a low target will run right underneath your barrel and be completely blocked from your vision. You may not even see the target until it is way out in the field and about ready to hit the ground."

The philosophy of holding a lower gun is, as we will see later, the same as that used in sporting clays to prevent the barrel from blocking one's visual acquisition of the bird. Woodhouse recommends shooters adjust in the following manner.

"There are five marks on the front of the trap house, facing the shooter," he explains. "Each mark locates the center trap for that particular station. It also marks the point at which the targets from the right- and left-hand traps will cross on the field. This is a physical mark, and most successful shooters will hold their muzzle right on that mark to make sure that the target always comes out above the gun."

The extreme angles that can be thrown require that shooters adjust their foot position or natural point of aim as well.

"Most shooters will have a wider swing range to the off side (swinging to the left for a right-hander) and still be able to stay with the gun, meaning keeping their cheek firmly on the stock and their head down. A long swing to the strong side (right swing for a right-hander) will often cause the gun and shooter to separate," states Woodhouse. "For this reason I recommend that the natural point of aim be moved slightly to the strong side. I would suggest that a right-handed shooter take a natural point of aim six inches to the right of the house mark and then swing the gun back to the mark when calling for the target. The reverse would be true for a left-handed shooter. This helps increase the swing range to the strong side to accommodate the severe angles in international trap."

## Second Shots

Another factor that American shooters find both fascinating and at times disconcerting is the second shot that is allowed should their first shot miss. The second shot is, unbelievably, a difficult habit to accept for ATA trap shooters. When the shot is fired in that game, whether the bird is hit or missed, well-taught shooters will dismount their gun. This becomes an automatic, subconscious response and it can be difficult to change. The second shot in international trap must be a subconscious response, in and of itself, and that has to be learned through practice, too.

Many international shooters train to force their second shot, even if the first hits. This way the second shot becomes as automatic as the first. Here is how Coach Woodhouse suggests this be done: "I encourage shooters to fire both barrels, even if the first barrel scores," he explains, "but only under certain conditions."

Woodhouse says that if you get into the habit of breaking the target with the first shot, and not shooting the second (because there is no reason to), then you become complacent. "You start coming out of the gun," he says, "pulling the gun away from your cheek after the first shot. If you miss the target with the first barrel, then you are doomed because you are coming off the gun and the target will get away from you.

"However, just triggering the second shot after you break the target with the first one is no good either because it conditions your subconscious to shoot at nothing. You don't have a target. I tell my shooters to do one of two things. If you hit the target with the first barrel, then pick a piece of that broken target and follow it with your eyes and gun until it hits the ground. If you are in a good position and feel very confident that you can break that piece of target, then shoot it. If not, and you don't feel confident, then just follow it down."

Either way, Woodhouse feels the shooter is now alert, "with" his gun and still following targets in the target zone. "If you ever require a second shot," he says, "this becomes a perfect rehearsal for those times, because it makes you keep the gun alive and the shooter stays ready to shoot. Lastly, breaking a little piece of target the size of a quarter at 40-plus yards is a tremendous confidence-booster. It's a very positive thing for the shooter."

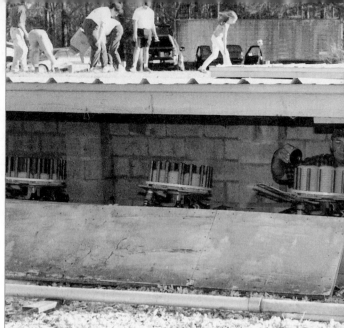

The view inside the international bunker and from the outside looking in. The variety of possible targets that can be thrown makes anticipating the exact angle and speed extremely difficult.

## Double Trap

If international trap sounds like a tough game, there is an even tougher version called "Double Trap." This game is now incorporated into international competition for both men and women.

Double trap uses the same 15-trap layout as the singles game, but only the three trap launchers on station three (numbers seven, eight and nine) are used. As competitors rotate between stations, the angle at which they are shown the targets from the center machines will change the nature of their shots.

Three basic setups, or schemes, can be used in this game. Each uses only two of the three traps, with a pair of birds launched simultaneously.

The "A Scheme" uses trap launchers seven and eight. Trap seven is fixed at an angle five degrees to the left of dead center with station three, and at a height of 3.5 meters at a point measured 10 meters in front of the trap house. Trap eight is set at zero degrees (a dead straightaway from station three) at a three-meter height. Both targets travel 50 meters, which means their speeds are slower than international trap. They more resemble ATA target speed and their speeds are constant throughout the round.

The "B Scheme" uses traps eight and nine. The number eight trap is a dead straightaway at a 3.5-meter height, while the number nine trap is set at a three-meter height and five degrees to the right.

The final or "C Scheme" uses traps seven and nine, with a setting of five degrees left and right, respectively, and at a three-meter height.

The speed of double trap targets is the same, regardless of the scheme.

A round of double trap consists of 25 pairs, or 50 targets. In competition, this is repeated three times for 150 birds, which is followed by a 25 pair shoot-off round for the top shooters.

"Although this game is relatively new," says Coach Woodhouse, "it is here to stay in international competition."

## Double Trap Tactics

Double trap requires a slight change in tactics compared to those used in standard international trap.

Since all targets come out of the trap house at a rising angle, a shooter can use the higher gun hold favored by ATA shooters. Because the speeds are slower and the angles and target order are known to competitors, the first bird can be jumped on quickly. Most shooters opt for a relatively open Modified choke with the #8 ½-shot international load for the first barrel. The second barrel will be choked tighter with a #7 ½-shot load.

"In all schemes," Woodhouse explains, "the targets will appear essentially as leading and trailing birds. Just as in sporting clays, I advise my shooters to take the trailing target first and then swing through to the leading target. This avoids the shooter standing there with a 'dead gun,' or having to make complicated changes in gun direction and speed."

Although that sounds uncomplicated and straightforward, double trap is not easy. In fact, if you compare the score percentages that are used to rank shotgun competitors into various classes for the different games, you will see that a shooter can miss a lot more double trap targets and still be a Master (AA) class shooter than at any other game.

This is what makes double trap so challenging.

# CHAPTER 7

# TOP GUNS FOR TRAP

Practically all clay target games, trap included, began as an attempt to duplicate field shots on actual game birds. To an extent, the current game does that just fine. However, it only applies to flushing birds moving quickly away from the gunner and rising as they do so. Birds having that flight pattern include the occasional pheasant, quail, sharp-tail grouse, Chukar partridge and perhaps woodcock. The fact that trap targets are launched at a speed far higher than any game bird can achieve on the flush (at least 42 mph for singles and 39 mph doubles) actually makes modern trap an optical illusion. Real birds rise in flight, but they do not do it very quickly.

What a trapshooter gets when he calls for a bird is a target that appears to be moving away from him, either as a straightaway or at a quartering angle, yet is actually rising quickly.

This means that shooters need a gun that will place the shot charge above the actual point of hold to compensate for the sharp climb of the target. If the gun shoots "flat," as we would want for skeet, sporting clays, or perhaps a hunting gun, then a shooter must actually cover the target with the muzzle of the gun, swinging right up through the target and blocking it out. Since that causes a shooter to lose sight of the target at the critical moment he triggers the shot, a flat-shooting gun becomes a factor that will decrease the shooter's score.

As a result, guns that win in trap are those that place the center of their pattern above the point of aim. In some cases, depending on the shooter, that might be as little as three inches at 40 yards. Other shooters favor a much higher shooting gun, as much built-in elevation as 18 inches at that range.

This "hold over" can be achieved simply by installing a different rib on the barrel or experimenting with sight beads and their placement. Others choose to modify their stock, replace the fixed stock with an adjustable stock or add a padded cheek-sleeve…others simply take lessons and practice.

Some shooters force the gun to shoot high by having a certified gunsmith bend the barrel ever so slightly upwards. Although it is not obvious to the naked eye, such a micro-bend will elevate the shot pattern. All things considered, however, having the barrel bent is less desirable than purchasing a new barrel-rib combination or having the rib replaced. Bending the barrel of an expensive shotgun would almost certainly be foolish, and with barrels varying in expense but cost-

ing in some cases less than $150, it would be more satisfying to purchase a new barrel for a relatively inexpensive brand.

The most common way to produce a high-shooting gun is to raise the comb height. This effectively raises your eye, which functions as the rear sight, and the gun will then shoot higher. This is accomplished with either a detachable cheekpiece or with a high-combed stock. Most guns marketed as trap guns will have a drop at comb of 1 ⅜ inches, instead of the 1 ½ inches that is almost standard for field-grade guns. On the other hand, the Browning Citori XT Trap over/under with a tapered, floating top rib has a 1 ⁹⁄₁₆-inch drop at comb, thus showing perhaps that every "rule" is made to be broken.

Another factor that determines an effective trap gun is its handling quality. Stand behind a skeet shooter addressing a mid-field crossing bird and you will see him swing the gun through a degree of lateral movement that will cover a range of up to 15 yards as he tracks and breaks the target. Stand behind a trap shooter, and you will see that even the most extreme bird angle will not cause him to move the gun more than a few degrees from his starting stance. That movement must be very quick and forceful, and must drive through the target. That driving motion has proven to be best accomplished with a longer, heavier gun, the inertial force helping swing the gun. The most effective trap guns are those with barrels in excess of 30 inches in length and with a weight of 8 ½ to 9 ½ pounds. Again, the Browning Citori figures at the lower end of that weight scale, coming in at 8 ½ pounds, but only with the 32-inch barrel; the 30-inch barrel weighs only 8 ⅜ pounds.

Trap shooters also favor tighter chokes than those pursuing skeet and sporting clays. A fast trap shooter, shooting from the 16-yard line, might get onto a target when the bird is at a range of 25 yards. More likely, it will be 30 yards. If he or she is a little slower, the bird could be 35 to 40 yards away from him. A Modified choke is considered to be a relatively open choke for trap, although it is probably the best-all-around choice for the 16-yard game if the shooter is using quality, hard-shot loads. The handicap and doubles games are best played with Improved Modified or even a Full choke constriction.

An experienced competitor engaging targets from the 27-yard handicap line is looking at shots of 40 to 50 yards and may even opt for Extra-Full choking.

If a shooter plays the doubles game or international trap, he needs a gun capable of firing two shots. If he just shoots 16-yard and handicap singles, a single-barrel gun works just fine. Those who play all the trap games sometimes use a two-barrel set: an over/under receiver that is fitted with a single barrel and a set of double barrels.

The ardent trap shooter can end up with a gun that has a very limited application for any other shooting game or actual fieldwork. Long, heavy and tightly choked, the trap gun is a specialized tool for a specialized game. If you want to win this game, you will need one.

A note of caution before proceeding to the guns section. Numerous companies, both manufacturers and importers/distributors, advertise that they have trap guns in their line-up. Some truly do and some truly do not. A "trap gun" usually incorporates a few special design items that help one shoot rising birds flying straight away at high speed:

- built to shoot high to catch a fast-rising bird – high tapered, adjustable ribs and high or adjustable stock comb
- a longer barrel – up to 35 inches
- heavier, to help swing through the pitching clay
- available with fixed or interchangeable Full or Extra-Full chokes

Manufacturers naturally want to please their customers and increase their loyal following, and thus they want to appeal to all shooters and all games. Realizing that the primary element in breaking clay is the shooter and the secondary element is the gun (or, some would argue, the load), any gun might do—even though we have not discussed pump guns in the gun-specific copy—and thus some guns labeled as "trap guns" are simply a company's standard field or sporting gun with a different label.

So the caution is to differentiate between truly specialized guns and those which are probably excellent shooters but do not incorporate any of the elements that help a shooter break fast rising and going-away birds. Watch for the guns that will give you the advantage, that will take your form or style and enhance it for better scores.

## Off-the-Rack & Custom Guns

While top trap-shooting outfits tend to be expensive and specialized on the long and heavy side, you do not need a specialized trap gun if you just want to go out and shoot for fun. An aerial target is an aerial target. It flies, you shoot it. That can be done quite nicely with any shotgun, although it does get a little tough with the sub-gauges, especially the 410 and 28-gauge.

If you want to take your Mossberg, Winchester or Remington hunting pump gun out to the trap range, do it. For that matter, try trap with any make or model shotgun you happen to own. If it has only a fixed Improved Cylinder choke, don't worry about that either. If you miss the bird, though, do not blame the gun and choke. Just remember on the next shot to swing through your target. Use a 1 ⅛-ounce 12-gauge trap load. If you decide that you want to be a serious trap competitor, then you can consider a specialized trap gun, but you do not need it to start.

When you are ready for a specialized trap gun, here is a look at the best ones currently available. Unless otherwise noted, all are chambered for 12-gauge shells. A number of recognized and quality custom manufacturers are not included, but can easily be located with an internet search even if, as in the case of Alfermann USA, they do not have a web site.

First, a word about shotgun ribs. All new shotguns come with a rib. Find a shotgun without a rib and it will probably be a venerable old gun, someone's "truck gun." A rib is a sighting alignment device of the sort we refuse to acknowledge as important in shotgunning where we talk about pointing rather than aiming. If this were strictly true, if we were pointers instead of aimers, we would not need ribs or the beads or aiming devices on the ribs.

Most trap masters shoot from a pre-mounted gun. Before calling "pull," they consciously use the rib and the traditional front and middle beads to ensure correct placement of the head against the stock and hence, proper alignment of the gun. Exclusive trap shooters are easily recognizable in the club house because their guns are the ones with extremely high ribs. Their high rib lowers the barrel's bore axis and may reduce felt recoil, especially to the face, and almost any modification that reduces (not "eliminates," because I would argue that some recoil is necessary to good shooting) recoil is going to increase your scores.

Last, a word about choke on European guns, which is often indicated by stars or asterisks. CYL indicates true cylinder or none at all, since the bore diameter nine inches forward of the breech is the same as at the muzzle. Otherwise, * = Full choke (0.9-1.0mm constriction); ** = ¾ (0.7-0.8mm); *** = ½ (0.4-0.6mm) and **** = Improved Cylinder (0.2-0.3mm).

## Baikal (Remington-Spartan, EAA)

www.baikalinc.ru
www.remington-spartan.com
www.eaacorp.com

Baikal shotguns are built in Russia by Izhevsky Mekhanichesky Zavod, IMZ. Once imported by European American Armory (EAA), Remington took that franchise and began bringing them into the U.S. under the Spartan label. EAA advertised if you want a pretty gun, one that costs so much that it virtually requires you to carry it in a fancy case, you should "buy the competition's gun." Remington Spartan suggested that farmers might purchase them for predator shooting because the guns were "made specifically for the more cost frugal shooter." The point (and this is reinforced by commentary in on-line chat rooms) seems to be that the Russian guns are quite serviceable, without being too fancy or too expensive.

On the other hand, the MP-39 over/under 12-gauge from Baikal is a good looking gun although the English translation of their web site swears it is ideal for every type of shooting. The trap version, Baikal says, is also excellent "for waterfowling at passage," presumably indicating longer distance shooting than jumping a grouse in the quakies. The M-39 has a single selective trigger unit, and the chrome-plated trap barrels measure 750 mm or 29.5 inches. The top barrel is choked Extra-Full and the bottom choked Full. The forend and stock are walnut. The MP-39E offers a selective ejector that can be switched on or off. Baikal says this gun is quite similar to the MP-27M, which comes in all gauges.

Curiously, the Remington-Spartan.com Internet site explicitly states, "This site is not affiliated with the manufacturer. This website is a privately owned company that retails the products of the manufacturer." Nevertheless, there is an over/under Russian shotgun in the Remington-Spartan line that is very similar to the MP-39—the SPR 310, which features nickel plated or blued steel receivers, cross bolt safety systems, cocking indicator, titanium coated trigger, checkered walnut stock and forends. In addition, the forged barrels—28 inches in the 12-gauge configuration—are chrome lined and the gun includes a single selective trigger and a rubber recoil pad, and retails for around $500.

Baikal's Remington SPR100 is a single barrel 12-gauge that will be good for singles trap shooting. Its 29 ½-inch barrel gives it a 44 ½-inch overall length. The SPR weighs only 6 ½ pounds, but has a 3-inch chamber and comes with four chokes: Cylinder, Improved Cylinder, Modified and Full. A look around on the Internet finds the 12-gauge SPR100 for $110, although the 20-gauge and 410-bore go for about twice that.

## Beretta

www.berettausa.com

The operating principle of Beretta's new UGB25 Xcel semiautomatic with break-open barrel is short recoil, designed to keep internal parts of the gun clean even after prolonged use. The short recoil helps compensate for muzzle jump, with quicker and easier realignment for a follow-up shot. The low barrel axis transmits recoil in line with the shooter's shoulder, thus minimizing felt recoil.

The UGB25 Xcel's cartridge carrier holds a second cartridge on the right-hand side of the receiver, making it immediately ready for use. It chambers automatically through the feeding port after the first round has been fired. The design of the cartridge carrier button and its position on the receiver ensure easy removal of a cartridge on the carrier.

The ejection port is in the bottom of the receiver. The ejector expels spent hulls downward, away from the shooter and nearby competitors, and is user-friendly for both right- and left-hand shooters.

With 30- or 32-inch chromed barrels, this new 12-gauge semi-auto with break-open barrel is—uncharacteristic for Beretta —chambered for 2 ¾ shells. A fully-adjustable stock for length of pull (14.09 to 14.88 inches) and comb height is caped with a GelTek recoil pad. The gun weighs 8.1 to 9.0 pounds.

Beretta's DT10 Trident 12-gauge over/under with 3-inch chamber ($7,400) has been in Beretta's line-up for several years. Barrels in 30 or 32 inches are available and the DT10 comes with five interchangeable chokes. The gun is sold in a padded, hard-sided case and features a gold-plated single selective trigger (adjustable for length of pull), field removable trigger group, palm swell and adjustable comb. The stock and forend are gloss finished checkered walnut. Drop at comb is 1 ½-inches; drop at heel is 2 ¼ inches on the straight comb and 1 ½-inches on a gun with a Monte Carlo stock. The flat 10x8 rib includes a white front bead and steel mid-bead; weight is 8.8 pounds. The DT10 can be special ordered with left-hand cast, including a left-hand palm swell and trigger shoe.

The Beretta 12-gauge 682 Gold E Trap over/under with an adjustable stock carries a suggested retail price of $4,425. This Italian gun's Optima-Bore barrel has a "long forcing cone and over-bored internal bore diameter." Barrels are available in 30 or 32 inches. Four chokes are included as is a hard-sided case with room for the gun, choke set and spare parts. The gold-plated trigger is adjustable for length of pull and the 682 Gold E comes with two trigger shoes. The progressive step rib is ⅜ by ⅜ inch.

The 682 Gold E has a 3-inch chamber, low profile box lock action, and features a checkered Monte Carlo walnut stock and forend. The adjustable comb is complemented by a palm swell and can be special ordered with left hand cast, including left hand palm swell and trigger shoe. Drop at comb is 1 ½-inches and drop at heel is 2 ¼ inches. The 682E weighs 8.8 pounds. A serious over/under gun for serious shooters, this model is built for versatility and durability, right down to replaceable bearing shoulders on the monobloc and hinge pins.

The 12-gauge 682 Gold E Trap Unsingle ($4,825) is

designed for American Trap. The single-barrel-only version is available solely with the 34-inch barrel and adjustable rib. Two combo versions are available, each with a 34-inch adjustable bottom single: over/under barrels in 30- and 32-inch lengths. Barrels have a white front bead and steel mid-bead.

All 682 Gold E Unsingle models are equipped with a factory adjustable comb with and adjustable trigger shoe. The Unsingle has a low profile improved box lock receiver built with nickel-alloy steel for strength and durability. Chambered for 3-inch shells, the Unsingle has a checkered walnut stock and forend. Dimensions in inches are drop at comb 1 ½, drop at heel 2 ¼ and weight 8.8 pounds.

The suggested retail price of Beretta's 12-gauge, 3-inch AL391 Teknys Gold Trap autoloader is $2,200. This gun comes with three chokes and a choice of 30- or 32-inch barrels. The AL391 is a semiautomatic, gas-operated gun with self-compensating exhaust valve. The checkered stock and forend are oil-finished walnut and the receiver features colored enamel inserts. Drop at comb is 1 ⅓ inches and drop at heel is 2 ⅓ inches. The Gel-Tek recoil pad consists of a soft polymer shell and an inert, recoil-absorbing silicon gel core that is unaffected by temperature or time.

The AL391 is "accessorized" with a gold-plated trigger that contrasts with the satin, nickel-finished receiver and its raised flat rib is ⅜ by ⁵⁄₁₆ inch. This rib is interchangeable with an included tapered rib especially for trap. The barrel is topped with a white front bead and a steel mid-bead. Fitted into the buttstock is an 8 ½-ounce recoil reducer. This gun weighs 8.0 pounds.

## Blaser

www.blaser.de

www.blaser-usa.com

Technically, it is Blaser Jagdwaffen GmbH in Isny im Allgäu, Bavaria in extreme southern Germany. These guns are imported through Blaser USA in San Antonio.

Blaser's F3 line, launched in 2004, includes both competition trap and American trap models. The American trap gun comes in 12-gauge, 3-inch over/under, unsingle or combo versions. Briley Spectrum Choketubes are included: for the over/under Impoved Modified (.025) and Full (.034), and for the unsingle, Full (.034).

Over/under (32-inch) and Under-Single or unsingle (34-inch) barrels are factory set to throw 60-40, "based on the classic Figure 8 sighting plane." The free-floating rib on the F3 Under-Single is fully adjustable both at the muzzle and at the rear elevation point. This allows not only for adjustment of the pattern by lifting or lowering the bead, but also allows the competitive shooter to adjust the angle of the rib by raising or lowering its rear end for achieving the preferred sighting-plane. The pattern of the Under-Single barrel can be increased from 50/50 to 10% by adjusting the rib. Lifting the bead changes the pattern downwards while lowering the bead changes the pattern upwards.

The F3 American Trap has a high Monte Carlo walnut stock and weighs about 9 pounds. Length of pull is 14.6 inches.

Blaser is one of the few companies that, in its Competition Trap (Olypmic and DoubleTrap) model offers 34-inch over/under barrels as well as the standard 28-, 30- and 32-inch barrels. Barrels are topped with either a tapered 10.5mm to 8.5mm rib or a 10.5mm parallel rib.

The Blaser "balancer" in the stock is a threaded rod with two weight cylinders and it replaces the normal stock nut inside the stock. The balancer allows individual adjustment of weight distribution and compensates for possible differences in the wood density. Expect to pay $7,500 or more for a new Blaser F3.

## Bowen Custom

www.bbguns.net

Bruce Bowen builds custom single-barrel trap guns, and custom guns from any special builder are not for the novice. After all, Bowen likes customers to travel to his factory in Sturgis, South Dakota, for a custom stock fitting. His plant has an indoor shooting and testing range. Alternatively, interested shooters should make an appointment to meet him at a national event for a personal measurement before valuable maple is cut for a stock.

A 9-pound Bowen custom trap gun is available with all the bells and whistles. The elevated, ventilated trap rib may be ordered with a choice of point of impact: 100%, 80%, 70% or 60%. The .740-inch bore 12-gauge barrel is available in 32- through 35-inch lengths and comes only in a Full, fixed choke version. Bowen will build a custom gun with either a standard pull or release trigger, but both are included in the base price of $16,500.

Stocks, too, are custom-built to a customer's interests and measurements. Bowen cuts each block of walnut by CNC to a rough dimension and then hand shapes and polishes the stock to the individual measurements required by a shooter. Straight or Monte Carlo stocks are available from custom English or Claro walnut. If desired, Bowen will build adjustability into your comb. Engraving is available and can be individually designed and the price negotiated.

## Browning

(www.browning.com)

Any shotgun will break a clay target. Certain throws of the trap, however, are best approached with guns that incorporate specific, small details. The devil is, as

Browning's 12-gauge 2 ¾ BT-99 is a very serviceable though modestly priced single-barrel, break-action shotgun with either 32- or 34-inch barrels. Its high post ventilated rib is just right for handicap trap where one makes longer shots.

they say, in the details. Browning offers a bucket-load of shotguns in every gauge—although at times their gauge seems to be stuck on 12—and they are all serviceable weapons. Some, indeed, border on the superior and all will bust a number on a bird.

Before attending to the stock guns in Browning's catalog, it is worthwhile mentioning that a group of "non-cataloged" trap-ready shotguns is designated for Omaha, Nebraska's Guns Unlimited (www.gunsunlimitedomaha.com). Although described as "unadvertised," these Citoris are also available in the regular lineup. Go figure. Their specified drop at comb is usually 1 %16-inch; drop at heel, two inches. Tapered, high post ribs are ¼ to ⅜ inches wide. Browning's Triple Trigger system allows you to adjust a Citori's 14 ⅜-inch length of pull and switch between three gold-plated trigger shoes: wide checkered, narrow smooth, and wide smooth canted. The optional adjustable comb has ⅝-inch height adjustment and a right-hand palm swell. Includes highly polished Full, Improved Modified and Modified interchangeable, stainless steel screw-in Invector-Plus choke tubes.

Citori XT Trap Combo: A 12-gauge with 2 ¾-inch chamber, this Citori has .742 back-bored, factory ported barrels for increased shot velocity, more uniform patterns and reduced recoil. It is available with 30- or 32-inch over/under, 32- or 34-inch single barrels and either Monte Carlo or adjustable comb stocks. In Grade I, a 30-inch over/under with a 32-inch single barrel is $3,295 with Monte Carlo stock; an adjustable comb is an additional $200. The Golden Clays version of this gun is $4,595.

Citori XT Trap Unsingle Combo: As the name suggests, the unsingle barrel is fired by the under-barrel firing pin. The unsingle barrel thus sits low in the receiver, which, in theory, results in reduced muzzle flip and perhaps in less felt recoil. With this unsingle combo, introduced at the 2006 Grand American, a shooter can dial in rib adjustability from a 60/40 point of impact to a 90/10 point of impact. The combo comes with a hard case and a choice of either Monte Carlo stock or adjustable comb. It is available with 30- or 32-inch over/under barrels and 32- or 34-inch single barrels.

Expect to pay $3,795 for Grade I and $5,095 for Golden Clays; an adjustable comb is $200 extra.

Browning introduced its single barrel, 2 ¾-inch chambered smoothbore BT-99 trap gun, in 1969. Although it was originally a less expensive alternative to a gun like the Citori, it is now available in styles and prices from the no-frill Conventional model at $1,329 to the Golden Clays version with adjustable stock and comb at $3,989.

Available with either 32- or 34-inch barrels, with a high-step ¹¹⁄₃₂-inch-wide floating rib, these guns are back-bored and fitted for the Browning Invector-Plus choke tube system with three choke tubes supplied. With the 34-inch barrel, the 51-inch BT-99 weighs eight pounds, five ounces. The stock configuration is conventional, with a length of pull of 14 ⅜ inches; drop at comb 1 ⅜ and a drop at heel from 1 ⅝ to 2 inches, depending upon the model.

A BT-99 redesigned in a lighter, smaller package that Browning says is ideal "for smaller-framed shooters," the BT-99 Micro is available with a 32- (seven pounds, 13 ounces) or a 30-inch barrel. Although other dimensions remain the same as the standard BT-99, the length of pull has been shortened to 13 ¾ inches. MSRP is $1,549.

The $3,539 Cynergy Classic Trap has an engraved silver nitride receiver and gloss-finished Monte Carlo walnut stock with right-hand palm swell. The forearm is a modified semi-beavertail forearm with finger grooves. This 12-gauge comes with three stainless steel Invector-Plus chokes which extend beyond the barrel for easier installation and removal. The floating rib is tapered from 8 to 11mm and topped with a HiViz Pro-Comp fiber optic sight and mid-length bead. The Classic Trap is chambered for 2 ¾-inch shells and is available with 32- or 30-inch ported barrels in weights of 8 pounds, 12-ounce and 8 pounds, 10 ounces respectively. The 1 ¹⁄₁₆-inch drop at comb is complemented with a 2-inch drop at heel and 14 ⅜-inches length of pull. Three gold-plated triggers are included. The Cynergy Classic Trap is also available as an unsingle combo with or without an adjustable comb.

## Charles Daly

www.charlesdaly.com

Charles Daly is not an original manufacturer, but an importer that brands the items they bring into the U.S. Often their guns and scopes are made in Turkey.

The Charles Daly Model 206 Trap ($1,062) is a 12-gauge over/under. It features a ventilated 10mm rib and ventilated side rib. The 30-inch barrel is factory ported and comes with a mid bead, front fiber optic sight and five multi-chokes. Expect single selective automatic ejectors. The 206 Trap weighs 7 ½ pounds and other dimensions (in inches) are: overall length is 47, length of pull 14 ⅛, drop at heel 2 ½ and drop at comb 1½. The walnut Monte Carlo stock and forearm are satin finished.

In gas guns, the Superior II Trap ($739) is a 12-gauge with a 30-inch factory ported barrel topped by a 10mm rib with a red, fluorescent front sight and a mid-rib bead. Three screw-in extended choke tubes are included. The Monte Carlo stock and forearm are glossy coated walnut. The Superior II Trap weighs 7 ¼ pounds and other dimensions (in inches) are: overall length is 49 ⅞, length of pull 14 ⅜, drop at heel 2 ⅛ and drop at comb ¹³⁄₈.

## DeVault Industries

(www.devaultind.com)

While there are many custom stock makers, Dennis DeVault is one of a few custom builders specializing in complete trap guns. "One hundred percent of the work is done in house, too," he says. And DeVault's interest is as much in rib design and quashing recoil as it is in grades wood.

The 12-gauge Infinity is the standard DeVault trap gun. It is based on DeVault's original, 10 ½-pound MachOne, which dates from 1992. Infinity steel barrels are 33 inches long with .740 bores. They are built for extended Briley chokes, three of which come with a purchase (Modified .020, Improved Modified.025 and Light Full.030).

DeVault also specializes in ramped ribs and offers five different adjustable and interchangeable ribs for an infinite point of impact: ¾-inch sloped to ⁵⁄₁₆ or ½, ⅞-inch sloped to ⁵⁄₁₆, and 1 ¼-inch sloped to ⁷⁄₁₆ or ⅝. DeVault says it was the first company to build with a free-floating rib design that is adjustable and also interchangeable.

The single barrel Infinity ($10,900 includes custom fitting at a nearby shooting range in Ohio) follows current shotgun design with a small profile receiver: 1 3/8 inches thick and only 2 ¼ inches high. "With the radius on the top of the receiver your viewing area around the gun is greatly expanded," says the DeVault web site. "This low profile sets the barrel further

**The Infinity from DeVault Industries can be ordered with a variety of ribs designed just for trap shooters. Such otherwise highly stylized ribs give trap shooters a choice of point of impact, important when shooting rising, going-away birds.**

down in the receiver allowing recoil to came straight back and not up in the face." Receivers are 100 percent machined from 17-4 forged stainless.

Stocks with four-way adjustable combs are built to custom specifications from English or Claro Walnut, "as supply allows." The stock has no bolt hole and this allows for a generous 1 ¾-inch depth of cut comb. "With no bolt hole," DeVault says, "we dropped the pistol grip down and we can now put as much toe out, offset and heel drop for a deep drop Monte Carlo as a shooter needs. Many people have asked why the gun is lighter and kicks less. With no bolt hole, the recoil does not travel back the bolt and transfer the recoil to the shoulder. The wood acts as a buffer and absorbs some of the felt recoil through the wood density."

Devault's new Ultra Rib is for the shooter that needs a 22- to 26-inch POI. "This allows the guy with the long neck to get his head up-right and in perfect position," says DeVault. The Ultra is available in two POI (point of impact) configurations, from 80-20% to 140%.

## F.A.I.R.

www.fair.it

Here is another shotgun from Brescia, Italy. In business since 1971, the 2 ¾-chambered trap over/unders—Master de Luxe, Master and SRL 802—are available in either 12- or 20-gauge. The 29 ¾- or 30-inch barrels have ventilated upper and side ribs. Topped with an interchangeable bright dot sight , the top rib is 11mm on 12-gauge guns and 9mm on the 20-gauge. Guns come with a gold-plated single trigger, automatic ejectors, fixed single triggers, straight pistol-grip-style walnut stock and forend. A rubber, ventilated recoil pad is standard. Depending upon gauge and barrel length, F.A.I.R. trap guns weigh between 6 ½ and eight pounds.

F.A.I.R. lists its Jubilee Trap in 12- or 20-gauge as a luxury gun. Typically with European guns, this means the action is the same, but the walnut stocks and forends are a fancier grade and the engraving is more elaborate. The 12-gauge has a 30-inch barrel while the 20-gauge barrel is ¾ inch shorter.

(Typical of European websites, and even though they want to sell product in the U.S., the F.A.I.R. site is translated awkwardly from Italian to English, and confusing on points such as choke size, longer barrel availability and interchangeability.)

## Renato Gamba

www.renatogamba.it

Click on the British flag, indicating the English translation for this Italian gun maker's web site, and the first word you notice is Automatici, indicating the automatic ejectors of the Concorde Trap over/under. Apparently, the Concorde is available in 12- or 20-gauge with either 2 ¾- or 3-inch chambers. Barrel lengths are 28, 30 and 32 inches, with fixed or interchangeable chokes. The Concorde over/under weighs slightly less than eight pounds.

At Renato Gamba, "our arms, also those with a big mechanical production, are never anonymous objects, but have a formal cure and great personality and a general tweak that just the hands of expert craftsman can make."

Now, all of that is well and good, but if a fine company cannot communicate clearly with its customers—and a company that names one of its guns the "Daytona," certainly has Americans in mind—it is not going to develop a strong following. It seems that they could easily afford to hire a copywriter who specializes in American English to interpret their site (and sales personnel who, charming and well informed as they may be, speak intelligibly in the target country's "mother tongue").

And another complaint, just to get it out in the open, is that European gun owners apparently desire expensive guns with gorgeous engraving. Perhaps that is because relatively few Europeans, primarily members of the wealthy class, enjoy or can afford the cost and leisure time of shooting.

European manufacturers apparently do not understand America, where shooting and hunting are more democratic activities. Of course, a democratic approach lowers the average price of a gun, but shooters in North America are more concerned about performance than fancy, gold plated engraving. The web sites and literature should reflect this difference.

## Cesar Guerini

www.gueriniusa.com

Guerini shotguns are produced in Brescia, Italy, and three bear the trap designation, the Magnus, Maxus and Summit.

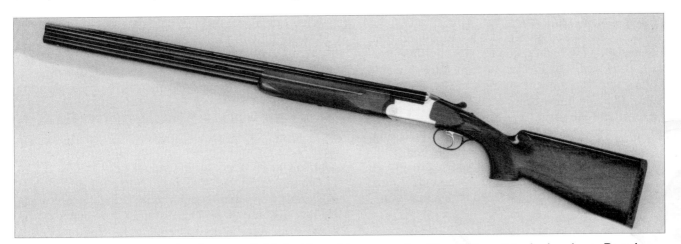

The Concorde from Renato Gamba is available in 12- or 20-gauge with either 2 ¾- or 3-inch chambers. Barrel lengths are 28, 30 and 32 inches, with fixed or interchangeable chokes. The simple, but dignified Concorde over/under weighs eight pounds.

The 12-gauge Magnus Trap may be the most common in the U.S. and comes as an over/under with 30- or 32-inch barrels or as an unsingle with 32- or 34-inch barrels. The .735 over-bored barrels have 5-inch forcing cones, chrome lined chambers and bores, screw in chokes, and antiglare satin finish. Guerini's Maxis chokes are extra long, extending into the barrel "to enhance patterning and ballistic performance in the tightest constrictions such as Light Full, Full, and Extra-Full, a very desirable quality when shooting in competition from the 27 yard line." Maxis chokes are built with a conical-parallel contour, crowned muzzle end, clear markings and tight tolerances for constriction and concentricity. The unsingle comes with three chokes and the over/under with five.

The 12mm tapered barrel rib allows point-of-impact adjustment from 60-40 to 120 percent. Adjust the rib by turning an elevation wheel with positive detents and clear incremental markings. Once the best rib height and angle is obtained, lock it in place with a locking screw. The mid-section of the rib has a dampening bushing to eliminate vibration and noise.

The trigger is a simple non-selective system with adjustments for length-of-pull, take-up and over travel. Factory-installed release triggers are an option.

A multi-axis comb on the Turkish Circassian walnut Monte Carlo stock allows for the adjustment of offset, cast, comb height and comb drop. Comb hardware is light but simple and strong; designed with an index system, it will stay exactly were it is set.

Guerini shotguns have increased in price as their desirability has increased. The MSRP for an over/under or an unsingle (top or bottom) is $6,350; the combo set retails for $8,395. There is an additional $200 charge for a left-hand stock.

## Khan

www.khanshotguns.com

Turkey's Khan Shotguns builds a competition trap gun featuring the highest quality, gloss finish Monte-Carlo stock and Schnabel forend from Turkish walnut. As for engraving, a deer hunting scene is on the right, with gold inlaid duck scenes on the left. The underside, top lever and the trigger guard are also furnished with gold plated flowers. A 12-gauge with 3-inch chamber, the gun's rib is high and ventilated, in the high-shooting trap style. Barrels are 28 inches, giving the 45-inch gun a weight of a little more than six pounds. Five interchangeable chokes are included with a new gun.

## Kolar

www.kolararms.com

For 11 years, Kolar has built a Competition Trap gun in Racine, Wisconsin. Available as an over/under (30-

or 32-inch barrels), bottom unsingle only (34-inch barrel) or combo, the 12-gauge 2 ¾ T/C comes standard with a .750 bore barrel, adjustable ramp rib and adjustable comb. Barrels utilize a unique mid and front hanger system that allow for precise point of impact (POI) adjustments. Two rib configurations are available allowing POI adjustment from 60/40 to 100 percent on both over/under and un-single barrels, but barrels are pre-set 70/30 at the factory.

An unsingle Kolar allows for the addition of over/under barrels at a future date. As with the T/C gun both standard height and X-Hi rib configurations are available, allowing for POI to more than 100 percent.

Kolar's interchangeable trigger group is mechanical, selectable, coil spring driven and features seven different positions for length adjustment. The factory release trigger option comes with four hammers. This trigger can also be reconfigured as a single or double release or a pull trigger in seconds, using only the supplied Allen wrench.

In order to meet the needs of most shooters, Kolar Trap guns are also supplied with 6-way adjustable combs. All guns come in an aluminum airline case.

Kolar standard over/unders begin at $9,595 and build to $25,590 with superior engraving and grades of walnut. The combo—over/under and unsingle—begins at $12,595 and ends around $28,590.

The Max T/A comes as an over/under, a bottom unsingle or an over unsingle. A weight kit is available to meet specific balance requirements when choosing the over-single barrel. The standard rib is adjustable from 60/40 to 100 percent and the X-Hi rib is adjustable from 100 to 140 percent.

Kolar Max T/A combos—over/under and unsingle bottom or over—begin at $13,995 and end around $29,990.

## Krieghoff

www.krieghoff.com

Krieghoff, with Perazzi and a couple of the U.S. specialty manufacturers, perhaps Ljutic and Bruce Bowen, is probably the high end of the competitive shotgun world. The reason, other than hefty price tags, is the high degree of individual hand fitting, unlike mass-production guns with interchangeable parts. Critical components such as sears, the trigger system and receivers are machined in the rough and then finished by skilled craftsmen to produce an individual gun.

The same care then extends to fitting the gun to the customer. Mass-market guns come with standard stock dimensions; not these. The customer determines exactly what measurements are required for length of pull, pitch, drop at comb and heel, cast, rib height and even width. The result is a handcrafted, precisely tailored shotgun.

Krieghoff is located in Ulm, Germany, and U.S. offices in Ottsville, Pennsylvania, was founded in 1886. The K-80 12-gauge and the K-20 in 20-gauge are the primary guns known in the U.S.

The K-80 was introduced in 1980 and is available as a single barrel gun, an over/under or in a combo-pack. The theory was that a single high quality, hand finished receiver could, with the simple attachment of a different barrel and/or stock combination, shoot any competition game or go to the field for pheasants. Your gun could thus handle anything from a 410-bore over/under in the morning and a 34-inch "unsingle" barrel in the afternoon.

Chambered for a 2 ¾-inch shell, K-80 receivers are engraved in a classic scroll pattern, case hardened and plated in durable satin nickel. They are available in traditional blued, brilliant coin or the classic case-colored finish. Trigger pull is adjustable between 3 ¼ and 3 ¾ pounds. The K-80 has a wide, smooth trigger shoe with deeply curved profile. It is adjustable for best length of pull. Release triggers are available in both single and double release configurations.

In lengths from 30 to 32 inches, K-80 barrels are not joined by a rib. Thus, Krieghoff says, they heat and cool independently. This reduces weight and wind resistance, Krieghoff suggests, when swinging on a crossing target. Additionally, the impact point of the bottom barrel of an over/under can change using different hanger attachments or spacers: nine separately sized hangers are available for fixed choke barrels, six for adjustable choke barrels. The barrel hanging system allows adjustment of the pattern ratio for the bottom barrel from a flat-shooting 50-50 to as high as 70-30. For trap, the bottom barrel is customarily set at 70-30 at the factory.

Although there are no joining ribs between barrels, the K-80 has four different matte-finished, adjustable and interchangeable top ribs and one of them, tapering from 12mm at breech to 8mm at muzzle, is specifically designed for trap. These top ribs allow changing to as much as 90-10. Ribs have a white pearl front sight and metal center bead.

Krieghoff barrels are engineered with a long forcing cone and are over-bored to reduce recoil and produce more uniform patterns. Fixed choke barrels have a Full choke on top and Improved Modified on bottom. Barrels with interchangeable chokes come with five chokes from Extra-Full to Improved Cylinder.

The unsingle barrel is fired with the under-barrel firing pin. It sits low in the receiver for less muzzle flip and felt recoil. The unsingle barrel point of impact adjusts by hand without tools via two coin-slotted screws and a small wheel.

Five stock designs are available for American trap

shooters, three Monte Carlo and two straight, each with equal drop at comb and heel. Krieghoff stocks can be custom made, even from a person's own chunk of wood. Impervious to moisture "stock stocks" are shaped from European select walnut with ambidextrous palm swells and are finished in satin. Stocks remove easily with a stock wrench. Standard length of pull is 14 ⅜ and the K-80 weighs 8 ¾ pounds. A fitted aluminum case is provided with each gun.

Krieghoff's single barrel 12-gauge trap gun, the KX-5, is available with 34- or 32-inch barrels with interchangeable chokes. The KX-5 has a fully adjustable tapered ⅞₁₆-⁵⁄₁₆ rib which allows quick adjustment of point of impact and is calibrated at the factory to achieve a 65-35 pattern. By altering the height of the rib via a dial at the muzzle, one can vary the pattern from a flat shooting 50-50 to nearly 90-10. Once the desired rib height is reached and the set screws are tightened, the adjustable comb can be raised or lowered to match the shooter's preferred sight picture.

The 2 ¾ chambered KX-5 features an adjustable trigger and new forend iron design with a push button lock, providing a stronger latch to the barrel. In addition to strength, this gives the receiver a more elegant streamlined look. For quick target pick-up with reduced heat distortion, the KX-5 has a ventilated tapered step rib. Trigger pull is easily adjustable for both weight and sear engagement. A release trigger is also available. With the standard Monte Carlo stock and adjustable comb, the KX-5 weighs 8 ¾ pounds.

## Ljutic

www.ljuticgun.com

(Ljutic is pronounced "lutik.")

Its original "claim to fame," the Mono Gun single barrel trap gun, is available from Ljutic in six models for $7,495: standard rib, medium rib, medium rib with screw-in chokes, Olympic rib (with or without screw-in chokes) and Deluxe PR03. The medium rib height is half that of the Olympic rib. Expect to pay $8,495 for a stainless version. All models come in American walnut and are offered with custom detailing, with the exception of roll over combs, cheek piece stocks and extreme cast on and off which carry added labor charges. You may also select English walnut and upgrade the wood grade and the standard checkering patterns. Release triggers can be installed on the Mono Gun. Barrels are available in 32-, 34- and 35-inch lengths and Ljutic charges an additional $300 for screw-in choke barrels. Guns are delivered in a hard-sided Americase.

The Pro 3 single barrel trap gun is available in alloy steel for $8,995 or in stainless steel for $9,995. The 34-inch .740 barrel is factory ported and comes with four Briley Series 12 chokes. An aluminum baseplate with interchangeable two-pad system and adjustable comb is included. These hand-made guns are built in a family business still owned by founders Al and Nadine, both ATA Hall of Fame competitors. "Everything is machined," Al says, "nothing is stamped or cast, from solid steel billets." For the Pro 3 with screw in hinge pin and Ljutic internal flush mount or extended chokes, expect to pay an additional $900.

## Perazzi

www.perazzi.it

"The history of Armi Perazzi is the history of Daniele Perazzi, a poor but doggedly determined young man who chased the myth of a perfect gun and dreamt about becoming a gunsmith. At 16 he finally got a job…[and in] 1957 at the age of 25, Daniele Perazzi founded Armi Perazzi and established his own factory, of which he remains the President." A bit over-written, the Perazzi viewpoint coincides with their arguably over-hyped image in the shooting sports.

Because most high end shotguns are built by hand to individual specifications, it is unusual to see a new Krieghoff, Perazzi or Ljutic on the shelf at your local gun dealer. Only rarely are they made with "standard" dimensions for off-the-rack sales. On those occasions, a customer will not have the option of selecting a butt-stock with different dimensions or even an adjustable buttstock, although a stock-fitter can shape a pre-existing stock to one's preferences.

Generally, an ultra-expensive gun on a dealer's rack is used and they sell fast. Folks who favor upper-end guns hang onto them. Very expensive guns (and that is, of course, a relative term) are generally purchased from authorized distributors or sales representatives who help a customer order the measurements and features he or she requires. While each of these makers offers a number of different models, the true differences are typically in rib and stock configurations and the quality of engraving. The heart of the gun, the action, even the barrel, will essentially be the same. Various model designations are simply a way to describe differing small features, grades of walnut, or beauty and complexity of engraving plus gold and silver inlay.

Perazzi of Brescia, Italy, is barely 50 years old and normally employs only 100 or so people to produce a scant dozen shotguns a day. Still, these guns are made available almost one-by-one with individualized, customized parts and options.

As a manufacturer, Perazzi has built an enviable reputation for expensive, world-class guns in single barrel, double barrel and combo sets. Options include adjustable-impact ribs, adjustable stocks and a wide variety of barrels and chokes.

Perazzis are among the elite on the international competition circuit and are easily among the favorites of top-ranked U.S. shooters. One look at the high quality, lusciously engraved field scenes, or scenes from history or mythology will convince most U.S. competitors to pull on gloves prior to handling.

The MX15 is a 12-gauge trap gun with 32-, 34- or 35-inch barrels and either fixed Full choke or interchangeable chokes. The $^7/_{16}$-$^9/_{32}$ tapered rib is adjustable with six notches and topped with a white front bead and steel mid ramp bead. The trigger group with gold-plated trigger is removable. Stock and forend are selected walnut and the comb is adjustable.

Other Perazzi single-barrel trap guns—the MX10, MX2000, MX2005—are versions of the MX-15 with slightly different styles of adjustable rib. Only the MX8 has a fixed rib.

The MX2005 is typical of Perazzi combo sets. The lower single barrel is 34 inches while the over/under barrel set is 31 ½ inches long. One orders the MX2005 with a fixed choke size in mind or with interchangeable chokes. The single barrel rib is adjustable with five notches and tapered $^7/_{16}$-$^9/_{32}$. The gun can be ordered with fully ventilated or half-ventilated side ribs. With the adjustable comb and rib, point of impact is highly adjustable.

And yes, it is possible to pay nearly $200,000 for the most beautiful shotgun in the world. Though hesitant to touch it, I have seen one at a business trade show—and yes, it is a Perazzi.

## Remington

www.remington.com

The venerable and seemingly unchanging Model 1100 Trap uses Remington's basic gas gun design for the 1100-series, and this has made it extremely popular in the field and among casual trap, skeet and sporting clays shooters. In its Classic Trap mode, this 12-gauge holds four shells in the magazine and one in the 2 ¾-inch chamber. Its 30-inch barrel is topped with a light, contour vent rib and front sight bead. Standard issue are Singles (.027), Mid Handicap (.034) and Long Handicap (.041) Rem-Chokes. The overall length is 50 ½ inches and length of pull is listed as 14 ¼ inches with a 1 $^7/_{16}$-inch drop at comb and two-inch drop at heel. The 1100 weighs 8 ¼ pounds and the high gloss wood Monte Carlo stock is graded semi-fancy American walnut. The trigger is gold plated and MSRP is $1,159, though ImpactGuns.com listed it new for $987.

Almost any of the breed of 1100s will work well for trap shooting because their reputation for reliability is understood. Still, the longer, 30-inch barrel in 12-gauge is preferred unless one becomes a trap master, in which case fancier and more expensive guns tend to appeal. Still, the 1100 Competition with half-inch ad-

**Italy's Perazzi has a well-deserved reputation for producing high quality shotguns such as the MX15 Trap, guns which, with routine maintenance, will afford a shooter high quality results for many years.**

justable stock and extended ProBore Full choke would be a premier shooter on the trap circuit.

For shooters who want their trap experience to replicate their field experience, Remington recommends its slide-action Model 870 Wingmaster Classic Trap pump. The 870's dimensions are similar to the 1100, except that its weight is four ounces lighter. This 870 has a walnut Monte Carlo stock and forend with deep cut checkering and a high-gloss finish. The 30-inch light contour vent rib target barrel has twin bead sights (ivory front bead and steel mid-bead) and a new purchase includes three RemChokes: Singles, Mid Handicap and Long Handicap (MSRP $1,039).

In Remington's Premier Competition STS line, over/unders with 30- and 32-inch barrels will bust any kind of clay including trap. This gun comes with fixed or adjustable combs on Monte Carlo walnut stocks in those longer barrel lengths. Expect over-bored barrels, a right-hand palm swell and gold-plated trigger. Five extended ProBore choke tubes are included so one can switch between trap and other shotgun games quickly. At $2,890 MSRP, this is Remington's most expensive shotgun.

## Rizzini

www.rizzini.it

Several Rizzini companies are building shotguns. The expensive ones are F.lli Rizzini, but of the other Rizzinis, the B. Rizzini guns are generally considered to be the best. A brand new S2000 will set you back about $3,800 right now, although this generally depends on the relationship of the dollar to the Euro, so for the next few years anything can happen!

A check of the Rizzini-USA site (www.rizziniusa.com) does not list a specific trap gun, but the Italian site is entirely different, although with the same gun names and specifications. There, the Vertex Trap, Premier Trap, S2000 Trap and S790L Trap are all listed. All Rizzini models are 2 ¾ over/under 12-gauge with chrome-lined barrels. The Premier is also available in 20-gauge; the S2000 has a completely chrome-plated action; and the S790L has hand-worked engraving.

The Vertex comes with automatic ejectors and a single trigger. Barrels are 29 ½ (75cm) or 30.7 (78cm)

inches in length and can be purchased with fixed or interchangeable chokes. The ventilated rib is 10mm and the pistol grip stock and beavertail forend come in select walnut, hand checkered and polished oil finish.

## Seitz

www.silverseitz.com

The Silver Seitz trap gun is manufactured by Aim, Inc. in Parkton, Maryland. Aim claims that it is "one of the nation's leading manufacturers of precision components and assemblies for military and commercial use" and carried on the Seitz trap gun tradition after Tom Seitz died. They decided to name the new gun the "Silver Seitz," "Silver" for the Silver Dollar Trap Club in Odessa, Florida, and of course "Seitz" to honor Tom Seitz.

Silver Seitz 12-gauge single barrel trap guns come with a buyer's choice of pull or release triggers guaranteed to remain crisp with a very fast lock time over years of shooting. Receivers are made of stainless steel or titanium steel for weight reduction. A titanium coating reduces wear and adds durability, and a high grade English walnut stock with an adjustable comb is standard. Barrels come in 33, 34 or 35 inch lengths. Seitz offers three types of adjustable ribs: 60-40 to 90-10, 80-20 to 120 and 110 to 140. Custom fitting is available. In a custom aluminum carrying case, a new Silver Seitz will cost about $14,500 and with custom engraving and select walnut, to $22,000 or more.

## SKB

www.skbshotguns.com

SKB was derived from the Samurai family name Sakaba by dropping the vowels. The company was formed in the Ibaraki province of Japan in 1855. Guns are imported into the U.S. through Omaha, Nebraska.

New, low-profile box-lock 85TTR trap guns—12-gauge with 3-inch chambering—can be ordered as an over/under ($2,330), unsingle ($2,800) or in a combo set ($4,050). All come with either fixed stocks or for an additional $200, adjustable combs. Stock dimensions are: length of pull 14 ⅜; drop at comb and drop at heel 1 ½.

Barrel lengths for the 85TRR are: over/under 30 or

The 12-gauge, 2 ¾-chambered TT-09 from TriStar includes a walnut Monte Carlo stock that is drilled for an aftermarket recoil reducer. The raised target rib sits atop a 34-inch factory ported barrel; ideal for handicap trap.

32 inches, unsingle 32 or 34 inches long. Barrels are factory designed for SKB's Inter-Choke System and come with Improved Modified, Full and Full Trap. Ribs are topped with a center post and interchangeable Hi Viz competition fiberpipe.

The 12-gauge CG7 trap gun may be ordered as a top single or an unsingle in 32- or 34-inch barrel lengths or a combo in a combination of barrel lengths including 30 inches. Barrels are chromed and bored to 735. The top single rib is tapered from 9mm-7mm while the unsingle is tapered from 12mm-9mm. Available with either Monte Carlo or straight stocks, the CG7 weighs between 8 ½ and nine pounds.

## TriStar

www.tristarsportingarms.com

TriStar Sporting Arms of N. Kansas City, Missouri, calls itself "The Value Expert" and its new TT-09 Mono Trap ($999) is dedicated to trap shooters. "This gun may resemble other brands," TriStar says, "but it sells for a fraction of the price."

The 12-gauge, 2 ¾-chambered TT-09 includes a Monte Carlo stock with "TriStar select wood." The stock is drilled for a recoil reducer. The raised target rib sits atop a 34-inch factory ported barrel, fiber optic front sight and brass mid-bead. The TT-09's receiver is acid-etched and equipped with shell ejectors. As with any TriStar firearm, the TT-09 comes with a 5-year warranty. Three extended Beretta choke tubes (Modified, Improved Modified and Full) are included. Stock dimensions in inches are: drop at comb 1 ⅛, drop at heel 2 ¼ and length of pull 14 ⅜.

## Winchester

www.winchester-guns.com

Winchester has not promoted its trap gun like it has its new SXP speed pump, which Xtreme Sport Shooter Patrick Flanigan now uses in demonstrations and nine-time world welterweight Ultimate Fighting Champion Matt Hughes endorses. Perhaps Winchester and these young bucks see trap as "old school." Nevertheless, the company has replaced the older over/under name Select Energy Trap with the only slightly modified Model 101 Pigeon Grade Trap.

The 12-gauge, 2 ¾ Model 101 has a wide 10mm steel runway rib, and comes from the factory with a mid-bead sight and TruGlo Tru-Bead interchangeable fiber-optic front sight for what Winchester calls a "truer, more technical sight picture." The lightweight, .742-inch back-bored barrels are polished, have factory porting and vented side ribs. An included adjustable trigger shoe helps fine-tune length of pull.

Available with 30- or 32-inch barrels, the 101 uses Winchester's screw-in Invector-Plus choke system. These chokes protrude from the barrel and are marked at the tips for easy identification. Chokes included are Extra-Full, Full and Improved Modified. The 30-inch barrel gives the gun an overall length of 47 ¾ inches; 14 ¾-inch length of pull; 1 ⅜-inch drop at comb; 2 ½-inch drop at heel; and weight of 7 lb. 8 oz. Other measurements are the same, but the 32-inch barrel increases length to 49 ¾ inches and weight to 7 lb. 12 oz.

Like the Select Energy Trap, the Belgian-made 101 is available with either a fixed raised comb ($2,289) or an adjustable comb ($2,429). Adjustable combs allow individual height and cast on/off customization. These stocks, says Winchester, are carved from beautiful Grade III/IV walnut. A molded ABS hard case is included with each new purchase.

## Antonio Zoli

www.zoli.it

Neither the Italian manufacturer Zoli nor its North American distributor in New York carries a specific trap gun in its inventory, but the Z-Gun in its trap model is a popular all-around shooter and would certainly perform superbly in the right hands.

The 12-gauge Z-Gun is available in barrel lengths of 34 inches single or 32 inches over/under with long forcing cones and slightly over-bored to .731. Barrels are topped with an 11mm straight rib and fiber optic foresight. Triggers are adjustable and detachable; stocks and forearms are Turkish walnut. Adjustable comb and length are optional. Approximate stock measurements in inches are 1.18 drop at comb, 1.65 drop at heel, 14.8 length of pull, 0.160 cast at heel and 0.24 cast at toe. Base price with minimal engraving is $5,200.

# CHAPTER 8

# TRAP LOADS

Loads for trap are simple and straightforward, whether you are purchasing them at the range, at Wal-Mart or even building them in your garage, and the more you burn through shells, the more you will be attracted to handloading. Most high handicap shooters, in fact, rely on just a few load combinations.

The heaviest load allowable for shooting sanctioned ATA targets is a 12-gauge, 3-dram equivalent, 1 ⅛-ounce load of #7 ½ shot. This formula has become such a standard that loads in this combination are invariably referred to as "trap loads," and every ammunition manufacturer offers them.

Trap loads may be simple, but they are some of the most highly refined shotshells in the clay sports game. A reloader ought to be able to save money by purchasing supplies in bulk and load enough shells for the month in only a few hours—it doesn't take long with today's multi-stage loaders. Any reloader who thinks he can beat the performance of factory trap loads and stay within the rules, however, is faced with a challenge. Probably the best an occasional reloader can hope to do is to equal their performance.

Loaded trap shells have the power to break any target on a trap field, even the occasional 50-yard-plus bird you will see from the 27-yard handicap positions. If a shooter wanted to standardize on one load and one load only for this game, he could not go wrong with 1 ⅛-ounces of #7 ½.

All that power is not always needed, however, and all the recoil is never welcome. In fact, a number of experienced shooters have found that switching to lighter loads and, sometimes, smaller shot, can actually improve their scores.

Number 8 shot will reliably break a clay target out to about 35 yards. By the time the target gets to 40 yards, the breaking power of a load of #8 is questionable, though. While practically every shooter on the 16-yard line breaks his target inside 35 yards, there is no reason not to use #8 shot for that event, and there are some very good reasons why you should.

According to Winchester, a 1 ⅛-ounce load of #7 ½ shot (.095-inch diameter) contains about 350 individual pellets. The same charge of #8 shot (.090-inch diameter) will have about 410. Consequently, #8 puts a significantly larger number of pellets—17 percent more—in the pattern.

Smart shooters take advantage of increased shot density by using a slightly more open choke, which increases the diameter of the gun's effective pattern. If

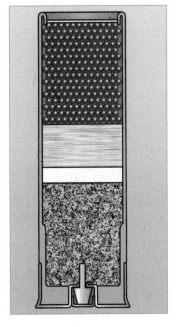

The Shotshell Cartridge Shotgun shells have evolved gradually from muzzleloader days. The components of a shell are designed to be a one-piece shot rocket and all parts, from the primer to the crimp, must work efficiently for superior and safe shooting. Today, most wads and shells are plastic while the powder is a highly evolved propellant that burns at a controlled rate.

you are not scoring as well as you would like at the 16-yard line with a Full-choked gun and a load of #7 ½, shifting to an Improved Modified or even Modified choke and #8 loads can give you a few more birds. You will have a larger usable pattern (more room for error) and the individual pellets still have enough energy to break the target.

## Shoot Lighter Loads

Another option with #8 shot is to drop to a lighter load. A 1-ounce load of #8 contains about 410 pellets, still more than a 1 ⅛-ounce load of 7 ½. The lighter shot charge should, if the powder charge is the same, result in slightly less felt recoil, yet will put the same number of pellets in the air. Many savvy shooters shift to one-ounce loads of #8 for 16-yard work simply to reduce the cumulative effects of recoil during an extended match. That can pay dividends by keeping them a bit fresher at the end of the day, and they are not really sacrificing pellet count or pattern size over the heavier 1 ⅛-ounce #7 ½ load.

While the 3-dram load is fairly standard in trap, many shooters opt for lighter, 2 ¾-dram loads with the same 1 ⅛-ounce shot charge. The heavier dram load moves at about 1,235 fps, but the reduced 2 ¾-dram still accelerates from about 1,120 to 1,165 fps, depending upon the powder used. From the 16-yard line, no medium shooter will be able to detect the slight reduction in velocity; it will make no difference in a shooter's score, just in the recoil he or she will absorb. The lighter loads are softer shooting. When moving back to longer handicap distances, however, most serious trap shooters still favor the full 3-dram, 1 ⅛, #7 ½ loads.

Another performance option is a 1-ounce, 2 ¾-dram load of #8 ½ shot. This one moves at about 1,180 fps, and one-ounce of #8 ½ carries about 480 pellets. This is as soft a 12-gauge load as you can shoot that still has enough energy to get the job done. In fact, in an 8 ½- or 9-pound gun, this load will produce less recoil than most 7-pound 20-gauge guns, or 5 ½- to 6-pound 28-gauge guns.

The drawback to this load, of course, is that #8 ½ pellets begin to lose their target breaking power at a range of just over 30 yards. A quick shooter, though, will break 16-yard targets at under that range. Increased pellet count allows the use of a Modified choke to increase pattern size with a very significant reduction in felt recoil.

Fine scores from the 16-yard line can be shot with the #8 ½ shell in a Modified-choked gun. You cannot ride the target and take your time, though. This load works well, but only when you get on the bird quickly. Still, the incredibly soft-shooting qualities of the #8 ½ (or any other 2 ¾-dram one-ounce package) make it worth your time to experiment with it from the 16-yard line.

Some reasonably good shooter at every range will swear by #9 shot with an open choke and a fast shot. Forget it, because #9 runs out of consistent target-breaking power right around 25 yards, and that is an awfully close range at which to break all your 16-yard targets. Some days it works, but often it does not.

My own trap load selection runs like this: Anything beyond the 20-yard handicap line calls for the full 3-dram, 1 ⅛-ounce load of #7 ½ shot; inside that, I am comfortable with the 2 ¾-dram, 1 ⅛-ounce loads. At the 16-yard line, most days, I have no problem with a 1-ounce load of #8, or the same load of #8 ½.

## The Official Trap Rule

According to ATA rules (Section XI: Paragraph G), a competitor can not use:

2. Loads that contain nickel or copper coated shot or tracer loads. However, the use of lead, steel, bismuth, or other composite nontoxic shot materials shall be allowed. Any gun club allowing shot materials described in this Rule, other than lead, shall be required to cover or shield all hard surfaces on trap fields which are known, or reasonably believed, to cause pellet ricochet with material which will prevent the shot pellets from rebounding and/or ricocheting.

3. Any load with a velocity greater than 1290 FPS (Feet Per Second) with maximum shot charge of 1 ⅛

ounces, or 1325 FPS with a maximum shot charge of 1 ounce, or 1350 FPS with a maximum shot charge of ⅞ ounces or less, as measured in any individual shotshell. These velocities are maximums and no individual shotshell shall exceed these limits for the designated shot charge. In addition, no load containing more than 1 1/8 ounces or any shot larger than Number 7 ½ can be used. Shot charges are maximum and no charge may exceed the charge amount by more than 3%.

4. Any shell loaded with black powder.

## Factory Ammunition

Here is a look at shotshell offerings from the major ammunition makers in 12-gauge trap loads.

First, a note about shooting trap in the sub-gauges. Fewer factory loads are available in those gauges because the game becomes exponentially more difficult—much more so than skeet and on a par with sporting clays—when switching to smaller bore and shell sizes. If you choose to shoot trap with a 16- or 28-gauge, for instance, it will be a good idea to look into reloading because cost and availability will become issues right away.

### Eley Hawk

www.eleyhawkltd.com

England's Eley Hawk says its antecedents date to 1828. Nevertheless, it is owned by an international conglomerate called UEE...not only faceless, but nameless! Still new to the U.S. shooting scene, Eley or Eley Hawk reports that it is capable of producing "well in excess of 10,000 cartridges per hour."

Eley has a somewhat incredible eight lines of clay target shotshells—perhaps because hunting in the UK and much of Europe is a rich man's sport—each designed in a slightly different configuration. Eley does, however, specify the percentage of antimony. These English shells are specified in grams: 24 is 0.8466-ounce or ⅞, 28 is 0.9877-ounce or 1.0, 32 is 1.1287-ounce or 1 ⅛ and 36 is 1.2699-ounce or 1 ¼.

Note also that Eley gives both muzzle velocity and "observed velocity" for shot. According to the UK's Jonathan Spencer, observed velocity is the average velocity of a shot charge over the first 20 yards of flight. Thus an observed velocity of 1070 fps is approximately equal to a muzzle velocity of 1320 fps.

The Eley First brand is an entry level, 3-percent antimony cartridge in 24- or 28-gram loads of #7 ½, #8 and #9. Priced for value-conscious shooters. Plastic or fiber wads in each load. Muzzle velocity 1350 fps; observed velocity 1050 fps.

The new Eley Trainer training cartridge was developed in conjunction with the country's top shooting grounds. The light load fibre wad cartridge—24- (1300 fps) or 25-gram (1350 fps), #7 ½ or #8—gives novice shooters "performance, clean breaks and therefore confidence in their ability to shoot clay targets," Eley says. Trainer cartridges use the unique Eley Kleena wad to reduce recoil "whilst realistic speeds are achieved."

What is really new in the Eley line, however, is their new Hush Power cartridges. Due to the increase in noise complaints, the company says, and more shooting grounds coming under pressure because of environmental issues, Hush Power cartridges are developed to use an extremely fast burning propellant with the Kleena wad system. Thus, they are "probably the quietest clay cartridges available on today's market whilst still having the ability to break clays at long distances." Available in 12- and 20-gauge in 3-percent antimony #7 ½ and #8, 1050 fps.

Most Eley competition brands are set for velocities that exceed ATA maximum specifications (1 ⅛-ounce = 1290 fps, 1-ounce = 1325 fps and ⅞-ounce = 1350 fps): Eley Competition Trap (for the 20-gauge); Eley Blues (observed velocity is 1050 fps, but muzzle velocity is 1400 fps); Eley Superb Competition (5-percent antimony); Eley VIP (7-percent antimony and the "flagship of the Eley range") and Eley VIP Sporting.

## Federal

www.federalcartridge.com
www.federalpremium.com

Federal has built shells in Anoka, Minnesota, since 1916. In 2001, it was purchased by ATK (Alliant Techsystems). Today Federal/ATK manufactures loads for every size smoothbore (10, 12, 16, 20, 28 and 410), every shotgun option from lead for trap to steel for waterfowl, and every need including plenty of low recoil options and high velocity for high handicap shooting.

You can shoot a round of trap with virtually any load the range will accept, perhaps even with buckshot, though you would not expect to break many clays with a barrel full of double-ought, at least not in the air. Still, remember that official ATA competition loads have limitations on shot speed and shot size. So here are a few of the offerings to help illustrate the differences between the various Federal brands.

In its Gold Medal Target – Plastic line, Federal has loads for all the common gauges, 12 to 410-bore, plus high velocity handicap, extra-light, low recoil and even paper hulls. T116 is a good example of the true trap load—1200 fps, 1 ⅛ ounces of #7 ½, #8 and #9—and reloaders will ask for your hulls. N110 International Plastic offers a muzzle velocity of 1325 fps with 7/8 ounces of #8 ½. (N110 also comes in #7 ½, but they are disallowed for competition trap because they are copper plated.)

For the Paper line, Federal promotes three loads, all for 12-gauge. T118 throws its 1 ⅛-ounce load at 1200 fps with a 2.97 dram equivalent of powder, but T117 will accomplish the same task with only 2.72 drams and at the end of the day, the lighter load may be well worth the measly 55 fps loss of shot string speed. Federal promotes T172 Extra-Lite Paper as a low recoil load for those long trap events, as its 2.51 drams only give the 1 ⅛ ounces of shot an 1100 fps rap on the shoulder.

Federal says its Game-Shok small game shells are cost-effective and H121 might be an excellent trap load, especially if you use it for bird hunting and use trap more as an off-season stay-in-shape sport. The 12-gauge H121 offers the maximum 1 ⅛-ounce velocity of 1290 fps in #7 ½ and #8 with 3.25 drams.

Top Gun shells are advertised for "the volume shooter like you who needs consistent performance at a reasonable price," but then again, Federal or any company for that matter, rings up more bling with a finished shell than it does with components for reloading. The TG12 12-gauge fires a very reasonable 1200 fps with 1 ⅛ ounces of #7 ½ and #8. TG20 is the Top Gun 20-gauge shell.

According to Federal, it developed its TGM123 subsonic load—900 fps with 1 ⅛ ounces of #7 ½—"for use in conjunction with the Metro Barrel system" such as the one Federal demonstration shooter Tom Knapp uses in performances. Combined with the subsonic load, Federal says it is quiet and effective. With only 1.6 drams, this may be a fine load from the 16-yard line for a fast shooter.

## Fiocchi

www.fiocchiusa.com

Manufactured in Ozark, Missouri, since 1986 and in Italy since 1876, the colorful Fiocchi catalog offers quite a range of hard, uniform shot that is designed with functional, one-piece plastic wads.

In their Shooting Dynamics Target line, Fiocchi has a dozen 12-gauge loads with ⅞-, 1- and 1 ⅛-ounce, all featuring 3-percent antimony shot in #7 ½, #8 and #9.

Of 12 loads listed in the Paper Target line, 10 meet ATA specifications for speed and size: 1 and 1 ⅛ ounces of #7 ½ and #8. Two loads meet International 24-gram specifications for 1350 fps and Focchi has even invested in the 1 1/16-ounce #7 ½ (372 pellets) and #8 (436 pellets) cartridges. Multiple 1- and 1 ⅛-ounce options are available in Fiocchi's line-up for every trap position and angle.

For sub-gauges 20-, 28- and 410 multiple cartridges have been developed, but it is their unusual 16-gauge shells that make Fiocchi stand out. With an ounce of #7 ½ (#16VIP75) or #8 (#16VIP8) at 1300 fps, this Italian-American brand has introduced one of the only 16-gauge clay target shells available, and that is a fine thing.

## Kent Cartridge

www.kentgamebore.com

Established just in 1996, Canada's Kent Cartridge purchased Activ (West Virginia, 1997) and Gamebore (England, 1998). Kent's founders wanted to develop a "nontoxic shotshell to equal or exceed high quality lead shot for waterfowl." Their Tungsten Matrix shot still contains, Kent contends, the "only true alternative to lead," but it is nevertheless their lead competition line that is designed for clay shooting and endorsed by shotgun phenom George Digweed.

Demonstrating the environmental consciousness seeping through the manufacturing ranks, in 2009 Kent's sister division Gamebore has introduced an environmentally friendly 2 ½-inch Bio-Wad with a fibre shot cup and a varnished paper hull, the first fully degradable shot wad in some of its loads. The Bio-Wad protects the barrel of a gun (especially when firing steel shot) and immediately starts to break down after firing.

Kent has revised the line-up of target shells in its Velocity series and is now quite versatile. The company says its Diamond Shot is "highly polished" lead and that it uses B&P wads and Cheddite hulls. It has #7 ½, #8, #8 ½ and #9 shot-filled 12-gauge cartridges in 1 ⅛- and 1-ounce as well as 24-gram for international trap.

Neither has this Canadian-American-English company neglected the sub-gauges. Its 20-gauge Velocity cartridge shoots 1240 fps with ⅞ ounces of #7 ½, #8 or #9. Same-size 28-gauge loads with ¾-ounce are clocked at 1200 fps.

One of its most interesting packages is #K122SL32, a "spreader" load which clocks 1250 fps with 1 ⅛ ounces of #8. Cut open one of these shells and one finds a thin-walled X separating most of the shot into four equal compartments with only a thin layer on top. According to Ballistic Products, which sells the X-Steam Spreader Insert, the theory is that a thin layer of shot on top fills the center-section of a pattern, while the pellets below, in the chambers, are evenly dispersed toward the outside of the pattern. Results are more consistent and wider patterns (by about one choke) and fewer deformed, fly-away pellets.

New loads also highlight Gamebore's High Performance 12-gauge Competition series in which there are three types of shells: White Gold, White Gold XLR and Blue Diamond. Several White Gold loads have paper hulls. Their #GBRP1232 for example is available with 1 ⅛ ounces of #7 ½ or #8 and shoots 1280 fps. Gamebore also sells a 20-gauge shell: #GBCO2024 at 1280 fps with ⅞ ounces of #7 ½, #8 or #9.

## Remington

www.remington.com

Remington Arms is owned by Cerberus Capital Management, and that's not a name consistent with our hunting and shooting heritage. Nevertheless, Remington, now headquartered in Madison, North Carolina, is the only U.S. manufacturer who produces both guns and ammo inside the U.S. In addition, they are the oldest continuously operating manufacturer in the U.S., having been founded in Ilion, New York, in 1816 by Eliphat Remington.

Remington's line-up for the target shooter is extensive and includes five separate lines: Premier STS (Skeet-Trap-Sporting), Managed Recoil STS, Premier Nitro 27 Handicap Trap, Premier Nitro Gold Sporting Clays and the economical Gun Club line.

The Premier STS line is available for all gauges, but in the 12 you can buy it in standard, low recoil and handicap versions in #7 ½, #8 and occasionally in #8 ½ and #9. Reloaders should note that Remington brags about hull durability for the STS, by the way. The Premier STS Light Handicap, for instance, #STS12LH, uses a 3-dram powder charge with 1 ⅛ ounces of #7 ½ or #8 for shooting 1200 fps (rated velocities measured three feet from the muzzle) from 19 (ladies and juniors) or 20 (men) to 27 yards.

Only two loads are offered in the Managed Recoil STS line, one for 12- and one for 20-gauge, but are rated at 1100 fps with ⅞-ounce of #8 ½ shot pushed along by 2 ¾ drams of powder. Perhaps the idea is that anyone shooting a sub-gauge is automatically the beneficiary of reduced blast and recoil. Remington says the 12-gauge load, RLSTS1285, reduces recoil by 40 percent and is thus "ideal for new shooters and high-volume practice."

Remington says Premier Nitro 27 Handicap is designed for "back fence" shooting, in other words, avid trap masters with high handicaps. Thus, to achieve the maximum 1290 fps in #STS12NH1 (1 ounce of #7 ½ or #8) and 1235 fps in #STS12NH (1 ⅛ ounce of #7 ½ or #8), it lists the drams equivalent of powder simply as "HNDCP."

The Gun Club line has three 12-gauge 2 ¾-inch shells (GC12) useful for trap. The GC12L has 2 ¾ drams equivalent and 1 ⅛ ounces of #7 ½, #8 or #9 for 1145 fps. GC121 loads down to 1 ounce of 7 ½ or #8, thus boosting the velocity to 1185 fps. Finally, GC12 is hyped to 3 drams in #7 ½ and #8 for a 1200 fps shot string. Remington says the Gun Club line allows many shooters to get "acceptable reloading life while stretching their shooting dollar."

## Rio Ammunition

www.ableammo.com

This American subsidiary of the Spanish corporation UEE has shotshells that it specifically designates as trap loads in 1 ⅛, 1 and ⅞ ounces of #7 ½ and #8.

Trap load TLT32 is a 2 ¾-inch shell with one ounce of #7 ½ or #8 lead and 2 ¾ drams equivalent for 1150 fps at three feet from the muzzle. Its lighter, 1-ounce

TLT28 fires 1210 fps, but its Top Trap TT32 load is rated at 1250 fps for longer-distance handicap shooting. Top Trap lead is mixed with a five percent antimony rather than the standard three percent.

Rio has sub-gauge shells available for 20-, 28- and 36-gauge (the 410). For the 20, TT20 gives a 1250 fps velocity with ⅞-ounce of #7 ½, #8 or #9. For the 28, RC28 gives 1300 fps with ¾-ounce of #7 ½, #8 or #9. And for the 410, RC36 gives 1200 fps with ½-ounce of #7 ½, #8 or #9.

Paper cartridges are the latest addition to Rio's product line. Why so many manufacturers are returning to paper is a puzzle though in an era when pennies count, paper must be less expensive. As to there being a "ground swell" of support for paper hulls, the true questions would be "Is that so?" and "Why?" In my experience, there is no substantial reason to request paper over plastic and paper is generally less durable and offers fewer reloading possibilities.

Nevertheless, paper shells offer "a traditional cartridge" loaded with one ounce (28 grams) or 1 ⅛ ounce (32 grams) of shot in #7 ½ or #8. These are combined with UEE's Bossi wad and CSB powders in shells such as #TLTP32, a 1 ⅛-ounce trap load of #7 ½ or #8 with 1150 fps performance. The low recoil 1-ounce is #TLTP28, but it shoots 1210 fps. Go figure!

### Winchester/Olin

www.winchester.com

Individuals at a cocktail party who learn that you shoot and/or hunt will soon get around to telling you they know that Winchester has gone out of business, as if this is a sign that you have horns growing out of your head or are simply an ignorant, gun-loving lout. Like Remington, which was owned by DuPont and then by Clayton, Dubilier & Rice and now is part of some other faceless financial group, Cerberus Capital Management, Winchester was bought by Olin in the '30s, reformed in the '60s, incorporated as U.S. Repeating Arms in 1980 and is today part of the Belgian FN Herstal.

This Alton, Illinois company has been through numerous owners, but it has built shotshells since 1886 and, today, the Winchester Double A (AA) and economical Super-Target (TRGT) loads are a standard at any shooting line.

There are 36 AA hard shot target loads. Introduced almost a half century ago, shells with the "HS" or high strength designation are eminently reloadable, Winchester says. All of the standard loads are present in the AA line from a 2 ¾-inch shell as straight-forward as #AA127 with 2 ¾ drams equivalent and 1 ⅛ ounces of #7 ½ (1145 fps) to the 24-gram, #9 International #AANL129 (1350 fps).

Shells of particular interest in the AA brand are those in sub-gauges, because, as you grow in proficiency and handicap, the urge will be to begin honing your shooting skills by blowing trap with 20-, 28- and 410-bore. AAH208 is Winchester's 20-gauge standard, 1-ounce of #8 at 1165 fps. AA288 is the 28-gauge standard, ¾-ounce of #8 at 1200 fps. And for the 36-gauge .410 ask for AA419 with ½-ounce of #9 at 1200 fps.

In the limited 1 ⅛-ounce Super-Target 12-gauge shotshell line (#TRGT…), Winchester has designed two value-priced shells in #7 ½ and #8 shot sizes. The 3-dram equivalent shells are rated at 1200 fps while the 2 ¾-drams are rated 1145 fps. Super-Target shotshells are intended for the "high-volume, cost-conscious shooter" who does NOT want to reload.

In 2009, Winchester added a 12-gauge, 2¾-inch, 1-ounce load in #7 ½, #8 and #9, all at 1180 fps, to the Super-Target line. This shotshell is designed for both performance and value. Winchester Shotshell Product Manager Brad Criner said the company had long recognized a shift in demand from 1 ⅛- to lighter 1-ounce loads. "The #TRGTL12 is a light load with consistent patters and very little recoil."

The Super-Target line carries two 20-gauge shells. Loaded with ⅞-ounce of #7 ½ (#TRGT207) or #8 (#TRGT208), these clay-busters are designed to shoot at 1200 fps.

## Reloading for Trap

Shooters who prefer to load their own shells will find a wealth of good load recipes in any number of loading manuals. One of the most comprehensive is this publisher's own *Reloading for Shotgunners, 5th Edition* (Krause, 2005). Even though manufacturers are forced to add colorful new packaging, change names every couple years and flip between paper and plastic, little changes fundamentally in the trap reloading world. As it includes several components which are no longer sold but are still in circulation, this remains a valuable and comprehensive all-gauge tool for hand loaders.

The powders, wads, hulls and shot change slowly. Federal, Winchester and powder manufacturers like Hodgdon, Alliant and IMR (now owned by Hodgdon) offer informative volumes on loading data for their components. These days, most of the information can be accessed through their Internet sites.

A few observations on trap reloads are in order, but realize that the price of components mirrors the price of finished shells, having practically doubled in the past five years.

### Shot

It is an accepted point of shotgunning faith that, all other factors being equal, the harder the lead shot (higher antimony content, six percent plus) the tighter the load will pattern, the more uniform and evenly-distributed the pattern will be, and the shorter the shot string.

In theory, hard shot suffers less deformation in the barrel as it is fired, and round, un-deformed pellets fly truer and maintain a more consistent velocity.

Softer shot pellets (low antimony is usually in the 3-5 percent range and is often referred to as "chilled shot"), it is suggested, do not make it out of the barrel in a perfectly round condition. This causes a number of pellets in the load to veer away from the main pattern, becoming what smoothbore shooters call "fliers." Fliers offer greater resistance to the atmosphere, resulting in their losing velocity faster than the round pellets. This causes them to fall behind the main shot charge, and this extends the shot string. The farther shot has to travel to a target, the more air resistance it meets, the slower it moves and the more the pattern falls apart.

In actuality, many reloaders and those conscientious at the pattern-board dispute this conventional wisdom, which is promoted by manufacturers, distributors and retailers because they charge more for hard shot. Many individual experimenters say they find it does not matter, either for eventual scores or for pellets in the pattern paper. So this is your call. The difference in a bag of high antimony shot versus chilled shot is still only a dollar or so.

Nevertheless, trap is not a close-range game. Twenty yards is a very short shot and it takes a real expert to get on a bird that quickly. From the 27-yard handicap line, shots of 50 or more yards are common. Serious trap shooters, the guys who take home the trophies and perhaps a little cash, simply cannot afford fliers, patchy patterns or long shot strings.

So if you load your own trap shells, I recommend using top quality, high-antimony shot. It costs a little more, but it may be the quickest way I know for a shooter to increase his score. Here are representative loading costs from www.midwayusa.com in Columbia, Missouri, as of March 2009:

- Seven pounds of #7 ½ Hevi-Shot cost $170 ($24.29/pound). Hevi-Shot, a non toxic pellet made from tungsten alloy, nickel and iron that is denser than lead and is not known to deform, is a legal ATA load as long as the club takes ricochet prevention seriously. Five years ago, Midway was selling bismuth at $13.29/pound as their non-toxic alternative.
- An 11-pound bag of #7 ½ BPI nickel plated lead shot was $51 ($4.64/pound). Five years ago, this shot was $2.27/pound. Nickel plating results in hard, round shot and, while it is not allowed in ATA competition, Europeans shooting live released birds seem to prefer it. Copper plated lead is not allowed either but, just for comparison, a 10-pound bag of Lawrence #7 ½ was $33 ($3.30/pound).
- A 25-pound bag of Lawrence # 7 ½ magnum lead shot fetched for $32 ($1.28/pound).] Again, for com-

Studies by the U.S. Fish & Wildlife Service indicate that the build-up of lead shot is not an environmental hazard on shooting ranges. Still, states face increased pressure from various environmental groups to outlaw lead shot and move toward "non-toxic" options.

parison and realizing that the shot itself is a minor part of the reloading equation, a 25-pound bag of Star #7 ½ from www.wideners.com in Johnson City, Tennessee, was $2.50 ($.94/pound).

## Powder

Powder selection for trap loads is extremely wide, and a number of powders of different burning rates will work quite well.

A check, for instance, of the Hodgdon reloading data at www.hodgdon.com for 1 ⅛-ounce of lead in 2 ¾-inch Cheddite plastic hulls, 12-gauge, returns 17 loading options using their Clays powder. Introduced in 1992, Hodgdon says Clays is clean-burning with soft recoil. While all of the loads are velocity-suitable for ATA shooting, depending upon primer and wad, powder weights vary from 15.9 to 20.5 grains and bore pressures from 7,700 psi to 11,500 psi.

I tend to avoid quick-burning powders. My experience has been that they tend to provide a slight increase in recoil, more of a sharp rap than the softer push I prefer, and of course, some of them can be rather dirty-burning, leaving lots of powder residue in the gun. Owners of semi-auto gas guns who use fast powders may find that they need to clean their bores and receivers more frequently.

Powders with a slightly slower burn rate will deliver the same velocities at lower pressures, and are easier on the shoulder. You may not notice the difference in recoil immediately, but it will become apparent after a couple of boxes of shells.

Whether you buy 'em or load 'em, contemporary trap loads are simple to select. The key is to try as many as possible, pattern what you use and then use the one that works best for you.

# CHAPTER 9

# THE EVOLUTION OF SKEET

The clay target game we call skeet got its start shortly after the turn of the century when three avid Massachusetts wingshooters got tired of missing game birds in the field.

You could probably win a trivia bet on this one, but it was C.E. Davies, his son Henry, and shooting buddy William Foster who invented the game that ultimately grew into what we know today as skeet. They realized that the game of trap would not duplicate the angles and flight patterns of all game birds. So, they bolted a trap machine to a plank and, by altering their position in relation to the trap and setting it at high and low elevations, they found they could re-create the flight of virtually any bird, and have a heckuva lot of fun in the process!

The original shooting layout was a full circle with a 25-yard radius. The circle was marked off like the face of a clock, with shooting stations located at each hour. The launcher was positioned at 12 o'clock and threw the targets at six o'clock. Two rounds were fired from each of the 12 stations, with the 25th shot fired from the middle of the field and the target flying right over the shooter's head. This original version of skeet was referred to as "shooting around the clock" and lasted in that form for a couple of years.

The obvious drawback to a 360-degree shot fall zone was overcome in 1923 when Foster, then editor of the bygone National Sportsman magazine, conceived the idea of two traps set within a semi-circle rather than one trap in a full circle. Not only did this allow the game to be played on much less land, but it also earned the gratitude of the spectators and those who drove automobiles to the shoots.

Unfortunately, the new version of the game did not have a name, so Foster sponsored a contest to create one. From more than 10,000 entries, the name "skeet," a derivative of the Scandinavian word for "shoot," was selected. Mrs. Gertrude Hurbutt of Dayton, Montana, submitted the name and won a $100 prize for her effort.

Skeet was originally developed as a bird hunter's game and it even required a low gun position when calling for the bird. It has evolved into a formalized competitive event—sporting clays has followed this track as well—and winning has gotten to be very tough. In the first national championship match held

The game of skeet evolved in the US in the twentieth century when wingshooters realized that the practice they were getting did not prepare them for dove, quail, grouse and woodcock. (*Photo courtesy Ed Oehmig*)

in 1927, the winning team missed eight targets out of 125. Today, a top-ranked shooter who misses eight targets out of 1,000 should consider taking up golf!

This level of perfection often intimidates new shooters, but it should not. I certainly do not intend to take anything away from those steely-eyed AAA and AA Class shooters who run 100 straight targets and consider it nothing more than a warm-up. They are true masters of the game and their form and timing is practically perfect. To be brutally honest however, skeet lends itself to that type of performance. Of all the clay target games available today, skeet is by far the easiest. A look at a skeet field will show you why.

## Field Layout

A skeet field is laid out in a semi-circle with trap houses located at both ends, at three o'clock and nine o'clock. The left-hand house is called the high house and launches the bird from a distance of 10 feet above the ground, and at a slight upward angle. The right-hand house is the low house and sends the bird out at a more abrupt upward angle from a position three feet above the ground.

The launchers are locked into a fixed position and throw the bird to the exact same spot every time. When properly regulated, they will launch the bird at about 42 to 45 mph and the bird must travel between 58 and 62 yards through the air, landing at a predetermined spot under "no wind conditions."

Seven shooting stations are set in a semi-circle around the outside of the field. Station one is directly under the high house, with the following stations moved 26 feet, 8 inches to the right of the previous station. The last station, number eight, is located in the center of the field, midway between the two houses.

Ten feet forward of station eight is a white stake called the "Eight Post." Launchers are regulated to send the bird directly over the top of this stake.

The speed and flight path of the bird are fixed. The shooter knows precisely where it will come from, where it will go, how fast it will be traveling and when it will be launched. The shooting positions are fixed and each shooter will see the same speed and angle of the bird for each presentation from that station.

Each shooting position will show the shooter a different angle, but once the shooter learns the proper lead and technique for each of the stations, he has all the information he needs to break every target consistently. After that it is simply a matter of biomechanics or, as a former Olympic gold medal winner said, "Making your body work like a machine."

The shooting format for standard skeet is simple. A squad, composed of up to five shooters, starts at station one and works around the field to station eight. At stations one, two, six and seven, each shooter is given four targets: a single bird from the high house followed by a single from the low house and finally a pair of doubles where both the high and low house birds are launched simultaneously. When shooting singles, the high house target always comes first. In doubles, the outgoing target (regardless of which house it came from) must be shot first, then the shooter swings back to pick up the incoming bird. At stations three, four and five, the shooter will get only a single target from each house (no doubles), with the high house coming first. At station eight, he will shoot the high house, then the low.

## Four Gauges

Competitive skeet is shot as a four gauge event. In a registered match, where scores are kept for classification purposes, the 12-gauge event will be open to all gauges 12 or smaller, using shot loads not exceeding 1 ⅛-ounces of shot. The 20-gauge event is open to all guns of 20-gauge or smaller, with a shot charge not to exceed 7/8-ounce. The 28-gauge event can be shot with either the 28 or the 410 and a shot load of not more than 3/4-ounce. The 410 event requires the 410 with no more than 1/2-ounce of shot. Regardless of the gauge actually used, all scores will be recorded under the gauge in which the event is officially scheduled.

The only restriction on shot size is that no shot smaller than #9 (2mm) may be used. However, some ranges will have individual restrictions on shot size, based upon the size of their shot fall area.

This does not mean that in order to shoot skeet one must have four gauges. You are quite free to enter only a specific gauge event, if you desire, and to shoot non-registered practice rounds with whatever you want, a pump or side-by-side if you like.

Nor does it mean that if you are an inexperienced shooter that you must go head-to-head with the experts. The skeet classification system is designed to pit shooters against those of similar abilities. In skeet, that system is based on the percentage of registered targets you have broken.

## Etiquette and Procedures

A round of skeet consists of 25 shots. However, it is advisable to have an extra half-dozen shells with you, because it is possible to break both birds during a doubles presentation with one shot. In this case, you have to shoot them over again. It is also common to get a broken bird ("no bird") out of a house in doubles and not be able to stop yourself from shooting in time. "No birds" are also re-shot. Therefore, you can use more than 25 shells in a round and nothing is more irritating to those waiting their turn to shoot than to have a shooter run back to his car for more shells. (Generally, in this case, someone in the squad will toss you a shell, but don't expect this generosity twice!)

A skeet squad can be as many as five shooters. The reason for limiting it to five is that most traps do not hold enough birds for more than that. The sign-up sheet determines your shooting rotation in a squad. It is your responsibility to know which shooter you follow.

On the skeet field, a gun is never loaded until the shooter actually steps onto the three-foot-square shooting pad to take his turn. The rest of the time the gun must be visibly unloaded. With pumps and semi-autos, rack the action open and lock it there: break open double guns. This is only common sense and it not only guarantees that the gun is unable to fire, but it lets everyone else in the squad confirm that at a glance. Skeet shooters are among the friendliest and most gregarious members of the shooting community. I have yet to see an experienced skeet shooter who did not genuinely want to see everybody have a good time and do all he or she could to help inexperienced shooters learn the game. However, nothing will turn this same shooter into a rampaging demon faster than discovering that one of his squad mates is wandering around behind him with a loaded gun.

Skeet shooting is one of the safest participant sports there is. In fact, more people are injured while bowling, playing golf, jogging and swimming than are ever hurt on a skeet field. Strict adherence to the safety rules keeps it that way.

While waiting for your turn to shoot, do not crowd the shooter already on the pad. Be in line and prepared to take your place when the time comes, but the only person who should be within 10 feet of the shooter on the pad is the target puller/referee.

Some skeet ranges have a rule that as soon as a fired shell hits the ground it becomes the property of the range. It is advisable to check to see if that rule is in effect before you start a round. If it is, you must abide by it. Most of these clubs collect those shells and sell them to shotshell reloaders to help offset the cost of operating the field. If there is no such rule, it is perfectly permissible for the shooter to pick up his empties as he leaves the shooting station, as long as it is done expeditiously. The only time on the skeet field that is truly "yours" is the time you are on the pad shooting. Causing delays at other times is infringing on the time another shooter has paid for.

When you step onto the pad to shoot, it is generally accepted that the target puller will release the target at the first sound from you. If you are not prepared for the target, it is a good idea to say nothing. When you call for the bird, do so in a loud enough voice that the puller can clearly hear you. It makes little difference what command you give: "Pull," "Yaaah!," "Now!" Whatever you are comfortable with is perfectly acceptable. Just be consistent in the command and you will help yourself by making the puller's job easier. With a smoothly functioning squad, a round of skeet should be completed in no more than 20 minutes, often less.

## Skeet Accessories

All shooters wear eye protection. It is mandatory. Don't even think of stepping out toward the line without ballistic eyewear. Many shots in skeet are incoming birds and when the shooter breaks the bird, the pieces can keep coming. A piece of broken clay bird traveling at almost 45 mph can cost you an eye. It is common to get pelted with a few shards during the course of the round, whether from birds you have broken yourself or from birds others have shot; maybe even from the adjacent field. Any shooter not wearing eye protection on a skeet field is taking an unnecessary chance with his vision.

Once, hearing protection was an excellent idea. Now, it is a mandatory pre-condition for shooting. Not only does it protect your hearing, but it will also go a long way toward guarding you from recoil fatigue and flinching brought on by continued exposure to high noise levels. A jumpy, tired shooter will not perform well. Muff-type protectors can be uncomfortable for some, especially in warm weather, but there are a number of excellent molded plugs designed to fit comfortably inside the ear that do not interfere with bringing the gun to your cheek. Even an inexpensive set of throw-away foam plugs is better than nothing.

You also need some effective way to carry your shells as you move around the field. If you are saving hulls for reloading, you will need a place to put those empties also. Many shooters favor a shooting vest with large pockets to hold both. These can be purchased with a small amount of padding in the shoulder area to help dampen felt recoil. Belt pouches are also available. These have divided compartments that perform quite well and are both inexpensive and comfortable. Either the vest or the belt is preferable to lugging a box of shells around in your hand or trying to stuff 30 12-gauge shells into your Levis.

Gun breakdowns can occur on the range and most are not quickly repairable, so there really is not much point in carrying a tool kit with you.

There is one little item, however, that can help, a shell knocker. It is possible for a fired shell to lodge in the chamber or for a "squib load" (either a reload or a fresh factory round, it happens with both) to leave a wad stuck in the barrel. A cleaning rod will remove either, but cleaning rods are cumbersome to tote. A simple solution is a piece of brass rod about six inches long. If you shoot all four gauges, its diameter should allow it to slip down a 410-bore tube. Pushed forcefully down the barrel, it will dislodge most obstructions and it can be carried easily in your back pocket. It is annoying for a squad member to have a jammed chamber or an obstructed barrel when it is his turn to shoot and not have anything handy with which to clear it. Toting a shell knocker will make you a popular squad member.

The governing body for skeet competition in America is the National Skeet Shooting Association (NSSA). You will find a full copy of their current rules printed in the back of this volume.

Skeet is a simple and enjoyable game. Best of all, most shooters will have an easy time finding a skeet range near where they live.

# CHAPTER 10

# SKEET SIMPLIFIED

Of all the clay target games, skeet is without a doubt the easiest to learn. Unlike trap and sporting clays, where targets may take varying trajectories when released, the path of every skeet target is fixed. Shooters know precisely when the target will be launched, what path it will take and how fast it will be going.

Once the shooter learns the proper body and gun position for each station, along with the required lead, he has all the information required to break every target consistently. This chapter will provide that information, but before that, we will take a moment to review the two most effective shooting techniques: "fast-swing" and "sustained lead."

## Lead Techniques

With the **fast-swing technique**, the shooter begins with the gun behind the target. The shooter then swings the barrel quickly through the target at a speed faster than the target is moving. One shotgunner described it as "painting the bird out of the sky with the muzzle." As the muzzle overtakes the target, the shot is triggered when the shooter sees the required amount of lead.

The advantage to the fast-swing technique is that it is the most effective way to handle almost any aerial target, including trap, sporting clays and feathered game. Because the gun must be moving much faster

Among the various methods for making the shot automatic, the fast swing is perhaps the most popular. The shotgunner triggers the shot at the appropriate instant as his barrel swings through a flying clay.

On skeet station five, use about a three-foot lead on both the high and low house. Shooting with good form and stance, this competitor is well prepared.

than the target, the shooter has an almost automatic, built-in means of compensating for targets moving at varying speeds: the faster the target is going, the faster the shooter swings the gun to catch it. On the skeet field, a fast-swing shooter has the specific advantage of getting onto the target more quickly than the sustained lead shooter. This is an advantage on windy days when targets sometimes dance to their own tune. The faster you can break it, the better off you are.

The disadvantage, if it can rightly be called such, is that it is impossible to explain precisely what length of lead is required for each station because no two fast-swing shooters will see the same lead. Individual reaction times and swing speeds vary. One shooter may swear he sees only two feet of lead at station four, while the next may claim it takes four feet. Mastering the fast-swing technique requires practice and repetition in order to program your mental computer. It is,

however, time well spent because it will make you a better and more versatile shooter. It will also be to your advantage should you take up trap or sporting clays, and it will certainly increase your gamebird average in the field.

**Sustained lead** on the other hand requires that the gun muzzle start ahead of the bird and never get behind it. Once ahead, gun and target speed are matched while the shooter seeks a precise lead before triggering the shot.

This works well in skeet because you know every lead in advance. The disadvantage (other than being a poor choice for targets of varying speeds whose precise lead is unknown) is that it requires more time to get onto the target than the fast swing. This does not at all hurt the shooter on the easy, lazy incoming targets and indeed, many fast-swing shooters will revert to the sustained lead technique on them. It can result in a shooter "riding" an outgoing target too long and may cause problems if there is a stout breeze. In doubles, because you have to fast-swing through the second bird, you cannot use this technique.

If skeet is the only shotgunning you do, the sustained lead technique can make you a AAA-ranked shooter. Unfortunately, it sometimes causes problems in other wingshooting areas and then shooters have to go through the traumatic experience of "unlearning" this technique. That said, all of the leads given in the balance of this chapter dealing with the fundamentals of skeet are sustained leads, since those are the only leads that will be essentially the same for every shooter. For those who wish to learn the more effective fast-swing technique, cut these leads in half as a starting point. You will quickly see if you need to increase or decrease your body rhythm.

## A Station-By-Station Look at Skeet

### Station One

This station positions the shooter directly under the high house and presents four targets: high and low house singles, and one pair of doubles (one bird from each house).

The high house target is easy but deceptive. It appears to be a straightaway shot, but because it is launched from above the shooter and has a slight upward angle, it is not. You must actually lead this target by shooting underneath it. If you shoot it like a straightaway, you will miss it by going over and behind it every time.

To break this target, take a comfortable shooting position that aligns gun and body on the Eight Post. This advice will hold for virtually every station on the field, because it is advantageous to have your body set for the best shooting position at the point at which you will actually break the target. Since every target on the field is calibrated (if the trap machines are properly adjusted) to send the bird directly over the Eight Post, it makes sense for this to become your focal point. If the Eight Post is where you set up, you will be in position to break every station, with the possible exceptions of high house two and three, low house five and six, and station eight, which we will explain as we reach them.

Once you are positioned, bring the muzzle up to about a 30-degree angle above horizontal and call for the bird. As soon as the bird appears over the muzzle, swing down and through the bird, triggering the shot when you see a six-inch lead below it. Take this bird as quickly as you can, because if you allow it to get beyond the Eight Post it starts to drop rapidly and becomes a much tougher shot. "Riding" this bird will occasionally cause you to break the low house bird also with the one shot, when shooting doubles at this station. That results in a "do-over."

If you are having trouble with high house one, increase the gun angle to 45 degrees. This will cause you to swing faster to catch the bird, and it often helps.

Low house one is easy. Again, align your body on the Eight Post and then bring the gun back to a point about four feet to the outside (left) of the house. On any incoming skeet target, never align the gun directly on the trap house opening where the bird will emerge. This will temporarily blot out the bird as it emerges and will interfere with your ability to pick it up quickly.

Once the bird is released, swing smoothly with it; yet do not be in a hurry to break it. Veteran skeet shooters want to break this target (along with low house two and high houses six and seven) in the same place they will break it during doubles. Let the target reach a point about 45 degrees off your left shoulder and take it there. The lead for this target is one foot.

If you get into the habit of shooting station one singles in this manner, doubles are easy. You take the high house quickly and, when you come back for the low house, you will find it right where you normally break it as a single.

### Station Two

Station two presents four targets: high and low house singles and one set of doubles. This station, however, is not as easy as station one.

The high house shot is one of the tougher targets on the field. It is a vicious quartering angle that must be taken quickly and with a lot of lateral body movement. Right-handed shooters have trouble with this station because the body does not swing as well to the right as it does to the left.

Start by positioning on the Eight Post or maybe just a bit to the right of it to give yourself a little more room to uncoil. Pivot the body to bring the gun about two-thirds of the way back to the house. If you come too far back toward the house, you may not catch this target. Put the gun at the same elevation at which the bird will appear. Once the bird comes out, get onto it quickly with about 2 ½ feet of lead. You must follow through on this shot. Any slowing or stopping of the swing will result in a miss. This is true of any skeet target, but especially so on high house two.

Low house two is much easier. Treat it just like low house one and extend the lead to between 18 and 24 inches. Let the bird fly to a point almost equal with your position. That is where it will be during doubles.

Doubles are the same as at the last station. Get on the outgoing target (high house) quickly, and come back to find the incoming low house right where you normally break it as a single.

If you have a problem with high house two, the answer is to swing faster and shoot quicker. You must be aggressive on this target.

## Station Three

During a standard round of skeet, the shooter takes two targets at this station, both singles, one each from the high house (first) and one from the low house. The high house is an outgoing quartering shot similar to high house two, but you have more time and it is an easier shot. Position on the Eight Post or a bit to the right of it and give the bird three feet of lead.

The low house is an "incomer," similar to low house two, but becomes more of a crossing shot due to the distance. Position as with low house two and give this target 3 ½ feet of lead

One problem with station three (along with four and five) is wind. If there is a breeze, these targets can do some serious dancing. It pays to develop the habit of getting onto these birds quickly. That will also help you when you shoot doubles and find yourself taking doubles at these stations.

## Station Four

Like station three, the shooter is presented with two singles. Both are direct crossing shots and are the longest one will see on a skeet field. These birds are 21 yards away from the shooter when they cross the Eight Post. The lead for the birds from both houses is four feet.

I prefer to position on the Eight Post for both houses and try to break the pigeons as they cross the post. Some shooters use a different foot position for the high and low houses at this station (as well as three and five), but I do not concur because it causes problems when you shoot these stations in the doubles game. As long as you position your natural point of aim on the Eight Post, you have all the range of movement you require for both singles and doubles.

Until this point, shooters have been seeing new angles and shots at each station. As you move to station five, however, things begin to become familiar.

## Station Five

This is nothing more than station three in reverse, with the high house becoming the incomer (and still shot first) and the low house becoming the outgoing target.

Take the high house using the same 3 ½-foot lead used on low house three. Take the low house with the same three-foot lead as high house three. Positioning on the Eight Post is the same.

The biggest difference is that the low house takes a more abrupt upward angle because of your proximity to it and you must rise with it. Other than that, every bit of practice you take at station three helps you with station five, and vice versa.

## Station Six

This is the reverse image of station two. Shoot the high house first. It is a gentle incomer like low house two. Body position is the same, as is the 18- to 24-inch lead used on low house two.

Low house six becomes the outgoing target and is a sharp and rapidly rising target. For right-handers however, it is easier than the "Demon High House Two" because the body uncoils better to the left. Shoot it the same way, using the same body position and 2 ½-foot lead.

For doubles, shoot the outgoing low house first and take the incoming high house as it draws in to a 45-degree angle to the shooter's right.

Shoot station six the same way you shot station two.

## Station Seven

This is the easiest station on the field. Shoot the high house first, but let it get close, and use a one-foot lead.

The low house looks like a dead straightaway and, if you have a little upward angle in your initial gun position, it is. This target can be broken with no gun movement. Position the gun and your body on the Eight Post, elevate the gun barrel to a point about eight feet above it and, if the launcher is regulated properly, the target will "appear" right over your front bead.

Pull the trigger—dead bird.

Doubles at this station are so easy one wonders why they even bother. Take the outgoing house with no gun movement and let the recoil ride the gun up to perfectly pick up the incoming bird.

If you are introducing a new shooter to skeet and you want to build their confidence quickly, take them to station seven first.

## Station Eight

Having completed a trip around the outside, it is now time to step inside and face two of the most intimidating targets on the field.

High and low house eight targets are not "gimmees," but they are not nearly as tough as they appear and you have more time to shoot them than you might think.

The reason these two targets are intimidating is that they are close. In years past, some shooters even used special "spreader" loads to handle them. Once shooters found out how easy these targets were to break, however, the station eight birds lost their intimidation factor.

Take high house eight by positioning gun and body right on the trap house opening, then moving the gun four feet to the right of the trap house. As the bird comes out, swing quickly up and through it, triggering the shot just as the gun muzzle passes the bird and shows just a hint of daylight between bird and muzzle.

**Station One, High House:** This deceptive target looks like a straightaway, but shooters must actually trigger the shot with the barrel below the target if they are to score.

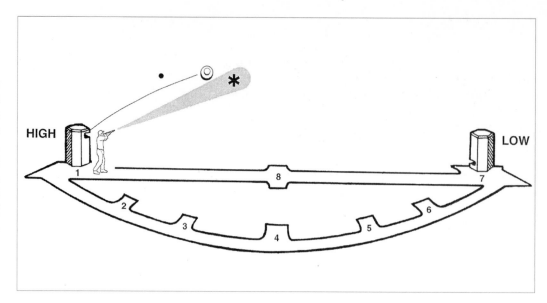

**Station One, Low House:** Smart shooters are in no hurry to break this easy shot and allow it to reach the same point where they will shoot it as a double. It is easier to find it when you always look for it in the same place.

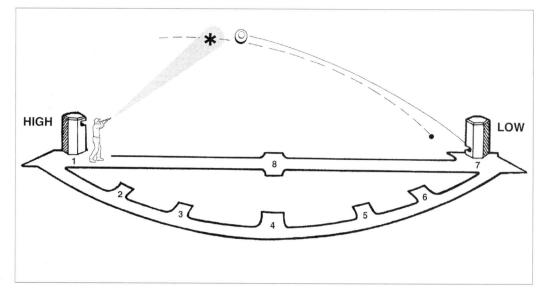

**Station Two, High House:** A tough shot for right-handed shooters, this requires a lot of lateral body movement, and a shooter must drive forcefully through the target. Get sluggish here and you will miss.

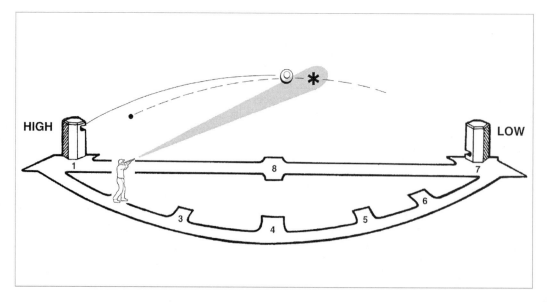

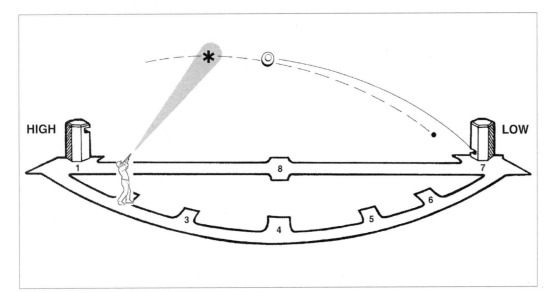

Station Two, Low House: This is very similar to the low house target from station one. Shoot it in the same place with just a slight increase in lead.

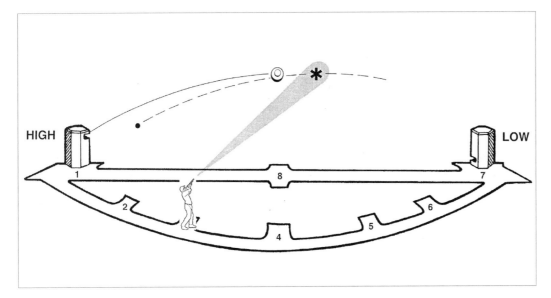

Station Three, High House: An easier angle than station two high house, this requires another foot of lead but gives the shooter more time to get onto the bird.

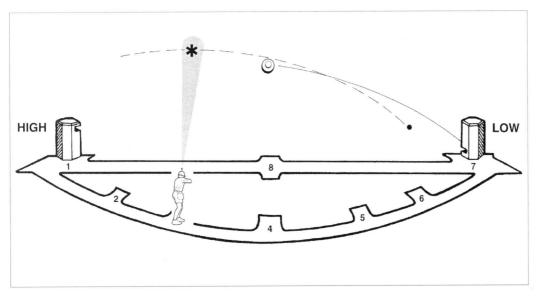

Station Three, Low House: This is one of the easier targets on the field when taken as a single. The shooter has plenty of time to find it and establish the correct lead.

Station Four, High House: This is one of the longest shots you will see on a skeet field and it tricks many sustained lead shooters who do not believe they need a four-foot lead on a 21-yard target. Fast-swing shooters can cut that lead in half.

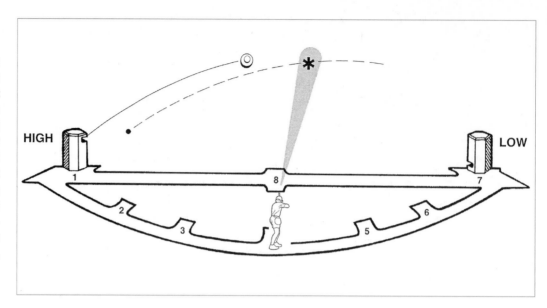

Station Four, Low House: Virtually the same shot as from the high house, but in a different direction. If you break both station four targets near the "Eight Post," you do not have to change foot position.

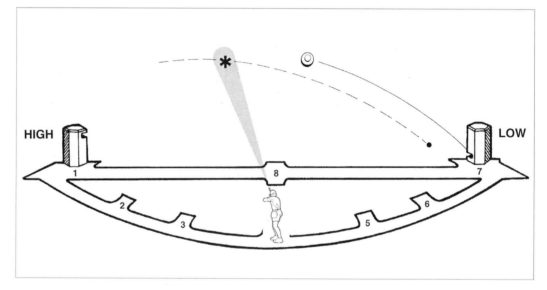

Station Five, High House: This is almost the mirror image of the station three low house. The lead is the same.

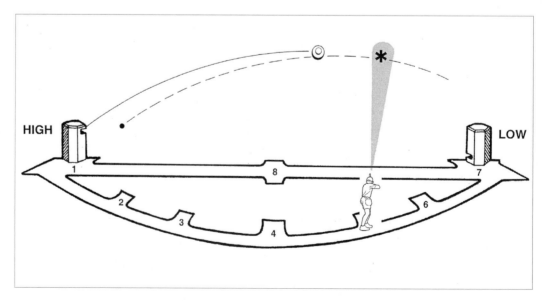

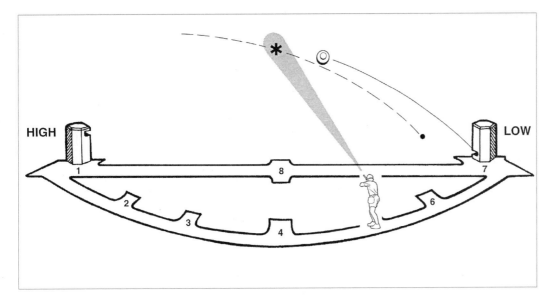

Station Five, Low House: Very similar to station three high house except that the target is usually climbing a little more. The leads are the same and the shooter must concentrate on swinging up and through the target.

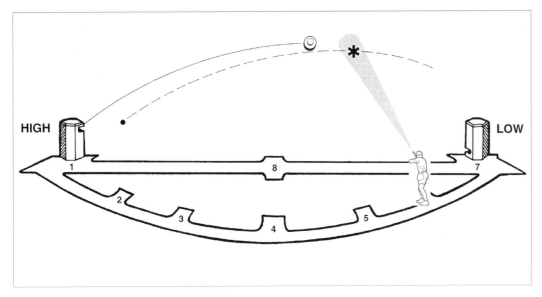

Station Six, High House: This is an easy as the station two low house shot, although the target is often falling slightly, depending on wind direction.

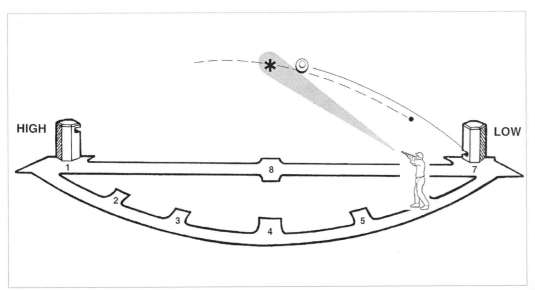

Station Six, Low House: Left-handed shooters have the same problem with this target that right-handers do on the station two high house. You must swing quickly through this target and trigger the shot as soon as you have your lead. If you hesitate, you will lose this bird.

Station Seven, High House: One of the easiest shots on the field, this target should be broken in the same place you will see it as a double.

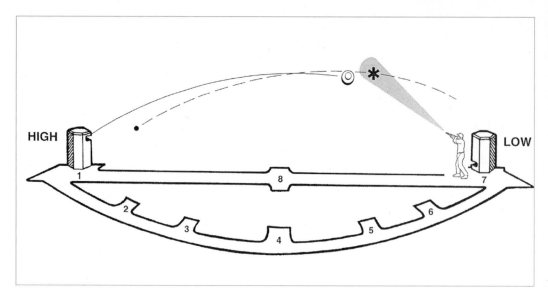

Station Seven, Low House: This is the only target on a skeet field that can consistently be broken with no gun movement. "It's a true 'gimme,'" says co-author Chris Christian.

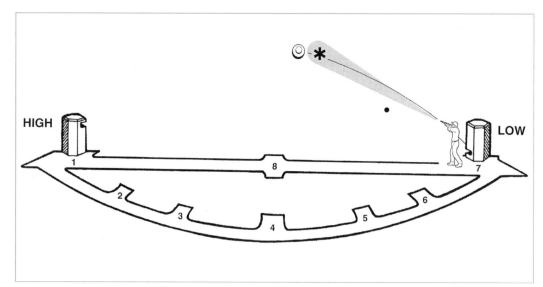

Station Eight, High House: More intimidating than it looks, shooters should swing fast through this target and trigger the shot as soon as the muzzle reaches the leading edge of the bird.

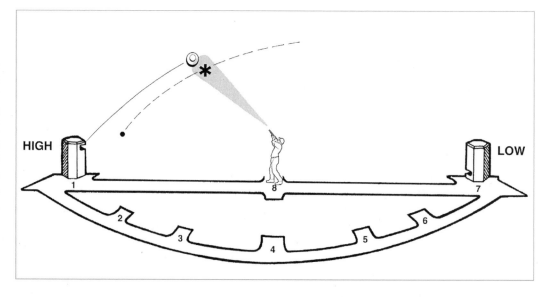

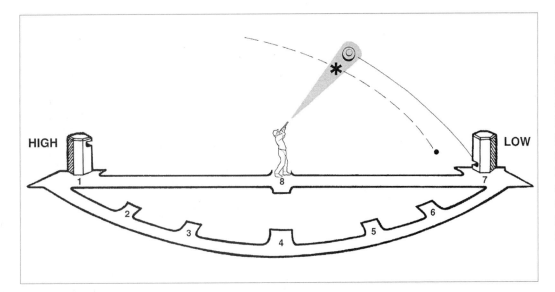

Station Eight, Low House: The closest shot on a skeet field, with many birds broken only four yards off the muzzle. Fast-swing through the target and trigger the shot as soon as the muzzle blots out the bird.

Shoot the low house by positioning on the opening and then moving the barrel three feet to the left of the house. When the bird comes at you, swing up and through and break the shot the moment the muzzle blots out the bird.

These targets are that simple.

If you have been counting shells, you know that we have only fired 24 of our 25 rounds. The last round is called the "option round" and it is fired at the first target missed during the round. If you get to low house eight without a miss, you may fire the last round as a second shot on that station. If you have never run 25-straight skeet targets before, this is the toughest shot on the field. If you make it, it is also the most satisfying.

Getting to that point, however, takes proper equipment and intelligent practice.

## All-Important Practice

The foregoing angles, leads and body positions provide all the information required to break every target on the field consistently. To make use of this information though, a shooter must see enough of those targets and break them to build the positive subconscious images needed for success. There are good and bad ways to arrive at that point.

In the opinion of many good skeet shooters, the worst possible way to start is for a new shooter to simply fall in with a squad and start shooting. This is because a new shooter sees new angles and shots at each station. Before he can begin to understand and master them, he is whisked off to the next station where what is new begins all over again. Along the way he or she will get a lot of well-intentioned advice from the other shooters on the squad, yet much of it will be confusing, hard for a novice to understand and sometimes even contradictory. This makes for a poor learning environment.

The most effective way to learn skeet and the most efficient in terms of time and ammunition spent is to start with one particular shot and work on it until it is burned into the subconscious. Then, move on to the next shot presentation.

At first, begin working on the easy incoming shots and ignore everything else. This builds a shooter's confidence and demonstrates the symmetrical nature of the game.

Start at station one and work on the low house until you become proficient. This sometimes takes as few as four or five shells. Once the shooter has a solid feel for that target, move to low house two. It is virtually identical, except for the lead, and the positive experience with low house one is a benefit at low house two. Then go to low house three and do it again. Stations five, six and seven require work on the incoming high houses until the shooter has a firm grasp of all these shots.

When you reach this point, move to station four to work on both high and low houses. The leads are identical and these shots are similar to those the student has already learned at stations three and five. This also gets the student used to swinging quickly on fast-moving targets, because until now all shots have been lazy incomers. Station four is the perfect spot to make the shift from deliberately taking incomers to aggressively pursuing outgoing birds.

After that, it is back around to stations three, two and one, and then over to five, six and seven for work on the outgoing targets. Station eight comes next and the final lesson is putting it all together with doubles.

Using this approach, the time required to give a new shooter a solid, working knowledge of the game is reduced from months to weeks. I have seen students expend as few as 10 boxes of shells in practice, then go out and pop 23 birds the first time they shoot a complete round!

Assuming you find a competent instructor, progressive lessons like this can also prevent the shooter from acquiring bad habits at the start. Bad habits will do some serious damage to a shooter's scores.

## Common Errors

To achieve a good score in skeet, which I have said was perhaps the easiest shotgun game; a shooter must still execute the fundamentals properly. Sometimes this does not happen, though. There are three very common ways to miss even the easiest skeet target and they will, on occasion, plague shooters at almost any level of skill.

The most common mistake is lifting the head from the gunstock. Not surprisingly, this seems to be the bane of new shooters as well as those who have taken significant time off from the game. Under these conditions, targets seem to be the size of aspirin tablets moving at about the speed of a Patriot missile and new shooters will often pop their heads off the stock to get "a better look" or simply locate the target. When the head comes off the stock, the shot charge goes high every time.

There is no quick and easy cure for this, other than to continually remind yourself to "Love Thy Wood." Take plenty of care when mounting the gun to assure a proper cheek weld with the stock. That cheek weld is critical to successful wingshooting. Maintaining a

A Remington 105CTi auto-loader held tight against the cheek and shoulder allows one's eyes to come into good sight alignment along the barrel rib.

| Individual Skeet Classification | | | | | |
|---|---|---|---|---|---|
| Class | 12-gauge | 20-gauge | 28-gauge | .410-bore | Doubles |
| AAA | 98.5% and over | 98% and over | 97.5% and over | 96% and over | 97% and over |
| AA | 97.5-98.49% | 97-97.99% | 96.5-97.49% | 94.7-95.99% | 95-96.99% |
| A | 96-97.49% | 94.5-96.99% | 94-96.49% | 91-94.69% | 91-94.99% |
| B | 93.5-95.99% | 91-94.49% | 90.5-93.99% | 86-90.99% | 85-90.99% |
| C | 90% to 93.49% | 85.5-90.99% | 85.5-90.49% | 80-85.99% | 80-84.99% |
| D | 85.5-89.99% | under 85.5% | under 85.5% | under 80% | under 80% |
| E | under 85.5% | n/a | n/a | n/a | n/a |

cheek weld is a shooting basic that the shooter must continually work on and reinforce.

Stopping the swing is another quick way to blow a target and, surprisingly, this often seems to affect mid-level shooters the most. This error can be especially prevalent among shooters who rely completely on the sustained lead technique since it can, at times, encourage indecision and hesitation.

New shooters see targets moving so swiftly that they must swing very quickly to catch them and this forces them to swing through the target. Once a shooter gains some experience however, two things happen at about the same time: the targets suddenly grow much larger and they slow down.

The experienced shooter knows he has plenty of time and becomes more concerned with getting "just the right lead." The gun swings through the target, the correct lead is obtained, analyzed, trimmed up a bit, and then the subconscious says, "We've got it! Pull the trigger."

Then, just as the trigger gets slapped, the gun stops and the shot charge sails harmlessly behind the target.

The best way to avoid this is to think of wingshooting in the same light as many other sports: one must follow through. If a golfer stops his swing the moment his club makes contact with the ball, or a bowler stops his arm movement when he lays the ball down on the alley, or a tennis player quits the instant his racket strikes the ball, what would the results be? Nothing. Zip. Nada. No follow-through equals no good results.

Shotgun shooting is not any different. To hit an aerial target, the gun must be moving at the moment the shot is triggered and it must continue to follow right on through the target. If stopping your swing troubles you, try following the broken pieces and mentally take a second shot. If you develop the habit of staying with the broken pieces after the shot, even if for just a fraction of a second, you will not have to worry about stopping your swing.

The last of the common problems is simply not being ready when you call for the bird. Unbelievably, this can often sneak up on experienced shooters without warning.

What happens is this: you have broken that target hundreds, maybe thousands of times. You could do it in your sleep, and with one hand tied behind your back. You never miss that bird. Then, you step on the shooting pad and let your mind drift. Bingo! When the bird comes out you are unprepared. Your timing is completely off and the bird sails away unscathed.

I watched a terrific shooter lose his concentration at a national championship once and he admitted his gaffe afterward. He stepped to the shooting pad, took a moment to admire an airplane flying overhead, called for the bird and found his mind was still on the airplane. He missed.

Everyone will develop a little routine when he steps onto the pad. Some people squiggle around. Some adjust their shooting vest or glasses. I sweep all the little bits of broken target off the pad with my foot. The point is that we all do something. While our small habits may look a little quirky to others, they are actually an important part of our shooting game. These individual quirks are our subconscious mind's way of preparing us to execute the shot. Let the subconscious do its job. If you have a comfortable "pad routine," do not deviate from it or you may short-circuit your own success.

When you are about to conduct a complicated movement that requires a number of coordinated body movements and mental decisions, all happening in about 1.2 seconds, your subconscious mind is the best friend you have. Do not get in its way.

Combine your personal routine with an understanding of proper leads and angles and an effective practice regime that lets your subconscious absorb them, and you will find that skeet can indeed be as simple as it is fun.

# CHAPTER 11

# SHOOTING SKEET DOUBLES

There was a time when you did not have to survive a shoot-off to win a trophy at a skeet championship, but if you want to take home something for the trophy case today you will have to be good at doubles. For that matter, if you are looking for the "High Overall" (HOA) trophy, you will have to shoot doubles anyway, so you may as well prepare.

There are stations in skeet where doubles (a pair of targets launched simultaneously from the high and low house) are shot. This is a normal part of the game, and one that any shooter will learn to handle simply by shooting skeet. When you get to the actual game of doubles however, you will find that it is slightly different and that you will shoot two different versions of it: regular doubles and shoot-off doubles.

Regular doubles is a scheduled event in any skeet tournament. The program will usually say "25 Pairs" or "50 Pairs." The former means it is a 50-round match, while the latter listing calls for 100 rounds. One shoots regular doubles as a 12-gauge event, although that does not stop shooters from using smaller gauges. In fact, the 20-gauge is the tool of choice among

top shooters. Shooting the 20-gauge sharpens their hand-eye coordination and handicaps these shooters in a way that gives them extra pride in their ability to bust birds. Like everyone who has achieved proficiency in some public sport, shooting the 20 allows them to show off, too. It is a perfectly natural and reasonable thing to do.

## Regular Doubles

You shoot regular doubles as follows: shooters start at station one and are presented with the same pair of doubles seen in standard skeet. You shoot the high house bird first. At this station, you only shoot the one pair. Moving to station two the shooter sees the same thing, basic skeet doubles, with the high house again shot first. You have fired four shots, and move to station three where the game changes.

In standard skeet, station three is a pair of singles, one from the high and one from the low house. In doubles, you get both at once and you will want to shoot the high house first. Move to station four and the situation repeats.

Station 7 may be the easiest of all in skeet for a right- or a left-hand shooter. No purpose is served by altering your shooting style from standard skeet at this station or on stations one, two or six. Shoot them as you always do.

**This doubles shooter's aggressive, ready posture with plenty of weight on her forward foot should ensure that she has no trouble swinging through a bird on station seven.**

That completes the first half of a doubles round. It requires 24 shells. The second half is identical except that we now finish on station one, instead of two, in order to get rid of those last two rounds.

## Shoot-Off Doubles

Shoot-off doubles is a condensed version of regular skeet doubles. Here, shooters move between stations three, four and five with the order of the targets the same: high house always first at three, low house always first at five, and alternating between high and low house at four. This will continue until one shooter has not missed and he or she is the champion.

Shoot-off doubles was created when skeet scores began to become so perfect that a standard 100-bird match would see several shooters with a perfect upper level score. It was simply a way to decrease the amount of time it would take to conduct a shoot-off and determine a winner in the event. What makes shoot-off doubles so tough is the fact that one shoots it in the gauge class the shooter used to get to the shoot-off.

If several shooters tie in the 410 class, they will have to shoot doubles with the 410. Some clubs will run a standard round of doubles first, and then shoot-off doubles for any shooters who survive that. In the 12-, 20- and 28-gauge events, you can expect to go directly to shoot-off doubles in those gauges.

## How to Shoot Doubles

Doubles intimidates many shooters, but it should not. In fact, regardless of the doubles game you are shooting, shoot-off or regular, only three stations offer anything different from what you have already seen in standard skeet: stations three, four and five. For that reason, no purpose is served by altering your shooting style for stations one, two, six and seven: shoot them like you always do. You will want to make some changes for three, four and five, however.

At station three, your normal foot position on the three mid-field crossing stations (three, four and five) would have the body aligned to break both birds over the center stake. Some top shooters, when shooting these stations as singles in the regular round, shift foot position for each of the two birds, but I do not recommend that unless you have shot long enough to know it benefits you.

On station five, you again have two birds at once, but this time take the outgoing bird (now the low house) first. Stations six and seven offer one pair of doubles, the same as a standard skeet round.

Of course, we have not fired all of our shells yet, so we now make a reverse trip around the field. From station seven, we go back to six and repeat the doubles presentation there; then we go back to five and do it again.

When we reach station four again on the return swing a major change takes place. The rules require you to take the low house bird first, and this can be one of the toughest shots on the skeet field. The reason is simple. This is the only time you will ever shoot the low bird first on station four and it does terrible things to your subconscious computer.

Moving back to three, things get back to normal and you shoot the high house first as you do at station two.

With the body aligned on the Eight Post, you are in position to utilize your full range of body movement to break each single over the stake. Unfortunately, in doubles, this foot position can hinder you. I have not seen more than a handful of shooters that can shoot fast enough to take both the first bird and the second with their body aligned on the stake. The second (low house bird) is invariably going to get beyond the stake. If you align your body with the stake, you may have trouble picking the target up and catching it.

This is a situation where you know the second bird is going to be tough. Experienced shooters will usually fudge their body position to favor that bird.

It becomes a matter of individual reaction time and shooting style, but every shooter will benefit by shifting his basic station-three-position in the doubles round toward the high house side of the stake. I normally start new shooters with an alignment almost halfway back to the high house and see where we need to fine-tune it from there. This will bind the body slightly on the outgoing first bird (high house), but it gives perfect position on the second. Some shooters can handle the slightly restricted swing on the high house and some cannot. Those who have trouble catching the high house bird may have to start easing their gun position back toward the stake.

You do not have to wait to shoot a doubles round to find out if this is the case with your shooting rhythm. You can practice this while shooting standard skeet. Simply adjust your initial gun position back toward the high house on singles at station three until you find the point at which you are too bound up to take high house three. Once you find what your body's limitations are, you can begin adjusting your gun position to give you the best shot.

The first time we visit station four we encounter a similar situation. Shoot the high house first and the low house can get away from you. I recommend that you make the same readjustment of the body to the high house side of the field.

The second time we see station four it is a different situation. Now the low house is first. If you discount the subconscious reaction to shooting the low house bird first, this is actually not as tough a shot as shooting the high house bird first. The reason is that when you take the high house second, its normally higher trajectory tends to keep it in the air longer than the low bird. Many shooters find they can use a normal "align on the stake" position here and get away with it. Others find that only a slight fudging toward the low house is all they need to get back smoothly on high four for the second shot.

**Station One Doubles:** The high house target is taken first with normal lead and the gun is swung back to break the low house target at an angle of about 45 degrees to the shooter's left.

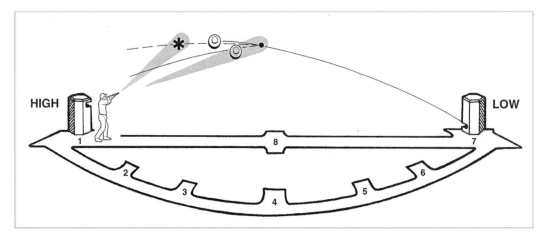

**Station Two Doubles:** Shoot the high house target first and break the low house target at the same point it would be taken during singles.

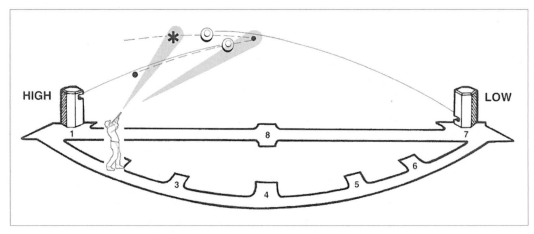

Station four is however, one skeet station where a heavier second load is a major asset. Regardless of where you catch the second bird at station four, it is going to be one of the longest shots you will ever see on a skeet field. You are pushing the range at which #9 shot will reliably break a target. I favor a 1 ⅛-ounce 12-gauge load of #8 ½ shot or a one-ounce load of the same if I am shooting the event with a tubed 20-gauge.

The heavier shot pellets will get you an extra bird now and then and that is sometimes enough to win.

A number of shooters who routinely opt for the 20-gauge in this event use a full one-ounce load of #8 ½ for all of their doubles shots, simply to remove the possibility of confusing different shot size loads during the pressure of a shoot-off. They know the importance of a heavier load for the second shot on the

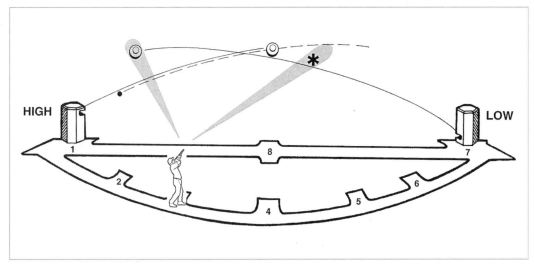

**Station Three Doubles:** The high house target must be taken quickly in order to get the gun back to the low house target. Shooters often fudge their natural point of aim to the high house side of the field in order to have sufficient swing room for the low house target, which is usually taken beyond its normal position when shot as a single.

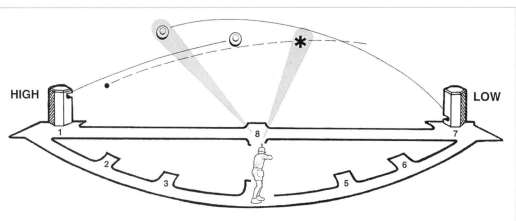

**Station Four Doubles:** This is considered the most difficult station in doubles since the high house is taken first the first time the station is shot and the low house taken first the second time through.

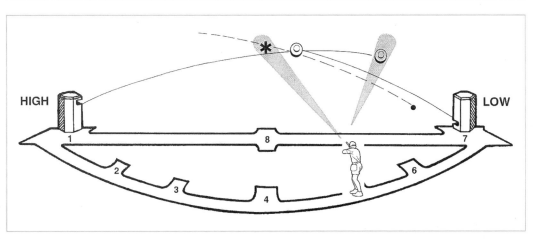

**Station Five Doubles:** The low house is taken first, and many shooters will shift their natural point of aim to the low house side of the field to increase the swing distance on the second bird. A tail wind will cause the high house bird to hunt the ground quickly, requiring the shooter to speed up his timing.

**CHAPTER ELEVEN** SHOOTING SKEET DOUBLES **77**

**Station Six Doubles:** The low house target is taken first and the incoming high house broken at about a 45-degree angle to the shooter's right. This can be a difficult shot for left-handed shooters.

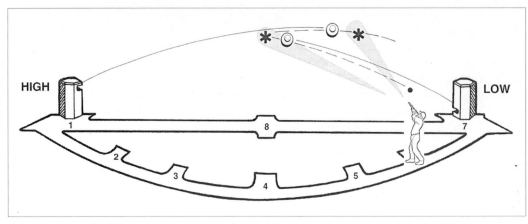

**Station Seven Doubles:** This is the easiest doubles shot on the field. With proper gun hold position, the low house bird can be taken without moving the gun, and the recoil will lift the gun into the perfect position to pick up the high house target.

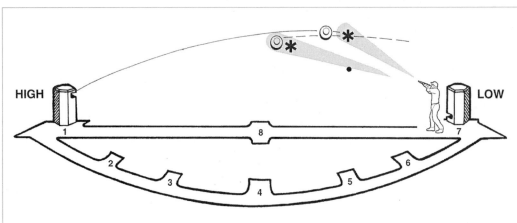

middle stations and do not want to take the chance of not getting one in the gun. For the same reason, many experienced competitors have a few #8 ½ loads made up for the 28-gauge and 410 as well. They may not use them in regular skeet, but if they do have a good day in those gauges, they know they will have to run them in the shoot-off and the heavier loads can come in handy.

Station five is similar to station four on the second swing-through. The high house becomes the second bird and its trajectory favors the shooter. You do not need to fudge as much toward the low house from a basic "align on the Eight Post" position, but some shooters find it does help to edge to the low house side slightly.

This shift in body position is a purely individual matter. There is no one correct foot position for every shooter because body shapes, swing speeds and reflexes are different. You accept the fact that favoring the second bird is a good idea, and then begin experimenting with foot position until you find the one that works best for you.

One way you can definitely help yourself in the doubles game is to change the way you shoot singles in regular skeet. If you have ever watched a top shooter,

you will see that he or she takes every mid-field crossing shot as soon as possible. In fact, these competitors try to break them before the clays get to the stake. This is obviously an asset in the doubles game, because the faster you can break the first bird the more time you have for the second and the less you have to fudge your gun position for it.

Fast shooting also becomes an asset on a windy day. It takes a strong wind to affect the flight path of a skeet target before it gets to the stake because it is still under the influence of the launcher's velocity. By the time it gets to the stake, however, the wind will catch it and you may find that terrible things happen. If you shoot doubles in a laid back, "ride the target forever" mode and the wind comes up, you are going to get murdered. You have to be a little excited and pumped up to shoot good doubles.

Doubles is a different game, but not radically. It is no more difficult than standard skeet. In fact, classification scores show that over the course of 100 rounds, doubles is only about one bird harder.

Doubles is a game one will have to master to advance to the upper levels of the shotgun sports. If you are going to win any trophies in skeet today, you will have to do it in a shoot-off, and doubles is the game.

# CHAPTER 12

# INTERNATIONAL SKEET COMPETITION

The game we shoot as American skeet has been called, correctly, the easiest of the various clay target games to master. That lack of challenge has not rested very well with our English and European counterparts, though. As a result, they have modified the game to a slightly different and infinitely more difficult version for international competition. In this chapter, we will review what our shooters face in World Cup and Olympic competition.

You shoot international skeet on the same field as the American version, with all distances and dimensions identical, but the target order and the speed are different.

## Firing Order

On station one, international shooters first take a high house single and then a pair of doubles. As in American skeet, you shoot the high house first. There is no single target from the low house, which is one of the easiest shots in skeet. Moving to station two, you repeat the same procedure with a single high house and a pair of doubles.

At station three, the shooter must deal with a single from each house and then a pair of doubles, with the high house target taken first. On station four, the procedure is the same. At station five, we again get a

International shooters look at our American skeet game as somewhat tame. The international venue requires shooters to begin from a low gun position, so do not expect to shoot many 100-straight birds. *(Photo courtesy Winchester)*

Unlike American skeet, the International game requires that you call for the bird from the low gun position. International skeet requires a permanent, contrasting strip on your vest "from the side to the front of the outer shooting garment placed at the top of the shooter's hip line." The stock of the gun must touch this line at the low gun "ready" position.

pair of singles, with the high house target taken first and then a pair of doubles, with the low house taken first.

Moving to station six, the shooter sees a single from the low house and then a pair of doubles, with the low house taken first. At station seven, shoot the single targets first and then one pair of doubles, with the low house shot first.

On station eight, the shooter loads one shell and takes a single from the high house. At that point, the shooter unloads the gun, turns completely around to the low house (turning to the outside of the field in a clockwise direction), loads a single shell and takes the low house single. There is no "option round" as there is in American skeet.

Thus, the international course of fire deletes the easiest shots in American skeet (low houses one, two, seven and high houses six and seven) and replaces them with the toughest shots on the field, which are doubles from three, four and five. In effect, it takes away the "gimmees" and incorporates shoot-

off doubles into the basic round. This alone tends to prevent a lot of perfect scores, but wait... it gets even tougher!

## Gun Position

International skeet requires shooting from a low gun position, and when they say low they are not kidding! Competitors must have a permanent contrasting strip (about one inch wide and 9 ¾-inches long) from the side to the front of the outer shooting garment placed at the top of the shooter's hip line. The stock of the gun must touch this line at the low gun "ready" position, and you cannot move the gun from it until the target actually appears. You have the gun butt on your hip when you call for the target and, as in sporting clays, the target release device is equipped with a variable delay of up to three seconds.

Compared to the ready gun position in sporting clays, international skeet is much lower and requires more gun-handling skills.

International rules allow competitors to bring the

gun to their shoulder for a brief pre-target sight picture only at stations one and eight. They must then immediately return to the ready position before calling for the target.

## Target Speed

Field managers also crank up international skeet targets to a higher speed. They move about five mph faster than American targets. This requires that they be more stoutly constructed to take the higher launch velocity and, in addition to being made from harder materials, they have a reinforcing ring on the throwing ring. How tough are they? Lloyd Woodhouse, coach of the U.S. Shooting Team (USST) told me of a picture

Since international skeet is very fast, developing a fluid gun mount is critical. "We find that a leading-arm elbow position of 45 degrees gives the best compromise for effective movement in all directions," says acclaimed coach Lloyd Woodhouse.

he has from a competition in Cuba that shows him standing with all of his 195 pounds on one foot atop a target, and the target is just fine!

It is not uncommon to find unbroken targets on an international field, clays that have a few holes punched completely through them. It takes a solid, center-pattern hit to get that all-important "visible piece" in this game.

The last significant differences between the two skeet games are the load and gauge. International skeet is shot almost exclusively with the 12-gauge, while American Skeet uses the 12, 20, 28 and 410. The maximum allowable load for international is a mere 24 grams (about ⅞-ounce) with a maximum shot size of #7 ½.

In former years, many USST shooters favored Federal Cartridge international loads in size #8 ½. A couple of the shooters however, opted for the #7 ½ load for the second shot on doubles from stations three, four and five. The #8 ½ shot incidentally, is an excellent doubles load for American skeet, as well as for many shots in sporting clays. Despite the diminutive shot charge, this load is an awesome performer and it will really crush a target. Recoil is light and its 1330 fps velocity gets it to the target fast.

## Guns and Gear

Guns for international skeet are little different from the 12-gauge guns used for our version of the game. One sees both over/unders and gas-operated semi-autos in competition, although the stackbarrel guns do predominate. The standard skeet constriction of .004- to .005-inch is considered the best bet. The preferred barrel length for the over/unders falls right within the 28- to 32-inch range that we see on skeet fields in this country. One difference is that ported guns may not be used in international competition, but given the gentle recoil of the 24-gram load, they are not really much of an asset.

The only significant difference in guns between the American and the international games is the recoil pad. Because of the extreme low ready position, the pad needs to be smoothly radiused at the top to aid in a smoother gun mount. Most shooters also round off the inner edge. This is also common in sporting clays. Some competitors go a bit farther and apply a slick-surfaced PVC or Teflon tape to the sides and sometimes to the top of the pad to remove that sticky "pencil eraser" feel that can cause drag on the shooting vest with some types of rubber pads.

When it comes to selecting a shooting vest, the international style, which has a slick-faced shooting pad extending completely down the gun-mount side, is the overwhelming favorite.

Eye and ear protection is mandatory and, as in American-style skeet, is a superb idea because you can get pelted with an occasional target piece during a round. Some competitors are taking a page from their sporting clays counterparts and opting for electronic ear plugs. These contain an electronic cutoff circuit that shuts out noise levels above a certain decibel level, yet amplifies low-level sounds. Many instructors wear them because it makes their teaching job easier and allows better communication with their shooters. On the international and sporting clays fields, they have one additional valuable advantage: they can amplify sounds enough to let you actually hear most trap machines release the target. To my way of thinking, that is of no small importance!

The variable target delay of up to three seconds can result in a significant change in the timing of a shooter who is used to having the target appear immediately when he calls for it. On an international field, the target may come immediately or it may be delayed long enough to bring on the jitters. With conventional ear plugs the only target acquisition device the shooter has is visual. In the real world, we tend to blend all of our senses into one system. With the amplification powers of electronic ear plugs, we can now use both sight and sound to acquire the target. These can be a real advantage to some shooters and they are now commonly accepted at sporting clays events. This technology will certainly work its way onto the international fields as well.

## Shooting Tips for International Skeet

International skeet is far more complex and challenging than the American version. Not surprisingly, it can create problems for shooters used to the tamer American sport.

"The biggest problem for new international shooters is getting the smooth and consistent gun mount down pat," says Lloyd Woodhouse, who taught our Olympic shooters the finer points of scattergunning for more than a decade. "Gun handling is critical in this game and it must become a subconscious learned response. That can take a lot of practice, and a lot of shooting."

Interestingly, Woodhouse and his assistant coaches have developed a training system that works on the principle of starting with the easy shots to build the shooter's confidence and gradually progresses to the more difficult shots. Woodhouse calls it "stage training."

"The theory," Woodhouse has explained, "is to set the stage for success, and this works well to develop gun handling skills. We start a new shooter off with a pair of low house station one single targets. This is a very easy shot and gives the shooter 1.4 to 1.6 seconds to mount the gun. Then we move to station two and shoot low houses again. Once the shooter is comfortable with this, we move to stations six and seven and shoot the incoming high houses. All of these are easy targets that give the shooter the maximum amount of time to mount the gun. This insures that the shooter experiences success."

On the next stage, Woodhouse continues, his shooters return to station one and start working their way through the stations taking just the low houses. "As we reach stations four through seven, we gradually decrease the 'time look' at the targets and require the shooter to increase the speed of the gun mount. Nevertheless, we start with the easy targets and build the shooter's confidence before we begin asking more of him, or her. There is a significant difference in the time element for gun mounting between a low house one and a low house six."

By slowly decreasing the amount of time the shooter has to consciously think out and execute the gun mount, he notes, USST coaches get the mount so rigidly built that it becomes a subconscious learned response. That lets the shooter keep the conscious mind on important things like acquiring the target and executing a smooth swing and follow-through.

Developing a fluid gun mount is critical in this game, as well as in sporting clays. It is easier if one starts with the proper hand position on the gun. In that respect, regardless of the type of shotgunning one does, the following advice from our former Olympic Team coach is well worth studying.

"Biomechanically," Woodhouse has explained, "if you put the elbow of your leading hand directly below the gun, like a rifleman's stance, you have the greatest leverage for moving the gun up and down, but the weakest leverage for moving the gun from side to side. If you move that elbow out to a 90-degree angle from the gun, you now have the maximum leverage for side movement, but the weakest leverage for up and down movement. We find that an elbow position of 45 degrees gives us the best compromise for effective movement in both directions, and that is where we like to start a shooter. After that, we can fine-tune the position over time."

The same is true for moving the hand forward and back on the forearm, he continues. "If the hand is way out on the forearm, the elbow is almost straight. If you move it back almost to the trigger guard, then the elbow is bent too much. In that position your arm can support a lot of weight. If you move the hand forward and straighten your elbow, then you will not be able to hold as much weight. The farther back your hand is on the forearm, the heavier the muzzle seems and the more it has a tendency to whip. If the hand is moved way out on the forearm you have very positive control over the muzzle, but minimum strength to move it. By starting with the 45-degree elbow position, you automatically adjust the forearm hand to the best compromise position."

Woodhouse adds, "Many American-style skeet shooters not only have the forearm elbow out to almost a 90-degree angle, but stick the trigger hand elbow out the same way also. They can get away with this because from a pre-mounted gun position they really only have to move the gun on a horizontal line unless, of course, the wind is blowing and making the targets rise and fall above and below their normal track. When that happens, the wind eats these shooters up because they don't have the biomechanical leverage to quickly and precisely adjust their elevation."

Another problem many American-style shooters have with international skeet is in their initial body position when calling for the target. As in American skeet, the international shooter will take his natural point of aim where he expects to break the target. That will vary with the targets, although the center stake (Eight Post) is a good place to start for singles on stations one through seven. For doubles on stations three, four and five, it does not hurt to fudge that natural point of aim toward the more difficult target, which will be the second bird. The problem arises when the shooter pivots his upper body back to the house for his initial acquisition of the target.

"I have yet to see an American-style skeet shooter who shoots a sustained lead, which is what I teach my shooters, who didn't have to make adjustments in that body position for the international game," says Coach Woodhouse. "Normally, you would adjust your visual acquisition point a little farther out from the house because the targets come out a little quicker. Many American shooters will take an initial gun hold position on a line just about parallel with the face of the house, or a little inside that. We recommend they increase that to about 10 to 20 degrees farther toward the center of the field."

Fast-swing shooters will find that is not always necessary. They can often take their normal position.

The exception to this is station eight. This is one case where increased target speed combined with low gun position requires the shooter to compensate. Both the high and the low houses will send their targets to the boundary stake in about 6/10-second. Shooters must take the target inside that, normally in about 4/10-second. That is not much time to mount the gun, acquire the target and see the lead. Adjusting your foot position can help here.

"One problem right-handed shooters have with station eight," Woodhouse says, "is that they often

| International Skeet Classification | |
|---|---|
| Class | Average |
| Master (AA) | 95.00% and up |
| A | 87.00 - 94.99% |
| B | 81.00 - 86.99% |
| C | 75.00 - 80.99% |
| D | below 75.00% |

face too far into the house. Your natural point of aim comes into play big-time here, because these shots are subconscious. There is no real time for thought. If you were to take the distance from the center stake back to the house window and divide it into thirds, two-thirds of the way back to the stake is where most people break those targets. That should be the natural point of aim, that circle of air two-thirds of the way back to the stake. The initial acquisition position should have the upper body pivoted back to a point just outside the house. Many shooters tend to look into these houses, crowding them too much and it will hurt on these targets."

One area where shooters will not have to make many adjustments is on their leads. Despite the targets' increased speed, the leads remain virtually the same. The increased gun speed required to align with the target, whether the shooter uses the sustained lead or the fast-swing technique, will compensate for the increased target speed.

Surprisingly, one of the biggest factors that can adversely affect skilled shooters making the transition from American skeet to international skeet is not physical, but mental.

"One of the most important things a shooter has to condition his mind to accept in this game is that he is not going to shoot many 100 straights," Woodhouse has stated. "In American skeet, if you shoot a 99x100 in a major match, you can go home. There will be shooters who have shot perfect scores and they will settle things in a shoot-off. This is not so in international skeet. You can miss a target and still win the match. Even the best will miss. A shooter must accept that and develop the mental discipline to miss a target and still maintain his focus. That shooter must realize that he or she is still in contention, and get right back down to business. I spend a lot of time working on just that mental aspect with our shooters, and it is very important if you want to win."

While international skeet is not nearly as popular in this country as our more sedate version, it is much more challenging. This game will truly test your skills.

# CHAPTER 13

# GUNS THAT WIN AT SKEET

Hunters created skeet as a hunter's game, a serious game, however. Since the inventors were essentially northeastern upland bird shooters who occasionally dabbled in ducks, the game reflected common bird-shooting situations. Shots are naturally quick and close, similar to those one would commonly see when hunting grouse, woodcock and small-pond mallards. In fact, the longest shot you will encounter on a skeet field is 27 to 30 yards and that length only rarely. The closest shot will be less than four yards and most will range from that to about 20 yards.

The way the original game, "Shooting Around the Clock," was played, it more closely resembled sporting clays than contemporary skeet. The gun had to be off the shoulder when the bird was called for—the "low gun" position, as it is called today. Given the nature and range of the targets, a lightweight, fast-handling smoothbore with a wide-open choke was a distinct asset.

In fact, a specific degree of choke, called Skeet 1, was developed for this game. For a 12-gauge, that is a constriction of .004 to .005 inch and is intended to place the entire shot charge within a 30-inch circle at 25 yards. An additional choke, sometimes called Skeet 2 or, more commonly, Light Modified, is about .012-.014-inch constriction and was intended to provide a slightly denser pattern for the longer, second shot. (An over/under choked Skeet 1 and Skeet 2, by the way, is also an extremely effective upland bird gun.)

For all practical purposes, however, a standard Improved Cylinder choke (.009-inch constriction in a 12-gauge) will deliver just about the same performance on a skeet field as either of the skeet chokes. If you have a gun that is choked Improved Cylinder and want to shoot some informal skeet, do use it. It will do the job just fine.

## The Modern Skeet Gun

Today, skeet is shot from a pre-mounted gun position, with the gun at the shoulder when one calls

Skeet was originally a hunter's game that began in the U.S. and while it provides excellent practice for fast crossing shots in the field, it now has all the hallmarks of having a full life of its own. Complex, even "rigid" rules. All-American teams. International competitions. And guns designed for quick, steady movement from bird to bird.

"Pull!" This removes the requirement for serious gun handling ability and the radiused buttpads commonly found on sporting clays guns. This practice has also encouraged the use of longer barrels with more muzzle weight that promote a smoother swing. As recently as a dozen years ago, a 26-inch barrel was standard for skeet over/unders. Today, 28 inches is about as short as many shooters require, and some even opt for barrel lengths in the 30- to 32-inch range. Interestingly, the shift to longer barrels is probably a result of knowledge gained from shooting sporting clays.

If you want to use the skeet range as a means to tune up for fall hunting season, just use an open-choked hunting gun of any sort—semi-auto, over/under, pump or single shot—although, as two clays are thrown, a gun that will deliver two shots is quite preferred. That

Tubes are a relatively inexpensive alternative to buying multiple guns in different gauges. Contemporary skeet masters often tube a 12-gauge for 20- and 28-ga. and .410 and omit shooting the 12-gauge entirely.

much still applies. If you want to win a major skeet tournament, however, you are going to have problems shooting your truck gun.

Competition skeet has become as ritualized and stylized and over-regulated as any clay target game in the world and, as one might suspect, there is a specialized breed of gun that wins.

Competitive skeet is shot as a four-gauge event—12, 20, 28 and 410. You can, of course, shoot in only one of those gauges, but you will be confined to winning (or losing) in that class only. After a while—after you become proficient—that will not be satisfying. A High Overall match winner will have to shoot all four.

The four-gauge ability can be accomplished in a number of ways.

Years ago, competitors actually showed up at a skeet field with four different guns, whch occasionally were an unusual mix of pumps, semi-autos and double-barrel smoothbores. Others might have selected what could be termed a "matched" four-gun set. Remington offered its excellent Model 1100 semi-auto in that manner for a number of years and even included barrel weights for the smaller gauges that would give all of the guns the same weight and even the same feel.

Winchester offered its over/under Model 101 as a four-gun set, and other makers followed suit.

The four-gun approach has fallen out of favor today, however. A method that still enjoys great popularity is an over/under with four separate barrel sets. This is a bit pricey, with the more expensive brand guns, and even cumbersome, and there has been a strong move to lightweight tubes for barrels.

## Barrel Tubes

Still another approach, which has been used by past champions, is to opt for a lighter-recoiling 12-gauge gas-operated semi-auto for that class, and use an over/under with interchangeable sub-gauge tubes (a 20-gauge gun with 28-gauge and 410-bore tubes) in the remaining classes.

Contemporary masters, however, have a quite different approach. They use a 12-gauge over/under, but with 20, 28 and 410 tubes, and omit the 12-gauge shell entirely.

Competent skeet shooters have found that an individual of even reasonable skill does not require the full 1 ⅛-ounce 12-gauge shot charge to break a skeet target. They elect to use the 20-gauge (usually with 1-ounce loads) in the 12-gauge event, shifting to the prescribed 20-gauge ⅞-ounce load for the 20-gauge event, and then following up with the 28 and 410 shells and tubes for those events.

The NSSA rule in Section II-B-1-a is explicit: "Twelve gauge events shall be open to all guns of 12 gauge **or smaller** [emphasis added], using shot loads not exceeding one and one-eighth (1 ⅛) ounces." Subsequent paragraphs specify this policy for each sub-gauge.

What they get with that approach is a three-gauge capability where each gauge has the exact same balance, weight and "feel" as the others. There is an old adage that goes, "Beware of the man with one gun because he probably knows how to use it." That applies to skeet, and it is most certainly true. The only difference in gun feel between the different gauges, when set up in this manner, is the recoil generated by the different gauges, which of course is lighter as the gauge gets smaller.

Sporting clays shooters who shoot in sub-gauge classes occasionally use the same system.

This requires an explanation of sub-gauge insert tubes. Chuck Webb of Briley Manufacturing, probably the largest and most respected maker of these tube sets, gave *Gun Digest* the following comments a few years ago, and they are still accurate.

"Insert tube sets have come to dominate the skeet market in the last dozen years, he says, "and they are popular with sporting clays shooters as well.

"These tubes, at least the ones we make, are constructed of 6061 aircraft aluminum, with the chambers made from titanium and secured to the barrel via threading.

"We can make tubes with a fixed choke, but normally we supply them with interchangeable stainless steel choke tubes, four per gauge. You can certainly order additional tubes. Briley makes one of the widest selections of constrictions in the industry. The interior and exterior aluminum surfaces of the barrel are hard-anodized and, if the tubes are used properly, they will last the life of the gun."

What you have with insert tubes are interchangeable barrels-within-a-barrel, complete with their own interchangeable chokes. This shooting option may be especially appealing if you are traveling to a foreign country and do not wish to take your primary firearm.

If your shotgun is a standard make and model, Briley may have tubes in stock manufactured to your gun's specifications. If it is a custom gun or an older or unusual model, it may need to be sent to Briley for measurements by their gunsmiths. That is required because the tubes will be precisely fitted to your barrel. In most cases, the fit is so close that a tube for the top barrel will not go into the bottom barrel of the gun.

While skeet and sporting clays shooters using over/

Tubed 12-gauge guns for sub-gauge shooting are an excellent – and economical – way to enjoy varying the gauge ... and the challenge.

unders are the biggest customers for these specialized accessories, they can be fitted to any break-action shotgun including side-by-sides and single shots.

According to Briley's Chuck Webb, the company long ago tested their tubes with target-sized steel shot and found no problems with their use. If there is a way to damage the tubes, it is when a shooter attempts to insert them into a gun for which they were not fitted. For shooters of even minimal intelligence, that should not be a problem, because the tubes are serial-numbered to the gun.

"If your 20-gauge tubes are inserted into a different 12-gauge shotgun," Webb says, "you might possibly split the tube on firing; there will be no chance of injury to the shooter however, just the tube. The 28-gauge and 410-bore tubes (because of the smaller inside diameter and greater amount of metal) could probably be shot on their own as individual barrels (at least once!), but the 20-gauge does need the support of the barrel to which it was fitted. That's about the only way you can mess up a tube set."

Sub-gauge tubes will add 10 to 14 ounces of weight to the barrels of the gun. Many shooters find the added muzzle weight an advantage when it comes to executing a smooth swing. After all, when shooters are fitted to a gun by a professional, they often end up adding specific barrel weights and thus tubes may accomplish the same thing: a slower and smoother swing onto the target.

Knowledgeable shooters who know they will "tube" a gun often opt for a model with a weight of around eight pounds. By the time the tubes are installed, this brings the total gun weight to a bit less than nine pounds and makes a comfortable package. If the tubes are added to an already heavy gun, the additional weight might be uncomfortable.

While tubes are the way to go if you want to win, shooters who just want to enjoy the game of skeet on an informal basis can get by very nicely with just one gun and gauge. Any shotgun in 12-gauge—or even in 20-gauge—will be a good choice, and probably a fine skeet performer and a good pheasant or duck shooter.

## Skeet's Top Guns

Competitive skeet shooters will also find sporting clays over/unders to be excellent choices as the basis for a tubed skeet gun set. If a wider range of choices is required for those lucky shooters who get bitten hard by the skeet bug, here is what some of the major manufacturers offer in their specialty models.

### Benelli

www.benelliusa.com

Founded in 1967, Urbino, Italy's Benelli has been owned by Beretta since 2000. Benelli USA is headquar-

Almost any good field gun can run the table in skeet if the shooter is capable. An open-choked gun like the Weatherby Athena III Classic Field in 12- or 20-gauge with a 26- or 28-inch barrel should give you scores to be proud of right away.

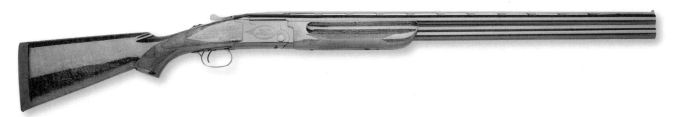

Ruger's Red Label over/under is available in 12-, 20- and 28-gauge. You can order this gun with a pistol or straight grip. A .410 tube set is available for the 28-gauge.

The Remington Model 332 over/under puts in regular appearances at the skeet line. Three barrel lengths – 26, 28 and 30 inches – and a narrow, eight mm vent rib make this an extraordinarily versatile gun in the field and for clay shooting.

tered in Accokeek, Maryland. It is allied with Franchi, Stoeger and Uberti.

For high performance competition shotguns, Benelli recommends its 12-gauge SuperSport and Sport II autoloaders. Even a casual study of the Italian's catalog and web site, however, will demonstrate that this Italian manufacturer is not well-represented in shoot-offs for competition championships. Indeed, the folks from Urbino are best known perhaps for turkey hunting, slug guns and military and police arms.

You will be able to identify the black $1,979 SuperSport in 12- or 20-gauge on a skeet line because its looks are so unusual—it's black! The "ComforTech" stock is carbon fiber with imprint checkering in the pistol grip and a soft gel comb insert that mounts against the shooter's cheek. Benelli says this smooth, cushioned surface eliminates the "neck snapping impact of comb against cheek." The stock is split diagonally from the heel of the buttstock to a point just behind the pistol grip. Eleven synthetic "recoil-absorbing chevrons" fill the holes in both sides of the stock. According to Benelli, the result of the redesign and materials selection is a lighter weight gun with as much as 48 percent less felt recoil than similar shotguns. In addition, you

can adjust the SuperSport's length of pull (drop and cast) with a "shim kit." Drop at heel is 2 ¼ inches and drop at comb is 1 ⅝ inches.

Two gel size pads are routinely available for the SuperSport, standard 14 ⅜-inch length of pull and shorter 14-inch length of pull. Differently shaped pads are available for left hand and right hand shooters. As part of the ComforTech stock system, Benelli says muzzle climb is reduced significantly compared to a hard stock and butt pad and this puts you back on target faster for a second shot.

SuperSport factory ported barrels are available in 28- and 30-inch lengths. You can carry as many as five shells: four in the magazine and one in the chamber. With the 30-inch barrel, the SuperSport is 51.6-inches long and weighs 7.93 pounds. Each barrel is topped with a high visibility red bar sight on the tapered (10 mm to 8 mm), stepped rib. Benelli says its hammer-forged barrels are cryogenically treated, frozen to -300 degrees Fahrenheit, to smooth out the molecular structure and make barrels easier to clean.

Five extended chokes—Cylinder and Improved Cylinder included—are part of each purchase. Longer choke tubes allow a more gradual constriction of the

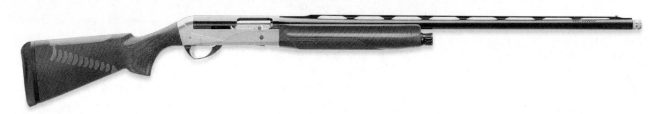

The Benelli SuperSport 12-gauge with ComforTech synthetic stock is designed to bring felt recoil with any shell to a minimum. Benelli extended CrioChokes help reduce pellet deformation, and the ported barrel is intended to minimize muzzle climb for fast second target acquisition.

shot charge, further reducing pattern-destroying pellet deformation.

The $1,699 Benelli Sport II is built with a satin walnut stock and fore-grip and can be purchased with 28- or 30-inch barrels in 12-gauge; 28-inch only in 20-gauge. Otherwise, specifications for the Sport II are identical (length of pull, choke tubes provided, etc.) to the SuperSport.

## Beretta

www.berettausa.com

Rugged military firearms to delicate self-defense pistols for petite ladies, this Italian manufacturer nevertheless has a superb reputation in the competition arena and offers several models in their skeet gun line. As I have said with most shotguns, however, almost any Beretta over/under with a relatively open choke will work as a skeet gun, but several are specifically designated and worth mentioning.

After many years in the line, the 12-gauge DT10 Trident Skeet is typical Beretta. Beautifully wood grained walnut with checkered stock and forearm; low-profile box-lock chambered for a three-inch shell. The comb is adjustable so that you can develop a personal sight picture, but drop at comb is nominally 1.375 inches; drop at heel 2.125; and an 8-pound weight. This model has a blued and polished receiver and your choice of 28- or 30-inch blued barrels. The single trigger is gold plated and adjustable for length of pull while the trigger assembly can be removed without tools for cleaning or maintenance.

The flat tapered rib is ⅜ x ⁵⁄₁₆ inches. A white front bead and steel mid-bead give the shooter fast aiming points. The DT10 comes in a hard-sided carry case with five interchangeable choke tubes. Expect to pay $7,900 for this high grade shotgun.

At $4,275, the 682 Gold E Skeet is less expensive, but still offers an adjustable comb so that you can make this gun fit more comfortably and securely against your cheek. This over/under has a low-profile box-lock action, 2 ¾-inch chambers and ventilated side ribs. The 12-gauge barrels are 28 or 30 inches long. The Gold E Skeet has polished, blued barrels and a handsome, polished aluminum receiver with futuristic engraving.

The 682 Gold E is chambered for three-inch shells and comes with five choke tubes: Improved Modified, Modified, Improved Cylinder and Skeet 1 and 2. Drop at comb is 1 ½ inches and drop at heel is 2.36 inches. The flat tapered rib is ⅜ x ⁵⁄₁₆ inches. This fine gun weighs 7 ½ pounds and comes in a black, hard-sided carrying case. A palm swell is standard and the 682 can be special ordered with left hand cast, palm swell and trigger shoe.

If the softer pounding of a semi-automatic is more appealing, show up for skeet with a Urika 2 Parallel Target RL and you won't be disappointed. According to Beretta, the "improved gas system" of the Urika 2 reduces felt recoil and improves second shot recovery. The improvement is actually the addition of a "spinning and self cleaning action." In theory, as gas pressure feeds into the gas cylinder, a series of mechanical fingers on the spinning piston expand outwardly to scrape and clean the gas cylinder as the action cycles. Carbon deposits are thus dislodged and removed from the gas system.

The Urika 2's adjustable drop and cast system ensures a custom fit, even for the next owner when you trade up to a Teknys Gold or even the new, break-barrel UGB25 Xcel (discussed in the Guns for Trap chapter). An optional Recoil Reduction System device can be installed in the walnut stock.

## Browning

www.browning.com

With shotguns made in Belgium and Japan, Browning offers shotguns for every shooting option and virtually all of them have good reputations—better than good. A shooter should have no trouble finding a 12-gauge Browning that is just right for skeet or a gun that can be very nicely tubed for sub-gauge shooting. Several models are offered in all four gauges (12, 20, 28 and 410).

In half a dozen years, the only thing that has changed about the Citori XS Skeet over/unders are the prices, having climbed about $100/year. Its critical dimensions are length of pull 14 ⅜ inches, and drop at comb and at heel, 1 ¾ inches. The XS Skeet is available with either a fixed ($2,829) or an adjustable ($3,139) comb. With a 30-inch barrel tipped with a HiViz Pro-Comp front sight, the XS weighs around eight pounds.

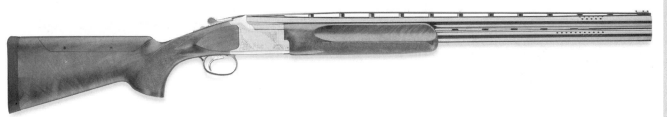

Browning makes its Citori XS Skeet in 12- and 20-gauge with 28- or 30-inch barrels. It is also available with an adjustable comb.

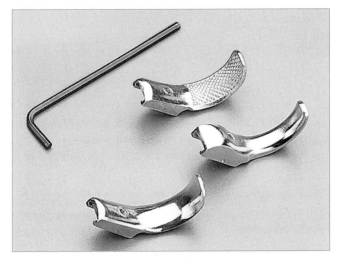

All Browning Sporting Clays, XT and XS Series Citori shotguns come equipped with the "Triple Trigger" System which allows its shooters to adjust the length of pull and switch between a wide/checkered, a narrow/smooth and a wide/smooth canted trigger shoe.

This 2 ¾-inch gun, with either a fixed or adjustable comb, can be ordered with a 30- or 28-inch barrel in 12- or 20-gauge editions; two Browning's Invector chokes are included: Skeet and Improved Cylinder. All barrels are back-bored with chrome-lined chambers and are factory ported to reduce recoil and barrel bounce, and to make your second shot easier. The silver-nitride receiver is lightly engraved.

The walnut stock and forend are given a satin finish and side ribs between the twin barrels are ventilated. The XS Skeet features a primary top high post rib for quick sight alignment. The right-hand model has an exaggerated palm swell and the trigger is gold-plated. The standard XS is not checkered.

Browning's Silver Lightning gas operated auto-loader in 12- or 20-gauge with three-inch chamber would be a fine choice for someone interested in a semi-automatic gun for skeet. I believe the back-bored 28-inch barrel is to be preferred to the 26-inch, as this will give you more front weight for a steadier swing through a bird.

The Silver Lightning has a 4+1 shell capacity and, even though two is all you will need at any moment at a skeet station, this will also be a fine field gun should you choose to hunt with it. Shooting dimensions are: 48 ¼ inches overall length, 14 ¼ inches length of pull, 1 ¾-inch drop at comb and two-inch drop at heel. Loaded, the gun will weigh about 7 ½ pounds and it comes with three chokes: Full, Modified and Improved Cylinder.

This semi-auto has what Browning calls a "self-adjusting Active Valve gas system" that uses gas from fired shells to operate the action, instead of recoil like most gas guns. So, they say, when shooting light loads, like those for skeet, most of the gases are diverted to operate the action. With magnum loads, however, because only a small amount of gas is used to operate the action, the majority of the gases are vented through the Active Valve—out the top of the forearm and away from the action. Browning says this keeps combustion gases from fouling the chamber and reduces recoil "without the need for heavy hydraulic recoil dampers, sticky gel pads and gimmicky gel inserts." The Silver Lightning costs $1,089 MSRP.

## Charles Daly

www.charlesdaly.com

Charles Daly and partners were importing hardware and miscellaneous sporting goods into New York during the administration of President Ulysses S. Grant, in 1875. When they were purchased by KBI more than a century later, in 1996, they included over-under and side-by-side shotguns from Italy and Spain, and most recently from Turkey, in the Charles Daly line-up.

The 12-gauge Superior II Sport ($709) semi-auto is available with polished black 28- or 30-inch interchangeable barrels and three chokes. Overall length with the 30-inch barrel is 49 ⅞ inches. The 10mm ventilated rib is topped with a brass, mid-bead center and red fluorescent bead front aiming points.

The high gloss Superior II Turkish walnut stock and forearm are checkered and drop a heel is 2 ½ inches while drop at comb is 1 ½ inches.

Differences between the target and hunting versions of this gun are minimal, but the hunting version includes 20- and 28-gauge.

The Charles Daly 206 over-under ($884) is new to the line. It is available only in 12-gauge with a single

The Superior II Sport VR-MC 12-gauge semi-auto is built with Turkish walnut buttstock and forend. You can choose from 28- or 30-inch factory-ported barrels. Three chokes are included. The 10 mm ventilated rib has a mid-bead center sight and fluorescent bead front sight.

The most popular Perazzis on the skeet fields are the MX8 and MX2000/8. Each is available with a detachable trigger group, interchangeable or fixed chokes in both barrels and a number of different rib configurations. Essentially, a Perazzi is expensive because it has a reputation for superior shooting and because it is personally fitted to the buyer.

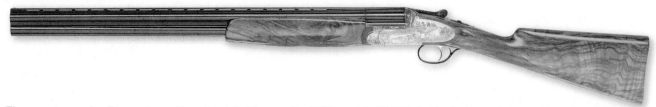

Tristar imports several models of European semi-autos and over/unders such as this SC 512 in its Valmet series. The 512 is available in three clays-shooting models, any of which would be fine for skeet: 12-gauge Sporting, 12- or 20-gauge Youth/Ladies and 12- or 20-gauge Field. Barrels are backbored and chrome-lined with three-inch chambers.

selective trigger, extractors and multi-choke tubes, or with selective automatic ejectors. Expect chrome-moly barrels and checkered Turkish walnut stocks.

The Sporting model—few guns are specifically denoted for "skeet" in Charles Daly or any other line because all the game requires is a reliable gun and an open choke—comes in 28-or 30-inch ported barrels with a wide 10mm ventilated rib and side ventilated ribs. Our Trap model comes with the same 10mm top rib and side ventilated ribs. Competition ribs have a mid-brass bead and front fluorescent sights.

### F.A.I.R.

www.fair.it

As the U.S. is increasingly incorporated into the European economy, expect to see more Italian guns on the shooting line—guns other than the established Perazzi. The Italian gun-maker F.A.I.R. builds an over/under in three models specifically labeled for skeet

shooting: Master, Master de Luxe and SRL 802. These guns may be ordered in 12- or 20-gauge with 26- or 28-inch barrels. Barrels are vented at top and side and are chrome-lined for corrosion resistance. The top rib is 11mm on the 12-gauge gun and 9mm on the 20-gauge. Look for an automatic extractor and a fixed, gold plated single trigger. Price varies by the amount and quality of engraving and whether the receiver housing is simply blued like the barrels or is finished in silver. Adjustable stock and trigger are optional.

Although price range in current U.S. dollars is sometimes difficult to establish with guns that are manufactured outside the U.S. and imported on a very limited basis, you would expect to pay around $3,000 for a new F.A.I.R. shotgun, if you could find one in the U.S., and if you do, be sure to inquire about warranty repairs. If the gun must be sent to Italy for warranty work, it may be worthwhile to look at some other mid-range brand.

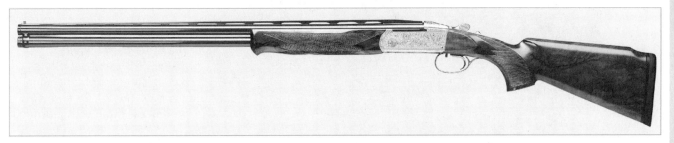

The Krieghoff K-20 20-gauge over/under is built with "all the technical refinements made in the famed K-80, adapted to the smaller receiver," the company says. It can also be fitted with 28-gauge and .410 barrels.

With a 28-inch barrel, the Winchester Model 1300 Sporting/Field is a versatile pump-action shotgun that can really open up to shoot the short range action in skeet. Working the pump however will test if you are fast enough – and accurate enough with all that extra upper body movement while you are aiming and following through.

The Jubilee 702 from FAIR may be ordered from Cabela's in 12- or 20-gauge with 28- or 30-inch barrels.

## Ithaca

www.ithacagun.com

So, you want to buy a new shotgun, one you can use on the weekends to shoot a little skeet with some friends and later take to the field for dove or woodcock. And of course money is tight.

There are two schools of thought. If you buy an inexpensive gun, you are probably going to be discouraged because it may shoot very well or it may shoot erratically, and the guys with the $25,000-Perazzis—even the $2,000 Berettas—will look down their nose at you. And of course, once you shoot it, you're stuck with it—a cheap gun, one you may or may not be proud of. It would be hard to use your cheap gun to trade up because it has little value compared to a new one; best hang it in the pick-up's gun rack and use it for feral hogs and rabid dogs.

The second school of thought is to buy a solid mid-priced, but still somewhat inexpensive—or perhaps even a pre-owned—smoothbore and see if you enjoy the shooting games before thinking about trading up. What do you have to lose? If, once you try it, skeet shooting bores you, then a budget-busting amount of money is not on the table. If, on the other hand, you love the game, you can easily trade up and use the less expensive gun for hunting or as a back-up.

If you decide to give the inexpensive gun route a try, why not look for an Ithaca? These pump guns—true, Ithaca is experimenting with producing an over/under—are entirely made in the U.S., now in Upper Sandusky, Ohio, and have a good reputation that is, coincidentally, identical with your financial condition.

The ubiquitous John Browning worked on the design of the famous Ithaca Model 37, which began life as the Model 17 Remington. Ithaca waited for the patents to expire and introduced their version in 1937; hence the name Model 37. Today, it has a reputation for having the longest production run ever for a pump shotgun model.

The Model 37 Deluxe pump 12- or 20-gauge, the Featherlight, with three-inch chamber will do just about everything you want. It both loads and ejects spent shells from the bottom, a feature that everyone—lefties and righties—can appreciate. Even though the

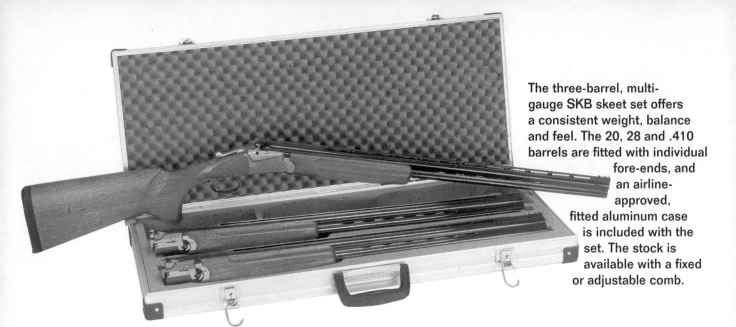

The three-barrel, multi-gauge SKB skeet set offers a consistent weight, balance and feel. The 20, 28 and .410 barrels are fitted with individual fore-ends, and an airline-approved, fitted aluminum case is included with the set. The stock is available with a fixed or adjustable comb.

folks with the gas guns and over/unders will probably eat your lunch at the shooting line, you are there to learn and enjoy—not necessarily expecting to beat the guys with the Krieghoffs.

The versatile Model 37 Featherlight pump has a steel three-inch receiver for shooting 2 ¾- or three-inch shells, checkered black walnut stock and forend, vented rib and black Pachmayr 752 Decelerator recoil pad. The Ultralight version of the Model 37 is built to the same specifications as the Featherlight but has a machined aluminum receiver and is thus lighter by a pound in any version: 6 ½ versus 7 ½ pounds in the 12-gauge, 5 ⅘ versus 6 ⅘ in 20-gauge.

Ithaca 37's solder-less barrels are "steel shot capable" with lengthened forcing cones. They are available in 26-, 28- and 30-inch lengths with vent ribs and three included flush mount Briley choke tubes: Full, Modified and Improved Cylinder. Barrels are topped with a red TruGlo fiber optic.

Stock specifications are generalized: length of pull is 14 ¼ inches, drop at comb 1.4 inches and drop at heel 1.6 inches. Overall lengths are: 45.6 inches with the 26-inch barrel; 47.6 inches with the 28-inch barrel; and 49.6 inches with the 30-inch barrel. For shooting later in the dove fields, the Model 37 has a five-shot capacity (4+1) with red safety follower and duck plug. With bottom loading and shell ejection, this gun is delightfully ambidextrous.

## Kemen USA

www.fieldsportltd.com

Unlike Americans, the Europeans prefer a single expensive gun—fancy walnut for the stock, beautiful engraving, an action that closes "ker-chunk" like the door of a Mercedes than "clink" like a Volkswagen—that, with reasonable care, could last a lifetime. On the other hand, their societies have highly stratified class systems with princes and queens and individuals with inherited wealth and titles, who think noth-

The 12-gauge SKB skeet guns are fitted with a 9.5 mm ventilated, sloped rib. The rib has three center channel grooves bordered by two raised, matted surfaces. The rib for small gauge skeet models is 8.5 mm.

ing of paying $25,000 for a shotgun. We, the common people, are discouraged from shooting.

Manufactured in Spain, Kemen has a lot in common with Perazzi and Krieghoff. It is a high quality name—primarily in Europe, of course—based on a high-quality product that has won international competitions for many years.

Writing for the English Sporting Gun magazine, Jason Harris suggests that Kemen is a major gun manufacturer in Spain, producing between 300 and 350 guns a year…! Harris says the word "going around" is that Kemen shotguns are often rumored to be exact copies of Perazzis and that Kemen barrels, forend and trigger parts are interchangeable with that Italian manufacturer's guns.

The eight-pound Kemen KM-4 ($8,500) has been a Kemen mainstay for years. This high-end 12- or 20-gauge over/under features a drop-out trigger assembly, various rib options including flat or stepped and high-grade walnut for the Schnabel fore-grip and the stock. The stock dimensions with pistol grip and palm swell are shaped to a customer's specifications. Length of pull is 14 %/16 inches. The KM-4 has a single, non-selective trigger.

Barrels are 28, 30 or even 32 inches with vented side ribs. The 11-7mm flat top rib is vented. A set of five Briley extended chokes is included.

Kemen shotguns are imported from Spain by Fieldsport in Traverse City, Michigan, and your purchase includes a hard-sided case.

## *Krieghoff*

www.krieghoff.com

The K-80 series is advertised for "Trap, Skeet, Sporting," so it is perhaps not surprising that, wherever you travel, it has earned a reputation as one of the top competitive shotguns in the game. Handled with skill, a Krieghoff will be a top performer on any course.

As each skeet shooter deals with the fundamental challenge that is unique to the clay game, namely how to achieve similar gun weight, feel, sight picture and balance in all gauges in order to shoot consistently round after round and event after event, Krieghoff offers a variety of options to suit the particular need. The weight of any gun combination is approximately 8 ¾ pounds and essentially varies only with barrel length.

K-80 skeet guns are distinguished primarily by their barrel configuration, which features the purchaser's choice of ribs, chokes and weight. To that end, K-80 skeet guns come as over/unders or two-barrel sets for the shooter who prefers a "heavyweight" or a "lightweight" concept. Typical skeet configurations are 28- or 30-inch barrel length, fixed chokes or choke tubes, and a choice of 8mm rib (called the "gentle taper") or 12-8mm tapered flat rib. Barrels have a white pearl front bead and metal center bead.

You can order the K-80 in 12-, 20-, 28-gauge or 410-bore. Krieghoff gold-plated single triggers are adjustable for trigger length and pull (3 ¼ to 3 ¾ pounds). In March 2009 the standard grade K-80 Skeet with 28- or 30-inch barrels, case and full-length sub-gauge tubes was listed at $9,945 from Allem's Guncraft in Zionsville, Pennsylvania.

Krieghoff pistol grip stocks and forends are cut from select European walnut, hand checkered and finished in satin epoxy. Ambidextrous palm swells are standard and a stock can be removed quickly with a standard stock wrench. All Krieghoffs are delivered in an aluminum carry case.

## *Mossberg*

www.mossberg.com

For those who want to take their venerable Mossberg hunting shotgun to the skeet range and toss some lead or even steel—go right ahead! Pump and gas operated guns from this Connecticut company are not commonly found in competition, but we know that breaking targets is not all the competition on the line. Just let the fancy gun owners look down their noses at your "no-name" hunter and you go ahead and show them how to bust targets "with a real gun."

Still one of Mossberg's most popular models, the 500 is available with wood or camouflaged synthetic stock and fore-grip. The 500 is a pump-action shotgun that comes in either 12- or 20-gauge or 410-bore and plenty of choke tubes are available. Barrels are interchangeable—24-, 26- and 28-inch lengths—and the gun is chambered for three-inch shells. Length of pull is a short 13 ⅞ inches with a drop at comb of 1 ½ inches and drop at heel of 2 ⅜ inches. Approximate weight

**Realistically, there is no reason that your field gun, your 12-gauge Mossberg 935 Magnum with 22-inch barrel for instance, will not shine on the skeet field. Its pattern will be wide open, but its construction may not be adequate for thousands of shots on clays and you may feel a little odd with this style gun, but hang in there and smoke 'em!**

The Bernardelli name has been associated with firearms production in Italy since the 1600s and the modern factory is in Brescia. The Mega Silver 12-gauge semi-auto has a 3-inch chamber, so after a round of skeet you can take it to the field for pheasant or grouse.

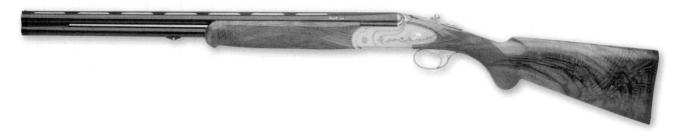

A shotgun such as this Fausti Stefano Class SL over/under that fits for the field will, with proper choke or shotshell selection, score well at skeet and sporting clays. Fausti, incidentally, dedicates this gun to the worm-eating woodcock which the company refers to as the "queen of the woods."

Marlin now owns the name "L.C. Smith" and for several years built side-by-sides in the Smith pattern in the U.S. They now import "models worthy of the great Smith name" from Europe. The Model LC12-OU features 3-inch chambers, a single selective trigger, selective automatic ejectors, automatic safety, three chokes (IC, M, F), 28-inch barrels with ventilated rib and bead front sight. It has a checkered walnut stock with a fluted comb and recoil pad and features case-coloring on its receiver and sideplates.

is 7 ½ pounds with the 28-inch vent rib barrel. Holds 5+1 shells. Expect to pay about $300 for this gun out of the box.

Enough with Mossberg, right? No—there is a surprise!

Mossberg now imports a line of over/unders and side-by-sides in a Silver Reserve Series. The Combo Field with three-inch chamber is available in a 12/20-gauge or 20/28-gauge combo, with 26- or 28-inch barrels. This gun is 46 inches long with the 28-inch barrel: 14 ¼ length of pull, 1 ½ drop at comb and 2 ¼ drop at heel. Ventilated rib with front bead sight atop a black walnut stock and forend, it weighs seven pounds.

Chambers and bores are chrome plated and five chokes are included per barrel. Mossberg's price is $1,012, but it usually sells for $150 less than that as all manufacturers except custom or very high end builders set their prices artificially high.

## Perazzi

www.perazzi.it

"Some things never change."

Of course, we know that is not true. All things change, even as we watch, yet often so slowly that we might not recognize it in our lifetime. And thus, on international skeet fields, this high-grade Italian gun maker still enjoys a world class reputation, and among all the companies who claim they or their products are world class, Perazzi's identity is secure. American skeet shooters will find the handling qualities and legendary reliability of these Italian guns benefits them almost continuously.

The most popular Perazzis on the skeet fields are the MX8 and MX2000/8. All Perazzi differ slightly in weight and balance as chosen blocks of wood are slightly different, but with the Perazzi line that is easy to change, since interchangeable stocks allow a shooter to precisely custom fit the gun to his dimensions and style, and to whatever clay target game is preferred. Each gun is available with a gold detachable trigger group, interchangeable or fixed chokes (in one or both barrels), a number of different rib configurations and barrels in the unusual lengths of 26 ¾-,27 ⁹⁄₁₆-, 28 ⅜-, and 29 ½-inches.

The stock and forend are superior grade walnut. These guns come as a two-barrel set with a lightweight spare barrel designed for gauge reducing tubes. On the 12-gauge, the fixed rib is flat parallel ⁷⁄₁₆-⁷⁄₁₆ or tapered ⁷⁄₁₆-⁹⁄₃₂ inches with half ventilated side ribs. On the 20-gauge, look for flat parallel ⅜-⅜ or tapered ⅜-⁹⁄₃₂.

The critical fitting dimensions of a gun from the Perazzi line are whatever a customer/shooter wants them to be, and overall weight will vary as barrel and stock dimension changes. Expect some sticker shock if you are upgrading from a Browning Citori or even a Beretta DT10 Trident.

These Perazzi skeet guns can be yours for a cool $10,000…or ten times that much. My thought is that if you have to ask about the price, you can't afford it because if it gets a scratch on the gun rack, you are liable to lose your mind. A stash of Daniele Perazzi's legacy might be a wonderful hedge against inflation and hard times, though. So now might be excellent time to invest in pre-owned Perazzi shotguns because, as far as I know, their price is never going down.

### Remington

www.remington.com

Competition shotguns are not Remington's strong suit. In their heart of hearts, they prefer the hunter models—moving in Benelli's direction featuring men with beards down to here slogging through a Louisiana bayou and women who have apparently just changed the oil under the truck—rather than Browning's cleaner styling, to folks dressed for a relaxed day at the range.

Properly choked, Remington shotguns will bust a clay target as well as guns that cost a hundred times as much. Nevertheless, the company now located in Madison, North Carolina, has chosen to follow the hunting market instead of trap, skeet and sporting clays, and their shotgun line-up—even the venerable 1100 semi-auto—pales a bit compared to the truly fine shooters in the competition market.

Still, you could do worse than the new Model 105 CTi II 12-gauge semi-auto even though it is really a field gun and not a flashy high end skeet buster. Remington says it is the "softest-shooting 12-gauge semi-auto" they have ever built and that means that an average shooter will notice the difference in their cheek and shoulder at the end of a 100- or even a 50-bird day.

Remington has wrapped the #105's "skeletonized titanium receiver" in a layer of carbon-fiber which takes a few ounces of weight away from the center of the gun and, the company says, adds to the gun's durability.

It appears, however, that the innovation which will be most heralded by competitors is the bottom feed-and-eject mechanism. Remington calls it the "Double-Down" system, because it eliminates peripheral distraction from ejecting shells. In addition, Remington says the #105's "simplified gas system has very few moving parts, requires less cleaning and there's virtually nothing to wear out or replace."

Along with reducing felt recoil, over-bored 26- or 28-inch barrels enhance pattern consistency. Each gun comes with three, flush-mount ProBore chokes: Full, Modified and Improved Cylinder. With a 28-inch barrel, the seven-pound Model 105 CTi II has an overall length of 48 ¼ inches. For a custom fit of the checkered walnut stock and forearm, Remington's Adjustable Length-of-Pull Kit allows a full ¾-inch length-of-pull adjustment from 14 ¼ to 15 inches in ¼-inch increments. MSRP is $1,559.

It is worthwhile mentioning that Remington's Premier STS Competition over/unders now have an adjustable-comb model available with 30- or 32-inch barrels, and a 32-inch barrel option with a non-adjustable-stock. The barrels are over-bored (0.735-inch) with lengthened forcing cones to enhance pattern consistency and lessen felt recoil. These guns have a 10mm target-style rib with ivory front bead and steel mid-post. A set of five ProBore choke tubes with knurled extensions comes with each gun, including Skeet and Improved Cylinder.

### Ruger

www.ruger.com

Ruger, "Arms Makers for Responsible Citizens," is located in Southport, Connecticut, where it employs several thousand people. Officially Sturm, Ruger & Co., its Red Label over/unders, in 12-, 20- and 28-gauge, are excellent competition-grade guns in the low-to-middle price range. And if you enjoy shooting the 410, Ruger sells a fitted tube set for its 28-gauge gun.

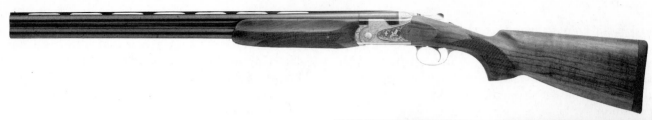

The new Beretta SV10 Perennia over/under 12-gauge has a 3-inch chamber, titanium trigger and choice of 26-, 28- or 30-inch barrels with longer forcing cones. Other features are a chrome-lined bore and chamber, selector switch for automatic ejection or shell extraction, and oil-filled hydraulic shock dampeners in the stock to cut recoil by 70 percent.

Little Skeeters are a mini-tube gauge reducing shooting system for shotguns. They come in 10-, 12-, 16-, 20- and 28-gauge carrier tubes. Testing 12-gauge carrier tubes with the step-down gauges 20, 28 and 410, the velocity matched factory published velocities for skeet target loads.

We discuss their Red Label as a "skeet gun" because it is a durable, popular model with an excellent reputation. Truthfully, depending upon the choke and your personal fit, this gun can be shot for any clay game and taken successfully into the woods for feathered game as well.

The Red Label has been around since 1978. Its 20-gauge is chambered for three-inch shells and comes with a choke tube wrench and five steel-shot compatible chokes: Skeet 1 and 2, Full, Modified and Improved Cylinder. You can order a Red Label with a hammer-forged, back bored alloy steel barrel in lengths of 26, 28 or 30 inches, all topped by a dovetailed, free-floating

rib that is stress-relieved, contour-ground and silver-brazed (not soft-soldered) to the finished monoblock. The overall length of the 30-inch gun is 47 inches and its weight is 7 ¾ pounds. Length of pull is 14 ⅛ inches.

Red Label cut-checkered stocks are shaped from premium grade American walnut and two styles are offered, pistol grip and the less-popular—at least in the U.S.—straight English-styling. Each gun features a drop at comb of 1 ½ inches and a drop at heel of 2 ½ inches. You can also purchase a Red Label with a "Target Grey All-Weather" stock, but this feature is available only in 12-gauge.

Ruger has systematized pricing for Red Labels. The standard charge for a Red Label with walnut stock, stainless steel receiver and blued steel barrels is $1,956. Order an all-weather synthetic stock with low-glare, stainless steel receiver and barrels and you will pay the same thing. Add $224 per gun for factory applied, scroll-engraving with either a gold pheasant, grouse or woodcock (pistol-grip style stocks only).

### SKB

www.skbshotguns.com

The initials "SKB" were derived from the Samurai family name Sakaba.  The vowels were simply dropped and the company was formed in the Ibaraki province of Japan (north and east of Tokyo on the Pacific coast) in 1855.

The SKB Series 85 has been in the line for some time and is still available as an excellent quality gun. Barrels are back-bored, which means that the interior bore of the shotgun is slightly enlarged beyond normal dimensions. For instance, the SKB 85 over/under is opened

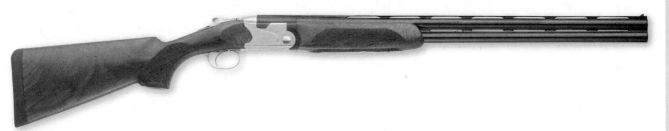

Beretta's new 12-gauge, 3-inch SV10 Prevail is something of a "plain Jane" in the Beretta line. With one tool, however, you can remove the stock and trigger group for cleaning or repair: 26-, 28- or 30-inch barrels, five extended chokes and a ventilated 10 x 8mm top rib.

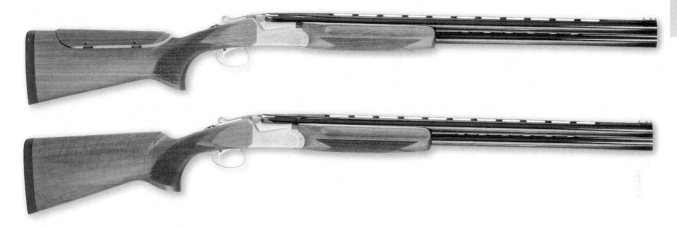

The "performance tuned" 85TSS skeet over and under from SKB is available in 18 models: four gauges, fixed or adjustable combs, Monte Carlo or fixed combs and a finger-groove fore-end. The 12-gauge barrels are backbored and chrome-lined with lengthened forcing combs. Automatic ejectors are standard.

Rizzini's new Premier 12-gauge over/under with a 28-inch barrel is an excellent gun for skeet shooting. Barrels are chrome-lined and the rib is vented top and side.

or over-bored at the factory beyond the SAAMI standard of .729 to .735. Oversize bores allow the wad of a shell to spread slightly, reducing friction as the wad travel the length of the bore. The benefits are a denser and more evenly distributed pattern with fewer deformed pellets, and a reduction in felt recoil.

The standard features of the "85" include: a low profile receiver with a box-lock action, manual safety, single selective trigger, automatic ejectors and a matte sighting plane equipped with a nickel plated center post and white front bead. All skeet style buttstocks, regardless of gauge, are fitted with a radiused butt pad from Pachmayr for a fast, sure mount. 12-gauge models are performance-tuned which includes oversized bores, lengthened forcing cones and a Briley

competition series tube system. Skeet models are available in the following three grades: 785, 585 Gold, and 585 Standard.

The performance-tuned 85TSS skeet over/under is available with a fixed or an adjustable comb. The three-inch fixed comb 85 is available in 12-, 20- and 410; the 28-gauge comes in 2 ¾. A multi-gauge set is available in two models. The three-barrel multi-gauge set delivers consistency in weight, balance and feel.

The 85TSS skeet models feature a new semi-wide, 9.5mm ventilated sloped target rib with three center-channel grooves with matte-finished outer edges fitted with a nickel center post and Hi-Viz Litepipe competition sight (optical quality, injection-molded plastic). This sighting plane aids fast target acquisition and

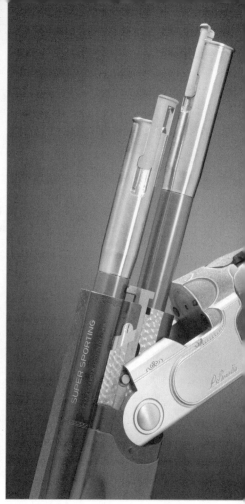

A tubular insert for an over/under provides a chamber end portion with a smooth outer surface. The complete shotgunner will compete in all gauges and rather than buy four separate guns, perhaps the answer is a single 12-gauge with a size-matched set of 20-gauge barrels and a set of tubes for 28-gauge and 410-bore or 36-gauge.

proper alignment and, in a game like skeet where people shoot all day and rarely miss a single bird, this sighting plane may give just the small advantage you need.

The 20- and 28-gauge and 410 barrels are fitted with individual forends and an 8.5 mm ventilated sloped rib. An airline-approved, fitted aluminum case is included with the three-barrel skeet set to protect your investment.

The 85TSS 12-gauge barrel group is available with "Pigeon Porting" by Mag-Na-Port. This porting process is accomplished by Electrical Discharge Machining (EDM) that ensures smooth incisions of exact dimensions. "Pigeon Porting" reduces perceived recoil by as much as 20 percent and muzzle lift by 60 to 80 percent.

The SKB 85TSS is available in fixed or adjustable comb options. The adjustable comb version has a maximum adjustment range of one-half inch laterally and vertically. Length of pull on the fixed comb is 14 ⅜ inches. Drop at comb is 1 ½ inches and drop at heel is 2 ³⁄₁₆ inches.

A 12-gauge with a 30-inch barrel chambered for

three inches weighs eight pounds, four ounces with a fixed stock.

Like many specialty shotguns, the cost of an 85TSS varies depending on the options. Expect to pay $2,500 for the 12-gauge with a 30-inch ported barrel and fixed comb. Add $180.00 for an adjustable comb.

While the above-mentioned guns are all suitable for competitive skeet, they are by far not the only choices available. As I mentioned earlier, all you really need is an open-choked gun that will fire two rounds and with the wide availability of factory guns fitted with interchangeable choke tubes, it is quite easy to find a quality hunting shotgun that can do informal double duty on the skeet fields.

Though side-by-side doubles are seldom seen on the skeet range in the hands of serious competitive shooters, you will see them toted by a number of bird hunters warming up for the fall season. If you happen to own a fine side-by-side like the Merkel Model 200E, or the American Arms Brittany or Gentry models, there is no reason not to spend an afternoon on the skeet field with it. If you do, you will find afternoons in the fall bird fields much more productive.

# CHAPTER 14
# SUCCESSFUL LOADS FOR SKEET

Like trap, skeet does not require a diverse selection of loads. While competitors may be required to obtain shells and loads for four different gauges, the maximum permissible shot weight per gauge is tightly defined and, with the exception of the 12-gauge and one application of the 20, nothing is to be gained by deviating from it.

The 12-gauge is allowed a maximum of 1 ⅛ ounces of shot, with the 20-gauge carrying ⅞-ounce, the 28 holding ¾-ounce and the 410 only ½-ounce.

Shooters are allowed some latitude in shot size, but again, the nature of the game pretty well dictates that little is gained by using any shot size other than #9.

Skeet is a close-range game. In fact, the farthest shot a shooter will see on a skeet field will be about 27 yards. In standard skeet, this would only occur if the shooter really hesitated on an outgoing target and let it get so far out that such poor form would likely dictate a miss anyway. In the doubles game, it is possible to see longer shots on the second bird at stations three, four and five than you would see when shooting them as singles. These birds can often be "shot out of position" and may present longer than normal shots, but they do not approach the range at which trap targets are routinely broken. In contrast, many shots will be quite close—low house eight for example is commonly broken only three yards off the muzzle—and the majority of shots on the remaining stations do not exceed 20 yards.

Since #9 shot will reliably break any target inside 25 yards, it has become the almost universal choice for skeet. With a pellet count of about 585 per ounce (Winchester standard shot size), that gives 1 ⅛-ounce 12-gauge loads a pellet count of over 650 individual pellets! The 20-gauge packs 510; the 28-gauge packs 435; and the diminutive 410 packs 292.

That means the ¾-ounce #9 load in the 28-gauge is carrying a lot more pellets than a full 1 ⅛-ounce load of #7 ½, which holds only 390.

Number 9 shot will do the job, but there are two instances where shifting to #8 ½ shot can help.

1. The first is on the second shot in the regular doubles game. With any shooter hesitation, these targets can get out far enough that they verge on being close to the outer limits of #9 shot's reliable break range. I find that a few #8 ½ loads in my pocket are confidence boosters, since I know they will consistently break targets five to 10 yards farther than #9 shot.

I generally use #9s for standard skeet and the first bird in doubles, with the #8 ½ load reserved for the second shot. Other shooters opt for a lighter load of #9s for the first shot and a heavier load of the same size shot for the second, theorizing that the increased pellet count provides multiple hits to add striking energy at those outer range limits. I would not argue with that approach, but my doubles scores have improved and become more consistent after switching to the larger pellet for the second shot. It may be strictly psychological. I know the shells will break the target in any legal position, so I am not inclined to hurry or change my rhythm. Maybe #9s would work just as well, but the mental game is every bit as important as the physical game, and if the larger shot makes me feel better, there is no reason I should not use it in that situation. The decrease in pellet count between #9 and #8 ½ is not significant enough to make a serious difference.

2. The second situation where I favor #8 ½ shot is in ½-ounce 410 loading. This little rascal needs all the help it can get!

Bird in the air! Skeet was developed by upland bird hunters. At first, the game was shot in a circle, but it became much more popular – and viewer friendly – when it changed to the semi-circular format today. Because of the close-shooting action, #8½ and #9 shot is usually prescribed.

Early in my shooting career, when I was still searching for the "magic load," a veteran shooter advised me not to even bother patterning the 410. "It's too frustrating," he stated. After ignoring his advice and running many test patterns, I have to admit he was right.

My experience with the ½-ounce 410 load indicates that consistent patterns are rare. Even the best factory loads will occasionally throw one with a few holes that a bird could slip through, or maybe be struck by only one or two pellets and not crack open and that may not be enough to give the shooter that all-important "visible piece." My solution to that has been to increase the shot size to provide more striking energy per pellet. By going to #8 ½ shot for the 410, I decrease overall pellet count from about 290 to around 240, but each individual pellet packs more punch. It takes fewer #8 ½s to break a bird than it does #9s. Since I cannot control pattern density, the only thing I can do is get more punch from each individual pellet, and #8 ½ gives me that.

That increase in pellet size is not something that will be a night-and-day difference, but it will get me an extra bird or two, and that is more than enough reason to use it. I tend to think of it like chicken soup for a cold: it cannot hurt.

Although shot weights for the 20, 28 and 410 are pretty much carved in stone (nobody in his right mind opts for lighter loads with these), a number of shooters find that lighter 12-gauge loads are a plus. The less recoil one absorbs during the day makes him or her a better shooter at the end of the day. Many shooters find the one-ounce load to be as much shell as is required. Others opt for the security of the full 1 ⅛-ounce load, but select one of the 2 ¾-dram "Lite" versions.

Some shooters load the three-dram, 1 ⅛-ounce load, but it is rare because it is not needed. In fact, some top shooters do not even bother with the 12-gauge at all: they shoot the 12-gauge event with their 20-gauge. One obvious reason is decreased recoil. Skilled shooters do not need more than ⅞-ounce of #9s to break a skeet target anyway.

Another reason is convenience. Most top shooters today shoot over/unders fitted with sub-gauge tubes. In order for the tubes to fit properly, the barrel must be clean. If a shooter has a good score in the 20, 28 or 410 event in the morning segment of a tournament, he knows he faces the possibility of a shoot-off in the same gauge at the end of the day. If he pulls the tubes and starts running 12-gauge rounds through the gun he will have to scrub the barrel in order to reinsert the appropriate tubes later; not a big chore, but a chore, nevertheless.

Thus, the 12-gauge has somewhat disappeared from the competition skeet fields, at least in the hands of skilled shooters. Instead, a lightweight skeet load is becoming perfectly acceptable—the one-ounce 20-gauge. It is legal to use in a 12-gauge event because even though the shooter may be using a 20-gauge, he is still allowed the 12-gauge maximum shot charge of 1 ⅛ ounces.

Here's what the ammo makers offer for those who favor factory fodder.

## Factory Ammunition

### Eley

www.eleyhawkltd.com

You do not see many Eley cartridge boxes discarded after an American skeet event; they are more common at high end sporting clays events. Still, this English shell with the graphically-challenged boxes are available in a variety of light shells, and trying them will be an adventure to the shooter who expects, from long experience, to leave the range with a sore shoulder.

The American skeet shooter accustomed to the foot-pound-inch system ought to learn metric conversion to use international loads and perhaps accustom himself (or herself) to the European concern for "head" size in millimeters (mm), type of wad (plastic or fiber) and such interesting though inessential—at least in skeet shooting—measurements as muzzle velocity versus observed velocity. Several European manufacturers, like Eley, even give the percentage of antimony (85 percent of which comes from China, by the way) in each load selection too, something that is almost never found in standard American catalogs.

Eley First is the entry level cartridge for the price conscious shooter, which just about includes everyone these days. These four types of 2 ½-inch shells will fire just fine from a gun with a 2 ¾-inch chamber. Loaded with 24- (⅞ ounce) or 28-grams (1 ounce) of #7 ½, #8 or #9, they will bust clays without busting your shoulder. A similar set of shells, also with three percent antimony, is available in Eley Blues, only they are true 2 ¾s.

Stepping up to a 5 percent antimony shell, Eley Superb Competition is still a lightweight #9 at 1-ounce. The 32-gram or 1 ⅛-ounce shell is not available in #8 ½ or #9. A variety of 20-gauge shells is available in the Competition Trap line: 3 percent antimony and #9s. The 12-gauge-only Eley VIP shells have 7 percent antimony in ⅞- or 1-ounce for #9s.

### Federal Cartridge

www.federalcartridge.com

For effective skeet shooting, we are looking for a good load of #9s and perhaps an occasional #8 ½ in all competitive gauges: 12, 20, 28 and 410.

The 12-gauge probably represents more than half of all shotguns and shotshells sold in the U.S. It has a "ballistic advantage" because its shot column, certainly compared to smaller gauges firing the same amount of shot, is shorter. What I mean is that one ounce of shot in a chunky 12-gauge shell makes a shorter stack than it does in a thinner 20 gauge shell. In theory, a short shot column results in fewer shot deformed by friction on their quick trip through the forcing cone, down the barrel, and out through the constriction of the choke. One ounce of shot in a 12 gauge has a .690-inch column. For a 20-gauge, an ounce of shot results in a .968-inch column; in a 28-gauge, it measures 1.21 inches.

According to Chuck Hawes, who writes an on line shotgunning column, what this means is that a 12-gauge will pattern better than smaller gauges with the same amount of shot, or maybe just as well with more shot. The advantage is particularly noticeable at longer range, as in handi-cap trap shooting or long range water fowling. It will not be so noticeable in skeet where shots are close and relatively fast.

All things being equal, the patterns of all gauges are the same size, based on the accepted measure-ment inside a 30-inch circle at 40 yards. In any gauge, a Full choke is supposed to put 70 percent of its shot inside of that 30 inch circle. But because bigger 12-gauge guns toss more shot than the sub gauges, more pellets wind up inside that circle. Seventy percent of #9 shot at 40 yards—and remem-ber that such a distance is far beyond the normal skeet shot:

    12-gauge (1 ⅛ ounce = 658 pellets) 461
    20-gauge (⅞ ounce = 512 pellets) 358
    28-gauge (¾ ounce = 438 pellets) 307
    .410-bore (½ ounce = 292 pellets) 204

Minnesota's Federal Cartridge makes at least one of everything. In the 12-gauge shell, there is much to choose from in the Premium Gold and Top Gun lines. A standard 2 ¾-chamber offering such as the Top Gun TGL12 which will give you 1,145 fps with 1 ⅛-ounce of #9, a slight shoulder-saving load over a load over a 1,200 fps load of Gold Medal T118. All of these loads

are plenty fast for skeet. For #8 ½, look for Federal's T113 (1 ounce, 1,180 fps) or T114 (1 ⅛-ounce, 1,100 fps: an Extra Lite, shoulder saving load).

Federal has one designated shell for each sub-gauge in Premium Gold. The 2 ¾ Gold Medal Target-Plastic T206 for 20-gauge guns loads 7/8 ounces of #8s or #9s at 1,200 fps. (This shell is also offered in the Top Gun Target line as the TG20 at 1,210 fps.) The 2 ¾ TG280 for 28-gauge loads is ¾ ounce of #8 ½ or #9 at 1,230 fps. The 2 ½ T412 for 410 loads ½ ounce of #8 ½ or #9 at 1,230 fps.

### Fiocchi

www.fiocchiusa.com

For Fiocchi, let's look at the sub-gauge loads first, because they are very specific. The 2 ¾-inch 20-gauge uses ⅞-ounce of #7 ½, #8 or #9 high antimony lead while the 28 and 410 come in #8 and #9 only. All three loads achieve 1,200 fps.

Now, in the 12-gauge series, there are a dozen load possibilities to choose from. With Fioc-chi, as with so many companies, the differ-ences are not only very small, but the types of powder burned to give a hotter or faster or perhaps a slower burning load. Again, the differ-ences are so small as to be insignificant except perhaps to a chem-ist. Your task is to find a shell that works best in your gun and with your shooting form.

In one-ounce, 2 ¼ high antimony lead loads, Fiocchi offers four shells that are graduated in velocity from light to heavy: 12TL Target Light (1,150 fps, 2 ¾ dram: #7 ½, #8, #8 ½, #9); 12 TH Target Heavy (1,200 fps, three dram: #7 ½, #8, #8 ½); 12TX Little Rino (1,250 fps, handicap load: #7 ½, #8, #8 ½) and 12CRSR Crusher (1,300 fps, maxi-mum load: #7 ½, #8, #8 ½, #9). With some minor differences, the same type shell progression is available in 1 ⅛-ounce loads.

### Kent Cartridge

www.kentgamebore.com

Kent's 2 ¾-inch Diamond Shot loads are available for #8 and #9 shot, but only in 12- and 20-gauge loads. Their new 12-gauge shell K122GT32 for #7 ½, #8 and #9 is loaded with 1 ⅛ ounce and 2 ¾ drams. At 1,145

> *The differences between loads must be carefully examined be-fore shoving into the chamber. In the excitement of a day in the field, it is easy to make a mis-take with shot size or shotshell length if one shoots multiple gauges, several types of guns and perhaps reloads at home.*

fps, it is plenty for skeet. Dropping down 1/8-ounce in shot to the K122GT28 in all sizes will raise your speed to 1,200 fps and perhaps give your shooting shoulder a rest as well.

In the 20-gauge shell, both one-ounce (#6, #7 ½, #8) and ⅞-ounce (#7 ½, #8, #9) shells are offered with 2 ½ drams.

The Gamebore loads are strictly designed for field use in loads #5, #6 and #7, but here loads are available for all four gauges.

### PMC (Precision Made Cartridges)

www.pmcammo.com

PMC does not currently offer an #8 ½ shell, but they have plenty of #8 and #9. Their Field & Target Specific loads are offered in their Bronze Line and all gauges are covered somewhere.

For 12-gauge guns, PMC's FT128 #8s and FT129 #9s are chronographed at 1,230 fps with 1 ⅛ ounces and a full, three-ounce dram equivalent. These same shells are offered with only one ounce of lead and the speed rises to 1,250 fps.

If you are shooting a 20-gauge, you have a choice of #7 ½, #8 and #9 shells at 1,230 fps. All are fully loaded with ⅞ ounces and 2 ½ drams. The 28-gauge and 410 are equally served at 1,220 fps in #7 ½, #8 and #9 shot in the PMC FT loads. (In the Gold line, PMC loads up their sub-gauges with shot and powder. For instance, their HV419 for 410 is three inches long and carries ¹¹/₁₆ ounces of #9 shooting 1,135 fps.)

### Remington

www.remington.com

The Gun Club target loads are Remington's economical line. They offer a couple 2 ¾-inch loads of #9 shot, one for the 12-gauge (GC12L: 1 1/8 ounces, 2 ¾ dram equivalent, 1,145 fps) and one for the 20-gauge (GC20: ⅞ ounces, 2 ½ dram equivalent, 1,200 fps).

Because we are concentrating on current offerings in the #8 ½ and #9 size, Remington offers a variety of shell options in its Premier STS target loads. The folks in Madison, North Carolina, say that these shells are loaded with extra-hard, target-quality shot. Although Remington says its Low Recoil load (STS12LR) for 12-gauge is designed "specifically for the avid skeet shoot-

er," it is not offered in # 8 ½ or #9. The closest shell is the 2 ¾-inch STS12L, Light Target load in #7 ½, #8, #8 ½ and #9 with a full 2 ¾ drams of powder and 1 ⅛ ounces of shot rated at 1,145 fps.

In sub-gauges, Remington has several loads for the 20, 28 and 410. The 2 ¾ STS20LR is loaded with 2 ½ drams and ⅞ ounces of #8 or #9 at 1,135 fps. The 20-gauge STS20H shell has a full ounce of #9 and spins the shot out at 1,200 fps. In 28-gauge shells, look for #8s (STS28SC) or #9s (STS28), each at 1,200 fps with ¾-ounce of shot and two drams of powder. For the 410 or 36-gauge, Remington's 1,200 fps offerings are in #8 ½ or #9 with ½-ounce of lead and the maximum allowable drams of powder.

### Rio Ammunition

www.ableammo.com

Rio Ammunition is an American company headquartered in

**Remington's Premier STS is their "reduced recoil" shell. These clay loads feature the STS mouth design where skive depth is increased to one-half inch. Thus, it travels beyond the hinge point of the crimp and greatly reduces the angle of taper.**

Kent's Diamond Shot loads for #8 and #9 are currently available for 12- and 20-gauge.

Rio 12-gauge 2 ¾-inch shells with 1 1/8 ounces of #8 are an inexpensive shell that is often sold by clubs and ranges for clay shooting.

Houston, Texas, the offspring of a Spanish company that has been producing shotshells since 1896. Today, they say, their shotshells are sold in more than 70 countries.

Rio's 2 ¾-inch 12-gauge designated skeet loads contain #9 shot. Load 24 has ⅞ ounces, Load 28 has one ounce and Load 32 has 1 ⅛-ounce. Loads in #8 ½ are not available, but #8 loads are plentiful. Rio says that their target loads feature a three percent antimony alloy while their top target loads have five percent.

A 2 ¾-inch target load is available for smaller gauges as well in #7.5, #8 and #9. The 20-gauge is loaded with ⅞ ounce (1,250 fps), the 28-gauge with ¾-ounce (1,300 fps) and the 410 with ½ ounce (1,200 fps).

### Winchester

*www.winchester.com*

While many of the 12-gauge "Double A" Winchester loads are offered in #9, it does not at this time offer any #9s in its more economical Super-Target line. You can choose the AA SuperSport line even though it is designated for sporting clays shooting, but the hotter powder and speedier shot (1,300 fps minimum) is not an asset in skeet shooting. There is no special reason that a single designated shell, the AAL12 Xtra-Lite, in either one ounce of #8 ½ or #9 should not be a fine load for all skeet shooting challenges. At 1,180 fps it is plenty fast enough and it will be easier on the shoulder than the AA12 (1,145 fps) which carries 1 ⅛-ounce of shot.

Winchester has easy-to-remember designations for its sub-gauge shells, which are all rated at 1,200 fps. The 2 ¾ AA20 for 20-gauge loads 2 ½ dram equivalent with ⅞-ounces of #8 or #9. The 2 ¾ AA28 packs

two ounces of powder with ¾-ounce of #8 or #9. The 2 ½ AA41 packs the maximum powder charge and ½-ounce of #9s.

According to Winchester its HS (for High Strength) shells are excellent for reloading.

## Reloading for Skeet

Most serious skeet shooters are reloaders, and the reason is simple economy. If you do a "best buy" by case-lot of the four different gauges, you will find that the 12, 20 and 410 cost virtually the same, while the 28-gauge generally runs about 20 bucks more. Considering that the 410 carries less than half the shot of the 12-gauge (with the 28-gauge running about 65 percent) and that both use less powder, it is difficult to explain why they should cost as much as or more than a larger 12-gauge shell, but they do.

Skeet shooters who load their own can realize a savings of about fifty to sixty percent on the smaller shells, and around forty percent on the 12- and 20-gauges!

Shot selection for skeet loads is not quite as critical as for trap. I favor hard shot for everything in trap, but do not mind the less expensive chilled shot for the 12- and 20-gauge loads. In fact, novice shooters might actually be helped by softer shot in these two gauges. You have more than enough #9 pellets in even the ⅞ ounce 20-gauge load to break the close-range targets. The drawback is that it is difficult to get the load to open up. Soft shot does that better than hard shot.

The 28-gauge is an under-appreciated little jewel. It is such an efficient shell that good hard shot can make it every bit as effective as a 1 ⅛-ounce 12-gauge load. Indeed, a number of shooters find they can carry the same average with both. Not surprisingly, many shooters opt for the 28-gauge as their practice load because it is truly an effective skeet shell. Inside 30 yards, it will break anything the heavier 12- and 20-gauge will, and with softer manners. It just makes sense to give it the best.

With the 410-bore loading, hard shot becomes mandatory. While I do like the miniscule shell (and even do some bird hunting with it), it needs help and cannot really tolerate soft shot even though many budget-conscious shooters do load it with that. I have a preference for #8 ½ shot in this shell, but I know that many skeet shooters familiar with the 410 swear by standard #9 loads.

While handling the loading chores for four different gauges may seem like a complex endeavor, it is not—two sizes of shot, two different grades in size #9 if you prefer, the appropriate wads, and just a couple of different powders are all it takes to give you your best shot.

Winchester's AA Super Sport for the 12-gauge is offered in 11/8-ounce of #9 shot in its #AASC12 load. Shorter barrel, open choke and this load means vaporized skeet clays!

# CHAPTER 15

# SPORTING CLAYS: CHALLENGING AND FUN

Sporting clays or hunter clays, as it has sometimes been called, is not the rigidly programmed predictable clay target game we find in trap and skeet (although it is tending in that direction, pushed by the men and women who prefer shooting for score rather than shooting for pleasure). Neither is sporting clays a game that lends itself to perfection. Even the world's greatest shots miss, with surprising regularity, and a perfect score in a tournament is virtually unheard of.

This is a game where everybody will miss, and most will laugh about it and go on to the next shot. This is probably why it is well on its way to becoming the most popular shotgun game in the country.

That has not always been the case. In fact, just 25 years ago sporting clays ranges were about as common as good manners at a punk rock concert. In those days, the sport was already well established in Europe, though, and it was beginning to make its presence felt on these shores. Today, it is safe to say that the majority of new shotgun ranges being constructed or those

When you advance to a new station on a sporting clays venue, your squad has a right to call for a bird. Be alert, because this is your opportunity to see the flight path and make a decision about the break point before the shooting starts.

Everyone on the squad plus the puller and scorer want to huddle near the shooter and watch the action. The advantage of shooting second or later is that you can watch the first person and get a strong indication of where you want your pattern to kill the bird.

under re-construction are either primarily sporting clays or they incorporate sporting clays into their program.

For shotgunners who are bored with the unvarying fare of trap and skeet, the first taste of sporting clays is a smorgasbord! Targets zip by at speeds and angles previously unseen on American ranges. Sometimes a single clay leaps from a hidden trap and disappears behind a conveniently situated tree before the surprised gunner can even react. Just about the time the gunner has that target figured out, the boom of his shotgun sends another target speeding across the field. Targets might be crossing, climbing, incoming, outgoing, quartering, streaking high overhead, falling … or any combination of the above.

When the shooter, having shot the course previously, starts to get comfortable with that selection, a sneaky range operator will change the speed or angle

on the trap or even move the shooting stand, leaving the hapless gunner to face an entirely new set of challenges.

For many wingshooters, this game is as much fun as you can possibly have with a shotgun.

## Sporting Clays Origins

Sporting clays began its popular rise in England just about the same time that skeet was becoming the favored new game in America, in the early 1920s. It would be incorrect to say it was an immediate success. Over the last 25 years or so, it slowly grew into the most popular shooting game in England.

Historians credit Orvis with sponsoring the first sporting clays match in the United States, in 1983. The game had been played here before that, however. Remington Farms, in Maryland, had a version of hunter clays in the late 1960s. The firm lured British course designer Chris Craddock to these shores and, using the hilly, wooded terrain of Remington Farms, he was able to lay out an impressive course.

In 1985, an interested group formed the United States Sporting Clays Association and in 1989, the National Sporting Clays Association (now affiliated with the National Skeet Shooting Association), became the dominant, governing body for the regulated game in the US.

## How Sporting Clays Works

Sporting clays takes trap and skeet several steps further. While a sporting clays shooter will see some of the same angles that he might on a trap or skeet field, that is about as similar as the three games get. There are significant differences between sporting clays and trap and skeet:

1. Like other games, the shooter calls for the bird. However, in sporting clays the puller may wait up to three seconds before he releases the target. Some launching controls even have a built-in variable delay, similar to international skeet.

2. Formerly, when calling for the bird, the regulation game required the shooter to have the gun in a low position, meaning the entire buttstock had to be visible below the armpit. Often, shooting vests incorporated a special stitch indicating such a line and, in addition, you could only mount your gun when the birds become visible. Pushed by the bean counters in our games, those who shoot for other reasons than simple pleasure, this is unfortunately no longer the case and this changes the entire nature of the game. While those who shoot from a low- or un-mounted position are still in the majority, you may expect this to change as years go by and the game becomes fossilized like trap and skeet: NSCA: IV-I-4. Shotgun Mount and Posi-

A target on the ground! Both ends of the running rabbit station. In photo on left, the bird is away and visibly bouncing while in photo on right, the shooter sees the target and takes aim. This is a target presentation you will never see in trap, skeet, crazy quail or hélice!

tion—The shooter may start with a low gun or a pre-mounted gun when calling for the target.

3. Other shotgunning games provide for alibis. If a gun or ammunition malfunction occurs, the rules allow a shooter to re-shoot the target. This is not always the case in sporting clays. Alibis are allowed but are more limited and the rules applying them are stricter.

4. Shotguns of 12-gauge or smaller are allowed. Shooters may use different guns at different stations and guns fitted for multiple barrels with different length barrels and chokes are permitted. Shooters may also change barrels or choke tubes between stations. Sporting clays is occasionally referred to as "golf with a shotgun" and some shooters bring along a full bag of guns.

5. Trap and skeet use one target. In sporting clays, five different targets may be incorporated in a single round:

A. The standard clay bird;

B. A slightly smaller (90mm) bird that throws or flies faster;

C. A 60mm bird (about the size of a tennis ball) that really gets moving;

D. A Battue target, about ¼-inch thick and very flat, that takes some highly unpredictable paths during flight; and

E. A thicker, tougher version of the standard clay target used as a ground-bouncing rabbit. This sturdier target takes a harder hit to break.

6. Targets may be presented as singles, true pairs (when both targets are launched simultaneously),

following pairs (the second target is launched immediately after the first, at the puller's discretion and often with a time lag) or as report pairs, where the second target is launched at the sound of the shooter's first shot.

7. If this is not confusing enough, there are also "poison birds," targets of a separate and clearly discernible appearance that may be inserted at random anywhere in the match. A shooter firing on this target is rewarded with a miss. Shooters who refrain from shooting at these targets score an automatic hit. You never know when or where one will pop up except that they are never thrown as true pairs.

## Terrain Hazards

As you can imagine, these rules give course designers a tremendous amount of latitude and they are encouraged to use it. It is common for courses to use existing terrain features to place obstructions deliberately in the path of a shooter. For example, some targets may fly through trees or brush and only give the shooter a small window of visibility. Alternatively, there may be two or three windows available on a given shot and each will change the basic nature of the shot. It is then up to the shooter to determine which might be to his best advantage.

The use of natural terrain features can also result in targets presented below the shooter, as he stands on a hilltop or targets that fly uphill from the shooter. In most cases, shooting cages are required to restrict the shooter's range of movement and require him to break the target within a relatively confined area.

The result of this course latitude means that sporting clays courses, like golf courses, will differ across the county. No two will be the same. If this were not difficult enough, course managers are encouraged to make frequent changes in their target presentations just to keep things interesting. What results is one of the most challenging and enjoyable shotgunning experiences possible.

## Sporting Stations

Since courses vary considerably, there is no standard sporting clays range as in trap and skeet. Shooters see a wide variety of target presentations and this has made sporting clays a thinking shooter's game. You cannot react your way around a sporting clays course. You must think your way through it, analyzing each individual station as you come to it. Here are some of the target presentations you are likely to see.

### The Rabbit Run

Sporting clays traces its roots to hunting and that flavor lingers. Virtually all of the various sporting clays target presentations represent a situation that will occur in the field. They are invariably named after specific "critter" shots.

Sporting clays courses around the world are often designed to reflect the local hunting traditions as well as a geographical adaptation of the terrain. Many American wingshooters learn from an early age not to shoot rabbits while bird hunting because they may run the risk of hitting one of the bird dogs … or worse, teach the dogs bad habits. This is not necessarily the case in Europe. Rabbits are fair game in any "rough" or "walk-up" hunt and thus, the rabbit target has become a staple of many sporting clays courses.

The rabbit is a ground-bouncing target using a sturdier, specially made clay. The rabbit launches from a special machine so that its flat edge hits the ground and bounces across it. Sometimes field managers place a piece of carpet at the first contact point the clay makes with the ground to help cushion that initial blow. These targets are not as easy to break as standard clay because of their heavier construction. There is no way to predict precisely what path the target will take after it first hits the ground.

Course managers may create a short, narrow opening for the target to pass through or they may let it sweep across open ground. Sometimes this target launches as a following target or a report target in conjunction with an aerial bird. The rabbit may run

A low crossing shot across a pond at Cherokee Rose Sporting Clays south of Atlanta. This bird is deceptively fast and, when thrown as a pair of crossers, the second can quickly get out to 40+ yards.

The high, fast crossing shot is popular and, depending upon your shooting window, can be fun and easy – or fun and difficult, but in sporting clays, the emphasis is always on safety and fun.

Shots over water are usually wide-open and the tendency is to take your time, but depending on the distance to the target, the spacious shooting situation may cause you to shoot late and behind the bird.

Many ranges – trap, skeet, sporting – have guns for rent so, when traveling for fun or profit, take time to bust a few birds! Birds Landing, California, is a scenic, 1200-acre sporting clays course in the vicinity of Napa Valley.

partially on the ground and then bounce smoothly into the air. The most common range to shoot this target is 15 to 40 yards.

This is a quick-sweeping shot that demands a strong follow-through and last minute corrections to account for erratic movement. Not surprisingly, this is a tough target, even more so because many American shooters must overcome an ingrained mental block that prevents them from shooting a target on the ground.

## Woodcock

This is usually a low overhead or extremely hard crossing throw that only gives the shooter a quick glimpse of the target. Doubles might be thrown here. The range is generally 20 yards and under.

Some ranges may throw these targets from multiple traps located at various positions in front of the shooter. This is quick, fast shooting with a wide-open choke.

## Duck Tower

The duck tower is often a 40- to 70-foot tower with as many as five stations laid out around its base. The tower may be behind the shooter with birds going away or quartering away and falling off to the side. There is often one station where the target may be a sharp incoming angle. The targets may be standard, 90 mm or 60 mm unless you have a truly devious course manager, in which case who knows what you will get. Some managers install an oscillating trap, add a "poison bird," or something even more radical. Expect to shoot this one anywhere from as close as 20 to over 60 yards.

## Dove

Doves can be similar to the duck tower with birds launching from an elevated position. Often however, they will be incoming angled shots unless the course manager puts out extra shooting stations along the flight path and thus creates overhead crossing targets.

The incoming Dove Tower at Cherokee Rose in Griffin, Georgia, had a cage that limited the downward position of the gun. The target house is dead ahead of the shooter and throws what looks like a high house eight skeet shot, except the birds are almost 15 yards up and traveling as true pairs. It is possible to start behind both birds, swing through them and take the trailing bird first, then continue the swing to get the lead bird. You just have to shoot this fast and there is not much room for error.

## Grouse Bluff

This is the most charitable name you will hear this difficult ulcer-maker called. It is generally set up as hillside shot with the shooter looking down into a gully. Some stations may have crossing shots and often stick a tree or two along the flight path to make you think

about the shot. Others may have a more "away" angle. Some stations combine both by putting in two different shooting platforms that will alter the angle from crossing to outgoing. Regardless, if you see the word "grouse" on a station, expect it to be tough!

## Blue Bill Pass

This is similar to a low-angle duck tower. The purpose, I suppose, is to simulate a passing shot on a lesser scaup bluebill duck. They often skim low and fly faster than hell. That is what these targets do. Some shots may have a slight outgoing angle, but many will be hard crossers. If the course manager has a sense of humor, there may be four or five shooting stations scattered along the flight path, each of which changes the angle, distance to the target and the lead. This station may be shot from 20 to 50-plus yards, and the longer shots are some of the toughest.

## Duck Boat

Our favorite course designer has been drinking too much again, and this time dragged home an old boat. You get into it to shoot. Sometimes it actually floats in water, other times it lays on a bed of very wobbly truck tires. Just getting a steady shooting position in the boat is tough enough, but hitting the targets, which may be incoming, crossing, or outgoing at 15 to 40 yards, is even tougher.

## Springing Teal

This trap is angled skyward and the birds go almost straight up. You will get the full range of presentations here: singles, true pairs, report and following doubles. Do you try to hit them on the climb at relatively short range or wait until they peak out or try to hit them as they fall? If you wait too long you may have a 60-plus-yard shot!

## Rising Sharptail

This event often uses the little 60 mm target and throws it away from the shooter at a rising angle. Because of the speed and the small size of the target, this can often call for a Full choke and a high velocity load, even though the birds may be taken inside 40 yards.

## Whistling Bobs

This simulates the close range flush of a quail with the target heading quickly away from the shooter and, just like its namesake, heading quickly to cover. This calls for fast shooting with an open choke.

## Sneaky Snipe

This can be similar to the rising sharptail, except the targets may not achieve a great deal of height. The window on this station can be quite small, with the target often starting out against a wooded background, zipping across a small patch of open sky, and then back across the background.

### Duck Pond

Another crowd favorite, this station has three strategically placed traps that can throw incomers, outgoers and settling crossing shots to a shooter on a small stand that juts out into a pond. You do not know what you are going to get when you call for a bird.

### Rising Ringnecks

This is a steep-climbing bird, similar to springing teal, but at a shorter range. Often there is another bird, quartering away, that joins the first.

### Modified Dove Tower

Sometimes seen as a component of a standard dove tower, this station has targets coming from behind the shooter on a high, going away angle. It looks a lot like a skeet high house, one on steroids.

The foregoing is a basic look at some of the presentations offered on courses around the country, but it certainly is not all-inclusive. Sporting clays is not a universally scripted game and veteran shooters do not want it to be. If course design and target presentations ever reach the point where shooters begin to run clean scores, things will change. That is the nature of sporting clays.

## Etiquette and Procedures

Sporting clays is a laid-back game and the procedures are similar to skeet. A squad of two to five shooters proceeds through the course with a course guide/puller. The shooting rotation within the squad may be set by the course guide or left up to the shooters. If shooters want to change the rotation of that shooting order, there is nothing in the rules to stop them.

Like skeet, each shooter steps onto the shooting station as his turn comes. The first shooter to take the station has the right to "see" the targets, to call for birds to be thrown without firing, so he and the other members of the squad can actually see what they are up against.

"Seeing targets" is an important step. If you are in a squad where the first shooter ignores this factor, remind him between stations. The first shooter has a responsibility to call for birds to be shown and every shooter on the squad benefits. If he continually forgets, change his rotation and get somebody in the first spot who is more considerate.

When a visible piece is knocked off, targets are scored as a hit. Doubles are treated differently than in skeet or trap. If the shooter manages to break both birds with one shot—a very rare occurrence—he is credited with both and saves a shell.

When shooting doubles or pairs, if the shooter misses

Guns are loaded only when the shooter steps onto the cage to take his turn. Violating this rule will get you thrown off any course in the U.S – and rightly so.

the first target he has the right to fire his second shell at it or try to get both targets with the second shell. If the shooter breaks both targets with either the first or the second shell, he gets credit for both.

If a target in the air is broken by pieces of another target, it is treated like a "no bird." When this happens, the shooter receives whatever score he got on the first shot and the doubles are thrown again. The shooter must attempt to hit the first target, but he will already have that scored. It is only the second target he is shooting for score.

Scorers call missed birds as "lost." If the shooter disagrees with the call, he must make his protest before firing another shot. The scorer then must poll the other shooters, or even the spectators, and can change his call based on that input. If he does not change it, his call stands.

In the event a gun is acting up, the shooter can ask the puller/referee for permission to test-fire it. Other than that, every round fired is for score.

Like skeet, know your rotation order in the squad; be ready to step to the shooting pad when your turn comes; and do not crowd the shooter on the pad.

## Accessories You Will Need

A good sporting clays course is like a golf course; you will do a lot of walking. Some ranges have golf carts available, but you will have to tote all your necessary items with you.

A shooting vest is an excellent idea. You will want some place to put the five to fifteen shells you use on each station. You may want divided pockets in the vest to keep #7 ½, #8 and #9 shot separate. As we will see later, changing loads for different targets can be a big plus. Since NSCA sporting clays no longer requires a low gun starting position, you will no longer need a vest of the international style unless you are shooting

FITASC. Remember that these do not have a distinct shoulder pad to catch on the recoil pad during the mount. Instead, they have a smooth face, often with padding on the shooting side to allow a sloppy gun mount to keep the buttstock where it belongs.

Vests made for sporting clays shooters often have loop-type holders or small pockets to hold extra choke tubes and a tube wrench. You will most likely have to change tubes as well as shot loads during an event. A good sporting clays vest will keep everything where you can find it in a hurry.

A standard round of sporting clays is either 50 or 100 birds and that is a lot of shotshells to carry. In addition, experienced shooters carry between three and five—or even more—different loads. It is easy to see that stuffing everything in your vest pockets is going to leave you exhausted by the end of the round. That is a lot of weight to wear throughout the round. Instead, get a tote bag to carry your shells, shell knocker, choke tube lube, spare eye and ear protection, maybe a plastic bottle of water, lens cleaning paper and other items you want.

The only time you will have to lug a separate shell bag is between stations. The rest of the time, toss it on the ground and let Mother Earth pack the load. You would be surprised what a difference that can make by the end of the day, especially in warm, humid climates. Four or five boxes of shotshells weigh a bunch!

If you are shooting a course that does not offer golf cart transportation between stations, consider the shoes you are wearing. There can be a lot of walking involved, and toting a shotgun and a lot of shells means you are wandering around, up hill and down, dragging 20 or more pounds. Jogging shoes are a good idea. The more comfortable your shoes, the better you will feel.

A round of sporting clays takes a lot longer than a round of trap or skeet, and there is more physical exertion involved. You might want to carry an energy snack and drink. Dried fruit is great, since its sugar gets to work quickly and does not give you false energy like the refined sugar in candy.

That is a lengthy list, but sporting clays is a complex game. It is a thinking shooter's game, one that will test the versatility of both your equipment and your shooting technique. It is also a heckuva lot of fun and certainly can be addictive!

**When you first try sporting clays, you may want a simple and compact plastic case such as the 100-Round Shotshell Case from MTM as you walk from station to station. This case has a removable choke tube holder and space inside for four boxes of shells.**

# CHAPTER 16

# GETTING STARTED

Unlike trap and skeet, sporting clays is not and should not be a game that can be learned by rote and then shot on reflex. The variation in target speeds, distances, angles, target sizes and the different multiple target presentations inherent in sporting clays make that impossible.

For example, it is easy to tell a skeet student what the best foot position and the proper lead are for station four. That target will be the same whether you shoot it in Maine or California. The ATA has rigidly prescribed its speed, flight path and distance. This is anything but the case in sporting clays.

You might find one course's rabbit target a rather simple shot, thrown from a slow-speed manual trap at a modest 15 yards from the gun. The next course may zip a rabbit target from a higher-speed electronic trap at a range of 40 yards! You cannot even use the same choke for the two shots, let alone the same lead. That is what makes sporting clays such a challenge.

The successful sporting shooter does not necessarily "learn" to shoot this game. Instead, he learns a well-rounded selection of shotgun techniques, and then applies the correct technique for the target presentation he is facing on that particular station. Sporting clays is a thinking shooter's game.

## Gun Position and Handling

Traditionally, a round of sporting clays began with the gun in a low gun position before calling for the bird. In standard sporting clays, the butt had to be visible below the shooter's armpit. It could not be shouldered until the bird actually left the trap.

Unfortunately, this has changed. Today, pre-mounted guns are allowed, just like skeet and trap. Apparently, the bean counters won, the men and women who see their image magnified in trophies rather than the folks who shoot because it is a thrill to bust a clay and spend a day with friends or who compete for the simple pleasure of being outside with a gun and ammo. It is too bad....

Mounting a gun in the traditional manner, starting with it on the side of the body, was what separated sporting clays from automatic games like trap and skeet, what made the game special. And mounting the gun properly was—and perhaps still is—the most over-

looked area of sporting clays instruction, especially if the shooter has had some experience at trap and skeet where the targets are called for from a mounted gun position.

Proper mounting is still one of the most important aspects of good field shooting and the reason should be obvious: unless the gun is mounted to the same position each time, it will not shoot where you are looking each time. If you fail to achieve a consistent mount, your body position, target lead and shooting technique

Classic sporting clays began with the gun in low position, the butt visible below the shooters armpit. It could not be shouldered until the bird left the trap. Today, that has changed and one may begin with a pre-mounted gun.

**There are only a million reasons to introduce your youngster to shotgun games, but here are four: the unbreakable bond you will form, the lifetime skills your youth will learn, the opportunity to teach respect for firearms and safety, and the chance to pass on our firearms and shooting sports heritage.**

become moot points because you will not be on the bird even if you do all of the other things correctly.

If you doubt the truth in those words, watch what happens to a skeet shooter that has some skill (B Class and above) the first time he tries to shoot a round of skeet from the sporting clays low gun position. His score will drop markedly. Trap shooters will likely fare even worse. Yet every one of those shots and angles are ones he will have seen many times before. He knows the leads and techniques. It is just a question of mastering gun-handling skills, and that is just one of the things that is going to be lost with the rule change.

Nevertheless, to be a really great sporting shooter, a great shotgunner, you must learn and then practice good gun-handling skills. It also helps if your equipment is properly set up. Let's study this from the position of one who shoots without a pre-mounted gun, a participant who really wants the most out of his experience. Otherwise, almost any of the cast-aside gear from trap or skeet will work ….

A well-fitted shotgun is a tremendous asset, and one reason why experienced sporting clays shooters have typically gone to the time and trouble to have it done correctly. It also helps if the heel of the recoil pad is smoothly radiused to prevent snagging as the gun comes up. Some shooters also put a slight radius on the inside edge of the recoil pad to further reduce drag. The toe of the pad also gets a smoothing. This aids in a smooth dismount of the gun because, as we will see later, traditional shooters will sometimes dismount the gun between shots on some target pairs.

When selecting a vest or shooting shirt for sporting clays, you will want one with an international-style shoulder pad that extends down the front of the vest. Those made for conventional trap and skeet have a small pad that often catches the gun's recoil pad and makes a mess of the gun mount. The fewer things you have on your vest or gun to snag, the smoother and more consistent your gun mount will be.

Stance also plays a role. Trap and skeet shooters can exhibit some of the most uncomfortable and exaggerated stances one could imagine. Some of the semi-crouch, feet-stuck-together, body-wound-up-like-a-spring stances make a consistent gun mount a real feat!

A novice should learn to stand up straight with the feet opened to about shoulder width. There should be no exaggerated crouch and one should not lock the knees. Some shooters are more comfortable with their weight spread evenly, while others like just a touch more weight on the leading foot. This provides better balance, a smoother swing and wider swing arc. Novice shooters often tend to take a classic "rifleman's" stance, with weight on the back foot. This is not good because it restricts the swing. The only time back foot weight is good form in sporting clays is when a high incoming target must be taken almost directly overhead.

The shooter's grip on the forend of the gun is another overlooked point. You should move your hand around on the forend until you find the point where you can mount and dismount the gun without strain using the forend (leading) hand only. That point is usually a bit farther back than the shooter started with, especially if he has been shooting trap or skeet from a pre-mounted position. This will alter the weight distribution between the shooter's hands and make for a much smoother and more consistent gun mount.

Additionally, there is the matter of an erect head. When mounting the gun, always bring it to the face; never bring the face to the gun! To do the latter encourages a lot of bobbing and weaving of the head and, since your eye is essentially the rear sight on your shotgun, you can imagine what that does to your score.

Proper gun handling techniques give you a comfort-

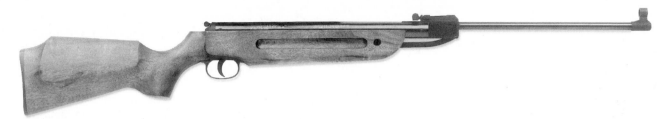

Many shooters testify that the finest way to ease your children into a shotgun is to start them with a BB gun or a pellet gun such as this Winchester by Daisy.

The smart shooter will slip his gun into a soft-sided case between stations and certainly between events. A hot gun will attract dust and the build-up of grime can suddenly cause an unnerving halt in your shooting day. For less than $50, you can buy a fine portable slip case and, given the cost of a quality shotgun, that is cheap insurance.

able stance with a maximum range of movement. Your eyes will lock onto the bird and the gun will come up smoothly without a great deal of conscious thought and in a consistent manner.

Master the traditional gun mounting process and you are well on your way to becoming a good sporting clays shooter. Neglect it and you will have more trouble scoring than you need … unless you move to a pre-mounted gun.

One final matter concerns where to position the barrel before calling for the bird. There are only two hard and fast rules:

(1) The muzzle should be within your range of vision so that it and the bird can be viewed simultaneously before the mount is begun; and

(2) The muzzle should never be held above the flight path of the target. If the bird leaves the trap and ducks under the barrel, you will temporarily lose sight of it and your focus on it. You then have to re-acquire it, and that wastes time you do not have.

This obviously means that there is no single correct gun hold position. A ground-bouncing rabbit requires a lower gun hold than a high, incoming dove. In pairs involving different targets, like a rabbit and a snipe, the hold should be correct for the first target you will engage.

## Body Position

In the skeet section, we discussed the importance of aligning your body to its natural point of aim. For most skeet targets, that will be near the Eight Post, since all targets are directed toward it. The principle of natural point of aim is still valid in sporting clays, but it is tougher to define and changes with the shot.

Determining body position starts with figuring out where you want to break the target. Every target has an ideal break point on its flight path where it fairly screams, "Kill me!" Not surprisingly, this is called the "kill zone." Given differing abilities and reaction times among different shooters, the best kill zone for each shot may vary among shooters. You have to figure out where it is for you, and position your shooting stance to it. This, in effect, becomes the sporting clays shooter's Eight Post. It may be nothing more than a small circle of air.

Multiple targets can complicate that, since a perfect position for one target may not be so for the other. Because lifting the feet to shift position while a bird is in the air is virtually guaranteed to cause a miss, you will have to do the same type of fudging that occurs during skeet doubles. Give yourself enough swing room to break the first target and fudge your body position toward the second. This is one reason why an upright, fluid stance is so important in sporting clays and you get a head start on breaking two birds when the show birds are thrown for the first shooter in the squad.

Equally important is the point to which you pivot your upper body to get your "first look," the point on the flight path where you first visually acquire the target. New shooters tend to come back much too far toward the trap. This often causes the bird to get by them, and then they have to really unwind to catch it.

Given the variety of target presentations, there is no hard and fast rule here either. Top shooters prefer to come back to the trap hard enough to put some coil in the body and this makes them unwind a bit when moving to the bird. This generates gun speed during the mount. If the bird is consistently outrunning you however, you may have to position yourself even more toward the kill zone.

Exceptions to that are some extremely quick and close crossing shots. Sometimes it can be to the shooter's advantage to take a first look point close to the house because it will make you swing like hell to catch it. At times that is exactly what is needed to break that target! Time and experience will also alter your first look point.

The more proficient you become, the more you can fudge to the kill zone. Depending on the shooting technique you use, your first look point can also be altered.

## Shooting Techniques

Sustained lead and fast swing were both explained in the "Skeet Simplified" chapter and there is not much point in discussing them again here. Both have their uses in sporting clays and they pretty much parallel those in skeet. Sustained lead is a good way to handle incoming targets that have a little angle away from the shooter, while the fast swing is generally a superior technique for crossers, out-goers and quartering shots.

The biggest disadvantage to the sustained lead in sporting clays is that it requires you to know the lead. You must have handled that distance and angle successfully in the past and have filed the amount of daylight you see between muzzle and target away in your little on-board computer. Some experienced shooters who have virtually seen every shot can make good use of the sustained lead in a far wider variety of presentations than most shooters. The technique does not work nearly as well for novices and intermediate shooters in this game as it does in skeet. The problem is that we see new leads and angles on each new course.

Another factor is target speed. The velocity of skeet and trap targets is fixed. Sporting clays use machines that throw at different speeds, and the size and shape of the targets also produce different speeds. All of this complicates the game for a shooter using a technique that requires the exact lead to be known and is relatively unforgiving if target speed and distance are misjudged. With the fast swing, the speed of the target

will tend to accelerate your gun speed and that in itself can help compensate for varying target speeds.

I believe that makes the fast swing the bread-and-butter technique for sporting clays. The faster the target is moving, the faster you have to move to nail it. There is however another technique that can be extremely useful. The individual who explained it to me called it the "pull-away" and I will use the same explanation, although I'm certain some shooters might poke holes in this definition.

The pull-away came about as a direct result of the low gun position used. It is not especially effective from a pre-mounted position, nor is it easy to accomplish. It works because of the body's natural tendency to lock eyes upon an aerial target while the upper body uncoils to track it in flight. If one executes the proper gun mount technique, the eyes never leave the target and the gun comes up to look exactly where the eyes are looking. Since the body is moving while you are mounting the gun, gun speed has already been generated. Once the gun is mounted, it is still moving at body speed, which is moving at target speed. At that point, the gun speed is quickly increased and the shot triggered.

In practice, it works like this: take your natural point of aim in the kill zone, pivot the upper body to the first look point, call for the bird and, as it appears, swing with it as the gun comes up. When the gun hits the cheek and shoulder, it is on the bird, not at a point behind it as with the fast swing. As soon as you see the bird picture, the body accelerates the swing and triggers the shot as soon as the lead is recognized. For all practical purposes, you trigger the shot within milliseconds of the gun mount.

This particular technique results in two very positive things for the sporting clays shooter. The first is a reduction in lead. The sudden acceleration of the gun, which is essentially moving at target speed, creates a faster swing than possible with other techniques. Going back to the skeet field, from a low gun position you need about four feet of lead to break a station four crossing shot with the sustained lead. With the fast swing, the lead decreases to a bit more than two feet. With the pull-away, it is cut even further, to about what appears to be 18 inches. It is worth remembering that this is a 21-yard direct crossing shot on a 45 mph bird. Some of the closer, slower targets on a sporting clays range can be broken by virtually shooting at the bird.

The reduction in lead is primarily why the pull-away technique achieved its popularity.

It is common in sporting clays to have crossing shots in the 40-plus-yard range. If you shoot a sustained lead, you will need more than 10 feet at 40 yards. That is too much for most human brains to compute and hold because you have no real frame of reference. The pull-away cuts those long leads down to something with which we can be more comfortable and consistent.

Another factor enters the picture with sustained leads that are long, and that is which way the target is crossing. A right-handed shooter will have the gun to the right cheek and the right eye looking down the rib. The left eye, assuming the proper "both eyes open" technique, will be looking down the left side of the barrel. If the target is crossing from the left, both eyes can easily see and track it. This provides the binocular vision we humans require for accurate depth perception.

If the target is a right-to-left crosser however, the left eye can be blocked from seeing it by the gun. Holding a precise lead is extremely difficult with only one eye if the lead exceeds more than a couple of feet, and doubly tough if the target is rising.

There are some outstanding sporting clays instructors who recommend that right-handed shooters use the pull-away on all right to left crossing shots (the reverse being true for left-handers) just because of this, and teach the fast swing or sustained lead for targets going the other way.

Regardless of the circumstance, the pull-away can greatly reduce the lead required on a target. Another advantage is the control it gives a shooter over where he breaks his targets.

Because one fires the pull-away almost simultaneously with the mounting of the gun, the only restriction on how quickly you can break the target is how fast you can mount the gun. Conversely, by delaying the mount, you can comfortably break targets at different ranges.

Going back to skeet station four, a standard shot that any shooter can duplicate, you will find that from a low gun position you cannot break the target with a sustained lead in a consistent manner until it has gone 10 to 15 feet past the Eight Post. The fast swing lets you take it on the Post and the pull-away lets you break it 10 to 15 feet in front of the Post. So you can break it anywhere along the flight path you choose just by delaying the gun mount. Some of that control can be had with the fast swing, but the pull-away offers a larger degree of control. When you have to break a bird in a narrow window in trees or brush, or take one bird in a pair very quickly in order to get a reasonable shot on the second, the pull-away is worth its weight in gold. When you have to make a shot quickly, regardless of the speed, distance or angle, the pull-away can be lightning fast.

## Multiple Targets

Once a shooter has a handle on proper gun mount, stance, body position and shooting techniques, he now must consider how to handle the gun on multiple targets.

A single target is just that. Shoot the thing, reload and call for the next presentation. Pairs however, require some thought about how you will deal with them.

"Following pairs" are one bird launched within three seconds of the shooter's command with a second bird launched at some time within three seconds of that, at the puller's discretion. Shooting from a fluid, low gun position, experienced shooters find the act of mounting the gun itself to be an integral part of the shot-making process. So what do you do after you break the first bird and are waiting on the second? Smart shooters drop the gun from their shoulder! This makes both shots the same. That is also why these shooters radius the toe on their recoil pad. It makes the dismount as smooth as the mount.

You do not have to drop the gun back to the original starting position. It is easier to just push it slightly away from the shoulder and drop the butt slightly to unlock the cheek.

Once a shooter becomes accustomed to this, he will

Paired trap machines can make your sporting afternoon a challenge. Doubles can be thrown simultaneously, or in sequence or as report pairs (the second being flung immediately after you shoot the first one).

find it also works on "report pairs," where the second bird is launched at the sound of the shot fired at the first. You do not have as much time, but you do not need it. You are not going back to a rigid low gun position, merely dropping the buttstock. You do not have far to go to remount the gun and with a bit of practice the partial dismount becomes as smooth as the mount.

In both cases, it beats the heck out of smoking the first target with a fluid gun mount and then standing there with a dead gun locked into your shoulder while you try to find, and then re-establish, swing speed on the second target.

"Simultaneous pairs" present a totally different challenge. If they are different targets (Fur & Feathers, for example), some skilled shooters still do a slight dismount after the first bird. If they are true pairs, there are few shooters skilled enough to do it. Most of us cannot, at least not if we want to shoot the second bird in the same county as the first. You have to analyze the flight path of the birds and determine how you can best swing through the first to get the second without slowing the gun.

Sometimes that means taking the trailing bird first and then accelerating to catch the lead bird. It works on some stations. Other times, you may have to take the lead bird first, recover from recoil, and catch the second with a classic skeet shooter's pre-mounted fast swing.

Every now and then, if the Good Lord is smiling on you and the course designer had an off day, you may find one point in the flight of that pair where you can kill both with one shot. This usually happens after they have gotten out a bit. If you happen to miss, well ... you now have an even longer shot on the second bird. This is a gamble, but sometimes it can be worth it. Smart shooters will watch the targets at viewing to see if it is feasible. If you can pull it off, it impresses the heck out of the other shooters.

These gun handling techniques are markedly different from those used in conventional trap or skeet. However, trap and skeet ranges are the best place to learn them. The reasons are time and money.

Most shooters have to travel a good bit farther to find a sporting clays range than a trap or skeet setup. Sporting clays also takes a lot longer to shoot. A round of 50 birds can take a squad most of the afternoon. A round of sporting clays also costs a lot more than trap or skeet. On the shaded courses at Deer Creek Sporting Clays (www.deercreeksportingclays.com) north of Tampa, Florida, for instance, a non-member pays $.46 per clay (cart rental is $20 and gun rental is $15). Annual individual ($200) or family ($300) memberships qualify for 10 percent target discounts. Thus, a 50-bird round of sporting clays will run about $25.

## Cross Training Practice

To learn fluid gun handling and the various shooting techniques, a shooter needs to see a lot of targets and a variety of angles. It is fast and cheap to do it on a skeet or trap range. It is also valid practice, because you will find virtually every angle presented to you in trap or skeet at some point on a sporting clays field.

At most skeet clubs, it is common for a few sporting clays aficionados to open their own field and play their own games ... under the watchful eye of the range safety officer, of course. They shoot between the existing stations to look at new angles, and frequently back up 10 or 15 yards from the mid-field stations to practice long crossers.

Sporting clays shooters also practice on trap ranges by starting at the 16-yard line, then moving progressively forward until they are standing right behind the trap house. When you get on a sporting clay field, you will see those same shots represented as quail, pheasants and rising sharptails, and you will have a far better handle on them than you would if your experience with those angles has been limited to a few expensive rounds of sporting clays.

Because you will see more targets in less time, you can hone your gun mounting technique more quickly if that is the way you prefer to shoot. There is nothing in anybody's trap or skeet range rules that says you cannot call for a target from a low gun position, so why not take advantage of that to fine-tune your gun handling skills?

For that matter, why not take advantage of cross training to master shots that are giving you fits on the sporting clays fields? Bonnie McLaurin, a world-class female shooter, has remarked, "Shooting sporting clays is a lot like fighting a forest fire. Just when you get a problem solved in one spot, something flares up in another area."

That sort of thing happens all the time. A perfect example is one particular tower shot on a local sporting clays range. It is not a difficult shot. I have been looking at skeet targets like that for years. Essentially, the bird comes off a 20-foot tower to the right and angles out into the field to the left at about 45 degrees. The target is very visible and is normally broken at about 20 yards, slightly to the shooter's right side.

This is a simple shot and one I did not think needed to be rushed, at least not until they threw a true pair with the birds in trail. Then the smooth rhythm I had been using to take the singles resulted in my second shot being at a 30-yard falling bird. Not my cup of tea!

The singles were easy, but the pairs were killing me. So I decided to speed up my shot rhythm, and promptly screwed everything up. Now they were all eating my lunch.

I solved the problem at a skeet range. I backed up about 10 yards from a point midway between stations two and three to duplicate the angle and distance on the shot and began practicing what could be called a slight variation of the pull-away shot. Upon seeing the bird, I would mount the gun, get spot-on the bird, and immediately accelerate forward. The amount of lead was nothing. I triggered the shot as soon as the acceleration began. It did not take a full box of shells to get the timing right. With pairs, all I had to do was mount on the trailing bird, fire, and swing smoothly through the first.

I invariably run that station now, and it only took 15 minutes on a skeet range to figure out how to do it.

Another station that was giving me fits was also deceptively simple. The trap was located behind and to the right of the shooter. Three singles would come out at angles varying from a moderate quartering angle to a dead straightaway. Pairs launched at the moderate right-to-left angle. The shot was not difficult. The problem was the lack of time because the birds were in the bushes within 25 yards.

I first started shooting this station by screwing my body all the way around to the right to stare right at the trap house. I found I did not have time to catch the birds though, and was missing some easy singles because of it. I adjusted by moving my first look point farther out into the field and found that caused me to shoot as soon as the gun hit my shoulder—almost spot or snap shooting. This resulted in my shooting behind birds with any angle on them.

That took four boxes of shells shooting from low gun from the 16-yard trap line to correct, and it was quite an interesting experience. I think I broke only eleven birds my first round. I had no problems with the extreme angled shots; I was missing the gentle angles. I discovered that I was rushing the shot and shooting behind the birds. Once I altered my timing to mount the gun slightly behind the bird and then move smoothly and unhurriedly through it, I started popping 22 to 23 per round.

That slight bit of practice and a little change in timing was all it took, and I now run that sporting clays station regularly. I have no idea how long it would have taken me to discover that solution by just shooting that one sporting clays station until I got it right, but four rounds of trap cost less than one round of sporting clays!

Another problem with which cross training has aided me greatly is the building of speed on those close, quick, "in your face" targets that many Southeastern sporting clays ranges love to throw. If you measure distance and angle, a lot of these targets are not that tough. Add increased speed and stick some trees and bushes on the field for them to duck behind periodically though, and things get a bit more complicated.

You have to jump these birds quickly. Having learned my clay target style as a sustained-lead American skeet shooter, I just was not getting the job done.

Swearing off the slower American skeet targets for a while and shifting over to the international skeet range worked wonders on my speed. In fact, if I had to pick one clay target game that would benefit sporting clays shooters the most, that would be it. If you are just out to practice, not shooting registered targets, you do not need to adopt the gun-on-the-hip starting position: use your normal sporting clays low gun position. The faster speed of the international targets will certainly improve your speed.

Combine that with a few rounds of trap, maybe some selected skeet stations, and you will find lovely things happening to your scores.

You can even practice your techniques for following and report pairs simply by telling the puller what you want him to pull.

The only realistic sporting clays practice you cannot get on a trap or skeet range is trailing true pairs or perhaps the bouncing bunny. With this "intensified" training regime however, the first time you do step onto a sporting clays field you will have a working knowledge of the various techniques you will need.

As you step up to a new station, view the target presentation and then analyze the shots with the following factors in mind:

(1) What is the range at which you will be engaging the targets? This will determine your choke and load selection for that station.

(2) Then, if pairs are presented, which bird will you take first? Which shooting technique will be most effective for each? This is not something you should try to figure out after the birds are in the air!

Sometimes you will have no choice in the order. At other times you may have wide latitude, including taking a trailing bird first and driving through to the lead bird or taking the lead bird first and then executing a fast swing on the trailer or maybe even taking both with one shot. Planning how you will shoot is important because it will determine your kill zone and that will determine your initial stance and gun hold position. Remember to note the flight path of the first bird you will shoot, and make sure your gun hold is correct for it.

After that, sporting clays is just a matter of properly executing your shot plan. Now, that is often easier said than done and is one reason why sporting clays is the most challenging shotgun game around.

# CHAPTER 17
# SPORTING CLAYS' TOUGHEST SHOTS

Hitting aerial targets is nothing more than matching their combination of speed, angle and altitude. That much holds true regardless of the clay target game. Veteran trap or skeet shooters will see many of the angles they are familiar with the first time they step onto a sporting clays field and the reverse is true.

What separates sporting clays from other games is that, while you may be getting a familiar target speed, angle and altitude, you get those features in targets of widely varying size, weight and construction.

Launch two dissimilar targets from the same trap at the same angle, speed and altitude, and you will get two targets with dissimilar flight characteristics. That is something only seen in sporting clays, because all other games use a single standardized target. It exhibits standard and consistent flight characteristics, unless affected by the wind. You can predict its movements.

The bottom line is that the sporting clays station you shot yesterday can be radically different today due to nothing more than a change in the targets loaded in the trap machine.

Another factor that separates sporting clays from other games is the array of target presentations. When you factor in the mix of different targets and combine that with the possibility of seeing those targets as singles, following pairs or report pairs, and even simultaneous (true) pairs, then you can have a tremendously varied shot presentation.

## Clay Targets

That is why the game cannot be learned by rote and shot on reflex. Every station must be thought through, not only the flight path of the targets, but also how different targets might fly from the same launcher.

### Standard Target

This is the same target used in trap and skeet. It has a relatively stable flight path. It is 110mm in diameter and even casual shooters are familiar with its performance. We will use it as a yardstick to measure the performance of the other clay targets commonly encountered in sporting clays.

### Midi Target

This bird has the same configuration as the standard but, at 90mm, is smaller in diameter. It has the same

The targets used in sporting clays come in several sizes and each has its uses: standard and the thinner battue (110 mm in diameter), midi (90 mm), mini (60 mm) and ground-running rabbit.

flight characteristics as the standard, but can be one of the more frustrating targets on the field.

The reason is that determining the distance to the target is very important in figuring lead, as well as the choke and load. The midi target is often mixed in with standards, but because it is smaller it is deceptive. It can fool a shooter into thinking it is a standard target just at longer range.

Its speed can be deceptive, too. Because it is smaller and lighter, it can leave the trap faster, yet because it is lighter it will slow down faster than a standard bird. Throw it with a standard target as a pair, as is often the case, and it may be the lead target for the first portion of the flight and then be overtaken by the standard. This can play real hell with a shot plan! The challenge for the shooter is to be able to identify the target as a midi quickly and understand the difference it will display in flight. It can require a different shot plan than when facing two standard targets as a pair.

### Mini Targets

This 60mm saucer is the smallest target normally thrown in sporting clays. Like the midi, it is just a scaled-down version of the standard. Unlike the midi however, it is seldom misinterpreted. When this one

There is only one gun presentation like this in clay shooting – the Running Rabbit. Thrown across the ground, the rabbit will dance and jump and roll unexpectedly and often in a most aggravating manner!
*(Photo courtesy Winchester)*

is thrown, there is little doubt. It is like shooting at an aspirin tablet traveling at Mach 1.

The problem with minis is that their light weight really makes them zip out of a trap and their small size can make it difficult to get an accurate fix on the range. Because of their size, they can slip through pattern gaps easily so they can require a denser shot pattern.

Another item to factor in with minis is that most of the time the target is completely black and they are generally thrown as a part of a pair. The pair might be two minis, or a mini in combination with a midi or a standard. It is easy to lose sight of this target and concentrate on the brighter one. They tend to get out there fast and blend into any vegetation in the background. This means the shooter must concentrate on finding the best visual window and take the target as quickly as possible.

When range operators throw this target in tight, tree-lined quarters it can be extremely difficult to pick up and hit.

### Battue Targets

This is a very different target than the three previous ones. It is a 110mm target, but only ⅜-inch high and with a slight center dome. Its flight characteristics do not resemble any other target. Because of this, it is a very difficult bird to hit and it calls for a lot of discipline from the shooter. Not only will this target's unusu-

al shape cause it to change attitude in flight, but it will also change profile!

The most common presentation for battues is as pairs, generally as crossing shots; sometimes with a very slight outgoing or incoming angle. As they launch, they present a very slender profile to the shooter: they are edge-on flat! Some shooters call them "flying razor blades" and they can be difficult to hit early in their flight. At a point somewhere around mid-flight, they begin to turn on their edge and present a fuller profile. This is called "development" and the target is now easier to find with a shot pattern. This "development" continues until the shooter sees it as a round disc. Unfortunately, by the time the bird gets that far it is generally beginning to drop quickly and actually picking up a bit of speed again as it falls.

The shooter must wait until enough of the target "develops" to be hit, yet not waste too much time. Since range operators normally throw battues as pairs, the second bird is a difficult shot. Farther away and falling, it can be a frustrating target.

### Rabbit Target

This standard-sized 110mm target is always presented as a ground-bouncer rolling on its edge. Since the ground is uneven, the target path may vary considerably. Some "rabbits" may zip across flat, some may bounce high and wild, and others may do both. No two targets will be perfectly alike in their running path. Because the rabbit target is thrown into the ground— even if the first and hardest bounce is on a section of carpet—it is beefed up to avoid breakage. Therefore, it may require a shot charge heavier than the range would indicate in order to be certain of a break. Rabbits may be thrown as the only target on a station or they may come as singles or as following or report pairs. Operators seldom throw these as true pairs. They are often the first target of a "Fur & Feather" presentation, with the second target (usually a standard) as an outgoing or quartering away target in about the same general distance range.

Reading the type of target and understanding what it will do is only part of the process. You also must determine exactly what it is doing in relation to the shooting stand.

Terrain, trees, elevation changes, and landscaping can paint a deceptive picture of what the target is actually doing. Shadow and light can play tricks on the shooter, too. Good range operators will use all of these to create serious optical illvusions. Some targets may look like they are true crossing shots, yet have some incoming or outgoing angle on them. A target launched downhill may appear to be rising when it is actually falling. One that appears to be rising may actually be losing speed and falling.

Gil Ash of Optimum Shotgun Performance Shooting School says to wait for a target to turn slightly in the air and present its underneath cupped side, which it will do, rather than try to take it on its edge, a much smaller target.

An inventive range operator can create more illusions than a magician. If you shoot without thinking through the illusion, you will likely miss.

## Developing Shot Plans

Another consideration in sporting clays is having a shot plan for true pairs. Many expert shooters are convinced that if they miss the first target, they should fire at it again instead of shifting to the second bird. This often happens among shooters with a hunting background or with experience in a game like international trap. There are some valid points to that argument.

A shooter firing at a target is already concentrating on that target. It has been acquired, tracked and engaged. If the shot misses, the gun is already traveling with that target and it sometimes takes only a slight correction in point and hold to nail it with a follow-up shot. For some shooters, this is an effective way to salvage at least one bird out of a pair when the first shot misses.

Some shooters are not mentally geared to go after one bird twice though. Skeet shooters are an excellent example. They shoot doubles as a regular part of the game and only get one shot per bird. Skeet doubles invariably requires that the gun track be radically altered for the second bird. Shoot-off doubles, for example, from stations three, four and five, demand that the gun direction be quickly reversed to acquire a target moving in the opposite direction. It becomes a fluid, learned subconscious response to leave the first target, whether it is hit or not and immediately go after the second bird.

For shooters with this mindset, it may be well to stick with your shot plan to fire one round per bird, regardless of the results. Changing a preconceived plan that you have executed countless times before is very difficult to do in the millisecond you have to make the decision.

With the above in mind, here are some thoughts on developing shot plans for the more common target presentations we see on the sporting fields.

Thousands – perhaps millions – of shotgunners enjoy a few clay rounds each year. A small percentage of them is particularly interested in shooting for score. The rest are shooting one or more of the clay games as a tune-up for field shooting.

### Incoming Tower Shot

This kind of station simulates incoming ducks or doves, and the towers may be as high as 100 feet.

On singles, the best bet is to be patient. Put some weight on your leading food and wait for this target to come to you, but do not be in a hurry to take it. Give the shot time to develop and wait until it approaches a direct overhead shot, then mount the gun only when you are about to shoot. This gives you the largest possible target surface to shoot at and makes the shot a relatively simple one. The shooter swings through the bird and triggers the shot as soon as the barrel passes the leading edge. A skeet choke and #9 skeet load are usually the best choice, as most of these shots are within 15 yards of the gun.

Following and report pairs are shot the same way, and the gun should be slightly dismounted between shots. True pairs are a little tougher. If the pairs are taking the same track, consider taking the trailing bird first and then continuing the swing through the first bird. Leads are minimal and the recoil of the gun will help move you from the trailing bird to the leader. That, of course, assumes the shooting cage gives you enough room to get on the birds quickly and that the birds are traveling within five or six feet of each other. If not, take the leading bird first, leave the gun mount-ed, and then fast-swing through the second target. Often when a shooter faces an incoming tower shot, he will find his gun angle restricted by the construction of the shooting cage to prevent his shooting the trap machine.

If birds are launched on separate flight paths, take the most direct incoming bird first and as quickly as you can. This gives you time to acquire the second bird, which will now be an incoming shot with some angle away from the shooter. Some shooters prefer to dismount the gun after the first shot and then remount for the second. Dismounting between shots gives you a better visual acquisition on the second target and, if you have worked on your gun handling skills, the remount and shot will be almost simultaneous. Leads are minimal in either case, since the targets are closing on you. I have never seen this shot presented where a Skeet choke and #9s were not the best bet.

### Springing Teal

This target is thrown fast, almost straight up to a height of about 70 feet, and may be traveling slightly toward or away from the shooter. It intimidates many shooters with trap or skeet experience but surprisingly, shooters with little shotgun experience find it easy. The reason is that they wait until the bird gets to the top of its flight, and then they shoot it as a stationary target as the bird hangs there. They forget about lead. That is the way to do it.

One of the toughest bird presentations in sporting clays is the springing teal. It is thrown fast, almost straight up to a height of 70 feet or so. To shoot it successfully, delay your mount until the target has almost reached its apex, and then mount and shoot it at the momentary pause at the top of its flight.

One cruel course designer placed the trap machine on top of a high tower and forced the shooters below to take an outgoing, overhead dropping shot. Photos of the final Seminole Cup at the TM Ranch, Orlando, Florida.

To shoot springing teal, your gun hold point should be high, with weight on the front foot. Delay your mount until the target has almost reached its apex. Then mount the gun, perch the bird on top of the bead and take it. When dealing with true pairs, take the target that hits the lower apex of its flight first and then let the recoil swing you up to the second.

Dealing with this presentation takes some timing. If you are off, hitting the bird at the last portion of its upward flight is the better choice. Once it starts to fall, it becomes a very difficult target.

### Outgoing Overhead Dropping Shot

This simulates a dove coming in from overhead and behind, and it confuses some shooters. If you are one of them, go to a skeet range and spend a box of shells shooting the high house one target. That is all these are, although they do look like a high house one on steroids.

The first checkpoint for this shot is almost directly overhead, with a little weight on the back foot. Shift your weight to the front foot as you acquire the target. The gun muzzle is high. Pick up the target as quickly as you can, mount the gun with the muzzle either spot-on or slightly behind the bird, then swing down and through it. Trigger the shot when you see about six inches of daylight between the muzzle and the bird. Take this shot as quickly as you can because, if you do not, it becomes a long-range dropping target. It will then become one of the toughest shots you will

A typical fur and feather presentation is a rabbit followed immediately – or worse, simultaneously – by a crossing shot. If the course designer is imaginative, and many are, the crossing shot will be in the opposite direction as the running rabbit. To make a smooth swing and follow through, you are required to pay close attention to the call-birds and any shooters who may be in line before you.

ever see. Hit it quick, and it is relatively easy. You can handle this shot well with an open choke and either #9s or #8 ½ shot.

This presentation is almost never seen as a true pair, but if you encounter it as such, take the trailing target first and drive through to the second, doubling the lead for the second bird. For following or report pairs, dismount the gun between shots and bring the upper body back to the initial first look point.

### The Driven Shot

This is very similar to the incoming tower shot, except the birds start at a lower elevation and rise. The procedure however, is not that different. You still need to swing quickly through the bird and trigger the shot when the muzzle passes it. If there is a difference, it is that the lead is a bit less. If the birds are close, you can nail this presentation as soon as the muzzle blots out the bird. A skeet choke and #9 shot are the best bet. Spreader loads will help if the birds are within 20 yards.

If you face simultaneous pairs in this presentation, you must acquire the targets as quickly as possible and nail the first bird fast. In this case, taking the leading bird first is the best bet. You may not have time to take the trailer and then catch the lead bird. Let the recoil carry your gun to the following bird. Regardless of the pair presentation, this is fast, close shooting. It pays to get pumped up for this one!

### Fur and Feather

This gives you a rabbit for the first target, followed (as a report, following or simultaneous pair) by an aerial target, which is usually a standard. The gun hold point on this must be for the rabbit, which you should take as quickly as is comfortable. Resist the temptation to rush the first shot to the point where you miss it though. Make sure you get the rabbit, and then let the other target take care of itself. Rushing is the biggest mistake new shooters make on this presentation and it costs them the rabbit. You will not get far if you always miss the first target in a pair.

The best advice for true pairs is, "Kill the first target every time!" The second target will, through practice and repetition, break on its own.

On following and report pairs, dismount the gun after the rabbit. That gives you better visual ability to pick up the aerial bird. This is normally not a difficult shot, being usually a mild quartering-away or a gentle crosser. Open chokes, with #8 ½ for the rabbit and #9s (maybe a spreader, because these are often close-range shots) for the bird, are good choices.

### Going Away Shots

You will see these shot profiles a lot. Most of the time there will be some quartering angle on any singles targets and on one bird in a pair. The other bird in a pair will often be a dead straightaway that has some rising angle on it.

The range at which these targets may be engaged can vary considerably, from 10- to 35-plus yards. Regardless of the range, it is important to have weight on the front foot and pick up the first bird as soon as possible.

The choke and shot size depend upon the range. This is generally Skeet 1 or Improved Cylinder territory, with shot in the #8 ½ to #8 range: the narrower profile of these targets will give you fewer pellet hits and they need to be larger pellets to get a visible piece.

For a second or so on a rising target, there will be a period where it levels out and flies almost straight. That is the time to break it. If you wait too long and the target starts to drop, you have a much tougher shot.

On true pairs, take the straightaway as fast as you can. It may be a dead straightaway or slightly rising. Then move to the quartering bird. It pays to fudge your natural point of aim to the second bird.

### Crossing Shots

These can be of the most varied shot presentations you will see in sporting clays. You may get crossers at 12 yards moving through a screen of trees or brush. You may get them at more than 40 yards sailing across a relatively open area. It is the same angle and target speed, but vastly different techniques are required to break them.

Many hard-crossers in sporting clays will be in the 15- to 25-yard range. These require a lot of lateral body movement, due to the closeness of the launching platform to the shooter. Some of the best possible practice you can get for these is to spend a day on a skeet range working on the outgoing targets from stations two, three, five and six. You have to get the first look position close to the house, and then uncoil rapidly as you swing through the target.

The best shooting technique for these is the fast swing-through. Few shooters can pinpoint the target quickly enough to execute a good pullaway shot.

Leads are often minimal. The faster the target is moving, the faster the gun has to swing to catch it. The faster the gun is moving, the less apparent lead is needed. Targets within 15 yards can often be broken, even by a somewhat lazy-swinging shooter, by shooting as soon as the muzzle meets the bird.

With report and following pairs, a gun dismount between shots is the best bet. On true pairs, swing through and take the trailing target first and then continue your gun movement to swing through the leading target. It is a good idea to fudge your natural point of aim a bit toward the direction of the second target (leading bird) when dealing with true pairs. You

This competitor is taking a breath and focusing on the path of the birds – this was a long going-away shot – with his gun at the low-gun position before calling for the throw.

A tightly confined shooting lane over the palmettos and between the pines means these shooters have to plan for a crossing shot.

may need the extra swing room, because the second bird is likely to be taken out of the position where you would expect to break it under less strenuous presentations.

This is nothing more than aggressive shooting. You have to go after any close-range crossing target aggressively; if you lay back, you are finished! It is pure reflex and speed of swing. The story is a little different on long crossing shots.

A target that makes you really coil up and unwind at close range gives you a lot more time at longer range, even if it is the same speed and angle. The increased distance between you and the target allows your field of view to become greater and you can acquire the target with less body movement. For many, there seems to be a discrepancy between apparent speed of crossing targets at ranges inside 25 yards and those beyond that. I do not have to move as much to take a station five hard right-angle shot in trap from the 27-yard line as I do from the 16-yard line. The increased distance to the target means less body movement for the shooter and the same holds true here in sporting clays.

Since I have that extra time, I tend to shoot all 30-plus-yard crossing shots with the "pullaway" technique instead of the fast swing. It works for me and gives me an apparent lead on a 40-yard crossing target of about four to five feet, as compared to the more than 10-foot lead I would see with a sustained lead, or the six- to seven-foot lead I would see with a swing-through. There is plenty of time to dismount the gun between shots on following or report pairs and, if you are using the pullaway, you will want to do so.

I would use this procedure for anything except true pairs. There, I would fudge my natural point of aim to the direction the target is traveling, take the trailing bird first with a pullaway, and then swing through the lead bird.

If you face battue targets on this presentation, you may have to fudge your body position even more to the target direction side, since experienced shooters wait longer for these targets to "develop" enough to be consistently broken.

# CHAPTER 18
# SPORTING'S OTHER SIDE

Sporting clays is still growing as the hottest shotgun game in America and it is a rare clay target enthusiast who has not shot at least a few rounds.

A traditional sporting clays course takes a lot of land. It could require as much land as a 9-hole golf course. While the shooting stations themselves do not require that much room, one has to plan for shot fall areas, and #7 ½ shot (the largest size allowed) can travel almost 340 yards through the air. The areas where it lands cannot, in a very practical sense, be used for anything else. That means a good sporting clays course can eat up a deceptively large amount of property and property is not cheap or, in some areas, readily available. Deer Creek Sporting Clays, on valuable development-prone land north of Tampa, Florida, sits on 300 acres

Another drawback is that the game is both time- and labor-intensive. As with golf, it takes a fair amount of time to negotiate a course and a squad will require the services of a course guide/puller. If manual traps are used on any station, someone has to be paid to operate them.

## 5-Stand Sporting

The brainchild of Scottish-born Raymond Forman, this shotgun game is a computer-driven contest that can be set up on existing trap or skeet fields, even using some of the traps already in place. 5-stand can be run by one operator and shooters can be cycled through in little more time than it takes to shoot a round of trap or skeet. Nevertheless, this game can offer virtually every shot found on a full-sized sporting clays course. Some of the country's top range operators feel this may be one of the most significant things to happen to sporting since it arrived on these shores.

"The 5-stand game is a real money-maker for us," one operator noted. "Our emphasis is on corporate and group entertainment. We needed a game that could be shot day or night, rain or shine, 365 days a year. That is not feasible with sporting clays. You cannot afford to cover walkways and shooting stations on a full-sized course, and lighting them up for night shooting would take a huge bank of lights."

The new games use so little space that he can both cover the shooting stations and light the field economi-

**5-Stand sporting clays is a great way to shoot a variety of target presentations in a limited space. Shooters stand side-by-side and rotate to their right after they shoot. Target presentations can be changed quickly, even between squads.**

Competitors who are not accustomed to the caged feeling and standing in line with their squad members may have some initial difficulty with 5-Stand shooting, but when they begin to focus on the fundamentals, they quickly overcome these obstacles.

cally. "We do not get weathered out like we do on our full-size sporting course," the course operator said, "so this has become a commercial range operator's dream set-up."

For an idea of just how economically beneficial these games can be, I talked to Skeet Hall of Fame shooter Danny Mitchell, who operates the Wolfe Creek Gun Club near Atlanta, Georgia. Danny reported that on one recent weekend a few years ago his range threw sixteen rounds of trap, 174 rounds of skeet (which required opening six fields, with personnel to run them) and 97 rounds of NSCA 5-stand sporting. One man, on one field, handled all the sporting rounds! That is an enormous labor-saving reduction in cost and, in an era where we are all pinching pennies, makes the difference between profitability and bankruptcy.

While the new 5-stand games have logistical and economic advantages for the range operator, do not be lulled into thinking they are just cheap, "fast-food" versions of the real game. They are not. In fact, they can be every bit as challenging as traditional sporting clays or even harder.

There are a number of versions of the 5-stand game. One is the original Raymond Forman version that is still seen on some ranges. This utilizes the "Birdbrain" computer to operate four to eight trap machines. The machine throws the same five shots for each shooter in random order. Five shots from each of the five stations

As in sporting clays, 5-stand simulates bird hunting shots. Shooters in squads of one to five people move from station to station with a predetermined menu of shots and combinations. This is the 5-stand set-up at Flint Oak (www.flintoak.com) in Kansas.

make a convenient 25-target round. The shooter does not know what target will emerge when he calls for the bird. The game has three different levels, with three degrees of difficulty. On Level One, the shooter will see all singles. Level Two throws three singles and one simultaneous pair. Level Three offers two true pairs and one single and it will tax even an experienced shooter's abilities.

Forman's game was never standardized. The last time I shot it was at Cherokee Rose in Griffin, Georgia, and here is what was offered: As you stepped onto the field you were confronted with five shooting stations arrayed in a straight line, each with its own shooting cage. Each shooter started at one station, received five targets, and moved to the next. As you changed stations, the angles changed and the shots varied considerably. On the far left side of the field, trap one launched a rabbit target across the middle of the field and a snipe target that took a similar crossing angle. Farther out from it was a grouse trap that launched a hard-angled shot that, depending where you were on the stations, could be a fast outgoing, quartering target or a long-range crossing shot. Trap three was located just forward and below shooting station three and was a wobble trap that simulated flushing quail on outgoing angles. Trap four, located outside the edge of the field on the right-hand side, was a teal trap throwing high birds that settled into the middle of the field. Inside of that trap, on the right, was trap five, a fast-climbing pheasant. Trap six was located on the roof and threw a high, outgoing dove.

These targets were tough to master even with repeat practice. What made it tougher was that they were thrown randomly, and you had to change stations every five rounds.

The only time you knew which target to expect was when the trap threw a broken "no bird" target. It would then repeat that presentation.

5-stand was one of the first mini-sporting games.

## 5-Stand Standardized

In 1992, the National Sporting Clays Association (NSCA) purchased the rights and trademark to 5-stand sporting and made a few changes. The biggest was that the random order of the targets was dispensed with and targets are now thrown in a known order that can be read from a menu posted at each shooting station. They also began a campaign to bring more standardization to the game. About what you would expect from the organizational bean-counters ....

The purpose of some standardization is to establish NSCA 5-stand sporting as a game that can be shot anywhere in the country and scores compared and equated. This is important for competition with registered targets. If there is going to be any consistency in sporting clays, at least one version of the game must become standard. That is not to say however that it must become rigid, although it will.

The criteria for sanctioned NSCA 5-stand sporting are not tightly drawn. The field must have either six or eight individual traps and, except for one specialty trap, they must be automatic. Hand-set, manual traps can create a safety hazard on the small field where the same situation would not exist on a larger sporting clays course.

To qualify as a sanctioned course, the following targets must be presented in the array: a tower outgoing bird; an incoming bird; a right-to-left crosser (or quartering away); a left-to-right crosser (or quartering away); a rabbit and a vertical "teal-type" target. If the range is using eight traps instead of the minimum six, the extra two traps can greatly increase the options in target presentations.

Three levels of difficulty are retained (Level One, singles; Level Two, three singles and a true pair; Level Three, one single and two true pairs), but the order is known and posted on a menu at the shooting station. That order, however, can be changed on a daily basis by changing the number of the trap, the angle of the

Will Fennell demonstrates proper low-gun technique, weight forward, hands in proper gun-hold position. The shooter never sees the same shot more than twice on a typical Parcour.

**FITASC sporting or Parcours de Chasse shooting is commonly held to be more difficult than what we normally shoot in the U.S., which is a version of "English sporting." All FITASC competitors must stand inside a small hoop or box in order to shoot.**

trap, or even by moving the trap. For example, if a Level One shooter is going to get a single from trap one (all traps are clearly numbered and these numbers are visible to the shooter on each station), it might be a rabbit today and an outgoing tower tomorrow by simply changing the trap number. It allows a lot of variation in the basic field.

The field can also be set to play different games just by changing trap angles, although those changes will not be called sanctioned NSCA 5-stand sporting. One can even configure the traps to regular sporting clays rules and have a registered sporting clays match.

Although the NSCA-sanctioned version does have a set of criteria, there is some versatility built into the equipment layout, and it can be quickly configured to a variety of other games.

Because of the cost and versatility and the small amount of space required, NSCA 5-stand sporting is popular. Many gun clubs that do not have the room for a full-size range do have the space required for this game.

A number of ranges have what they refer to as a "5-stand" range, although they often do not meet NSCA standards. These are often quite varied in their target fare and can be a lot of fun to shoot.

Because the targets and angles are known, the NSCA version is perfect for television and spectator coverage.

## FITASC

While mini-games are ideal for ranges with limited space, there is another game that is making inroads onto the U.S. sporting scene: FITASC.

FITASC stands for Federation Internationale de Tir aux Armes Sportives de Chasse and it is one of the two world bodies (the other is the International Shooting Union or "UIT") governing international shotgun competition. The FITASC version of sporting clays is to that game what international skeet and trap are to the American versions of those games—a bit more challenging!

This game centers on the Parcour or layout. In traditional FITASC, a Parcour is a 25-target station with three different shooting positions for each station. In a 100-bird round, shooters visit four different Parcour.

There are no shooting cages in this game. There is a shooting pad (or circle or square—often an old-fashioned hula-hoop), about a meter square in size. In the traditional version, targets were thrown in a 360-degree arc around the shooter. For obvious reasons, participating as a spectator was not encouraged. The newer version deletes the 360-degree target arc, adds a fourth shooting position to the Parcour, and keeps shooter firing more restricted. Thus, it is more spectator-friendly.

In the Americanized version of sporting clays, each station may have a number of traps, but will throw only a few birds per trap. The English version uses fewer traps, but shifts shooters around the layout more and throws more targets from each trap. Many English stations use only two traps, but keep things very interesting by presenting a lot of different angles. FITASC falls more in line with this design.

The major difference between FITASC and American sporting clays is the degree of varied presentations a shooter will see as he moves to the different shooting positions on each Parcour. The shooter never sees the same shot more than twice. Generally, the first time it will be a single and, at the second presentation, the same target will be incorporated into a pair of doubles.

By moving shooting positions radically, the angle on the shots can change considerably and what might be a relatively easy target from one position may be extremely difficult from another. The wide spectrum of target presentations includes greatly varying ranges. It is quite common to have targets as close as 10 yards and as far away as 60 yards from the same shooting position. This poses an interesting problem for the shooter, because once he steps onto the shooting position he cannot change his chokes. All shots must be handled with what is in the gun.

A varied load selection is far more important in FITASC than in standard sporting, and some competitors carry as many as five or six different loads of varying shot sizes, weights and velocities. Since shooters may also shoot twice at any single, it is common for competitors to tote 100 or more rounds for a 25-bird shoot.

Another difference in this game is the gun position when calling for the bird. Traditional sporting and the various 5-stand games allow the butt of the shotgun to either be off the shoulder and visible below the armpit, or pre-mounted. FITASC competitors are required to have a stripe on their shooting vest that extends 25 cm downward from the top of the shoulder toward the hip. The gun butt must be visible below the bottom of the line. In World Class matches, they measure the vest line. (And this is the way American shooting ought to remain.)

Like NSCA 5-stand sporting, the trap order in FITASC is known and displayed on a menu at the shooting position. As the squad moves to a new position, the first shooter is allowed to have the targets thrown one time for viewing. Once on the shooting pad, the shooter engages all his singles. Then he or she is followed by the next shooter. When the singles are done, shooters return to the pad for doubles, and the second shooter in line now becomes the first. This rotation continues in order that every member of the six-man squad is required to shoot first for at least one new presentation.

This game requires about the same amount of land as a full-sized sporting course, so it is not growing rapidly. It is growing in individual popularity however, as many veteran sporting shooters seek new challenges. A number of established sporting clays ranges have incorporated the game on available space.

In the U.S., the governing body for FITASC is the National Sporting Clays Association.

Though each of these various games is similar enough to sporting clays so that the same equipment and techniques can be used, each is different enough to increase the challenge to the shooter. The fresh look of a game such as 5-stand sporting should ensure its popularity for years to come.

The 5-stand sporting station at Quail Creek Plantation near Okeechobee, Florida is popular because one gets a great deal of shooting without having to walk great distances in the sub-tropical heat and humidity.

## CHAPTER 19

# THERE'S MORE TO LIFE THAN A 12-GAUGE

Most of what one sees or hears about sporting clays centers around the 12-gauge. That is understandable. It has been the dominant gauge in competition since the sport's inception, and will continue to hold that position. Plus, it is far and away the most widely sold gauge in shotgunning—some experts even estimating that more 12-gauge shotguns are sold than all other gauges combined. Still, it is not the only bore size seen on the sporting fields.

Many people shoot sporting clays strictly for fun and have no real interest in registered competition. As they are discovering, you can have just as much fun with the smaller gauges as you can with the 12-gauge, and each passing year sees more sub-gauges making their way to the sporting courses. This has not gone unnoticed by course managers. In fact, some are now utilizing bits of extra land to set up shorter, less demanding courses that not only allow shooters to use smaller gauges, but serve a second purpose by providing a slightly less challenging course to introduce new shooters to the game.

The interest in sub-gauges has not escaped the notice of the ammo makers, either. In a move that should clearly demonstrate how strong that interest actually is, several have brought out special sporting clays loads for the 20, 28 and 410 guns.

In fact, there is enough interest in sub-gauge sporting that the NSCA now incorporates sub-gauge classes into registered competition, as has long been done in skeet.

Sub-gauge sporting is not a passing fad or fancy. It is here to stay and is certain to grow in popularity because it adds an extra dimension of challenge. A number of insert tube manufacturers say that sporting clays shooters are now starting to have their 12-gauge guns "tubed" to smaller gauges in the same manner as skeet shooters.

How effective can the little gauges be at this demanding game? To be perfectly honest, the 12-gauge will always be the best choice if breaking the maximum number of targets is your goal. The smaller gauges cannot of course match the load versatility and long-range power of the bigger bore; they just cannot carry the shot to do it. With that obvious statement out of the way, however, it must also be said that the sub-gauges offer surprising performance when target

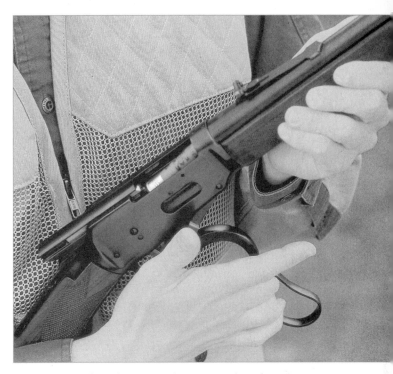

If you begin this chapter with a sense that the 12-gauge is a "Real Man's Gun," a serious gun for competition and hunting and that the other, smaller gauges – 20, 28 and .410 – are just toys or are not serious, well, read on. The difficulty of breaking targets increases arithmatically as you step down in gauge, but you will soon discover that the feel is one of geometrically increasing difficulty! *(Photo courtesy Winchester)*

distances are kept at less than 35 yards. Many of the shorter, sub-gauge courses do that.

Getting the most out of sub-gauges is not quite as easy as with the 12. The load selection, whether you buy them or build your own, is so varied in that gauge that many shooters no longer do much in the way of choke tube changes, they just change their shells to adjust patterns. That approach is less effective in the smaller gauges. Pattern control becomes more important and it is best achieved by balancing both load and choke.

If your favorite 20, 28 or 410 is not fitted for interchangeable choke tubes, the biggest favor you can do yourself is to have it done. Hastings, Briley, Seminole,

Clearview and others can perform this work. Though I do not use a large selection of choke tubes in the 12-gauge, when I head out with a 28-gauge or 410 I want to be carrying Skeet, Improved Cylinder, Modified and Full tubes. They will be needed.

You will also want to fit the gun to yourself with the same care you would apply to your favorite competition 12-gauge, maybe more. The smaller gauges do not give you much margin for error; so good gun fit is critical.

On the plus side, these additions will make the gun a much better performer in the game fields. In addition, a few rounds of sporting clays before bird season will certainly improve your ability to bust feathers instead of clays!

Here are the rules, as specified by the NSCA for registered events (rule IV-E-4-b also notes these as maximum loads):

### IV-C. GAUGE SPECIFICATIONS

1. Twelve gauge events shall be open to all shotguns of 12 gauge or smaller, using shot loads not exceeding one and one-eighth (1 ⅛) ounces.

2. Twenty gauge events shall be open to all shotguns of 20 gauge or smaller, using shot loads not exceeding seven-eights (⅞) of an ounce.

3. Twenty-eight gauge events shall be open to all shotguns of 28 gauge or smaller, using shot loads not exceeding three-quarters (¾) of an ounce.

4. Four-ten events shall be open to all shotguns of .410 bore, using shot loads not exceeding one-half (½) of an ounce.

## 20-Gauge

Although the 20 qualifies as a sub-gauge, a reasonably skilled shooter is not handicapping himself or herself very much on any targets inside the 35-yard mark. The 20 is plenty under those conditions, and its lower recoil level and lighter weight are often an asset to small-framed shooters.

There is a wealth of top-quality 20-gauge over/unders on the market. Many have been introduced specifically for sporting clays, with back-bored barrels, long choke tubes and ported barrels in the preferred 28- to 30-inch range.

For maximum recoil control, it would be hard to beat guns like the popular Remington 1100, Beretta Teknys Gold or the Browning Gold. Their gas-operated actions alter the recoil impulse noticeably and produce a soft-shooting smoothbore. Have one of them properly fitted to the individual shooter, add a basic selection of choke tubes and you will have a fine tool for sporting clays.

Experienced 12-gauge shooters have learned that care in selecting the right load for the target distance can boost their scores. The same approach is even more important with the sub-gauges.

For ultra-close ranges (10 yards and under), any ⅞-ounce load of #9 shot that will open quickly is an asset. Look for something like a felt-wad 20-gauge that opens a bit faster than a plastic shotcup. Several products referred to by names like "brush wad" are available in 20-gauge and create excellent short-range loads when stuffed with an ounce of soft #9 shot. Another alternative will be any of the softshot promotional loads. Generally, they are available in size #8 as the smallest 20-gauge offering, but they spread pretty quickly and that is what counts here.

Moving to the 15- to 25-yard range, it is hard to argue with any 20-gauge #9 skeet load. This is exactly the range where they were designed to offer optimum performance. Look for one-ounce skeet loads in #9. These loads are intended for skeet shooters who use the 20 in 12-gauge events and they are an excellent choice for 20-gauge sporting (in the 12-gauge event, of course) factory load for this range. When a company offers this same load with their premium hard target shot in sizes #7 ½, #8 and #8 ½ as well, you probably have the best sporting clays lineup for the 20-gauge. It would be hard to think of a more complete load selection.

Beyond 25 yards, we start to see a decrease in the breaking ability of #9 shot. A proven way to increase that power, while maintaining as much pattern density as possible, is to shift to #8 ½ shot. A ⅞-ounce load in this size becomes my first choice for shots in the 20- to 30-yard range, but it is a combo you will have to load yourself. About as close as you can come to the ideal load is #8 shot in a ⅞-ounce target load. There are some one-ounce field loads in the same shot size if shooting up in gauge. The target loads, by virtue of their harder shot, generally produce better results, despite carrying fewer pellets per shell. Results can also depend on how well your individual barrel handles the full load. It is worth taking time to do some test patterning here. A good ⅞-ounce load of quality #8 shot is a consistent target-breaker out to 35 yards. Some very smart shooters handload a ⅞-ounce nickel-plated #8 shot load for over-30-yard shots, and they do marvelous work beyond 35 yards. The ability of nickel shot to maintain tight patterns and short shot strings improves 20-gauge performance at this range.

Beyond 40 yards, the 20-gauge starts to become marginal. Reloaders have the option of going to #7 ½ nickel shot in either ⅞-ounce or ¾-ounce loads, depending upon which patterns best in their barrel. If your gun has a three-inch chamber, there are magnum versions of acceptable loads available that pack 1 ⅛ ounces of #7 ½ nickel for the 12-gauge field. Other long-range alternatives are any of the premium copper-plated, buffered field loads offered by several companies in size #7 ½.

Although it has recently grown its reputation for police and tactical operations weaponry, Benelli's $1,435 Legacy 20-gauge, with its 26-inch barrel appropriately choked, will perform well at skeet and sporting clays. It accepts both 2¾- and 3-inch shells.

Ruger builds its Red Label shotguns in 12-, 20- and (pictured) 28-gauge. It also offers a tube insert for the 28 that allows you to shoot .410 shells.

The 9410 is Winchester's lever-action 410. The 2½-inch chambered 9410 was introduced in 2001. It comes equipped with the Invector Choke System and will shoot everything from high performance shotshells to slugs.

## 28-Gauge

Inside 30 yards, this little jewel does not really take a back seat to the bigger gauges. Between 30 and 40 yards, it does need some help (perhaps nickel shot) and beyond 40 yards it does help if a shooter has a sense of humor. That is not a knock on the 28-gauge. It just points out that there is a limit to what you can expect from ¾-ounce of shot, no matter how efficient the shell, or how carefully constructed the load.

Moderately priced 28-gauge guns of the clay target persuasion are becoming more common. Depending upon how you define the term "moderately priced," of course, one that I can think of is the classic Remington 1100 autoloader (actually the Remington "sporting clays" version although the difference is strictly in the advertising), because it is a sweet little shooter. Remington has also chambered their 870 pump for the 28, and if you like pumps you will certainly like this one. Browning offers a 28-gauge pump in their BPS Hunter line for about $609, and these are quality guns as well.

Moving up in price we find the Browning Citori White Lightning for $2,039 and the Ruger Red Label with a straight or pistol grip for $1,956. Beyond these,

28-gauge guns get a bit pricey, yet they are certainly exquisite.

The lack of affordable guns is almost matched by the availability and price of ammunition. For some inexplicable reason, perhaps only extent of national demand, 28-gauge shells run about $20 a case more than 12-gauge. You will also find a rather limited selection of shells, and this is one situation where it can really pay to reload. Not only can you save a significant amount of money on your shells, but also you can greatly expand the versatility of this small round.

In the ultra-close-range area, the best choice among factory rounds are the standard ¾-ounce, 1200 fps, #9 skeet loads offered by everybody that makes a 28-gauge load. A better choice by a wide margin is a softer 28-gauge "brush wad" with ¾-ounce of soft #9 shot. It is strictly the province of handloaders, but inside 15 yards you would think you were shooting a 12-gauge. (Beware, however, that FITASC shooting prohibits spreader loads and reloads. If you become too accustomed to them for NSCA sporting, you could be handicapped in the international game.)

From that range out to almost 25 yards, you will be well served with a standard skeet load using good hard

Winchester's AA Super Sport is available in all gauges and just the right shot sizes (#7½ #8, #8½ and #9) to help a young or small-frame shooter get used to smoothbore recoil. The 12-gauge shell is available in one and 1 ⅛ ounce, the 20-gauge in ⅞ ounce, 28 in ¾ ounce and 410 in ½-ounce.

Doublechecking your reloading equipment settings occasionally is an exceptional idea, especially the amount of powder headed for sub-gauge shells.

shot. The little 28 is an extremely efficient shell and will break under 25-yard targets just as well as a 12- or 20-gauge. In fact, many skeet shooters carry as good an average with the 28 as they do with the 12-gauge.

Beyond 25 yards, out to almost 35 yards, #8 ½ shot becomes the best choice. In factory shells, this is available from Federal as the ¾-ounce and from Remington, which also offers a 28-gauge sporting load. Kent Cartridge has a 2 ¾-inch 28-gauge shell with ¾-ounce of shot that is offered in #7 ½, #8 and #9. Even Rio Ammunition offers a 28-gauge target load in #7 ½, #8 and #9 rated at 1300 fps at three feet. For reloaders, shifting to hard target-grade #8 or #8 ½ shot in your standard skeet load recipe will accomplish the

same thing for a little more than half the cost of factory shells.

Pushing the 28-gauge beyond 35 yards is not easy, because you really do not have enough shot to work with. Winchester offers a load in sizes #6, #7 ½ and #8. For factory ammo shooters, whichever load patterns best in your gun is your best option. My solution is to go at least to a 1200 fps, ¾-ounce handload of #8 of very hard shot, perhaps even nickel.

I have mentioned nickel-plated shot quite a bit, because it simply gives the best pattern performance at extended range in any gauge. It is certainly more expensive than standard chilled shot, but in the case of the 28-gauge it is money well spent. When you factor the cost of nickel shot reloads against the cost of factory rounds, the nickel shot loads are not only cheaper but they are more effective. If you develop an affection for the 28-gauge and you really want to wring the most out of it, becoming a reloader is the way to go.

## 410-Bore

Whoever designed the 410-bore (or "36-gauge," as it is often called in Europe) was either extremely drunk or had a wickedly twisted sense of humor. In fact, no one even seems to want to own up to creating it. The best I have been able to find in any reference work is the fact that the shell "just sort of appeared" at some point in history!

The big problem is the extremely small diameter of the hull in relation to the shot column length. This encourages a lot of pellet deformation and long shot strings. Even with a Full choke and hard shot, 410 patterns fall apart by the time they reach 35 yards and they become noticeably patchy as close as 20 yards. This shell also operates at higher pressures than its larger cousins, which aggravates the shot deformation problem even further. Getting consistently smooth and even patterns from a 410 is tough. Nevertheless, there is a certain appeal to this miserable little rascal.

Inexpensive 410 shotguns are common. Even the heaviest loads have recoil levels that could only be described as minuscule and a fair selection of shells can be found virtually anywhere ammunition is sold. A knowledgeable shooter would conclude that if the 28-gauge was as readily available in affordable guns and ammo as the 410, the latter would probably fade from the scene—but they are not, and so it is not going to!

Although I am not a fan of pumps, nor a real devotee of the 410, I admit that one of my favorite fun guns is an old and well-worn Mossberg 500 pump. It is light, cute and fun to shoot. A few years ago, Hastings installed interchangeable choke tubes in that gun, and subsequent experiments with loads and chokes were remarkable.

When it comes to spreading a pattern quickly at close range, the 410 has no peer, unless the other guns are loaded with spreader wads. Using the basic Skeet choke tube, this gun will produce a circular pattern of about 25 inches at 15 yards with a three-inch #9 shot load. By comparison, a soft-shot 20-gauge field load from a similar choke will create a pattern of about 19 or 20 inches at that range. That 410 pattern will be uniform enough to consistently get the job done. The pattern will go completely to hell by 20 yards, but inside 15 yards it is a clay-busting little fool!

Once the range increases beyond about 15 yards, I am through with the Skeet or Improved Cylinder tubes. The patterns are too patchy with any load. This is where the .009-inch Modified tube makes a big difference. Even though it is technically a Modified choke in the 410, it does the best patterning job from 15 to about 25 yards. In fact, custom gunsmiths in the skeet game have come to the almost universal conclusion that the most effective 410 constriction for skeet shooters is .008-.009-inch. Anytime you can get a half-dozen top gunsmiths to agree on the same thing, consider it a Universal Truth!

With the .009-inch tube in place, I like the standard #9, ½-ounce skeet load out to just beyond 20 yards, and shift to the same load in good hard #8 ½ shot for birds out to 30 yards. This is one case where less is better, as these ½-ounce loads will generally deliver better patterns than most three-inch loads. The short shot column and hard, target-grade shot produce less pellet deformation than the longer shot column in the

three-inch load. (Substituting nickel shot for lead can change that, though.) These loads are readily available from the factory in the skeet lines from Remington, Winchester and Federal, with the ½-ounce #8 ½ loads being found in the 410 sporting clays numbers from Federal (#T412) and Remington (#STS410SC). If a shooter confines his 410 endeavors to ranges under the 30-yard mark, he can get by quite nicely with these three different loads and a pair of choke tubes.

Beyond 30 yards the going gets tough with the 410. Choking the #8 ½ loads down through a full tube will produce a fairly tight center core pattern at 30-plus-yards, with little margin for error. If you do not point it like a rifle, you are going to miss. Even if you do, you start to run out of power to break targets at about 35 yards. Shifting to hard #8 shot in a ½-ounce load will produce a pattern that looks acceptable on paper, but just does not seem to work in real life. There is not enough shot in the charge to compensate for the inevitable effects of shot stringing, which do not show up on a stationary patterning board. Shot stringing will produce more than a few holes in actual practice. That often results in gaps in the pattern that cause the bird to be hit with just one or two pellets, and that may not be enough to get that "visible piece." Although #7 ½ shot works well with larger gauges because it increases the striking power of individual pellets, it does not seem to help here. You just do not have enough pellets in the load to do the job. The pattern density is not there.

I have spent a lot of time looking for a 35-yard 410 load and will be the first to admit that, even with a full choke tube, I have not found one I like. All the three-inch factory loads use shot that is just too soft to take the abuse it receives in that long, small-diameter shot column. If you are stuck with factory loads, the best bet is to pick a three-inch #7 ½ load and hope you can get a couple of pellets onto the bird. Do not even bother to pattern the loads; it is too frustrating. Shoot for real. Alternate between a Modified and Full tube, and keep track of which performs best for you.

If you reload, you have a better option with three-inch loads of #8 nickel shot. It is not perfect, but it is the best choice I have found when you have to push the 410 into the 30- to 40-yard range. You will not ever confuse this load with a 12-, 20- or even a 28-gauge load, but it will give you about as much as you can expect from a 410.

It helps to have a sense of humor any time you take a 410 onto a sporting clays range. You are going to need it.

Give the sub-gauge guns a try if you shoot for fun. They will provide that in spades.

Even a small youngster with confidence can handle a .410 and probably a 28-gauge, if the crowd is supportive of his efforts. On a sporting clays course, the .410 is a challenge for even a mature shooter, so a 28 may be the minimum if parents expect a youngster to score enough targets to stay happy, interested and progressing.

# CHAPTER 20

# THE ALL-AMERICAN

Bobby Fowler, Jr., who lives in Houston, Texas, was 38 years old when we first talked by telephone—and he had already been shooting competitively for half his life. The excitement and zeal for shooting and the intensity that has made this international champion a shooting sports star were still loud and clear in his voice, though.

Bobby's Internet site at www.eliteshooting.com lists his competitive sporting clays victories from 1995, and they are extensive. Terms like Team USA, All American, HOA Champion and FITASC Champion are sprinkled through his resume like grains of salt on your

All American sporting clays shooter Bobby Fowler, Jr. of Houston, Texas, gives demonstrations, competes actively and teaches shotgunners the fundamentals and mechanics of successful shooting. "When you approach one of the basics carelessly," he says, "you miss."

Saturday morning scrambled eggs. More than you want to count. The man knows his game and has a passion for winning, but his biggest thrill these days is passing on his knowledge to other shooters.

"Anymore, I get the biggest kick out of promoting my sponsors and helping my students build their skills," he says. "I guess it's like a daddy being there to help his kids grow up."

According to Bobby, the very best way to move upward in the ranks of sporting clays top shooters is to work hard, continuously on the fundamentals. Whether you are a many-time sporting clays All American like he is or a novice approaching his or her very first competitive event, such basics as stance, gun hold, weight distribution, focus and follow through are the foundation of success at any level.

## What Bobby Teaches versus What Bobby Practices

"I'm an active competitor, but I also travel to give demonstrations and teach the techniques of good shooting," Bobby Fowler says. "There are two levels of instruction. In a typical first-level school, students learn and practice the basics under my direct supervision. The basics are the things every shooter needs to understand and put into practice before he pulls the trigger. I want students to understand stance, gun hold and orientation to the target break point and make them an unforgettable routine, every shot, without fail. When you forget something basic or perform it carelessly, you more often than not fail, so this is what we work on in the lower-level school."

Bobby teaches Double-A shooters as well as introductory classes. These are often men and women who are older than him and have as much shooting experience, but rarely have as much course savvy and nowhere near his success. "Double-A and Masters shooters know the fundamentals very well, so we build on them. There are only so many shot presentations you will see in sporting clays—incoming, outgoing, crossing, teal (straight up) and running rabbit (on the ground)—and we learn how to orient or position for each of them so that when the school is over, they can practice effectively."

Bobby teaches his students that sporting clays is as much a mental as a physical or gun handling game. In a sense, he teaches the mental fundamentals.

"A lot has been written about the mental aspect of competition," he says, "and most of it is true. Mental

Shooting coach and frequent High Over-All competitor Bobby Fowler, Jr. says the mental game is just as important as the physical game. "I teach people to concentrate on the next shot," he says, "to leave the success or failure at the last station behind them." In this respect, he admits that he does not follow his own advice. "I like to know where I am in the standings," he admits. "It helps motivate me."

toughness is the ability to concentrate on a single objective or task to the exclusion of all other thoughts. To become a champion, you have to be focused. You cannot be thinking of the next station, the next joke to tell your squad or the things your spouse asked you to pick up on your way home. If you want to win on a consistent basis, you can only concentrate on putting a shot string exactly where it has to go to bust a bird."

Because shooting a good clays course may take several hours, Bobby realizes that the average person cannot keep tightly focused for that long, with as many natural distractions as there are along the way, and not collapse in exhaustion. "Teach yourself to relax between stations," he says. "If you have done well, be happy. If not, laugh about it and recall the fundamentals. Whatever you did 'back there' is done. You can't really take it with you and you can't re-do it. It's over. Look forward. Relaxing some between stations helps you save energy for what you might call a 'burst of concentration' for the next pair of birds."

For Bobby, the mental game involves a stand-up act, a consistent approach to breaking one bird—or two in the case of doubles—at a time. He has a pre-shot routine, loading.

"I take between eight and ten seconds to load," he says. "I put the shells in and then line them up to the exact same orientation every time. Since shells are cylinders, this may seem silly, but I line up the type on the bottom of the shell casing the same way every shot. What this little ritual does is slow me down. There's no hurry. This helps me establish a methodical pace and

it puts me in a familiar place. It reminds me to think of the fundamentals. 'Holding the gun firmly against your cheek. Where are you going to break this target? Remember to follow-through.' I have trained myself to perform this little ritual before every shot. It works for me, so I drill the idea of developing a familiar routine into my students' heads in class."

Speaking of routine, Bobby says he gets nervous before every big shoot and has had to adjust. "I expect to be nervous and have learned how to make that loose energy work for me," he says. "I use it to focus, to think positive no matter what else is happening in my life. I translate the butterflies in my stomach into kind of a visioning process." Bobby has learned to accept his nervous stomach before a shoot, to think of it as his body's way of getting prepared.

Actually, Bobby Fowler, Jr. experiences two nervous points: before and during a shoot. Everyone who is shooting seriously and wants to win rather than just show up is tempted to look ahead he says, especially if they have run a station or two. Use this natural anticipation—which, after all, is just another term for nervousness—to focus on the shot problem you have immediately before you. Never think of such things as how close you might be to winning your division. (This is not easy, but that is why it is called 'discipline.' Everyone's mind wanders, even a trained yogi. This is natural. Accept it and gently guide it back to the station you are on. It is like hunters learning to concentrate on picking a spot rather than staring at the deer's antlers.) During the shoot, many things can cause your mind to drift off, a lost bird or a stuck wad, for instance, but as you build your skills you will be able to stay focused and channel your anticipation more thoroughly.

In one area, Bobby's routine varies significantly from the advice he gives his students. Unlike many shooters, he keeps score. He keeps up with his position on the leader-board. "I like to know where I am in the standings, know what I have to shoot for," he explains. "For a young shooter or a new shooter of any age, this amounts to pressure they can do without. I don't recommend paying attention to anything other than the shot you are making right now. Let your score surprise you. So, yes, I actually don't practice what I teach on this point."

## Notes About Practice

Many AA and Masters shooters break 1,000 targets a week, and Bobby has gone through years when he has shot 1,600 in some weeks. "You want to make everything you do automatic," he says. "You want your movements and even your thoughts to become repetitive and totally predictable. So when you get to the shooting line in something of a machine-like trance and begin breaking everything that is thrown at you, you know you have arrived in the zone. Nothing will get you to this point faster than a shooting coach and hours of practice breaking birds."

These days, Fowler practices three to four times a week with his ported, extended choke 12-gauge Browning over/under and the same Winchester Super Handicap shells that he takes to a clays venue. His selections are three-dram #7 ½ and #8 loads. "Shot size selection is important," Bobby says. "The smaller the pellet the less energy it carries at distance, but the larger the pattern will be. So, for close shooting I use the #8 and as the bird gets out to 40 yards or so I switch to #7 1/2."

This Texas All American believes that, after you understand how your gun patterns, choke selection should be a big part of your learning curve and practice as well as your game-day ritual. While drams of powder and shot size control energy delivery, choke controls pattern size. At less than 20 yards, use an open choke. At 20 to 35 yards, he suggests Improved Cylinder or Light Modified. From 30 to 50 yards, the Modified is about right and at 50 yards, switch to Full.

Unlike much advice about practicing with smaller gauges to make your 12-gauge shooting more effective, Bobby says he practices with every gauge. "I compete in sub-gauge events," he says, "but I don't substitute practice with them for practice with the 12-gauge. The guns are different and they feel different. Nevertheless, whatever gauge you are using, if you approach the shot with proper fundamentals, you can be challenged. Watch the target. Stare a hole in it, like a base-

Even in tight shooting spaces like this one, Bobby Fowler teaches that there are only half a dozen shot presentations in sporting clays. One trick to mastering any shot combination, even in tight quarters, is to approach the station with a plan and then to work the plan.

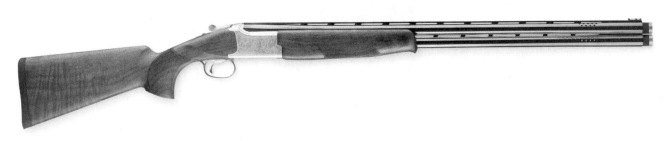

Bobby Fowler, Jr. shoots the Browning Citori 525 Sporting. The 525 comes with a beautiful silver nitride receiver with intricate scroll engraving and a walnut stock and Schnabel-style forearm. It is available in 12, 20 28 and .410. In the 12- and 20-gauge models, the comb is adjustable. Expect a comfortable right-hand palm swell, gold-plated trigger and five choke tubes.

ball pitcher staring his pitch over the plate and into the catcher's glove. Think of the old Superman serials on television where he had laser-like light rays coming out of his eyes. That's the concentration you want. In a sense then, the gauge you shoot doesn't matter."

Every gauge has its merit, but the fundamentals of shooting a 20 or 28 or even a 410 are not different from a 12-gauge, he says. "You just have to remember that you have a lot less shot available so you have to be smoother in your presentation. A 28 or 410 give you less room for error. For 12-gauge practice, I often step back to handicap distances or shoot doubles in other games like skeet and trap. When I get tired of that, I tighten the choke. After a miss or two, the constricted shot string wakes me up."

## The Elements of Bobby's Game

Because he typically uses the sustained lead shooting technique, it seems to many observers that Bobby's shots are relaxed and unhurried.

This is good, but it is a bit of an illusion, he says. Switch from sustained lead to the "come from behind and push through" style of shooting and it can seem—because there is much more gun movement—that the shooter is hurrying his or her shot. But this is all a matter of perception caused by a particular style of shooting. However they see and manage lead, effective shooters are smooth and learn good follow-through.

The mental game is extremely important, but it is not complete without a complementary physical game.

Bobby believes in staying in shape and says that physical conditioning, especially when you are shooting sporting clays, is more important than most people realize. "In trap or skeet, unless the day is extremely hot, it is possible to come off the line without much strain. This is not the case in sporting clays. In clays you walk and lug ammo and guns and so on from station to station for what can feel like miles."

Perhaps it helps that Bobby married a fitness instructor, but today he works out at least three times a week.

"I had a really good year in 2000 and then decided to take some time off from exercise," he says. "That phase lasted about a year and a half, and during that time I didn't do as well. I began to feel sluggish after a day of shooting. Now that my wife acts as my fitness instructor, I lift weights and walk the treadmill regularly. When I finish a course these days, I'm not as winded. I still have energy at the end."

The games have become so competitive that Bobby does not know if the average shooter can compete effectively at the highest levels of sporting clays without professional coaching.

"When you are ready to make the move from the level of just another good shooter to elite status, the guy people point out on the range," he says, "it is important that you train with a professional coach. A professional will pick your shooting game apart and help you put it back together seamlessly. Your coach should be someone who has 'been there and done that,' but also someone who is a good communicator as well as a good shooter."

Bobby not only keeps the stock of his Browning Citori firmly in place on his cheek, he is able to teach the fundamentals and beyond, as evinced by students like Cole Storey, All American First Team member who has worked with Bobby for two years and Nadim Nasir, a current Second Team All American.

"There is a difference in levels when selecting a coach," he says. "A person who is a good shooter and a reasonably good communicator can work with almost anyone and help them shoot better. However, a shooter who is trying to bust the 80 out of 100 mark will have to build a different program than say an elite shooter who is trying to raise her or his average from 90 to 94. There are a lot of reasonably good coaches out there for the first step. For the second step, do yourself a favor and choose a professional, because if you really listen to their advice and put it into practice, it will occupy hours of your time over months and maybe over years. Sporting clays is not the cheapest game in town, so you want somebody who can help you get it right."

# CHAPTER 21

# SPORTING CLAYS' TOP GUNS

Sporting clays is a game with its roots firmly planted in the hunting fields, so one would assume that any field-grade shotgun would be an acceptable choice. That assumption is correct, but it relies heavily on one's definition of the term "acceptable."

If your reason for shooting sporting clays is to tune up for some fall bird season, then, by all means, use the gun you intend to carry into the field. If you want to learn the capabilities and limitations of your favorite smoothbore, or perhaps identify the shot angles you have the most difficulty making, there is no better way to do it than by spending a few summer weekends on a sporting clays range. It makes no difference what gauge you shoot or what type action your gun has. If it will spit out two shells, it becomes an acceptable choice.

If your goal is to play the game for the game's sake, however, to score and improve at all angles and speeds, you might be disappointed with your favorite field gun.

## Top Gun Requirements

Sporting clays is a demanding and varied game. You will encounter targets, distances, angles and presentations that appear in no other clay target sport, and all in the same day of shooting. To master this game, if such a thing is possible, you need a gun equal to the challenge. Fortunately, the game has been in existence long enough in the U.S. and Europe that top competitors understand the combination of features that characterize an effective gun. Here is a butt-to-muzzle look at what the experts think works best and why.

Formerly, the first concern was mounting the gun quickly and smoothly to your shoulder. This is no longer the case, however, since rules of NSCA sanctioned tournaments now say that, "The shooter may start with a low gun or a pre-mounted gun when calling for the target." (IV-I-4 Shotgun Mount and Position)

It is the international game, F.I.T.A.S.C. (Federation

The often-imitated saying among architects is that "form follows function." In the field of shotgun design and especially coupled with the demands of innovative sporting clays courses, this is especially true. *(Photo courtesy Browning)*

Internationale de Tir aux Armes Sportives de Chasse), that requires beginning each station with an un-mounted gun: "With the heel of the gun touching the body under a horizontal line marked on the shooter's jacket. This line will be indicated by a tape of contrasting color fixed to the jacket by some permanent means. The horizontal line shall be located 25cm (9.85") below an imaginary line drawn over the top of the shoulders along their axis. The shooter will maintain this position, with the gun not pre-mounted, until the target(s) are in sight." (A-5 Shooting Position)

Although regulation sporting clays allows shooters to begin with a pre-mounted gun, many high achieving shotgunners prefer the un-mounted position, believing this is the way the clays game is supposed to be played, as a game that replicates the sudden flush and/or flight of a bird or two. So bringing the gun smoothly to the shoulder and cheek is important and no one wants the recoil pad to catch or squeegee to a stop on the shooting vest.

A recoil pad with sharp edges or a lot of deep serrations on the face is going to inhibit fast mounting by catching and dragging on your clothing. If you fumble a gun mount and do not lock it in, you can pretty well kiss the targets goodbye! For this reason, a more rounded pad with a relatively smooth face is a major asset.

Having the buttstock properly fitted to your physical shape is also very important if you begin to take the shooting game seriously. If you cannot snap the gun into a smooth and consistent mount, then everything else becomes uncertain. Numerous stock fitters are available at major tournaments around the U.S., and most have "try guns" on which almost everything is adjustable. For a fee, such a shotgun professional will help you design a gun stock—drop at comb, palm swell, length of pull and so on—that will exactly meet your body build and shooting style.

Although actual "bird picture" over the barrel is a matter of individual preference, most sporting clays shooters want a relatively flat-shooting gun that has its pattern impacting equally above and below the bead. This is another element of shooting that can be adjusted depending upon an individual shooter's style or preference.

Rib and bead arrangement is another matter of personal preference. Some fine shooters choose not to have any beads on their rib. Their contention is that if the gun is fitted properly—the role of the professional stock fitter—beads are nothing more than a distraction. Other shooters fare well with a step in the rear of the rib and a single front bead. Some prefer a large bright bead or a fiber optic, while others favor something smaller and more subdued.

I shoot best with a flat rib and double gold bead arrangement. This may sound like nitpicking, but the picture you see over the sighting plane is a critical part of your subconscious triggering mechanism. When you find the set-up that makes you most comfortable, you will shoot better. Changing bead arrangements is a relatively simple matter, and worthy of experimentation.

When sporting clays first became popular in the U.S., shooters opting for over/unders often settled on relatively short barrels of 25 to 26 inches on the theory that the lighter guns, with more between-the-hands balance, would get on targets faster. Time and experience have shown that not to be the case. Stack-barrel shooters today invariably opt for barrels in the 28- to 30-inch range, and even longer, because folks have come to understand that additional weight forward promotes a stronger, smoother swing with less chance of stopping the gun.

I shoot the 30-inch-barreled Ruger Sporting Clays Red Label noticeably better than my standard Red Label with 28-inch tubes. That two inches of barrel may not sound like much, and with applied weights, both guns have the same overall weight, but the longer-barreled gun balances 3/8-inch forward of the hinge pin, while my standard gun balances right at the hinge pin. I believe that small difference is worth a few extra birds, especially late in each round when my muscles become just a bit tired.

Those who favor semi-autos or pumps say they find the 28-inch barrel a bit more effective than 26-inch tubes.

Given the need for quick follow-up shots, many shooters have found barrel porting to be an aid because those tiny holes in the barrel reduce muzzle jump and gets you back on target a bit faster.

The ability to gain improved pattern control over the widely varying ranges one sees in sporting clays has given rise to a serious interest in custom barrel work designed to enhance shotshell performance. Many of today's sporting clays guns have lengthened forcing cones, back-bored barrels and long chokes.

Given the need for frequent choke tube changes (barrels may be changed between stations and chokes after birds are thrown for the first shooter) many manufacturers produce tubes with knurled ends that protrude from the barrel. This allows them to be quickly changed without the hassle of a wrench. A very nice touch on any interchangeable tube intended for sporting clays is an identifying system that allows the shooter to determine what tubes are in the gun by simply looking at the muzzle, instead of having to unscrew and remove the tube to find out. Extended tubes are more than a "nice convenience," I believe, and will be

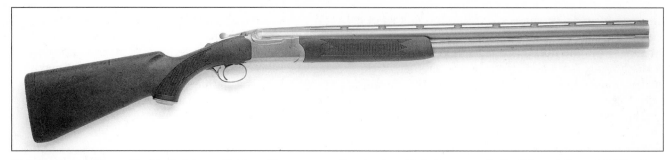

The 12-gauge Ruger Red Label is available with a composite stock, which Ruger calls its "Target Grey All-Weather Red Label Shotgun." This gun is available only with a pistol-grip stock, but you have a selection of 26-, 28- or 30-inch barrels.

The Weatherby Orion Super Sporting Clays 12-gauge has a cast-off stock from top to bottom of the butt (three to six mm) to provide a better fit against the shoulder and improved balance and feel. It also features a schnabel forearm and three barrel lengths: 28, 30 and 32 inches.

Here is a 12-gauge semi-auto from Weatherby. The SAS Sporting Clays comes with 28- or 30-inch barrels. It features a walnut stock and ported barrel and includes five extended chokes.

Perazzis have interchangeable buttstocks that can be ordered in a wide range of dimensions for length of pull, drop at comb and heel, cast-on/cast-off or straight comb with sloping field pistol-grip stock or a Monte Carlo stock. This customizing prohibits publishing final suggested retail prices, but with a Perazzi, if you have to ask, perhaps you can't afford it!

Winchester's Select Energy Sporting is distinguished by the oval checkering pattern on the pistol grip stock and forend. It is sold with 28-, 30- or 32-inch barrels and a TruGlo competition front sight and mid-rib bead.

worth the extra dollars they may cost. In the heat of competition in the middle of a long course, it is just too easy to forget what tubes you have in the gun.

## Sporting Clays Guns

Guns with all of the above features were not common in years past. Today, however, sporting clays remains the hottest game in the shooting sports, and every shotgun maker has models specially designed for it— and those same "competition" guns make excellent field guns! Here is a look at who is producing what in the 21st century.

### *AYA*

www.aya-fineguns.com

Even if you cannot pronounce the Spanish manufacturer Aguirre y Aranzabal and have never imagined visiting Eibar, Spain, you probably know these fine shotguns as AYA. In the Basque Country of northern-most Spain, this small company has been in business since 1915 with sales of more than a million guns, mostly side-by-sides.

Like so many of the European guns, AYA is not particularly interested in business from the common shooter and this is immediately obvious in the catalog, though not because of the price of the guns. The AYA catalog does not show a complete gun, only the engraved sections and the beautiful specialty woods— "Who cares about the rest!"

AYA also sells specialty boxes for its accessory items. Velvet covered wood with leather straps and brass nameplates. Apparently, the way an instrument looks is more important than how it shoots and, even though the action and mechanics of the lower priced and higher priced guns are practically identical within genres, the higher price AYA can be many thousands higher because of fancy engraving, highly grained woods and gold inlays. These Spanish gunmakers ask for an eight-month (or greater) leeway, by the way, to specially craft an AYA to your specifications.

According to AYA, its Model #37 is the most famous over/under ever made in the Basque Country, and at one time was the most expensive shotgun made in Spain. Patterned after the German Merkel, the #37 was described by the American gun expert, Col. Charles Askins, as "the best over-and-under made in Europe."

Like the Merkel, the 12-gauge Model #37 has a three-piece walnut forend, pistol-grip stock and true side-lock action, with internal gold-plated cocking indicators and "gold washed" internal lock parts standard. AYA makes barrels from "chopper lump chrome nickel steel," but maximum barrel length is 28 inches. Double trigger with hinged front trigger (optional selective or non-selective trigger). And for those shooting features so valued by our European cousins, "Fine rose and

scroll, game scene or bold relief engraving and gold initial oval."

In the recent AYA price list, the price of an A-Grade Model #37 was listed as $13,700 ($17,770 as of April, 2009) while the price of a C-Grade gun was $20,600 ($26,720): some taxes, tariffs and duties are not included in this price.

### *Bernardelli*

www.bernardelli.com

Here is another of those 300-year-old Italian manufacturers with HQ near Brescia. Bernardelli puts its name on a little of everything, high quality, of course, though distribution and sales in the U.S. are still thin. Unusual among Italian gun makers, however, over/unders are almost an afterthought in the Bernardelli line.

Their semi-automatics are especially nice, guns like the Mega Silver 12-gauge with three-inch chamber and barrels in 24-, 26-, 28- and 30-inch lengths with three flush-mount chokes. There is also a 24-inch slug barrel. The barrel is topped with a ventilated rib with fiber optic front sight and brass mid-rib bead. The stock is oiled and polished. Plenty of options are available in these gas guns, from shim kits to adjustable stocks, and prices vary by engraving and walnut quality.

As far as price goes, Bernardelli semi-autos are surprisingly affordable. A recent offer on www.cheaperthandirt.com, an SX801L Sporting 12 Gauge with 2 ¾-inch chamber and a 30-inch ported barrel noted a MSRP of $928.91. The asking price from a dealer, however, was $489.99. The receiver is aircraft aluminum and barrels have extended forcing cones, and a raised 9mm vent rib with Hi-Viz sight. The gun comes with four TruLock extended chokes. The Monte Carlo stock is oil-finished checkered Turkish Walnut.

### *Beretta*

www.berettausa.com

You see a lot of Berettas at the sporting clay shooting stands because they offer a fine selection of very solid guns at a variety of price levels—and they look good, too. Beretta recently renamed its "Competition" line to its "Victory Shooters" line. Go figure.

Perhaps the most interesting gun to premier in the Beretta line—which tends to be very solid, but a bit ho-hum—is the new $4,025 UGB25 XCEL 12-gauge, a break-action semi-auto. The operating principle is based on short recoil, which keeps the internal parts of the gun clean even after prolonged use. Beretta believes that the short recoil (and low barrel axis position) "almost completely compensate for muzzle jump during firing, with quicker and easier realignment of the barrel on the target for the next shot. The low barrel axis position transmits the recoil forces in

Skeet and sporting clays allow you to bring your turkey gun to the course and expect to walk away with a respectable score. You will probably not win a tournament, but if you are a good shot, your Mossberg pump will not embarrass you. *(Photo courtesy Mossberg)*

line with the shooter's shoulder, thus minimizing felt recoil."

The UGB25 Xcel cartridge carrier receives the second cartridge on the right-hand side of the "light alloy" receiver. It chambers automatically through the feed port after the first round has been fired. The ejection port is in the bottom of the receiver. The ejector expels the spent hull downward, away from the shooter and nearby competitors, and is user-friendly for both right- and left-hand shooters. This is not ho-hum.

Beretta's barrels in 30- or 32-inch length are fully chromed inside and topped with a ¼ x ¼ ventilated rib. The trigger guard-mounted button safety is reversible for left-hand shooters. Stock and forend are checkered walnut and, with the adjustable comb, length of pull and drop are adjustable. At between eight and nine pounds, this gun is a little on the heavy side, but ought to be a winner on the range.

For lovers of semi-autos, Diane Sorentino won the 20th NSCA National Championships at the National Shooting Complex in San Antonio, Texas, with a Beretta Teknys Gold Sporting ($2,050). Gas guns like the Teknys will throw lead accurately while softening the felt recoil of a shot. Shoot all day and the next and you may well prefer that than the generally harsher pounding of an over/under.

The Teknys has over-bored 12- and 20-gauge barrels 28 or 30 inches long with flat, floating ribs. The Teknys comes with a white front bead and steel mid-bead. Triggers are gold plated and stocks and forends are select walnut. These guns are built with a three-inch chamber and the 12-gauge Teknys models are fitted to accept a special 8 ½-ounce stock recoil reducer.

Near the top of the line is the $6,975 Trident Sporting with over/under three-inch chambered barrel lengths available in 28, 30 and 32 inches. This eight pound 12-gauge gun has a high gloss pistol grip walnut stock and Schnabel style forend. Look for a field

removable trigger group with gold-plated single selective adjustable trigger. Rich, floral engraving decorates receiver. Barrels have a raised, flat top rib (3/8 x 5/16) and both top and side ribs are vented to promote rapid heat loss. The standard aiming points are a front white dot and mid-rib bead. Drop at comb is 1 ½-inches; drop at heel is 2 1/3-inches; adjustable for length of pull. Five chokes are included as is a fitted hard-sided case.

For all-gauge shooters, the EELL Diamond Pigeon Sporting ($7,675) is available in all gauges. Expect a low profile, box lock action, three-inch chamber for the 12 and 20, 2 ¾ for the 28 and 410. Single selective, gold-plated trigger. Barrels are available in 28-, 30- and 32-inch lengths with a ³⁄₈x⁵⁄₁₆ flat rib, front bead sight and weight between six and seven pounds that varies by gauge. The stock and Schnabel-style forend are checkered and oil-finished walnut. Length of pull is adjustable while drop at comb is 1 ½ and drop at heel about 2 ⅓. Most new Berettas come with a fitted, hard-sided plastic carry case.

After these over/unders, Beretta steps its over/under line down gradually, reducing the sticker shock and the elegance, but perhaps not the performance of a gun. Expect to pay $4,075 for the Gold E Sporting 12-gauge, and $2,175 for the handsome White Onyx Sporting.

### Browning

www.browning.com

A dozen years ago, Browning designers and managers from its Utah marketing facility met with parent FNH managers from Belgium and manufacturing partners Miroku from Japan to begin re-thinking (tinkering with) the basic shotgun mechanics in their popular Citori brand. Eventually the Browning team put several ideas into steel: a reverse-type hinge system, a low-profile receiver and double firing pin concept (which became a "reverse striker ignition system") to provide fast lock times. The result was Browning's Cynergy

The Model 2000 semi-auto 12-gauge from Stoeger is a value-priced gun that, with the appropriate choke in place, will handle most shooting chores on the competition line.

The Cynergy Sporting 12-gauge from Browning is available with a walnut or a composite stock and forearm. Barrels are back-bored and factory ported. Note the stylized stock, recoil pad and forend.

Browning's Gold Sporting Clays 12-gauge semi-auto has long been a favorite among value-conscious fans of repeaters. It features a 28- or 30-inch ported barrel, front HiViz TriComp sight with mid-bead and comes with three chokes.

shotgun line which that corporation believes represent "the first major rethink of the over and under concept in nearly a century."

Whether one prefers the newer Cynergy to the older Citori is a matter of personal preference, but the Classic Field/Sporting Combo ($4,355) in the Cynergy line ought to be just right for shooters who like a few weekends on the clays field each year, but might just as well be hunting plantation quail or pheasants on Corps of Engineers Missouri River land.

This 12-gauge comes with two sets of barrels. One set is 28-inch field barrels with three-inch chamber and ventilated top and side ribs. The other is a set of ported sporting 30-inch barrels with 2 ¾-inch chamber and ventilated side with floating tapered top rib. Field barrels are designed for three Invector Plus chokes (F, M, IC) and ivory front and mid bead sights. The Sporting barrel set uses three Invector Plus Midas Grade chokes (M, IC, SK) with a HiViz ProComp fiber-optic front sight and ivory mid bead.

Cynergy receivers are steel with a silver nitride finish, ultra-low profile and monoblock hinge. Brown-

ing says the action is "Reverse striker ignition system; Impact ejectors; Top tang barrel selector/safety." This gun has a walnut stock with gloss oil finish and sporting-style recoil pad.

Even a cursory look at Browning shotgun's turns over the "Cynergy Euro Sporting Colored Composite, Yellow" ($2,800). Why is a plastic gun produced in Halloween colors worth that much cash? And would you be laughed off the range if you showed up with one?

The "Euro Yellow"—just could not resist—is a 12-gauge with 2 ¾-inch chamber and 30-inch barrels. It is the stock and forearm, however, that get all of the attention, for they are composite in solid yellow with black rubber over-moldings and the comb is adjustable.

The workhorse of the Browning line, the Citori, is a step down in price from the Cynergy, and Browning recommends several Citori over/unders for sporting clays. The $2,648 Citori XS Special 12-gauge ($2,570) is available with 30- or 32-inch ported barrels. Top and side ribs are ventilated. The floating top rib tapers from eight to 11mm and comes with a HiViz Pro-Comp sight

Ithaca pump-action shotguns like the New Classic Model 37 which you use for jumping woodcock and ruffed grouse out of heavy cover are fine for most stations in sporting clays, especially with the 28-inch barrel and the three, flush-mount choke tubes included. Ithaca calls this distinctive fore-end a "ringtail" style.

Charles Daly 12-gauge over/unders are imported from Italy. Barrels are honed, chromed and polished in 28- or 30-inch lengths.

Beretta's DT10 Trident L Sporting 12-gauge has rich floral engraving around the receiver beautiful walnut stock and Schnabel grip, gold-plated trigger and your choice of 30- or 32-inch barrels.

and mid bead. Five extended chokes are supplied: M, LM, IC, C and S. The satin finish on the adjustable stock and forend plus a silver nitride receiver and gold-plated trigger make this a handsome gun. It is chambered for 2 ¾-inch shells—all Citori chambers (not barrels) are chromed to reduce fouling—and weighs about 8 ½ pounds.

In the Citori line of over/unders, the Lightning is available in all gauges—12, 20, 28 and 410-bore. You can order the 12- and 20-gauge models with an adjustable comb and three extended chokes are supplied: M, C and S. Lightnings are available with 28- or 26-inch barrels. All four gauges have a 14 ¼-inch length of pull. Expect an oiled finish on the walnut stock and foreend and a lightly engraved, silver nitride receiver. The cost varies for the Lightning by grade of walnut and engraving in this interesting and unusual manner as described at www.ableammo.com:

• Grade IV: $2,430 for 12-, 20-gauge with three-inch chambers and $2,720 for 28- gauge (2 ¾-inch chamber) and 410 with three-inch chamber.

• Grade VII: $3,860 for 12-, 20-gauge with three-inch chambers and $4,50 for 28- gauge (2 ¾-inch chamber) and 410 with three-inch chamber.

• The Real Deal: The value gun in the Browning Lightning line is the all-blue in all gauges which retails for $1,580: same mechanics, quality production—just different eye appeal. The MSRP is listed at $1,879.

In the semiautomatic line, Browning's Gold Sporting Clays guns come only in 12-gauge with a 28- or 30-inch ported barrel, chrome-plated chamber, ventilated rib and three choke tubes—M, IC, S. Each gun includes two interchangeable gas pistons for optimal performance with light or heavy loads. These pistons can be changed in minutes without tools, Browning says.

The Gold "Golden Clays" gun has a 14 ¼-inch length of pull, a silver nitride receiver with handsome engraving and costs $1,941—an increase of about $75 per year since we last researched this book. Drop at comb 1 ½ and drop at heel 1 ¾.

## Cortona

www.cortonashotguns.com
www.kalispelcaseline.com

Cortona is manufactured exclusively for Kalispel Case Line, an enterprise of the Kalispel Indian Tribe in Cusick, Washington. The original Italian manufactuer is F.A.I.R., which has been building shotguns since 1971 and has a very good reputation.

The Remington 1100 semi-auto may have been in every shooter's sights at one time. This long-lived gun model has proven itself as a rugged and versatile gun. The good ol' 1100 in the Sporting 28"-barrel flavor features a fiber optic front sight and steel mid-rib bead for fast target acquisition.

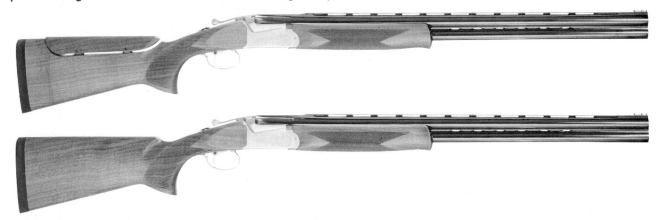

SKB says that mastering sporting clays requires a shotgun that provides a responsive fit, is well balanced between the shooter's hands, has a smooth swing, a fast sighting plane and a crisp trigger. Its 85TSS is designed for "fast target acquisition and hard-hitting patterns without producing shooter fatigue."

The Cortona Grandé Sport is the sporting clays model featuring 30- and 32-inch chrome-lined barrels, a silver finished receiver with gold inlay, gold-plated adjustable trigger, adjustable comb on the 12-gauge model and a comfortable palm swell.

Designed with the clay shooter in mind, the Grandé Sport is made in both 12-, 20-and 28-gauge with Anson style forend iron an easy-to-use barrel selector. The stock is hand-rubbed, checkered Turkish walnut finish (MSRP $2,995-$3,200). All Cortona shotguns carry a lifetime warranty for the original purchaser.

### Charles Daly

www.charlesdaly.com

In "the old days," a company like Charles Daly could get a start by importing lines of guns—going high end and expensive, or low end, down and dirty—to compete with U.S.-made products. Once the guns were in the U.S., the company would act as a distributor, setting up a network of dealers and then hope the gun's name or some virtuous shooter-benefit took hold. Today, practically everyone is an importer and that sometimes makes it difficult for a company like Charles Daly—in business as an importer/distributor since the late 19th century—to find the right shooting niche.

This Pennsylvania firm imports fine 12-gauge over/

unders from Italy and semi-automatics and pump-action guns from Turkey and then brands them with the Charles Daly name. Their 12-gauge 206 Sporting($999) is available with a single selective trigger, extractors and multi-choke tubes, or with selective automatic ejectors. Look for 28- or 30-inch ported, chrome-moly barrels with 10mm ventilated top and side ribs, and checkered Turkish walnut stocks and forearm. Competition ribs have mid-brass bead and front fluorescent sights. With a 30-inch barrel, the 206 Sporting is 47 inches long.

Length of pull is 14-⅛: drop at heel 2 ½ and drop at comb 1½.

The Charles Daly Superior II Sport 12-gauge semi-auto ($709) has internally honed, chromed and polished barrels acceptable for lead or steel shot. Look for factory porting, a 10mm ventilated rib with front fiber optic and mid-point aiming beads plus multi-chokes (F, M, IC) for 28- or 30-inch barrels. Gold-plated triggers and Turkish walnut stock and forend. With the 30-inch barrel installed the gun is about 50 inches long.

### Diamond Guns/ADCO Sales

www.adcosales.com
www.diamondguns.com

Diamond imported shotguns is a division of ADCO

Sales, headquartered in Massachusetts. You may be familiar with the ADCO name from its well-advertised red dot sight. Modestly priced, gold engraved Diamond semi autos are occasionally seen at sporting clays shooting stands. At this time, Diamond imports 12- and 20-gauge semi-autos and pumps, but the company says that 28s and 410s are on the way.

Under the ADCO name, the Diamond Doubles Imperial over/under in 12- or 20-gauge can be purchased with 28- or 26-inch barrels, ventilated top rib and deluxe single trigger with ejectors. Stock and forearm are walnut. Comes with five choke tubes at a price of $639 direct from ADCO.

A Gold Series Diamond semi-auto costs $549 at full retail, that price having not changed for nearly five years! Pay 50 bucks less for a synthetic stock. The stock and forend can be ordered in Turkish walnut or black matte polymer. The gun handles 2 ¾- or 3-inch loads and the chrome-lined, 28-inch barrel comes with three slotted, flush-mount choke tubes and a choke tube wrench.

### Caesar Guerini/Guerini USA

www.caesarguerini.com
www.gueriniusa.com

Italian shotgun manufacturer Guerini is making a run at the U.S. market, but there is a limit because of its philosophy: "… modern firearms that combine technical and aesthetic features with performance and beauty. Today, the market offers firearms of all types but most, despite being effective, are neither aesthetically pleasing nor distinctive. However efficiency is no longer enough for those outdoorsmen who consider hunting as an art form and not just the harvesting of game. These discriminating hunters also see their firearms as an extension of that art form."

The Summit Limited is available in all four shooting gauges—12, 20 and 28 with a 2 ¾-inch chamber, and the 36 (410) with three-inch chamber. Chrome-moly barrels with long dual forcing cones are available for these guns in lengths 28, 30, 32 and 34 inches. The barrel rib is ventilated for rapid cooling, 10mm for all guns except the 410 which is only 8mm. Look for automatic ejectors with oversized cams. Barrels and chamber are chrome-lined. Each Summit comes with six extended, screw-in competition chokes tuned for sporting clays (conical-parallel interior design, crowned muzzle, polished interior, knurling and thread design that prevents them from coming loose during use). Guerini USA says that each gun is balanced approximately one centimeter in front of the hinge pin for stability.

The Turkish walnut stock and Schnabel-style forearm of the Summit are checkered and oiled to a high luster. The 14 ¾-inch stock is cut to a pistol grip design

The SKB 85TSS receiver is produced in two sizes: a standard frame for 12-gauge and smaller for others. It is cut from a forged steel ingot by computerized CNC to precise dimensions marked in thousandths of an inch. The final result is a low profile box lock receiver with a modified "Greener" style crossbolt lock at the top of the receiver.

with a right-hand palm swell. Guerini says an included stock wrench allows you to remove the stock without removing the recoil pad.

A 12-, 20- or 28-gauge Summit Sporting is $3,295 while the 410 is $3,450. The 20-28-410 combo is $6,450. Expect to pay $200 for a left-hand stock and $295 for a factory installed adjustable comb.

Guerini USA has several warranty programs. The Pit Stop: original owners can send their guns to Guerini in Cambridge, Maryland, once a year for up to three times for free servicing and tune-up. Turnaround time is five to seven days and the owner's cost is only shipping. In addition, there are original manufacturer and distributor warranties and a purchaser would want to understand these for ultimate gun care.

### F.A.I.R.

www.fair.it

Something tells me it isn't fair making fun of international web sites—but I don't have a web site so they can't return the favor. F.A.I.R., based in Bresica, Italy, says its new Carrera Sporting over/unders are "the result of a deep research and shooting in top-range competitions, for the purpose of designing an appealing gun with excellent performances."

The 2 ¾- or 3-inch chambered Carrera comes with 30-inch barrels though that length can be custom ordered at 28, 32 and even 34 inches. Barrels are factory ported, topped with a ventilated, checkered rib and,

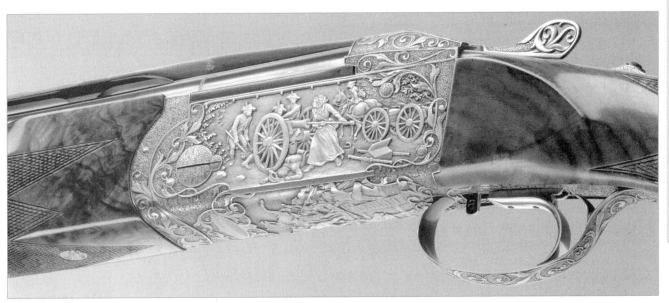

Krieghoff delivers fine, expensive guns with intricate engraving. This K-80 features the latest in the "Patriot Series," inspired by legendary Molly Pitcher who carried on with her husband's work at the cannon after he fell mortally wounded in the Revolutionary War. According to legend, General George Washington made her a sergeant in the Continental Army the next day.

In a similar manner to the area around Brescia, Italy, the Basque country in northern Spain is home to a tradition of custom gun manufacturing. AYA Excelsior over/unders for trap and sporting clays are built there in 12- and 20-gauge. Barrel lengths available are 28-inch, which is standard, or 29 or 30.

F.A.I.R. says, "made of high-resistance materials." One hopes they are steel.

Stocks and forearms are walnut with laser-etched checkering. Stocks are adjustable for "height, right and left cast-off and dip." The front sight is a fiber optic with three interchangeable color light pipes. Gold-plated triggers are adjustable to 15mm. Guns come with two extended, knurled TechniChokes, automatic ejectors and single selective triggers.

F.A.I.R. offers at least seven over/unders for sporting clays. Depending on the model, they are offered in 12- and 20-gauge: Jubilee 702 (12/20), Jubilee 700 (12/20), Master de Luxe (12/20), SRL 802 (12/20), LX 600 (12), LX 692 (12) and Premier (12). The 28-inch ported barrels are vented at top (11 mm for 12-gauge, nine mm for 20-gauge) and side. The pistol-grip stock and forend are hand-checkered walnut. Interchangeable chokes are available on request.

### Franchi

www.franchiusa.com

These fine Italian guns began showing up in the U.S. after World War II. Today, Franchi is part of the Benelli USA business family with Uberti (classic reproductions) and Stoeger. The new 20-gauge 720 Competition auto-loader with three-inch chamber has a 28-inch barrel with front and mid beads and 50-inch OAL. The walnut stock has a gel-filled recoil pad and it comes with three extended chokes: C, IC and M. It weighs 6.2 pounds and costs $1,149 MSRP. Length of pull 14 ¼, drop at heel 2 ¼ and drop at comb 1 ½.

The I-12 Sporting is the new 12-gauge competition

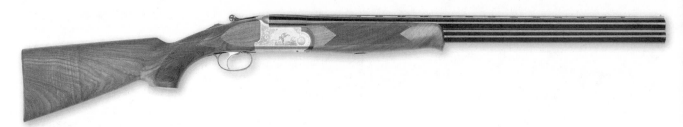

As the U.S. is increasingly incorporated into the European (and perhaps the world) economies as an equal partner, you can expect to see more international shotguns banging away at clay birds than just Perazzis or Krieghoffs. FAIR imports the Italian-made LX 600 Sporting in both 12- and 20-gauge models.

The Rizzini Artemis DeLuxe 12-gauge for sporting clays features a pistol-grip stock with palm swell and target fore-end in extra-select walnut. It comes cased in a cloth sleeve. Barrel lengths are 28, 29, 30½, or 32 inches.

shotgun. It has a three-inch chamber, walnut stock and forearm and MRP of $1,379. I-12s are "inertia driven," which means they will reliably cycle anything from light field loads to 3 ½-inch magnums. Because it has an aluminum receiver, this gun weighs only 6 ½ pounds.

This system has only three primary and moving parts: the bolt body, the inertia spring and the rotating bolt head. With few moving parts inertia systems are fast and clean. Gas, smoke and burnt powder stay in the barrel instead of being channeled into the gun's mechanism as they are in gas systems. It is the first inertia driven shotgun with an elongated forcing cone.

The I-12 has a 30-inch barrel with 10-mm tapered target rib and red bar sight. The barrel is ported to control muzzle climb and uses extended choke tubes. Five chokes are provided: C, IC, M, IM, F and a wrench. Specifications for the 51-inch gun are LOP 14 ½, drop at heel 2 ¼ and drop at comb 1 ½.

Franchi says the I-12 Sporting is the first of an innovative line of fast, reliable auto-loader shotguns designed specifically for clay shooters.

The company is also making a move in the over/under market with the new 12-gauge three-inch Renaissance Sporting ($2,249). It has 30-inch ported barrels with extended, knurled choke tubes for easy fitting and removal: C, IC, M. The forcing cones have been lengthened to ensure uniform shot patterns and to reduce back pressure and felt recoil.

Weighing in at eight pounds, this Franchi uses an extra-strong, stainless steel box-lock action. The receiv-

er is enhanced with scroll engraving and gold embellishments. The walnut stock features cut checkering and is enhanced with an adjustable comb and a patented, recoil-reducing recoil pad with gel insert. With a 30-inch barrel, the gun is 46 ⅝ inches long with a 14 ½ LOP, 1 ½-inch nominal drop at comb and two-inch drop at heel.

### Ithaca

www.ithacagun.com

The folks at Ithaca Gun now do their manufacturing in Upper Sandusky, Ohio. With new ownership came a streamlining effort and many of the newer guns—the Deluxe and Classic series, for instance and the Sporting Clays model—were sacrificed.

Now, you can have a lot of fun shooting competition games with one of their pumps and, besides, it is excellent practice for the field. Pump-action guns are not shot in serious clays competition, although a national pump-gun competition would be fun, but you do see them in the friendly rounds when friends shoot on weekends. So with that in mind, here is the Ithaca classic pump.

The Model 37 Featherlight was originally designed by John Browning and John Pedersen. Hundreds of thousands of this gun in several variations have been produced.

Today's Model 37 has bottom eject action and is thus suitable for either left- or right-hand shooters. Available in both 12- and 20-gauge, the Featherlight has a steel receiver; its cousin, the Ultralight has an alumi-

Barrel porting – drilling a series of small holes toward the muzzle – is designed to bleed-off some of the hot gas behind the shot pellets before they leave the barrel. Porting is supposed to make follow-through to a second shot easier by reducing "muzzle jump."

num receiver and is thus, Ithaca says, nearly a pound lighter. Expect these features in either model: 4.5-6-pound trigger pull, gold-plated trigger, lengthened forcing cone, vent rib, three-inch chamber, red front sight, black walnut stock and forend, black Pachmayer Decelerator recoil pad, and three screw-in Briley chokes (F, M, IC) with a choke wrench.

The 12-gauge Model 37 weighs 7.4 pounds with these dimensions in inches: LOP is 14 ¼, drop at comb 1.4, drop at heel 1.6, OAL 49.6 with 30-inch barrel. Barrels are also available in 28 and 26 inches.

The 20-gauge Model 37 weighs 6.4 pounds. Other dimensions are the same as the 12-gauge.

## Khan

www.khanshotguns.com

Turkey, like Italy and Spain, has a center of gun manufacture, and for the Turks that is in the neighborhood of Konya in the southwestern quadrant of this large country. Established in 1985, Khan began exporting shotguns to the U.S. and elsewhere 15 years later. Regardless of the quality which one may or may not find in their Khan shotgun, the company has not yet established a "presence" in the U.S. and guns can thus routinely be purchased for less than $500.

The High Class HC-12 over/under is available in 12- or 20-gauge with 28- or 26-inch barrels, five interchangeable chokes and a three-inch chamber. Overall length is 45 inches and weight about 7 ½ pounds. Expect hand-made scroll engravings with a gold inlaid eagle figure on a gloss finish silver receiver. The top lever and the trigger guard are furnished with an unusual gold flower design.

Kahn's Fireball II Field gas gun semi-auto is offered in 12- and 20-gauge with three-inch chamber. The Fireball features a chrome lined barrel with an 8mm ventilated rib. Receivers are AA 7012-T6 aircraft grade aluminum with a hard chromed bolt assembly. High grade Turkish walnut with hand cut checkering is used for stocks and forearms in all models. A synthetic stock is also available in 12-gauge. The Fireball can be purchased with a magazine capacity of 4+1 (4 in magazine, 1 in chamber) or 3+1 (3 in magazine, 1 in chamber). Guns feature gold colored triggers and trigger guard that are large enough to suit gloved fingers.

## Kolar

www.kolararms.com

For many years, the manufacture of high quality custom competition shotguns was limited to several overseas gun makers. The discerning clay target shooter had few choices when looking to purchase a gun that would withstand the rigors of heavy clay busting. Kolar says that is no longer the case.

Kolar Arms of Racine, Wisconsin, introduced its quality line of American-made skeet, sporting and trap shotguns in 1995, after four years of extensive research and testing. Having won numerous World Skeet, National Sporting Clays and ATA Grand American titles, Kolar has met its objective of being a competitive force with the fine European shotgun manufacturers.

The introduction of the .750 Semi-Lite factory choked barrel on all models compliments the standard weight .740 bore barrel. Without question, this allows Kolar shotguns to be soft shooters. The new ramp taper rib and expanded selection of factory stock configurations are a step forward for Kolar.

The Kolar shotguns are available in skeet, trap and sporting clays. The clays model features a neutral weight distribution and balance. Careful selection of stock and forend density assures this critical aspect of performance. The specially designed stocks optimize gun fit, whether you choose to pre-mount or shoot the low gun FITASC discipline. Available with 28-, 30-,

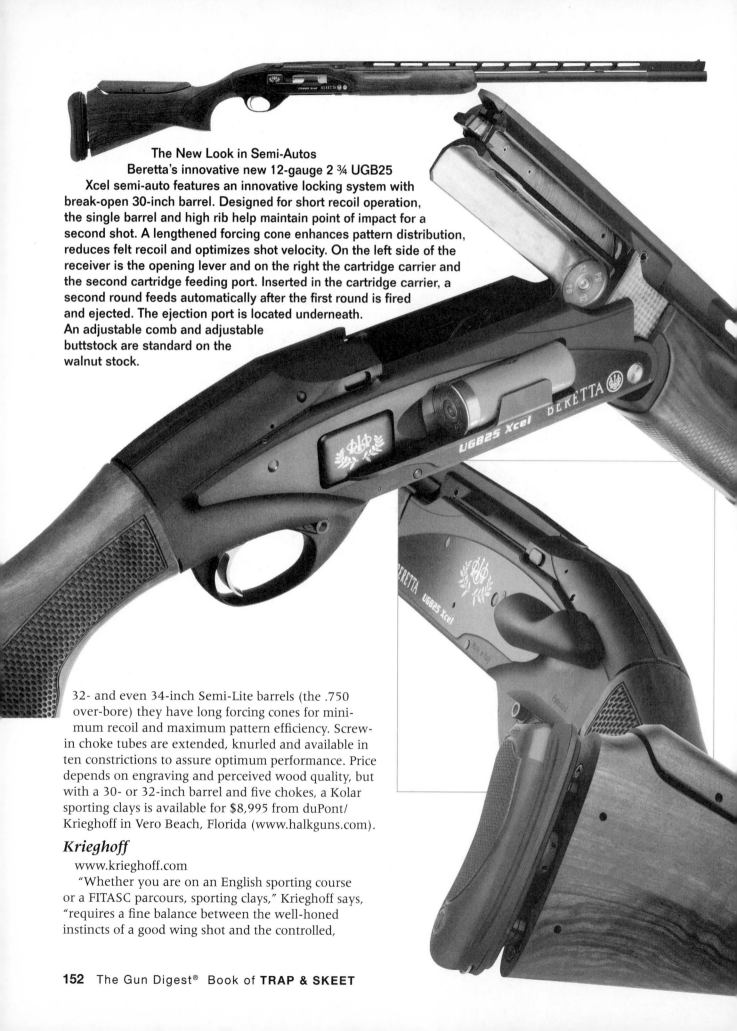

**The New Look in Semi-Autos**
Beretta's innovative new 12-gauge 2 ¾ UGB25
Xcel semi-auto features an innovative locking system with break-open 30-inch barrel. Designed for short recoil operation, the single barrel and high rib help maintain point of impact for a second shot. A lengthened forcing cone enhances pattern distribution, reduces felt recoil and optimizes shot velocity. On the left side of the receiver is the opening lever and on the right the cartridge carrier and the second cartridge feeding port. Inserted in the cartridge carrier, a second round feeds automatically after the first round is fired and ejected. The ejection port is located underneath. An adjustable comb and adjustable buttstock are standard on the walnut stock.

32- and even 34-inch Semi-Lite barrels (the .750 over-bore) they have long forcing cones for minimum recoil and maximum pattern efficiency. Screw-in choke tubes are extended, knurled and available in ten constrictions to assure optimum performance. Price depends on engraving and perceived wood quality, but with a 30- or 32-inch barrel and five chokes, a Kolar sporting clays is available for $8,995 from duPont/Krieghoff in Vero Beach, Florida (www.halkguns.com).

## *Krieghoff*

www.krieghoff.com

"Whether you are on an English sporting course or a FITASC parcours, sporting clays," Krieghoff says, "requires a fine balance between the well-honed instincts of a good wing shot and the controlled, measured performance of a clay target veteran."

The newest sporting clays shotgun offered by Krieghoff is the new Pro Sport model ($10,695 from duPont/Krieghoff in Vero Beach, Florida in March 2009). Introduced at the 2008 Sporting Clays National, it is available in 30- and 32-inch barrels with extended, knurled titanium choke tubes, and topped with a new higher, floating rib and higher stock. With the higher rib, a shooter maintains a higher head position and broader sight picture. The floating rib provides the option to raise the POI (point of impact) from the factory setting of 50/50 to 60/40.

This manufacturer's K-80 Sporting 12-gauge over/under, chambered to accept either 2 ¾ or 3-inch shells, is available with a host of options and personal adjustments. The single selective trigger is adjustable for length of pull and weight (from 3 ½ to 4 pounds). This gun weighs 8 ¾ pounds and comes with a fitted aluminum case with slots for extra barrels. A standard grade K-80 Sporting—if any Krieghoff can be said to be "standard"—with five choke tubes and a hard-sided case cost $9,870.

Three barrel lengths are available for the K-80 Traditional Sporter: 30-, 32- or 34-inch. Both barrels take choke tubes and five are provided (steel, not titanium on the traditional models): S, two IC, M and IM. Other choke constrictions are available from Krieghoff. You may choose from two rib configurations, tapered flat (10- to 6mm) or 8mm. Ribs have a white pearl front and metal center bead.

Krieghoff stocks are cut from walnut in multiple standard configurations. The Sporting International stock has 14 ⅜-inch length of pull, drop at comb of 1 ⅝ inches and drop at heel from between 2 ¼ to 2 ¾ inches. The forearm is Schnabel-styled.

You can shoot sporting clays with a K-20 over/under as well. This standard grade 20-gauge is $8,595.00. Just for fun, the K-20 with three-barrel set (20-, 28-gauge and 410), five choke tubes per barrel and three barrel case is $16,105.00.

## Lanber

www.lanber.net

A 40-year-old manufacturer in Bizkaia, Spain, Lanber is well represented in England and Australia, but has yet to identify a niche in the U.S. Nevertheless, several of its 12-gauge over/under smoothbores are certifiable clay-busters. The Model 2097 Sporting ($885 at Skip's Firearms in Ooltewah, Tennessee: www.skips-firearms.com) comes with 28- or 30-inch barrels and 2 ¾- or 3-inch chambers. Its pistol-grip stock and Schnabel forearm are cut from polished walnut. The 7.7-pound gun is 44 ½-inches long, has a 14 ⅝-inch length of pull, 1 ⅜-inch drop at comb and 2 ⅛-inch drop at heel. The front sight on the vented rib is a white bead

and the side rib is vented. Lanber opens the spaces between the barrels as much or more than most other manufacturers.

Lanber offers seven semi-autos in its 12-gauge Victoria line. The Victoria II (LCH – INT: $605 at Skip's in Tennessee) with internal, flush-mount chokes has a blued receiver and a choice of 26- or 28-inch barrels and 2 ¾- or 3-inch chambers. Its OAL with a 28-inch barrel is 48 ⅜ inches and weight a little less than seven pounds. In addition to the rear-of-trigger button safety, a button mounted on the forward part of the receiver allows for control and unlocking of the carrier. Lanber says this gives shooters "greater safety in loading and unloading operations."

## Miroku

www.browningint.com/miroku/

In Nankoku, Japan, Miroku builds solid shotguns under its own label and also for Browning and Winchester, though Miroku guns generally sell for $1,000 or less in the U.S. The handsome MK38 Sporter Teague over/under shotgun is well-thought of internationally and has achieved some success in competition. With a satin varnished wood finish the MK38 weighs about 7 ¾ pounds. Length of pull is 14 ¾ inches and drop at comb/heel are 1.4/2.2 inches.

The 12-gauge MK38 comes with 32-inch back-bored barrels—from .724- to .740-inch—and three extended Invector+ chokes (listed as ¼, ½ and ¾), which according to the Browning research department reduces recoil by six percent. The barrel is topped with a 10mm rib.

Back-boring barrels, by the way, is designed to ensure that there is less friction between the shot and the wall of the barrel as the pellets rush forward at upwards of 1200 fps, driven by burning hot and expanding gas. With back-boring, or opening the barrel slightly—in this case only .016 inch—instead of having to overcome friction, more of the energy generated by gunpowder gases serves to propel the shot, thus increasing the shot velocity while the shot retains its ballistic quality. With back-boring, the force of contraction or the pressure exerted by the immovable steel barrel wall on the load of softer lead shot is reduced, thus reducing the number of deformed pellets.

Browning/Miroku posts this note as an attachment to its MK38 page: "All hunting or sporting shotguns (over-and-under or semi-auto guns) by Browning, Winchester and Miroku fitted with the original chokes (Invector, Steel Invector Plus, Stainless steel Invector Plus, Teague, Briley, Midas, Diamond, Signature chokes) can fire 'high performance' steel shot cartridges. Tested at the Liège test bench (high performance 1370 bars) in accordance with European law on the use of steel shot."

Exhibition shooter Patrick Flanigan's Super X3, Winchester's newest semi-auto 12-gauge has distinctive red anodized metal parts and black rubberized (Dura-Touch Armor) coating to keep the stock from slipping in your hands. Flanigan's magazine tube is modified to hold 11 shells.

## Mossberg

www.mossberg.com

Although this Connecticut company is not known for shotguns for shooting clay targets, their 12-gauge 930 All-Purpose Field auto-loader (MSRP $568) with American black walnut stock and forearm ought to do very well busting birds. Mossberg includes an adjustable stock drop and cast spacer system and the butt has a black rubber pad. The 28-inch barrel is factory ported and topped with a ventilated rib and additional barrels in 24- and 26-inch lengths are available for the field. Three Accu-Chokes are included: Full, Modified, ImpCyl). A three-inch chamber will handle all shells for clays. The 930 AP Field weighs about 7 ¾ pounds, is 48 ½ inches long (with 28-inch barrel) and has a length of pull of 14 inches: drop at comb is 1 ½ and drop at heel two inches.

For kicks, you could take your black synthetic stock Mossberg 930 Special Purpose and shoot or even your old Mossberg pump. If you are serious about shooting sporting clays, however, there are much better guns—although Mossberg has chosen not to build them—although to be argumentative, a $600 shotgun that will break any clay its user can hit can be viewed as a great bargain, the cost for busting per clay being fractions of the cost of an expensive gun! This American company has a marketing plan that calls for reliable, affordable shotguns (and now, rifles) that can be taken to the field and used hard, guns that you will not worry about scratching while stalking through the brush or getting wet in a duck blind.

Still, should you choose to shoot guns with synthetic stocks, understand that they are about 1/3 lighter than walnut, and yet are stronger. Ram-Line stocks (www.ramlinestocks.com), for example, are GFN, glass filled Nylon 6/6, although other materials are routinely used by other companies. Nylon is significantly strengthened by the addition of glass-fibers. The added glass provides stability and rigidity, but reduces non-lubricated wear properties. Synthetic stocks will not bend or absorb water and swell. They are scratch-resistant with a non-glare finish.

## Perazzi

www.perazzi.it

Arguably the most idealized name in top-end competitive shotguns, Italian gun-maker Perazzi offers what amounts to custom fitting even in basic over/under guns (all three in 12- or 20-gauge), the MX8 ($12,000), MX12 ($12,000) and MX2000S ($14,000). The prices quoted are for a gun with minimal engraving and should be considered base cost. Upgrading to SC3 Grade engraving for instance for the MX8 quickly raises the price to $18,394 and moving farther upward in design and execution including gold inlays brings the cost of this gun to $31,275 and it steps up eventually to $100,449!

Barrel lengths are available from 27 ⁹⁄₁₆ to 34 inches. Interchangeable or fixed chokes are optional in one or both barrels. (No modern shotgun with interchangeable chokes should ever be fired without chokes securely in place in both barrels.) Perazzi choke tube designations are marked on the tube for quick identification. The flat tapered barrel rib and the side ribs are "half ventilated." The 12-gauge measures ⁷⁄₁₆ by ⁹⁄₃₂ while the 20-gauge is ³⁄₈ by ⁹⁄₃₂.

Critical stock dimensions on a Perazzi are essentially whatever you want them to be, because if you can afford one of these fine, but expensive guns, you can probably afford the trip to Brescia, Italy, to have the gun fit to you personally.

Perazzis have interchangeable buttstocks that can be ordered in a wide range of pull lengths, drop at comb and heel, with cast-on or cast-off, or straight comb with sloping field pistol-grip stock or a Monte Carlo. In effect, you are custom-building the gun when you buy it. Obviously then, the overall length and weight can vary widely with barrel and stock selection.

These Italian shotguns are not the kind of equipment you buy off the rack at the local firearms emporium. Those who can afford them swear by them, however. There is an old story that goes around every now and then, and which I recently read again in a Sporting Clays magazine forum, about why German FITASC competitors shoot Perazzi rater than Krieghoff: "If we buy a Kreighoff," they supposedly say, "and put 60,000 rounds through (normal for them in a year) the gun is shot out and worth next to nothing. The Perazzi by contrast is just being broken in and we can sell it for close to what we paid." After spending $25,000 or more on a fine shotgun, this could be something to keep in mind.

## Remington

www.remington.com

There are other guns in the Remington line than the long-lived 1100 gas gun. In fact, Remington has a set of over/unders that have a small, but growing reputation as fine shooters and it calls them its Premier Competition guns.

The Italian-made Premier Competition STS 12-gauge has .735-inch or slightly over-bored barrels with lengthened forcing cones. Barrels are offered in 28-, 30- and 32-inch lengths. The receiver is nickel-plated and barrels are topped with a 10mm ventilated rib with ivory front and steel mid beads. The STS comes with five extended, knurled ProBore chokes: S, IC, LM, M and F. The barrel selector is integral to the thumb safety.

"For added comfort," Remington says, "there's a right-hand palm swell, and the lustrous satin wood finish is complemented by a gold [plated] trigger and [lightly] engraved receiver." Otherwise, expect a Schnabel forend and premium hard case. Overall length with the 30-inch barrel is 47 ¼; drop at comb 1 ½ and at heel 2 ⅜.

The MSRP of the Premier STS Competition is listed as $2,540. Add an adjustable comb and the price climbs to $2,890. It must be said that this list price is considerably greater than you will find at a neighborhood gun store. In April, 2009, Big Sky Guns in Great Falls, Montana, was selling the same gun for $1,971 plus shipping and handling to a dealer near you.

According to Remington, the Model 105 CTi II (MSRP $1,559) is "The lightest, softest-shooting 12-gauge semi-auto we've ever built." And that says something considering I have shot the 1100 successfully for years and almost always found it an excellent gun for the money. The Model 105 CTi II is built on what Remington calls "the industry's only skeletonized titanium shotgun receiver" which is then wrapped with a carbon-fiber shield to create the "ultimate fusion of toughness and reduced weight." The receiver has the Remington-exclusive semi-automatic bottom feed and eject mechanism, what the folks in Madison, North Carolina, call the "Double- Down" system. It produces no peripheral distraction from ejecting shells—a feature that trap, skeet and sporting clays shooters will certainly like.

The Model 105's simplified gas system has few moving parts to require cleaning and there's virtually nothing to wear out or replace. Along with reducing felt recoil, the over-bored barrel enhances pattern consistency. For a custom fit, the new Adjustable Length-of-Pull Kit allows ¾-inch length-of-pull adjustment from 14 ¼ to 15 inches in ¼-inch increments. Barrels are 26 or 28 inches long and this seven-pound gun is 48 ¼ inches long with a 28-inch barrel. Comes with three ProBore chokes: IC, M and F.

Of course, no discussion of Remington shotguns would be complete without mention of the venerable and versatile (and valuable…) 1100 semi-auto. The 1100 is now available in a 12-gauge, 2 ¾ Competition model with 30-inch .735 over-bored barrel, 10mm ventilated rib, front ivory bead and mid-rib steel rib. Internal receiver components are either nickel-finished or Teflon-coated. At 51 inches long, this 1100 as a LOP of 14 ¼ drop at comb of 1 ½ and drop at heel of 2 ¼. The Competition 1100 was $1,277 in April, 2009 at www.ableammo.com or $1,413 with an adjustable stock.

## Rizzini USA

www.rizziniusa.com

Like many high quality manufacturers, most Rizzini over/under shotguns are used very successfully on clay targets. Still, Rizzini, with U.S. offices in Connecticut, has been building over/unders for nearly half a century and five of them are specifically designated as sporting clay weapons.

In Rizzini's standard line of sporting over/unders, all have the same specifications as the Vertex, the only difference being the type of engraved side-plates … and the cost.

The Vertex is a 12-gauge chrome-plated box-lock, with 2 ¾- or 3-inch chambers. Barrels are 30 or 32 inches long and made of chrome-moly steel. Bores are chrome-lined, topped with a 10mm ventilated rib and come with either fixed or interchangeable chokes. Stock and forearm are polished, oil-finished walnut with the following measurements: LOP 14 ⅝, drop 1 ¼ and 2 ¼. Look for a single selective trigger, extended five-inch forcing cones and a weight of about 7 ¾ pounds.

Differences in the line are the new BR320 which is also available in 20 gauge, and the S790EL which has a 34-inch barrel option. Otherwise, for engraving, the Vertex has "light scroll," the BR320 has the Rizzini name in gold, the S2000 has photo-engraved borders and English scroll, the Artemis DeLuxe as a hand-finished game scene and English scroll with pierced top lever and the S790EL has "completely hand-made [engraving] with names in gold and pierced top lever."

Rizzini is justifiably proud of its optional 360-degree adjustable comb, which adjusts up and down, side to side and allows for the actual pitch of the comb to be adjusted also.

In a more versatile vein, guns in Rizzini's Field and Premier lines should make excellent sporting guns and, indeed, it is difficult to understand why the company—and it is not alone in this regard—makes artificial differences between "field" and "sporting" guns, but it does. Consider the low profile, box lock Artemis Classic with hand-finished game scene with gold figures.

Mechanically, the Artemis Classic ($3,109 from www.impactguns.com in the spring 2009) is available in all gauges including 16! Guns have chambers appropriate to their gauge and chrome-lined, glossy blued barrel lengths of 26, 28, 29 and 30 inches. Look for full side and ventilated top ribs. The top rib for the 12/16 is 7mm and for the 20/28/410 is 6mm. Chokes can be ordered as fixed or interchangeable. Automatic ejectors, single selective trigger. Prince of Wales pistol grip stock and Schnabel forend in middle-quality select walnut, hand checkered with a polished oil finish. LOP 14 ⅝, drop 1 ½ and 2 ¼ inches.

### Ruger

www.ruger-firearms.com

Not cheap or terribly expensive as shotguns go, Ruger's Red Label over/unders are positioned above shotguns from most box stores in price but below the guns you must have custom fitted and hence are very popular on sporting clays fields. The suggested retail price for one of these Connecticut smoothbores is $1,956. As with any MSRP or manufacturer's suggested retail price, expect to pay much less when you negotiate your own purchase at a local gun store. (Bud's Gun Shop in Lexington, Kentucky, sells the non-engraved Red Label for $1,406, delivered!)

You can order a Red Label in almost as many styles as are possible with shotguns and to include a variety of options. The standard gauges are available, 12, 20 and 28; and Ruger builds a 410 tube set for their 28-gauge guns should you really wish to face a sporting challenge.

A Red Label is built with straight grain, fully-seasoned American walnut for stocks and forearms, and either the customary pistol grip or straight English-style grip. A pistol grip and rubber recoil pad are standard on the 12 and 20 models; the 28 has a plastic butt plate. Stocks and forearms are deep-cut checkered 20 lines to the inch for secure gun hold. All wood surfaces are sealed with a satin weather-resistant finish.

Red Label 12- and 20-gauge over/unders are chambered for three-inch shells and the 28-gauge is chambered for 2 ¾-inch. Rugers are shipped with shell ejectors which eject spent, but not unloaded shells. These can be deactivated so that you can manually remove or extract all shells. (Reloaders usually prefer this option because on most ranges, if a shell hits the ground it belongs to the range.)

Ruger over/unders feature barrel-firing selection. The letters "T" (Top) and "B" (Bottom) appear to the right and left of the safety thumb-piece, and indicate which barrel is to fire first. The safety must be "on" (the letter 'S' visible, safety moved to rearmost position) before the barrel selector feature can be used. If the thumb-piece is then moved to the right so that "B" appears, the bottom barrel fires first. If the thumb-piece is moved to the left so that "T" appears, the top barrel fires first.

Receivers can be ordered plain or engraved. Factory engraved side plates have "Tasteful scrolling and gold-inlaid bird, appropriate to each model, on both sides of the receiver." Engraved 12-gauge guns have a gold-inlaid woodcock taking flight: the 20-gauge features a grouse and the 28-gauge a woodcock. If you order a gun with a factory-engraved receiver, expect to pay an additional $224. Plain receivers have a brushed finish.

Set into stainless receivers, barrels are hammer-forged steel and back-bored for softer recoil and more uniform patterns. Available barrel lengths are 26, 28 or (12-gauge only) 30 inches. A choke tube wrench and five, steel-shot compatible flush-mount choke tubes are included: two Skeet #1 (one for each barrel), Improved Cylinder, Modified and Full. The dovetail, free-floating rib (stress-relieved and contour-ground) has a single gold bead aiming point.

The Red Label has a 14 ⅛-inch length of pull. Drop at comb is 1 ½-inches, drop at heel is 2 ½-inches and a 12-gauge with a 28-inch barrel is 45 inches long and weighs about eight pounds.

### SKB

www.skbshotguns.com

SKB still says mastering sporting clays requires a shotgun that provides a responsive fit, is well balanced between the shooters hands, and has a smooth swing, a fast sighting plane and a crisp trigger. It also needs the performance features that allow fast target acquisition, and hard hitting patterns without producing shooter fatigue. Hence, this century-and-a-half old Japanese manufacturer claims, the continuing need for its 85TSS over/under, which is available in 18 models with multi-gauge sets available for eight models.

The 85TSS Sporting Clays models are available in 12, 20, 28 and 410. The 12-gauge 85TSS is chambered for a three-inch shell and features your choice of barrels: 28, 30 or 32 inch. Small gauge models are available with either 28- or 30-inch barrels. Clay barrel sets are available in 12/20, 20/28, and 20/28/410 gauges, all with 30-inch barrels.

Barrel length determines the precise weight of the gun at approximately an ounce an inch. The "85" with a 32-inch barrel, for instance, weighs eight pounds, nine ounces. Each top barrel carries a nickel center post and bright Hi-Viz CompSight. The ventilated step rib is 12mm wide. Barrels are available with Mag-Na-Port's "Pigeon Porting" as an option (about $200). A system of screw-in chokes is available and three (S1, S2, M) are included.

All SKB shotguns have lengthened forcing cones which provide a relatively gentle transition for the shot column. The lengthened forcing cone leads to better downrange performance by diminishing pellet deformation and is responsible for a reduction in felt recoil. (The forcing cone is the transition immediately forward of the chamber. Typically, a shotgun has an abrupt diameter change from the chamber into the bore.)

All 12-gauge "85" over/under barrels are backbored. In other words, the interior bore is slightly enlarged. In a 12-gauge, the nominal SAAMI bore diameter is .729. SKB 12-gauge "85" over/unders are over-sized to a nominal bore diameter of .735, like Remington. (Instead of starting with a .729 bore and removing metal to create the larger diameter, SKB manufactures a .735 bore to begin with. SKB claims that this maintains the barrel's strength.) Over-sized bores allow the wad to spread slightly, reducing friction as it burns along the length of the bore. The benefits are denser and more evenly distributed patterns and a reduction in felt recoil.

The walnut stock of the "85" is available with a fixed or an adjustable (a little less than $200) comb. The stock and essential dimensions are: 14 ½, 1 ⅝ and 1 ⅝ inches. A high grade walnut stock costs an additional $400.

SKB's GC7 Clays Series over/unders are re-engineered, multi-discipline, competition grade target shotguns with American black walnut stocks and come in all gauges. They provide sporting clays and skeet shooters a blend of performance features. The new clays stock has a longer length of pull, greater drop dimensions, and a longer pistol grip allowing for better low mount and pre-mount applications. The 8.5mm top ventilated rib or tapered top ventilated rib reduces barrel weight while improving target acquisition speed. The clays series is fitted with Briley X2 extended chokes.

## Stoeger

www.stoegerindustries.com

Stoeger has an interesting history. In 1923, Austrian immigrant Alexander Stoeger issued a price list from his New York City shop, announcing that he was the "sole authorized importer" for the U.S. and Canada of the Mauser and Luger Arms and Ammunition.

The next year, he issued his first catalog and by 1931, he proclaimed the company was "the only exclusive gun house in America."

In the 1990s, Stoeger was purchased by Finnish rifle manufacturer Sako. In 2000, Sako was acquired by Beretta and Stoeger was placed under the ownership of Benelli USA, where it remains today.

Stoeger's Condor over/under ($600) comes in 12- or 20-gauge editions with a gold-plated single, selective trigger, automatic ejectors and a three-inch chamber with black non-engraved receiver. The Condor Competition Combo ($829) is a two-barrel 12- and 20-gauge set, with 30-inch barrels that fit the same receiver. Stock and forend are checkered walnut, and the standard stock has a vertically and horizontally adjustable comb. Choose a right-hand or left-hand palm swell.

Combo barrels are 30 inches for both 12- and 20-gauge. The ported barrels are topped with a vented rib, brass bead and silver mid-bead. This shotgun comes with Improved Cylinder, Modified and Full screw-in chokes. Overall length is 47 inches; LOP is 14 ½; drop at heel two inches; drop at comb, adjustable.

If you are looking for a 410 or a 16-gauge, Stoeger offers these bores in its Condor line. Both bores have fixed chokes. The 410 comes with a 26-inch barrel and the 16 offers a choice of 26 or 28 inches.

The Model 2000 semi-automatic 12-gauge ($500) has a satin-finished walnut stock and forend, or can be purchased for the field in Realtree or Advantage camo. The Inertia Driven system has only three moving parts in the bolt—the inertia spring, the bolt body, and the rotating locking head—for more reliable operation. Stoeger says, "The operating system is mostly contained in the receiver, giving the Model 2000 a trimmer forend with better balance. Plus, with no propellant gas venting into the operating system, the Model 2000 stays cleaner."

The 2000's chrome-lined 26-, 28- or 30-inch barrels are proofed for steel shot and use a red bar sight on top of a vented rib as an aiming point. Equipped with the 30-inch barrel, it is 51 ¼ inches long and weighs 7 lb 3 oz. It will accept 2 ¾- or 3-inch shells and has a 14 ½-inch length of pull and drops at comb of 1 ⅜, drop at heel of 2 ½. The Model 2000 comes with five flush chokes: Cylinder, Improved Cylinder, Modified, Improved Modified and Full chokes.

A cavity is designed into the butt stock of the Stoeger Model 2000 to allow installation of an optional, mercury-filled recoil reducer.

## TriStar Sporting Arms

www.tristarsportingarms.com

TriStar calls itself "The Value Experts," which means that you will want to take a look at their shotguns because they will not be terribly expensive per shot, especially if you are only an occasional shooter.

The gas gun series is called Viper, though what that moniker might have to do with sporting clays is puzzling. Nevertheless, the Viper 12- or 20-gauge semi-auto ($519)—either with 3- or 2 ¾-inch chamber—has a gloss finish on the wood stock and forearm. It comes with three choke tubes (F, M, IC), a 28- or 26-inch chrome-lined barrel and matte, ventilated rib with front bead. The 6 ½-7-pound gun has these specifications: LOP 14 ¼, drop at comb 1 ½ and drop at heel 2 ⅜. This gun is also available in black synthetic ($469) or carbon fiber ($589) stocks/forearms.

TriStar is importing a new group of over/unders. Its Sporting Clay shotgun, it says, "goes target to target against the competition in price, features, performance and warranty." For $839, the Sporting has a three-inch chamber in 28- or 30-inch chrome lined barrels with extended forcing cones and ventilated top target and side rib. The front sight is a fiber optic and barrels have a brass mid-bead. Expect a single selective trigger, steel receiver, selective auto ejectors, walnut pistol grip stock and semi beavertail forend. Five extended Beretta-style chokes (SK, IC, M, IM, F) are included.

## Weatherby

www.weatherby.com

Founded by Roy Weatherby in the 1940s, Weatherby was not a name in shotguns until Roy's son, Ed, took over the company and began expanding the offerings. Today, Weatherby is headquartered in California, but its semi-automatic shotguns are made in Turkey. They feature self-compensating gas system to reduce felt recoil and a safety button on the rear of the trigger guard.

The SA-08 Upland semi-auto ($700) is built for Weatherby in Turkey. It is chambered for a three-inch shell and available in 12- or 20-gauge with 28- or 26-inch chrome-lined barrels and vented top rib. With a checkered walnut stock and forearm and a 28-inch barrel, OAL (overall length) is 48 inches and weight is 6 ¾ pounds. The 20-gauge weighs about six pounds. Length of pull is 14 inches: drop at comb is 1 ½ and drop at heel 2 ¼.

A good cook will carefully remove the shot pellets before serving breast of pheasant. A good field gun will break clays, too. The author prefers pheasant marinated in wine and baked with apples!

Three extended steel Multi-Choke tubes and a choke wrench are standard: Improved Cylinder (.013), Modified (.022) and Full (.040). The tops of the chokes are notched for identification, although this is requires memorization and familiarity, and all-in-all I much prefer that Weatherby soon change to extended screw-in chokes with the choke recognizably stamped on the leading, knurled end.

The Weatherby trigger system drops out for cleaning by pushing two pins in the 7075 T-6 alloy aluminum receiver. It snaps back and locks into position just as easily.

Weatherby offers two lines of Italian-made over/unders, Orion and Athena, which will be excellent for sporting clays shooting. There are differences between models as noted, but generally, as one climbs in price the difference is increased quality of standard factory engraving and nicer looking walnut.

- Orion I ($1,700): In 12- or 20-gauge with 26- or 28-inch barrels and a three-inch chamber. All metal-work is blued and polished.
- Orion II ($1,900): Adds a chromed and lightly engraved receiver and upgraded walnut. A 28-gauge with 2 ¾-inch chamber is available for $1,979.
- Orion III ($2,200): Upgraded walnut and receiver engraving features a gold grouse in flight.
- Orion SC ($2,600): An adjustable stock for improved sight alignment and faster target acquisition. This model only, ported barrels in 28-, 30- and 32-inch lengths.
- Athena III ($2,600): Upgraded engraving.
- Athena IV ($3,100): Also in 28-gauge with 2 ¾-inch chamber, 26- or 28-inch barrels.
- Athena V ($4,000): Features, Weatherby says, "old world Italian custom craftsmanship traditionally reserved for guns costing thousands more."

## Winchester

www.winchester-guns.com

"Winchester." Just the name brings to mind cowboys and Indians. John Wayne. Without embellishment, the name needs no special explanation in the U.S. or for that matter in much of the world, for even the anti-hunting, anti-gun, anti-everything crowd recognizes it. If I had another son, I would name him Winchester.

And yet the marketing people at Winchester, a division of U.S. Repeating Arms—and God bless them, for the company itself has been around the block a few times lately—are deeply involved in "creative writing," as are, to be absolutely fair, the marketing people from most other companies from guns to automobiles.

Apparently it is now against the marketing rules to give straight-forward names and explanations. Butt pads are not rubber, but are "special polymers"—Inflex Technology. Stocks are "synthetic," which, unless you are a chemist, means plastic. The rubberized coating on the stock and forearm is Dura-Touch Armor. The extended, knurled chokes are Invector-Plus. The people who run these companies are seemingly scared to death of the words "rubber" and "plastic."

Winchester's newest semi-auto 12-gauge is a duplicate of the very distinctive red and black Super X3 ($1,459) shot by pro staff headliner Patrick Flanigan in live shows except, Winchester adds, that Flanigan's magazine tube is modified to hold 11 shells. Light and responsive, the Super X3 allows faster follow-up shots because its Active Valve system, "which allocates gases in a clean, precise manner," reduces felt recoil.

The 28- or 30-inch barrels are .742 back-bored. Working with extended and knurled Invector-Plus chokes, this is designed to provide consistent, dense patterns. A black, rubberized (Dura-Touch Armor) coating keeps the stock from slipping in your hands, and the stock is adjustable to fit your shooting style and body type. The Inflex recoil pad has a hard heel insert for quick, no snag shouldering.

Manufactured in Belgium and assembled in Portugal, the Super X3 is 51 inches long with the 30-inch barrel. LOP is 14 ¼ inches; drop at heel and comb are 1 ¾ and two inches. Nominal weight is seven pounds, eight ounces. It includes an additional gas piston to allow the use of a full range of loads from the lightest one-ounce target loads to heavy three-inch magnums.

For shooters who may want to carry a Winchester, but are not in love with the red and black circus look, Winchester makes the Super X3 in a Walnut Field model ($1,159) that is mechanical similar but includes two stock spacers for length of pull adjustments.

Winchester's Select Model 101 Pigeon Sporting ($2,579) over/under 12-gauge is new for 2009. Its lightly engraved silver nitride receiver is offset by a checkered walnut stock with a slight right hand palm swell and forend. The adjustable comb will move from 1 ¼ to 1 ¾ inches, thus accommodating many shooting styles quickly, including cast-on/cast-off.

The Model 101 features a 10mm, tapering runway rib, mid-rib bead and TruGlo Tru-Bead front fiber optic aiming point. Back-bored .742-inch barrels are ported to tame second-shot recoil, have vented side ribs and are available in 30- or 32-inch lengths: also 28 inches in the more standard 101 Sporting ($2,139).

Chambered for 2 ¾-inch shells, five Invector-Plus choke tubes and a choke wrench are included: Light Full, Modified, Improved Modified, Improved Cylinder and Skeet.

The overall length of the 101 Pigeon with a 30-inch barrel and fixed comb is 47 inches. Length of pull is 14 ¾ inches; drop at comb is 1 ¾ inches; and drop at heel is two inches. The trigger is adjustable for length of pull. This gun weighs about seven pounds.

# CHAPTER 22
# BEST LOADS FOR SPORTING CLAYS

Here is a summary of what NSCA rules say about sporting clays loads for registered tournaments in IV-4. Ammunition:

1. All shot shell ammunition including reloads may be used.
2. Maximum ounces of lead by gauge: 12 – 1 ⅛, 20 – ⅞, 28 – ¾ and .410 (2 ½-inch maximum) ½.
3. Plated shot is permitted.

NSCA All-American Wendell Cherry, captain of the 1st All American Team, shoots #7 ½ exclusively. No matter what the presentation or angle or type of target, he sticks with this single load. The top barrel of his Perazzi MX 2000 is choked Full while the bottom barrel is choked Improved Modified. Wendell kicks butt with this load even when others in his squad may be shooting #8 ½ or even #9. It worked for him—in 2008 he won the U.S. Grand Prix, the Masters Cup, the Gamaliel Cup and much more—but it may not work for everyone.

Unlike other shotgun games, there is no single load that is perfect for sporting clays … in any gauge. Whether you are shooting our conventional English sporting or the supposedly more difficult FITASC, 5-Stand or Compak Sporting, you have a diversity of loads and shells that can do the job. Millions of skeet shooters swear by their 1 ⅛ ounce of #9, about 650

Whatever loads and chokes you find suitable to your gun and your shooting style, some type of vest or even a bag or box such as this heavy-duty nylon Bob Allen four-box shell carrier will be your new best friend on a long sporting clays course.

round pellets per shot for a 12-gauge. The occasional shooter will chamber #8 ½ for the second shot in doubles if he or she is just a touch slow or methodical getting on the bird. Trap shooters typically rely on loads of #8 (461 pellets) for the closer birds and #7 ½ (about 393 pellets) for those that get out beyond 40 yards. Registered trap targets and trap tournaments are regulated by velocity for 12- and 20-gauge: 1290 fps for a 1 ⅛-ounce load or 1325 fps for 1-ounce and 1350 for ⅞-ounce.

In trap and skeet, you know where a bird is coming from, where it is going and at what speed. Precisely. Sporting clays is different.

Every clays course sets its traps to give you seven fundamental shot presentations—running rabbit, crossing left-to-right and right-to-left, springing teal, straight-away, high incomer and looping bird or "chandelle"—and yet they are different on every course, too. This is why sporting clays is occasionally referred to as "golf with a shotgun," perhaps referring to the diversity of opportunity one encounters on a course. Except for the loud "bang" after one pulls the trigger, that description is apt. No other shotgun game matches the mixed bag of shots, speeds, distances and angles one sees in sporting clays, and one can shoot it in a regulation manner or totally for fun.

The variety of possible loads is one reason that some sporting shooters end up with pockets full of shells.

Sporting clays competition may be the most exciting shotgun sport in the world unless you are a fan of the more expensive European import, hélice. Fortunately for shooters who scalp from their local BoxMart and for those who prefer premium loads, there's a great deal of ammo to choose from.

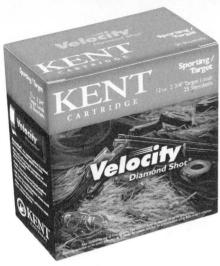

Kent Velocity Diamond Shot is available for 12-, 20- and 28-gauge. This is a versatile load for the 12-gauge. #K122SL32-8 uses a spreader wad for 11/8 ounces of #8 lead.

Remington's Premier STS Target and Premier Nitro Gold Sporting Clay Target Loads are developed specifically for clay shooting and are available in all loads needed to bust birds with consistent success.

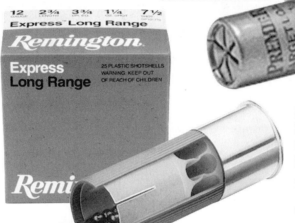

Remington's Express Extra Long Range Loads are available from 12-gauge to .410 in #7½. The 12- and 20-gauge are also available in #9.

"Oops, I thought I put #9 in the left pocket and #8 in the right pocket and the #7 ½ in my …. Aargh! Where are the 7 ½?" Your #9 may still have concentrated enough BBs in its shot string, but not enough dynamic energy left to break the 50-yard crossing shot, but for a quick 15-yarder, the 7 ½ is not normally the most efficient load. So, what this all means is that with courses often a mile long, this option for shell diversity becomes a boon to bag and cart (or big, double-stitched pocket) manufacturers.

## Load Selection Is Important

Most sporting clays shooters are aware of the need to be equipped with a selection of interchangeable choke tubes to handle varying distances. Knowledgeable shooters are also becoming aware that in order to increase the number of birds they smash they must give equal thought to the selection of shells they carry. In fact, quite a few experienced shooters feel that a minimum of three different loads—short-, medium- and long-range—is a minimal approach. Some even favor five distinctly different loads, varying their shot size, payload weight, velocity and even shot hardness, though this seems a bit extreme.

For shooters seeking to build a versatile shell selection, you can certainly find it represented within the offerings of the major ammo makers. Often, however, for reasons I will mention below, simply buying someone's "sporting clays" shell may not give you the best load for the job. Here is an overview of loads that are commercially available for the various shot problems you will encounter on a thoughtfully laid-out sporting clays course.

## Ultra-Short Range Shots

Although extremely close-range shots (under 10 yards) are not as common in sporting clays as they are in skeet, they certainly can occur, and the most effective shell is not hard to define. You need one that

opens the pattern quickly. A shooter with a 12-inch pattern will have considerably greater chance to break a tight target than one with a five-inch pattern. Shot size is not a critical requirement here: any size target pellet will do. Since #9 shot packs the largest pellet count per load, it is the odds-on favorite, though. Because larger, sturdier pellets tend to pattern tighter, this size shot is a doubly good choice for short range shooting.

Regardless of choke, and without resorting to custom "spreader" wads, wads with internal divisions for the shot, there are three basic ways to increase close-range pattern spread:

1. Use softer shot, which tends to deform under firing pressures and produces a lot of out-of-round pellets that become fliers. A chilled shot of two percent rather than a magnum or high antimony 5-6 percent antimony load;

2. Increase shot velocity, which results in essentially the same thing if less than ultra-hard shot is used, and will even encourage some pattern spreading with #9, regardless of its hardness. Stepping up, for instance, from Federal Gold Medal Target Paper at 1145 fps to Gold Medal Target Plastic at 1200 fps may not be a noticeable difference to the human eye, but the additional 55 fps can make a difference on short, fast birds. Conversely;

3. One could opt for shells with fiber wads—very popular in Europe and with some hand-loaders—instead of modem one-piece plastic shotcups. These will also open your patterns (though they may actually slow it down a bit).

All shotgun sportsmen are aware that lead is an environmental contaminant. At this time, steel is rarely used on sporting clays courses and, except in rare instances, not at all in trap and skeet shooting. Still, the occasional sale or closing of a shooting range with tons of lead on and in the ground causes a great deal of debate and discussion among sportsmen, in government and in environmental circles. The use of steel or composites in all shotgun loads and the abandonment of lead may not be that far out on the horizon.

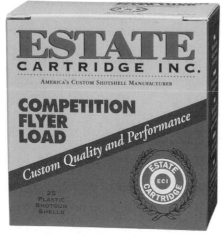

Estate extra hard shot cartridges are a division of ATK in Anoka, Minnesota. Estate target loads are available for all gauges.

Any one of these factors alone can increase pattern size. Combine a couple of them, and it can make a very noticeable difference at close range.

One easy way to accomplish this is to stock up on the ubiquitous promotional ("Dove & Quail") loads from WalMart at the beginning of each fall season. These generally toss a one-ounce charge of shot that is not as hard or as precisely formed as the premium target loads, at velocities from about 1250 to 1300 fps. Their inability to deliver tight patterns is legendary and that makes them an excellent and relatively inexpensive choice for ultra-close sporting targets. The fact that

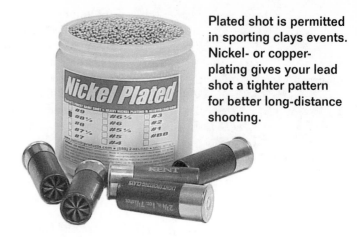

Plated shot is permitted in sporting clays events. Nickel- or copper-plating gives your lead shot a tighter pattern for better long-distance shooting.

they only carry a one-ounce charge makes no difference, because there are more #9 pellets in a one-ounce load than you need at ultra-close range anyway. All you have to do is get the pattern to open quickly and these are some of the fastest-opening factory-loaded shells available. Their patterns may be as full of holes as a rusty bucket at 30 yards, but they work very well up close.

Another option would be any of the high velocity (1,300-plus fps) target loads carrying one-ounce or less of plain lead shot. Not as effective as Dove & Quail loads, these are a much better bet than premium target loads that are intended to throw dense, uniform patterns.

Practically any of the skeet #9 or #8 ½ loads will work well for ultra-close shooting, especially with an open choked gun and a shell that is fitted with a brush-style wad that allows the pattern to open immediately.

## Close Range

A lot of shots on a sporting range will fall within 10 to 20 yards, and effective shells are easy to find. Select any good #9 skeet load because this is precisely what they were designed to do. No clay pigeon is designed to withstand a hit at this range, even from such a small pellet, and birds will obviously chip or vaporize. Again, those loads that we have talked about in the skeet chapter will be especially useful.

## Medium Range

Unless you are terribly slow to get on a bird, 20 to 30 yards probably represents the majority of the shots found on a sporting range and good shells are equally easy to find. Trap loads like those discussed in the chapter on successful loads for trap shooting are ideal and can be purchased at retail or hand-loaded cheaply.

This is the range at which #8 loads were designed to operate at their best. On the shorter shots, some feel a 1- or 1 1/8-ounce load of #8 ½ shot is hard to beat. They have plenty of target breaking power to a range approaching 35 yards. On the longer shots, especially if you are a methodical shooter or just learning the game, consider switching to #8. It will do the job out to about 40 yards. In either case, one benefits from the increased pellet count over loads using #7 ½.

Some ammo makers offer #8 loads with a fiber wad, and they are also effective within this area. The Eley VIP Sporting line, for instance, offers both 1- and 1 ⅛-ounce loads with fiber wads in #7 ½, #8 and #9 for the 12-gauge. Of course, the problem with purchasing shells like the Gamebore Super Game High Bird in 12-gauge 2 ¾-inch with one ounce of #7 ½ at 1300 FPS and fiber wad is that, at $10.99 + shipping for a box of 25, they are a bit expensive!

## Long Range

At 40 to 45 yards you get into handicap trap ranges, so it only makes sense that a heavy three-dram #7 ½ trap load would be an excellent choice, and it is. On the shorter side of the range, the 2 ¾-dram, "Lite" 1 ⅛-ounce, #7 ½ loads will also work very well. Many manufacturers specify ultra-hard shot in fast cartridges for these ranges. Eley's VIP Sporting or Superb Competition, for instance, with relatively high seven percent antimony contents at are good choices.

## Ultra-Long Range

The 45-plus-yard shots are some of the toughest shots one will see on a sporting clays range, and not just because distant targets take a good punch to break. They also take a fast load and longer lead to catch! While the heavy handicap trap loads in #7 ½ are still a good bet, some shooters are finding that the International trap loads are just as good. Although they start with only 24 grams of #7 ½ (about ⅞-ounce), their special shotcups and plated shot pellets give them a very tight-patterning ability at extreme range. Since most of them are moving at 1300-plus fps, they are also an aid in cutting down the long leads required for those extreme distances. In addition, they normally exhibit very short shot strings and this gets the most out of their smaller shot charge. They are definitely gaining favor among sporting clays shooters when the targets get "way out there."

When it comes to breaking distant targets, the most effective shells other than your .22LR will generally be those packing nickel-plated shot. These are noticeably more expensive than shells containing other types of shot, but you will not need many of them in a round and they are well worth the extra cost when you do need them.

Lyalvale's High Velocity Competition (www.lyalvale-express.com) has not been mentioned, certainly but deserves notice. An English shell tested in internation-al competition, these were first introduced in 1986 and have been upgraded virtually every year. The heavy 1 ⅛-ounce, 2 ¾-inch shell comes in #7 ½, #8 and #9 and specifies Vectan A1 as a single base, clean burning powder for this low base (base measures ⁵⁄₁₆ inches high) 1400 fps speedster. Lyalvale thus not only describes the shell, but tells what powder is used and that is as informative as it is rare in the ammo manufacturing business.

## Reloads and Components

While NSCA rules prohibit reloads at many major matches and FITASC abhors them, they are allowed at the club level, at the discretion of the club. The individual club rules on reloaded shells will, understandably, vary, and shooters will certainly want to inquire about them before taking the time to roll their own.

If your club allows them, handloads let the sporting shooter create some specialty loads that you will not find readily available from the major makers. Dave Fackler of Ballistic Products (www.ballistic-products.com), an enthusiastic sporting clays shooter himself, has come up with a number of interesting wad designs and has found several more that he imports from Europe. They allow the reloader to craft effective custom loads and, coupled with BPI's Mica Wad Slick ($7.99 for an 8-ounce can) to dust the wad and hull, will get the most out of every handload combination.

For ultra-close-range shots, even the cheap, soft-shot promotional loads are not going to give a large pattern inside 10 yards, although they will open up a good deal more than hard-shot target loads. Getting a pattern to open up really fast, actually scatter the shot, is an advantage here. If you double the diameter of your pattern you do not just double your chances of getting the shot on target at close range, mathematically, you increase it by a factor of four. That is well worth the time spent making up some special "spreader loads," perhaps with a brush wad without a constricting shotcup.

Creating these specialty loads used to require inserting a separate component, either a cardboard X-spreader, or a spreader post, into a standard wad during the loading process. One can also cut the shot-protecting petals on a standard target wad back to about a quarter of their original length. These methods still work, but there are easier ways to do it today.

The Ballistic Products 12- or 20-gauge G/BP Dispersor X-12 wad ($8.99 for a bag of 200—a $2 increase in five years) is a one-piece, easy-to-load wad with an integral X-spreader molded right into the shotcup. As the wad leaves the muzzle, the specially-designed petals fold back and allow the spreader to really get the pattern open quickly.

Another option is the G/BP 12-gauge Brush Wad ($7.69 per bag of 200), which is nothing more than a standard plastic wad less the protective shotcup. This was created to counter the rules some clubs have against wads with an X-spreader. Either of these flexible wads can be loaded with one to 1 ⅛ ounces of shot, at various velocities. If softer grades of #9 shot are used they will more than double the pattern size of conventional loads. The Dispersor works at its best under 15 yards, while the Brush Wad works well out to 20 yards.

Another option that is particularly useful in the close-range area is the G/BP Piston Skeet wad ($7.49 per bag of 200). This is a conventional one-piece target wad, but uses a unique petal arrangement to promote fast-opening patterns in the 10- to 25-yard range. It is very popular with European international skeet shooters for that reason. Piston Skeet wads can be used with standard American components and makes a great skeet load. It is at its best with harder grades of shot and will throw some very wide yet uniform patterns from an open-choked gun. When loaded with #8, it becomes a very useful shell for longer shots in the 20- to 30-yard range.

Mid-range shots can be handled quite well with standard trap load recipes, and they will be discussed in the reloading chapter.

Effective extra-long-range loads (45-plus yards) can be difficult to assemble from conventional target components, so a full shotcup is usually recommended and this can be found in most manufacturer listings. This style will usually handle shot charges from one to 1 ⅛ ounces and is designed to produce maximum pattern density at extreme range. When loaded with #7 ½ nickel shot, it helps build a fine, extra-long-range load and will break 60-yard birds.

While toting a large and varied selection of shotshells may seem like a lot of trouble, it is one of the best ways to take the initiative on any sporting clays course. If you are going to "play golf with a shotgun," it just makes sense to have all the clubs in your bag.

## A Note About Plated Shot

Lead shot coated with nickel or copper will fly more accurately because it resists deformation. Smooth and aerodynamic, plated or coated shot maintains excellent pattern density at longer ranges than standard lead shot. Plated shot is harder and, for hunters, that means it also penetrates better.

Commercially, most major manufacturers offer loads that can be shot in sporting clays. Fiocchi (www.fiocchiusa.com), for example, offers four options in 12-gauge, 2 ¾ one-ounce #7 ½ (#12TXN75, 1250 fps) and #8 (#12TXN8, 1250 fps) shells in its Nickel Plated Target and Helice line.

The difficulty with plated shot is not availability, but price. Generally, it costs more than twice what standard lead—even magnum—shot costs, and sometimes the disparity is even greater than that. A box of Fiocchi 1255 fps 12-gauge 2 ¾, 1 1/8 ounce, #7 ½ lead cost $8.83 in spring 2009 through www.ableammo.com. Fiocchi's 1250 fps 12-gauge 2 ¾, 1 ounce, #7 ½ nickel-plated lead cost $68.90!

It would be awfully good to have a few long shot shells in one's pocket for a day of clays shooting, but it might be best to build them at the reloader's bench, or else use them sparingly.

Reloading is a relatively simple task for shotshells. Seat the primer in the base. Pour in the powder. Seat the wad and fill it with shot. Then, crimp the top tight. Follow the directions in your reloading manual and you are ready to shoot.

# CHAPTER 23

# SEMI-AUTOS VS. OVER/UNDERS

If your shooting goal is to knock more ducks and geese out of the clouds or to learn to get your gun up faster on thunder chickens, then you should probably shoot the gun you hunt with for every clay sport. There is no better way to learn what to expect from your gun and any combination of chokes and loads than by actually putting it all to the test in trap, skeet and sporting clays. It is why policemen practice clearing buildings again and again.

If, however, you intend to pursue any of the shotgun games for the fun and the challenge of quality competition, you will very quickly discover that there are only two shotgun types that will take you into the winner's circle, a gas-operated semi-automatic or an over/under. That is not a knock on pumps or side-by-side doubles, just a simple statement of fact. These guns in fact sometimes have their own shooting events.

To excel in the conventional game, a shooter needs a gun that will reliably fire two shots, while allowing total concentration on the target. Pump guns such as the fine Remington 870 Express ($383) require the shooter to manually chamber the second round. Some experienced scattergunners can do that with remarkable skill. Exhibition shooter Tom Knapp, who travels for Benelli and Federal Cartridge, has been making a living with short-barrel, fast-action pump guns for years. On the competition range however, even the best shot will score a couple of targets less per round with a pump than they would with a gas gun or over/under.

Side-by-side doubles such as a fine Merkel Model 47SL ($3,650 at www.hallowell.co.com) can be lively handling smoothbores. They can get off two rounds very reliably. Unfortunately, the broad sighting plane

Over/unders such as the Krieghoff K-80 that author Rick Sapp (right) is shooting have the reputation of being better handling smoothbores than most semi-automatics. On the other hand, semi-autos demonstrably transfer less recoil to the shooter.

offered by the twin barrels is proven to give less precise leads on targets traveling on a largely horizontal plane, and that includes most game targets.

That pretty much leaves us with gas guns and over/unders, and the debate over the relative merits of each action type can be lengthy. Often that debate will generate far more heat than light. So which is the best choice, if there is one?

## Recoil

The uncomfortable but inescapable fact of recoil is one of the two biggest reasons shooters select a gas-operated semi-auto in preference to an over/under. The gas gun is commonly believed to have less felt recoil. If you are talking about factory guns right out of the box, that statement is almost certainly true.

When the normal gas-operated semi-auto is fired, a small amount of propellant gas is bled off from the barrel through one or more small holes drilled into the barrel. The gas acts to operate a piston mechanism within the forend that mechanically forces the bolt to the rear. An extractor mounted on the bolt grips the rim of the fired shell to pull it out of the chamber as the bolt recoils. When the bolt has drawn the shell back far enough to strike a fixed piece of metal called the ejector, the shell is automatically kicked out of the gun. While all of that is going on, a new shell is released from the tubular magazine onto the shell carrier below the bolt. As the bolt moves forward under spring pressure the carrier rises to position the shell, and the bolt rams it into the chamber for the next shot.

A lot of mechanical events are taking place at one time.

Actual recoil depends on the weight of the gun and the power of the shell. Obviously then, an eight-pound 12-gauge firing a 2 ¾-dram, 1 ⅛-ounce load will have less recoil than the same gun firing a 3 ¼-dram, 1 ¼-ounce shell. And an eight-pound gun will absorb a lot more recoil than a lightweight six-pound gun.

The gas gun does not necessarily reduce the actual reaction from the exploding powder. What it does is retard it, spread it over a longer period and use a little of the gas to cycle the action. This makes a gas gun feel like it is a softer kicking gun. You get a shove instead of the sharp rap that would be produced by a fixed-breech gun, an over/under or side-by-side, for example, of the same weight firing the same load.

With that said, I will now point out that my 12-gauge Ruger Red Label over/under delivers less recoil punishment to my shoulder than my 12-gauge Franchi Prestige gas gun, when firing the same loads. With the Franchi, which is a very soft shooting gas gun, 100 rounds in an afternoon will have me reaching for an aspirin bottle as I leave the range. With the Red Label, I do not need the aspirin. How can this be so?

The reason is the difference between actual recoil (which can actually be measured in foot pounds of energy) and perceived or "felt" recoil, which is how our bodies understand and perhaps react to the recoil. The latter is the more important of the two, and is dependent on a number of factors including shooting form, how well the gun fits the shooter and what cushioning material is present between the shooter and the gun.

Put another way, a heavyweight boxer who delivers a solid left hook to your jaw with his naked hand would injure you and perhaps his own hand severely. If that boxer is wearing a 16-ounce boxing glove, however, he will probably just knock you down and give you a headache. Nevertheless, the actual foot-pounds of energy (kinetic energy = ½ mass x velocity2) in the punch would be the same.

That is the case with my Red Label. It was fitted precisely to me by stock fitter Jack West, and has a thick KickEeze recoil pad and his padded comb. The Franchi has a KickEeze pad as well, but no padded comb. The Franchi feels slightly softer on firing, but the Ruger feels better over the long run.

Any shotgun can have its felt recoil reduced noticeably in this manner. If the stock treatment is done to a gas gun, it will probably be a bit softer shooting than an over/under, but both can be made to produce less felt recoil than they did out of the box.

That is why the question of recoil between the two guns, in my mind, only comes into play if we are dealing with unaltered factory guns. In that case, the gas gun wins the recoil war. However, that should not be the reason for selecting one over the other. Each can be made to shoot soft enough so that any shooter can enjoy them.

It is no longer appropriate to call every semi-auto a "gas gun." Take

The X-Coil all-weather Recoil Pad from Browning is a lightweight composite that can easily be fitted to your stock when you find your gun's recoil unacceptable. The X-Coil has a radiused heel for fast mounting and a surface texture that prevents slipping when you shoot in the rain.

the new Beretta UGB25 Xcel, for example. This break-open barrel gun's operating principle is based on short recoil, which, Beretta says, keeps the internal parts of the gun clean even after prolonged use. And the break-open design gives other shooters confidence that the gun is unloaded moving between stations. A second round is no longer hidden inside the magazine's tube, but is always visible in its side cartridge carrier.

The short recoil (and a low barrel axis position) compensates for muzzle jump during firing, with quicker and easier realignment of the barrel on the target for the next shot. The low barrel axis position transmits the recoil forces in line with the shooter's shoulder, thus minimizing felt recoil.

In addition, with the cartridge carrier for the second cartridge on the right-hand side of the receiver, a new shell chambers automatically through the feeding port after the first round in the cartridge chamber has been fired. The design of the cartridge carrier button and its position on the receiver ensure easy removal of the cartridge on the carrier.

And for this new gun, the ejection port is in the bottom of the receiver. The ejector expels the spent hull downward, away from the shooter and nearby competitors, and is user-friendly for both right- and left-hand shooters.

## Balance and Handling

This is one area where over/unders have a perceived advantage. The twin barrels poking out past the forend give more forward weight than the single barrel on a gas gun. This promotes a smoother swing, and one that is more difficult to stop once started. As a result, the targets are hit more often because follow-through is more effective.

The balance and handling qualities of any shotgun are determined by the way the weight of the gun is distributed. If there is a bit more muzzle weight, the gun tends to swing more smoothly. If there is more weight in the butt, the gun seems to mount quicker, but can be a little more "whippy" or loose on the swing. Over/unders tend to have a bit more muzzle weight and thus swing a bit more forcefully and positively.

You can alter the balance of a gas gun to give you the same swing characteristics of an over/under, though.

If you want to add a little more muzzle weight, fill an empty shotshell with shot, crimp it, seal it with duct tape, and stick it in the forward portion of the tubular magazine in place of the wooden plug that is already there. A 12-gauge shell full of shot will weigh 2 ½ to three ounces. The weight will lie forward of the leading hand and will promote a smoother swing. Depending upon the gun, you can add up to three weights and customize each for your preferred balance.

However, what if you feel the muzzle is too heavy? Stick one or more of the shot-filled shells in the stock bolthole in the buttstock. It is that simple.

You can change the balance and handling qualities of the over/under as well. Just add weight where you need it, and there are many products on the market to make that easy. Meadow Industries "Barrel Buddy" attaches to the underside of the barrel and gives you the option of adding up to eight ounces of weight. It cannot be used with a semi-auto because it prevents the forend from sliding off the gun in the normal manner during takedown, but it works well for over/unders. Buttstock weight can always be added via shotshells (fired and shot-filled, not live shells) in the bolthole of the stock.

Few shooters will need to change the balance of their gas guns. Makers are adding a bit more muzzle weight to semi-autos as they bring out specialized models.

In short, if you do not like the way the gun balances as it comes from the factory, you do not have to accept it. It is so easy to change that the discussion of balance and handling between the two gun types essentially becomes moot.

## The One Choke Syndrome

If you shoot a gas gun, you have only one choke available at a time. If you shoot an over/under, you have a choice of two (if the gun has a barrel selector switch). This is often touted as a major advantage of the stack-barrel. Again, there is some truth in that, but not as much as many might suppose.

There are a number of clay target games where having only one choke is no handicap, such as ATA 16-Yard trap, and handicap trap. Every target is going to be broken within one relatively narrow range, and one choke is fine. Ditto for the close shooting in American skeet.

The ability to use different chokes is often cited as a reason for the twin-barreled gun's popularity in sporting clays, but in truth it is rare to find a station where the shots vary more than 10 yards in range difference. Regardless of whether they are singles, report pairs, true pairs, following pairs or simultaneous pairs, once you know the range you can generally find one choke that is right for both birds.

One game where the shot array may present targets at wildly varying ranges from the same station is FITASC (acronym for the Federation Internationale de Tir aux Armes Sportives de Chasse: one of two international governing bodies for shooting sports). Here, you step into a shooting station with your gun and loads, and must shoot whatever is presented with the chokes you have in the gun. You cannot change them

Randy Travalia, owner of the Horse & Hunt Club near Minneapolis, demonstrates another reason that most top shooters prefer an over/under. It's easy to carry!

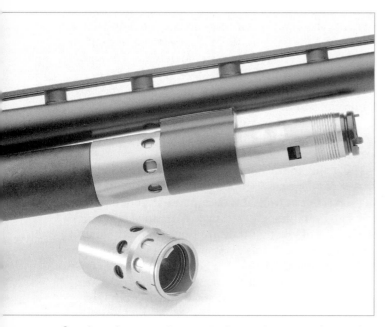

One knock on semi-autos is their relative mechanical complexity. If you take this gun apart for cleaning, unless you can do it blindfolded, perhaps you should label and tag the parts! In truth, giving a semi-auto a thorough cleaning is not that difficult, but it requires your complete attention.

once you step up to shoot. You may get a target at 15 yards and the next may be at 50. Shooting that game, it helps to have the versatility of two choke tubes readily available, but it is possible to make one choke serve multiple tasks.

How does a shooter make one choke do the work of two? Easy. By changing the loads in his or her shells. Many shooters assume that if they want the proper pattern for the range encountered, they must put the proper choke tube in the gun. That is not true. You can vary the pattern performance of your gun by simply changing your shells.

If that sounds confusing, consider this: in clay target games we do not grade the targets. All it takes to score a kill is to knock a visible piece off the target that the scorer can see. A target that is "ink-balled" (powdered) counts no more than a target that is merely chipped.

If your load gives you that visible piece, no matter how small it may be, who cares what your actual pattern looks like?

A growing number of shooters are doing more shell changing than choke tube changing, even if they shoot an over/under.

For example, you are facing a Fur & Feathers presentation on a sporting clays course. It gives you a rabbit target at about 15 yards and a quartering away aerial target that is supposed to be broken at around 25 yards. The ideal choke for this would be a straight Cylinder choke for the rabbit and an Improved Cylinder for the bird. Or you can shoot them both with the Improved Cylinder or a Skeet 1 choke simply by using a quick-opening load of #9 in the first barrel and a 1 ⅛-ounce load of hard, target-grade #8 in the second barrel. The first load could be an inexpensive promotional load with soft shot, a spreader reload using one of the Ballistic Products wads designed for that or perhaps a less expensive shell from the Remington Gun Club line, a GC12L at 1145 fps. Quick-opening shells give you as large a pattern as you are going to get at that range, regardless of the choke tube in the gun. The second load of hard #8 provides plenty of pattern density and individual pellet target-breaking power for the farther bird, even if you shot from a straight Cylinder choke and for this shot, you might want the higher grade Remington Premier STS121 at 1185 fps.

To take an extreme example, think of a FITASC shot where you might have one bird at a bit under 20 yards and a second at a little over 45. Many would choke Skeet 1 in the first barrel with a load of #9, and slip a Full choke tube in the second barrel with a load of #7 ½. The single choke shooter, however, can accomplish the same thing with a Full or Improved Modified choke (you have to choke for the longer bird) and then effectively open up that barrel to a Skeet 1 choke by using one of the fast-opening loads for the closer bird. The spreader-type loads will usually open a Full choke to about Improved Cylinder and a Modified choke to about Skeet 1.

More subtle modifications can be made by altering the velocity and shot hardness of the loads. Soft shot at high velocity will usually pattern one complete choke wider than the tube you are using. Hard, target-grade shot at moderate velocity will often pattern a one choke tighter.

Few sporting clays ranges throw shots beyond 30 yards, and a shooter with a single barrel gun can do just as well as a shooter with an over/under. If a farther target is thrown, choke for it, and use a spreader load—where the club allows them—to open patterns for any closer target.

The usefulness of spreader loads is the reason that a gas gun shooter is not at a disadvantage because the gun offers only one choke.

This covers the three most common reasons for making the selection of either an over/under or a semi-automatic gas gun. From my viewpoint, there is little real difference between them … at least so far. Now, let us get down to the real, nitty-gritty differences.

## Reliability

The over/under wins here. No argument. In fact, the very best any gas gun shooter can do is to make his or her gun as reliable as an over/under. The reliability factor is very important in all shotgun games.

In some games, if you cannot fire on the target for any reason, you lose it. Other games will give you a certain number of "alibi" birds and allow targets to be re-shot. Even then, there is a limit and beyond that you lose targets.

A gun malfunction can also deal a blow to your confidence and adversely affect your subsequent performance. It is very difficult for the subconscious mind to perform the tasks required to break a target if it is wondering if the gun will go off. A gun malfunction early in the game or in the key later stages of a match can cause you to miss subsequent targets even if the malfunction never recurs. A mind is a terrible thing to mess up and a malfunction can do it.

Because of the large number of moving parts and mechanical operations required, a gas gun will never be as reliable as a fixed-breech over/under. That is the biggest single reason why top competitors show a marked preference for the stack-barrel guns. If you can stuff the shell in the gun and close the action, the primer will be struck when the trigger is pulled. If the shell is any good, it will go off. Not so with gas guns. They can be working perfectly and still screw up.

The gas gun requires near-perfect ammunition, and the power level of the shell must be sufficient to operate the action, yet not so powerful that it generates too much gas energy. That can cycle the action too fast and result in a failure to feed a second shell. I have light target loads that will run 100 straight on the skeet range in my Ruger Red Label, yet will not cycle the action on my Franchi.

If you reload, you must make certain that every shell is as perfect as a factory load. A hull that is worn, slightly out of round, or has a poor crimp may fail to feed and fire. If it will just fit into the chamber, that shell will operate just fine in an over/under though.

Gas guns must also be kept scrupulously clean if they are to even approach stack-barrel reliability. This brings us to another factor, one often dreaded—unnecessarily—by those of us who as energetic, out-of-doors-oriented kids were forced to take regular baths: cleaning.

## Ease of Maintenance

Cleaning an over/under is simplicity in itself: unhook the forend, open the action, dismount the barrels, brush or swab them out and reassemble. A little light lube on the ejector/extractor arms and the barrel hinge, and the gun is ready to kill pheasants or shoot another tournament.

Gas guns are more tedious. The forend must be removed, the barrel slid out of the receiver—with care taken not to lose any of the little O-rings found in most gas-operated systems (and then to put them back in the same order when done). Then the piston has to come off and all the attendant parts laid out, and we are not done yet. Smart shooters also "drift" out the retaining pins that hold the trigger/shell carrier group in place (You do have a drift punch and small hammer, don't you?) and, for detailed cleaning, remove the bolt.

Now that the gun is disassembled, here are some potential problem areas:

1. The trigger/shell carrier. Flush it out with something like Outer's Crud Cutter and allow it to dry. Spray the assembly lightly with Break-Free or any similar lube before reassembling. The reason this part must be cleaned is that unburned powder flakes can work their way into crevices and tie up the shell carrier. Some powders are notorious for this. When that happens, your gun becomes a single shot. It is a common problem and an area many shooters neglect.

2. You will scrub the barrel, naturally, but that does not finish that job. Pay particular attention to the gas ports. They can become clogged with carbon, reduce gas flow, and cause a feed malfunction. You will also need to remove plastic fouling from the chamber. This is left by the outer surface of the shell itself from heat generated upon firing. If allowed to build up, it will

seriously impede the gun's ability to feed and extract shells. Standard bore cleaning solvents and brushes do not remove it. I use a bore brush wrapped with 0000 steel wool. Once you scrub the chamber, leave it slick and dry. Oil in the chamber contributes to both feeding and extracting malfunctions.

3. Follow the manufacturer's instructions for cleaning the gas system. Some have certain lubrication "do's

and don'ts." Remember to add some light lube to the action bars and the channels they ride in within the receiver. This is another area where unburned powder can cause the gun to foul.

That will handle routine cleaning. Every 10,000 rounds or so, it is advisable to take the gun to a good gunsmith for a thorough strip down and tank dunk cleaning.

Considering all of this, is it any surprise that most fine shooters who fire 10,000 to 30,000 rounds per year prefer over/unders?

## Durability

Another win for the over/under. At the risk of offending a few gas gun makers, the most expensive gas-operated semi-auto made will not even come close to the lifespan of even a moderately priced (but well-made) over/under. No one can predict how many rounds each type gun will handle before it is ready for the scrap heap, but the very top competition gas gun shooters consider replacing them annually and have one or more backup guns on hand.

## Ease of Repair

As a rule, the gas gun wins this one. This is especially true if you are shooting a well-known model that has been around for a few years, a gun like the Remington

Regardless of the type of gun or the manufacturer, things go wrong. Murphy said it and it is true. Wads stick. Guns jam. Chokes fall in the dirt. Approaching a malfunction with a sense of humor will help you cope and the people around you will rally to your assistance, even if you are in a neck-and-neck shoot-off with them.

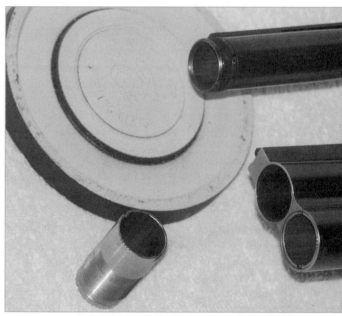

Whether to purchase a special gun for clays shooting comes down to a choice of over/unders with two barrels or semi-automatics with a single barrel. The over/under is a more prestigious gun and often more expensive. The semi-automatic has a reputation for softer recoil and its magazine holds more shells.

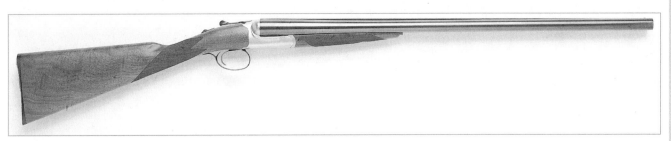

One thing all advocates agree on is that a side-by-side, regardless of its quality, does not usually provide the sharp sighting plane needed for competitive clay shooting. This Ruger Gold Label 12-gauge is a high quality side-by-side that is 45 inches long and weighs 6 ⅓ pounds.

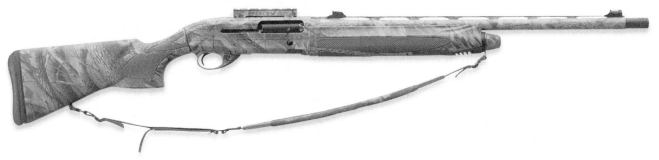

The cost of two styles of gun that will each accomplish the shooting task for clay games can be small or significant, even within the same product line. The moderately priced Beretta 686 White Onyx Sporting lists for about twice that of the corresponding semi-autos. The Xtrema, pictured in Realtree Hardwoods HD and tricked out for turkey hunting, is a similar gun to the Urika Sporting.

A father takes his three sons to learn shooting on a fine summer day. With pumps and semi-autos, the boys are learning skills that last a lifetime, and all are storing strong family memories.

The interior of the Fausti manufacturing facility in Italy – clean, well-lighted and highly computerized – illustrates just how focused modern gun producers are on building the very highest quality product for today's shooters.

1100 or the various Winchesters. You can likely find parts and service at your local gunsmith. He knows what small parts routinely break or wear out and keeps them in stock.

Since gas guns are designed for mass production with parts interchangeability, replacing parts is fairly easy. When over/unders need repairs, they are more complex. Generally, it is best to send them back to the factory. If the gun is an American-made model with solid repair facilities, turn-around time can be relatively quick, but expect four to six weeks. If you have an expensive European or Japanese model, repair time can sometimes stretch into many months, although most of these manufacturers now maintain U.S. service and repair centers.

On the plus side, over/unders seldom require minor repairs. When a well-made gun needs fixing it is generally after a lot of shooting, more than casual shooters will do in two or three lifetimes.

## Use of Reloads

The stack-barrel wins hands down on this one, for reasons that have already been mentioned. Another factor that comes into play, however, is that over/unders are easier on the shells and you can generally squeeze a few more reloads per hull from them. Their mechanism does not ram the empties around and then toss them all over the ground. You just simply pluck them from the chambers—extractors preferred to ejectors as catching hot shells in flight is tricky—and stick them in your pocket. That can be especially important if you are shooting on a range whose policy is, "When a shell hits the ground, it becomes the property of the club."

Since most serious competitive shooters, men and women who put a lot of rounds through the barrels in a given year are reloaders, this has become one of the strong points in the over/unders favor.

## Cost

The second biggest reason shooters choose semi-autos over over/unders is that they cost less to acquire than a good quality stackbarrel. The cost difference can be a significant factor for shooters on a budget, and that is something the shooter will have to decide. However, in some cases, that difference can be deceiving.

There are a number of budget-priced over/unders on the market, but they must be made with parts that are not the highest quality possible. In order to obtain an over/under with the quality needed to be a top competitive gun, you are looking at a suggested retail price of at least several thousand dollars.

A smart shopper can generally save a few hundred dollars if he looks for the best "street price," and the Internet is both a boon and a problem.

Quality gas guns like the Remington 1100, Browning Gold, Verona 692 Gold and Beretta models usually have a shelf price that is several hundred dollars lower than the MSRP, the manufacturer's suggested retail price, which is always inflated. The street price philosophy also applies to them. (See for instance www.ozark-guns.com.)

If you are thinking of entering serious competition,

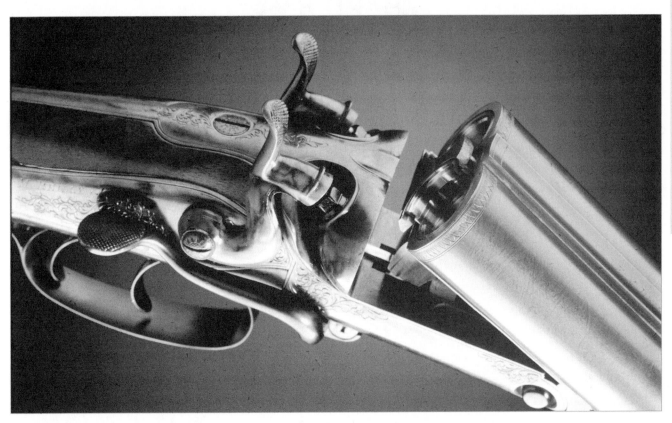

An organization called The Vintagers – Order of Edwardian Gunners holds special shooting events for collectors of vintage side-by-side shotguns. Members dress in the style of the Edwardian period and say they have far too much fun to keep score!

the total difference in price of $800 to $1,000 may not be worth the increased inconvenience of the gas gun. That price difference is, after all, only about the equivalent of six or seven cases of shotshells. When you are talking about a gun you may want to keep, shoot, and possibly even invest a bit of money in for custom fitting or upgraded walnut stock, that difference becomes a lot smaller. You are only talking about a few months supply of shells as the price difference on a quality gun you may well pass on to your children.

Over/unders also hold their value. If you decide you want to change guns after 20,000 or so rounds, you will get a much larger percentage of your original purchase price back if the gun you are selling is a well-made over/under that has been cared for properly.

Try selling a gas gun that has gone 20,000 rounds and most knowledgeable shooters will not even look at it.

These last are the real reasons why over/unders dominate competitive clay target games, but this is not meant to denigrate gas guns. With the exception of the reliability factor, they will hold their own with the over/unders when it comes to busting clay targets. Nevertheless, making a decision as to which type of shotgun to buy is more involved than that.

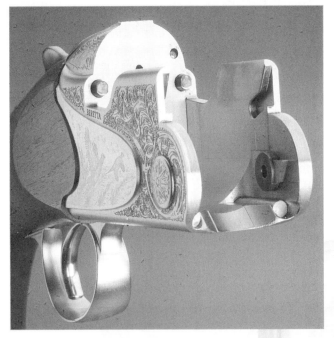

In extra fine shotguns, the wood of the stock fits so closely to the metal that the two seem naturally to flow into each other. When wood projects above the surface of the metal receiver, it is referred to as "proud." *(John Taylor, The Shotgun Encyclopedia)*

# CHAPTER 24

# FITTING YOUR SHOTGUN

We Americans, I believe, still tend to see ourselves as rough-and-tumble people of the frontier with a close, personal relationship with our guns. Unlike most other places in the world, we hunt in great numbers. Even our electronic entertainment, games and movies, are full of gunfire. We buy guns for home defense and even the most average guy on the street can play with guns. This becomes something of an ego problem when we confront the International versions of shotgun games, which tend to be a good bit more difficult than ours.

As Americans, we may have a tendency to jump to the "bang," the explosion, the result, the quick fix. By the millions, we go to the local Wal-Mart, buy a shotgun and a license and straight-away go out hunting. Consequently, the average shotgun owner rarely understands or has patience with the idea of fitting the gun to their body, their style or personal quirks, and their eyes. The idea of fitting is perhaps one of the details—like fine engraving and scrollwork—that does not seem to belong in our western egalitarian environment. In this case, however, we have a lot to learn from "old Europe."

When we see a seven-foot professional basketball player next to a retired five-foot computer programmer wearing a bow tie in a shoe store or an auto showroom, we naturally understand that they are buying shoes or vehicles built to different styles and patterns. One size obviously does not fit all. The basketball play-er needs a sport utility vehicle with plenty of room for his long legs and size 13 ½ feet. The computer programmer can get by very happily with an economical sub-compact. Why then is it a difficult concept that these two individuals would require differently fitted guns to consistently hit their target? One size gun does not fit all, either.

Manufacturers are not concerned about the basketball player's personal dimensions any more than those of the computer programmer. They build to a few standardized patterns, patterns that are "generally acceptable" to the public as a whole. Browning and Beretta do not know who has a 35-inch sleeve or who has one that only measures 29 inches. They cannot know who wears thick glasses and who has high, bony cheekbones. Except for the most expensive or custom-produced guns—an Italian Perazzi or even an American Ljutic, perhaps—the average manufacturer cannot make every purchaser wait in line for individual measurements and stock modifications before they purchase a gun.

Many shooters have, through trial and error, learned to adapt to these one-size-fits-all guns, figuring out how to crawl their body around on the stock to get everything lined up perfectly—at least, lined up most of the time, when they have time to think. They have also learned that they shoot better with some makes of guns than with others. This is because manufacturers do not all build to the same stock dimensions.

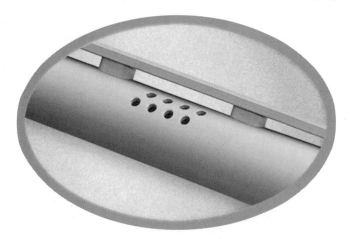

A ported barrel such as this Mossberg 500 pump will reduce "muzzle-jump" and help you get on a second bird faster than if all of the energy were in-line.

Pattern performance is crucial to shooting success, and any smoothbore operator who wants to get the most benefit out of every shot will spend time at the pattern board. *(Photo courtesy Mossberg)*

When a shooter finds a gun that truly fits or modifies one so that it fits, breaking targets becomes easier. Scores go up, and the world becomes a nicer place in which to live. The purpose of shotgun fitting is to allow you and your gun to see the very same sight picture and to make this as natural as possible. You break more targets and everyone is happy.

Master shotgun fitter Michael Murphy (www. murphyshotguns.com) says that having your shotgun properly fitted will improve your scores. Having a skilled individual help with this will get the shooter started on the right path much more quickly than if he or she tries to do it on their own. "And," Murphy says, "a better fit makes you a better shot. Surely, Butch Cassidy and the Sundance Kid would understand and approve. There is nothing soft, effeminate or old world about that!"

## Tests and Results

**TEST 1:** Any individual with even average hand/eye coordination can pass this test. Stand on any clay target range and have a pigeon thrown. Now, smoothly and without any effort, raise your arm and track the target with a pointed finger. You do not have to consciously work the finger into position; you focus on the target with the eyes and your finger finds it every time. Were that finger "loaded" you would probably break that target practically every time, too.

Swap your finger for a shotgun however, and the picture changes considerably. Now you are struggling with a heavy foreign object that you must place against your body with proper and consistent contact at four points—cheek, shoulder and both hands—before you can even begin to track the target. Unless that shotgun exactly fits those four spots the same way each time you bring it into position, it will not point at the same place every time. If that happens, you cannot hit the target every time.

Yet, if you switch back to your finger you are right on target. The purpose of fitting a shotgun is to turn it into a finger, and it does not need to be difficult to be effective—although it sometimes is. Three situations can complicate proper fitting:

- An experienced shooter who has definite opinions,
- A shooter who may be right-hand and left-eye dominant or vice versa, or
- An individual with a particular injury that makes good hold and fit a special challenge.

**TEST 2:** This from the forums on www.gunnersden.com. Make up a target approximately two feet square and place it down range, perhaps 200 yards away. Relax a few minutes and then pick up your shotgun. Snap point your shotgun at the target as if it were a grouse or a clay bird trying to get out of range. Repeat this procedure four or five times. If you had to make any adjustment whatsoever to get on that target, simply put, your shotgun stock does not fit you.

**TEST 3:** If the above does not work for you, then a test we informally refer to as the "bed sheet test" just might. To perform this test, get an old bed sheet and smoothly tack it up over a safe backstop. Use a felt-tip marker or a can of spray paint to mark a six-inch circle in the middle and then step back 25 yards. Put a Full or Improved Modified choke tube in your gun and grab a handful of your favorite target loads. Hold your gun in a low gun position and get your body set on the circle, just as if you were lining up to break a bird at a specific spot at the range.

Now, focusing on the dot, mount the gun smoothly and quickly. Fire as soon as the gun comes into position and you can see the circle over the barrel. Do not

Mike Murphy of Michael Murphy & Sons, Kansas, says that fitting is not rocket science and you can certainly do it yourself. However, he cautions, there are many options that should be considered before you begin sanding and cutting a fine walnut stock. Better to spend a few extra dollars with a coach and professional fitter, he believes, than to risk ruining your shotgun stock.

aim the gun or wiggle around on the stock. To do so defeats the purpose of this exercise.

The reason for using a bed sheet is because it will take a number of rounds to punch a clearly defined hole in it. Fire as many rounds as it takes to get one well-defined hole. The reason for using a Full choke tube at 25 yards is that it will punch a compact hole. The center of that hole is where your gun is looking when you have made a smooth mount, while your eyes are looking at the "bird."

Once you have punched a hole in the sheet, it is a simple matter to raise or lower the comb or move it a bit right or left until you and the gun are looking at the same bird. You can also use the bed sheet test to determine whether both barrels of an over/under or side-by-side are shooting to the same point of impact.

## Getting Started

According to Michael Murphy, fitting usually involves reviewing your shooting mechanics before altering the dimensions of your stock. If you approach the shooting station with an awkward stance or unusual gun-hold, you definitely want to review the basics before you begin cutting walnut.

Assuming your stance and hold are acceptable however, Murphy's approach is to train you—and the shotgun—to look at the same spot every time you throw the gun to your shoulder. His fitting sessions covers the dimensions built in to your shotgun by the manufacturer.

### Drop at Comb

Your cheek makes contact with the gun here and this measurement largely determines whether the gun places its shot charge higher or lower.

It works this way. Consider your eye to be the rear sight on a shotgun, and the height of the comb to be the means for elevation adjustment.

The higher the comb height (less drop at comb) the higher your eye is above the barrel. This leaves you looking at lots of rib and, with the gun at your cheek, actually pointing the barrel upward. The higher the comb height, the greater this effect will be and the higher the gun will shoot. On the opposite side, the lower the comb height (more drop at comb), the lower your eye is, the less rib you see, and the lower the gun will place its shot charge.

A change of about 1/8-inch in comb height will result in an elevation change of an amazing eight to 10 inches at 40 yards. You can easily get that degree of change just by having a face that is fatter or thinner than "average."

The "universal" drop at comb for a flat-shooting field gun (50 percent of the pattern above and 50 percent below the bead) is 1 ½ inches. Trap guns, where a

The GRACO "CTS" adjustable comb system on an SKB 85TSS. This system allows the shooter to adjust the comb for both height and offset. Base plates fitted in the comb are etched with ¹⁄₁₆-inch indicating lines for offset adjustment. The comb height is adjusted by sliding ¹⁄₁₆-inch vinyl washers over the support posts. Maximum adjustment is one-half inch vertically and laterally.

pattern impacting above the bead is desired, typically use a 1 ⅜ drop at comb, about ⅛-inch more height than a field stock. This is often referred to as a high comb.

"The point of adjusting comb height," Murphy says, "is to make the gun shoot where the eyes go and allow the shooter to adjust his mental 'bird picture' to the point of impact of the shot charge. This is a very individual thing, because different shooters may have a different subconscious bird picture ingrained over the years. Some shooters want the barrel covering the target, some want to see it just below the bird, and some may want to float the bird above it. Regardless of how much adjusting you do in the shop, this is something that must really be finished by actually shooting. That is the big advantage to an adjustable stock: the shooter can fine tune it himself."

Lateral impact of the pattern, which used to be adjusted with cast-on and cast-off of the stock, can now be more precisely adjusted with the lateral adjustment of the adjustable comb.

### Length of Pull

This is the distance from the face of the trigger to the center of the recoil pad. On factory guns, length of pull is most commonly falls between 14 and 14 ½ inches. If your sleeve length is around 32 inches and you usually shoot in light clothing, that length is about what you want. That, of course, is a big "if." With longer or shorter arms, you probably need a gun with a different length of pull to shoot effectively and you can either have the stock cut (for shorter arms) or have shims

Well-attended and well-advertised shoots attract manufacturer representatives, high test shooting coaches and professional triggermen. Big events are wonderful opportunities to pick up some tips that may help you bust into the next level and perhaps to get some shooting instruction and/or gun fitting first-hand. Working with a coach, our intrepid shotgunner shoots for a pattern, makes adjustments and shoots again. Between shots, the coach re-paints the pattern board and critiques his stance and gun hold.

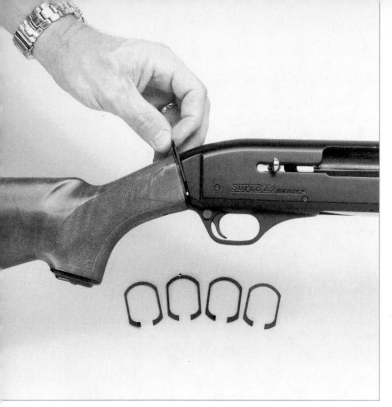

**Installing shims in a shotgun is not usually a difficult job. Shim spacers are used to adjust drop and cast to bring you close to a custom fit.** *(Photo courtesy Winchester)*

placed between the stock and the buttplate or recoil pad (for longer arms).

If you have a gun with a sloping comb (in contrast to a Monte Carlo-style comb that is level), a stock that is too short can cause you to shoot high. This is because your cheek (and your eye above it) seems to naturally slide farther up the comb to a higher point. It can also cause you to bang your nose with your trigger hand and that will just make life miserable in general. A stock that is too long, so that your cheek and eye slide or are positioned back toward your shoulder, can cause problems mounting the gun and makes it shoot low.

The rule of thumb for length of pull is what is most comfortable for the shooter. "Since we most often shoot a level comb," Murphy says, "length of pull has no real effect on the impact point of the shot charge, like it would with a sloping comb. I like to get the nose of the shooter no closer than one inch from the shooting hand, and not a lot farther back than that, either." It is a game of fractions.

### Pitch

Pitch is the angle at which the buttstock meets the shoulder. You can measure the amount of pitch by standing the shotgun against a wall with the top of the receiver contacting the wall and the buttpad flat on the floor. If the receiver and rib are in perfect contact with the wall, you have zero pitch. If the barrel is away from the wall, you have down or negative pitch. If the tip of the barrel contacts the wall before

the receiver does, you have up, or positive pitch. (Sights and beads can interfere with proper measurement.)

Most shooters benefit from down pitch, and normal down pitch on a factory gun will place the barrel two to 2 ½ inches away from the wall. It is easy to detect if you have improper fit. When you fire the shotgun, if it flips the muzzle up or down the pitch is wrong. With proper pitch, the shotgun will recoil straight back into your shoulder.

Determining the proper pitch for the stock is not a difficult process. "All the pitch angle does is to distribute the recoil forces evenly on the shoulder pocket," Murphy says. "If the pitch angle is not correct it will send most of the recoil force either to the top or the bottom of the shoulder and make the shooter uncomfortable. Pitch has no effect on point of impact with an adjustable stock, so you just make certain the angle is proper to let the pad lie evenly and comfortably on the shoulder pocket."

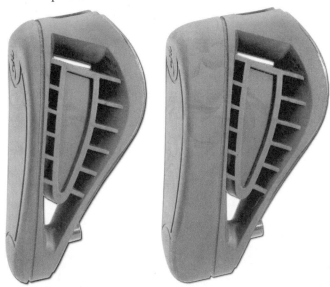

**Sometimes, fitting can be accomplished with the simple addition of or change of the size, shape or density of a recoil pad. Spacers are designed to help you adjust length of pull to your best shooting needs. These pads and spacers are designed for Browning's Cynergy Shotgun.**

## Cast at Toe

The toe of the recoil pad contacts the shooter's shoulder at an angle. One of the problems in making a smooth gun mount is that shotgun recoil pads often run straight up and down, while the shoulder pocket they are supposed to fit into is at a slight angle or is curved gently. The angle increases on a shooter with a heavy chest, and this person can benefit from an angled recoil pad.

## Cast-On/Off

Cast-off is a slight lateral bend in the buttstock that moves the comb away from the shooter's face and positions the recoil pad farther out on the shoulder. Cast-on is the reverse. The primary purpose of either measurement is to serve as a "windage adjustment" for the rear sight (your eye) and position the shooter's eye in perfect alignment with the center of the rib. If the eye is not perfectly centered on the rib, your patterns can impact to one side or the other of your aiming point.

Many English and European guns have some cast-off built in, on the theory that the shooter's eye should be moved into the comb to center the rib. American factory-made guns do not feature this.

# Hands-On

Once you understand stock measurements and what information they give you, Michael Murphy says, it is time to pick up and fit your shotgun. This is not a process like the aforementioned shoe buying. No one can just look at you and tell you what is right for you, Murphy says. Fitting is a process whereby an experienced person walks you through numerous possibilities and combinations, gradually, with your active participation, arriving at the right balance of variables that put you precisely on target. It is a matter of balancing effective shooting form with comfort.

Murphy, who works with shooters who travel to his home in Kansas and makes appointments during his travels to competitions around the U.S., says proper fitting takes a minimum of several hours. "If you think this can be done in half-an-hour, you're wrong," he says. "I can give you some tips in half an hour, but to work with your gun or guns and a try-gun can take a while, maybe all afternoon if you have a competition gun and a hunting gun or a semi-auto and an over/under. We will normally fire a lot of shells, so I recommend that students wear a light, comfortable pair of gloves to protect them from hot barrels and chafing from the checkering on the stock.

"Of course, you will also need to wear ear protection and shooting glasses, just like you would at the shooting range. I don't recommend muff-type hearing protectors though, certainly not the style with the hard plastic outer shell because your shotgun can knock against them when you're trying to make a good mount and that's pretty distracting. And of course, you have to have shooting glasses because at the distance we typically shoot the pattern plate, 16 yards, shot can come bouncing straight back at you almost as fast as it went forward.

"The problem with a quick fitting is that it can change if you change clothes; a thicker or thinner vest and shirt for example, can change your point of aim and impact. (Having two different sizes of buttpads or an adjustable butt pad can help here.) It can even change if you are having a bad day and grimace rather than smile. Remember that it just takes a millimeter or two at the point of the angle to change the impact point by three or four inches at distances between 20 and 25 yards.

"I find that experienced shooters who want to reach the next level and come to me for tips and fitting have often spent a lifetime adapting themselves to their guns. You have a fitting so that you can adjust the gun so that it conforms to you."

When a shooter makes an appointment with Murphy, he gets the stock roughly adjusted and then stands in front of the muzzle while the shooter mounts the gun to make finer adjustments. "What I am doing," he says, "is watching the shooter shoulder the gun and looking right into his pupil as he looks down the rib. You get the gun very close to 'on' in this manner, but the real final test is to watch the shooter break targets, and we finish the tuning from there."

# Some Do-It-Yourself

Adjustable combs and recoil pads are not gimmicks. Their advantage is that they not only make it very easy for you to fit a gun yourself, but they also allow you to alter fit to meet existing conditions.

There are times when having the ability to quickly adjust a stock can be advantageous. A trap shooter, for example, shooting into a strong wind knows it will make the target rise more quickly. Increasing the comb height slightly will raise the point of impact to compensate for the wind without the shooter having to alter his hold. In short, adjustable stocks give the shotgunner the same degree of control that finely adjustable sights give riflemen and handgunners.

The range of comb movement is considerable on an adjustable stock. In fact, most shooters should be able to get all the windage and elevation adjustment they require from one, with no further stock work. Combine that with an adjustable recoil pad and you have a wide range of adjustment that will allow you to fit your gun to virtually any normal dimension or shotgunning challenge.

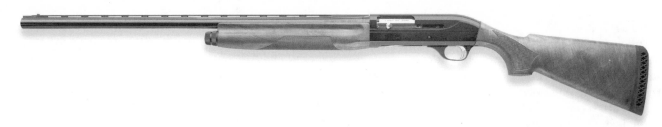

Semi-auto shotguns have a reputation for softer shooting than an over/under, but the typical automatic shell ejection feature can be problematic for a left-hander or if a sporting clays station is beside a tree. Pump shotguns eject below or out the side of the receiver; over/unders eject straight behind the barrels when they are opened, unless they are fitted with hand extractors – preferred by reloaders. For a left-hand shooter the typical semi-auto, built for right-handers, spits out a shell near your face. Look for a left-hand semi-auto like this Benelli Montefeltro in 12- or 20-gauge. It will shoot 2¾- or 3-inch shells comfortably.

## Stock Adjustment

One of the biggest problems with stocks made in the U.S. today is that the comb of the stock is high and you occasionally see shooters try to scrunch down into these stocks to get their eyes directly on target. While at first you may think a lot of wood has to be removed to correct this, you can lightly sand this area down by hand and keep checking for fit until it is comfortable to shoot. A telltale sign that the comb is too high is when the stock smacks you on the cheekbone when you shoot.

If you feel you need to shorten your stock, never cut off more than a quarter of an inch at a time before putting everything back together and checking for fit. This may take more time to get to that perfect fit, but it is better than trying to lengthen a stock after you cut it too short.

To properly cut a stock to keep it from splintering is quite simple, but requires a careful approach:

1. Make a pencil mark around the stock where you want to cut it.

2. Take a sharp utility knife and cut into the wood all the way around your stock, on your pencil mark.

3. Using a saw of fine kerf (small teeth set close together), cut the stock at the edge of where you cut with the utility knife. This method produces a clean cut with no splinters.

There is a quick and easy way, however, to lengthen your stock. While it does not give you the most appealing look, you can buy black and white plastic butt plate spacers and add these ahead of the butt plate or recoil pad. If you still need more length, try adding a slip-on recoil pad.

It sometimes does not take much in the way of stock adjustment to get a gun to shoot where you look. The cure is often simple. I have a Franchi Prestige 12-gauge on which I slightly lengthened the stock by simply changing the recoil pad. The Franchi is a sloping-comb field gun. Lengthening the stock moved my face down the comb a bit, which caused the gun to

shoot slightly low. An adjustable and detachable cheek-piece from Meadow Industries quickly corrected that. The pad attaches with Velcro strips and it raised the comb enough to return the gun to a 50/50 shooter (half the pattern above and half below the bead). The pad comes with inserts that can be quickly installed to raise the shot pattern in about eight-inch increments at 40 yards. This pad did not add any cast, so the lateral impact of the pattern remained the same. These pads are a simple way to make minor corrections, and there are a number of different models available.

## Pistol Grip Fit

Pistol grip fit is something that is not taken into consideration by manufacturers. This part of the stock should fit the shooter. If you have small hands, you will probably be better off with a narrow grip that lets you lock onto it. If you have a hand like a bear paw, you will need a thicker grip. A palm swell can also be a help. The only drawback is that if it is not in the proper position—so that it falls right into the perfect pocket of your hand—it can be a detriment.

Another easily overlooked item about a palm swell is a place for the meat of your thumb to rest comfortably. Some meticulous shooters hollow out a little spot for that, kind of 'melt' the thumb into the pistol grip.

Your pistol grip should feel good. When you slip your hand onto it, it should be like putting on a fine old glove.

## Master Eye

Almost everybody has one eye that is dominant. The dominant eye often overpowers the other eye in vision decisions. If you are a right-hander and have a right dominant eye, you have a good situation. Left-handers with a left dominant eye are equally fortunate. If you happen to have a dominant eye on the opposite side of your body from your dominant hand however, you can have problems with hand-eye coordination. The eye on the other side of your body is doing the looking, while the eye you have lined up on the rib is getting short-changed. Your gun will not shoot where you are looking.

Here is a quick test to see which eye is your master eye. With both eyes open, point your finger at a defined spot on a wall. Now close your left eye. If the finger stays on target, your right eye is dominant. If the finger moves off target when you close your left eye, but stays on target when you close your right eye, the left eye is dominant.

Some right-handed people with a strongly left-dominant eye (or vice versa) simply cannot shoot a shotgun from their normal side. In the long run, the best solution is to learn to shoot from the same side as your dominant eye. Sometimes that does not work, though. For these shooters, the solution is a strange looking contraption called a crossover stock. It features an extreme bend in the stock that, for a right-hander, will put the left eye in exact alignment with the barrel when you shoulder the stock to the right side. These are available from a number of stockmakers.

## Recoil Control

Once a gun is sighted-in, there are still a few things that can be done to fit it more comfortably to you. One area is controlling recoil.

According to Newton's Third Law, for every action there is an opposite and equal reaction. No one has yet repealed that law, but researchers have found some interesting ways to amend it.

Shotguns kick. Some kick more than others and that is not always dependent upon the gauge of the gun. I have seen some 20-gauge shotguns belt shooters harder than some 12s, and a few 28-gauges that would draw blood from the cheek.

Proper shotgun fit aids immensely in reducing felt recoil by evenly distributing the recoil forces to those areas most capable of handling them. A correctly shaped comb (especially a padded model) will further soften the blow. Too many shotguns seem to have combs designed to slice butter instead of cushion recoil. I have shot some of these and, although I did not feel pain at the time, they sliced my cheek open as effectively as a razor.

Another way to reduce recoil is to add weight to the gun, and many gunsmiths do just that. A 12-gauge competition gun in the nine- to 10-pound range has little recoil with normal target loads. Many kick less than 20-gauge guns in the 6 ½- to seven-pound range. Weight added to the barrel helps keep the muzzle down on recoil and prevents cheek slap. If barrel weights make the gun too muzzle-heavy, adding some weight inside the buttstock will restore the balance.

Another way to cut your punishment is to shoot a semi-auto. They can be set up with the same exact stock fit as any other shotgun and their gas systems usually make them noticeably softer to shoot.

You can add a recoil reduction device to almost any gun. There are plenty of these on the market. These are essentially shock-absorbers that use a spring-loaded, air/oil or special synthetic elastic polymer (such as "sorbothane") cushion to slow the recoil impulse and turn it into a gentle push instead of a shove. They all add weight to the gun and some smiths will tell you that the additional weight is what really does the job. Others will tell you they work just as they are advertised. Regardless of the reason, they do work.

Porting your barrel(s) is supposed to help cut recoil. I have a ported gun, and it does cut muzzle jump slightly (an asset on a quick second shot), but does not seem to otherwise reduce recoil with target-level loads. I also use this gun for ducks however, and the recoil reduction with stouter loads is noticeable.

Fit a gun properly, add whatever recoil reduction your gunsmith recommends, and you will likely find that shooting is not nearly as punishing as it used to be. If you enjoy the sport, you owe it to yourself to make it fun!

## Your Trigger

It is commonly accepted that shotgun triggers are stiff, gritty, and something no rifleman would tolerate. That is okay though, because you do not "squeeze" a shotgun trigger. You "slap" the trigger on a scattergun. Therefore, it does not make any difference if they are miserable.

I do not accept that reasoning.

If you shoot a heavy eight-pound, squishy trigger,

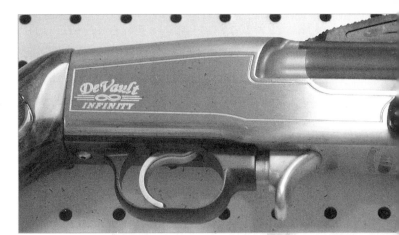

**Some alterations to a shotgun's trigger result in better shooting options: adjustability, different styles of trigger "shoe" for a different trigger feel. Others are strictly cosmetic, such as the gold plating found on many high end shotguns.**

think about having a good gunsmith tune it to a crisp 3 ½- to four-pound break. Your scores will soar! A good shotgun deserves a good trigger. The first time you try a good one on a shotgun, you will agree. There have been past (and current) champions that shot custom triggers in the one-pound range. If they were not an asset, do you think they would have used them?

A very few shooters, especially those afflicted with "trap-shooter's flinch" or "target panic" might even need to get more radical than that.

You most commonly see flinch in trap, but it can affect any shooter (competitor or hunter). It is the inability of the shooter to pull the trigger. It is not a physical inability, but a mental one. You just cannot make your finger trigger the round.

Just what is "trapshooter's flinch?" Coaches believe it is a response by the body to the cumulative effects of recoil. The body just gets tired of taking the pounding and the subconscious says, "That's it, I'm not pulling that trigger again!" The brain short-circuits the trigger finger. Your subconscious has a lot of authority in those areas!

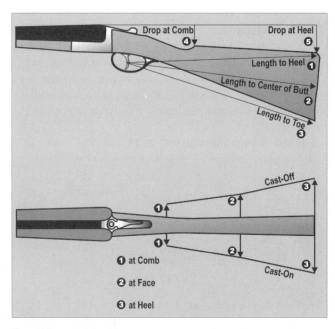

### Gun Measurements
**This diagram gives you the basic jargon of gun fitting. Not every person is built on the same physical frame, but manufacturers who sell to the general public must make "one size fits all" judgments based on average sizes. Fortunately, it is relatively easy to change some of your gun's specifications to conform to your body type and for the final minutiae of fitting, specialists are available to help.**

Once this happens to a shooter, he or she is in big trouble. One remedy is to just stop shooting for a while and let the subconscious get over its temper tantrum. Sometimes that works, just like laying off shooting in the middle of a slump will sometimes help. Other times it will not, and one item that has proven to help shooters in this situation is a "release trigger."

A release trigger works in reverse of a conventional trigger: pulling the trigger sets it, releasing the trigger fires the gun. On double guns, they can be set up to function as a "release-pull" trigger, pull to set, release to fire the first barrel, pull to fire the second. At least one Olympic trapshooter has used this in the games because he felt it was the fastest way to get off two shots.

Many gunsmiths will perform this work, but release triggers do have some controversy surrounding them. This is one of those subjects that few shooters seem to have a middle-of-the-road opinion on. You either love them or hate them.

I fall into a different group. I have played with them and personally do not like them, but if I had to use one I am certain I could. They have extended the shooting careers of a number of competitors that would otherwise have had to quit.

That said, "there oughta be a law" that every gun equipped with a release trigger of any configuration be so marked on the gun's buttstock in one-inch neon fluorescent letters. Release triggers are not inherently dangerous—not as long as the shooter remembers what he has and understands how it works. These triggers can be dangerous however, if a shooter picks up the gun without realizing it has a release trigger.

You load a round, call for the bird, pull the trigger and nothing happens. You subconsciously think, "Damn! I've got a misfire." Then you release the trigger and the gun fires! You have to hope that safe gun-handling doctrine has you pointing it down-range when you release. Nevertheless, it is most disconcerting and has the potential to be disastrous.

I am well aware that range courtesy and common sense would preclude a shooter from picking up and firing a gun that is not his. I am also aware that mistakes happen. Release trigger guns should be marked.

Other than that, release triggers are a matter of personal preference and can help some shooters. For that matter, so is shotgun fitting, on the whole, and one reason why it is worth the time and trouble. Remember to just turn your gun into your finger and smoothly point. It is not that hard to do.

# CHAPTER 25

# GETTING THE MOST OUT OF YOUR SHOTGUN

"High-performance shotgun" is a term that can mean different things to different shooters. Some will define it as how smoothly and quickly the gun gets on fast-flushing grouse. Others will consider it an indication of how well it hits with heavy steel shot loads on a distant goose or even how "hard" it smokes/vaporizes clay targets.

Oklahoma's Larry Nailon, president of Clearview Products gunsmiths in Oklahoma City, however, has a different and much more succinct definition. Although his study of recoil has now advanced far beyond the basics, he has offered these thoughts on getting to the first plateau of high performance shooting.

"When we speak about a high-performance shotgun," he explains, "what we are talking about is a gun that delivers the best down-range performance regardless of the load or distance. It is the combination of gun and load that delivers the maximum number of pellets in the load to the point of impact while simultaneously producing the largest useful pattern that has no gaps or holes a bird or clay target could slip through.

High performance is down-range performance. "To achieve that," Nailon says, "you must get every pellet, or as many as is humanly possible, out of the shell, through the bore and choke, and out the gun in a perfectly smooth, round and undeformed condition. Round pellets fly true and arrive at the target together. Pellets that have been partially flattened or deformed veer off course and even lag behind the main shot charge. Sometimes, they will be far enough away from or behind the main charge to be of absolutely no use. You may as well not even have fired them for all the good they will do you on that shot."

According to Nailon, it does not really matter how many pellets you start with in the load. "What counts is how well you take care of what you start with," Nailon says. "When we build a high-performance shotgun barrel, our goal is to get as many pellets out of the gun in as undeformed a condition as possible."

Nailon knows a thing or two about tweaking a shotgun barrel for improved performance. As the brains behind Clearview, he has earned a reputation among top-notch competitive shooters in every shotgun game

for his custom barrel and choke work; yet, Nailon does not consider what he does to be new or earthshaking.

## Critical Areas

"There are a number of modifications one can make to a shotgun barrel," he says, "that will result in a certain degree of performance enhancement. All I do is combine these proven enhancers into a total barrel work-over. Each of these modifications complements the others and results in a much greater increase in performance than you would get if you only opted for one or two of them." The whole, then, is definitely more than the sum of the parts.

Nailon is concerned with four key areas when he begins working with a barrel: chamber, forcing cone, bore and choke. Modifications to any one of them can improve performance. However, Nailon refines all four areas to harmoniously provide maximum performance. Here is his prescription for "tweaking" a barrel.

### Chamber

Modern mass-production methods work because of manufacturing tolerances. As a result, measurements need only be "within spec." It is possible, although not common, to get a factory shotgun chamber having incorrect dimensions.

With the sideplates and stock removed, the over/under is exposed as a relatively simple instrument. This cutaway from a Weatherby Athena clearly shows the sear-block safety design, the gold-plated single, selective inertia trigger and the automatic ejectors in place on the barrels. When it comes to a fine shotgun, "cleanliness is indeed next to godliness."

Most commonly, the chamber is shorter than required. The problem with a short chamber is that it may not allow the crimp to unfold fully without protruding into the forcing cone. If this happens, the wad and shot charge are restricted in their ability to exit the shell, and that occurs at the precise moment that maximum chamber pressure is reached. This causes shot pellets to deform and increases chamber pressure and recoil.

"Checking chamber dimensions is a standard procedure for us," Nailon notes. "I also like to increase the length of the chamber to .060-inch longer than normal, especially if the shooter is a reloader. As a shell is reloaded and fired it tends to stretch just a bit, not unlike a brass cartridge case, and a slightly longer chamber becomes an asset."

Excessively long chambers, however, are not a benefit.

"We have found," he explains, "that while 2 ¾-inch shells will function perfectly in a three-inch chamber, the down-range performance of the load can suffer. The shot column and wad has an extra ¼-inch run at its highest pressure point before it enters the forcing cone, and side pressure on the pellets at this point tends to beat up the pellets more than if they were fired in a chamber of the proper length for the shell."

### Forcing Cone

Directly ahead of the chamber is the forcing cone and, as its name implies, it acts as a funnel to guide the wad and shot charge from the chamber to the bore. The normal length of most factory forcing cones is between ½- and ⅝-inch. Nailon does not like that either.

"The length of a shot column is about one inch inside a light 12-gauge load and over 1 ½ inches in a heavy load," he explains. As the pellets at the rear of the load are rammed into the upper pellets, outward pressure is tremendous. This is highest at the moment the shot charge moves from the chamber to the forcing cone. Since the shot column is moving through a constricting area (the forcing cone) that is only about half the length of the shot column, with as much as 10,000 psi pressure behind it, it's pretty apparent that a significant number of pellets are being deformed before they even get into the barrel."

Nailon's solution is to lengthen the forcing cone.

"I feel a cone of 1 ½ inches is the minimum," he states. "My own patterning tests with our moving patterning board, where precise target speeds can be set and shot strings of up to 16-feet in length can be accurately measured, indicates that even a forcing cone length of over 2 ½ inches will help, not hurt."

Forcing cone lengthening is a custom technique that some major shotgun makers are incorporating into their better grades of guns, often those intended for

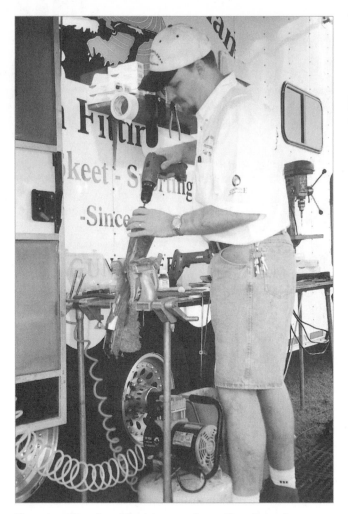

If you are handy with shims and recoil pads and resetting trigger positions (where possible), you could possibly fit the stock to your shooting dimensions yourself. Otherwise, you may need an experienced gunsmith, because the idea of proper fit is that your dominant eye lines up with the centerline of the rib precisely, every time you bring the stock to your cheek.

trap, skeet and sporting clays shooters.

"The standard short forcing cone can be an asset if one uses the older fiber wad shells," Nailon claims, "but with modern one-piece plastic wads, this is obsolete. All a short forcing cone does here is raise pressure, increase recoil and deform shot."

Some of the biggest offenders in the short, tight forcing cone area are the low- and mid-priced Italian and Spanish imports, because many shooters in their original market area still rely on fiber wad shells. European shotshell manufacturers usually specify whether the wad used in a particular shell class is plastic or fiber (or "fibre," as Britain's Eley Hawk specifies for its shells in its printed catalog and on its Internet site at www.eley-hawkltd.com).

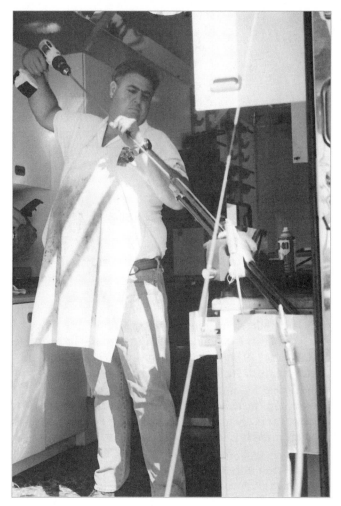

**Joe Morales, president of Rhino stainless chokes, works on a barrel in his traveling shop. "The purpose of porting is to cause suction on the wad," he says, "pulling it away from the shot stream before it collides with the individual pellets to cause 'flyers' in your pattern. A byproduct of ported, extended chokes is that they further reduce recoil and muzzle jump."**

## Bore

Larry Nailon is a big believer in back-bored barrels, the process of deliberately boring the barrel out to a larger diameter than is industry standard for that particular gauge. To understand why that is so, an understanding of choke is required.

The term "choke" is used to describe two dissimilar, but related factors: how the gun patterns and the constriction at the muzzle of the gun.

The first definition is commonly understood. A gun that patterns 70 percent is considered to have a Full choke. A 60-percent pattern is Modified, while 50 percent is Improved Cylinder. A Cylinder choke runs about 40 percent. A Skeet choke is very close to Improved Cylinder in performance. In terms of

measurement, a Skeet choke is intended to throw a 30-inch pattern at 25 yards.

The second definition is much less properly understood.

The actual muzzle constriction we refer to as "choke" is not completely dependent upon just the constriction at the muzzle. Actual choke achieved is the relationship between the constriction in the choke itself and the inside diameter of the barrel.

Barrel constriction is measured in thousandths of an inch. The British often refer to this as points of choke. For example, a measured constriction of .005-inch could be referred to as "five points of choke." A constriction of .019-inch would be nineteen points.

The degree of constriction required to produce different chokes varies from gauge to gauge. With the 12-gauge, for example, no constriction gives Cylinder choke, .005-inch produces Skeet 1; .009 is Improved Cylinder; .012 equals Skeet 2; and so on. Extra-Full and Super-Full chokes run from .045- to .089-inch.

From the above it might seem that we could grab a choke tube marked Modified, screw it into our 12-gauge and get a 60-percent pattern. Maybe, maybe not.

If our 12-gauge has a bore diameter of .729-inch, and if we have a choke tube marked Modified, that has an internal diameter of .710-inch, then we do have 19 points of constriction between the two and will get a Modified pattern, assuming the load is accurate and well packed. Suppose, however, that the actual diameter of the barrel is .745-inch. If we insert our .710-inch tube, our real constriction is now .035-inch, or 35 points! Regardless of what is marked on the choke tube, we have a Full choke. Shot charges cannot read, they can only respond.

If our 12-gauge barrel has a bore diameter of .720-inch, then our modified, .710-inch tube is actually giving us only .010-inch constriction, 10 points, or about Improved cylinder.

This should not sound farfetched. Every shotgunsmith I have ever talked to tells me it is common to measure factory barrels that are above or below standard bore diameter. In fact, they may vary from .710- to .750-inch in guns coming off the same factory production line.

That in itself does not explain why Nailon favors back-boring barrels. This however, will: "The degree of pattern control you exercise is dependent upon the inside diameter of both the barrel and the choke tube," he says. "If a 12-gauge barrel has an inside diameter of .725 and you put a .715-inch tube in it, you have an Improved Cylinder choke. If you have a barrel with an inside diameter of .750 and you want to install an Improved Cylinder choke, all you need to do is put in

Your length of pull is not right if you cannot settle on a spot for your cheek, if your trigger-arm feels cramped, or if your eye seems too close to the receiver. An aftermarket recoil pad such as the Remington R3 (pictured) can help you get the fit just right for a secure four-point hold.

If you know the precise diameter of your barrel, you should be able to develop an exact pattern with aftermarket choke tubes.

a tube with an inside diameter of .740-inch. "You have the same degree of constriction with either," he continues, "and you'll get the same pattern control. However, with a back-bored barrel, you get it with a bigger hole in the muzzle for the shot to go through. Once the shot pellets enter the choke constriction, they can do one of two things if they are lead: they can either reposition themselves (one pellet moving ahead of or behind another) or they can deform. With a back-bored barrel and larger choke tube in use, the pellets have more room to reposition and fewer are deformed."

With steel shot, especially the larger sizes, the situation changes. Pellets can either reposition, or damage the choke! Back-boring is even more important to waterfowl hunters than to lead-shot users.

How much to over-bore depends on the individual barrel. Nailon feels most will take between .010- and .015-inch without difficulty. Going over .015-inch can produce a slight velocity loss, but often results in larger useful patterns. Nailon has one 12-gauge back-bored to .750-inch (.021-inch over industry standard) and reports that one-ounce loads lack the pellets to fill the pattern, but that the gun shoots marvelously with 1 ⅛-ounce loads.

An additional advantage to back-boring is that Nailon and the customer now know precisely what that barrel's inside diameter is and that it is uniform from chamber to muzzle without high spots. Back-boring will also reduce recoil to some extent.

One additional step Nailon takes on the bore is to burnish it. "If the bore isn't perfectly mirror smooth," he has found, "it tends to accumulate fouling, especially plastic fouling from the wad, at a much higher rate. This fouling acts to increase friction as successive wads and shot charges move through the barrel, decreasing velocity and increasing recoil. In extreme cases it can actually impede the performance of the wad and cause pellet deformation."

Most manufacturers only finish a bore to "near smoothness." Complete polishing is a time-consuming job, and time is money in mass production or at a custom shop. Even if the bore is chrome-lined, that is no guarantee it is smooth. Chrome is only as smooth as the surface over which it was applied, and if the bore is not polished mirror-smooth before the plating you still have a rough bore.

Nailon polishes his bores with a set of specially designed hones running down to an ultra-fine #800 grit. If you are one of those smart shotgunners who routinely cleans his barrel with a brush wrapped in 0000 steel wool—the best way to remove plastic fouling left behind by solvents and brushes—you are doing a little burnishing every time you clean the gun. Nailon's method is just a lot quicker.

### Choke

Once Nailon has tweaked the bore this far, all that remains are the choke tubes. Once again, he disagrees with most manufacturers.

"Once the pellets enter the choke constriction they can again either reposition or deform," he explains. "My goal is to give them the maximum opportunity to reposition before they begin to deform.

"Most factory choke tubes," he continues, "are about 1 ½ inches long. That requires the shot to reposition within a limited amount of space. If you double the length of the choke tube, you double the time and distance they have to do that. All other factors being equal, longer choke tubes deform less shot and that is our ultimate goal with custom barrel work."

Nailon combines a three-inch tube length with an inner taper that combines a cone with parallel surfaces, instead of the more commonly seen cone style that places the maximum constriction at one extremely short point The addition of the parallel surfaces is a further aid in allowing the shot to reposition.

Making the longer, custom choke tubes is considerably more difficult than making factory-length tubes. It is more time-consuming and expensive because, as a machinist's rule of thumb, you cannot hold precise tolerances in high-speed production when boring more than twice the length of your diameter. To make his tubes, Nailon has to make a series of precise, fine cuts instead of getting it all done in one pass.

What the customer receives is a set of custom-made choke tubes sized precisely to the diameter of the gun's barrel. Nailon normally provides these in .005-inch increments, which assures a precise degree of pattern control. In past few years, he has cut it even finer than that.

"We find that a number of competitive shooters, especially sporting clays gunners, want to go to half-step chokes to increase their ability to really fine-tune their patterns for whatever conditions exist in their area," he notes. "We offer tubes in these half-step increments (i.e., .002-inch, 007-inch, etc.), and they really do make a difference. I have been shooting a .002-inch tube for close-range shots recently, and it does some amazing things. You'd be surprised the difference a simple .002-inch constriction can make over a straight cylinder bore. That small difference, in the more open chokes, makes a much bigger change in pattern control than the same .002-inch difference does in the tighter chokes."

If a shooter does not want to go to the expense of a full-blown barrel make-over, he can still benefit from custom-fitted choke tubes.

Nailon will make choke tubes in whatever reasonable incremental series a shooter requests, in any one of the various popular thread systems. This does, however, require that the shooter either have the barrel inside diameter measurements done by a competent gunsmith on a local level and supply them to Nailon, or simply send his barrel to Nailon, who would prefer to take those critical measurements himself

## Aftermarket Tubes

Another alternative to improved pattern control, albeit less effective, is for a shooter to simply add aftermarket choke tubes to his existing selection. However, factory-offered choke tubes are often rather limited in scope. Generally, you can get Skeet 1, Improved Cylinder, Modified, Full and, sometimes, Extra-Full.

If you are not satisfied with the pattern control your choke selection allows you to achieve, then adding tubes in Skeet 2, Cylinder, Improved Modified or Extra-Full may help correct the situation. If your actual barrel inside diameter is not .729-inch and, for example, your Modified tube is actually producing Improved Cylinder or Full patterns, going to some of the intermediate constrictions can help put those patterns back to where you want them.

There is, however, a pitfall with this approach if done incorrectly.

"There are a number of different choke tube systems on the market," explains Nailon. "More than one gun manufacturer may use the same system. For example, the Win-Choke system threads will fit a number of guns besides those that bear the Winchester brand. When you are talking about different choke tube systems, you are basically talking about the thread pattern they use and the length of the choke tube itself.

"Just because a Win-Choke may screw into the barrel of your gun," he continues, "does not necessarily mean the fit is exact. If the barrel diameter is not properly matched to the choke tube, you will not get the pattern you expect. You can also have a problem with the fit at the base of the choke. A barrel will expand slightly upon firing. That expansion can range from about .002-inch to almost .010-inch. To accommodate this, there is a small step at the rear of the choke that allows for the expansion and helps guide the wad from

Getting the most out of your gun means performance and also emotional satisfaction. Salvatore "Sal" Echel, a New York City "beat cop", had his Beretta 391 semi-auto – stock and forearm – painted with a wrap-around American flag by AnglePort after 9/11/01.

the barrel into the choke. In effect, it acts almost like the forcing cone does at the chamber.

"If the barrel diameter varies too much from the diameter of the rear of the choke, then you get a ridge that the wad can hang up on. If that ridge is large enough, the wad can jam, the pressure will build, and you'll blow the choke tube out the end of the barrel. That's expensive to repair. Shuffling choke tubes around just because they have the same thread system and will fit into the gun is not a good idea," Nailon feels.

In a best-case scenario, you will not get the down-range performance you expect. In a worst-case scenario, you may seriously damage the barrel.

This, of course, does not mean that aftermarket choke tubes are dangerous, just that they can be, even if the thread systems are the same and the chart says they will interchange. (For that reason, we are not going to include a chart showing the compatibility of the various systems. Though there are some systems that will truly interchange, the majority of them are just different enough that problems can arise, even if the tube seems to fit the gun perfectly.)

When you purchase aftermarket choke tubes—and there is absolutely nothing wrong with that—you will do yourself a favor if you tell the supplier precisely what the make and model of your gun is; better yet, give him the barrel inside diameter measurements, regardless of what the "chart" says your gun will take.

If your gun is not threaded to accept interchangeable choke tubes, then the best thing you can do for it is to send the barrel off and have them fitted. This is not a complex operation in a competent custom shop. A number of aftermarket companies do an outstanding job in this area and it is not just limited to 12-gauge guns. Any gauge can be adapted to the system.

The point is this: If your favorite smoothbore is not presently fitted to accept interchangeable tubes, you are wasting over half the gun's potential, regardless of gauge.

Interchangeable tubes can greatly increase your gun's performance, and there are no real mysteries to their use.

## Tube Installation

One key is in the installation of the tube. It should be fully inserted into the gun, completely bottomed out in the threads, hand-tight and not over-torqued. If a tube begins to back out from the threads even slightly, there is a very real risk of gun damage.

It is an excellent idea to check the snugness of your tubes before any shooting session.

Tubes should never be installed in the barrel without lubrication on the tube threads. Standard gun-grade or machine oil is not the proper lubrication because it provides no support for the threads. Far better choices are Never-Seez, Lubriplate or any of the many commercial choke tube tubes incorporating these ingredients. Improper lubrication is one of the biggest problems with interchangeable tubes. If you forget the tube, or use one that is inadequate, you may not be able to remove the tube from the barrel without the services of a gunsmith.

Barrels threaded for interchangeable tubes should never be fired without a tube in place. This is just about guaranteed to damage the threads and leave you with another costly repair bill.

It is also not a good idea to leave a choke tube in the barrel indefinitely, even with the best tube and lube. Even if you do not use a gun frequently, at least one time a year, pull out the tube, clean it, re-lube it and stick it back in. If you forget about periodic maintenance, the tube may find a permanent home in that particular barrel.

It is worth pointing out that interchangeable choke tubes, lengthened forcing cones, back-boring and long choke tubes are not new developments. Custom gunsmiths have been doing them for more than 30 years—far longer if you read the antique literature from Europe and China. What should be pointed out is that major gunmakers often include interchangeable tubes as standard equipment and most offer longer choke tubes, lengthened forcing cones and long chokes on their top-of-the-line competition guns.

You should never fire a shotgun without its replaceable chokes securely screwed into the barrels. Even soft or chilled lead shot can damage delicate choke threading inside a barrel. Before you load, check to be sure the chokes are secure, because over the course of a shoot, they can loosen.

# CHAPTER 26
# A PRIMER IN CHOKE TUBES

According to George Trulock, president of Trulock Chokes (www.trulockchokes.com), a choke is "simply a tapered constriction of the gun barrel's bore at the muzzle end. The exit end of the choke is smaller by some dimension than the actual bore of the barrel. This difference is the amount of constriction. For example, if the bore of the barrel is .730 inch and the exit diameter of the choke is .710 inch, you have a constriction of .020 inch."

George and his crew have dealt with practically every shotgun made in the past half century, and he says that the amount of constriction for a given type choke—Improved Cylinder or Full, for instance—varies between manufacturers. "As a general rule for standard chokes," he says, "the total range will be between .000 and .045 in thousandths of an inch. The length of the choke varies also, between 1 ½ and four inches, and this affects your shot pattern almost as much as the type choke you are using."

Chokes are grouped in three general types:

- **Fixed:** These are integral parts of the barrel and cannot be readily changed, except by a gunsmith. Any alteration is considered permanent.
- **Interchangeable:** Although these can be of the externally attached "screw-on" style or the internal "screw-in" recessed in the barrel, most are of the latter type. To change the degree of constriction, you simply remove and replace with a choke of a different diameter.
- **Adjustable:** This style choke—now, in practice, quite rare—is adjustable throughout the entire range of constrictions by turning a sleeve, which collapses or expands, thus changing the exit diameter.

The internal design of choke tubes can also be broken down into three main groups:

- **Conical Parallel:** These chokes have a cone that blends into a parallel section at the muzzle. This helps to stabilize a shot charge as it leaves the choke and the gun.
- **Straight Conical:** This type choke has a cone only. Where the cone stops is the point where the shot exits the choke and the gun.
- **Wad Retarding:** These chokes do not make use of constriction as either of the above design, instead using machined bumps or projections to alter the shot pattern.

## Shotgun Patterns

George Trulock says that patterns are normally expressed as a percentage, such as 50 percent or 70 percent and so on. This is a commonly accepted method for comparing pattern density. "A 50 percent pattern means that half of the pellets in the shell will strike inside a circle 30-inches in diameter at 40 yards," George says. "So, to find the percentage of any given load, divide the number of hits inside the circle by the total number of pellets contained in the shell. You can obtain the approximate number of pellets any given load will have from a shotshell reloading book or you can actually cut open a couple shells and count them."

Typically, pattern testing is done at 40 yards. Cylinder

New for 2004, Trulock's Ti (Titanium) Chokes are approximately ⅓ lighter than comparable steel chokes. They are extended, knurled and notched and each choke has a unique color, which makes them easy to identify. In addition, the heads are marked with the degree of choke and the body is marked with the exit diameter in thousandths of an inch. George Trulock, president of Trulock Chokes, says these are "perfect for long-barreled sporting clays guns." Trulock chokes come with a lifetime warranty.

Because steel is much harder than lead, make sure that any choke you buy is certified to accept steel shot without deforming. Damage to the choke can throw your pattern into disarray and eventually cause barrel damage.

Browning's Midas Grade Extended Tubes are designed for clay targets. Manufactured from stainless steel, they are finished with black oxide. Extended tubes feature easy installation and removal without a wrench. Browning says its "minimum gap geometry plus high-resolution 'RMS' finish reduce buildup of plastics in the shotgun bore." Available in all gauges for $49 or less each at your favorite retailer.

and Skeet 1 chokes in all gauges, however, and the 410-bore (all chokes for this small bore gun) are measured at 25 yards. The former because they are very open, spreading shot and the latter because they lack the power at distance required for good 40-yard patterning.

According to George, the purpose for patterning a shotgun is to allow you to select a choke that will throw a pattern that is as large as possible without having the pellets so far apart that the target can escape multiple hits. "For shooting both game and clay targets," he says, "you want a pattern that is perfectly even in pellet distribution over the 30-inch circle. Having said that, and after looking at thousands of patterns over a span of 25 years, I could count on my fingers the number of shots I would call perfect—and if these were measured with scientific accuracy, some of them would not have qualified. In this instance however, 'close' is good enough." (Two exceptions would be buckshot and turkey patterns, because with these you want a tight center cluster of pellets.)

George believes that the only consistency from gun to gun is that very few things are consistent. "Identical guns with the same degree of choke and using the same shell may not pattern the same," he says. "The same load between various brands of shells can pattern differently. Patterns can change when you change from hard to soft or chilled shot. Patterns can change when anything inside the shell changes: a different wad, a different powder or primer. What I am trying to get across is that when you change anything—brands, shot size or components—you need to check the pattern as it could have changed, sometimes by a surprising amount."

Once you find a choke and shell combination that gives you the pattern and results you want, it should remain reasonably consistent as long as nothing else is changed. For instance, if the manufacturer switches powder types, your patterns will probably change. George says that he, personally, is satisfied as long as the percentage of change is plus or minus five percent.

The associated chart shows the relationship between degree of choke, the percentage and constriction based on lead shot. These percentages are a guide only. What you actually want is a pattern that is dense enough to insure multiple hits on your target at the distance you normally shoot. You want to vaporize a bird, not have to argue about it later!

This chart should be used as a starting point only, and it is important to note that percentages vary between "experts." So select a choke and pattern it your way, then change chokes or loads as needed to get the pattern you want. When someone comes along and says "That's wrong—your Modified should score a 67 percentage in the 30-inch circle" just give them the thousand-yard stare and keep on keeping on, unless what you are doing is not working. Then be strong enough to change.

While there are other variables, for all practical purposes chokes will determine the density of the shot pattern. "I look at density from two different ways," George says. "The first is the pattern percentage. This is

## Lead Shot Choke Chart

| Name | Constriction (in inches) | Percent (at 40 yards) |
| --- | --- | --- |
| Cylinder | .000 | 40 (70 at 25 yards) |
| Skeet 1 | .005 | 45 (75 at 25 yards) |
| Improved Cylinder | .010 | 50 |
| Skeet 2 (Light Modified) | .015 | 55 |
| Modified | .020 | 60 |
| Improved Modified | .025 | 65 |
| Full | .030 | 70 |
| Extra Full | .040 | 73 |
| Turkey | .045+ | 75 |

simply a figure telling you how many pellets out of the total number of pellets that were fired at the target hit inside a 30-inch circle. For example, if 250 pellets are in a shell and 200 land inside the circle, divide 200 by 250 and you have 80 percent. Percentage is percentage and does not matter what size shot is used. The second way of looking at pattern density is 'pellet spacing.' Common sense tells us that a 1 ¼ ounce load of #8 shot will have many more pellets than a 1 ¼ ounce load of #4 shot. If both loads pattern at 70 percent, you have more #8 shot in the target than you will have with #4s. The #8 pellets will be as a rule, spaced closer to each other than the #4s."

## How to Pattern a Gun

George likes to use paper that measures four feet square. "Paper this size may be hard to find locally," he says. "If it is not available, try taping several sheets of butcher paper or newsprint together. Bruce Buck the 'technoid' of 'Shotgun Report' has suggested using red resin flooring paper. This is available at any home supply store and shows the pellet holes perfectly when viewed from the back. He notes that it is available only in 36-inch wide rolls but that it cuts and tapes easily. If you use small paper and your gun does not shoot to the point of aim, part of your pattern could be off the target. You would probably confuse this with a bad pattern. If it helps, mark the target center with spray paint for use as an aiming point."

When he is patterning, George prefers to use a shooting bench. At this point, he maintains, you are not checking the gun for fit and a rest helps to remove some of the variables. From the correct distance, he shoots at the center of the target. "I recommend shooting a minimum of five times on different targets with each shell or choke you are testing," he says. "Draw a 30-inch circle around the densest portion of the pattern on each target. If you intend to do much of this get a 30-inch diameter template, like a piece of Lexan [Plexiglas] or even a old-fashioned compass and string with a pencil on the end. You can easily move this around on the paper to find where to draw the circle. Count the pellets inside of the circle. Divide this number by the total number of shot in the shell and you have your percentage. Take the percentage from each target, add them and divide by the total number of shots fired for each shell or choke and this will give you the overall average for that test. Sounds like a royal pain doesn't it? It is, but there are no short cuts if you really want to know what your shotgun is doing."

After you have finished the shooting and the math, look carefully at each pattern for holes big enough to let targets slip through. You want a dense enough pattern to ensure multiple hits.

## Point of Impact

George says that he and the staff at Trulock are asked on occasion about chokes that do not center the pattern exactly on the aiming point. "Most shooters want a shotgun that centers the pattern exactly with the point of aim," he says. "In theory, most shotguns are manufactured to do this, but it is not unusual to find guns shooting high or low and to the right or left, or a combination of these."

Shotguns that pattern half above and half below the point of aim have what is commonly known as a 50/50 pattern. One that shoots three-quarters of the pattern over and one-quarter under the point of aim has a 75/25 pattern and so on.

Certain guns are designed to give patterns other than 50/50. Common reasons for off-center pattern—if the gun is not designed for that as are certain custom trap guns—are: a defective choke tube, a bent barrel, misaligned choke and barrel, a loose barrel, poor gun fit and flinch.

To check your gun for point of aim, use the following procedure:

1. Set up with a padded rest.

2. Make sure to get perfect bead alignment if your gun has a center bead. If it does not, the rib should be perfectly flat, with the bead visible.

3. Use the same load you use in the field or on the range.

4. Squeeze the trigger. (This is easier said than done, as most shotgun trigger assemblies give anything but a good pull.)

5. Use targets with a center aiming point.

6. Shoot several targets, change chokes and repeat.

George suggests following this procedure with several different chokes, and to test some of the factory tubes that came with the gun if you are using aftermarket chokes, such as his Trulock chokes. Here are the possible results:

1. If all of the chokes shoot to the same spot or at least very close to the same, you do not have a problem with the chokes.

2. If your point of impact changes with each choke you test, you certainly have a problem, but not the chokes.

3. If one choke shoots to a different point of aim and the others do not, that choke is probably defective and a call to the manufacturer is in order.

One other thing you should be aware of, George notes, is "point of convergence." This problem will be found only on side-by-side or over/under shotguns. Both barrels should shoot to the same spot. Again, what works in theory seldom works in practice at the range. Generally with over/unders the top barrel will shoot high. When testing for proper convergence you will find it easier if you use tight chokes. If the convergence is close, be happy, many are not. If you cannot live with the error, you should talk to the manufacturer.

## A Note About Steel Shot

If you use your competition shotgun for hunting, you need to be aware of the effect of steel shot on choke tubes and choke fit.

Much has changed over the years with steel loadings, George Trulock says. The quality and consistency of the shells has been greatly improved. However, the fact that steel shot exerts much more stress on choke tubes has not changed. The problem is that steel shot is much harder than lead. It transmits much more energy to the choke when it strikes the conical portion and if the tube is not of sufficient strength it will cause it to deform. This is known as "choke creep."

Over a period of time, choke creep can lock a choke in the barrel so that it is next to impossible to remove. When purchasing aftermarket chokes, look for chokes rated for use with steel shot and use a good tube lube. Birchwood Casey makes a non-evaporating, metallic base Choke Tube Lube (www.birchwoodcasey.com $7.20 for ¾-ounce) that prevents corrosion and galling in regular and stainless chokes due to high-pressure loads and extreme temperatures. This product and others that are similar are readily available at your local shooting supply store.

## Choke Cleaning

George recommends that you clean your chokes and the threads every time you clean your gun. Plastic fouling and powder residue build up in screw-in chokes much faster than in fixed choke guns. Powder fouling will also work between the choke and the choke counter bore in the barrel. Remove the choke and clean with a toothbrush using solvent. Trulock markets and uses a good solvent as a cleaner. Simply drop the choke into the solution for a short time and it will come out with the fouling dissolved. Clean the inside of the barrel with a cleaner/lubricant such as Clenzoil (www.clenzoil.com) making sure the threads do not have any residue. Then, lightly wipe the choke with oil and reassemble. Remember that rust can occur in the barrel and freeze a choke in place even if the choke is made from stainless steel.

## Choke Tightness

Although this seems like a "no-brainer," George believes there is a proper way to install a choke tube. When changing a choke in the field or at the range, wipe the choke with a clean rag first, he says. This keeps any abrasive from being ground into the threaded area of the choke/barrel. Finger-tighten and then

There are almost as many ways of marking chokes with their constriction as there are chokes. These days, it hardly makes sense to require a special wrench to remove a choke when extended chokes with rough or knurled surfaces can easily be removed by hand. If you cannot remove your chokes by hand, here is a tip: Buy two (or more) wrenches. You will drop or misplace one practically every time you use it. Guaranteed.
*(Photo courtesy Winchester)*

Remington's Express Upgrade Kit is available in 12- and 20-gauge versions. It includes Improved Cylinder and Full Rem Chokes, a Choke Tube Speed Wrench and a one-ounce bottle of Rem Oil. Comes in a rugged plastic box.

use a wrench that properly fits the tube to finish tightening using a moderate amount of pressure. This will help keep the choke from loosening when in use.

When a choke is not properly seated, the possibility of the shot charge striking the edge of the choke greatly increases. If this happens, a bulged barrel and a ruined choke are almost guaranteed. Most chokes will loosen and back out to some degree if they are left finger-tight. A perfectly clean, dry choke installed in a clean, dry barrel and moderately tightened with a wrench should not work loose though. Having said that, most shooters are better off making sure that there is a light coating of oil on the choke before installing as this will help prevent rust in the barrel. George recommends checking chokes for tightness on a regular basis.

## Frozen Chokes

"In our shop we have pulled frozen chokes of almost every brand," George Trulock says. "Normally by the time we get the barrel one or more people have attempted to remove the choke. Did you ever wonder where the saying 'Fixed Guns Repaired' came from? Frozen choke tubes is a problem that can be prevented 99 percent of the time by simply cleaning the choke and barrel on a regular basis. The number one problem is RUST in the threaded area of the choke/barrel. If you keep this from forming, amazingly you will not have any problems. The second problem is choke creep or expansion. This fortunately is much less of a problem than rust. It is caused normally by using large steel shot in tight chokes [Full or tighter]. Follow the manufacturer's suggestions when using steel shot and the odds are very much in your favor that you will have no problems."

If you experience choke creep, you will notice the choke becoming harder to remove and install and if you continue it will eventually lock in the barrel. If you find yourself with a frozen choke, George Trulock's first suggestion is to take it to a competent gunsmith—before you and your neighbor work on it in the garage. Make sure the smith has some experience in this line of work.

If you are going to try to remove a frozen choke yourself, however, first unload the gun! Now, these are the instructions from Trulock. Remove the barrel from the action and soak the muzzle in a can of penetrating oil for several days. Make sure the container has a sufficient amount of oil to completely cover the barrel as deep as the choke is recessed. Use a proper fitting wrench and try to work the choke back and forth in small increments. If this does not work, try letting it soak several more days. Heat applied to the choke area can be of help. Never get the barrel so hot that you cannot touch it with your hand for several seconds. Do not use a hammer of any kind to try and "tap" it. Soaking and low heat will get most frozen chokes out. ("Be patient when following this procedure," George says. "We have seen quite a number of barrels ruined because of apparent impatience.")

## Choke Storage

Trulock suggests that you keep chokes in a padded case especially designed for them. There are a number of quality cases on the market in the under-$20.00 range. The purpose is to keep them from hitting each other or any hard object that could cause burrs or deformation. Chokes are particularly susceptible to denting in the threaded area. "We have seen this occur on numerous occasions when chokes stored in plain boxes were dropped," George says. "We also urge you to clean all of the chokes that have used when you clean your gun. Alloy steel chokes need a light coat of oil prior to storage and stainless steel keeps its rust resistant properties best when it is free from contamination."

## Patterning The Shotgun

"Patterning" means understanding how your shot pellets disperse or spread out when shot through the muzzle of your gun. In the pattern on the left, an even distribution of pellets prevents clays or ducks from squeezing through any holes in your shot pattern. T gives you the best possibility of hitting what you are shooting at. If you shoot a pattern that results in something like the diagram on the right, however, there is a good chance that you may miss shots that you should be making with a more even distribution of pellets. You can often remedy an uneven pattern by experimenting with chokes and loads, or the off-kilter pattern may be a gun fitting problem. In the worst case, you will need to take your shotgun to a professional gunsmith or fitter for examination.

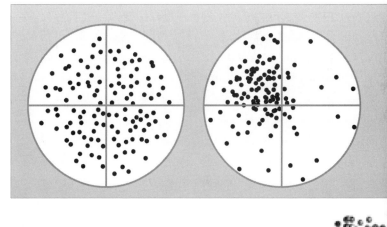

Innovative schematics from Federal of your shotgun's wad opening and the shot streaming out toward your target. To reach your target as a cloud without excessive holes or ragged diameter, this shot stream needs to be relatively compact and without flyers.

## CHAPTER 27

# TAKING CARE OF YOUR GUN

If you have had a chance to be involved in or even to follow the aftermath of any natural or man-made disaster that involved fire or explosion, and certainly the 9-11 tragedy is a terrible case in point, you know that the clean-up and restoration process can be an enormous amount of work. Dirty. Smelly. Time consuming.

So, imagine what happens when you pull the trigger of a loaded shotgun. A microscopic camera in the barrel would record an atomic-bomb-like flash followed by a devastating explosion, the result of combining a tiny spark and a compressed ounce or so of highly combustible gunpowder. In its own scale, the aftermath leaves as much charred debris lying about as a very nasty house fire.

There is good news however. Even though top-ranked gunners take care of their shotguns meticulously, routine or day-to-day maintenance is easy and not at all time-consuming. Barring a major break-down, just a couple minutes of effort performed religiously will virtually insure that your shotgun performs smoothly every time you take it out of its case or sleeve. In our experience, it does not matter whether the shotgun costs $500 or $5,000; regular attention with a swab, a brush and a cloth will maintain its efficiency and pattern. As the folks at Hoppe's (www.hoppes.com) say, "Be good to your gun and it will be good to you."

## First Principles

You want the bore of your shotgun to be so smooth and clean that, if it were a dinner plate, you would think nothing of letting your children eat from it. More good news. The more you shoot, and the more you scrub and clean the bore, the smoother and shinier it looks.

Shotgun sports are fun: they are designed to be fun. However, as you get into the games deeper, you will encounter many situations that are not ideal for the performance of your gun: blowing grit, rain, salt air and perhaps periods of inactivity. Maintaining your gun properly is necessary to stay at the top of the leader boards and to keep you from having an irritating afternoon when something goes wrong that could have been prevented with a half-hour of regular cleaning.

Why clean it at all? If you do not, you are apparently running the risk of metal corrosion from moisture build-up and of jamming due to the build-up of "gunk" in the action. This will eventually affect accuracy, cause jamming and shorten your gun's useful life. The problem for many of us is that powder residue and tiny irregularities in the barrel cannot be seen without a special bore scope. By the time you can see scratches or a marred surface finish with your "naked eye," they have already become problems.

Condensation is one of the most insidious ways that moisture attacks your gun. After a shoot in the rain, it is obvious that you must clean and dry the gun. What is not so obvious is when you are shooting outside on a cold day and then take your gun into the clubhouse. Bingo. Condensation immediately forms on all the metal surfaces, inside the gun and out. Any type of condensation or moisture (rain, fog, snow, salt water spray, etc.) will immediately start the rust-formation process. Therefore, the first rule of gun care is to wipe and dry your gun right away—especially if you are shooting a course (or hunting) near salt water. Even miles away, salt spray can be deadly to a fine metal finish.

Storing a gun for an extended period also requires some special care. I have heard shooters complain that, knowing they would not be shooting for a while—a "while" sometimes lasting for years—they cleaned and oiled their gun before they put it away. Then, when they eventually got around to shooting again, they pulled the gun out and … Ugh! It was a mess.

To store your gun for a significant period, it is important that it be kept in a clean, dry and, need we say, safe place. Even though you have cleaned it before putting it away, a gun should be stripped and cleaned periodically even if it is not being handled or fired. This is required because leftover oils from fingerprints and normal moisture inside the case around the gun cannot be 100 percent removed.

## Patches, Brushes and Solvents

Most guns you buy from a shooting sports retailer, especially those that are still in their original box, come with a very light coating of grease on all the metal parts. The idea of greasing a gun is to keep it from corroding while it sits on the retailer's rack waiting for you to buy it. (Of course, if you purchase a Perazzi and travel to Italy for a custom fitting, this will not be a problem.) Grease can slow down the action of the gun, and it has to come off. Use a clean rag and a solvent such as the famous Hoppe's No. 9.

Chances are that you will religiously clean a new gun after the first few times you shoot it. Then, after a couple months, a day will come when your spouse asks

you to pick up bread on the way home from the shooting range and you will forget the patches and solvent. Or some every-day pressure like washing the car or taking the dog to the veterinarian will suggest that you clean the gun tomorrow. Every day you wait, the job becomes more necessary than ever.

Here is step one. Before you begin any cleaning job, you need to be sure the gun is not loaded. Although this sounds simple, almost too simple for a veteran shooter, people are killed and permanently maimed each year by guns that were not thought to be loaded. And even though a load of low base #8 may not blow your leg off, you will certainly walk with a limp and terrible scars for the rest of your life, so why not be certain?

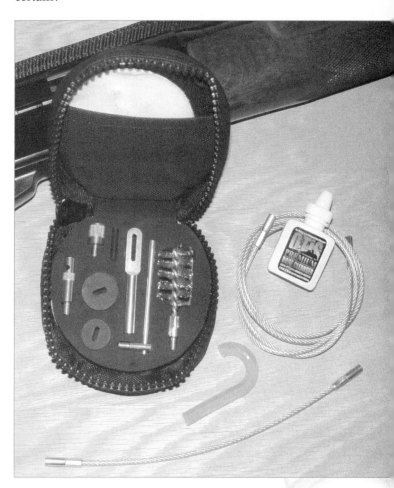

Perhaps the best way to learn about the care and cleaning of a shotgun is to buy a kit with a pamphlet and follow the directions. This Otis Shotgun Cleaning System kit will clean all shotguns from .410 through 10-gauge. Of course, the five ounce bottle of Bore Cleaner will not last long, but you should be able to use the rods, brushes and cable connectors for years. These small kits are the ideal size to take to the range or to the field for a quick cleaning.

One of the first principles of gun cleaning and care is to always pull the rods, cleaning swabs and brushes from the receiver to the muzzle, never in the opposite direction. For over/under owners, this is a simpler operation than for those with semi-automatics who should partially disassemble their gun for thorough cleaning. There is a temptation to clean semi-autos from muzzle to breech because it is quicker and easier. You have to resist this because you can cause irreparable harm to the finely machined lining of the barrel.

As you are running patches and brushes through the bore, you should be careful to never allow the rod to scrape against the bore itself. It is said that all firearms record their history and perhaps this is the reason people look down the barrel of a firearm. An experienced eye can tell the method of cleaning, make a close guess about the number of shots put through the barrel, and understand the gun maintenance routine applied to the firearm. When people carelessly allow the tip of the rod or the rod itself to scrape along the inside of the barrel, it leaves scratches.

Your first cleaning operation is to run a patch into the receiver, past the forcing cone, through the barrel, then past the choke and out the crown or muzzle.

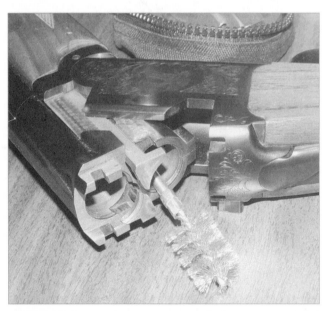

**The first step in cleaning after an afternoon at the range is to run a patch with an all-purpose solvent – one-way only – down the barrel. To remove any tough metal residue in the barrel or in the action, a solvent such as Birchwood Casey's Bore Scrubber works well. Remember that after spraying or wiping, you want the residue to run away from the action. Let the Bore Scrubber soak for a few minutes and then run a wire brush through the barrel about 10 times again, one-way only. Next, strip your gun of all foreign oil, residue and film using a Gun Scrubber Solvent/Degreaser-style product. Spray the brush clean before you use it a second time. You can spray this into hard-to-reach spots as it dries rapidly. Do not neglect the screw-threads for choke tubes and the choke tubes themselves.** *(Set-up photos courtesy Otis)*

**You cannot anticipate every possible problem. Sometimes things just break. They wear out. Structural flaws in the metal or the mechanism fail. These things cannot be helped. On the other hand, religious routine maintenance can prevent many ordinary problems.**

You want to soak this patch or swab with solvent, not so much that it will form a pool, but enough that the swab will cover 360 degrees of barrel. Too much solvent and it will drip down into the trigger mechanism and cause a gummy trigger and perhaps delayed firing. Too much will drain back toward the stock and damage the finish. This action lubricates the bore and prevents sand or dirt from scratching the muzzle end of the barrel because it is picked up on the patch and carried out.

After the first swabbing, run a dry patch through the barrel until you have absorbed the solvent and then use a brush. Select something perhaps a little oversized to clean the forcing cone and the barrel—especially backbored barrels*, which are honed to a diameter greater than SAAMI specifications.

*SKB's 12-gauge "85" over/under barrels are "backbored." This means that the interior bore of the barrel is slightly enlarged. For a 12-gauge, the nominal SAAMI bore diameter is .729 inches. SKB bore diameter is .735-inch. An oversized bore allows the wad to spread slightly, thereby reducing friction as it travels the length of the bore. In theory, the benefits are denser and more evenly distributed patterns, and a reduction in felt recoil.*

Never run the bore brush down through the barrel of any gun before using a lubricated patch. This would almost certainly damage your gun. Any dirt or sand in the muzzle end would adhere to the bristles on the brush. Then, when you bring the brush into the forcing cone, the dirt will be deposited in the chamber and forcing cone, which are relatively clean even following a shot. This is the exact equivalent of cleaning in the wrong direction (from muzzle to breech).

Do not forget to spray the brush clean with a solvent like Birchwood Casey's Gun Scrubber Solvent/Degreaser after use (www.birchwoodcasey.com). This Solvent/Degreaser is environmentally safe and dries rapidly leaving metal clean and free of film or grease. Solvent left on the brush is messy and can weaken the bristles. In addition, if the brush is used dirty when you are trying to clean your gun the next time, it can cause more harm than good.

After this, if you notice crud (miniscule lead or plastic fragments) inside the barrel, you will almost certainly see scratches as well. These scratches may be caused when the cleaning rod—either with a patch or a brush on the end—is moved back and forth on the false assumption that this is the proper way to remove grit and lead fouling. It also means that abrasive dirt from the muzzle was brought back into the chamber and forcing cone. (Conventional cleaning equipment does not clean the wider diameter forcing cone very well.) You are not in the kitchen scrubbing pots and pans. Run patches and brushes one way, the right way, from receiver to muzzle only.

Speaking of brushes, remember that brushes are designed to be run one way only through the barrel. Never reverse the direction while the brush is inside the bore: this will bend the bristles on the brush. This is the equivalent of bending a wire back and forth until it breaks. You will always ruin a brush if you reverse it while in the bore.

Dirt pulled backwards down the barrel causes abrasions, and understand that most of these are not visible on casual inspection. Scratches allow tiny lead and plastic fragments to adhere to crevices in the bore steel and, depending on their depth and the hardness of the eventual deposit, they become resistant to cleaning. Your pattern suffers.

So, if you clean the chamber and forcing cone by working only in the direction the shot is fired, the bore should never be scratched.

Otis (www.otisgun.com) makes a flexible steel clean-

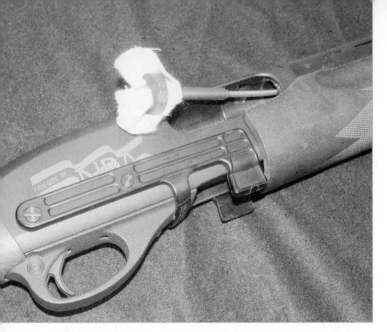

Cleaning a semi-automatic without disassembling the barrel requires a flexible cable – and some care not to scratch the inside of the barrel.

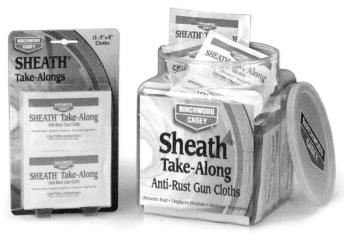

It is a handy thing to be able to run through the barrel, and to wipe down your barrel and the outside of the receiver with a rust preventive during a long day at the range. Guns attract dust and dust attracts crud build-up. These individual five-inch by eight-inch cloths are impregnated with Sheath Rust Preventive. Use once and toss. Products like Sheath are supposed to drive out moisture from metal pores and deposit a transparent coating to protect against corrosion.

ing rod that allows you to perform daily swabbing to your semi-auto without disassembly. Just open the action as you would to insert a shell, Otis says, and then run the flexible steel rod with lubricant-soaked patch attached down the barrel, pulling it out the muzzle end. This quick cleaning, while not complete, is very good and takes only a minute.

There is a tendency among shotgunners, especially those who have been casual about cleaning, to simply turn a patch over or even re-use it. You may be able to get away with turning it over depending on how you fold it and how dirty the swab has become, but swabs are so cheap, why would you risk using it a second time? The abrasive material that adheres to it, the very stuff you want to remove, will certainly scratch the forcing cone and bore at the breech end. This will cause lead and plastic buildup and defeat the purpose of the cleaning.

You can use a chamber-cleaning rod with oversized bore brush to clean the chamber and the choke tube threads. It is always desirable to clean the barrel first before changing the choke tube. This will prevent dirt from getting into the threads. If you find the choke tube does not easily screw in, do not force it. Remove it and clean the threads again carefully. Force a choke tube into place and a bulged barrel could result; and while that may not indeed alter your patterns, it will not make you proud of your work and there will be those questions from shooting partners. When you have cleaned the threads, immediately reinsert the choke tube.

After you have finished cleaning the bore, apply a small amount of lubricating or gun oil to a clean patch and run it through. Your barrel will now be clean and lightly lubricated, ready for the range or the field.

## After the Barrel

The action and trigger mechanism can be cleaned with solvent and scrubbed lightly with a brush. A fast-drying spray solvent works well here unless you feel certain that you can completely disassemble the mechanics of your gun and reassemble them as good as new. Few casual shooters feel this competent, especially with a semi-auto, and some parts of the action just cannot be easily cleaned or disassembled by us occasional shooters. (Always check your gun's Owner's Manual and "exploded parts list" before performing anything more than routine disassembly. Like your car engine, if there is one part left over or reinserted backwards, it just will not operate properly.)

After spraying and brushing using solvents and degreasers, wipe your gun as clean as possible and apply a light coating of oil. Very light, but very thorough should be the password to this operation.

The last thing to do is wipe the outer metal surfaces to remove any fingerprints or runny drips of solvent or oil. A clean cloth or even a clean patch with a light coating of Hoppe's No. 9 works fine.

If you are shooting in wet weather or perhaps near the seashore, a number of manufacturers offer specialty gun cloths and other products with ingredients that

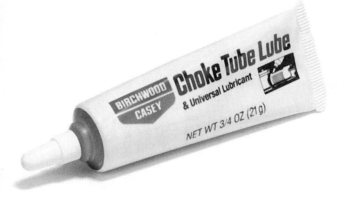

It is easy to forget or ignore the choke tubes. They are as subject to fouling as the barrel, especially the threads. A good anti-seize lube will prevent tubes from sticking in the barrel from corrosion, the high stress of steel shot, and the extreme temperatures and pressures from repeated shooting.

drive out moisture, lubricate and help prevent rust. It is a good thing to carry a few of these in your case to wipe down and run through the barrel right after shooting. Birchwood Casey's convenient and disposable Barricade Take-Along Gun Cloths, for example, are individual 5x8 cloths impregnated with Barricade Rust Protection and sealed in a foil packet for compact carrying. A 25-pack of these costs $7.80.

And what about the stock and forearm? Unless they are synthetic, these pieces are usually walnut and, even though shooters are usually very careful of their own and other shooters' guns, it is easy to bump the metal edges of a gun rack or scratch

against the tailgate of your pick up. A spot application of stock finish, followed by an oiling and, finally, a good rub-down with a clean cloth should once again bring out the gun stock's luster and original brilliance.

Barrelguard makes a super-lightweight tube (www.barrelguard.com) that should take much of the anxiety out of leaving your guns in the case for any extended period. The company's VCI (Volatile Corrosion Inhibitor) tubes slip into the barrels of your shotgun to replace more conventional treatments with cosmoline, grease, oil, preservatives, dessicants and waxed or barrier papers. Airtight packaging is not required for these tubes to work. Barrelguard says the VCI chemicals vaporize in the packaging environment and condense on

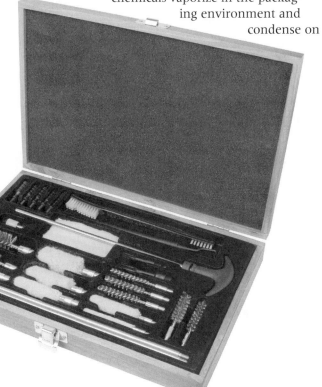

Indiana gunsmith Richard Clauss studies a 44-caliber 1858 New Army Remington revolver purchased from Pietta of Italy. A good gunsmith will be worth his weight in gold when you have a problem that cannot be quickly resolved with a good cleaning.

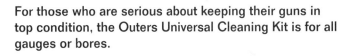

For those who are serious about keeping their guns in top condition, the Outers Universal Cleaning Kit is for all gauges or bores.

all metal surfaces to form a protective molecular layer that prevents moisture, salt, dirt, oxygen and other materials from depositing on the metal and causing corrosion.

For shotguns, Barrelguard tubes are 22 inches long and 0.4 inches in diameter. They will fit any size shotgun from 10-gauge to .410. These tubes do not require a snug fit. Barrelguard tubes are sold in packs of five and cost about $2 each. While the automatic replenishing action of the tube's chemicals may last for years, Barrelguard recommends that, for highest effectiveness, they be replaced annually.

# CHAPTER 28

# MISSING AND SHOOTING TO MISS

Courtesy of Bob Knopf (www.shootinginstruction.com)

Second to none, the biggest concern of both beginning and experienced shooters is missing. For many, it represents some sort of shooting failure. It triggers frustration, sometimes anger, and it places our egos on our sleeves. It ruins our calm, which is what we need most when we miss.

Missing is inevitable. Viewed correctly it can be a great teacher because, using our mind, we can learn how to shoot better when we miss. We can strive to improve our technique when we miss. We are forced to focus on hitting when we miss.

Misses are a great teacher on controlling the mental aspects of shooting because, if we don't control how we think when we miss, we continue to miss, and miss, and miss again. We need to use missing to make ourselves better shooters. If we use it right, we'll excel in our shooting.

Remember this. Shotgun shooting professionals, the best of the best, easily miss more targets in one week than most clays shooters or hunters miss in a month. Why? They shoot more. They know they'll miss. They calmly work to correct their misses, to minimize them. They work to deal with them mentally. And very importantly, when they miss, they learn to leave their misses behind them, so that one miss doesn't breed another.

For many shooters, missing one target causes additional misses more than any other single factor: More misses than poor shooting skills, more than improper choke selection, more than poor gun fit. When we miss, our thinking mind kicks in and tries to keep us

Bob Knopf is a National Sporting Clays Association (NSCA) certified instructor and chief instructor for his National Wing & Clay Shooting School. His book Wing & Clay Shooting Made Easy www.shootinginstruction.com is an excellent and fast-reading primer for shotgunning and for hunting.

*If you miss, do not focus on what you did wrong. Focus on what you need to do right to hit the target. Leave the miss behind. Quickly, get directed on hitting the next target.*

> *Common Mistake: For most shooters, on long crossing shots our mind will not easily accept the correct lead we must use. When missing a 35-50 yard shot, double your lead and tell yourself, "It's okay to miss in front."*

from missing again. Ironically, the opposite of what we want usually happens. Fluid gun motion becomes stiff, our timing becomes irregular, and our trigger pull becomes delayed. We think, we analyze, we miss again.

Therefore, when you miss, immediately focus on hitting the next target and shoot it with enthusiasm. Importantly, allow yourself some free misses without any thought as to why you may have missed. The target or game simply got away.

It is important to learn to view missing as a learning experience. That way we will keep our calm and our misses help us learn. The learning moment should begin with, "Okay, next shot I'll give the bird more lead," or "I'll swing more smoothly to the target." Then, as you prepare for the next shot, visualize yourself on one of those days you simply couldn't miss … and call for the next bird.

As much as we will not let misses upset us, we definitely want to minimize them at every opportunity. New shooters should focus on easier-to-hit targets. Keep it easy as you develop your personal style and technique. Don't go out with an experienced shooter and shoot all the hard targets. On a sporting clays course, shoot only the easier stations. Observe the more difficult targets and shoot them with your pointer finger (no gun). Allow yourself time to develop your technique before tackling the tougher targets first hand.

Experienced shooters, to get better, need to practice on their own personal "tough for me to hit" target list. When practicing these, and when you begin missing repeatedly, stop shooting for a minute. Determine why you aren't breaking the target. Do not focus on what you did wrong. Focus on what you need to do right. Resume practice considering some of the "miss" factors presented in this book. If you continue missing, make the target easier to hit. Move closer, reduce some of the angle. Don't force yourself into the, "I'm gonna shoot till I break it" habit unless you're calmly prepared to handle the additional misses that lie ahead.

The quickest, easiest and least costly way to become a proficient wing shooter is to hire a certified instructor. "The money you pay a qualified instructor will show immediate results and will save hundreds, perhaps thousands of dollars on ammunition and targets," says Bob Knopf.

*When you're missing, change something. Are you hesitating on your trigger pull? Are you being too careful? Pull the trigger as the sight picture develops or ¹⁄₁₀th of a second before you see the perfect sight picture.*

When missing regularly, be sure to change something. Alter your method, your gun hold point, or your target view point until you hit the target.

A good way to handle misses is to keep a list of targets you commonly miss. "Long crosser right to left." Quartering away from behind on left side." An instructor can get you hitting these problem shots, or spend a couple of sessions where you specifically practice them.

On tougher targets, getting a correct sight picture usually remedies the problem very quickly. When teaching, I commonly tell a shooter to miss intentionally. Perhaps to "miss in front" of a target. Or to "miss underneath." Many are surprised to see that when they double or triple their lead trying to miss in front, that they solidly hit the target. This is because often a miss is simply due to a wrong sight picture. But sometimes our mind won't easily let us change.

I've watched both experienced and new shooters alike hit a tiny quarter-sized spot every time in their shooting. The only problem, it was 10 feet behind the actual target or two feet over it.

If you're missing, make the shot easier, and spend some time hitting some easier targets. If you're an experienced shooter who is shooting with a novice shooter, don't let them shoot the harder shots. Very few new shooters get disgusted and give up shooting because they were overly successful.

To shoot successfully, we must learn to smile at ourselves when we miss. We must treat ourselves gently. This is not easy, and it, too, takes practice. The reward, however, is more hits than we ever imagined.

Professional shotgun shooting coach Bob Knopf says that each miss and each broken target or downed game bird must be viewed in terms of the three basic wing shooting fundamentals: moving (pointing) your gun to the target, obtaining your personal sight picture (correct lead) and pulling the trigger at the right time.

# CHAPTER 29
# HÉLICE: NEW GAME IN TOWN

Much to the dismay of the hundreds of sporting clay enthusiasts present, the TM Ranch east of Orlando, Florida, was going out of business—selling out to a real estate developer—and its famous Seminole Cup was ending. So 2004 was the last chance to see the highly-regarded shooting layout and enjoy the warm, February weather while busting ranch pigeons.

Just down the road from the headquarters and manufacturer display area however, before competitors reached the sub-gauge and 5-Stand competitions, was an open field where Ohio's Tom Veatch had set up a hélice shooting ring.

"We're not holding a competition," Veatch said. "We are just shooting for fun. We want to introduce all the clay shooters here to the newest, hottest game sweeping through Europe."

According to Veatch, who was a sales representative and distributor for Wells Hélice Equipment in the U.S. (www.helice.us), millions of plastic hélice targets are shot every year in Europe and the new game—some-times called ZZ Bird or Electrocibles—is at last making strong inroads in U.S. shotgun sports as well.

"Hélice isn't a side-game or some novelty," he says. "It is a prestigious, stand-alone sport. Statistics compiled over many years prove that hélice is actually more challenging than the live pigeon shooting it is designed to replace. Generally, in Europe and around the world where it has been introduced, hélice has been a highly accepted improvement over live birds. The flight of these targets is outstanding and there are no political repercussions from the anti-hunting crowd. Plus, the World Cup circuit now offers some of the most exciting and difficult hélice competition available to shotgunners."

Not only did this turn out to be the author's first opportunity to shoot these dipsy-doodle plastic flyers, but also Tom handed me his Perazzi. "Try my gun," he generously offered. It was quite a moment.

## Plastic, Not Clay

The U.S. Hélice Association (USHA, www.ushelice.com) sanctions hélice shoots. It gives points and awards for shooters seeking to be Team USA members and earn expensive paid trips to the Helice World Championships each year. The USHA notes that shooting its plastic target is not intended to be a clay game. Hélice is designed to replicate and replace shooting "Box Pigeon" or live birds, where that venue is still allowed.

Hélice is shot from a single station. Depending on a shooter's earned or observed handicap, it may be as close as 24 meters or as distant as 30 meters from a semi-circle with green boxes containing hélice 110-volt throwing machines, spaced an equal distance apart. There may be five boxes (spaced 4 ½ to five meters), or seven (2 ¼ to 2 ½ meters between machines #2 and #3 and #3 and #4) or even nine stations depending on the field and tournament layout.

Hélice targets are spun or thrown away from the shooter in a completely random pattern and order. This obviously differs from the highly regulated pattern of trap and skeet and to a great degree from sporting clays as well since it is impossible to guess the sequence. And no bird is thrown for general viewing before a shooter steps to the shooting stand, either.

A hélice is a two-piece target, an orange or red body with two angled wings and a white snap-on cap called the "witness." Struck by shot, the witness must separate from the spinning orange body and wings and fall

Unlike other shotgun games which are shot with clay targets (except for live pigeon shoots, of course), hélice is shot with a winged plastic flyer, the white part of which (the "witness") is knocked off when hit and reused. The standard load is 1¼ ounce.

within the area between the two semi-circles for the target to be scored.

Unlike a clay disk, there is no such thing as a "visible piece." The two parts of a hélice target are reusable, at least until they become visibly damaged (which happens quickly, sometimes after one shot, to the orange wings), and range operators collect the white witness and as many of the undamaged orange winged sections as possible.

The U.S. Hélice Association specifies that hélice targets are 28cm (11 inches) from orange-red wingtip to wingtip. The raised white witness in the center is 10.4cm wide and the lightweight target weighs a maximum of 70 grams. The wings must be built of a material fragile to impact (polystyrene) while the witness is specifically not fragile (50 percent polyethylene) and hence reusable. The throwing machines can be adjusted from between zero and 10,000 rpm.

These throwing machines or "hélice traps" are not universally standardized. As long as a target or machine performs within FITASC rules, they are allowed in a sanctioned match. In international competition, you may shoot Spanish machines and Spanish targets in Spain, Italian in Italy and French in France. The best advice is to do a little research—perhaps on the Internet—before heading off to a match. An hour of research may well be worth a target or two.

When participants are called to shoot, they advance to the designated shooting station with their gun empty. They load and call "Ready" when the range is declared clear. The operator must then respond with "Ready." The shooter will then call "Pull" and the target is thrown instantly by an automatic voice-activated system such as the Canterbury Voice Release (www.cvr.co.nz).

The shooter must hit the whirling hélice target before it reaches a second semi-circle marked by a fence placed 21 meters beyond the target-throw semi-circle. In hélice shooting, any safe preliminary gun hold is allowed. Shooters may wait with their gun down or fully shouldered. You may think that no one would want to wait with the gun in the down position, but many shooters find that it is easier to move on a target, especially when they do not know which target is launching it, and align their head properly with their gun at the un-mounted position.

Tom Veatch (left) and Frank Mowrey go down-range to replace targets on the hélice throwing machines. These machines can spin a bird into the air from zero to 10,000 rpm, but at this time, the plastic birds must be manually replaced after all the stations have thrown a bird.

Starting from a high gun position, the shooter calls "Ready," the range controller (inside the adjacent hut) responds with "Ready." When the shooter calls "Pull," the target is thrown instantly, triggered by a voice-activated system. Unlike trap or skeet, the birds appear in random order.

Hélice rules state that a 12-gauge is the largest gun allowed and that no credit will be given for smaller gauges. The maximum size lead shot used is #7 ½. The maximum shot load allowed by FITASC (which governs international hélice competition) is 1 ¼-ounce and it is standard for Hélice.

Shooters accustomed to 1 ⅛-ounce loads will find plenty of commercial options available, but often they are designated as small game loads. Federal, for example, offers 1 ¼ ounce loads of #7 ½ in its Game Shok or Wing Shok lines. Wing Shok Flyer #P153 contains 1 ¼ ounces of #7 ½ or #8 in a 2 ¾ shell for 1330 fps. Federal says this load is fine for turkey, pheasant, grouse, squirrel or rabbit—and, we might add, hélice!

When the shooter calls "Pull" a hélice target is thrown and the gunner then has two shots to separate the witness from the wings and have the reusable witness fall between the semi-circles.

USHA gives a range operator some latitude to develop his or her shoot format, but generally 25 or 30 targets a day make up a complete competition program. With one person shooting on one station at a time, the game proceeds slowly. Because there is not much squad rotation except on and off the stand—in a seven-machine competition, each shooter shoots five birds at a time, for instance—your entire shooting day can easily be over in an hour.

Major hélice competitions are frequently two to three day events and are often held at a range near some "destination" such as Las Vegas or Reno or Dallas or Shreveport. Although each day consists only of a 25- or 30-target main match, shorter 10- or 15-target events or "races," as they are called, often follow these matches. There are typically awards for Daily Champions, Ladies, Veterans and Juniors. In addition, there are High Overall (HOA) awards for the weekend (perhaps 75 or 90 targets).

Tom Veatch says that one of the exciting things about hélice is that shooters from all major disciplines are usually present. Champions from skeet, trap, sporting clays, flyers and even the Olympics can, and will, regularly attend and are surprised to learn that the HOA prize often goes to the person who breaks 86 out of 90 rather than the 100 out of 100 with a shoot-off as is common elsewhere.

The short shooting day may be fine—or not—depending on your finances. Hélice is expensive. Given the flexibility (and many would argue the necessity) of a venue to charge a little more to pay for the computerized infrastructure and all the natural variables, say $3 per bird, a round of 30 targets might well cost $90 plus options such as a $10 fee to USHA and ammo. A hélice event at the Dallas Gun Club, for example, often becomes as much of a fraternal event as it does a shooting event, with many side games and opportunities to spend—and win—money.

Why is hélice so expensive compared to shooting a clay game?

Hélice differs in numerous important ways from the clay sports, and target cost is one of them. Hélice

Helice "traps" are spun or thrown away from the shooter in a completely random pattern and order.

Many hélice set-ups in the US, such as the one pictured here, are still for demonstration rather than competition, because the game is new to the US. "It isn't a poor man's game," Tom Veatch says. "A cost of $13 per bird is not unusual, so a round of 30 targets may cost $390."

the base cost of the hélice target is much higher due to their more complex, non-polluting injection molded plastic components. Clay targets cost range owners in the neighborhood of five to seven cents each. Hélice targets cost between 70 cents and $1.00 each!

"Hélice is not a poor man's sport," Tom Veatch says, stating the obvious, "but in competition the return to winners tends to be high."

## Chokes and Loads

Hélice is most successfully shot with comparatively tight chokes and powerful cartridges. This is because chips (the famous "visible pieces") do not count. The white "witness" must be separated from its red-orange carrier and wings. All shots will be between 32 and 47 yards and an on-edge target presents a shallow (3.25 cm) profile. Light Modified or Modified will be the most open choke you want to use and then only for your first shot. When shooting a semi-automatic, .025 to .030 is about right, and with a double barrel a Modified and or even a Full set up should be preferred. The USHA specifies that the heaviest shot charge is 38 grams or 1 ¼-ounces.

supporters say the difference is not as bad as it appears, because Hélice competitions and even practice sessions require far fewer targets to be shot. Where a full competition day at sporting clays may require 100 to 200 targets (or more), a full day of hélice may only, as we have pointed out, be 25 to 30 birds. In addition,

# CHAPTER 30
# ACCESSORIZE, ACCESSORIZE

Shotgunning is like home ownership. Once you have bought the basics, a shotgun and a few boxes of shells to shoot a little skeet or trap or sporting clays, the sky is the limit on the fun you can have—and the accessories you can acquire. Of course, all these things cost money: some are not at all expensive and some can break a poor man's bank account in a hurry. Then too, there are a few that you absolutely must have, such as high quality eye and ear protection. If you are lucky, you will eventually be able to convince your spouse that the new golf car and trailer (and then the garage extension) are essential to your happiness—perhaps even to her happiness.

## Making The Case

### Hard-sided cases

The trick with a hard-sided case is to buy the best you can afford. After all, this case is going to protect your shooting investment and if it fails you may not be able to shoot, so settle for nothing that you do not really want. What do you look for in a hard sided case? Well, watch for such things as recessed hinges and locks that cannot be easily smashed by airport baggage handlers; steel-reinforced corners help prevent a cracked or damaged case if it is dropped; and when you think of carrying the case, a comfortable, sturdy, non-slip handle will make the difference between misery and suffering if you have to walk any distance with it. Check the locks and the seals because you want the case to be tamper-proof and moisture-proof. If you are a traveling shooter who uses several guns, you may want a case with wheels and perhaps a canvas cover, also.

Fortunately, there are plenty of excellent cases to choose from: handsome models from T.Z. Case International (www.tzcase.com), high-performance carriers from Hardigg Storm Case (www.stormcase.com), and the well-known and rugged cases from Plano Molding (www.planomolding.com).

For local travel, almost any case that is legal will do just fine. If you are traveling to a shoot in California or France, you want something solid and that means metal—heavier than plastic with foam, and more expensive—but consider a high quality case a once-in-a-lifetime purchase, and after you pay for it you will never regret it.

A good example is the 37-inch gun case (#1437) in Plano's Protector Aluminum line. Case walls, Plano says, are "nearly 3X thicker than competition" and it is reinforced with a durable hexagon railing. The handle is "comfortable" and four lockable latches are provided across the face of the case. Measuring 37 x 13 x 4.5, three layers of high-density foam to protect firearms inside. Unfortunately, this otherwise good looking gun case only needs a couple things to make it truly superior: a latch for an additional padlock and a seam or hinge across the back that is sturdier than just a couple of pop rivets. So even at $150 or less, this may only be a good local-use case.

Vanguard USA (www.vanguardusa.com) markets numerous cases for outdoor activities and several shotgun cases. The diamond tread exterior of the Commander Series is scratch and dent resistant. Dual layers of high-density foam hold firearms securely in place while tension springs hold the metal carrying handle against the body of the case. Rubber feet extend the life of the case by elevating it and inset Mylar wheels reduce friction resistance when pulling it through an airport.

The 52W Breakdown Shotgun Case has metal corners to prevent damage during travel and its inset butterfly pad lock latches stand up to airline treatment. Speaking of airlines, don't even think you can

**The aluminum Winchester Breakdown Shotgun case has impact- and scratch-resistant side panels and reinforced corners. Features four heavy-duty key locks and padlock receptacles.**

stuff this case in an overhead bin: outside measurements are 38 x 14 x 7 ⅛ and weight is a solid 18 ¾ pounds. In an era when airline fares are cheap but one is charged extra for luggage or bags of peanuts, the weight with an eight-pound gun inside will be a factor when flying to a shoot, but at some time in your shooting career a very solid case will save your shooting life.

The Winchester name in a case is usually a good bet, but "airline-approved hard-shell case" means the airlines understand their baggage handlers take exception to sturdy looking cases—thinking of them not as something to take special care with, but as a manly challenge.

The Winchester Bruiser holds two shotguns (or scoped rifles). A double-wall outer shell of textured, impact-resistant polyethylene structural resin has recessed handles and rubber wheels for portability without snagging. The full padded interior cradles your guns in high density and foam dividers can be extended upward to separate guns in transit and prevent them from rubbing: dividers may be pushed down flush with surrounding foam when not needed. A neoprene rubber gasket provides an air- and watertight seal that keeps dirt and moisture out. Integral, corrosion-inhibiting inserts also protect firearms from rust. An automatic purge valve equalizes pressure inside the case for ease in closing lid. Bruiser (56 x 19 x 6 ⅝) has rugged hinges, while four "bullet proof" latches and three, separate locking points for padlocks mean that, once this case is shut, it's not going to open until you

The Guardforce GDF Series has a durable polyester exterior for a semi-hard-sided case. Inside, thick padding to protect your breakdown shotgun. Weighs just six pounds!

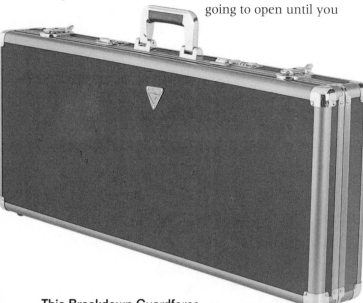

This Breakdown Guardforce Shotgun case by Vanguard features combination and key locks with metal-reinforced corners for the black, ABS plastic sides.

want it to. Cost is $233 at www.brownells.com.

There are several specialty case manufacturers in the U.S. and Canada like Dean Ziegel's Ziegel Engineering (www.ziegeleng.com) in California. Of particular interest is Ziegel's 15-pound Model 75 (6 ½ x 9 x 31), which is designed primarily for over/under skeet or sporting clay gun sets with 28-inch barrels. This heavy-duty aluminum case has reinforced corners and will accommodate four barrel sets and two receivers in a compact format. It has four barrel compartments in the lower section and all dividers are covered with high-density foam. A built-in inner leaf separates barrels from receivers: receivers are held in place with Velcro fastening straps. The Model 75 is lined with a black polypropylene fabric. It has one handle on each side and two catches. This case can be locked with padlocks through the stainless steel catches or with Dean's AC16 Locking Rod. The suggested retail price is $302 and that price has not gone up in five years!

Few manufacturers have more cases specifically dedicated to carrying a shotgun than Waxahachie, Texas' Americase (www.americase.com). Their catalog shows photos and diagrams and gives exact dimensions of dozens of cases designed for specific carrying tasks. In the Ameri-Lite line, for example,

#5031 is the 14-pound Skeet Tube Set (30-inch barrels) for $430. In the Premium line, high impact plastic sides with reinforced aluminum frame, #2001 is the Trap Single case (35-inch barrel) for $382. Or how about mixing and matching with #2018 from the Premium Line, the 22-pound Auto and Over-and-Under case for $435 and if you are strictly a pump gun or semi-auto fan, #3025, the Premium case for Two Take-down Pumps or Semi-Autos weighing 22 pounds, $435.

Americase offers customers several custom options and accessories. Because most breakdown shotgun cases are less than 38 inches long, an adjustable shoulder strap ($39) with a comfortable "Gel-Pad" is available. When you order a case with this accessory, two side-mounted D-rings for the strap will be attached to the case or case cover at the factory. Engraved name tags can be made and riveted to the case next to the handle or on the top side panel for a minimal fee and embroidery be sewn onto any velvet interior case: game animals, initials, the name of the shotgun manufacturer and so on. In essence, Americase will also custom-build your case.

## Soft-sided cases

Except for temporary storage and quick trips, soft-sided cases are not recommended; and they aren't good for long-term storage, either. While they are excellent when you want to reduce the bulk of a large, hard-sided case, they can trap moisture and introduce your gun to rust and corrosion.

The Boyt-Bob Allen connection (www.boytharness.com) has produced quite a number of good looking and serviceable soft-sided cases. You will find these excellent on the day you are car-pooling to the range and there just is not enough room in the trunk for everyone's hard-sided travel case. The Boyt that will catch your eye right away is the $180 #GC36 Boundary Lakes with leather handles, saddle, tip and butt. This model has an outside choke tube/accessory pocket. A two-way brass zipper and removable, adjustable sling are included. These cases are made with 22-ounce heavy canvas siding and soft, 40-ounce cotton batting

**A soft-sided, take-down shotgun case such as this one from Boyt is an excellent investment for protecting your gun. Made with a 22-ounce heavy canvas exterior, it is padded with 40-ounce cotton batting and a flannel lining. It has a leather tip and sling, plus an accessory pocket.**

**While soft-sided cases are not recommended for long-term storage, they are excellent for trips to the range and keeping your gun from becoming dinged or scratched between rounds. The Bob Allen "Two Gun Man" detachable double gun case fastens together by a full-length zipper for use as a double or a single case.**

with flannel lining. They are available in green and khaki in lengths from 46 to 52 inches.

Boyt offers many specialty cases. Two-gun cases like their $130 green canvas #GS150 Two-Gun Canvas Sleeve open from the butt of the case with a strap rather than a zipper in 48-, 50- and 52-inch lengths. The #GC214 Take-Down Canvas Case is made with the same 22/40 materials with a heavy-duty padded suede divider to protect your stock from the barrel lugs. This $129 green or khaki case comes with an accessory pocket, brass zipper and leather sling in three lengths: 28, 30 and 34 inches.

## Practice Traps

If you want to get in a few shots on the weekend or after work without going to the club range, Champion (www.championtarget.com) has a couple traps to consider. You can buy a lightweight hand thrower like their inexpensive Super Sport at almost any WalMart. It tosses one bird at a time and is adjustable for all size sporting clays targets, from standard to mini.

Throw two at a time like quail rising from the brush? Check out the EZ-Double Throw from MTM Case-Gard (www.mtmcase-gard.com). Its adjustability will allow you to throw "for countless horizontal and vertical separation choices," MTM says, and you can throw right or left hand. In red plastic, total assembled length is 31 inches.

When you become more serious about your practice and either do not live near a certified range or just want the convenience of shooting whenever you want to shoot, you will want to step up to a machine like Champion's High Fly string-release manual trap—and it is only $30! The adjustable High Fly launches one or two birds with the pull of a cord and features a target clip for secure placement and consistent flight path. You can stake this one in the ground or, Champion suggests, mount it on a tire.

If you have a place to shoot, you can easily get in a few shots at practice targets. The MTM EZ Double-Throw and a few clay targets are cheap compared to a highly qualified assistant!

Inexpensive hand throwers and boxes of clay targets are available at most BoxMarts. They make practice cheap, easy and fun.

Champion also sells orange clays: the 108mm standard, 90mm midi, 60mm mini and thick, 108mm rabbit. For real shooting fun, Champion suggests nesting a midi underneath a standard and throwing them together for a challenging doubles presentation.

If your shooting partner wants to sit down while he or she throws your birds, Champion and others have practice-style traps with seats attached. Anchored by the operator's weight, the Champion MatchBird ¾-Cock Trap comes with an orange plastic seat. Match-Bird seated traps provide multiple mounting positions for the easy-to-use ¾-cock trap. They throw targets up to 70 yards and quickly attach to a two-inch receiver hitch for clay tossing. They are available in singles and doubles options and throw all clay target sizes: standard, mini, midi and rabbits. The MatchBid throws rabbits, stacked doubles and side-by-side doubles ($199 and $294 doubles).

## Recoil Masters

After a full day on the range and perhaps a couple hundred 1 1/8 rounds, your shoulder has taken a pounding and the resulting dull ache makes you resort to the Extra Strength Tylenol and a shot of Jack Daniels. A good recoil pad can soften the blow.

Pachmayr offers a large line-up of its Decelerator pads (www.pachmayr.com) in skeet/sporting clays (straight to slightly convex face to prevent snagging on your clothes) or trap (concave from heel to toe to provide a positive, "hugging" grip on the shoulder) shapes. Pads are offered in black or brown. Face texturing can be light to maximize mounting speed for those who still choose to begin with an un-mounted gun (leather, lattice or ribbed), medium for field shooting (line-checkered, screen or stippled) or heavy, which is recommended for trap or live birds (basket-weave, pigeon or grooved). The ultimate choice of face pattern depends on your personal preference for mounting ease. Thickness ranges from 0.6 to 1.1 inches and several can be purchased with a decorative white line.

The cost of a Decelerator depends on its thickness and face style, but the 1.1-inch Deluxe #S325 skeet style ribbed face is $26. A do-it-yourself, pre-fit Decelerator pad for a Browning Citori, on the other hand, runs $40.50.

Pachmayr also makes slip-on recoil pads in small, medium and large. These work very well when more than one person uses a gun or when the gun is used for pre-mounted skeet, perhaps, and then for un-mounted 5-stand. The $37.98 (plus $6 shipping and handling) brown leather slip-on is held in place with a hidden Velcro strip and includes a soft rubber insert. Excellent for adjusting length of pull, these black or brown rubber slip-on pads cost $13.50 or $22 for the Decelerator with the Speed-Mount Insert.

Pads such as the SC-100 Sporting Clays with the hard rubber Speed-Mount heel are built for shooters who prefer beginning with an un-mounted gun. The smooth, hard heel tip allows the gun to swing to the shoulder with minimum interference by clothes.

100-Straight Products (www.100straight.com) advertises its $35.95 Terminator as the softest recoil pad available. A closed cell design means this pad is resistant to tearing and splitting. You can choose from black or brown with a flat or curved surface and four depths: ⅝-, ¾- 1- or 1 ⅛-inch. Coupled with 100-Straight's Polymer Buttstock Spacers, you can easily adjust length of pull. Spacers are available in black or white. The plastic material is easy to sand for a smooth, seamless fit on your gun and slotted holes make it easy to adjust to any central butt hole spacing or location. The cost varies for the straight spacers from $7 for the 1/8-inch to $7.25 for the ¼-inch to $10.50 for the ½-inch.

Black buttstock pitch spacers are ideal for altering pitch without cutting your beautiful walnut stock. You can order positive pitch (thicker at top) or negative pitch (thicker at bottom). Quarter-inch spacers (tapered ¼-¹⁄₁₆) are $8 and ½-inch spacers (tapered ½-¹⁄₁₆) are $9.00.

You can also order the Jones Stock Adjuster ($57) from 100-Straight. It provides the versatility of a stock adjuster while adding ¼-inch of length. Use it for as much as one-inch vertical drop, 22 degrees of left or right diagonal and ⁵⁄₁₆-inch horizontal offset of the recoil pad. It mounts with machined steel thread inserts and fits recoil pads with 3 ⅛-inch hole spacing.

## Point of Aim

If you do not like the mid-point steel bead and front dot sight that come on your shotgun, don't be afraid to change it. Uni-Dot, part of the Lyman Brands group with Pachmayr, TacStar, Trius and others (www.uni-dot.com) makes a unique Uni-Dot fiber optic front sight that is partially encased in a black, non-reflecting tube. In either bright red or fluorescent green, you can only see this dot, which now comes in 2mm, 3mm or 4mm diameters, when the gun is properly mounted and aligned with your aiming eye. The Uni-Dot lets you aim with both eyes open and focused on the target. The Uni-Dot promotes proper gun mounting and shooting technique, because if you mount the gun improperly or lift your head, the dot disappears. The carrier is made of high impact plastic and will snap on the rib anywhere along its length or there are designs for rib-less barrels. No tapping, drilling or gluing is required. Multiple sizes are available to fit most shotgun ribs, and prices vary from $20 to $40 depending upon style and use.

The services of a highly qualified fitting guru and shooting coach like Kansas' Michael Murphy (left) can save you countless hours, frustration, and, in the long run, probably a lot of money needed to reach your shooting goals. Instructors such as Murphy can help you make the gun comfortable and bring the rib and beads precisely in-line with your dominant eye.

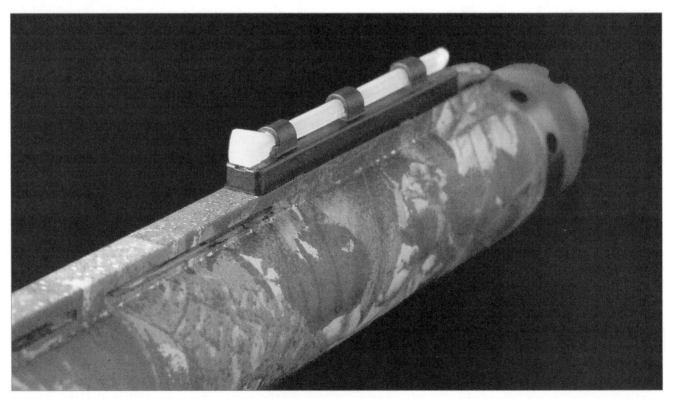

If you have difficulty using your front – or even your mid-point bead – sight as an aiming aid, it is easy to change. Many competitors and hunters find that they are attracted to bright non-electronic fiber optic technology.

## Barrel Restoration

If you have an older shotgun, chances are the barrel is pitted, scratched and has some moisture-related corrosion. Several manufacturers, including Teague Precision Chokes (www.teagueprecisionchokesltd.co.uk), have developed a process for restoring the shooting characteristics of the gun, if not the barrel itself, to its original capabilities.

Teague virtually creates a new barrel by machining the inner barrel wall and affixing a permanent, but ultra-thin wall liner from breech to muzzle. The liner restores the original bore dimensions, chamber length and gun characteristics. And yes, you can shoot the rejuvenated gun.

At the current 1.46 rate of exchange (U.S. dollars to British pounds sterling) and the current L 1,250 price (1,250 British pounds), the cost for a double barrel shotgun appears to be about $1,825 plus taxes (Britain has a VAT or value added tax) and, what Andrew Harvison at Teague calls CIF: carriage, insurance and freight. Obviously, this service is intended only for quite valuable and perhaps very old collector guns that you actually fire as in The Vintagers events (www.vintagers.org), for example, because for this price, you could purchase new barrels for many fine quality guns and, indeed, quite a few fine-shooting over/unders and semi-autos—lock, stock AND barrel.

## Shooting Bags and Shell Pouches

You must have one of these. It doesn't matter what brand or color, just so you do not have to carry a box of shells in your hand or a fist-full jammed down in your pockets. That is uncomfortable and … well, it makes you look like a beginner, and who wants that? Besides, we are not talking about much money for a shooting bag or pouch.

Boyt's #SC50 Shell Pouch (www.boytharness.com) comes with a heavy-duty web belt, zippered bottom and rugged but stylish green canvas trimmed in leather. For $59.00, you can buy one with two interior compartments; perhaps one for "live" shells and one for "empties" in case you reload or are just tidy.

The Bob Allen company is now part of the Boyt companies. At $28, the Bob Allen (www.bob-allen.com) Deluxe nylon divided pouch with belt (#425T) is backed with ¼-inch foam for rigidity and comes with an adjustable, two-inch web belt. The twin compartments hold one box of shells each. It is available in navy blue, green or black.

There is a very nice nylon mesh combo-pouch (#437T) available from Bob Allen for just $26 and you see a lot of these at a shooting event. It holds a box of shells on top and 100 empties on bottom. The bottom compartment has a spring-top opening that makes it difficult to spill your reloads. This mesh pouch comes in navy, green or black.

On a big sporting clays venue, you will walk for miles and shoot for several hours. Depending on the target presentation, you may well want several types of shells, chokes, extra sunscreen and something cold to drink. Many shooter bags hold eight boxes of shells and have various pockets for miscellaneous necessary stuff. However, do you really want to carry eight boxes of shells (200 shots) on your shoulder? Just because a bag will hold eight boxes does not mean you need to or even ought to carry eight boxes. Some people will though, just in case….

The $68 Bob Allen #500T Deluxe Sporting Clays Bag is made from heavy-duty nylon and has a central 14 x 8-inch inside compartment. It holds up to 12 boxes of shells and has a hard bottom and foam insert sides to add rigidity to your 25-pound load. The Deluxe has zippered front, back and side pockets. This bag is available in navy, green, black or, for the competitor who is also a hunter, Advantage Timber camouflage.

MTM (www.mtmcase-gard.com) makes a variation on the classic soft bag. Their hard plastic 100-Round Shotshell Case (#SW-100) holds four boxes of shells and has a removable choke tube holder that fastens to the top. MTM says you place open cartons of shells inside the case and the see-through choke-tube case holds chokes, lube and most factory wrenches. The case measures 7 x 10.6 x 6 inches and is carried with a swiveling plastic handle.

Shooters with a taste for the finer things in life will enjoy perusing the Filson line (www.filson.com), and the $110 Shooting Bag (#211) is designed for functionality and to make a statement. The belt is "genuine bridle leather," 1 ¼ inches wide with a belt loop and is made in the U.S. There are two side bellows pockets, each 9 x 10 x 1 ½, and a rear bellows pocket 10 x 11 x 2 ¼. The rear pocket is lined with coated nylon for easy cleaning. All pockets have flaps with one-hand snap closure. Fabric is oil finished tin cloth, 100 percent cotton duck, paraffin treated for maximum water repellency and vegetable tanned in green or tan.

## Vests and Harnesses

While most of us have, at one time or another, worn an adjustable harness to absorb some of our gun's recoil, it is my experience that most people do not find them entirely comfortable. Seems like the strap is always an irritant and that the protection offered by the padded section is minimal. Nevertheless, they are available from Boyt, Bob Allen and others. Bob Allen's adjustable $34 khaki Shotgun Absorb-a-Coil Harness (#399A) has a soft, visco-elastic polymer pad enclosed in a cotton pocket. The pad is supposed to absorb up

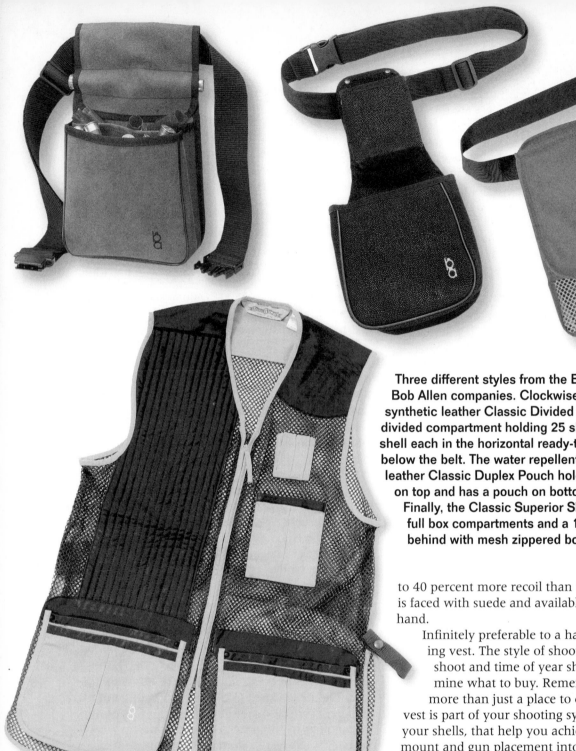

Three different styles from the Boyt Harness and Bob Allen companies. Clockwise from upper left: the synthetic leather Classic Divided Pouch with belt has a divided compartment holding 25 shells in each with one shell each in the horizontal ready-to-be-loaded position below the belt. The water repellent, distressed synthetic leather Classic Duplex Pouch holds a full box of shells on top and has a pouch on bottom for empties.

Finally, the Classic Superior Shell Pouch has two, full box compartments and a 100-hull mesh pouch behind with mesh zippered bottom.

**The Bob Allen #255M Series Mesh Shooting Vest** is made from soft, tightly woven polycotton twill base material. The International style pad is suede and it has a side tab adjustment, choke tube pocket, inside zippered pocket, side tab waist adjustment and two large front pockets. Cool, comfortable and convenient. Available for both left- and right-hand in two color styles and six sizes.

to 40 percent more recoil than the competition. It is faced with suede and available right hand or left hand.

Infinitely preferable to a harness is a full shooting vest. The style of shooting, the place you shoot and time of year should help you determine what to buy. Remember that a vest is more than just a place to carry your shells. A vest is part of your shooting system, no less than your shells, that help you achieve consistent gun mount and gun placement into the shoulder pocket. A vest is not necessary to good shooting, but in my experience, it helps.

When selecting a vest, consider the shotgun games you shoot. Vests can be purchased with a small gun pad of the style that is favored by those who shoot trap and skeet, where the gun is mounted before the bird is called for and the track of the bird is known to within a few degrees. Vests can also be purchased with a full front pad that is virtually mandatory in games where the gun does not have to be pre-mounted and where the gun butt can catch or snag on an abbreviated pad. Many shooters choose the International style; perhaps

**Every shooter experiences recoil. Begin taming a shotgun with a good quality shooting vest that has a padded shoulder. Relatively inexpensive, a vest is virtually mandatory for carrying shells and utility items for a few hours of shooting.**

most do, because it works well in any shooting situation.

Sporting clay shooters like vest styles with double divided shell pockets. This allows one to keep track of up to four different loads easily. It is not uncommon to carry several different loads to the shooting stand. Trap and skeet shooters need just one big pocket for the shells and one for the fired hulls.

Construction of the vest is important. In the hot, humid southeast, you rarely see a full front- and back-cloth vest. They are simply too hot, especially when loaded with shells. They quickly become sweat-soaked and wind up several pounds heavier than when they started the day. Hot weather shooters favor mesh vests for obvious reasons. Northern and cool weather shooters generally prefer fuller vests for warmth and because they compete well into cold weather. Vests are cheap and the answer—because a 100-degree day in Missouri or upstate New York can be absolutely stifling—is to have multiple garments available.

For $50 you can wear a Bob Allen #240M Series shooting vest made of tightly woven cotton twill and mesh for warmer weather. It features padded gun pads, a choke tube pocket and side tab adjustment for girth, with bellowed pockets and an extra two shell loops for spares. From this price point up to practically $136, you can purchase a vest with a variety of side tab adjustments, choke tube pockets, interior "security" pockets with zippers, a range of colors, towel loops and a gun pad and trim made from leather. The more expensive your vest, the more extras it will have.

## A Cart for the Field

Everywhere you go at a sporting clays tournament you will see people zipping around in golf cars. Major tournaments have dozens of golf cars on hand that you can rent for the weekend for a nominal fee. If you object to paying $50 to rent a car every time you shoot in a big sporting clays event, you could just buy a car.

Yamaha's four-stroke #G22A gas golf car has an 11.4 hp, 357cc engine and comes in a variety of colors. You can order one of these and have it shipped free for just $4,799 (in white) or $4,999 (in a variety of colors such as garnet or cobalt blue). They can also be purchased with electric drives, and for an extra $130 the folks at www.tntgolfcar.com (April, 2009) will attach a tinted, fold-down windshield. Light kits cost $165 for gas cars or $365 for electric cars and three-sided curtain enclosures start at $300. Built-in options include a radio and CD player, wood-grain dash, custom upholstery and a high speed upgrade!

Stepping down slightly to a more modest porter, many shooters enjoy the exercise of walking from station to station, while they pull a golf cart (cart, not car) that they have modified for shooting events. Now, these can be found practically anywhere online, at a golf retailer or the local golf course, but a basic, 10 ½-pound two-wheel folding Bag Boy #M-330 pull cart with adjustable handle will be less than $95, while the deluxe Sun Mountain three-wheel Speed Cart V2 is $180. Several adjustable, folding Sun Mountain carts have pneumatic tires, a dual-tube frame, and can be ordered in several colors and even with power assist.

Out in California, Dean Ziegel has designed a fine little field cart for shooters at sporting clays events where you often put on several miles while carrying your shotgun, shells, sunscreen, choke tubes and wrenches, a shell-whacker and numerous other essential items. This load seems to weigh about 100 pounds by the end of the day even though you have shot most of your shells. Dean calls his cart the Jackass Field Cart (www.ziegeleng.com). In price and versatility, it falls somewhere between the ease of riding and the more common push/pull golf carts.

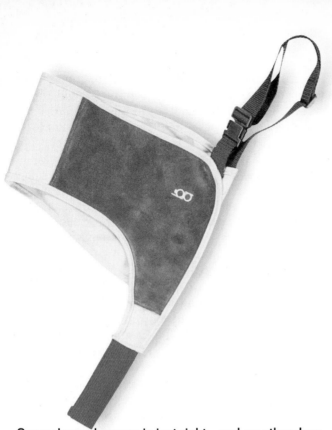

Some days a harness is just right – and on other days there is no way you can possibly squirm into one and feel comfortable. This lightly padded, adjustable harness is faced with a suede gun pad and available in right or left hand from Bob Allen.

Clyde Craddock and Brett Holcomb unlimber Clyde's golf cart for a sporting clays event. Clyde (no hat), who shoots a Krieghoff Parcours Special and owns the golf car and trailer, was a nine-year sporting clays All American. Brett was the 2003 Florida 20-gauge champion with his Browning 325.

Pull carts are everywhere on a sporting clays course. Based on the push/pull golf cart, these are far less expensive, but in some ways more versatile. Custom designs built on the golf cart principle have places for several guns, boxes of ammo and chokes, snacks and drinks. Three-wheelers are more stable than two-wheelers, but in any version, these carts can go places that the powered cars cannot.

According to Dean, "The Jackass uses the same kind of high quality machined aluminum materials you find on competition wheel chairs." The rear tires on a Jackass are 20 inches in diameter with 36 stainless steel spokes for stability over uneven ground. The 32-pound #J1-A model ($550) disassembles and folds into a compact unit to fit into an automobile trunk (approximately 11 x 23 x 23). It will hold three to five shotguns in carpet-covered, padded foam brackets and has a large aluminum front tray for your shells and gear or perhaps to support a cooler. Gun butts rest on a one-inch polypropylene high-density block covered with carpet to absorb shock. Casters and four-inch solid urethane wheels support the front. The upright handle of a Jackass resembles a standard hand truck, but the handle of the #J1-A is offset 30 degrees for easy pulling and is 42 inches above the centerline of the rear wheels. The #J3 economy model Jackass ($126) is built on a heavy-duty 300-pound capacity industrial hand truck so it is not particularly elegant. "Strong and simple," Dean says about the #J3.

One of the primary rules of shotgun games is, "Never go to the shooting line or station without hearing protection." When you wear earmuffs with safety compression circuits like these from Bob Walker, make sure they are sculptured so that when you bring your gun to your cheek, the stock does not clatter against the hard plastic of the cups.

# Chronograph

As if a simple score were not enough, everyone on the shooting line wants—no, needs—to know how fast they are shooting. Most shotshell manufacturers freely list this data by load. Reloaders have tables available depending on the powder used, the gauge, the amount and size of your shot. But for about the same price as a pair of good shooting glasses, you could own your own chronograph and then you would not have to assume: you would know.

Speed is important, and not so important. For sporting clays, you generally want a fast load. For skeet, one is shooting close and the difference of 50 or even a hundred feet per second may not matter. For trap, however, shotshell loads are regulated by not-to-exceed speeds:

XII.G.3. Any load with a velocity greater than 1290 FPS (Feet Per Second) with maximum shot charge of 1 ⅛ ounces, or 1325 FPS with a maximum shot charge of 1 ounce, or 1350 FPS with a maximum shot charge of ⅞ ounces or less, as measured in any individual shotshell. These velocities are maximum and no individual shotshell shall exceed these limits for the designated shot charge. In addition, no load containing more than 1 ⅛ ounces or any shot larger than Number 7 ½ can be used. Shot charges are maximum and no charge may exceed the charge amount by more than 3%.

Shooting Chrony (www.shootingchrony.com) has several folding portable models and they are all affordable for the individual. Every Chrony is made of 20-gauge steel, but weighs less than 2 ½ pounds. According to the company, "Every Shooting Chrony measures the speed of bullets, arrows, shotgun and airgun pellets, paintballs, et cetera, from 30 fps to 7000 fps and with better than 99.5 percent accuracy." They are powered by one nine-volt alkaline battery with a rated service life of 48 hours and are equipped with a large, ½-inch LCD readout. Folded, these chronographs are 7 ½ x4 ½ x 2 ¾ inches. All come with a three-year limited warranty but will, Shooting Chrony says, "last a lifetime."

The #F-1 is the stripped-down, entry level Chrony and it only costs $90. Of course, there are several upgraded features, but figure that for about $250 you can get a chronograph with absolutely all the bells and whistles.

The $200 M2 chronograph system from Competitive Edge Dynamics (www.cedhk.com) comes in a sleek, lightweight package. It is capable of reading velocities from 50-7000 fps, and has memory storage for over 1000 velocities or 500 shot strings. The M2 has the ability to take projectile speed readings in low light levels and new Data Collector software and USB interface allow you to download shot information to a PC.

The M2 comes with a main PC unit, two-foot mounting bracket, two sensors, sunscreens, side-arms, PC serial cable and software. Additional features include voice chip technology so results can be heard, back-up battery storage, low battery indicator and permanent memory back-up. The M2 measures high, low, average velocity; extreme spread; and standard deviation.

Bob Walker, founder of Bob Walker's Target Ear (and the popular Game Ear), actually began using hearing protection with safety compression circuits for turkey hunting. For hunting or clay target shooting, the theory and the circuitry are the same.

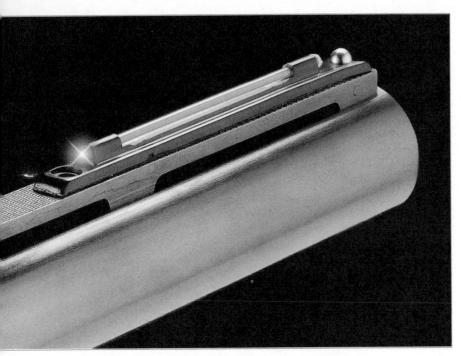

The TG-90 Univesal GloDot with .060-inch fiber optic pipe from TruGlo may help many clay shooters who need the extra point of reference near the muzzle of their shotgun.

## Miscellaneous "Must Haves"

Every shooter who has been at the line for a while has tried a toe rest. A shotgun is only eight or nine pounds, but after a day on a sporting clays course or even one hot hour at a trap shoot, it feels like it is pulling your arm down to about your knee. A toe rest looped into your shoe laces gives you a firm surface against which to rest your unloaded gun muzzle. Bob Allen's is made from heavy leather with a tab and snap to fit over shoelaces, and retails for less than $10.

At some time in your career, you will consider shooting with gloves. Some people like them and some do not. It depends on the weather and on your body's individual mechanics—sweaty or nervous hands, for instance. GripSwell ergonomic shooting gloves (www.gripswell.com) help absorb felt recoil and reduce fatigue while, GripSwell's Tosh Ono says, the padded goatskin gloves "provide a point of reference for a consistent mount" and act in the same manner as a palm swell on your shotgun's stock. Look for gloves in un-dyed natural leather that will not stain or absorb heat. Sizes available are small through XXL from $45 per pair, matching plain, to $70 for their winter insulated palm swell gloves. Unlike golf gloves, which wear out quickly due to the extreme friction of your grip on a wrapped shaft, these shooting gloves could last for years.

When you finally get your beautiful new shotgun home, are you going to keep it under the bed? Perhaps this is another reason to buy a cheap gun, but every gun owner needs a secure place for his or her firearms. The best place—other than the short-barrel Benelli you do keep under the bed for home defense—is a stand-alone safe.

At the lower end, a Cannon Patriot 6-12 gun safe costs about $930 from www.gunsafes.com, although you should have your head examined if you purchase from other than a reputable local sporting goods dealer who can provide movement to your room of choice and set-up. Otherwise, it is you and the spouse and kids … and that sounds more like a week on the sofa than an enjoyable shooting-related experience.

The Patriot is available in three sizes and has a one-inch steel composite door, 12-gauge uni-body construction and built-in fire resistance. Look for electronic locks, upholstered adjustable interior, internal hinges and active locking bolts. An electric humidifier is optional.

RedHead Premium Shooting Bags by Bass Pro have a reputation for quality accessories that fit practically any individual style. Water- and mildew-resistant RedHead shell carriers provide specific 24-ounce canvas exteriors and 3mm leather pouches, sleeves, pockets and bags for whole boxes, individual shells, multiple shell types and spent hulls.

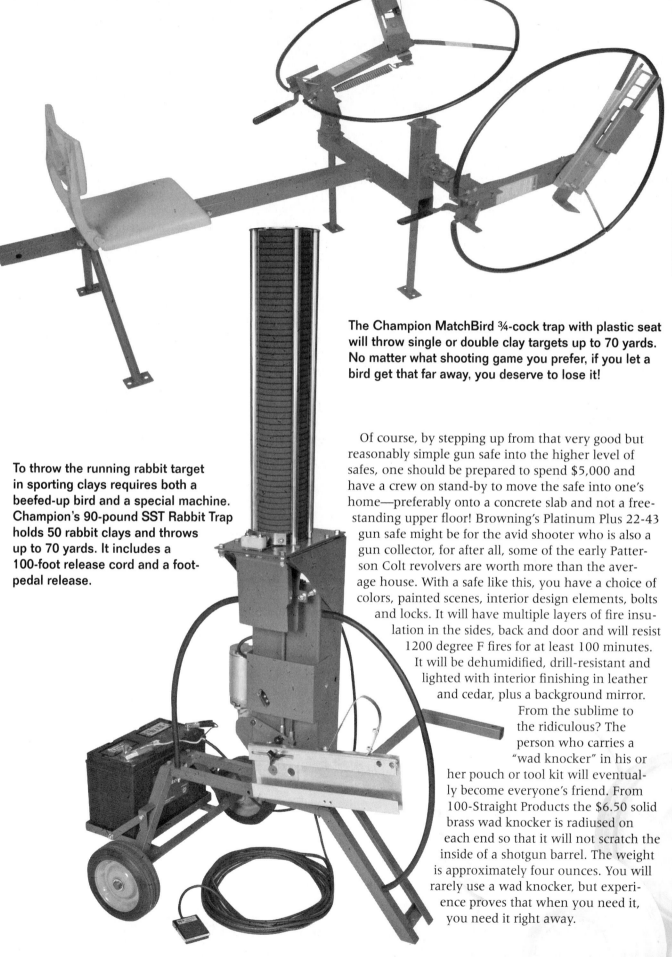

The Champion MatchBird ¾-cock trap with plastic seat will throw single or double clay targets up to 70 yards. No matter what shooting game you prefer, if you let a bird get that far away, you deserve to lose it!

To throw the running rabbit target in sporting clays requires both a beefed-up bird and a special machine. Champion's 90-pound SST Rabbit Trap holds 50 rabbit clays and throws up to 70 yards. It includes a 100-foot release cord and a foot-pedal release.

Of course, by stepping up from that very good but reasonably simple gun safe into the higher level of safes, one should be prepared to spend $5,000 and have a crew on stand-by to move the safe into one's home—preferably onto a concrete slab and not a free-standing upper floor! Browning's Platinum Plus 22-43 gun safe might be for the avid shooter who is also a gun collector, for after all, some of the early Patterson Colt revolvers are worth more than the average house. With a safe like this, you have a choice of colors, painted scenes, interior design elements, bolts and locks. It will have multiple layers of fire insulation in the sides, back and door and will resist 1200 degree F fires for at least 100 minutes. It will be dehumidified, drill-resistant and lighted with interior finishing in leather and cedar, plus a background mirror.

From the sublime to the ridiculous? The person who carries a "wad knocker" in his or her pouch or tool kit will eventually become everyone's friend. From 100-Straight Products the $6.50 solid brass wad knocker is radiused on each end so that it will not scratch the inside of a shotgun barrel. The weight is approximately four ounces. You will rarely use a wad knocker, but experience proves that when you need it, you need it right away.

# CHAPTER 31
# RELOADING FOR FUN AND PROFIT

No matter how you slice it, clay target shooting is not the most inexpensive sport in the world. In addition to guns, range fees, travel and all the other associated costs, you have to factor in the shells. There are only two ways to acquire those shells: you either buy factory fodder or roll your own. At some point, every clay target shooter will have to decide whether reloading is in his or her best interest. In some cases, it may not be. While reloaded shells are always welcome in a fun game and often accepted in regulated sporting clays events, they are specifically prohibited in FITASC shooting.

It is commonly accepted that you can save considerable sums of money reloading compared to buying factory ammo. Those mysterious savings however depend on how you buy the factory shells.

If you walk into your local gun shop or Wal-Mart and ask for a couple of boxes of target loads, you can expect to pay full list price. That does not mean the shop owner is gouging you. He has overhead, inventory costs and other expenses that must be recouped to stay in business. He also does not have the buying power to make big lot purchases at lower prices. The larger discount chains do, and that is why you will likely find the same shells for less there, assuming of course, that the discount store carries the particular load you want. Often they will not stock anything other than lower-priced soft-shot field loads unless there is strong clay target interest in their area and the store manager is smart enough to realize it. Do not count on the discount stores having a steady supply of target loads on hand when you need them, though, particularly the specialty loads.

Sometimes, however, the chains have worthwhile buys. I remember that several years ago the local Wal-Mart received a large quantity of Remington's promotional loads. These normally would not excite target shooters, but in this case (for some inexplicable reason) these shells were loaded in Remington's target-grade Unibody hull, which is an excellent hull to reload. They cost only $80 a case then and local skeet shooters cleaned out the store. Not only did they get a case of shells to shoot, but also good hulls to reload, and at only a slight increase over what it would have cost them to reload that same case with their own components.

If you find a bargain like that, it is worth buying as much as you can afford.

## Buy by the Case

Smart clay shooters buy factory shells through their club in case lots. Most clubs will take orders for case lots from members when they restock targets. That way, they save a considerable amount on freight and can offer the shells at what amounts to wholesale.

Target loads now run more than $100 for a case for 12, 20 and 410, with the 28-gauge running about $120. That is $5-plus per box for the first three and over $6 for a box of 28. It represents what I would call an average best case price. That price can vary around the country because of freight costs. Shotshells are heavy and expensive to ship. The farther you are from the manufacturer, the higher the cost.

Although $5 a box may sound cheap to someone buying retail one box at a time, you can cut that cost further by selling the empty hulls. Among skeet shooters, the going prices for once-fired brand-name hulls are: 5¢ per 12-gauge; 6¢ per 20; 8-10¢ per 100 per 28; and 10¢ for the 410. Trap shooters have no interest in anything other than the 12 and most sporting clays shooters are not especially enamored with the smaller gauges, so those prices are contingent on having a buyer.

What that means is that a full box of 410 shells costs $5 and the box of once-fired empty hulls is worth $2.50. Your cost to shoot factory 410s is around $2.50 per box. You can reload them for less than that, but not a lot.

The 28-gauge runs a buck a box more, and you can save money there. Even selling the empty hulls, you can realize a savings of $35 or more per case if you reload this gauge. The savings on 20-gauge shells is a bit less, while the 12-gauge will be similar in cost to the 20, unless empty 12-gauge hulls are worth more than 5¢ each in your area. At a trap range, that will likely be the case.

Another way to buy ammo, and a good one for the casual shooter, is to purchase it at the range. Many ranges operate under the assumption that they are there to sell clay targets and that is where their profit is. Since it takes shells to shoot targets, they will often sell top quality target loads for only about one dollar mark-up over their costs, which can be on the low end of the scale. Buying a single box of 28-gauge shells at my club (the most expensive shell they sell) runs $8.50, and the empties are worth about $2.50 a box. That brings the box cost to $6; and while you can reload them for about $4 a box, if you only shoot a dozen boxes a year, there is no point in it.

No, not every shooter needs to reload. In fact, some trap shooters who belong to active clubs and can expect to be able to purchase a fresh case every month (and be assured of a market for selling their empties) have quit reloading. Why tie up their money in the equipment and components, not to mention the space it takes to set up and load, or the time required to do it, when each box of factory shells costs them only about $2.50 more?

Similarly, many skeet shooters who reload the other gauges have stopped loading the 410. Why create extra work when the reward is not worth it?

On the other hand (and it's a big hand!), circumstances may make reloading far more attractive. My situation is not unusual.

## Reasons to Reload

I no longer shoot skeet on a regular competitive basis, but still bum a lot of rounds at that game, in addition to trap. I also shoot a fair amount of sporting clays, primarily with the 12- and 28-gauges. In the case of the latter, reloading is mandatory if I want to realize the full potential of this gauge on the sporting clays course. That means I need a loading press, primers, shot in four sizes (#7 ½, 8, 8 ½ and 9) and a place to set up the press.

Adding the 12-gauge to that requires only a set of dies, a couple different cans of powder, some additional wads and, of course, empty 12-gauge hulls. Everything else interchanges.

If you have already made the decision to load one gauge, then there is no reason not to load the rest. After all, you have already made the most significant investment on equipment for the first gauge.

Loading all of your own shells also simplifies things. I can purchase top-quality, nickel-plated, long-range sporting clays loads in 12-gauge. But if I only need three or four boxes a year (you do not use that many of these specialized long-range shells in an average round of sporting clays), why have a whole case sitting around? Ditto for the spreader loads; the #8 ½ load I like on the second shot of skeet doubles; or any of the other non-standard loads that, while being a major asset when you need them, just are not used that often. Nor do you suddenly find yourself out of a favorite load just before a match. You can always make more without having to wait for a bargain.

Yes, there are a number of shooters who do find reloading very worthwhile, both in terms of cost and shell performance. Rolling your own loads is not difficult.

## Reloading Basics

As with metallic rounds, all the reloader is doing is sizing the hull back to factory specs to fit the chamber, and then replacing those components expended on firing. With a shotshell that means the primer, powder, wad and shot charge. Accomplishing this requires a loading press and a set of dies for that gauge.

A number of companies offer quality shotshell loading equipment. At the moment, the big players in the game are Hornady (www.hornaday.com); MEC or Mayville Engineering Company (www.mecreloaders.com); Ponsness/Warren (www.reloaders.com); Dillon Precision (www.dillonprecision.com) and Lee Precision (www.leeprecision.com). In years past, there have been a number of companies other than these, but they have either merged into larger companies or gone out of business. A great deal of their equipment is still around, and still in excellent operating condition. You can probably find some of it for sale on the used market at a gun club or gun show, but I do not recommend it. Buying a loading press that is not currently manufactured can present a major problem if a part breaks and you need service. You may not be able to replace it, and if you cannot have it custom-made, then your press is useless. Parts break on occasion or just wear out, and if you cannot fix it, there is not much point buying it, no matter how attractive the price.

Expect to pay between $150 and $500 for a quality shotshell loader set up to load one gauge. Virtually all of them will offer interchangeable die capability, meaning that once you bite the bullet for the first purchase, adding other gauges is not expensive.

## Press Types

There are essentially two types of loading presses in use, single stage and progressive.

The single stage press requires that each hull be manually moved through each of the loading stations. On my no-longer-made Hornady 155, that means I move the shell to station one to de-prime and re-size it, station two to prime it, and station three to drop a powder charge, seat a wad and add the shot. At station four, I start the crimp, and station five finishes it. It sounds slow, but it is not that bad. I can load 50 to 60 rounds per hour.

The advantage to the single stage press is that every loading operation is fully monitored and it is hard to make a mistake—easier when one becomes comfortable with equipment and loads and approaches the job mechanically. The quality of the ammunition loaded on this (or other single stage presses) is high and uniform from shell to shell. I use this press when making test rounds or when I just need to run off a couple boxes of specialty rounds. Another advantage to the single stage is that they fall into the lower end of the price spectrum and changing to different gauge dies is easy. If you only shoot a couple hundred rounds a month and do not mind spending a few hours loading them, a quality single stage press will serve you well.

If you need more shells in less time, the answer is a progressive press. Feed shells into station one and each time you cycle the handle it will automatically re-size, de-prime, move the shell, prime, drop powder and shot, and do all the other things. All you have to do is feed in an empty hull, insert a wad, and you get one reloaded shell with each pull of the handle. They can crank out several hundred rounds per hour. Some of the expensive ones do not even require you to operate the handle.

The drawback to the progressive press, other than the cost and the fact that it is not as easy to shift to other gauges, is that it requires a lot more attention on the operator's part. It is not difficult to forget to insert a wad or drop shot or leave out the powder, or neglect something else. You will find out quickly if you messed up when you go to range and a shell fails to fire. One wag has observed that progressive press users who suffered from Attention Deficit Disorder invented shell knockers!

All the different manufacturer's presses do the same thing, just in a slightly different way. I happen to be very partial to Hornady and Ponsness/Warren equipment, but that is because their machines fit my style. All of them will work, and they come with complete instructions. In the case of the MEC equipment, they even have an information line to call for help when you need it.

## Heed the Data

Load data for shotshells is far more varied than for metallic rounds. With the latter there are really only a half-dozen powder, bullet and primer combinations that will produce decent results with any given cartridge. That is not the case here. Different makes and models of shotshells will have different internal volumes and shapes. These differences affect how they will react with any given wad and powder combination. For that reason, many shooters like to use just a couple of different hulls since this cuts down the number of different wads they require. Put the wrong components in the hull and you can have a lousy load, even a dangerous one. That has been amply illustrated by a test conducted by Dave Fackler at Ballistic Products (www.ballisticproducts.com). He took six different hulls and used exactly the same wad, primer, powder charge and shot charge to load each. Here is what happened to velocities and pressures with these mid-range hunting loads.

Any pressure over 11,500 LUP (Lead Units of Pressure) is excessive in a 12-gauge shell. Any pressure under 6,500 LUP may not let the shell fully perform by burning the powder charge properly and cleanly.

It is obvious from the test that not all hulls are created equal, and a combination of components that may produce a beautifully performing load in one can be hazardous in another. This is not a knock on any particular maker's shell, because all will work very nicely with the proper components and load data.

This test points out that anyone attempting to load shotshells should have current, tested data. That data is easy to come by. Remington, Winchester, Federal and other shell makers who also offer components have good loading data information and it is yours for the asking. Companies like Ballistic Products, which sells components, or Hodgdon, which sells powders, have plenty of data on their loads. It is available for a phone call, a letter or often on their Internet site. Some sell

reloading manuals full of recipes, and the most recent Reloading for Shotgunners from Gun Digest Books is a veritable bible of shotgun reloading information. Do not start shotshell loading without good data. Otherwise, you are asking for trouble.

Once you have the data that gives you the proper combination of wad, powder, primer and shot charge for a given hull, it is not advisable to deviate from it. Simply changing the make of primer can raise or lower pressure enough to turn a good load into a poor performer. You can, however, fine-tune your gun's performance by choosing the right load for the conditions, and one major factor in that respect is the temperature at which you will be using the load.

## Shotshell Pressures

Each shotshell recipe provided by the ammo or component makers will provide the tested working pressure for that load, expressed in psi or LUP. These are the two ways of measuring shotshell pressure and they are slightly different, but not enough to make much difference unless you are one of those who would rather pick nits than bust clays. As mentioned earlier, any pressure above 11,500 is excessive in a 12-gauge. It will not blow your gun, but it might well blow your pattern, and it will certainly increase the wear on your gun, not to mention your shoulder. Any pressure below 7500 (according to ballistic experts) will result in a shell that is not operating at full efficiency. I am not sure I fully agree with that, however. At the risk of sounding like a nitpicker myself, I have found that 12-gauge loads can function nicely down to about 6,500. The smaller gauges should be 8,500 or above.

Within the acceptable pressure range, the higher the pressure, the more recoil and shot deformation, and the lower the pressure, the less. When I am working with 12-gauge target loads, I prefer those that operate from 7,500 to 9,000 LUP. In the smaller gauges, I feel the range needs to be between 8,500 and 10,000 LUP.

On the surface, that would seem to make it a simple matter to find a good load. It is not always that simple.

It is the accepted industry standard to pressure-test loads at a uniform 70 degrees Fahrenheit (F) temperature. The reason is that for each 10-degree rise (or fall) in ambient temperature, there will be a corresponding increase or decrease of 1,000 LUP pressure.

In other words, select a load that pressure-tests at 10,500 LUP and that is what you will get at 70 degrees. Walk onto a sweltering 95-degree skeet field on a late August afternoon and you now have a load that is probably cracking 12,500 LUP! This is not good for your gun, your patterns or your shoulder. On the reverse side, select a conservative 7,500 LUP load and shoot it in 40-degree weather and some of the rounds may not even ignite! They are called "bloop" loads because that is just what they sound like when they go off. When that happens, tilt the barrel downward and pour out the shot that never left the barrel. Then, drop a shell knocker down the barrel to remove the stuck wad (fail to do this and the next round disassembles your gun for you!) and then hope all that unburned powder does not find its way into the action and bind up your gun.

This is one area where reloaders have an advantage over factory-round shooters. The factories must load to some uniform pressure, even though they have no idea at what temperature those shells will be shot. You know where and when you shoot and can load accordingly.

For cold weather 12-gauge loads, I pick one in the 10,500 LUP range. For hot weather conditions, I will go with one in the 6,000-7,000 LUP range. By the time I actually get them on the range, they are at about the temperature and pressure I want them, a fact much appreciated by my gun, my shoulder and my scorecard.

## Components

Another area where the reloader has a considerable amount of control is in the shot he elects to stuff into the shell.

Generally, the harder the shot, the better the load will pattern and the shorter will be the shot string. The degree of pattern control a shooter can exercise by simply varying the type of shot is about 10 percent. That is about one full degree of choke.

Top-quality nickel-plated shot (which can be used in sporting clays unless specifically prohibited during a regulation shoot) can tighten your patterns even more, a fact that has not been lost on world-class international trap competitors or clever sporting clays shooters.

If you want solid long-range patterns, go to hard shot. If you need to open a pattern quickly, use the cheap soft stuff. You can also open patterns by loading to higher velocity and pressure.

The type of powder you use can affect recoil and reliability. Some powders burn dirty. I do not shoot fast-burning flake powders like Red Dot because it gums up my gas guns. Sometimes you will get them in factory loads. In fact, just a week ago I was running a very good make of factory ammo through my old Franchi Prestige and the gun was a bit dirty. Early in the second skeet round the gun failed to feed a round. My Prestige just does not do that. It is one of the most reliable gas guns made. The culprit? Flake powder residue in the action temporarily bound up the shell carrier. Racking the action vigorously a few times cleared it and I was able to continue. In sporting clays that would have been a lost bird. Even on the skeet range, where gun malfunctions are a legitimate excuse to reshoot, it was enough to interrupt my concentration.

IMR PB, Royal Scot, Hodgdon Clays and International Clays are all clean-burning powders. They load to target velocities beautifully and will not foul a gas gun. In the smaller gauges, you can add 800-X to that list, although it does require a hot primer like the Federal 209A to light it off well in cool weather. With the 410, I consider

H-110 to be the best bet, with Winchester 296 a good second choice.

These moderate-to-medium powders, PB and 800-X in particular, also seem to deliver more of a shove than a jolt. They are softer shooting at the same load velocity than many other powders.

One last advantage reloaders have is the ability to create loads that do not exist in factory offerings. There is no doubt that factory loads are good these days though. In fact, reloaders will not be able to better the performance of many of them. That includes all established trap loads, many skeet loads and some long-range international loads. Nevertheless, you can equal them, and do it for less money. You can also create loads that are not available from the factory. As far as this shooter is concerned, those are more than enough reasons to spend time at the loading bench.

## Pattern Testing

Testing what you have created requires patterning the gun and load combo. There really is no other way to be certain you're getting an effective load, because each shotgun barrel, even from the same maker, is its own "musical instrument," and a load that does a beautiful job in one gun can be a marginal performer in another. It is traditional to pattern the 12-, 20- and 28-gauges at 40 yards, with the 410 being shot at 30. I test them my own way.

I make up specific loads to operate with a specific choke tube within a specific range. That's where I pattern them—where I will be shooting them. To me, it makes no sense, and provides no information, to test-pattern a 15-yard spreader load at 40 yards just because it happens to be a 12-gauge. Pattern it at 15 yards instead. The same holds true for a mid-range load or a high-performance nickel-plated long-range load.

My procedure is to pattern spreader loads at 15 yards, Skeet or close-range sporting loads at 21 yards, and 16-Yard trap loads (which are mid-range sporting loads) at 30 yards. Handicap trap loads and other long-range loads get tested at 45 yards, although I might take a look at them at 55 yards as well. I may not be able to improve their performance, but at least I'll know what to expect of them and that may be one of the biggest reasons to reload.

## Thoughts on Spreaders

Most scattergunners want their shot patterns as dense and uniform as possible. Still, there are times when a quick-opening pattern can be an asset.

This is especially true in sporting clays. Here, shooters may be faced with a number of real "in-your-face" target presentations at ranges between 10 and 15 yards. Most of these shots will be at quick crossing birds. Sometimes they will have a slight incoming or outgoing angle. It does not take a mathematical genius to see that a shooter who can only generate a 10-inch-wide pattern at that range has to be far more precise with his aim than one who uses a load that gives a 20-inch diameter pattern. In fact, the larger pattern does not give you twice as much surface area to hit the target with; it gives four times as much. When you are swinging like crazy on an orange blur, a larger diameter pattern can help your score dramatically. As a result, there has been a resurgence of interest in 12-gauge "spreader" loads.

These loads have been around for quite a while now, but they have not traditionally garnered much favor with competitive trap and skeet shooters. They were primarily hunting loads designed to open the shot charge from a modified or full choke to what might be achieved with improved cylinder choking.

Often called "brush loads," they were intended to allow a shooter with a fixed choke (which was the rule rather than the exception a decade or so ago) to have a quick and convenient way to open his patterns if he happened to wander into tight quarters. Hence the moniker "brush load."

There are a number of ways to open the pattern on a shotgun without changing the choke. Shooting softer chilled shot at high velocity will usually open a pattern one choke degree over harder shot at more moderate velocity. Wad inserts are also available to help spread the shot. These may be a simple X-divider or a post and base. They are placed into the wad prior to dropping the shot, or inserted into the shot charge after it has been dropped.

A couple different spreader devices are available, such as the Dispersor-X 20-gauge. Many small-bore shots are, by nature, tight and fast. As a shooter, you can use the most open choke available and in some cases that's still not enough.

Designed specifically for these in-your-face flushing bird shots, the Dispersor-X utilizes a central "X" shaped tower to separate pellets into four distinct chambers. When the shell is fired, the pellets are pushed not only forward and out the barrel, but outward as well. Divided, even pressure on all compartments delivers a consistent, wider fringe pattern, a distinct advantage in flushing and fast, incoming shots.

New reloading recipes for the Dispersor-X-20 have been developed and tested with popular hulls and are available for free from Ballistic Products. A pack of 200 spreaders is $6. The original intent of the spreader load was to turn a Full or Modified choke into an Improved Cylinder or Cylinder choke, and spreader wads will certainly do that.

I have tested #9 spreader loads in my Ruger Red Label with Briley long choke tubes in modified and Skeet 1. It showed that from the Modified tube it would produce patterns of almost identical dimensions and density to those achieved by a standard Federal #9 Skeet load from the Skeet-choked tube.

In short, it does just what a spreader load is intended to do. It makes the #7 ½ load a good item to have in your pocket in the hunting fields if you are using a more tightly choked barrel and suddenly find you need an open choke.

That makes spreader loads worthwhile additions to the contemporary factory shotshell lineup. A spreader load is not needed in the field that often—although I can think of times when hunting ruff grouse or woodcock when they were handy—and one bag is likely to last for years. Competitive shooters may not find them that valuable however, because of their quick-change choke options.

In doing some testing to find the best close-range load for my own shooting, I tested the spreader load against several standard #9 skeet loads that are not only less expensive, but more readily available. The results were eye-opening.

Patterning at 15 yards from the Briley Cylinder tube on my Red Label, I found that the spreader load produced a usable pattern of about 22 inches in diameter. The term "usable pattern" is a better reflection of the load's actual performance on targets than is a pellet count and pattern percentage figure. The usable pattern area is determined by simply using a felt marker to draw a circle around the portion of the pattern that is dense and evenly distributed enough to consistently break a target. Individual flier pellets, or small groups of two to four shot pellets outside this area might get you a target every now and then, but you cannot count on them.

A 22-inch pattern at 15 yards is nothing to sneer at! That is three to five inches larger in diameter than you can get with a Skeet 1 choke, and twice as big as what you get with a Skeet 2 (light modified) choke. It is about as much as you can open a pattern at that range and still maintain enough density with 1 ⅛ ounces of shot to prevent a bird from slipping through. In short, the spreader load is probably the best bet for "in-your-face" targets.

Patterning the Federal paper-hulled 2 ¾-dram, 1 ⅛-ounce #9 skeet load from the same cylinder choke at the same range, I got a usable pattern of about 21 inches. That pattern was more evenly distributed than the spreader pattern, which had a couple of thin areas.

The next load I tested was the Federal plastic-hulled #9 skeet load in the three-dram size. Shotshell ballistic theory says that the heavier powder charge would tend to open the pattern a bit more quickly and it did. The three-dram, 1 1/8-ounce load produced a pattern of about 23 inches. Again, it had better pellet distribution than the spreader load.

Cobbling up a quick reload on my Hornady press using an old Victory hull, 19 grains of Clays (about a 2 ¾-dram charge), Federal 209 primer and a purple PC wad (a one-ounce wad that leaves about ⅛-inch of the shot charge unprotected) I got patterns that equaled the three-dram Federal load, but with a bit less recoil. I could probably open that load a bit further by shifting to softer chilled shot, but I happened to be out of it at the time.

The results of my impromptu and, I admit, unscientific tests convinced me that, with my Briley Cylinder choke tube in place, an expensive spreader load is simply not necessary. I am getting the same pattern diameter and slightly better density with either an easily available factory load or a quick and inexpensive reload.

Interestingly, shortly after these tests I ran into shooting champions Bill Whitehurst and Bonnie McLaurin at a local sporting clays range and asked them how they felt about spreaders. Their response was, "Use a cylinder choke and #9 and you get the same thing."

So for my money, when I have an "in-your-face" target, I stick with Cylinder chokes and #9. That will spread me as thin as I'm going to get, and remember that spreader loads—indeed any hand-loaded shells—are no longer permitted in an official FITASC shoot.

## Bigger Is Not Always Better

There is a definite and very noticeable shift among competitive 12-gauge shotgunners toward high speed one-ounce and ⅞-ounce loads for most shooting, reserving the traditional 1 ⅛-ounce loads for longer ranges.

That trend began in a rather unusual way. Many years back, shooters competing in the demanding game of international (bunker) trap were allowed to use full 3 ¼-dram, 1 ¼-ounce loads; many did. This was punishing to the shooter because shooting two shots at a target is the rule, not the exception. Shooting 75 targets in a day means 150 shots with a heavy load.

The UIT Rules Committee decided to spice up the game and changed the rules to allow a maximum of 1 ⅛ ounces of shot. That brought predictable howls from the competitors who were convinced that their scores would go down. That did not happen, though.

A few years later, they changed the rules to allow a maximum of one ounce of shot (28 grams). Again the howls, and again the same results. Scores did not go down; indeed, they went up!

How could a smaller shot charge improve scores? The answer is recoil! The less punishment a shooter absorbs, the better he or she will shoot. The experience of the UIT bunker trap shooters proved this conclusively. In fact, when they made their most recent change to allow a maximum of 24 grams of shot (⅞-ounce), there were very few howls. The shooters had been educated.

Many of those same shooters have also realized that if an ounce of shot is enough to handle a high-speed, stoutly constructed bunker trap target, it will certainly handle the slower standard targets.

Earlier in this chapter, I provided loading data for a mild, actually an ultra-light, one-ounce, 12-gauge load that is an excellent American skeet load. Most one-ounce shooters favor higher velocities. An increase in velocity provides an increase in the target breaking power of the individual pellets, which means you get a good break with fewer pellet hits. I have watched one-ounce loads of #9 shot at 1,300 fps absolutely crush the sturdy international skeet targets, while an ultra-light load at 1,100 fps would merely dust them or make them wobble, but they would not produce the visible piece required to score a hit. Higher speed is one of the keys to making one-ounce loads effective beyond skeet ranges and loading data for these high-speed loads is available. Here is the data for some of the one-ounce loads that I have found effective.

With the Remington Unibody hull, load 22 grains of Hodgdon International powder and a Federal 209 primer. Use ⅞ ounce of shot in the Federal 12SO wad or one ounce of shot in the purple PC wad. Velocity of both is in the 1,280-1,300 fps range and recoil is very mild. Either of these is an excellent close-range load with #9 shot and my favorite for close sporting clays shots.

If you happen to prefer Green Dot powder, you get the same performance with 21.5 grains. If you use the Federal 209A primer, use 20.5 grains of Hodgdon International.

For Federal Gold Medal hulls, the Federal 12SO wad with the standard Federal 209 primer puts up a lovely one-ounce load with the same powder charges listed above. It has low recoil and a velocity of about 1,250-1,280. I like this load very much with hard #8 shot as an all-round load. With a modified choke, it is eminently suitable for 16-yard and double trap. Shift to an improved cylinder choke and it does a fine job on sporting clays targets to 35 yards. Switch to #8 ½ shot and it is a great international skeet load, although not legal in sanctioned UIT matches. I use #7 ½ shot for handicap trap and bunker trap, not to mention dove, quail and woodcock. It is a very versatile load.

Every now and then I run across a supply of Fiocchi hulls, and these create some logistics problems because they do not work well with the Federal wads I normally stock. However, they are good hulls and I want to use them. I use them to make an excellent one-ounce load with the purple PC wad and 20-21 grains of Green Dot. An advantage here is that I can load these with a different shot size than my standard loads, say #7 ½, and use them when I want a little extra punch. Their distinctive color makes it impossible to confuse them with other loads in the heat of battle.

If you are used to shooting full 2 ¾- or three-dram, 1 ⅛-ounce loads on a steady basis, the shift to one-ounce loads will surprise you. They will do pleasant things to your score, your cheek and shoulder as well. When it comes to busting clay targets, bigger is not always better.

# BY-LAWS AND RULEBOOK

# AMERICAN TRAPSHOOTING ASSOCIATION (ATA)

(Updated November 1, 2008)

## SECTION I

## ORGANIZATION OF THE AMATEUR TRAPSHOOTING ASSOCIATION

The following is an informative summary of the organization of the AMATEUR TRAPSHOOTING ASSOCIATION (ATA). Complete, and controlling, details are as contained in the Official Rules, Articles of Incorporation and the By-Laws of the Corporation. The Official Trapshooting Rules of the ATA govern the shooting of registered targets and the conduct of shooters and the duties of shoot management. The ATA has the responsibility for the formulation, regulation and enforcement of these Rules. These Rules are contained in this booklet.

Whenever and wherever used in this compendium, the terms: Rules, Official Rules, Official Trapshooting Rules or any similar derivative thereof, shall be interpreted to include the intended construction and application of the ATA Official Rules and/or ATA Articles of Incorporation (as may be amended) and/or ATA By-Laws (as may be amended) and/or changes made at the direction of the Board of Directors and/or the Executive Committee. The ATA Board of Directors and/or the Executive Committee reserves the right to make alterations in, or amendments to these Rules at any time, whenever it is deemed to be in the best interest of the ATA.

### *A. PURPOSE OF THE ATA*

The purpose of the ATA is to promote and govern the sport of amateur trapshooting throughout the world.

### *B. MEMBERSHIP*

Membership is divided into two (2) classes (Life and Annual), both of which have full shooting rights and privileges. The 2009 target year runs from November 1, 2008 through August 31, 2009. All shooters are considered amateurs and shall be entitled to all rights as set forth in these Rules.

### *C. STATE ORGANIZATIONS AND ATA DELEGATE ELECTIONS*

Shooters in the various States and Provinces are organized into State and Provincial Associations, which under the auspices of the ATA, control shooting in their own territories and conduct State and Provincial championship tournaments. Shooters are required to pay any fees and dues which may be set by these State/Provincial Associations in their place of residence in order to be considered members in good standing of that State/Provincial Association. Such associations receive assistance from the ATA in the form of trophies and cash refunds. This assistance is explained in Rule X., C.

At each annual State or Provincial championship tournament sanctioned by the ATA, a business meeting will be held on a date and time specified in the program for the tournament. The meeting date must be one of the last three (3) days of the tournament, held no earlier than 8:00 a.m. and no later than 9:00 p.m. If, however, the meeting is held on the last day of the tournament then it must commence no later than 12:00 noon. At the business meeting all members of the ATA residing in that State or Province, who are present in person at the meeting and are also members of their State or Provincial Association, who have been active members (e.g., having registered targets) in any two (2) target years, shall be entitled to vote for a State or Provincial Delegate and for not over two (2) Alternate Delegates.

A current (paper) Average Card, the form of which shall be determined by the Board of Directors or Executive Committee, shall evidence ATA membership, Life and Annual. No membership shall be effective until after receipt of proper application at the General Office of the Corporation, approval, issuance of an Average Card, and receipt by the member. A member shall not be qualified to cast a ballot for a State or Provincial Delegate or Alternate Delegate(s) until properly qualified in accordance with this Paragraph.

A shooter who has paid his/her dues and exhibits the receipt for payment may participate in registered shoots.

The criteria for election as a State Delegate or Alternate Delegate are:

- actual physical residence within the boundaries of the State/Province of representation, and
- in receipt of life membership certificate from the ATA, and
- a member in good standing of the State/Provincial Association of the State/Province of representation, and
- ATA member in good standing for at least five (5) consecutive years, and
- active participation as evidenced by registration of at least 3,000 targets total (Singles, Handicap and Doubles combined) in current and previous four (4) years, and of at least 500 targets each year in the current and previous four (4) years, and
- shall not have been suspended within the prior five (5) years or for a period of one (1) year or more.

Target registration may be waived for shooters with an extensive target history who because of documented physical problems are not currently able to participate.

Selection of the State or Provincial Delegate, and the Alternate Delegate(s) should be given the utmost consideration. Delegates (or in their absence Alternate Delegates), in a properly called meeting, constitute the Board of Directors of the ATA and as such have the responsibility of overseeing the operation of the Association. Only those persons who are responsible dedicated individuals should be considered.

### *D. ZONES*

The Zones are comprised of the following States and Provinces:

CENTRAL - Illinois, Indiana, Michigan, Iowa, Minnesota, Nebraska, North Dakota, Ohio, South Dakota, Wisconsin, and the provinces of Manitoba and Saskatchewan, Canada.

EASTERN - Connecticut, Delaware, Maine, Maryland, Massachusetts, New Hampshire, New York, Pennsylvania, Rhode Island, Vermont, New Jersey and the Provinces of Ontario and Quebec, Canada and the Provinces in Canada lying east thereof (Atlantic Provinces).

SOUTHERN - Alabama, Florida, Georgia, Kentucky, Mississippi, North Carolina, South Carolina, Tennessee, Virginia and West Virginia.

SOUTHWESTERN - Arkansas, Colorado, Kansas, Louisiana, Missouri, New Mexico, Oklahoma and Texas.

WESTERN - Alaska, Arizona, California, Hawaii, Idaho, Montana, Nevada, Oregon, Utah, Washington, Wyoming, and the provinces of Alberta and British Columbia, Canada.

### *E. BOARD OF DIRECTORS*

The Corporate Powers of the ATA under Illinois law are vested in the Board of Directors, which consists of a Delegate from each State and Province. The Board of Directors meets annually during the Grand American World Trapshooting Championships and at other times when properly called by the Executive Committee or as provided by the By-Laws.

### *F. EXECUTIVE COMMITTEE AND ATA EXECUTIVE DIRECTOR*

1. The Executive Committee consists of a representative from each of the five (5) zones elected each year to the Executive Committee at the annual meeting of the Board of Directors. One (1) member of the Executive Committee is designated President and the other four (4) are designated Vice-Presidents.
2. The Board of Directors has delegated direction of the affairs of the ATA to the Executive Committee between meetings of the Board of Directors.
3. The Executive Committee employs an Executive Director to handle the daily affairs of the ATA. The ATA Executive Director implements the policies set forth by the Board of Directors and/or the Executive Committee and follows their directions.
4. The main office and records of the ATA are located at 601 West National Road, Vandalia, Ohio 45377-1036, phone (937) 898-4638, Fax (937) 898-5472, www.shootata.com.

### *G. CONSTITUTION AND BY-LAWS*

The ATA is organized under the Corporate Laws of the State of Illinois and has a Illinois Charter and Corporate By-laws formulated in accordance with Illinois law, as a not-for-profit public charitable corporation. The ATA has also been recognized and approved under Internal Revenue Code (IRC) as a fully tax exempt 501(c)(3) charitable entity.

### *H. JURISDICTION*

The ATA has jurisdiction over all affiliated Associations regardless of location

## SECTION II

## INFORMATION FOR SHOOTERS

### *A. PROCEDURE FOR JOINING ATA*

1. ANNUAL MEMBERS

Application for Annual Membership may be made at any registered shoot by filling out an application and the payment of $20.00 dues to the ATA. Sub-Junior and Junior Annual Members shall pay $12.00 dues to the ATA. A temporary receipt will be given to the shooter upon receipt of a proper application. The temporary receipt should be retained as evidence of payment and be used in lieu of an Average Card until the Average Card is received. The ATA will issue an annual Average Card in the normal course of business. This card will be marked to indicate the shooter's handicap yardage. Full membership rights are effective upon receipt by the member of the Average Card.

Annual Members have all the shooting rights and privileges of Life Members, but may hold no office in the ATA. Annual Members, who have been active members (e.g., having registered targets) in any two (2) target years, are entitled to vote for the State/Provincial Delegate and Alternate(s), at the annual business meeting of the State or Province.

Annual Memberships are renewable by mail or at any registered shoot. To renew by mail send your complete name, address, including zip code, and $20.00 ($12.00 for Juniors or Sub-Juniors) to ATA, 601 West National Rd., Vandalia, Ohio 45377-1036.

2. LIFE MEMBERSHIPS

Life Memberships are obtained by the submission of a properly completed application and the payment of $500.00. Senior Life Memberships for those 65 years and older are $250.00. Life members pay no annual dues thereafter. Upon approval of the application, the ATA will issue a Life Membership Certificate and the Life Membership is effective upon receipt by the Member. Life Members are entitled to vote for State Delegates and Alternate Delegates to the ATA. Only Life Members may hold office in the ATA.

PLEASE NOTE: If a shooter pays dues at a shoot, he/she must retain his/her receipt until receipt of an ATA Average Card. Unless the shooter can show evidence of membership fee payment, he/she may have to pay again. Shooters must record all scores before receipt of an ATA card and then transfer these scores to the new card.

If a shooter does not receive an ATA card within four (4) weeks, he/she should send a letter to the ATA, 601 West National Rd., Vandalia, Ohio 45377-1036, advising the ATA that an application was made on a certain date and give ATA the name of the gun club that received the application and payment.

### *B. TARGET YEAR*

The 2009 target year runs from November 1, 2008 thru August 31, 2009; after that the target year shall be September 1, thru August 31. Scores shot at any tournament ending after October 31, 2008 regardless of starting date, will be included in the following year's averages.

### *C. RULES OF CONDUCT OF AN ATA SHOOTER*

Each member will be furnished a copy of these Official Trapshooting Rules, and it is assumed that the member will read and understand each rule. Members are strongly encouraged to know these Rules and abide by them for their own benefit and for the benefit of other shooters.

1. By entering the competition, every contestant agrees to accept all official decisions and to abide by these Rules.
2. It is the responsibility of all shooters to see that they are handicapped and classified properly in accordance with these Rules and/or the official program. Any errors made by the classification committee and/or the shooter must be corrected before shooting or the shooter may be subject to disqualification and may be subject to further disciplinary action.
3. When making entry at any registered shoot, shooters should produce their plastic identification card and Average Card so that names, addresses, and membership numbers are properly noted and errors in record keeping are prevented. Shooters not having a plastic card should always list their ATA number, entire name and address on entry forms.
4. The Average Card is intended to provide classification personnel at registered shoots with current data on a member's shooting ability. Shooters not having their Average Cards up to date may be put in a higher class or otherwise penalized. Failure to accurately record scores, or the falsification of scores, can lead to disciplinary action including suspension from the ATA.
5. Any member who;

Submits false information for any reason to a participating club, ATA, or shoot management; or
Who causes false scores or other information to be recorded; or
Who commits an act of theft; or
Who commits acts which result in artificially low scores; or
Who encourages or assists others in such acts is subject to disciplinary action.

# SECTION III

# REQUIREMENTS AND RECOMMENDATIONS FOR CONDUCTING A REGISTERED SHOOT

### A. APPLICATION TO CONDUCT A SHOOT

Proper blank application forms, obtained from the ATA, or local State secretaries, should be filled out and provided to the State secretary for approval prior to the scheduled shoot. If there are club dues or other obligations to the State, these must be enclosed with applications. Registered league dues of $25.00 per league must be submitted to ATA with the appropriate league application.

If the application is in order, the State secretary will approve and forward it to the ATA for the certification of registration provided that the date(s) requested will not conflict with the dates of a registered event and/or tournament granted to another club or association in close proximity. The question of close proximity is left to the judgment of the officials of the State association. State and Provincial Associations shall not unreasonably withhold approval of shoot dates from affiliated clubs. In the event the State association is unable or unwilling to decide the question of close proximity, the question will be referred to the ATA State/Provincial Delegate who has the duty to make the decision, and whose decision is final. The Delegate has no duty, responsibility or authority of the ATA to decide any shoot dates until the question of close proximity has been referred to the Delegate by the State/Provincial association.

Upon receipt of the approved application form, the ATA will issue the registration certificate, provided all conditions of the application have been met. A record of the issuance of the certificate of registration will be kept on file in the main office of the ATA, and prior to the holding of the registered event and/or tournament, necessary office supplies for the proper recording of scores will be sent to the club or association.

### B. PREPARATION AND PROGRAMS

1. An official written program for every shoot must be published or posted. (Note: the program may be handwritten or in email form.) The program must, at a minimum, list all fees, events, options, trophies, penalty classification and handicap (if used) for the shoot. It is required that ATA shoot programs indicate the specific amount of fees collected on behalf of the ATA. ATA fees must be set apart from all other fees and charges made by shoot management and are to be escrowed for payment to ATA. Programs should be made available and/or sent to an up-to-date list of shooters.

2. All shooters must be charged the same target and option fees. An exception may be made for special category shooters, (i.e., charging Junior and Sub-Junior shooters half price).

3. Shoot Management should ascertain that the gun club facilities are in good condition prior to the shoot and that an adequate supply of materials and supplies needed to conduct the shoot are available. ATA assumes no liability, or responsibility, if Shoot Management does not adequately comply with this, or any, ATA suggestion and/or directive contained in the Official Rules.

### C. CHECKLIST FOR THE SHOOT

1. Shoot Management should arrange for:
   a. capable classifying and handicapping personnel who shall classify and handicap all shooters in accordance with the Official Rules; and
   b. competent cashiers who will calculate purses and options correctly and pay off as many events as possible before the close of the shoot; and
   c. squadding personnel (Note - at small shoots, all three (3) of the above may be done by the same person or persons), and
   d. referee/scorers who know the ATA Rules, and who have been adequately trained to call all targets, or only the lost targets as directed, and to record the scores correctly on the sheets provided; and
   e. referee/scorers must be provided with an unobstructed view of shooters. It is improper at an ATA shoot for shooters to supply their own referee/scorers. (Note - one (1) person may serve as referee/scorer. If the person or persons serving in these capacities is negligent or inefficient, the Management shall remove him/her or them.); and
   f. provide appropriate hearing and eye protection to firing line personnel. This includes all employees who perform duties on or near the trap field. Shoot Management is required to enforce this provision, failure to do so may result in disciplinary action; and
   g. any additional help needed to conduct the tournament efficiently, such as squad hustler, scoreboard recorder, score sheet runners, and enough personnel to properly operate a shooting facility.

2. Management shall confirm that all participants are ATA members in good standing who have paid their annual dues or are Life Members before accepting their entries. If shoot management accepts entry from a contestant and it is subsequently determined he/she is not an ATA member in good standing and his/her annual dues had not been paid, Shoot Management must make every effort to collect those dues. If Shoot Management, ATA or another club is unsuccessful in collection of the unpaid dues, Shoot Management will be assessed an amount equal to each unpaid entry. Notice of unpaid dues will be mailed by the ATA to each participant and club responsible. Failure to timely pay assessments may result in a club's registered shooting and/or shoot application(s) being denied or held in abeyance until payment is made.

3. Shoot Management of any registered event and/or tournament, at its discretion, may reject any entry, or refund any entry. In all cases except as may be otherwise provided in these Official Rules, the authority of the Management of a registered shoot is not subject to appeal and all contestants must abide by its rulings. No entry shall be rejected on the basis of gender, race, religion, sexual orientation, or disability unless such disability renders the contestant incapable of complying with these Official Rules or results in an unsafe condition, which endangers any person or property.

4. Shoot Management shall appoint a judge or judges to be called upon for ruling on official complaints when the occasion arises. If a judge has not been appointed, the president of the club, or in his absence, the secretary shall act as judge. The referee/scorer must call upon a judge to settle any controversy regarding a score or when he/she has made an error by being ahead or behind in his scoring. Officials of the ATA will not change the decisions of these judges made in accordance with these Rules, or change the report of any shoot held in accordance with these Rules.

5. No shooter will be allowed to repeat any portion of the regularly advertised program (i.e., shooting more than once in an event) except as permitted in Section VII. Par., A., 8.

6. Additional events (not included in the official program) may be held and the scores registered provided that shooters have been notified of such events by shoot management, that the event is announced and posted, and that at least three (3) participants shoot and complete the event. (see Rule IV, A., 2., c.)

7. The sponsors of registered events and/or tournaments are responsible for the payment of all added money, guaranteed money, purses, and/or prizes advertised or offered in their shoot programs. If the Management of a registered shoot does not meet the above obligations, the ATA will not be responsible for such payments and will not be liable in any manner whatsoever. Sponsors and/or Shoot Management, for and in consideration of the privilege to conduct any registered shoot, shall knowingly and willingly hold harmless and indemnify the ATA for any and all disputes or causes of action arising hereunder.

8. Shoot Management must make every effort to see that the Average Cards of any shooters earning yardage are punched. If for any reason an Average Card is not punched at the shoot, Shoot Management shall inform the ATA, the shooter, and the shooter's State ATA Delegate in writing, of this omission.

### D. FOLLOW UP DUTIES

Following the conclusion of a registered shoot and/or tournament Shoot Management is responsible or will delegate the responsibility for:

1. Completing and sending to the ATA office the following items:
   a. The ATA report form with complete names, addresses, ATA card numbers, and accurate scores of all shooters for all events.
   b. The earned yardage reports.
   c. A trophy list and shoot - off results for all ATA registered events that qualify for All American points.
   d. Names and addresses of those paying ATA dues at the shoot.
   e. A check for ATA daily fees or league registration fees collected at the shoot or league.
   f. One (1) copy of the official shoot program or league Rules. This must be done within 8 calendar days following the last day of the registered shoot or league to avoid a $25.00 late shoot report fine for the first offense and a $100.00 late shoot report fine for second offense in a target year, which, if not paid, will be deducted from that state rebate. A third offense will dictate cancellation of registered shoot privileges until delinquent shoot reports and or money are properly received by ATA. Any check(s) presented to ATA and subsequently dishonored is equal to a third offense and must be paid, including bank charges, before further registered shoots are permitted.
2. Sending State fees collected to the State Association.
3. Sending a report of the results to the Trap & Field Magazine.
4. Reporting shoot results to the local radio and TV stations and the local newspapers as practicable.

### E. KEEPING SHOOT RECORDS

Shoot Management is required to keep the records from all registered shoots for at least one (1) year. This includes all shoot cashiering information (entry and options) and actual squadsheets that were used on the field.

# SECTION IV

# ATA TOURNAMENTS

In these Rules the words "shoot" and "tournament" are intended to include "leagues" throughout these Official Rules with exceptions only as noted.

### A. REGISTERED SHOOTS

1. The ATA governs the conduct of all shoots registered with it. Only clubs affiliated with their State/Provincial Association will be permitted to hold registered shoots.
2. To constitute a registered shoot the following requirements must be met:
   a. all contestants must be members of ATA at the time of their entry, and
   b. each contestant must pay ATA daily registration fee of $2.00 for each day of competition at each shooting location ($1.00 fee for Big 50 events), and such other Zone or State Association fees as may be charged, and
   c. at least three (3) or more contestants must compete in and complete the same event on the same day of competition.
3. No daily fee charges shall be permitted except those assessed by the ATA, the Zone, or the State in which the tournament is being held.
4. A shooter is not required to be a member of any club or facility to participate in a duly authorized registered shoot. (See Section IV A ,2.b payment of state/provincial dues)

### B. WHO MAY PARTICIPATE

Only ATA Life or Annual Members may participate in an ATA registered trapshooting tournament event and/or tournament. Shooters must be members of the State/Provincial Association in their place of residence to compete in registered shoots in that State or Province.

### C. MEMBERS OF OTHER SHOOTING ORGANIZATIONS

Targets shot and registered with any shooting organization other than ATA shall not be counted toward any published minimum target requirement, for any purpose, at any tournament where ATA trophies are awarded.

### D. FIRING POSITION AND SHOOTING ORDER

1. There shall be five (5) firing positions (posts), numbered 1 to 5, left to right, spaced three (3) yards apart, and sixteen (16) yards from Point B (Diagram I on page 56).
2. The referee/scorer shall not throw a target unless all contestants are in the correct positions.
3. At any registered trapshooting competition, no person shall be permitted to enter and take part in any completed or partially completed event or events after Squad No. 1 has completed sub-event 1 of any new event. At tournaments shot "bank system" with several squads starting at the same time on several traps, the procedure shall be construed to be the same as if all squads started on the same trap.

### E. SUB-EVENTS

A sub-event is any number of targets shot on any one field at one time, with one full rotation on all five (5) posts by each shooter, such as 25 or 50 Singles or Handicap targets or 10 pairs, 15 pairs, 25 pairs of Doubles. An event is the total targets of a specific type (16 yard, Handicap, or Doubles) such as 200 16-yard targets, 100 Handicap targets, etc. for which separate entry is made. It is not necessary to change traps after each sub-event. Events of less than 50 targets may not be registered.

### F. RECORDING SCORES WINS AND TIES

1. All 16 yard, Handicap and Doubles scores are required to be accurately and legibly entered on each member's Average Card in the spaces provided at the completion of each registered and/or tournament event.
2. It is the duty of each ATA member to record all wins and ties in 16 yard and Doubles events on his/her Average Card. The intent of this rule is to properly inform classification and handicap committees of prior wins and ties in 16 Yard and Doubles events.

Failure of any member to strictly comply with these rules may lead to penalty classification, disqualification and/or suspension from membership in the ATA.

### G. SQUADDING, SQUAD LEADER RESPONSIBILITIES AND TARGET OBSERVATION

1. In all ATA events contestants shall shoot in squads of five (5) except:
   a. When there are less than five (5) contestants available for the last squad of any program.
   b. When yardage differences in Handicap events make it impractical or unsafe.
   c. When there are withdrawals from a squad after the competition has begun and squads scheduled.
   d. When in the opinion of shoot management, the harmony of the shoot may be enhanced by squadding less than five (5) contestants.
2. In Handicap there shall be no more than two (2) yards difference between adjacent shooters in the squad, and no more than a total difference of three (3) yards in a squad. When squadding 18 yard shooters, there shall be no more than one yard difference between adjacent shooters in the squad and no more than a total difference of two yards in a squad.
3. It is illegal for more than five (5) shooters to be in a squad.
4. The squadding of practice shooters with those shooting registered events shall not be allowed, nor shall anyone be allowed to shoot registered events on a non-registered basis. This Rule shall not apply during Registered League Shooting or Big 50 events.
5. For each squad, the shooter who has been assigned to start on post 1 is designated the "Squad Leader". If post 1 is empty, the role of the Squad Leader passes to the shooter assigned to start on post 2, and so on. The Squad Leader has the following duties:

a. After all squad members are present at their assigned positions on the trap field, the Squad Leader should ascertain that all squad members are ready to begin the sub-event. After doing so, the Squad Leader only may ask that target(s) be thrown for the squad's observation. For regular 16-yard Singles and Handicap sub-events, the Squad Leader may ask for one (1) target only. For regular Doubles sub-events, the Squad Leader may ask for one (1) pair of Doubles. For Shoot-offs in 16-yard Singles and Handicap events, the Squad Leader may ask for two (2) targets. For Shoot-offs in Doubles events, the Squad Leader may ask for two (2) pairs of Doubles.

b. If the target(s) thrown for observation are broken, irregular, or illegal, the Squad Leader may ask that another target (or pair of Doubles as applicable) be thrown. The squad has the right to see a legal target (or legal pair of Doubles as applicable) before

commencing the sub-event.

c. The Squad Leader should check and initial the score sheet at the completion of each sub-event.

d. The Squad Leader shall have the responsibility to carry the score sheet, on which more than one (1) sub-event is recorded, from trap to trap until completion of the event.

6. During a sub-event, if there is a delay due to trap or gun malfunction, the contestant in turn may ask to see a target (or pair of Doubles as applicable) thrown before he/she resumes shooting.

7. Should a trap be throwing targets that, although not necessarily illegal, appreciably vary from trap to trap, any shooter may request that management reset the trap even though prior squads have shot. The final decision as to whether or not a trap is to be reset will be made only by shoot management.

8. During a sub-event, if a contestant is subjected to a single no target event, the contestant shall have the right to see a legal target (or legal pair of Doubles as applicable) and adjust the voice release mechanism (if present) before shooting resumes.

### H. SHOOT-OFFS

1. Shoot-offs shall be considered and interpreted the same as registered events and all applicable ATA Rules shall apply unless mutually agreed upon by all contestants. The management of a tournament may rule that ties shall be carried over to the first (or more if needed) sub-event of the next like event. However, when there are ties in a Handicap event and any tying shooter earns yardage and consequently will be shooting farther back in the subsequent Handicap event, all tying shooters must agree to the carry over.

2. All ties whenever possible shall be shot off and in such a manner, as shoot management shall designate. Unless otherwise specified by the management, ties on single target events shall be shot off in 25 target events and Doubles in 10 pair events.

3. Ties for High All Around Championships (HAA) shall be shot off 20 Singles, 10 Handicap, and 5 pair of Doubles. Ties for High Over All (HOA) shall be shot off in such a manner that the Shoot-off represents as closely as possible the same proportion of Singles, Handicap and Doubles targets as the High Over All program contains but keeping the Shoot-off to 50 targets or less. The Singles, Handicap and Doubles portion of the Shoot-off shall be shot in the order that the events occurred in the program, or as determined by shoot management.

4. When squadding shooters for Shoot-offs for High Over All (HOA) and High All Around (HAA) the shooting order shall be the order in which they shot in the last event involved except where such order would be inadvisable or dangerous because of yardage differences. This order shall remain through each portion of the Shoot-off.

5. The following method shall be used for rotation of shooters: Starting posts to be used shall be as follows except where handicap yardage makes it unsafe.

If 1 shooter - post number 2.
If 2 shooters - post numbers 2 and 4.
If 3 shooters - post numbers 2, 3 and 4.
If 4 shooters - post numbers 2, 3, 4 and 5.
If 5 shooters - post numbers 1, 2, 3, 4 and 5.

If more than 5 shooters are involved in the tie, they shall be divided as equally as possible into two or more squads as directed by the management.

In subsequent Shoot-offs the post shall be rotated in a clockwise manner, with the shooter from post 1 advancing to post 2 and the shooter from post 5 rotating to post 1 or to the post dictated by the number of shooters remaining, but always in clockwise rotation.

6. The practice of banking targets in advance of commencement of a shoot-off is not permitted unless all tying shooters are notified and are in unanimous agreement. Exception: banking of targets is permissible for telephonic shoots held in multiple locations.

7. It is recommended that shooters involved in shoot-offs be given no more than three five minute calls to report for a shoot- off. First call, second call and final call.

### I. SAFETY

Shoot Management may disqualify a contestant for violation of these Rules, and violations may also result in further disciplinary action.

1. It is the shooter's responsibility and shoot management's responsibility to conduct a shoot in a reasonable and safe manner.

2. It is Shoot Management's responsibility to remove any competitor who is conducting himself/herself in an unsafe manner. (Repeat violators should be reported to the Executive Committee for further action.)

3. It is Shoot Management's responsibility to instruct the trap help in the proper and safe conduct of their respective duties.

4. All trap help must have a flag or other warning device to warn of any person(s) exiting from the trap house.

5. Trap personnel should be thoroughly instructed of the potential danger of the trap (particularly the target throwing arm).

6. Movement and exposure on adjacent traps should be kept to the minimum.

7. The practice of tracking targets behind a shooting squad is unsafe, disconcerting to the shooters, and is not permitted.

8. Alcohol and drugs impair judgment and the ATA Rules pertaining to the usage of alcohol and/or drugs must be enforced by Shoot Management. This Rule shall be strictly complied with and shall apply to practice shooting as well as registered and tournament events. (Rule XII, B., 2., a.)

9. A gun, which for any reason fails to fire as intended, must be promptly opened without any subsequent determination by the referee/scorer of the cause of the Failure to Fire.

10. All guns must have the action opened and contain no live or empty shells at any time, except while the shooter is on the firing line. A break open gun's action may be closed when it is in a gun rack but it shall not contain a live or empty shell. Repeat offender(s) of these Official Rules will be given a 30 day suspension upon a second violation of these Rules; a third violation of these Rules will result in a 90 day suspension; and further violations will be reviewed by the Executive Committee for further disciplinary action.

11. As a safety precaution, test shots will not be permitted under any circumstance.

12. A contestant shall place a live shell in his/her gun only when on a post facing the traps. In Singles and Handicap shooting he/she may place only one (1) live shell in his/her gun at a time and must remove it or the empty shell(s) before moving from one post to another. In Doubles shooting he/she may place two (2) live shells in his/her gun at a time and must remove both live or empty shells before moving from one (1) post to another. In changing from one (1) post to another, the shooter shall not walk in front of the other competitors.

13. Snap caps or recoil reduction devices may be excluded from the above only if colored a safety orange as to permanently identify them as not being a live or empty shell.

14. A contestant may hold his/her gun in any position when it is his/her turn to shoot. The contestant must in no manner interfere with the preceding shooter by raising his/her gun to point or otherwise create an observable distraction.

15. All guns used by contestants must be equipped, fitted and utilized so as not to eject empty shells in a manner that substantially disturbs or interferes with other contestants.

16. All persons including competitors, referee/scorers, and trap personnel must wear appropriate eye and hearing protection while on the trap field. Failure to comply may result in disqualification.

17. No shooter shall be permitted to participate in any ATA event while seated in or otherwise using a golf cart on the firing line. Single passenger conveyances are the appropriate means for participating should one require assistance due to permanent or temporary disability.

18. While not prohibited, the practice of resting the muzzle of a shotgun on a shooter's toe is ill-advised and is discouraged.

### J. SPECIAL CATEGORIES

All Ladies, Juniors, Sub-Juniors, Veterans, and Senior Veterans must declare their special category at the time of their entry in any registered event. Without such declaration the shooter will not be allowed to compete for the applicable special category trophy. No shooter will be allowed to declare a special category after the first shot is fired in the event by the contestant. No exceptions to this rule are allowed. Lady, Junior, Sub-Junior, Veteran and Sr. Veteran shooters who declare such eligibility shall be so designated.

1. All female shooters shall be designated as Ladies, because of age they may also be designated as Juniors, Sub-Juniors, Veterans or Sr. Veterans.

2. A shooter who has not reached his or her 15th birthday will be designated as a Sub-Junior.

3. A shooter who is 15 but has not reached his or her 18th birthday will be designated as a Junior.

4. A shooter who is 65 years or older will be designated as a Veteran.

5. A shooter who is 70 years or older will be designated as a Sr. Veteran.

6. Age based categories are established on the birthday of the shooter. For purposes of determining age category for HOA and HAA awards the category declared by the participant on the first day he/she shoots shall be used.

7. Shooters who become eligible for new age based categories during the target year may elect to continue to compete in the previous category for the remainder of that target year. (For example a shooter reaching age 70 may elect to continue to shoot as a Veteran for the remainder of the current target year.) However, once a shooter has elected to move to the new category that decision is irrevocable and he/she may not again declare eligibility for the previous category. Junior shooters reaching the age of 18 may continue to declare Junior category for the remainder of the current target year. (Note: Shooters will become eligible for new age based categories on September 1, 2008 for the 2009 target year)

Note: Age based special category shooters that are in contention for or desire to achieve All-American Team recognition should review the All-American Team policy on page 57 prior to declaring a new special category.

a. When there is no Sub-Junior trophy Sub-Juniors will be included in the Junior category. Senior veterans will be included in the Veteran category when there is no Senior Veteran trophy.

## SECTION V
## SINGLES AND DOUBLES EVENTS

### A. 16 YARD SINGLES

This event must be shot 5 or 10 shots at each post from 16 yards with each shooter in order shooting at one target until all have shot 5 or 10 times, and then rotating in a clockwise manner to the next post.

Should Shoot Management elect to change to 50, 16-yard targets per trap (10 per post) after a shooter has made entry, the shooter must be allowed the option to withdraw and be refunded or change his/her option entry.

### B. DOUBLES

This event must be shot from 16 yards, with each shooter in order shooting at two (2) targets thrown simultaneously from the trap house until all have shot the specified number of times, then rotating in a clockwise manner to the next post. A Doubles event may be shot by having each squad shoot successive alternating 15 pair and 10 pair sub-events on the trap or traps being utilized, or Shoot Management may elect to throw Doubles in sub-events of 25 pairs.

### C. CLASSIFICATION

1. For 16-yard targets and Doubles, shooters should be placed in three (3) or more classes, according to their established average and/or known ability. A new shooter may be assigned to any class in 16-yards and Doubles events, at the discretion of classification personnel until the shooter establishes his/her known ability.

a. To arrive at known ability the following should be taken into consideration as far as such information is or can be made available:

(1) Official registered targets (abnormally low scores should be disregarded). Averages of all registered shooters are compiled and published annually.

(2) Non-registered scores including Shoot-off scores, nonregistered events, practice scores, etc.

(3) Any other information bearing on a shooter's ability to shoot and break targets.

2. For 16-yard events the following systems are established:

SIX CLASSES
98% and over AAA
96.25% and under 98% AA
94.75% and under 96.25% A
93% and under 94.75% B
90% and under 93% C
under 90% D

FIVE CLASSES
97% and over AA
94% and under 97% A
91% and under 94% B
88% and under 91% C
Under 88% D

FOUR CLASSES
95% and over A
92% and under 95% B
89% and under 92% C
Under 89% D

THREE CLASSES
95% and over A
91% and under 95% B
Under 91% C

3. For Doubles events the following systems are established:

SIX CLASSES
96% and over AAA
92% and under 96% AA
89% and under 92% A
86% and under 89% B
82% and under 86% C
Under 82% D

FIVE CLASSES
93% and over AA
89% and under 93% A
85% and under 89% B

78% and under 85% C
Under 78% D
FOUR CLASSES
90% and over A
85% and under 90% B
78% and under 85% C
Under 78% D
THREE CLASSES
89% and over A
83% and under 89% B
Under 83% C

4. If Shoot Management desires to use different classification it may do so by printing the modified classification in the program of the shoot.

5. For better classification of shooters it is suggested that the following method be used.

a. If the shooter has less than 500 targets on current year's Average Card, use the previous year average and known ability.

b. If the shooter has between 500 and 1,000 targets (inclusive) on his/her current year's Average Card, use the current average and known ability or the previous year's average and known ability, whichever is higher.

6. Foreign shooters who shoot DTL or doubles in their home associations will be classified either by those averages (or their ATA averages, at the discretion of the handicap committee.) For classification purposes, a DTL average of 95 will be considered the same as an ATA singles average of 95 and the same equivalence for doubles will be used.

### D. PENALTY CLASSIFICATION

Shoot Management may establish penalty classification for 16-yard targets and Doubles, if target requirements are printed in the program.

# SECTION VI
# THE ATA HANDICAP SYSTEM

The ATA Handicap system is the method whereby shooters whose ability to win or compete at a level of accomplishment has been demonstrated and shooters whose ability is unknown are handicapped by shooting a greater distance from the trap house. The minimum handicap is 18.0 yards and the maximum is 27.0 yards. A shooter's yardage is determined by Rules governing new shooters, by yardage earned, or by his/her established handicap yardage, which is based on known ability and 1000 target reviews, thereafter. At each State or Provincial shoot the handicapping and classifying shall be the responsibility of a State or Provincial shoot committee appointed by the State Association with the ATA Delegate as chair.

### A. HANDICAP EVENTS

This event must be shot 5 or 10 shots at each station as directed by shoot management from 18 to 27 yards with each shooter in order shooting at one target until all have shot 5 or 10 times as directed and then rotating in a clockwise manner to the next post. Should shoot management elect to change to 50 Handicap targets per trap (10 per post) after a shooter has made entry, the shooter must be allowed the option to withdraw and be refunded or change his/her option entry.

A contestant must stand on the highest whole yardage punched on his/her card. For example, if a card is punched at 20.5 yards, the shooter will stand on 20.0 yards. However, if one-half (1/2) yard is then earned, the card must be punched to 21.0 yards and the shooter must stand on the 21.0 yard line.

A shooter may not stand on a higher yardage than he/she is punched, unless assigned penalty yardage by shoot handicap personnel.

When a Handicap marathon event consisting of more than 100 targets is shot, each 100-target sub-event must not begin prior to the awarding of earned yardage based on the previous 100 targets. Shooters earning yardage must shoot subsequent sub-events from the new yardage. It is not permitted to have more than one 50 and/or 75 target Handicap event in a registered tournament in any one (1) day.

### B. CENTRAL HANDICAP COMMITTEE (CHC)

1. The Central Handicap Committee, made up of a chair and five (5) or more members, is appointed at the sole discretion of the Executive Committee. It is the responsibility of the Central Handicap Committee, under the direction of the Executive Committee, to oversee the handicap system and control the assigned yardage of all members of the ATA.

2. Any Central Handicap Committee member may increase a shooter's yardage at his/her discretion when applying the Known Ability Rule. The only other ATA Officers authorized to increase a shooter's yardage are voting members of the Executive Committee.

### C. HANDICAP YARDAGE ASSIGNMENT

A shooter will be handicapped between 18 and 27 yards and at the highest yardage punched on his/her Average Card, unless he/she is required to shoot penalty yardage.

1. New lady shooter - new lady shooters will be assigned a handicap of 19.0 yards.

2. New sub-junior shooter - a new male shooter who has not reached his 15th birthday will be assigned a handicap of 19.0 yards. A male shooter upon reaching his 15th birthday will be assigned a handicap of 20.0 yards unless he has previously earned or been assigned greater yardage. (Note: If a male sub-junior has been reduced to the 18.0 yard line by the review process, upon reaching his 15th birthday he will remain at the 18.0 yard line until additional yardage is earned)

3. New male shooter - a new male shooter, 15 years of age or older, will be assigned a handicap of 20.0 yards.

4. After a lapse in membership any shooter reapplying for membership in the ATA, who had been assigned a previous handicap yardage, shall resume shooting at the previously assigned yardage. The only exception is if the shooter was previously assigned a yardage based on age; because of present age the shooter may be required to shoot at a longer yardage. Failure of a shooter to shoot previously assigned yardage will result in disqualification and any and all scores and prizes, including money, forfeited thereby.

5. Rules for members of other trapshooting associations;

a. If a shooter is a member of any other trapshooting association or was a member of such association the preceding year AND shot targets in such association in the current or preceding ATA target year, he/she will shoot from the handicap yardage of whichever association shows the greater yardage.

b. A member who, at any time has previously been a member of another trapshooting association but has not shot targets in such association in the current or preceding ATA target year must shoot his/her last assigned yardage in that association (if it is greater) unless the shooter has received an ATA 1000 target review and been granted a reduction.

c. It will be the responsibility of the shooter to notify the shoot handicap committee if he/she holds or has held a card of another trapshooting association. Failure to notify the shoot handicap committee of another trapshooting association card may be cause for penalty action resulting in forfeiture of entry fees and all monies, including prizes, and possible suspension from all ATA shoots for one year.

### D. EARNED YARDAGE

1. Yardage will be automatically earned by shooters of high scores in all ATA registered events, according to the following table. This additional yardage is indicated by punches on the shooter's Average Card.

#### EARNED YARDAGE TABLE

High Scores (and all ties)

| Entries | 1st | 2nd | 3rd | 4th |
|---|---|---|---|---|
| 15-39 | 1/2 yd | | | |
| 40-69 | 1 yd | | | |
| 70-124 | 1 yd | 1/2 yd | | |
| 125-249 | 1 yd | 1 yd | 1/2 yd | |
| 250-499 | 1 1/2 yd | 1 yd | 1/2 yd | |
| 500-1499 | 2 yds | 1 1/2 yds | 1 yd | 1/2 yd |
| 1500 and up | 2 1/2 yds | 2 yds | 1 1/2 yds | 1 yd |

2. Any score of 96 will automatically earn 1/2 yard provided it does not earn at least that much under the earned yardage table.

3. Any score of 50x50 or 75x75 in events of that length will automatically earn 1/2 yard provided it does not earn at least that much under the earned yardage table.

4. The State/Provincial Handicap Champion will automatically earn 1 yard provided the score does not earn at least that much under the earned yardage table.

5. Any score of 97, 98 and 99 or winning a total of $750.00 or more (option and added money) in a single handicap event will automatically earn 1 yard, and a score of 100 or winning a total of $1,200.00 or more (option and added money) in a single handicap event will automatically earn 1-1/2 yards provided these scores do not earn at least that much under the earned yardage table.

6. In marathon Handicap events comprised of more than 100 targets, each 100 targets (or remaining part of 100 targets) shall constitute a separate event for earned yardage purposes and shall be reported as a separate event on the shoot report form.

7. When multiple Handicap events are shot during the same day with fewer than 15 contestants, yardage will be awarded the high score(s), under the earned yardage table, by combining the total number of different individual shooters in all events with fewer than 15 shooters. For example:

Event 1 - 14 shooters, Event 2 - 20 shooters, Event 3 - 12 shooters (3 of whom shot Event 1), Event 4 - 13 shooters (5 of whom shot Event1 and/or Event 3). Event 2 stands on its own because it has more than 15 shooters. Combining Events 1, 3, 4 total of 31 different shooters (14, 9, 8). The high score among those 31 shooters will receive a ½ yard punch based on the earned yardage table.

8. The earned yardage table applies to events of 50, 75 or 100 Handicap targets.

9. A shooter's card will be punched from the yardage actually shot (including penalty yardage if applicable). For example, if a shooter earns yardage shooting from 22 yards penalty he/she will be punched from the 22 yard line and not his/her normal yardage assignment.

It is the duty of each ATA member to have his or her Average Card punched if yardage is earned. The Average Card must be punched to the correct earned yardage on the day the yardage is earned and before leaving the tournament grounds. If a member is required to leave the tournament grounds prior to the completion of a Handicap event, it is the member's duty to determine if his or her score qualified for a yardage increase and to have his or her Average Card punched to the correct yardage prior to entering any subsequent registered event and/or tournament.

10. The number of contestants starting the event will be the number used for the earned yardage table.

### E. PENALTY YARDAGE

Shoot Management may establish penalty yardage based on numbers of registered targets if those target requirements are printed in the program. In no event shall any shooter be assigned a handicap of less than the minimum yardage appearing on his/her Average Card.

### F. SPECIAL HANDICAP RULES

1. A shooter must continue to shoot from the last yardage assigned or earned until he/she receives a new Average Card with his or her reduced yardage indicated on it regardless of the length of time that has elapsed since that yardage was assigned or earned. The ATA Shooter Information Center is not to be used to evidence of a reduction; only an Average Card with the new yardage will be accepted.

2. A shooter's handicap yardage may be reduced only as a result of a 1000 target review or a special review. No reduction may be made in the field. The shooter's new Average Card will be noted with the word "review".

3. A shooter's handicap yardage may be increased at any time during the year including immediately before and during the Grand American World Trapshooting Championships:

a. because of earned yardage, or

b. as a result of a review, or

c. at the discretion of a member of the Central Handicap Committee or voting member of the Executive Committee.

4. A shooter at all times shall have the right to appeal any Central Handicap Committee action(s) to the Executive Committee.

5. Earned yardage of 1.5 or more yards for any single event will not be removed in part or whole by 1,000 target review for a minimum period of two (2) years from the date the yardage was earned. This restriction on reductions may be removed after one year for a shooter by the State Delegate sending a request to his or her Zone Central Handicap Committee Member who will make the final decision.

6. If a shooter earns yardage while a reduction is in process the reduction shall automatically be void.

7. When multiple 100-target Handicap target events (marathons) are shot in the same day, only 2 100-target events may be considered as a maximum per day towards reduction. The 2 events considered out of the marathon must be those 2 in which the highest scores are registered.

### G. REVIEWS

#### 1. 1000 Target Review

The shooting record of each member will be automatically reviewed for possible yardage changes after each successive 1000 or more registered Handicap targets shot in the current and previous year if no yardage was earned.

a. A shooter with a low purified handicap average (the average with abnormally low scores deleted) accompanied by a relative 16 yard average, will receive a one yard reduction, EXCEPT

(1) No shooter will be reduced more than 3 yards in any target year.

(2) The known ability rule will be used in assessing a shooter's record.

b. A shooter with a high-purified handicap average may receive a "Special Review" for possible yardage increase.

c. If a yardage change is made, the shooter will receive by mail a new Average Card with the new assigned yardage noted with the word "review."

#### 2. Special Review

a. "Special Review" is an evaluation by the Central Handicap Committee generated by a high-purified average on a 1000 Target Review or initiated by a shooter through his/her State Delegate or a member of the Central Handicap Committee. The results of a Special Review shall be agreed upon by the Central Handicap Committee and the shooter's State Delegate. If a disagreement in yardage assignment exists between the State Delegate and the Central Handicap Committee, the matter may be directed to the Executive Committee. A Special Review may be used:

(1) To determine possible yardage increases for shooters showing high-purified handicap averages on a 1000 target review.

(2) To determine possible yardage reduction for a shooter because of advancing age or physical disability. A shooter through his/her State Delegate may initiate this review.

b. Other shooting organizations' registered handicap scores may not be used in the Special Review process to determine possible yardage changes, and such scores may be used only insofar as they may indicate known ability.

### 3. Assigned Yardage Increases

a. A member may appeal an assigned yardage increase by writing to the ATA office, to the attention of the Executive Director after having shot 500 targets at the assigned yardage. After receiving a reduction based on such an appeal for any further reduction 1000 additional registered Handicap targets must be shot.

b. There will be no yardage increase by shooter request beyond 25 yards. Subsequent to a shooter receiving an increase in yardage by request he/she will be ineligible for reductions from that yardage assignment based on 1000 target reviews for a period of 2 years.

c. The only persons authorized to increase a member's handicap yardage are member(s) of the Central Handicap Committee or voting member(s) of the Executive Committee.

# SECTION VII

# OFFICIAL SCORING

## A. PROCEDURE

1. The official score is the record kept by the referee/scorer on a sheet furnished him/her by shoot management. The referee/scorer's decision on whether a target is dead or lost is final, subject to review only by the shoot committee or other governing body. The score sheet shall show the scores earned in the event or sub-event. The score sheet shall not be smaller than 11 inches by 17 inches (for four sub-event score sheets) in any tournament in which ATA trophies are provided. The larger format score sheet is recommended for all tournaments. During Handicap events the first sub-event of each score sheet shall be annotated with the yardage assignment of each contestant.

2. The referee/scorer shall keep an accurate record of each score of each contestant. If he/she rules "DEAD" or "LOST," the referee/scorer shall promptly mark / or X for "DEAD" and 0 for "LOST" on the score sheet. Any target scored other than clearly with /, X or 0, or which appears to be scored, with both an X and 0, shall be "LOST", unless the word "DEAD" is clearly printed beside it. The scores of the competition shall be official and govern all awards and records of the competition.

3. The referee/scorer shall distinctly announce, "Lost" when the target is missed and "No Target" when no target is thrown or a target is thrown broken. The referee/scorer shall call the result of all targets, or only the lost targets, as directed by shoot management.

4. When the referee/scorer calls "No Target" for any contestant, the next contestant shall not shoot until the first shooter has shot and the referee/scorer has ruled "Dead" or "Lost."

5. Should more targets be fired in a sub-event than the event calls for, then the excess targets of the sub-event will not be scored.

6. It is the duty of the referee/scorer to see that the shooters change posts at the proper time; however, any targets shot after failure to move at the proper time shall be scored.

7. Inadvertently skipped posts. A shooter is required to shoot the requisite number of targets from each post (5 or 10 as specified by shoot management). If a shooter inadvertently skips a post he/she or any member of the squad shall not be deemed to be out of turn but will be required to shoot the specified number of targets from the skipped post. While the shooter is shooting the skipped post the remainder of the squad will remain behind the trapline and will not proceed to the next trap.

8. A contestant that inadvertently shoots ONE post at the incorrect yardage shall be allowed to move to the correct yardage and reshoot only those targets scored "DEAD" on that post. Targets shot at the incorrect yardage and scored "LOST" shall remain "LOST". Targets shot at the incorrect yardage on more than one post shall be LOST.

9. To preserve the harmony of the competition, no member of a squad shall move toward the next post or leave the field until the squad member who is last has fired his/her final shot of the current post's specified number of targets.

10. The official score must be kept on the score sheet in plain view of the contestant. If contestant's view of the score sheet is obstructed for any reason, he/she may refuse to shoot until he/she has been provided an unobstructed view of the score sheet.

11. It is an error if the referee/scorer fails to properly mark the results of any shot in the section of the score sheet where the results should be recorded. In such cases it is the duty of that contestant to have any error corrected before he/she has fired the first shot at the next post or in the case of his/her last post before leaving the trap. If the shooter fails to have the score corrected, the recorded score(s) shall remain unchanged and no valid protest will be entertained.

12. Every contestant in a squad shall be permitted to examine his/her score before the sheet is sent to the bulletin board or to the cashier's office. The score sheet should be checked, confirmed, and initialed by the Squad Leader. The Squad Leader is encouraged to verify that any targets changed during a sub event are correctly noted as either dead or lost. After the completion of the last sub-event the score sheet will be handled as directed by shoot management.

13. Errors in the recorded details of the official score can only be corrected in strict accordance with the aforementioned Rules, but an error made in the totaling or compilation of targets shall be corrected whenever the error is discovered. Shoot management must correct scores recorded in error by field personnel as a result of misapplication of the Rules.

14. Any protest concerning a score or scores must be made before or immediately after the close of the competition to which such scores relate. A valid protest may only be made by a contestant who competed in the event.

## B. BROKEN OR DEAD TARGET

A target (called "Dead") is one that is fired upon and has a visible broken piece from it, or one that is completely reduced to dust. The referee/scorer shall record a target dead when it is broken in the air.

## C. LOST TARGET

The referee/scorer shall rule, "LOST":

1. When the contestant fires and fails to break the target whether missed completely or when only dust falls from it. A "Dusted Target," is a target from which there is a puff of dust, but no perceptible piece is seen; it is not a dead target; or

2. When a whole target appears promptly after a contestant's recognizable command and is within the legal limits of flight and the contestant voluntarily does not fire; or

3. When an illegal target, a freak target, or a target of a markedly different color is fired at and missed. A contestant may refuse illegal, freak or off-colored targets, but if he/she fires at the target the result must be scored; or

4. When a contestant voluntarily withdraws from, or is otherwise disqualified, and takes no further part in a sub-event after having fired at 1 or more targets of a sub-event and does not fire at all the targets in the sub-event, the referee/scorer shall rule all targets not fired upon "LOST" targets and they shall be scored and reported accordingly. When the shooter is prevented by reasons beyond his/her control from completing a sub-event, the scores for that partial sub-event shall not be recorded or reported. Example: shooters have shot 61 targets of a 100-target event when a storm permanently stops shooting. The management should report the scores for the first 50 targets only; or

5. When a score sheet is delivered to the office with one or more targets that are not properly scored either "DEAD" or "LOST," they shall be scored as "LOST" targets by shoot management; or

6. When a contestant deliberately fires at the same target twice in Doubles Events. This rule is not applicable to a gun "doubling" or "machine-gunning", see Rule VII, D., 3.; or

7. When a commonly called "soft load" occurs, and the shot is fired but no part of the over powder wad or shot remains in the barrel and the target is missed. A soft load where the over powder wad or shot remain in the barrel shall be deemed a "Failure to Fire" and the "Failure to Fire" Rules apply.

## D. FAILURE TO FIRE

The following procedure shall be followed in all tournaments:

1. A contestant shall be allowed two (2) failures to fire in Singles and Handicap events, for any reason other than stated in Paragraph C., 2. above, during each sub-event regardless of the length of the sub-event. When the first or second allowable Failure to Fire in any sub-event occurs, the contestant shall be allowed to call for and fire at another

target, and the result of the shot will be scored in accordance with these Official Rules. During shoot-offs for All Around and High Over All events shooters will be allowed 1 Failure to Fire in each of the three (3) disciplines (Singles, Handicap, Doubles).

2. A contestant shall be allowed 2 failures to fire, for any reason other than stated in Paragraph C., 2., above, during each Doubles sub-event if the Failure to Fire occurs when the contestant attempts to shoot the first target of a Doubles pair, or when the contestant attempts to shoot the second target of a Doubles pair after the first target has been fired at and broken and would have been scored "DEAD". When the first target of a Doubles pair is fired at and missed and that target would be scored "LOST", there shall be no allowable Failure to Fire at the second target. (See exception in VII., E., 11., f.) When a pair is ruled lost there shall be no "Failure to Fire" charged. When the first or second allowable Failure to Fire occurs in any Doubles sub-event, the contestant shall be allowed to call for and fire at another pair of targets and the result of the shots at the new pair will be scored in accordance with these Official Rules.

3. Machine-gunning or doubling only occurs when in Doubles Events both shotshells fire simultaneously in a break open gun, or two (2) shots are fired with a single operation of the trigger in an autoloading gun, rendering the competitor incapable of firing at the second target because both shotshells have fired. When a defective gun malfunctions and doubles or machine guns, whether or not the first target would have been scored "DEAD" or "LOST" and whether or not either target is legal or illegal, the referee/scorer shall rule this occurrence a Failure to Fire and score it accordingly.

4. Whenever an allowable Failure to Fire as provided in this Rule occurs, the referee/scorer shall mark a large legible F1 on the score sheet in the space where that target is scored along with the score for that target, and also place the same mark beside the total sub-event score. After F1 and F2 is in the place where individual targets are scored, any subsequent Failure to Fire in the same sub-event and for any reason, when a target is called and the target appears promptly and within the legal limits of flight, shall be ruled "LOST" and shall be scored accordingly. Cumulative application of the rule is prohibited (failures to fire do not accumulate from sub-event to sub-event), and "sub-event" shall be as defined by Official Rule IV, E.

5. Shoot Management is required to examine each score sheet before the score is posted, and any target scored as a Failure to Fire after two (2) allowable Failure to Fire as set forth above, shall be scored "LOST" whether originally scored as "LOST" by the referee/scorer or not.

## E. NO TARGET

The referee/scorer shall rule "NO TARGET" and allow another target(s) in the following instances:

1. When an allowable "Failure to Fire" as described above occurs.

2. In single target events when the target is thrown broken, regardless of the result of any shot fired.

3. When a whole target appears on the call of the shooter along with target debris.

4. When a contestant shoots out of turn. All contestants must shoot in regular order or sequence according to his or her position in the squad. A contestant who does not shoot in regular order is "out of turn" and the results are not scored.

5. When two (2) contestants fire at the same target.

6. When the trap is sprung without any call of pull, or when it is sprung at any material interval of time before or after the call of the contestant, provided the contestant does not fire. If the contestant fires, the result must be scored.

7. When two (2) targets are thrown at the same time in single target events regardless of whether the contestant fires.

8. When an "illegal" target is thrown, which is a target that is not within the prescribed angle or height limits for single target shooting, or what is known as a "flipper" or "freak" target is thrown, which is a target that may have slipped out of the carrier of the trap or one not properly placed on the trap, provided the contestant does not fire at it. If the contestant fires, the result must be scored.

9. When a target whose color is markedly different from that of the others is thrown, and the contestant does not fire. If the contestant fires, the result must be scored.

10. When firing, the contestant's feet must be behind the firing mark at 16-yards, or behind the mark for the Handicap yardage assigned to him/her, depending upon the event being participated in. The contestant must stand with at least one foot on an imaginary line drawn through the center of the trap and continuing through the center of the post, or have one foot on each side of the line. Exceptions to the rule contained in the second sentence of this paragraph may be granted by the referee/scorer due to inequalities in the shooting platform, and shall be granted for wheelchair contestants. Wheelchair contestants shall position their chair so that the center of mass of their body is over the place where they would stand as required by this rule if no chair were used. If a contestant fails to follow this rule in its entirety, the referee/scorer shall rule any target fired at and broken a "NO TARGET," but if fired at and missed, the referee/scorer shall rule the target "LOST."

11. In addition, in DOUBLES EVENTS, the referee/scorer shall rule "NO TARGET" and allow another pair of targets in the following instances ONLY:

a. When only one target is thrown.

b. When more than two targets are thrown.

c. When both targets are broken by one shot.

d. When one or both targets are thrown broken even though the contestant fires at one or both targets.

e. When one or both targets are not within the prescribed angle or height limits and the contestant does not fire at either target.

f. If the contestant fires at an illegal first target and the second target is legal, he/she must also fire at the second target, and if he/she fails to do so, the legal second target shall be ruled, "LOST." After a contestant has fired at either a legal or illegal first target, he/she is not required to fire at an Illegal second target, but if he/she does fire, the result must be scored.

# SECTION VIII

# PURSES AND OPTIONS

## A. COMPULSORY PURSES

No compulsory purse and/or option of any type shall be permitted in any tournament in which ATA trophies or ATA added monies are provided.

## B. OPTIONS AND MONEY DIVISIONS

Failure to comply strictly with these Rules shall result in disciplinary action by the State or Provincial Association and/or the Executive Committee.

1. Added Money. No tournament promoter or other person responsible therefore shall in any advertisement or program mention any purse or money in excess of the money actually added or guaranteed. Examples of money divisions may be included provided it is clearly stated that the amounts listed are only examples and not guaranteed amounts. The word "example" must be included. Failure to observe the above provisions shall be grounds for disciplinary action by the State or Provincial Association and/or by the Executive Committee. The ATA does not guarantee and it assumes no responsibility whatsoever, for actual payment and receipt of added money, guaranteed money and prizes advertised or offered at any shoot except the money, prizes and trophies directly supplied by and/or authorized by ATA.

2. At every registered tournament the cashier, or other official in charge, is required to post on a bulletin board available to the participants the names of all contestants who have entered any purse, options or any other monies, with each type of entry and contestant noted in an orderly and discernable fashion. Purses, options, etc., may be entered by and for contestants only. Any club or cashier may deduct up to one-half (1/2) of one percent of the gross amount of purse and options to help defray costs of computations. Breakage accumulated by rounding off is to be considered part of the one-half (1/2) of one percent. The one-half (1/2) of one percent may be deducted from the gross amount of monies collected from purses, options, Lewis Class purses, guaranteed purses, or otherwise, but in no event shall Hall of Fame contribution awards be included in the computation or deduction. The deductions mentioned above shall be made in such manner that no individual purse, option, Lewis class purse, guaranteed purse or otherwise shall be reduced in any amount greater than the percentage that particular item bears to the whole amount of monies collected.

All monies collected shall be returned to the shooters in the same event in which collected unless otherwise noted in the program. In such cases the program must state clearly the circumstance under which the money will be paid. This rule shall not apply to any monies collected above the actual costs of any merchandise or other such prizes, for which a separate fee is charged. Any excess monies of that type shall not be required to be returned to the shooters provided specific notification of non-return of such monies has been conspicuously inserted into each program indicating where and under what circumstances such monies are to be collected.

3. The cashier shall post on the bulletin board the amount to be paid each purse or option winner. In the event payment is made by check after the shoot is over and the contestants have left the ground, a payoff sheet for un-posted events must accompany each check indicating the amount paid for each individual purse and option included in the payment.

4. Any reasonable request to inspect the cashier sheets must be honored by the shoot management. Any shooter or gun club must file a written complaint to validly contest any payoff or trophy award within thirty (30) days after the competition of the registered shoot and/or tournament or forfeit the right to do so without right of appeal.

### C. CALCUTTAS

The ATA does not encourage Calcuttas or similar events at any registered ATA tournament. ATA Rules concerning payment or nonpayment of monies shall not be applicable in any manner to any dispute involving Calcuttas or similar events.

## SECTION IX
## REGISTERED LEAGUE SHOOTING

The following Rules shall apply to League Shooting only:

A. Registered League Shooting shall apply only to 16-yard Singles targets and Doubles targets.

B. Registered League Shooting shall be subject to and governed by official ATA Rules. In the event of any conflict between any Registered League's Rules and any official ATA Rule, official ATA Rules shall take precedence and shall govern in all aspects. The Official ATA Rules shall govern all complaints of ATA Rules violation or any Registered League's Rules violation, as a result of which any contestant or league is subject to possible disqualification, suspension or expulsion.

C. The ATA will maintain and publish Registered League Targets history, and all Registered League Targets shall be counted for purposes of target attainment accomplishments.

D. All Registered League Targets shall be counted toward target requirements for the Grand American World Trapshooting Championships and for all other ATA Registered Tournaments.

E. Registered League Target Averages shall be reported in the annual Average Book, separate from ATA Target Averages, and shall be maintained on a separate column on the ATA Average Card.

F. The following conditions are required to be met before any league targets will be registered:

1. A League must elect to become a Registered League.

2. Any member of a Registered League electing to register scores must be a Life or Annual Member of the ATA.

3. Applications for Registered League Shooting must be made on application forms approved and supplied by the ATA, and each form must be fully completed before submission to ATA. An application fee of $25.00 for each Registered League must be paid at the time of submission of the application to the ATA office. The application must be approved in writing by the State or Provincial Association Secretary before the form is submitted to the ATA.

4. Each Registered League's total score will be registered upon payment of a fee equal to the standard ATA Daily Fee charged for registered tournaments. Registration will be made when the designated league representative provides shoot reports to the ATA office containing the total number of targets thrown and broken for the League, and the total number of targets broken by each individual League participant, along with the required fee.

5. League shoot reports are required to be sent to the ATA office within eight (8) calendar days after the date of the last shoot of the League. Failure to comply with this deadline shall result in a penalty of $25.00 assessed against the defaulting League. In the event the penalty is not timely paid, the $25.00 penalty shall be deducted from the State Association's annual rebate (see section X., C.).

6. In the event any League fails to comply with the requirements set forth in this Rule, League scores for the League and for individual participants in the League will not be registered.

## SECTION X
## STATE AND ZONE SHOOTS

### A. RESIDENCE

No person may compete for ATA trophies or titles in State, Provincial or Zone tournaments, unless he/she, for the immediately preceding six (6) months, has been a bona fide resident of said Province, State or Zone, and a member in good standing of the State or Provincial Association and the ATA. No person may compete for any such ATA trophies or titles in more than one (1) State, Province or Zone each target year. However, nothing shall preclude a shooter from returning to the former State, Province or Zone residence and competing for trophies in the event he/she has not been a bona fide resident of another State, Province or Zone for the immediately preceding six (6) month period prior to such competition. In case there is a dispute with respect to the residence of a shooter attending a State, Provincial or Zone tournament, it shall be the duty of the State or Provincial Association (for a State/Provincial Shoot) or the Zone Officials (for a Zone Shoot) in which the shoot is being held to rule as to said shooter's right to compete as a resident shooter. The ruling of the State, Provincial Association or Zone Officials shall be final.

### B. LINE REFEREE/SCORERS

At all shoots where ATA trophies are furnished shoot management is encouraged to provide a line referee.

### C. ATA SUPPORT FOR STATES

The ATA in its commitment to build strong state and provincial associations aids them financially. From the $20.00 annual membership, $3.00 is returned to the state or provincial organization. No portion of the $12.00 annual membership for Junior and Sub Junior members is included in the state rebate. From the $500.00 life membership, $250.00 is returned to the state or provincial organization over a 10 year period and part is retained in a special ATA emergency fund. From the $2.00 daily fee, 20% is returned to the state organization. These refunds are made to the State/Provincial Association ten days prior to the State/Provincial Shoot, provided such shoot is held and provided the State or Province turns into the ATA at least $200.00 from annual membership dues and registration fees. From this refund, there is deducted an amount equal to any fines due because of late shoot reports. On or before January 1 of each year the ATA shall inform the Secretary of each State/Province of the approximate amount of refund to be paid to that State/Province. This information must be printed in the program for that annual State/Provincial shoot.

### D. ATA TROPHIES

1. Only one (1) ATA trophy shall be awarded to any one (1) person in any separate event. This means a contestant may not win a special category trophy and an ATA event champion (runner up etc) or ATA class trophy. Trophies not provided by ATA to States/Provinces or Zones are exempt from this rule. Please see paragraph E. and H. of this section.

2. A contestant whose score qualifies them for more than one (1) ATA trophy must notify shoot management as to which trophy he/she desires to accept or shoot for. The shooter must make his/her declaration as specified by shoot management after the last scores for that day's event(s) are posted and before entering into any shoot-off/carry-over. The maximum time allowed for such declaration shall be made by shoot management, within a range of 15 to 45 minutes, and published in the shoot program. If not published in the program, the time shall be 15 minutes. This declaration should be made at a place specified by shoot management.

3. Any category shooter who is tied for event champion may shoot-off/carry-over for champion only. Shooters failing in the champion shoot-off/carry-over may elect only one of the options listed in Paragraph D., 5. (a) or (b).

4. Any category shooter who is high or tied for place, class or yardage group and also high or tied for his/her category, may elect only one of the options listed in Paragraph D., 5. , (a) or (b).

5. Options available to category shooters:

(a) Take out right or shoot-off/carry-over for his/her category forfeiting any place, class or yardage group trophy.

(b)Take outright or shoot-off/carry-over for place, class or yardage group trophy forfeiting any category trophy. If the shooter fails to make a declaration within the specified time, shoot management shall declare for the shooter and place the shooter as mandated by Paragraph D., 5., (a). If a shooter is placed in more than one category, shoot management shall place and declare if required:

(a) Sub-junior or Junior over Lady

(b)Lady over Veteran or Senior Veteran

(c)Chair over all categories

Once any declarations have been made either by a shooter or shoot management, the declaration is final and cannot be changed. There shall be no exception to this rule.

When there are both Junior and Sub-Junior trophies, the Junior must take the Junior trophy, and the Sub-Junior must take the Sub-Junior trophy regardless of the high score between the two. Likewise, this rule also applies to Veterans and Senior Veterans.

### E. STATE ATA TROPHIES

The ATA will also donate the following trophies to each State and Provincial Association holding a State or Provincial shoot:

Singles
Singles Champion
Singles Runner-up
Lady Singles Champion
Veteran Singles Champion
Senior Veteran Singles Champion
Junior Singles Champion
Sub-junior Singles Champion
Handicap
Handicap Champion
Handicap Runner-up
Handicap Third
Handicap Fourth
Handicap Fifth
Handicap Sixth

Class Champions, which may be utilized in the Singles or Class Singles Championship. (AA, A, B, C, D) awarded in Class or Singles Championship.

Doubles
Doubles Champion
Doubles Runner Up
All Around Championship
All Around Champion
Doubles Class Championships (AA, A, B, C, D) in Class or Doubles Championship

### F. CHAMPIONSHIP EVENTS AT STATE TOURNAMENTS

The 4 State championships shall be determined on the following:

Singles-200 targets
Doubles-50 pair
Handicap-100 targets
High All-Around - the sum of the above, 400 targets

Ladies, Junior, Veterans, Sub-Junior, Senior Veterans and any other championships not listed above may be determined on a lesser number of targets at the discretion of the State Shoot Management.

### G. ATA SUPPORT FOR ZONES

The ATA donates $3,000.00 in added money to be awarded at each Zone tournament. Zone officials may determine the division of the ATA added money for Zone tournaments in the Singles and Doubles class championships and in the championship events of Singles, Handicap, and Doubles. It shall be made available to all ATA registered shooters regardless of location unless the money is specifically restricted to Zone residents at the discretion of the various ATA Zones and it must be so stated in the Zone programs.

### H. ZONE ATA TROPHIES

The ATA will donate the following trophies to each Zone for its Zone Tournament:

| | |
|---|---|
| Singles | Doubles |
| Singles Champion | Doubles Champion |
| Singles Runner-up | Doubles Runner-up |
| Singles Championship | Doubles Championship |
| AAA, AA, A, B, C, D | AAA, AA, A, B, C, D |
| Lady Singles Champion | Lady Doubles Champion |
| Junior Singles Champion | Junior Doubles Champion |
| Sub-Junior Singles Champion | Sub-Junior Doubles Champion |
| Veteran Singles Champion | Veteran Doubles Champion |
| Senior Veteran Singles | Senior Veteran Doubles |
| Class Singles | Class Doubles |
| Singles Class Championship | Doubles Class Championship |
| AAA, AA, A, B, C, D | AAA, AA, A, B, C, D |
| Handicap | All-Around |
| Handicap Champion | All-Around Champion |

Handicap Runner-up
Handicap Third
Handicap Fourth
Handicap Fifth
Handicap Sixth
Lady Handicap Champion
Junior Handicap Champion
Sub-Junior Handicap Champion
Veteran Handicap Champion
Senior Veteran Handicap Champion

### I. CHAMPIONSHIP EVENTS AT ZONE TOURNAMENTS

Zone championships shall be determined on the following:

Singles-200 targets
Doubles-50 pair

Handicap-100 targets
All-Around, the sum of the above, 400 targets

Class Singles and Class Doubles-a minimum of 100 targets (not to be shot concurrently with the Singles and Doubles Championships).

Zone tournament programs shall call for a minimum of 600 registered targets.

### J. CONCURRENT STATE AND ZONE SHOOTS

When a State or Provincial shoot is held concurrently with a Zone telephonic shoot a shooter may win both an ATA state trophy and an ATA Zone trophy.

## SECTION XI
## GRAND AND ALL AMERICAN QUALIFICATION

### A. GRAND AMERICAN QUALIFICATION

No participant shall be classified to shoot Handicap events at less than 25.0 yards unless he/she has a minimum of 1000 registered Handicap targets in the current year. The 1000 handicap targets must have been registered beginning the first day after the last day of previous Grand American World Trapshooting Championships through the last day of

preliminary week of the current Grand American World Trapshooting Championships. However, participants who fail to meet Grand American Handicap qualification as described above shall have the choice of shooting targets only from their assigned yardage provided they waive and forfeit all rights to trophies, options, purses, and added money. Handicap target requirements are waived for Senior Veterans, making them eligible for trophies and monies.

Shooters who do not have a total of 1000 16 yard targets registered beginning the first day after the last day of previous Grand American World Trapshooting Championships through the last day of preliminary week of the current Grand American World Trapshooting Championships will be advanced (1) class or more at the discretion of the Handicap Committee. Shooters with less than 500 registered singles targets will be placed in class B or higher at the discretion on the Handicap Committee.

Shooters who do not have a total of 1000 doubles targets registered beginning the first day after the last day of previous Grand American World Trapshooting Championships through the last day of preliminary week of the current Grand American World Trapshooting Championships will be advanced (1) class or more at the discretion of the Handicap Committee. Shooters with less than 500 registered doubles targets will be placed in class B or higher at the discretion on the Handicap Committee.

### B. ALL-AMERICAN TEAM REQUIREMENTS

| | 16's | Hdcp | Dbls |
|---|---|---|---|
| Men | 3000 | 2500 | 1500 |
| Women, Juniors, Veterans | 3000 | 2000 | 1000 |
| Sub-Juniors, Sr. Veterans | 2000 | 1000 | 500 |

1. Qualified competitions are the Grand American, Satellite Grand Americans, Annual Resident Zone Tournaments, Annual State or Provincial Tournaments or any other ATA Registered Tournament where total entries in the Singles Championship Event, Doubles Championship Event, and Handicap Championship Event, individually or in any combination, total at least 600 entries.

2. Shooters must have competed in qualified tournaments in at least three (3) states. (State of residence may be included.)

## SECTION XII
## DISCIPLINARY ACTION, DISQUALIFICATION AND REINSTATEMENT

### A. PAYMENTS AND OVERPAYMENTS

Any club, which conducts a registered event and/or tournament, should make payment of all added money, purses, options, and other monies to the shooters as promptly as possible. Failure to do so within fifteen (15) days may result in the cancellation of registration privileges of that club for the remainder of the year, and no further registration shall be granted to that club until all monies due to shooters, the ATA and State organizations have been paid in full. The person(s) responsible, and/or officer(s) of such delinquent club(s), shall be barred from shooting registered targets until such payments have been made. Any ATA member who is due payment of money from a gun club and is requested to, but refuses to provide his/her Social Security Number or Tax ID Number is not protected by this fifteen (15) day Rule.

Any competitor at a registered shoot who, through error, has been overpaid on any purse, added money, option, or other awards, and who is notified of the overpayment by certified mail, must return the overpayment within fifteen (15) days. Failure to do so shall result in disqualification from participation in any ATA registered event and/or tournament until payment is made in full.

### B. DISQUALIFICATION

1. A shooter may be disqualified for an event or for a whole tournament at any time by Shoot Management, or at any time by the Executive Committee or such person as they shall designate for that purpose, or disciplined by the Executive Committee, whenever the following prohibited conduct is brought to their attention:

a. if in the opinion of Management or the Executive Committee the shooter disrupts the harmony of the shoot, or

b. Contestants not timely reporting for competition, including shoot-offs; or

c. if the shooter shoots at any place other than the regular firing line; or

d. if the shooter fails to shoot at his/her correct yardage in any subevent except as permitted in Section VII. Par. A., 8.; or

e. if the shooter has failed to have his/her Average Card punched for earned yardage at a prior shoot, and fails to report earned yardage at the time of any subsequent registration; or

f. if the shooter behaves in other than a sportsman-like manner such as physical abuse, verbal abuse or threats of any type directed to shoot personnel, other competitors, or any other person, whether on or off the shooting line, if such conduct occurs on gun club grounds and during any day when ATA registered trapshooting takes place; or

g. if the shooter interferes with the Management's procedures in conducting the shoot; or

h. if the shooter does not respond and report to the firing line in a timely manner when his/her squad is called to shoot; or

i. if the shooter does not abide by the Rules of the ATA, by the Rules set out by Management, and/or in the official program.

2. It is the responsibility and the required duty of Shoot Management to immediately remove and disqualify any contestant at any time during an ATA sanctioned tournament:

a. who is under the obvious influence of alcohol or drugs before starting or during any event, sub-event, shoot-off or practice, or who consumes any alcoholic beverage or drugs during participation in any event, sub event or between events or sub events held on the same day including shoot-offs and practice. For purposes of this rule, "drugs" shall mean any illegal drug, and shall also mean any prescription medication if that prescription medication affects the judgment or conduct of the contestant to a degree that renders the contestant incapable of safely participating in the sport of trapshooting, whether during a registered event and/or tournament or practice; or

b. who handles a gun dangerously on or off the firing line, or

c. who deliberately or carelessly violates gun safety precautions, Official Rules regarding safety, or in any manner endangers contestants, spectators, or gun club personnel.

3. Disqualification for a single event does not prevent a contestant from participating in other events in the same tournament and scores shot in other events are not affected. However, any disqualification pursuant to Rule 2., a. above shall include all events or practice on the same day after the time of disqualification.

4. If the infraction is severe the management may disqualify the contestant for the entire tournament and require him/her to leave the grounds.

5. Disqualification for a tournament does not prevent a shooter from participating in other tournaments.

6. All entry monies in events not competed in as a result of disqualification are to be returned in full. Events, which have been started, do not qualify for refunds due to disqualification.

7. Scores shot in a registered event and/or tournament for which a shooter is disqualified will not be registered, and any trophies or monies, which the contestant has received for an event for which he/she is disqualified, MUST be returned. Any shooter who is disqualified for any registered event or tournament and fails to return any trophies or monies which the shooter received in that event or tournament will remain disqualified and will be barred from shooting ATA targets or otherwise participating in ATA activities until all trophies or monies have been returned and written certification from the gun club involved is received at the ATA Main Offices.

8. When a shooter's Handicap score is disqualified and that score would have earned yardage under the earned yardage table, the shooter's average card must be punched to the earned yardage. Those targets that are disqualified will not become part of the shooter's target history.

### C. SUSPENSIONS, EXPULSIONS, AND REINSTATEMENT

1. The Executive Committee may at any time at its discretion suspend any member or discipline shoot management for any conduct specified in Rule XII, B., 1., and/or anyone who:

a. presents a check at any shoot for fees and targets, or has or allows his/her fees and targets to be paid by such check, that is returned or dishonored for insufficient funds or any other reason. Further, any person who presents such a check more than two (2) times shall be automatically suspended for a period of one (1) year. Suspension shall be timed after reimbursement is made. The Executive Committee may designate authority to the Executive Director to suspend any member for presentation of dishonored checks, on first and second offenses, until the gun club where the check(s) were written has been reimbursed and the reinstatement fee has been paid. Clubs receiving such a check shall report the name and address of the shooter or individual issuing the check to the ATA along with a copy and a statement that the check was for registered targets and/or fees. After having been reimbursed the club MUST immediately inform the ATA so that reinstatement proceedings may be initiated. Any ATA member who has been suspended for presenting a check that is returned for insufficient funds or other causes and becomes eligible for reinstatement shall be required to pay the sum of $25.00 to the ATA as a reinstatement fee. This fee must be paid before reinstatement will be considered; or

b. falsifies his/her scores; or

c. fails to have his/her Average Card properly punched for earned yardage or fails to report earned yardage at the time of registration for any subsequent tournament; or

d. fails to return any overpayment after proper notification; or

e. is convicted of any gun or firearms violation; or

f. willfully, deliberately, or repeatedly violates the Rules of the ATA as contained in the Official Rules; or

g. encourages, participates in or allows a willful rule violation by any minor of which he/she is parent or for whom he/she is acting as legal or actual guardian, either temporary or permanent. For purposes of these Rules only, a "minor" shall mean a person who has not attained his or her 18th birthday, and "guardian" shall mean a person who has actual physical custody or control of a minor, either temporarily or permanently and custody or control for the purpose of attending a single registered trapshooting tournament shall satisfy that definition of "guardian" for the purpose of enforcement of this rule only; or

h. engages in conduct or behavior, which constitutes cause for suspension in the opinion of the Executive Committee.

2. A member who is suspended for any reason is barred from shooting ATA targets or otherwise participating in ATA activities for the period of his/her suspension.

3. If the Executive Committee feels the violations warrant suspension for longer than three (3) years, or expulsion, the member shall have the right of appeal if he/she complies with the terms and provisions of the By-Laws of the Amateur Trapshooting Association.

4. Investigating Complaints

The procedure for investigations of complaints of any Rules violation, including those that may result in suspension or disciplinary action, is as follows:

a. All complaints of ATA Rule(s) violations(s) shall meet the following requirements:

(1) Shall be in writing and shall be signed by the complainant(s). Verbal or anonymous written complaints will not be accepted or considered.

(2) Shall be dated with the effective date that the complaint is made, and shall contain the exact date(s) of the alleged Rule(s) violation(s) in the statement of facts upon which the complaint is based.

(3) Specific Official Rule(s) alleged to have been violated shall be stated if known by the complainant.

(4) Full details of the incident(s) upon which the complaint is based must be made, and must include a statement of facts sufficient to describe the incident upon which the complaint is based, and sufficient to establish that violation(s) of Official Rule(s) occurred.

(5) The location and name and address of the gun club where the alleged violation occurred must be stated, and if a violation of Rule XII, B., l.e. is alleged then the exact location of the violation(s) must be described.

(6) Names and addresses of any witnesses to the alleged violation(s) must be stated.

(7) A complaint may only be made by an ATA life or annual member in good standing on the date the alleged violation(s) occurred, or by a gun club in good standing where the alleged violation(s) occurred and signed by an authorized officer or director of the gun club.

b. All complaints of violation(s) of ATA Official Rules must be made within thirty (30) days after the date on which the alleged violation(s) occurred. In the event a claim is made, or a defense is raised that a complaint was not timely made, the earliest of the following dates shall control:

(1) The date of receipt by the ATA Executive Director or other ATA Official as designated by Corporate Resolution; or

(2) The date of postmark of the envelope in which the complaint was transmitted; or

(3) The date of transmittal to the ATA Executive Director [supra-Throughout these Official Rules and/or By-Laws, the reference to Executive Director shall include any other ATA Official that has been legally authorized by appropriate Corporate Resolution to fulfill the responsibilities and/or duties herein impressed] by any electronic media, provided, that a hard copy showing date of transmittal can be printed, and provided further that the original signed complaint and hard copy of proof of electronic transmittal are mailed or delivered to the ATA Executive Director on the same date transmitted.

c. All complaints shall be sent or delivered to the ATA Executive Director at the ATA Main office, and any statement of procedure in any previous Rule stating otherwise is void and of no effect. Upon receipt of a written complaint the ATA Executive Director shall:

(1) Cause each complaint to be assigned a number, consecutive to the last complaint received in order of receipt, and consisting of the year of receipt and consecutive number of receipt, e.g. 99-01, 99-02, etc.

(2) Examine the complaint to determine it substantially complies with the requirements set forth herein.

(3) If the Executive Director determines that the complaint alleges a serious breach of safety he/she shall immediately notify the ATA President of the alleged violation. The President, after consideration of the allegation, may direct the Executive Director to issue an administrative suspension

of the member pending inquiry and action by the Executive Committee as set forth herein. While under administrative suspension a member may not participate as a contestant in any ATA registered events and/or tournaments. Notification of administrative suspension shall be by certified mail, return receipt requested or personal delivery.

(4) If the Executive Director determines that the complaint substantially complies with the requirements herein, he/she shall mail the complaint to the ATA State or Provincial Delegate representing the State or Province in which the alleged violation occurred, with instructions to proceed as required in accordance with ATA Official Rules.

(5) If the Executive Director determines that any of the following conditions exist:

(a) The complaint is directed against the ATA State or Provincial Delegate representing the State or Province in which the alleged violation occurred; or

(b) The Delegate has an obvious conflict of interest; or

(c) The Delegate recuses himself/herself, He/She shall assign the investigation to the Alternate Delegate(s) in succession. If one of the conditions described in (5.), (a.), (b.), or (c.) exist as to all available Alternate Delegates, then the Executive Director shall promptly notify the ATA President. Within ten (10) days after the receipt of such notification, the ATA President shall contact each voting member of the Executive Committee and, based on the majority vote of the Executive Committee, shall instruct the Executive Director who shall be assigned to conduct the investigation. In the event the person so assigned shall be unable or unwilling to conduct the investigation the ATA President shall repeat this procedure until an individual has been selected to conduct the investigation.

(6) If the Executive Director determines the complaint does not substantially comply with the requirements set forth herein, he/she shall return the complaint to the complainant with a letter informing the complainant of the reason(s) why the complaint does not comply with these Official Rules. Any defective complaint may be resubmitted at the option of the complainant, however, the time limit specified in Paragraph 4.b., above, is not extended and the time limitation is not tolled by this procedure.

d. Within fourteen (14) days after receipt of the complaint from the ATA Executive Director, the Delegate or individual appointed to conduct the investigation shall serve written notice of the complaint and a copy of the complaint on the alleged violator, by certified mail, return receipt requested or personal delivery. The written notice shall state the date and location of the alleged violation(s), the acts alleged to have occurred, the Official ATA Rule(s) alleged to have been violated, and shall inform the alleged violator that a written response is required within fourteen (14) days of receipt of the notice. A copy of the notice and a copy of the complaint, along with copies of any other documentation that is in the possession of the Delegate or individual appointed to conduct the investigation at that time, shall be sent to the Vice-President of the Zone in which the alleged violation occurred. The Delegate, Alternate Delegate or individual appointed to conduct the investigation shall thoroughly investigate the allegations of the complaint and shall obtain witness statements in writing, signed by the witness(es), whenever reasonable, possible, or practicable.

e. Upon receipt of any answer from the alleged violator, or if no such answer is received within fourteen (14) days after his/her receipt of the notice, or immediately upon receipt of notice of nonacceptance if the alleged violator refuses to accept the certified mail, the Delegate, Alternate Delegate or individual appointed to conduct the investigation shall confer with such State officers as deemed necessary, and then within twenty eight (28) days shall, in writing, recommend appropriate action to the Zone Vice-President. The entire file, including the return receipt or notice of refusal, and any response(s), answer(s), statement(s) or other documents relating to the complaint or investigation not previously sent or provided shall be delivered to the Zone Vice-President at the time the Delegate, Alternate Delegate or individual appointed to conduct the investigation makes his/her recommendation. Action recommended shall be specific, and shall not be general or left to the discretion of the Zone Vice-President or Executive Committee.

f. The Zone Vice-President, upon receipt of the recommendation(s), shall review the entire file, and within fourteen (14) days after receipt shall write his/her own recommendations, with supporting facts, to all members of the Executive Committee. Each member of the Executive Committee will be provided a complete copy of the file and all recommendations accompanied by an ATA Official Ballot.

g. All members of the Executive Committee shall, within fourteen (14) days after their receipt of the Zone Vice-President's recommendations, advise the ATA President of their agreement or disagreement with the recommendations of the Zone Vice-President, or any modification thereof. All Official notifications required under Section XII, C., 4., Subsections (e), (f), and/or (g), herein, may be effected by utilizing the Official Ballots as supplied or, in the alternative, scheduled for an adjudication hearing during any special or regularly scheduled meeting (teleconference or otherwise) of the Executive Committee, time requirement(s) permitting, subject to Section XII, C., 4., I.

h. After receipt of notice of agreement or disagreement from each member of the Executive Committee, or modifications approved by a majority of the Executive Committee, the ATA President shall cause reasonably prompt and appropriate action to be taken in accordance with the majority vote of the Executive Committee. Suspensions and/or expulsions made under this section shall conform to the applicable provisions pertaining thereto as fully set forth in the Articles of Incorporation and By-Laws of the Amateur Trapshooting Association.

i. Any time requirement set forth in this Rule may, for good cause, and after written request of a Zone Vice-President, be extended by the President or his/her designate.

5. Reinstatement

Any ATA member who has been suspended for any reason must pay a $25.00 fee to the ATA when his/her period of suspension is completed or when, in the case of returned checks, he/she has reimbursed the club where the check was written. This fee must be paid before reinstatement.

# SECTION XIII
# STANDARDS FOR TRAPHOUSES, TARGETS, TARGET SETTING, GUNS AND AMMUNITION

### *A. TRAP MACHINE*

A trap machine, which throws targets at an unknown angle, shall be used. All trap machines used to throw ATA registered targets shall be so manufactured, modified, or equipped as to interrupt irregularly the oscillation of the trap or otherwise assure the unpredictability of the flight of substantially all targets thrown.

Each gun club that throws ATA registered targets must have on file in the ATA main offices a signed Affidavit that the trap machines used to throw registered targets meet the requirements of this rule. The State/Provincial ATA Delegate is responsible for the enforcement of this Rule.

### *B. TRAPHOUSES*

Traphouses must adequately protect the trap loaders and shall not be higher than necessary for that purpose. It is recommended that traphouses constructed after September 1, 2003 shall conform to the following specifications:

1. Length not less than 7 feet, 6 inches, nor more than 9 feet, 6 inches.
2. Width not less than 7 feet, 6 inches, nor more than 9 feet, 6 inches.
3. Height not less than 2 feet, 2 inches, nor more than 3 feet, 0 inches, the height to be measured from the plane of the number 3 shooting position.

It is recommended that the throwing surface (throwing arm or plate) of the trap machine be on the same level as that of Post 3 and the target height setting pad.

### *C. POSTS*

The posts shall be 3 yards apart on the circumference of a circle whose radius is 16 yards. Handicap posts, when used, shall be prolongations of the lines given in Diagram I, commonly known as fan shaped. The distance between posts at 16-yards shall then be 3 yards.

### *D. TARGETS*

No target shall measure more than four and five-sixteenths (4 5/16) inches in diameter, and not more than one and one-eighth (1 1/8) inches in height. A target shall not weigh less than 95 grams or more than 105 grams with an allowable variation of plus or minus 5 grams per target lot. A target lot is defined as all targets with the same production lot number.

### *E. FLIGHTS AND ANGLES*

Singles targets shall be thrown not less than 49 yards nor more than 51 yards. Distance measurements are on level ground in still air. Targets shall be between 8 feet and 10 feet high, when 10 yards from Point B. The recommended height is 9 or 9 1/2 feet. The height at a point 10 yards from Point B is to be understood to mean height above an imaginary horizontal straight line drawn through the post and Point B. (See Diagram II) (See also the alternative to setting by distance – setting by speed - in Section F, following.)

Target height may also be set based on the height of the target at ten yards as measured above the level of the trap arm in the house rather than the height as measured from the number 3 shooting station. This is the recommended procedure at facilities where the installation of traps in the houses is inconsistent as to height. Point B is defined as the intersection of a line measured 1 foot 6 inches or 2 feet 6 inches from the outside vertical wall (farthest from the shooting stations) of the trap house and the centerline of the trap house. Please review Diagram I on page 55. Clubs constructing new trap house and fields should use the same point B measurement as their existing fields to keep all fields as consistent as possible.

In Singles shooting the trap shall be so adjusted that within the normal distribution of angles as thrown by the trap, the right angle shall not be less than 17 degrees measured to the right of center (3BF), and not less than 17 degrees measured to the left of center (3BF), with a total angle between outside target limits of not less than 34 degrees. (See Diagram II) Under no circumstances shall a Standard Model 1524 trap be set in less than the #2 hole. Any other trap machine shall be adjusted so as to throw not less than equivalent angles. Where terrain allows, a visible stake must be placed on the centerline of the trap on the arc of a circle that has a radius of 50 yards and its center is Point B (Point F, Diagram II).

To help in determining legal angles, stakes may be placed on the arc of a circle that has a radius of 50 yards and its center is Point B. One stake should be placed where a line drawn through Point A and Point B intersects this arc and another stake placed where a line drawn through Point C and Point B intersects the arc. These lines and stakes will assist in determining the required angles, but it is to be understood that the angle specifications apply when the target is from 15 yards to 20 yards from the trap rather than where the target strikes the ground. However, no target is to be declared illegal unless it is significantly outside normal parameters (e.g., more than 10 degrees outside normal).

In doubles shooting, targets shall be thrown not less than 44 yards nor more than 51 yards. Distance measurements are on level ground in still air. Targets shall be between 8 feet and 10 feet high when 10 yards from point B. The recommended height is 9 or 9 1/2 feet. The height at a point 10 yards from Point B is to be understood to mean height above an imaginary horizontal straight line drawn through the post and Point B (See Diagram II). The trap shall be adjusted so the angle of target spread is not less than 34 degrees. (See the alternative to setting by distance - setting by speed - in Section F, following.)

Target height may also be set based on the height of the target at ten yards as measured above the level of the trap arm in the house rather than the height as measured from the number 3 shooting station. The 17 degree angle will appear to be a straight-away from a point 3 1/2 feet to the right of post 1; the 17 degree angle will appear to be a straight-away from a point 3 1/2 feet to the left of post 5. This 17 degree angle refers to the flight line of the target from the house to 15 or 20 yards out and can be used for singles, handicap, and doubles targets.

### *F. RULES FOR THE USE OF RADAR GUNS AND CHRONOGRAPHS TO SET TARGET SPEED*

There are two types of radar guns, high-power and low-power. The practical difference between them is that high-power guns work reliably from the 16-yard line and low-power guns don't.

High-power guns (Decatur, Stalker, most "police radar guns" and similar) are to be used at the 16-yard line. The trap oscillation is stopped, and the target measured is a straightaway. The gun is pointed horizontally. The correct speed for a singles or handicap target is 42 MPH. The correct speed for the right target of a doubles pair is 39 MPH.

Low-power guns (SportRadar, Bushnell, and similar) are to be used at the back of the traphouse and at the level of the top of the traphouse. (Holding the gun higher than that will lead to a target which is too fast.) The trap oscillation is stopped, and the target measured is a straightaway. The gun is pointed horizontally. The correct speed for a singles or handicap target must be a minimum of 42 MPH. The correct speed for the right target of a doubles pair must be a minimum of 39 MPH. When a radar gun is used from inside the house, the correct speed for a singles or handicap target must be a minimum of 44 MPH. The correct speed for the right target of a doubles pair must be a minimum of 41 MPH.

A chronograph is to be used as close to the trap as practical and tipped up at approximately the same angle as the flight of the target. The correct speed for a singles or handicap target is 67 ft/sec. To set doubles with a chronograph, set a singles target to 76 ft/sec. and then switch the trap to throw doubles without changing the spring tension. Note: target speed may be set by distance as above or by speed as determined by a radar gun or chronograph. Target must be set by measured speed or distance.

### *G. GUNS AND AMMUNITION*

Any shooter violating any of these Rules shall be disqualified from competition in accordance with these Rules. Any such violator shall be referred to the Executive Committee for possible further disciplinary action.

A contestant cannot use:

1. A gun with a chamber larger than 12 gauge. Guns of smaller gauges are permissible in registered and tournament shooting, but no competitive consideration shall be given in recognition of that fact for handicap and classification purposes. A contestant may not use a gun capable of chambering more than one gauge of shells at the same time. For example, chambering 12 gauge and 20 gauge shells in the same gun at the same time is prohibited.

2. Loads that contain nickel or copper coated shot or tracer loads. However, the use of lead, steel, bismuth, or other composite nontoxic shot materials shall be allowed. Any gun club allowing shot materials described in this Rule, other than lead, shall be required to cover or shield all hard surfaces on trap fields which are known, or reasonably believed, to cause pellet ricochet with material which will prevent the shot pellets from rebounding and/or ricocheting.

3. Any load with a velocity greater than 1290 FPS (Feet Per Second) with maximum shot charge of 1 1/8 ounces, or 1325 FPS with a maximum shot charge of 1 ounce, or 1350 FPS with a maximum shot charge of 7/8 ounces or less, as measured in any individual shotshell. These velocities are maximum and no individual shotshell shall exceed these limits for the designated shot charge. In addition, no load containing more than 1 1/8 ounces or any shot larger than Number 7 1/2 can be used. Shot charges are maximum and no charge may exceed the charge amount by more than 3%.

4. Any shell loaded with black powder.

5. Shoot Management, ATA official(s) or any contestant may challenge the load of any other contestant. Any challenge shall be initiated so as to not disrupt the harmony of the shoot or interfere with other contestants not involved with the challenge. On receipt of a challenge management or ATA official(s) shall obtain a shell or shells from the challenged party, and if after examination, management or ATA official(s) find the contestant violated the ATA rule, he/she may be disqualified. Any such initiated challenges, determined to be abusive in nature, will be referred to the ATA Executive Committee for disciplinary action.

# OFFICIAL RULES & REGULATIONS

# NATIONAL SKEET SHOOTING ASSOCIATION (NSSA)

(Revised 2009)

## Skeet Welcomes You

The great sport of skeet shooting, designed in 1920 by a group of Andover, Massachusetts upland game hunters to improve their wing shooting, has rapidly caught the fancy of people in all age groups and both sexes. It is now a major sport, with its own international and state organizations. A dedicated group is guiding it carefully to even greater popularity and prestige.

Skeet has developed into much more than just an aid to better wing shooting or a substitute for hunting. It is now a competitive sport equaled by few in universal appeal. Matches are conducted for all gun gauges, and under skeet's universal classification system all shooters compete against others of like ability. (Note classification rules, Section V.) Competition is held for four gauges of shotguns, 12, 20, 28 and .410, though many people never use more than one. Guns must be capable of firing two shots since four sets of doubles are included in the regulation 25-shot round. In addition, competitive Doubles Events are offered at many tournaments. The gun may be a double barrel (side-by-side or over-and-under), a pump gun or an automatic, depending on the shooter's preference. Major manufacturers offer specially made skeet guns, and you should consult them or a good gunsmith before buying a shotgun for skeet. Details such as weight,

choke, drop and pitch and fit of the gun vary with shooters. It is actually better to try out several guns, all types if possible, before buying.

The National Skeet Shooting Association (NSSA) is a nonprofit organization owned and operated by and for its members, sportsmen and women who are dedicated to the development among its members of those qualities of patriotism and good sportsmanship which are the basic ingredients of good citizenship, and in general to promote and advance the interests, welfare and development of skeet shooting and related sports.

In addition to the present regulation skeet most commonly shot, the NSSA has an international division for those who wish to shoot under the rules used in international competition with low gun position and variable timing.

We believe that in skeet you will find the finest fellowship of sportsmen and women in the world. This is a rewarding recreational adventure where the best of sportsmanship prevails. You are welcome to this unique fraternity. Gratuities in skeet are not permitted.

National Skeet Shooting Association, 5931 Roft Road, San Antonio, TX 78253-9261
www.mynssa.com nssa@nssa-nsca.com (800) 877-5338 (210) 688-3371 Fax 210) 688-3014

# SECTION I

# EQUIPMENT

## A. TARGETS

Standard targets of good quality measuring no more than four and five-sixteenth (4-5/16) inches in diameter nor more than one and one-eighth (1-1/8) inches in height shall be used.

## B. AMMUNITION

1. Gauge Specifications - Lead Shot
   a. Shells commercially manufactured by reputable companies, which are clearly labeled and guaranteed as to lead shot sizes and weight are recommended for use in registered skeet shoots. However, NSSA will accept results of shoots and register scores where reloads have been used. NSSA assumes no responsibility in connection with the use of reloads.
   b. Gun Clubs are allowed to use alternate shot (other than lead) for registered shoots: alternate loads must meet industry standards for "target load" ammunition.

2. Reloads
   a. The maximum load permissible is described below. This table makes ample allowance for manufacturing purposes, but the use of a proper shot bar is cautioned (a 12 gauge bar designed for 7-1/2 shot will weigh approximately 11 grains heavy when No. 9 shot is used).

| Gauge | Ounces Lead | Grains Standard | Grains Maximum |
|---|---|---|---|
| 12 | 1-1/8 | 492.2 | 507 |
| 20 | 7/8 | 382.8 | 394 |
| 28 | 3/4 | 328.1 | 338 |
| .410 | 1/2 | 218.8 | 229 |

   b. No shot smaller than No. 9 (2mm) or larger than 7-1/2 shall be used in any load.
   c. Any shooter may elect to have his/her shells weighed by management before entering an event. The shooter must submit all shells to be used in said event. After one shell is selected, weighed and approved by these standards, the balance of the shells shall be stamped, approved and sealed by some suitable method and not be opened until on the field where the event is to be shot in the presence of the field referee. Failure to have the field referee witness the breaking of the sealed boxes or containers on their respective fields shall necessitate the shooter using factory ammunition or risk having his/her score disqualified. Any shooter using approved and sealed ammunition shall be immune from further checking.
   d. Challenge Rule: At shoots where shells have not been checked, any contestant may, upon formal challenge presented to shoot management, have the chief referee, who shall use timely discretion, select a shell from another contestant and have said shell checked against the standards listed in rule I-B-2-a. To prevent abuse of a shooter with this rule, shoot management shall make known the challenger and the individual challenged. Entire groups or squads shall not be challenged for purposes of anonymity.

3. Checking Factory Loads
   Any shooter found to be using commercial loads heavier than the maximum grains permissible as listed in I-B-2-a shall have his/her score disqualified for that event.

## C. FIELD LAYOUT

It is recommended and desirable for all NSSA registered targets to be shot on fields constructed according to the following specifications and the diagram shown on the centerfold of this book. Field layout deviation will not affect NSSA's consideration of scores. Under no circumstances will protests based on alleged irregularity of field layout be considered.

1. A skeet field shall consist of eight (8) shooting stations arranged on a segment of a circle of twenty-one (21) yards radius, with a base cord exactly one hundred twenty (120) feet, nine (9) inches long, drawn six (6) yards from the center of the circle. The center of the circle is known as the target-crossing point and is marked by a stake. Station 1 is located at the left end of the base

---

while standing on the periphery of the segment. Stations 2 to 6, inclusive, are located on the periphery at points equidistant from each other. The exact distance between Stations 1 and 2, 2 and 3, etc., is twenty-six (26) feet, eight and three-eighths (8-3/8) inches. Station 8 is located at the center of the base chord.

   a. Shooting Stations 1 and 7, each a square area three (3) feet on a side, shall have two sides parallel to the base chord.
   b. Shooting Stations 2 to 6, inclusive, each a square area, three (3) feet on a side, shall have two sides parallel to a radius of the circle drawn through the station marker.
   c. Shooting Station 8 is a rectangular area three (3) feet wide by six (6) feet long, with the long sides parallel to the base chord.

2. The location of each shooting station shall be accurately designated.
   a. The marker for shooting Stations 1-7, inclusive, is on the center of the side nearest the target crossing point.
   b. The marker for shooting Station 8 is on the center point of the base chord.

3. One target should emerge from a skeet house (called high house) at a point three (3) feet in back of Station Marker 1 (measured along the base chord extended), and ten (10) feet above the ground level. The other should emerge from a skeet house (called low house) at a point three (3) feet in back of Station Marker 7 (measure along the base chord extended), and two and one-half (2-1/2) feet from the base chord extended (measure on side of target-crossing point), and three and one-half (3-1/2) feet above the ground.

4. Mandatory markers (where geographically possible) shall be placed at points 44 yards and 60 yards from both the high house and the low house to indicate the shooting boundary limit of 44 yards. These distances shall be measured along a line and the flight of a regular target 60 yards from the opening (where target emerges) in skeet house through the target-crossing point. The 60-yard distance markers must be suitably marked to indicate Station 8 ground level where geographically possible.

5. The target-crossing point must be marked in a visible manner where geographically possible.

6. It is recommended to remove posts or box stands tangent to the front of the stations interfering with the shooter.

7. It is recommended and desirable that the side of the skeet house, from the bottom of the chute to the top of the house, be very light color or painted white where feasible.

8. It is recommended if more than one field is in line that a fence be constructed between fields.

9. Unusual or undesirable field variations must be corrected before contract negotiations are completed.

10. The pull cord will be a minimum length to allow the referee to reach all mandatory referee positions and will have high house, low house and doubles release buttons.

## D. MANDATORY POSITIONS FOR REFEREES

1. For shooting Station 1 (1R), stand six feet to the right and three (3) feet back of the front of Station 1 where possible.

2. For shooting Station 2 (2R), stand six (6) feet back and three (3) feet to the right of Station 2.

3. For shooting Stations 3, 4, 5 and 6 (3-4-5-6R), stand six (6) feet back and three (3) feet to the left of the respective station.

4. For shooting Station 7 (7R), stand six (6) feet to the left and three (3) feet back of the front of Station 7 where possible.

5. For shooting Station 8 (8R), stand on center line of the field, not less than six (6) feet from shooter (and not more than 10 feet).

6. During doubles shooting, as shooters are coming back around the circle, referees should stand six feet back and three feet to the right of Stations 5, 4 and 3. (See diagram on pages 30-31)
   Exception: A shooter may request the referee to move behind the station at Station 3 or 5.

## E. RECOMMENDED POSITIONS FOR SHOOTERS

It is recommended for courtesy to team members that shooters do not advance more than one-third of the way to the next shooting station until all shooters on the squad have completed the station. Furthermore, shooters should stand a minimum of six feet behind the shooter while waiting to shoot.

## F. RECOMMENDED PROCEDURE FOR SETTING DISTANCE ON TARGETS

It is recommended to adjust the skeet machine spring to a tension that will just reach the 60 yard stake, passing near dead center on the target setting hoop, under a "no wind" condition. This distance setting has a plus/or minus two (2) yard allowance, but should be as close to 60 yards as possible. Once this setting is made, it is unnecessary to change the spring tension during a tournament unless the spring becomes defective. The prevailing wind during a shoot may cause the targets to fall far short or long, but they are legal targets providing they pass through the setting hoop.

## G. USE OF A RADAR GUN

The use of a radar gun by shoot management for setting targets is permitted so long as the height and distance requirements specified under Rule III-A-4, Definition of a Regular Target, are complied with. Recommendations for the use of a radar gun are available from NSSA Member Services, posted on the NSSA website and are in the Gun Club Manual.

# SECTION II

# REGISTERED SHOOTS

## A. GENERAL

1. Identification of Eligible Shooters
Members shall receive a new classification card as soon as possible after October 31.
   a. This card will be of high quality paper and is to be used throughout the shooting year. Classification cards will be a different color each year for ease of identification. Replacement cards can be obtained from NSSA Headquarters if lost or accidentally destroyed.
   b. Presentation of a classification card, indicating a member's shooting record and paid membership status, and a NSSA membership card is required for entry in a registered shoot.
   c. Classification for the beginning of the year shall be indicated in the appropriate place on each classification shoot record card.
   d. These cards also shall contain columns in which the holders are to keep their up-to-date averages posted for each gun.

2. Open Shoot Registration

If a state or zone shoot is "Open" then gun titles and awards, both monetary and non-monetary, go to event winners, and the state title and awards are restricted to bona fide state residents. Two shoot reports must be submitted.

3. Night Shooting

Registered shooting at night is permissible. All scores recorded for night registered shoots will receive the same treatment as any other registered shoot. Participants in night registered shoots must accept the conditions at the club where the shoot is held and no protest concerning shooting conditions; e.g., light conditions, natural or artificial, etcetera, will be allowed. At night registered shoots, all orange targets will be used unless otherwise published in the program.

4. Shooting Order

The management shall determine the shooting order of the individuals in each squad at the beginning of the round, and the shooters shall adhere to this order. If the order is changed during any succeeding round of the same event, each squad member shall be responsible that his/her name be in the proper order on the respective score sheet, and that the change be plainly indicated for the attention of the final recorder. Each squad shall report to the field at its appointed time. Upon failure of a shooter to appear at the appointed time, where a regular schedule has been posted in advance, or after proper call, the squad shall proceed without the absent shooter and the offender be dropped to the first vacancy in the schedule, or if there is no vacancy, to the bottom of the list. Weather conditions shall not be deemed sufficient excuse for delay in taking the field or proceeding with the round, unless all shooting has been officially suspended at the discretion of management.

5. Squadding Restrictions

The squadding of practice shooting in a registered event shall not be allowed. It is permissible to squad Event 6 registered with regular registered events. Violations of this rule shall be sufficient cause for non-registration of all scores in the squad. Exception: If there should be a single entry in the last squad of any event, shoot management may allow no more than two additional shooters to shoot for practice, but only if requested to do so by the lone entry on said last squad. Pacer for lone participant on a field in shoot-off shall not be permitted.

6. Checks - Payments, Over-Payment

Anyone who presents a check at any shoot that is returned for insufficient funds or other causes, may not compete in any registered shoot until full payment has been made to the individual or club to which it was presented. Any club receiving such a check shall report name and address of the shooter issuing the check to the NSSA and to its own state, territorial or district association. Upon notification by NSSA, the shooter has 15 days to make the check good, or he/she will be suspended for six months. A second offense will result in indefinite suspension, and the shooter must petition the Executive Committee for reinstatement. The Executive Committee will determine penalties and suspensions as each case merits. Any competitor at a registered shoot who, through error, has been overpaid on any purse, added money, optional or other prize money and who is notified of the over-payment by registered mail, must return the over-payment within 15 days. Failure to do so shall result in disbarment from all registered shoots until repayment is made.

7. Club Qualifications and Responsibilities

a. Only clubs affiliated with NSSA with affiliation fees currently paid up for the year concerned shall be eligible to conduct registered shoots. Evidence of club's status in this regard must be displayed in the form of official NSSA membership certificate for the appropriate year. Only clubs also affiliated and in good standing with their state or territorial association will be permitted to hold registered shoots in areas where such associations are active. No registered shoot may be held at a facility which has been suspended or is in violation of NSSA rules.

b. Where state or territorial associations exist, application for a registered shoot must be made through those bodies, which, in turn after giving approval, will submit application to NSSA. NSSA will then issue proper certification and supplies on which to report scores, winners and make financial reports. When an area association does not exist, clubs will make application directly to NSSA.

1) The application form furnished by NSSA shall include the scheduled shooting dates and may not be altered without 10 days notice. Shoot applications, properly sanctioned, must be postmarked or received by NSSA at least 10 days prior to the shoot date. Note:

A registered shoot may take place over a maximum of a 31-day period. Any shoot conducted over 5-31 days must submit the event dates with their shoot report to NSSA.

2) Applications for night registered shoots must designate on the face of application that it will be a night shoot and all promotion by club shall clearly indicate that it is a night shoot.

c. Open shoots should be advertised to a majority of local contestants, and closed club shoots posted a minimum of seven days prior to the shoot date. Failure to so advertise may result in a disqualification of shoot scores. Exception may, however, be granted by the Executive Director on merit.

d. It shall be the responsibility of the management of the club, association or other organization granted a certificate of registration, to see that each shoot is conducted in accordance with the official rules of the NSSA

e. The group or club sponsoring the shoot shall check the NSSA membership of each shooter before accepting his/her entry and shall be responsible for the annual dues if they allow a participant to shoot when said participant's membership in NSSA has expired.

1) All individual shooters in all registered shoots must be members in good standing of the NSSA. It shall be the responsibility of the club holding a registered shoot to check cards of all participants and enforce this rule rigidly.

2) Management will be billed by NSSA in all cases where expired members are allowed to shoot. Management may seek reimbursement from said shooters.

f. Management shall check the shooter's classification card to ascertain the proper classifications in which he/she should compete and enter on the shooter's classification card the classification in which it is entering him/her in each gun.

g. Class winners must be reported if they are to be reported in the magazine.

h. Scores in shoots on which complete records are not made by shoot management will not be recorded and the national association shall not be liable to refund fees received in such cases.

i. It is the shoot management's responsibility to appoint a chief referee.

j. In the interest of safety, interference and time, only the club management's personnel shall be permitted to pick up empty shells from the grounds during a registered shoot, and extreme care must be exercised to prevent interference with other squads shooting.

k. Shoot management shall determine the number of targets to be shot on a field. When shooting background is fairly uniform, it saves time to shoot 50 or 100 targets on the same field.

l. Shoot management has the right to determine the rotation and shooting sequence of events in their program, as well as shooting mixed guns in squads, unless their state association rules otherwise. When a participant is allowed to shoot an additional increment of 100 targets above those shot in a program event, the first increment shot shall be the targets registered for the program event.

m. All two-man and five-man team events must be limited to club teams unless management exercises their prerogative of holding open or state team events duly announced in the program, or posted prior to acceptance of the first entry.

n. Shoot management has the right to change, add, delete from or correct the shoot program, provided the changes are posted at registration before the event has started.

8. Individual Qualifications and Responsibilities

a. Residents of a state or territory must be members in good standing of their own state or territorial association before they can register targets shot in that state.

b. It shall be the sole responsibility of the shooters to see that they are entered into all the events desired. The official cashier sheet/entry form or equivalent must be used. Once entered, clerical errors are the responsibility of shoot management.

c. Each shooter must verify his/her score and initial the official score sheet before leaving each field or accept it as the record. It shall be the responsibility of every shooter to enter in his/her proper class or classes at each shoot, including advancing himself in class when required by the rules based on averages at the completion of each representative event.

d. A shooter who fails to keep all of his/her correct scores posted on his/her card and shoots in a lower class than the one in which his/her record places him/her shall forfeit any winnings earned while shooting in the wrong class for the first offense, and for the second offense shall forfeit all winnings and also be disbarred from registered competition for one year.

1) A shooter winning trophies or money by shooting in a lower class or wrong class, including concurrent age groups than the one in which he/she was entitled to shoot must return his/her winnings within 15 days after notification by NSSA Headquarters that said winnings must be returned. Failure to comply within this 15 day period shall subject the shooter to suspension as an NSSA member and permanent disbarment from registered competition.

2) A shooter who enters, or allows himself to be entered in an event in a class lower than the class in which he/she was entitled to shoot forfeits all rights to any trophies or purses he/she would have earned shooting in his/her proper class unless the mistake is corrected prior to the distribution of such trophies or purse money.

e. It is the responsibility of the shooter to see that his/her safety is off and gun is properly loaded with unfired shells of proper size and loaded before calling for a target (for safety purposes).

## *B. STANDARD EVENT SPECIFICATION*

For the purpose of uniformity in records, averages, etcetera, the following provisions shall apply to all shoots registered or sanctioned by NSSA.

1. Gauge Specifications

a. Twelve gauge events shall be open to all guns of 12 gauge or smaller, using shot loads not exceeding one and one-eighth (1-1/8) ounces.

b. Twenty gauge events shall be open to all guns of 20 gauge or smaller, using shot loads not exceeding seven-eighths (7/8) of an ounce.

c. Twenty-eight gauge events shall be open to all guns of 28 gauge or smaller, using shot loads not exceeding three-quarters (3/4) of an ounce.

d. Four-ten events shall be open to all guns of .410 bore or smaller using shot not exceeding one-half (1/2) ounce.

e. A gun of larger gauge, which has been converted to take a smaller gauge shell may be used in an event for which it has been converted providing that the shell itself complies with the rule requirements for that event.

f. No shot smaller than No. 9 (2mm) or larger than 7-1/2 shall be used in any load.

2. Awards Eligibility

Anyone that participates in an individual gauge for a reduced entry fee (i.e. an new shooter or any shooter that shoots for targets only), where allowed by shoot management, shall not be eligible for tangible (i.e. purses, trophies) or intangible awards (i.e. event champion, sub-senior champion). Such shooter may not enter any concurrent events in this gauge where they entered for a reduced entry fee. This rule does not prohibit junior, sub-junior or collegiate shooter from participating in an event without paying that portion of an entry fee to be returned in the form of money, as outlined in II-C-4-b. Junior, sub-junior and collegiate shooters who elect not to pay into any purse, or who elect not to pay that portion of the entry fee to be returned in the form of money, are still eligible to win intangible awards (listed above) and tangible awards, except money. Shoot registrants who enter and pay the normal gun fees for each gun ARE eligible to enter the concurrent HOA and HAA and other concurrent events, even if there is not a separate entry fee for those concurrent events. Entry in open/class HOA/HAA is not required for entry in a concurrent HOA/HAA. However, entry in all of the individual concurrent events comprising the concurrent HOA/HAA is required.

3. Concurrent Events

a. Events designated for veterans, senior-veterans, super-veterans, seniors, sub-seniors, sub-sub-seniors, triple-sub-seniors, ladies, juniors, sub-juniors, military service, retired military, two-man team or five-man team may be shot concurrently with the corresponding event on the regular program or separately, at the discretion of the management.

b. No junior, sub-junior or collegiate shall be required to pay any part of an entry fee that is to be returned to the shooters in the form of money, including open purses and concurrent purses, but not to include team events if the involved junior, sub-junior or collegiate is shooting as part of an open team.

4. Concurrent Event Awards

Any shooter charged an entry fee for a regular event and an additional entry fee for a concurrent event shall be eligible to win in both events unless clearly stipulated in the written program.

5. HOA/HAA Titles

HOA/HAA titles must be an aggregate of all gauges offered in that registered tournament (preliminary events, Champion of Champions, not to be included) and will officially be recognized by the NSSA only when they include championships or title events in at least three of the four standard gauges and load divisions defined in paragraph No. 1 above and a total of at least 200 targets. Provided that the foregoing shall not be deemed to forbid local awards of special prizes for events of combination not recognized.

a. High Overall (HOA). HOA is the aggregate of all gauges shot in a registered tournament, excluding doubles, preliminary events and Champion of Champions.

b. High All Around (HAA). HAA is the aggregate of all gauges shot in a registered tournament, including doubles, but excluding preliminary events and Champion of Champions.

6. Minimum Number of Targets

No event of less than fifty (50) targets shall be designated as a championship or title event.

7. High Gun System

In explanation of the high gun system: If, for example, in a class, three should tie for high score and two tie for a second high score, the top three scores would divide evenly the monies for first, second and third places, and the two tying for second high score would divide evenly the monies for fourth and fifth places.

8. Method of Breaking Ties
In all registered NSSA tournaments, ties shall be decided in a uniform manner. In the absence of a shoot program announcing how shoot-offs will be conducted, or posting of notice of deviation conspicuously at the place of registration, thus informing all shooters of deviation before accepting entry fees, the following methods shall be used to break ties:
   a. Shoot management may elect to use regular skeet or a doubles event and shall follow NSSA rules for whichever event elected.
   b. All ties for championship titles, such as event champion, two-man and five-man teams, veterans, super-veterans, senior-veterans, seniors, sub-seniors, triple-sub-seniors, ladies, juniors, sub-juniors, junior ladies, military or any other concurrent title designated by the management, must be shot off by miss-and-out (sudden death). When the same individuals are tied for concurrent titles, such as event champion and senior champion, only one shoot-off will be held to determine both titles unless the shoot management announced in advance of the first shoot-off that separate shoot-offs will be held. Management may combine other shoot-offs only by approval of all the individuals involved in same.
   c. After determining the position of all persons involved in shoot-offs, all other awards shall be decided on the basis of the longest run in the event.
   d. Long runs in an event shall be determined by using the shooter's FRONT or BACK Long Run (WHICHEVER IS LONGEST). If longest runs are tied, the Long Run from the opposite end shall be used to break the tie. If Long Runs are still tied, miss-and-out shoot-offs must decide.
      1) A shooters FRONT LONG RUN is figured by counting all targets shot in the event before the first miss.
      2) To determine the BACK LONG RUN, count all targets broken after the shooter's last miss in the event. The optional shot must be counted in the proper sequence where it was fired.
   e. Long runs for team scores shall be the sum of the individual long runs for each team member. That is, the individual team member's front long runs will be totaled to determine the team's front long run, and the individual back long runs totaled for the team's back long run.
   f. All ties for all-around championship must be decided by a miss-and-out shoot-off using the smallest gauge gun of which the all-around score is comprised.
   g. All other tied scores for all-around awards shall be decided on the basis of the longest run from front or rear (whichever is longest) in that all-around event. If this also results in a tie, a shoot-off using the smallest gauge in the all-around event shall determine the winner of all places.
   h. Shoot-offs take precedence over long runs, so all persons competing in a shoot-off must continue to shoot off for all places beneath the event championship for which they may be tied.

9. NSSA Procedures for Shoot-offs
NSSA rules shall apply subject to the following:
   a. In employing doubles for shoot-offs a 50 target event is not required.
   b. Doubles shoot-offs shall be conducted doubles stations 3-4-5, miss-and-out by station. This means that a shooter must break both targets on a station in order to beat a shooter who only broke one target (i.e. if one shooter breaks the first target and another shooter breaks the second target, they are still tied).
   c. If shoot management has elected to conduct shoot-offs using total score of a complete round, the shooter with the highest score shall be determined the winner. Tied high scores must continue to shoot complete rounds until the tie is broken and the winners determined. Lesser place winners shall be decided by the highest scores and if a tie exists, long run from the front shall determine these winners; if still tied, continue to shoot until the tie is broken.
   d. In regular skeet miss-and-out shoot-offs, long run from the front shall determine the winners. Ties shall continue to shoot the round until the tie is broken.
   e. For team shoot-offs management may combine or separate teams for shoot-offs. Not all team members have to be present for the shoot-off. However, any team member not present will be moved to the last position(s) on the team shoot-off, and their targets will be scored as lost. Methods for different types of shoot-offs are as follows and should be noted in the shoot program. If not noted in the program, "miss-and-out by station" will be used.
      1) If "miss-and-out" team winners shall be determined by the full team shooting until the first miss and comparing this long run with other teams involved. Any teams tied with long runs shall continue to shoot their rounds until the tie is broken.
      2) If "miss-and-out by station", team winners shall be determined by counting a team's total score on a station and comparing it with that of the other teams involved. Any teams still tied shall continue until the tie is broken.
      3) If "total score", the total of the team scores shall determine the winner.
   f. Shoot management shall post notice of time of shoot-off as soon as possible during each event and shall also announce same by the public address system if possible.
   g. Contestants involved in shoot-offs forfeit all rights to the shoot-off if absent or if they do not report within five minutes of the time the shoot-off is called. However, any such person shall be entitled to any award he/she would have won by finishing last in the shoot-off. It shall be the shooter's sole responsibility to determine the time of the shoot-off before leaving the grounds. Shoot-offs may not be held prior to the completion of an event (registration for the event has closed and no possible ties or winners left on the field) or of events of that day UNLESS ALL PARTIES INVOLVED AGREE.
   h. If completion of shoot-offs is prevented by darkness, as defined in rule IV-C-4, the management and the contestants concerned shall determine the champion by a mutually agreeable method, but if no mutually agreeable method can be decided upon, then the shoot management shall determine in what manner ties shall be decided. Management should make every effort to schedule the last squad of the day early enough to permit normal shoot-offs.
   i. If shooters involved in a shoot-off offer management a mutually agreed upon method of determining the places, management may accept. If management does not accept, shoot-offs must continue and any shooter or shooters who refuse to continue forfeits as in paragraph "g" above.
   Declaring of event co-champions at the world championship shall not be permitted. Contestants must continue to shoot or forfeit.
   j. The shooting order for shoot-offs shall be the sequence of finishing the event, where possible. In team shoot-offs, team members shall line up adjacent to each other (i.e. shoulder to shoulder). Each leadoff person, or team, shall be dropped to the last position on subsequent rounds.
   k. Where shoot-offs are held under lights, all orange targets will be used unless otherwise published in the shoot program.
   l. A shooter involved in a shoot-off with a broken gun shall be allowed a ten minute time limit to repair or replace a broken gun, and then must continue in the shoot-off.

### C. ELIGIBILITY OF INDIVIDUALS

1. Membership
   a. All competitors must be members of NSSA in good standing, with current dues paid.
   b. Neither state champions nor provincial champions will be recognized by NSSA unless sanctioned by state organization, provincial organization, recognized with proper bylaws on record at NSSA.

2. Amateurs
Before participating in any event, NSSA shooters who might want to maintain their amateur status in any sport shall be familiar with associations they are involved with as to the definition of an amateur to maintain their eligibility. It is the shooter's responsibility to know those rules before entering any event where prizes consist of money or prizes over a certain limit.

3. Residency Requirements
   a. An individual must be a bona fide resident (permanent abode) of a state to be eligible for state championships or to shoot as a state team member and must be a bona fide resident of a state within the zone to be eligible for closed zone championships or to shoot as a zone team member. Persons with residence in more than one state must declare their eligibility by writing their state and club affiliation on the face of the current year membership card. Servicemen, by the same act, may choose their home state or the place in which they are permanently assigned for duty. Persons who change their official abode shall become immediately eligible to shoot as an individual in the state or zone shoot. They should contact NSSA for new membership cards reflecting change of address and present same before entering shoot. An exception to the residency requirements may be allowed to the individual residency requirements, providing all the following conditions are met:
      1) The individual resides in a state without an association.
      2) The individual joins the association of an adjacent state.
      3) The state association agrees to accept non-bona fide residents into its association.
      4) The state association notifies NSSA of these exceptions.
   b. An exception to the residency requirements may be applied for and granted by the NSSA based on circumstances and facts submitted; these requests will be ruled upon by the EC as individual cases, as long as both (incoming and outgoing) State and Zone associations involved approve the request prior to submitting. When a request has been approved, it will remain in effect until that shooter moves from his current domicile, or re-petitions the EC to be reinstated to his original state of legal residence. For purposes of determining State populations for NSSA representation, said shooter would count in the new State's numbers, not the numbers for his State of legal residence; further, said shooter is eligible to shoot as a resident in the new State/Zone Shoot, not his State/Zone shoot of actual legal residence. [Note: the procedure to apply for an exception is to write a letter with your justification/reasoning for a residency change. Submit letter in turn to both states involved then to the zones involved. If this residency change request does not involve more than one zone than the signature of only one zone would be required. Then send the letter with all necessary signatures to the NSSA Director at 5931 Roft Road San Antonio, TX 78253.]
   c. No person shall be eligible for more than one closed state or zone competition during the NSSA shooting year.

4. Concurrent Events
   a. A shooter's eligibility for concurrent events shall be determined by his/her age or status on 1 November. Exception: Military Reserve Component personnel may shoot in military concurrent events if they are on active duty during the shoot.
   b. No junior, sub-junior or collegiate shall be required to pay any part of any entry fee that is to be returned to the shooter in the form of money.
   c. Where shoot programs offer special concurrent events based upon age, shooters entering such special events must shoot in the one for which they are qualified by age, if such a class is available. Example: Seniors cannot enter as sub-seniors if a senior event is offered. However, sub-juniors can enter a juniors event if a sub-junior event is not available.
   d. In parent and child events, unless specifically stated otherwise in the shoot program, the child must be of junior or sub-junior eligibility age.
   e. A sub-junior is any person who has not reached their fourteenth birthday.
   f. A junior is any person who has not reached their eighteenth birthday.
   g. A collegiate shooter shall be defined as a full-time undergraduate student in an accredited degree oriented learning institution up to a maximum of five (5) years of eligibility. This category may include a shooter 18 years old or older, who is still in high school, for a maximum of one year. For one time only, a shooter is eligible to compete as a collegiate shooter prior to his/her freshman year as long as he/she produces a letter of acceptance from a degree oriented learning institution. At shoot entry, eligible individuals must provide a valid student I.D. card. The card must be valid on November 1.
   h. A triple-sub-senior is any person 18-39 years of age.
   i. A sub-sub-senior is any person who has reached their 40th birthday.
   j. A sub-senior is any person who has reached their 50th birthday.
   k. A senior is any person who has reached their 60th birthday.
   l. A veteran is any person who has reached their 70th birthday.
   m. A senior-veteran is any person who has reached their 80th birthday.
   n. A super-veteran is any person who has reached their 90th birthday.
   o. A military shooter is any member of the Army, Navy, Marine Corps, Air Force, Coast Guard, Reserve Component or National Guard/Air National Guard, who is on active duty and in possession of active duty orders or an active duty Armed Forces of the United States Identification Card.
   p. A retired military shooter is any retired member of the Air Force, Army, Coast Guard, Marine Corps, Navy or National Guard/Air National Guard.
   q. Where shoot programs offer special concurrent events for military shooters, retired military shooters are only eligible to compete in a retired military event, and are NOT eligible to compete in a military event, even if a retired military concurrent is not offered.

### D. TEAM ELIGIBILITY

The spirit and intent of these rules shall be interpreted to include all bona fide teams properly organized in pursuance of club and/or domicile requirements, and to exclude all teams of makeshift or pick-up character, organized on the grounds and seeking to take advantage of technicalities either herein or in program stipulations or omissions.

1. Team Representation
   a. The members of a team must be designated before the team begins the event.
   b. Team members shall be accredited by NSSA to the state in which they reside, but irrespective of residence, team members must not have represented any other club in a team event in any NSSA registered shoot at any time during the current year. A shooter who shoots on one club team, either two-man or five-man, shall by that act elect that club as the only club he/she shall represent in club team events during the current year. Exception: Service personnel who have, within this period, shot on teams sponsored by military organizations, such as division teams or teams representing specific departments of the same branch of the service, and have been required to do so as a duty assignment, may immediately shoot on teams representing individual military clubs, providing that said former teams have been definitely disbanded and also providing that they have been

members in good standing of the clubs they are about to represent for a period of at least 90 days prior to the shoot.

c. No individual may shoot on more than one team in any one event, even though both teams represent the same club, except in re-entry events where the program states that it is permissible.

d. Team members shall not be eligible to shoot for any state championships except in the state in which they reside.

2. State Teams

a. A state five-man team shall consist of five (5) individuals; a state two-man team, two (2) individuals.

b. Each member of a state team must have resided in the same state for at least ninety (90) days prior to the date of the shoot.

c. State teams may shoot in national competition, or in state shoots if approved by the state organization.

d. State Championship Team Events. Any out-of-state team whose membership complies with state residency requirements and rule II-D-3-b and II-D-3-d, may enter club team events but may be subject to a surcharge at the discretion of the state association.

3. Club Teams

a. A club five-man team shall consist of five (5) individuals; a club two-man team, two (2) individuals.

b. Team members must have been fully paid members of the club they represent for a period of at least 90 days prior to the date of the shoot (honorary, inactive, non-resident members or members whose dues or assessments are in arrears are not eligible).

c. No person shall reside more than 100 miles from the club he/she represents unless he/she resides in the same state in which the club he/she represents is located.

d. The club represented must be affiliated and in good standing with the NSSA with dues currently paid.

4. Exceptions to Domicile and Club Membership Requirements

The provisions of domicile and club membership of individuals on club teams do not apply to:

a. Shooters who have affected a bona fide change in place of domicile with resultant change in club membership affiliation.

b. Clubs organized within less than 90 days prior to the date of the shoot, provided that members representing such clubs comply with rule II-D-1-b.

c. New members of any club who have never previously fired in a team event in an NSSA registered shoot.

d. Privately operated clubs, which require no paid membership, may with the approval of NSSA be represented by either two-man or five-man teams if the members of such teams meet all of the other requirements except those applying to club dues and club membership. Such team members must be certified by management of such club as having been active shooters of the club for a minimum of 90 days before they are eligible to shoot for that club.

e. Former members of college teams and school teams who have become members of senior clubs after their graduation.

5. Open Teams (Definition)

An open team is one which is composed of members with no restriction as to club or domicile. Records established by open teams shall not be accepted to establish official records.

6. Five-Man Teams

a. Five-man club teams and five-man state teams must shoot shoulder-to-shoulder, unless management publishes otherwise in their program or same is posted prior to accepting the first entry. To be eligible for tying or establishing world records, any five-man team MUST shoot shoulder-to-shoulder.

b. Each five-man club team and state team shall designate a team captain who shall be the team representative.

c. At the completion of each round, the shooters shall view their respective scores and initial them. However, in the case of team shooting, the captain of the team may assume the responsibility for the shooters and sign for his/her entire squad.

7. Two-Man Teams

Two-man teams may shoot in separate squads.

8. Armed Forces Team Representation

For team representation, the domicile of members of the Army, Navy, Marine Corps, Air Force, Coast Guard or Reserve Component members shall be defined as the place at which they are permanently assigned for duty. One of the following two criteria must be met to be eligible to compete as a member of an inter-service team:

a. A military member as defined in II-C-4-o who is on active duty at the time of the shoot.

b. A Reserve Component or Retired Military member who is on active duty at the time of the shoot. Exception: If a Service does not have five active duty members entered in the shoot, shoot management may allow the team to include one retired military member as determined by his/her Armed Forces of the United States Identification Card. No team, so formed, shall be eligible to establish any world record scores.

9. NSSA World Championship Five-Man Teams

a. In the NSSA World Championships all members of a five-man team will shoot in the same squad through that particular event. If any team member fails to finish with his/her proper squad for any reason whatsoever, the team shall be disqualified as such but not the members as individual contestants.

b. Under no circumstances, however, will the provisions on broken gun and shooting up affect the requirement of shooting shoulder-to-shoulder throughout the five-man team competition at the NSSA World Championships.

c. Management may deviate from this rule if they deem it to be advisable to conduct five-man teams in more than one squad. For convenience in tabulating team scores, it is more desirable to keep a five-man team in one squad.

### E. PROTESTS

1. A Shooter May Protest:

a. If in his/her opinion the rules as herein stated have been improperly applied.

b. The conditions under which another shooter has been permitted to shoot.

c. Where he/she feels an error has been made in the compilation of a score.

2. How To Protest

A protest shall be initiated immediately when it is possible to do so upon the occurrence of the protested incident. No protest may be initiated by the shooter involved after thirty (30) minutes have elapsed after the occurrence of the incident for which a protest is desired to be made. Failure to comply with the following procedure will automatically void the protest. A protest involving the scoring of a target, if filed immediately on the station, a second shot, or shots will be fired and the results recorded and noted as a protest. The protest shall proceed in the prescribed manner.

a. State the complaint verbally to the chief referee. If not satisfied with his/her decision, then:

b. File with the shoot management a protest in writing, stating all the facts in the case. Such protest must be filed within 12 hours after the occurrence of the protested incident. If not satisfied with the decision of the shoot management, then:

c. File with the NSSA a written appeal, stating all the facts. Such appeal must be filed within 48 hours after the decision of the shoot management has been made known to the shooter. Protests in team events must be made by the team captain. Team members who believe they have reason to protest will state the facts to their team captain, who will make the protest if he/she feels such action justified by the facts. The shoot management may appoint a shoot judge to handle protests referred to it which have been handled in the manner stated above.

### F. DISQUALIFICATION AND EXPULSION

The shoot management shall upon proper evidence:

1. Disqualify any shooter for the remainder of the shoot program for willful or repeated violation of gun safety precautions which endanger the safety of shooters, field personnel and/or spectators.
2. Elect to refuse the entry or cause the withdrawal of any contestant whose conduct in the opinion of the shoot management is unsportsmanlike or whose participation is in any way detrimental to the best interests of the shoot.
3. Any shooter may be disqualified from a shoot for misrepresentation of his/her status under the eligibility rules.
4. Expel any shooter physically assaulting a referee or any shooter using extreme, abusive language to a referee upon adequate evidence presented by the chief referee.
5. The shoot management shall report to the NSSA all cases of disqualification and expulsion and the reasons for same. Subsequent action by the Executive Committee could result in being expelled and barred from further membership in the NSSA, after the shooter has had the opportunity to appear before the Executive Committee and present his/her case.

### G. OFFICIAL SCORES

1. All scores or records, to be recognized as official, must be shot under the official NSSA rules.
2. a. All scores shall be recorded as having been shot with the gun in which event they shot (e.g. scores shot with a 20 gauge gun in a 12 gauge event must be recorded as 12 gauge scores.) Such scores may not be included as part of a 20 gauge long run or average.

   b. When a shooter has started an event and realizes during or after the event the incorrect ammunition was used (e.g., 1 oz. 20 gauge shells in the 20 gauge event, etc.), that shooter must immediately notify the field referee or shoot management of the error. If possible, the competitor will be allowed to re-shoot the targets incorrectly fired upon and continue with the proper ammunition or re-shoot the entire event. If not possible, the shooter is disqualified from that event and the targets will not be registered. All targets incorrectly fired upon will not be reported to or recorded with NSSA.
3. Only the scores shot on scheduled dates, approved by NSSA, shall be registered. Scores made in shoot-offs shall not be registered; however, all NSSA rules shall apply in shoot-offs.
4. No shooter will be permitted to enter the same event more than once, even though his/her score has been disqualified. EXCEPT as noted and allowed in II-G-2-b. When a participant is allowed to shoot an additional increment of targets (50 or 100 targets) above those shot in a program event, the first increment shot shall be the targets for the program event.
5. The scores of any shooter who takes part in a registered shoot shall be considered official, and shall be registered with the NSSA even though the shooter had given notice that it was not his/her intention to have his/her score recorded.
6. While the management may refund the entry fees and permit withdrawal of shooters who would be required to compete under drastically changed and clearly intolerable weather conditions or darkness not confronted by a majority of participants in an event, scores of all shooters who do participate must be recorded. In the event of extreme weather conditions, power failure, trap failure or unusually early darkness, the shoot management may elect to continue the event some other time (e.g. the next morning or the following weekend) but must immediately notify NSSA, with a full explanation, who will sanction the change, provided it is deemed in the best interest of skeet.
7. If a contestant stops or withdraws voluntarily, or after disqualification by the management, his/her partial score for the round in which he/she is shooting shall be entered as his/her score of targets broken for that full round of twenty-five targets. He/she shall not be penalized; however, for any of the remaining full rounds of that particular event. Where such withdrawal is the result of sickness, injury or unrepairable gun, the shooter withdrawing shall be charged only with the targets actually fired upon in compiling and reporting his/her score. It shall be the shooter's responsibility to verify that the reason for this withdrawal is recorded on the score sheet. The target(s) and score(s), as reported, will then be used as an event for the purposes of classification. Withdrawal, regardless of the number of targets shot, is considered an event.
8. When a contestant stops or withdraws without finishing an event in which he/she has started, his/her partial scores shall be reported to the NSSA along with the other scores of the event.
9. The shoot management is responsible to see that each shooter's score is posted on the scoreboard within approximately 30 minutes after the last squad of each flight.

### H. REGISTERED SHOOT REPORTS

1. Reporting Requirements

It is the duty of each club or association holding a registered shoot to fulfill the following obligations. Payments and reports must be received by NSSA Headquarters no more than 15 days after the last day of the shoot.

a. Make payments of all money, purses and options to the shooters.

b. Submit fees and reports due to state association.

c. Two reports (Financial and Registered Target Official Report) must be made to NSSA on all registered shoots. Standard forms available from NSSA Headquarters, or equivalent approved by NSSA Headquarters, must be used. Rules II-H-3 and 4 outline required method of completing these reports.

2. Penalties

Failure to fulfill the reporting requirements shall carry the following penalties:

a. All shoot reports and wrap-ups MUST be received at NSSA Headquarters within 15 days of the last day of the shoot. A $25.00 DELINQUENT FEE will be charged to all clubs that have not submitted a registered shoot report and financial report (including all payments due) within the 15 days. For the second and all subsequent late shoot reports, a $100.00 fine will be imposed. Shoot reports received past November 15 will have the fine, plus additional fees imposed depending on the lateness of the report. Also, after the second offense, suspension by NSSA from further sanctioned registered shoots is possible at the discretion of NSSA.

b. Cancellation of all subsequent shoot dates for the offending club or association.

c. Denial of right to apply or reapply for any further registered shoot dates for a period of thirty (30) days in case of first offense, or ninety (90) days in case of second or subsequent offense or until obligations have been met.

d. Officers of any delinquent club or association shall be barred from shooting registered targets until all required obligations of said club association are met to the shooters, to the state association and to NSSA.

3. Financial Report

a. Daily Fees: List number of targets shot each day of shoot and remit to NSSA the required daily registration fee (in U.S. funds).

    b.   NSSA Dues Collected: Remittance (in U.S. funds) and duplicate copies of receipts for all types of NSSA memberships sold at your shoot must be attached. Membership applications must be completely and legibly filled out, including complete and accurate mailing address of purchaser. (Shooter buying membership receives original receipt.)

4.   Registered Target Official Report

An individual entry form/cashier sheet must be submitted on every shooter. These individual reports must include:

    a.   NSSA membership number

    b.   Full name or initials, corresponding to NSSA membership records

    c.   Member's complete address

        Note: All of the above information is included on the membership card. If an imprinter is not used, all information must be legibly written on individual shoot report form.

    d.   For each gauge in which the member participates (and HOA if appropriate) you must enter:

        1)   number of targets shot

        2)   number of targets broken

        3)   class in which member was entered (if member declares into a higher class at your shoot this information must be noted on shoot report form)

        4)   awards won. Regardless of what method was used in making awards, winners must be determined and reported under NSSA classification system. This applies even if no awards are made. Do not list winners above class champions unless such awards were made.

5.   are not REQUIRED to deliver or mail a copy of official shoot reports to the shooter. They are, however, required to retain copies of scoreboard and/or field score sheet on file for 90 days after the end of the applicable shooting year.

## I. RECOGNITION AND AWARDS

1.   High Average Leaders

    a.   For the purpose of determining yearly champions and High Overall Leaders on the basis of average alone, leaders will be recognized if they have shot the following standard requirements of registered targets.

| | 12 | 20 | 28 | .410 | Dbls |
|---|---|---|---|---|---|
| Open Team | 1000 | 800 | 800 | 800 | 500 |
| All Concurrents | 1000 | 800 | 800 | 800 | 500 |
| Sub-Jr/Sr-Vet | 700 | 500 | 400 | 400 | 300 |
| Sup-Vet | 500 regardless of gauge or Dbls | | | | |

    b.   That for the consideration for Annual High Average Leader (Open and Concurrent) recognition, only targets shot at registered shoots with ten or more entrants per event will be counted. Monthly targets and targets only are excluded from the calculation, except where a sub-junior, junior or collegiate shooter chooses not to pay the mandatory purse portion of an entry fee. This rule only applies to the seven (7) Jay Schatz Annual High Average Leader awards for open 12, 20, 28, 410, Dbls, HOA and Lady HOA.

2.   All-American Team

Candidates for All-American selection must have shot standard target requirements as defined for High Average selection in II-I-1 in the .410, 28, 20, 12 and doubles events.

3.   Long Run Records

    a.   Only scores shot in registered events, other than monthly targets or targets only, shall be included in official long run records. Scores shot with a smaller gun than the one for which the event is scheduled shall not be accredited as part of a long run with the smaller gun.

    b.   Shoot-off targets and other non-registered targets shall not be counted as part of a long run.

    c.   All long runs shall be compiled in the order in which the scoring appears on the official score sheets except the optional shot shall be counted in the proper sequence where it was fired. The sequence in which the official score sheets are posted must coincide with the sequence in which the scores were broken.

4.   High Overall Averages

For purposes of determining yearly all-around averages, divide by 4 the total of a shooter's year end averages in all four gauges.

5.   World Records

Current world records are listed in the NSSA Record Annual each year. Any shooter, or team, who feels they have tied or broken an established world record must follow the procedure outlined below for official recognition of a world record score.

    a.   Establish that the event in which the record was tied or broken was a part of the shoot program and available to all eligible competitors.

    b.   Establish that the shooter or team properly entered the event prior to firing the record score.

    c.   Submit application for recognition to NSSA Headquarters on the standard form which is available at NSSA member clubs. The form is also available from Headquarters, upon request.

    d.   In the event that more than one shooter or team should break a world record score on the same calendar day, and provided they have correctly followed the outlined procedures, they shall become co-holders of that record.

6.   Determination of Age Groups

Age or concurrent event status based on status as of November 1.

7.   Rookie is an individual who shoots NSSA standards for concurrent categories and was not a "classified shooter" in any gauge with receipt of their current classification card, and has never had an "initial classification" or "regular classification" in 2006 or prior years in any gauge. A shooter is only eligible to compete for Rookie honors for one shooting year in their lifetime.

8.   Honor Squad is comprised of those individuals who have shot NSSA standards in their open or concurrent categories in the current and previous year.

# SECTION III
# SHOOTING PROCEDURE

## A. DEFINITIONS

1.   Shooting Positions

    a.   Shooter must stand with any part of both feet within the boundaries of the designated shooting station.

    b.   Station 8 the designated shooting station is the half of the rectangular pad most distant from the respective high or low house.

    c.   Any shooter with one or both feet definitely off the shooting station should first be made to shoot over and, if he/she persists in standing off the station, he/she shall be penalized by loss of the target for each subsequent violation in that event. However, if the shooter missed the target while committing the first violation of shooting position, the result shall be scored "lost".

2.   Gun Position

Any safe position which is comfortable to the shooter.

3.   No Bird

Any target thrown for which no score is recorded, or failure of a target to be thrown within the prescribed time limit of one second. This permits the throwing of instant targets, but gives a short time period in order to prevent a contestant from refusing a target which does not appear immediately after his/her call. If a shooter fires upon a target which appears after one second has elapsed between his/her call and the emergence of the target, and also before the referee calls no bird, the result of his/her shot shall be scored. If he/she withholds his/her shot after such an alleged slow pull, the referee may declare the target no bird provided he/she, in his/her sole judgment, decides that the delay exceeded the one second time allowance. The pull is not required to be instantaneous.

4.   Regular Target

A regular target is one that appears after the shooter's call and within a period not to exceed one (1) second, and which passes within a three-foot circle centered at a point fifteen (15) feet above the target-crossing point. The target-crossing point shall be measured from the level of Station 8. The target, in still air, must carry to a distance equivalent, on level ground, to 60 yards from the skeet house when passing through the center of the hoop, with an allowance tolerance of plus or minus two yards.

5.   Irregular Target

    a.   An unbroken target that has not conformed to the definition of a regular target.

    b.   Two targets thrown simultaneously in singles. However, if by error or for mechanical reasons doubles are thrown, and the shooter shoots and breaks or misses the correct target, it shall be scored as in singles. It shall be the shooter's prerogative to elect to shoot or withhold his/her shot when doubles are thrown in the calling of singles.

    c.   Target thrown broken. Under no circumstances shall the result of firing upon a broken target be scored.

6.  Regular Double

A regular target thrown from each skeet house simultaneously.

7.   Irregular Double

Either or both targets of a double thrown as irregular targets or only one target is thrown.

8.   Proof Double

A repeat of a double.

9.   Shooting Bounds

For Stations 1 to 7, inclusive, an area forty-four (44) yards in front of the skeet house from which the target is thrown. For Station 8, the distance from the skeet house to a point directly over a line with Station 4, 8 and the target crossing point.

10.   Balk

Failure to shoot at a regular target or double due to the fault of the shooter.

11.   Malfunction of Gun

Failure of gun to operate or function through no fault of the shooter.

12.   Defective Ammunition

    a.   Defective Ammunition will be defined as:

        1)   Failure to fire, provided firing pin indentation is clearly noticeable.

        2)   When a target is missed in the case of an odd sounding shell, which in the sole judgment of the field referee does not deliver the shot the distance to the target, and therefore does not give the shooter a fair opportunity to break the target. NOTE: If a target is broken with an odd-sounding shell, it shall be scored dead regardless and will not be considered defective ammo. Odd-sounding shells where the shot does travel the distance to the bird and provide the shooter a fair chance to break the target will not be considered defective ammo and the results of those shots will be scored.

        3)   Brass pulling off hull between shots on doubles.

        4)   Separation of brass from casing when gun is fired (usually accompanied by a whistling sound as the plastic sleeve leaves the barrel).

    b.   Wrong sized shells or empty shells shall not be considered defective ammunition.

    c.   Repeated Targets - A target shall be repeated for each allowable instance of defective ammunition.

    d.   Number allowed - A shooter will be allowed only two instances of defective ammunition from the first box of shells used in that round. After two instances of defective ammunition in a round or a shoot-off round, a shooter may obtain a FACTORY box of ammunition and is then allowed two additional instances per box of FACTORY shells in that round. If shells are not changed in a round after two ammo malfunctions have been ruled, the third and all subsequent occurrences in that round will be excessive. EXCEPTION: If a shooter is provided a proof shell by the referee and defective ammunition is ruled on that proof shot, that instance will not count against the shooter as defective ammunition.

13.   Dead Target

A target from which, in the sole judgment of the referee, a visible piece is observed before the target hits the ground as a result of having been legally fired upon.

14.   Lost Target

A target from which in the sole judgment of the referee no visible piece is broken as a result of having been fired upon.

15.  Optional Shot

The shot fired after the first 24 targets have been scored dead in any one round (Station 8 low house only); or fired following the shooter's first lost target. In the latter instance it must be fired from same station and at the same house as the one first missed.

16.   Skeet Squad

    a.   A normal skeet squad is composed of five (5) shooters.

    b.   Any five (5) shooters may designate themselves as a squad. All shooters shall be formed into squads of five (5) shooters each, as nearly as possible. Less than five (5) is permissible for expedience, but more than six (6) should not be squadded for safety reasons.

17.   Round of Skeet

A round of skeet for one person consists of twenty-five (25) shots, the object being to score the greatest number of dead targets. Twenty-four shots are fired as described in III-B-1. The first shot scored lost in any round shall be repeated immediately and the result scored as the twenty-fifth shot. Should the first shot lost occur in a double, the lost target shall be repeated as a single with the result of this shot scored as the twenty-fifth shot. If the first shot lost should be the first target of an irregular double, then a proof regular double shall be fired upon to determine the result of the second shot, and then the first target scored lost shall be repeated as a single and scored as the twenty-fifth shot. Should the first twenty-four (24) targets of a round be scored dead, the shooter shall take his/her optional shot at low house eight only.

18.   Shooting Up

The procedure of a late shooter shooting out of turn to catch up with his/her squad (III-B-6).

## B. GENERAL

1. Squad Shooting Procedure For A Round Of Skeet
   a. A squad shall start shooting at Station 1 in the order in which the names appear on the score sheet. The first shot scored lost in the round shall be repeated immediately as the optional shot.
   b. The first shooter shall start shooting singles at Station 1, shooting the high house target first and the low house target second. Then, loading two shells, he/she shall proceed to shoot doubles (shooting the first shot at the target from the nearest skeet house and the second shot at the target from the farthest skeet house) before leaving the station. The second shooter shall then proceed likewise followed by the other members of the squad in their turn.
   c. Then the squad shall proceed to Station 2 and repeat the same sequence as on Station 1.
   d. The squad shall then proceed to Station 3 where each shooter will shoot at a high house single target first and a low house single target second before leaving the shooting station.
   e. The same procedure shall be followed at Stations 4 and 5.
   f. Upon advancing to Station 6 the leadoff shooter will shoot singles in the same sequence as at the previous stations. Then, loading two shells, he/she shall shoot doubles by shooting at the low house target first and the high house target second before leaving the station. The other shooters will follow in their turn.
   g. The same procedure will be followed on Station 7.
   h. The squad will then advance to Station 8 where each shooter shall shoot at a target from the high house before any member of the squad shoots at a target from the low house.
   i. The squad shall then turn to Station 8 low house and the leadoff shooter will shoot at the low house target.
   j. The shooter shall repeat the low house target for his/her optional shot before leaving the station, provided he/she is still straight (no lost targets in the round). The other shooters will follow in turn.
   k. At this time the shooter should verify his/her own score.
2. Rules and Procedures for Doubles Events
   a. No less than a fifty (50) target event.
   b. Shooting commences at Station 1 and continues through 7 and backwards from 6 through 5, 4, 3 and 2. Rounds 2 and 4 will end with doubles on Station 1 using the 25th shell from rounds 1 and 3. That is, rounds 1 and 3 will consist of 24 shots ending with doubles at Station 2, and rounds 2 and 4 will consist of 26 shots ending with doubles at Station 1.
   c. When shooting doubles at Stations 1, 2, 3, 5, 6 and 7, shoot the first shot at the target from the nearest skeet house and the second shot at the target from the farthest skeet house. When shooting doubles at Station 4 the shooter must shoot first at the high house target going around the stations from 1 through 7 and shoot at the low house 4 target first when coming back around the stations from 7 through 2 (or 1).
   d. The rules for doubles in a doubles event are the same as the rules for doubles in a regular round of skeet.
   e. All other NSSA rules apply.
3. Shooter's Right To Observe Targets
   a. At the beginning of each round the squad shall be entitled to observe two (2) regular targets from each skeet house and shall have the option of observing one regular target after each irregular target.
   b. Shoot management, state association, state chief referee and/or zone chief referee shall have the right, where topographically possible, to make it mandatory to use a hoop or other suitable device whenever a target adjustment is necessary.
4. Progress From Station To Station
   a. No member of the squad shall advance to the shooting station until it is his/her turn to shoot, and until the previous shooter has left the station. No shooter shall order any target or shoot at any target except when it is his/her turn. Targets fired upon while shooting out of turn, without permission of the referee, shall be declared "no bird."
   b. No member of a squad, having shot from one station, shall proceed toward the next station in such a way as to interfere with another shooter. The penalty for willful interference in this manner shall be disqualification from the event.
   c. No shooter shall unduly delay a squad without good and sufficient reason in the judgment of the referee in charge of his/her squad. A shooter who persists in deliberately causing inexcusable delays after receiving a first warning from the referee shall be subject to disqualification from the event.
5. Broken Gun
   When a gun breaks in such a manner so as to render it unusable, the shooter has the option of using another gun if such gun can be secured without delay, or dropping out of the squad until the gun is repaired and finishing the event at a later time when a vacancy occurs or after all other contestants have finished the event. Nothing shall prohibit the shooter from missing one round because of a broken gun, having the gun repaired and then rejoining the squad for all later rounds that the squad has not started. In that case the shooter will finish any or all rounds, starting with the shot where the breakdown occurred, that were not shot because of a broken gun, on the proper fields and in the first vacancy that may occur, or after the event has been finished by all other contestants.
6. Shooting Up
   a. Where a shooter has registered in but does not show up to start an event with his/her squad, he/she will not be permitted to shoot up after the first man in the squad has fired a shot at Station 2.
   b. He/she may join the squad for all later rounds, but the round missed because of lateness must be shot on the proper field in the first vacancy, or after all other contestants have finished.
   c. In the interest of conserving time the shoot management may modify this rule to meet special conditions, if it so desires.
7. Slow Squads
   It is suggested that shoot management use substitute fields when breakdowns or unusually slow shooting squads are disrupting the normal sequence of squads. Under normal conditions, a squad should complete a round in 20 minutes, including breaks between rounds. Squads using more time cannot object to being transferred to a substitute field.

## C. SCORING

1. The score in any one round shall be the total number of dead targets.
2. Targets declared no-bird shall not be scored.
3. One lost target shall be scored on:
   a. A balk or failure of gun to fire due to fault of shooter. Should this include both targets of a regular double, it shall be scored as first target lost, and a proof double shall be thrown to determine the result of the second shot only. If a balk should occur, or his/her gun fail to fire because of the shooter's fault, when a proof double is thrown and the result of the first shot has already been scored, the second target shall be scored as lost.
   b. Each excessive instance of defective ammunition, or excessive malfunction or malfunctions of gun.
   c. Doubles fired upon in reverse order.
   d. Target fired upon after it is outside the shooting bounds.
   e. Each target fired upon and allegedly missed because the shooter's gun had a bent barrel, or a bent compensator, or any other bent tube or accessory.
   f. Each successive foot position violation.
   g. Each successive time balk. It shall be considered a time balk if a shooter deliberately delays more than 15 seconds for each shot on a station and the referee shall warn him/her once each round without penalty.
4. If a shell having once misfired is used again, and fails to fire, the results shall be considered a fault on the part of the shooter and scored lost.
5. No claim of irregularity shall be allowed, either on singles or doubles, where the target or targets were actually fired upon and alleged irregularity consists of deviation from the prescribed line of flight, or because of an alleged quick pull or slow pull, unless the referee has distinctly called no bird prior to the firing of the shot. Otherwise, if the shooter fires the result shall be scored. The referee shall have final say as to whether he/she called no bird before the shooter fired.
6. If the brass pulls off a hull between shots on doubles, score as defective ammunition but do not score it as a gun malfunction.
7. During a regular round or a doubles event, if the brass pulls off a hull, or if defective ammunition occurs between shots on doubles, the referee shall rule that if the first target was a dead bird, nothing is established, and a proof double shall be fired upon to determine the result of both birds. However, if the first target was lost, it shall be so established and a proof double shot to establish the second shot result.

## D. GUN MALFUNCTIONS

The shooter must not be considered at fault if he/she has complied with the manufacturer's operating instructions for loading the gun, and the gun does not fire. In the case of a gun going into battery (locking closed) for the first shot on doubles or any shot on singles, if the shooter has closed the action in accordance with the manufacturer's instructions, and if the bolt appears visually to be closed, the failure of a gun to fire shall be scored as malfunction.

1. Semi-Automatics
   a. On a semi-automatic the shooter is not required to push forward or strike the breech bolt retraction lever to insure locking the gun. This is a normal gun function.
   b. The shooter must load the shell or shells into the gun and see that the action appears closed. If he/she loads two shells on singles or doubles, and if the second shell fails to go into the chamber or is thrown out of the gun, it shall be scored a malfunction unless a no bird is declared on the second shot.
2. Pump Guns
   a. The shooter is required to pump the gun, as recommended by the manufacturer, on doubles and to close the action completely forward (visually) on singles.
   b. If the shooter short-shucks the gun, the hammer will not be cocked, a fault of the shooter.
   c. If the lifter throws the second shell out of the gun it shall be a malfunction.
   d. It shall be a malfunction if between shots on singles or doubles the gun returns the empty shell to the chamber provided the hammer is cocked.
   e. The referee shall check for a malfunction as instructed under that title and shall then apply forward pressure on the forearm to see if the shell is lodged (a malfunction). However, if the gun closes smoothly, without jiggling, it is not a malfunction.
3. Double-Barreled Guns
   a. The shooter is responsible for loading a shell in the proper barrel, or two shells for doubles.
   b. The shooter must close the action in accordance with manufacturer's recommendations.
4. Shell Catching Devices
   Where any device is attached to a shotgun which must be adjusted or removed to permit shooting doubles, it shall be the shooter's responsibility to perform such adjustment or removal. Failure to fire a second shot on doubles, due to such device, shall not be an allowable malfunction, and the bird shall be scored lost.
5. Repeated Targets
   A target shall be repeated for each allowable malfunction and/or each allowable defective ammunition.
6. Number Allowed
   Only two malfunctions of any one gun in the same round or shoot-off round shall be allowable. The third and all subsequent malfunctions of the same gun shall be excessive. However, when more than one person is using the same gun in the same round, this rule shall apply to each person separately.
7. Loading Two Shells
   During the shooting of single targets, a shooter may load two shells except at Station 8 high house, or for the last single target on any station, or unless forbidden by club rules, and if the gun jams or malfunctions between shots, it shall be scored as a malfunction and the shooter permitted to shoot the target over. However, the shooter is still restricted to two allowable malfunctions with one gun in one round.
8. Malfunction on Singles or First Shot Doubles
   To establish that a malfunction has occurred the shooter must not open the gun or touch the safety before the referee's inspection.
   a. If the shooter is holding the trigger pulled, the referee, after seeing that the gun is pointed in a safe direction, will place his/her finger over the shooter's and apply normal pressure.
   b. If the shooter has released the trigger, the referee, after seeing that the gun is pointed in a safe direction, will exercise extreme caution not to jiggle or attempt to further close the action and will apply normal pressure to the trigger.
   c. The target shall be scored lost if the gun fires or is opened before the referee's inspection. A malfunction will be ruled if it does not fire and the referee's examination for ammunition, safety, barrel selection, etcetera, establishes that the shooter had fulfilled required responsibilities.
   d. For a gun modified with a release trigger, the referee will not require the shooter to pull and then release the trigger.
9. Malfunction Between Shots on Doubles
   If an apparent malfunction occurs between the first and second shot on doubles:
   a. The referee shall apply the same procedures as listed under malfunction on singles to determine if an allowable malfunction has occurred.
   b. During a regular round or a doubles event, if an allowable malfunction has occurred, the referee shall rule if the first target was a dead bird, nothing is established, and a proof double shall be fired upon to determine the result of both birds. However, if the first target was lost, it shall be so established and a proof double shot to establish the second shot result.
   c. If such malfunction is excessive (not allowable) and the first shot is a dead bird, it shall be scored first bird dead, second bird lost, but, if the first bird is lost then both birds shall be scored lost.
10. Fan-Fire

If a gun doubles or fan-fires while shooting singles or doubles the referee shall rule a malfunction, and during a regular round or a doubles event, if the first target was a dead bird, nothing established, and a proof single or double shall be fired upon to determine the results. However, if the first target was lost, it shall be so established and a proof double shot to establish the second shot result.

### E. DOUBLES OR PROOF DOUBLES

1. If the first target emerges broken, the doubles shall, in all cases, be declared no bird and a proof double shall be thrown to determine the result of both shots.
2. If a double is thrown but the targets collide, before the result of the first bird is determined, it shall be declared no bird, and the result of a proof double shall determine the score of both shots.
3. If the first target of a double is thrown irregular as to deviate from the prescribed line of flight and is not shot at, a proof double shall determine the score for both shots, whether the second target is fired upon or not. The referee shall be the sole judge of irregularity.
4. If the first target of a double is thrown irregular as to deviate from the prescribed line of flight, and is shot at, the result shall be scored for the first shot in accordance with III-C-5 and if the shooter is deprived of a normal second shot for any of the reasons in III-E-5 the second target only shall be declared no bird and a proof double shall be fired to determine the result of the second shot.
5. If the shooter is deprived of a normal second shot for any of the following reasons, the result of the first shot shall be scored even if an apparent gun malfunction may have occurred on the second shot, and the second target only shall be declared no bird and a proof double shall be fired to determine the result of the second shot.
   a. The second target is thrown broken.
   b. The second target is thrown irregular as to deviation from the prescribed line of flight and is not shot at.
   c. The second target is not thrown at all.
   d. The second target is not thrown simultaneously.
   e. Both targets are broken with the first shot.
   f. The wrong target is broken with the first shot. (For proof double ruling see paragraph 8 below.)
   g. The first shot is lost and a collision occurs before the result of the second shot is determined.
   h. The second target collides with fragments of the first target properly broken, before the result of the second target is determined.
   i. The result of the first shot is determined, and interference occurs before the second shot is fired.
6. There shall be no penalty for withholding the first shot when either target of a double is irregular. A proof double shall determine the score of both shots thereafter.
7. If a double is thrown and an allowable gun malfunction or defective ammunition occurs on the first shot, it shall be declared no bird, and the result of a proof double shall determine the score of both shots. If such malfunction is excessive, (not allowable), the proof double shall be thrown to determine the result of the second shot only.
8. In shooting a proof double after the first target (of a double) is lost, if the shooter fires at, or breaks the wrong target first, said proof double shall be scored as both targets lost. If, in such a proof double after the first target (of a double) is dead, the shooter fires at, or breaks, the wrong target first, it shall be scored as first target dead and second target lost.

### F. INTERFERENCE

1. Any circumstance beyond the shooter's control which unduly affects his/her opportunity to break any particular target is interference.
   a. If a shooter fires his/her shot, the appearance of a target, or a piece of target, from an adjoining field shall not be ruled as interference, unless such target, or piece of target strikes or threatens to strike the shooter or his/her gun. It shall be the final judgment of the referee to consider the evidence and determine whether a target or piece of target strikes or threatens to strike shooter or his/her gun.
   b. If a shooter withholds his/her shot due to what he/she considers to be an interference, and if the cause is observed and ruled interference by the referee, the interference may be allowed.
   c. If a shooter withholds a shot for safety purposes, the referee may give the shooter the benefit of the doubt and rule interference, providing he/she agrees safety was involved.
   d. Activities on other fields shall not be ruled as interference under any circumstance if safety to any person is not a question.
2. If the shooter shoots at a target, he/she accepts it. He/she must abide by the result unless the referee considers that there was legal interference. Following are a few illustrations of what may be considered legal interference:
   a. A target box being thrown out the door in the shooter's line of vision between the time of the shooter's call and the firing of his/her shot.
   b. Opening the skeet house door unexpectedly or suddenly under the same circumstances.
   c. Any sudden disturbance or exceptionally loud noise, except an announcement over the loud speaker.
   d. A bird flying directly across the target's line of flight just before it is fired upon.
   e. A child or any other person or animal running out on the field suddenly in the shooter's line of vision.
   f. A thrown object, or wind blown object, blown through the air so as to cause a conflict (a piece of paper being merely blown along the ground shall not qualify in this category).
   g. The sun shall not be considered as interference. It must be accepted as a normal hazard.
   h. Cell phones on or adjacent to a skeet field must be kept in the vibrate mode or off. No cell phone may be used on a skeet field to answer incoming or to make outgoing calls. A cell phone ring may be considered interference, except if it is the shooter's own.

### G. SAFETY PRECAUTIONS

The safety of competitors, field personnel and spectators is of primary importance and requires continuous attention and self-discipline. On any part of club grounds, as well as on the shooting field, particular attention must be given to the safety procedures outlined in the following paragraphs and to other safe gun handling techniques. Caution must also be used in moving about the field and club grounds. Where self discipline and attention to safety procedures is lacking, it is the duty of the field personnel to enforce them and the duty of competitors to assist in such enforcement.

1. Eye and Ear Protection - All persons (including shooters, referees and trap personnel) must wear some form of eye and ear protection on a skeet range at a shoot sanctioned by NSSA.
2. No gun shall be loaded until the shooter is on the shooting station. Loaded is considered as having any part of any shell in any gun.
3. As a safety precaution, test shots will not be permitted without permission of the field referee. Such permission shall not unreasonably be withheld.
4. The loaded gun shall be kept pointed in a direction that will not endanger the lives of shooters, field personnel or spectators.
5. When not on the shooting station, the gun shall be carried with breech open and empty. Pumps and automatics will have the bolt open. Fixed breech (double barrels including over-and-unders and side-by-sides) will be broken open and empty.
6. When the shooter is on the shooting station and ready to shoot and a delay occurs, such as equipment breakdown, the gun shall be opened and all shells extracted.
7. During the shooting of single targets, management may permit the loading of two shells. However, no one will be allowed to load two shells to shoot their last singles target on any station. Management cannot compel the loading of two shells in the shooting of singles.
8. The loading of more than two shells in the gun shall not be allowed at any time.
9. A gun may not be used that will accept more than one (1) gauge of shells at the same time.
10. A shooter will not be permitted to use a gun with a release-type trigger unless the referee and the other members of the squad are notified. Extra caution must be exercised if the gun is given to a referee who is unfamiliar with its operation. Guns with release type triggers must be clearly marked with designated safety stickers. Release trigger with instruction on placement are available from Headquarters. Please send your request in writing.
11. Any shooter whose gun accidentally discharges twice within one round for mechanical reasons shall be required to change guns or, if time permits, have his/her gun repaired, before continuing to shoot the round or subsequent rounds.
12. When a shooter intentionally fires a second time at the same target, he/she shall be warned by the referee. The second time the shooter intentionally fires a second shot at the same target in any event, the penalty shall be automatic disqualification from the event.
13. The placement of markers other than those specified in NSSA Rule Book shall be deemed illegal.
14. In the interest of safety, interference and time, only the club management's personnel shall be permitted to pick up empty shells from the grounds during a registered shoot, and extreme care must be exercised to prevent interference with other squads shooting.
15. No spectator shall be allowed on the skeet fields, and the referee shall be responsible for the enforcement of this rule.
16. The use of any drug, legal or illegal and including alcohol, prior to or during an NSSA sanctioned event by a registered competitor or referee is prohibited, with the exception of prescription or non-prescription over-the-counter medications that do not impair a shooter's or referee's ability to perform safely.

# SECTION IV

# REFEREES

### A. LICENSED REFEREE

1. NSSA official referees shall pass prescribed written examinations (with the aid of a rule book) and also eye tests, using glasses if necessary. For the eye test, a visual card system will suffice and save cost of a professional eye examination. Eye test cards are available through NSSA Member Services.
   a. These examinations will be given by their state associations or NSSA affiliated clubs.
   b. Applications for official NSSA referee cards and emblems shall be approved by the applicant's state association, where one exists, or by an NSSA affiliated club where there is no state or district association.
   c. It is recommended that all state organizations adopt the policy of using only NSSA official referees as chief referees.
   d. All applicants for referee licenses must be paid up regular members of the NSSA.
2. Referees for NSSA World Championship Shoots
   a. All applicants must be licensed NSSA referees for current year.
   b. Each applicant must be recommended in writing by two current officers of his/her state association or by one NSSA director from his/her state or zone.

### B. ASSOCIATE REFEREE

1. NSSA associate referees must meet all eligibility requirements specified for NSSA licensed referees (IV-A-1), with the exception of paid up membership in the NSSA.
2. An associate referee is eligible for an associate referee patch.
3. Application for associate referee status must be approved by applicant's state and/or zone chief referee.
4. An associate referee is not eligible to referee the World Championships.

### C. CHIEF REFEREE

When shoot management designates a chief referee, he/she shall have general supervision over all other referees and shall be present throughout the shooting.

1. It shall be his/her responsibility to appoint the necessary assistant chief referees and all other referees shall meet with his/her approval.
2. The chief referee shall designate and assign the referees to the fields and shall be held responsible for their conduct at all times during the shoot.
3. It is recommended that the chief referee also have the responsibility of instructing all other referees and being certain they are acquainted with the rules and approved interpretations.
4. It shall be the chief referee and/or shoot management's responsibility to stop a shoot or shoot-off when darkness or other conditions prevent a fair chance to shoot. This action must be carried out simultaneously on all fields. Example: Use of public address system or the shutting off of power; or a suitable signal, the significance of which is known to all referees. Use of the referee's eye test card - 5/16" dot at 21 yards - is MANDATORY. Eye test cards are available through NSSA Member Services.
5. Where practical, each state association should appoint a chief referee for its state. It is suggested that this chief referee be placed in charge of all referees in the state and that he/she conduct training courses to develop better referees.

### D. FIELD REFEREE

The field referee is responsible for the conduct of shooting on the field to which he/she has been assigned. On this field, he/she shall have jurisdiction over the area in rear of the field (that used by other shooters and spectators) as well as over the actual shooting area.

1. He/she shall be completely familiar with the shoot program and the NSSA rules.
2. He/she must be constantly alert, impartial and courteous (though firm) in the handling of shooters.
3. Upon protest, the referee shall rule upon the occurrence, and then without delay, proceed with the round as if nothing had happened. At the completion of the round, he/she shall notify the chief referee.
4. The referee shall distinctly announce all lost targets and all no-bird targets.
5. The referee shall see that each shooter has a fair opportunity to shoot in his/her turn, and if a shooter has been unduly interfered with while shooting, he/she shall declare no bird and allow the shooter another shot.
6. The referee shall declare no bird as soon as possible when:
   a. The shooter's position is not according to the rules. The shooter shall be warned by the referee of his/her illegal shooter's position, but if he/she continues to violate the position, he/she shall be penalized by the loss of one target for each subsequent violation in that event.
   b. Target does not emerge within the allowed time after the shooter's call.
   c. Target emerges before shooter's call.

d. An irregular target is thrown in singles, doubles or proof doubles.

7. It shall be the referee's first duty to declare "no bird" as quickly as possible when he/she determines that an irregular target has been thrown.
   a. If the shooter fires before the no bird call, the result of the shot shall be scored.
   b. In the case of doubles or proof doubles, if the referee's call of no bird occurs after the firing of the first shot the result of the first shot shall be scored and a proof double shall be thrown to determine the result of the second shot only.
   c. No result of firing on a broken target shall be scored.
8. The result of shooting at a target after it has been declared no bird shall not be scored and the shot will be repeated in all instances.
9. Dusted targets or perforated targets that are retrieved after landing shall be declared lost.
10. When the targets thrown from any machine are repeatedly irregular, the referee shall suspend shooting and order the machine adjusted or repaired. At shooter's request, after such repair or adjustment, the referee should allow shooter to observe a target, if such request is reasonable and not excessive.
11. The referee shall grant a shooter permission to shoot out of his/her regular turn where it is justified.
12. The referee shall disqualify, for the event:
   a. A shooter who in his/her opinion has willfully interfered with another shooter while the latter is shooting.
   b. Any shooter who repeatedly violates any of the safety precautions listed in Section III or for any act that in the referee's opinion endangers the safety of shooters, field personnel or spectators.
13. It shall also be the field referee's responsibility to supervise the keeping of correct scores and to see that all scores are verified by the respective shooters before the score sheet is taken from the field.
   a. Every regular target fired upon shall be shown on the score pad and it is recommended that the mark / or X be used to signify dead and O to signify lost.
   b. If an error in scorekeeping is discovered on the field, the field referee shall remedy it promptly at the time of discovery.
   c. In the event there is any question as to the correctness of a score after the score sheet leaves the field, shoot management shall check with the field referee and order the score corrected if it is determined that an error has been made.
   d. The referee's responsibility in seeing that shooters verify their scores is to announce after each round, Please check your scores.
14. The referee shall be the SOLE judge of decision of fact. For example, his/her decision as to whether a target is dead or lost shall be irrevocable, regardless of the opinion of spectators or other members of the squad.
15. It is better for a referee to continue to officiate at the same field.
   a. referees shall not take over the fields until the shooters have completed the round, except in cases of emergency, such as illness, etcetera.
   b. No NSSA official referee may be disqualified in the middle of a round but he/she may choose to disqualify himself.
16. Only assigned field referees, as designated by shoot management or the chief referee, may pull, score or referee registered targets. A voice release system may be used.
17. Whenever possible, have assigned field referees at registered shoots. However, in an effort to offer reduced shoot entry fees, shoot management may elect to have squads self-referee IF it is published in the shoot program and/or at the shoot registration desk. In such cases, the squad leadoff shooter shall be responsible for carrying the score sheet to and from the field, and having each shooter initial his/her final score at the end of the final round. In cases of any dispute or protest situation, these should be taken to shoot management immediately upon completion of the last round. Any protest to be filed must follow existing procedures as published in Section II-E.

# SECTION V

# NSSA CLASSIFICATION

### *A. DEFINITIONS*

1. NSSA Shooting Year
   The NSSA shooting year shall be any twelve month period running from November 1 through the following October 31.
2. Current Year
   The twelve month period November 1 through October 31 of the year for which classification is being determined.
3. Previous Year
   The twelve month period immediately preceding the current shooting year, (i.e. November 1 - October 31).
4. Gauge
   The term gauge used in this classification section includes International skeet and doubles as well as 12 gauge, 20 gauge, 28 gauge and .410 bore.
5. Class Assigned
   The assigned class of any shooter is the class he/she would be required to shoot in a subsequent event, whether or not he/she ever shot an event in that class.
6. New Shooter
   a. A new shooter in each gauge is any shooter who has not fired five registered events in that gauge during the current and previous three (3) years combined, even if he/she was previously a classified shooter in that gauge.
   b. The classification of such a shooter will follow the same pattern as in V-A-10, but will include the events and scores from the previous three (3) years until the five event limit is reached.
7. Classified Shooter
   a. A classified shooter in each gauge is any shooter who has fired five (5) or more events in that gauge in the current and previous three (3) years combined.
   b. If a classified shooter lacks the records to determine their proper classification, when they shoot their event after a lapse of a year or more, they may be permitted to shoot for "targets only" for that shoot only, while they obtain this data from NSSA records, by phone, fax, NSSA website or from a new classification and records card. The scorecard will then become their most current score when their prior shoot scores are obtained. Falsification subjects the shooter to action under rule II-A-8-d.
8. Running (Current) Average
   A classified shooter's running (current) average is the average of their most recent five events that they have shot in that gauge. It is the total of those five (5) scores divided by the total number of targets shot.
9. Event
   An event for purposes of classification is the gauge event as defined by the shoot program. This could be 50 or more targets as scheduled by the club for the event except in the case of monthly targets which must be shot in 50 or 100 bird increments. Thus a 200 bird shoot could be either one or two events as defined by the shoot program. Preliminaries and additional registered targets in any gauge will be considered separate events for classification purposes. However, the shooters' classification does NOT change between a preliminary and the main event. The changes are updated after the shoot; see V-A-II-e. Exceptions: Although the Mini-World is not considered a preliminary, you do not reclassify before shooting the Main World, but you do use it separately as a different event when reclassifying after the World. Note: Monthly Targets are events of 50 or 100 bird increments only. For League Targets, each league is an event consisting of the total birds shot for that league. Champion of Champion targets are not registered targets and none of the various gauge scores will be used in classification or reclassification.
10. Classification of a New Shooter
   a. The classification of a new shooter in each gauge is determined by the score shot in his/her first registered event. He/she is placed in the proper class for that event and for the next event of that gauge on the basis of percentage of targets broken using the classification tables.
   b. With each subsequent event in each gauge, both the targets fired upon and targets broken will be totaled, including all events of the previous three years if any, in that gauge to determine a running average until five (5) events in that gauge have been shot.
   c. The total number of targets scheduled for an event are to be used each time the running average is calculated for classification, whether 50 birds, 100 birds or more, and whether or not the event is spread over more than one day.
   d. The new shooter's class will "float" either up or down freely without limit based on that average until after the fifth event in that gauge. After the fifth event the now classified shooter's class can move upward without limit but not drop more than one class below where the fifth event placed him/her in each gauge during that shooting year.

Example 1: The first score was 85 putting him/her in class E for that shoot and the next shoot. The second event score was 89. His/her running average is now .8700 and is assigned to class D for the next shoot. The shooter next attends the World Shoot as a class D shooter, shooting only the 12 gauge, and shoots a 227/250. He/she has now shot three (3) events, totaling 401/450 giving a running average of .8911 and is still in class D. His/her classification card would look as follows for 12 gauge:

| Date | Place/Shoot Name | Class shot in | Shot | Broke Avg. | Class next shoot |
|---|---|---|---|---|---|
| xx/xx | xx/xxx | E | 100 | 85 .8500 | E |
| xx/xx | xx/xxx | E | 100 | 89 .8700 | D |
| xx/xx | xx/xxx | D | 250 | 227 .8911 | D |

Example 2: A new shooter has shot four (4) 100 bird 12 gauge events. He/she now shoots a 50 bird event. Having shot five (5) events, he/she now re-averages on the 450 targets of the five (5) events and is now a classified shooter. After the next event, he/she would be dropping the first 100 bird event and averaging the last five (5) events, the 2nd through 6.

Example 3: A new shooter has shot 100 12 gauge targets year before last with a score of 89, placed in Class D. Last year he/she shot 200 more 12 gauge targets, scoring 92 and 96. Average on these 300 is .9233 and this year's classification card will show that he/she is in class C for this year's first shoot. He/she fires an 88 in the first shoot this year. Average on four (4) shoots is now .9125 and he/she stay in class C. Since he/she is still a new shooter the class is still floating and he/she could possibly drop back to class D or E after the fifth event for the three (3) years combined.

   e. A new shooter may only declare upward to AA and if he/she does so may not shoot below AA for the remainder of the shooting year.
   f. A first time NSSA member who has been classified by another clay target organization in Class A or above, is required to declare a class no more than one class lower than their highest class held within the last three years. Such a first time NSSA shooter classified by another clay target organization below Class A shall follow the regular NSSA classification procedure for a NEW SHOOTER.
   g. It is the shooter's responsibility to maintain their records and averages, to determine their classification and reclassifications.
11. Reclassification of a Classified Shooter
   a. A classified shooter must keep a running average of their last five (5) events in each gauge, dropping the earliest event each time and adding the recent event, such that the running average is based on the most current five (5) events thereafter, regardless of how many actual targets were contained in these events.
   b. If the event is the classified shooter's first of the current year, he/she must use the last four scores of the previous year(s) to obtain the five scores necessary for re-classification, and then three scores, two scores, or one score as necessary, until five events have been shot in the current year.
   c. A classified shooter may reclassify upward by averaging without limit during the shooting year including into AAA, but may not reclassify downward more than one class during the year, and again at the end of the year. Downward reclassification may be declined by entering the higher class on the classification card in the blank for assigned class after reclassification. This will preclude later downward reclassification after another event for the remainder of the shooting year, since this is the equivalent of declaring upward. Note: If downward reclassification occurs as a result of the last event of the shooting year, the shooter starts the next year in the new, lower class. A downward reclassification at the end of the shooting year does not preclude a subsequent downward reclassification during the new shooting year, even after the first event of the year. The first downward reclassification may occur at any time during the year, but the second only at year-end.

Example: The shooter's annual classification card lists his/her last five shoots of the previous year in 12 gauge as:

| Date | Place/Shoot Name | Class shot in | Shot | Broke Avg. | Class next shoot |
|---|---|---|---|---|---|
| xx/xx | xxx/xxxx | B | 100 | 95 | B |
| xx/xx | xxx/xxxx | B | 100 | 94 | B |
| xx/xx | xxx/xxxx | B | 100 | 97 | B |
| xx/xx | xxx/xxxx | B | 100 | 97 | B |
| xx/xx | xxx/xxxx | B | 100 | 99 .9640 | A |

He/she then shoots 100 straight in first shoot of the current year. The new average and class are: (dropping 95 at the top of the list) 94+97+97+99+100=487/500=.9740 and is still in class A for the next shoot.

   d. A classified shooter who wishes to self declare into a higher class may do so, including into AAA. But thereafter may not shoot below the declared class for the remainder of the shooting year. When a shooter so elects, he/she must present their card at a registered shoot and have his/her card marked by management with his/her self declared class before competing in the event for which he/she is declaring upward, and be entered upon the official entry form as self declared.
   e. A shooter does NOT re-classify during a shoot after shooting in a preliminary registered

event in one or more gauges before the main event. It is a separate event however, and after the shoot the preliminary event score and the main event score should each be entered in order separately on the classification card. and then the average of his/her last five events and appropriate class resulting entered for each entry and gun.

12. Classification of Shooters from Others Clay Target Organizations
   a. Participants who have shot in another clay target organization must provide their shooting average and classification for all gauges from the previous three (3) years for all organizations, along with titles won, upon registration at a NSSA shoot.
   b. A first time NSSA shooter who has been classified by another non-skeet clay target organization (i.e. NSCA, ATA, NRA) in Class A or above, is required to declare no more than one class lower than their highest class held within the last three (3) years. Such a shooter may not reclassify downward, only upward, until the end of the current shooting year. Such a first time NSSA shooter classified by another non-skeet clay target organization below class A, or not classified in a particular gauge, shall follow the regular NSSA classification procedure for a NEW SHOOTER.
   c. For a shooter who is classified by another skeet clay target shooting organization (i.e., CPSA, ACTA, etc.), their NSSA class shall be determined as follows:
      1) If the individual is also a NSSA Classified Shooter (i.e., not a "NEW SHOOTER") they shall shoot in their earned NSSA Class.
      2) If the individual doesn't have sufficient targets to be an NSSA Classified shooter their NSSA class will be determined using their highest average for the past three (3) years in the other skeet clay target organization using the NSSA classification tables. Such a shooter classified by another clay target organization in Class A or above, may not reclassify downward, only upward, until the end of the current shooting year. Those classified below Class A, or not classified in a particular gauge, shall follow the regular NSSA classification procedure for a NEW SHOOTER.

13. Classification Cards
   a. As soon as possible after October 31 of each year, each PAID member will receive from NSSA a classification/shoot record card.
   b. This classification card shall include provisions for club designation, date, place and shoot name, class shot in, targets shot, targets broken, average and assigned class for next shoot in each gauge. It will be imprinted with:
      1) Member's name, address, membership expiration date and membership number, birth date and age concurrent and other concurrent status.
      2) The date and scores for the most recent five (5) events of each gauge in the previous three (3) years, the running average of these and the shooter's assigned class in each gauge for the first event of the current year.
   c. Any errors on shooter's new classification card, including those caused by failure of shoot reports to be received at NSSA Headquarters in time to be included on new card, must be promptly reported to NSSA by the shooter so that a corrected card can be supplied. This is also to insure proper inclusion in permanent record.

14. A New Shooter at their Initial Shoot
Shoot management may reserve the right to restrict such a shooter from entering purses and/or class options, but if they do, may not require such a shooter to pay any portion of the purse returned to the shooters in cash or other tangible awards. Such a shooter will not be eligible for cash or tangible awards for which they have not paid the required entry fee prior to entering the event.

### B. PROCEDURES

1. Maintaining Shoot Record Card
   a. Each shooter shall bear the responsibility of promptly and accurately entering his/her own score with the date, and shoot, in the proper gauge division at the conclusion of each registered EVENT in which he/she participates. Where a single EVENT extends more than one day, he/she should enter the total, not the day-today scores. When a shoot extends over multiple days, the score from each event will be recorded on the shoot record card on the date each EVENT is completed.
   b. Each shooter shall promptly update his/her classification in re-classification spaces on his/her classification card after each event of each gauge shot.
   c. The shooter is required to carry his/her card to each registered shoot and present it at registration. In the case of a lost classification card, or accidentally forgetting a classification card, the shooter may sign an affidavit attesting to his/her classification, subject to specified penalties. Such affidavit must be attached to the shoot report when it is forwarded to NSSA for tabulation. The score shot will become his/her most recent event score.

NOTE: Replacement for a lost card (including reported scores to date) may be obtained from NSSA upon request. If the original card is later found, the shooter should carefully consolidate the record, then destroy the extra card.

   d. In the space provided for club on his/her classification card, each member shall designate, not later than his/her first competition in such events, the club he/she has elected to represent in club two-man and five-man team competition.
   e. A shooter falsifying any entries or improperly using more than one classification card will be disqualified and reported to NSSA for action according to II-A-8-d.
   f. Targets Only are:
      1) Targets shot in increments of 100 targets, or 50 targets for 50 target programs, on the day of a registered shoot, or targets shot above the number scheduled for the event, and for which no winner is declared and no tangible prizes awarded. Targets only will be recorded on the day shot, and reported by the club with their report. You may not shoot 100 target increments during a 50 target event, nor may you shoot 50 additional targets during a 100 target event. Or,
      2) Those registered targets shot by a sub-junior, junior, collegiate or new shooter if they do not pay any portion of the mandatory purse. A new shooter, shooting targets only, is not eligible for any awards. (see II-B-2.)
   g. Monthly Targets are registered targets shot on all or selected days of the month. They must be shot in 50 or 100 bird increments, and will be recorded on the shooters' classification card and used for classification on the day and order shot. Monthly targets will be accumulated and reported by the club within 15 days after the end of the month. Monthly targets are shot for the purpose of acquiring lifetime targets, fulfilling annual minimum requirements, classification purposes and for fun.
   h. League Targets are targets shot during a regularly scheduled NSSA or club skeet league. The shooter must declare registering of his/her targets prior to the start of the league. All registered targets will count towards lifetime and annual minimum requirements, and will be recorded at the end of the shooting year for classification purposes. Multiple gauges and /or leagues may be shot during the year. Each gauge of each league is considered a single event. It is the shooters' responsibility to record all league targets on their classification card, in the order shot, as their final event or events for the year.

2. Classification Review
   a. A state association, director, club or shooter has the right to request a review of a shooter's record if it appears that he/she is unfairly competing in a class below his/her true level of ability. Upon review by a duly authorized national committee the shooter may be assigned a higher class and may be required to disregard certain abnormally low scores for the purpose of classification and reclassification only.
   b. If a shooter has been assigned a higher class because of a classification review, he/she will not be allowed to shoot below that class until removed from classification review by the committee.

### C. UNIVERSAL CLASSIFICATION TABLES

1. Use of the Universal Classification Tables shall be required for all registered shoots and shall be in accordance with the tables of averages shown below. Standard rounding procedures will be used to calculate an individual's average. Calculate the average to 5 digits and rounding to the 4th digit. If the 5th digit is greater than or equal to 5, then the 4th digit will be rounded up.
   a. A shooters correct class and average shall be posted on his/her shoot entry form.
   b. Classification in each gauge (including .410 and doubles) is independent and shall be treated without regard to classification in any other gauge.
2. Individual Classification

## CLASSIFICATION TABLES FOR OPEN INDIVIDUAL CLASSES

| 12 GAUGE | 20 GAUGE | 28 GAUGE |
|---|---|---|
| Class/Average | Class/Average | Class/Average |
| AAA/98.50 and over | AAA/98.25 and over | AAA/98.00 and over |
| AA/97.50 to 98.49 | AA/97.00 to 98.24 | AA/96.50 to 97.49 |
| A/96.00 to 97.49 | A/94.50 to 96.99 | A/94.00 to 96.49 |
| B/93.50 to 95.99 | B/91.00 to 94.49 | B/90.50 to 93.99 |
| C/90.00 to 93.49 | C/85.50 to 90.99 | C/85.50 to 90.49 |
| D/85.50 to 89.99 | D/85.49 and under | D/85.49 and under |
| E 85.49 and under | | |

| .410 BORE | DOUBLES |
|---|---|
| Class/Average | Class/Average/Doubles |
| AAA/96.50 and over | AAA 97.00 and over |
| AA/94.70 to 96.49 | AA/95.00 to 96.99 |
| A/91.00 to 94.49 | A/91.00 to 94.99 |
| B/86.00 to 90.99 | B/85.00 to 90.99 |
| C/80.00 to 85.99 | C/80.00 to 84.99 |
| D/79.99 and under | D/79.99 and under |

3. Compulsory Classes
Only Classes AA, A, B, C and D (and E in 12 gauge) shall be compulsory.
   a. Class AAA shall be optional and when AAA is not offered Class AA shall include all shooters who would be in Class AAA if it were offered.
   b. Class AAA is optional; however, it should be considered for use in any event where the number of entries exceeds 100, or where the number of entries eligible for AAA justifies doing so.
   c. It shall be the sole responsibility of shoot management to determine whether Class AAA shall be offered and its decision shall be published in the shoot program or posted before the shoot.
4. High Overall/High All Around
   a. Unless otherwise published in the program or posted at the shoot, a shooter's HOA or HAA class will be based on his/her 4 or 5 gun average, using the NSSA HOA/HAA Classification Table, at the time of their entry in the first event of the shoot and will not be changed as a result of a reclassification due to a preliminary event, except when a shooter's HOA or HAA class would be lower than their lowest gun class (see V-C-4-b).
   b. In no case will shooter's HOA/HAA class be any lower than his/her lowest gun class. For shooters who have voluntarily declared upward on any gun, or all guns, to calculate a HOA/HAA class, use the bottom percentage of the class in each gun.
   c. For a new shooter in one or more guns (see V-A-5 and V-A-7) who wishes to shoot HOA/HAA, simply calculate a HOA/HAA based on their current new shooter and/or classified shooter averages. A shooter who has never shot registered targets in any one of the required gauges is not eligible to enter these events.
   d. NSSA HOA/HAA CLASSIFICATION TABLES
   Use of these tables is not mandatory. However, if no other method for determining HOA/HAA is listed in the shoot program or prominently posted prior to beginning of registration, the tables listed below will be used to determine HOA/HAA classification. It is important for clubs to remember that the method for determining HOA/HAA classification must be posted or published in the shoot program.

### HOA/HAA CLASSIFICATION TABLES

| HOA | HAA |
|---|---|
| (4 guns, excluding Doubles) | (5 guns, including Doubles) |
| AAA 97.81 & over | 97.65 & over |
| AA 96.38 - 97.80 | 96.10 - 97.64 |
| A 93.88 - 96.37 | 93.30 - 96.09 |
| B 90.25 - 93.87 | 89.20 - 93.29 |
| C 85.25 - 90.24 | 84.20 - 89.19 |
| D 79.25 - 85.24 | 78.20 - 84.19 |
| E 79.24 & under | 78.19 & under |

Shoot Management has the discretion to offer, or not offer, Class E HOA/HAA as necessary.

### D. TEAM AND OTHER CONCURRENT EVENT CLASSIFICATIONS

1. Division of two-man team, five-man team, lady, junior and other concurrent events into classes is NOT MANDATORY. In cases where shoot management should desire to establish classes in these events, they may do so. When such classes are established, they should be designated by NUMBER rather than by letter, i.e., Class 1 (or I) XX - and over, Class 2 (or II) under XX.
2. Classification for team events shall be combined average of team member's scores, carried to the fourth decimal place at their most recent reclassification (i.e. - .9525). Standard rounding procedures will be used to calculate an individual's average. Calculate the average to 5 digits and rounding to the 4th digit. If the 5th digit is greater than or equal to 5, then the 4th digit will be rounded up.
3. The average for a new shooter competing in a team or other event that has been divided into classes shall simply be his/her current average for the gauge entered. A new shooter who has not shot his/her first registered event and thus has no classification in the required gauges is not eligible to enter these events.

### E. RECLASSIFICATION LIMITATIONS

Any shooter who believes he/she is entitled to compete in a lower class due to illness, accident, age, etcetera, may appeal to the classification review committee of NSSA after prior approval of his/her request by his/her state association. In the absence of a state association in the shooter's state, his/her appeal may be made directly to the classification review committee.

### F. ALTERNATE AWARD SYSTEM

Recommended for Small Shoots

This proposal represents an alternative method for small shoots to award tangible prizes (e.g. awards, trophies or added money). By cutting down the quantity, a club could increase the quality of awards and hopefully attract more shooters. Use of this system will not affect an individual's score as used for NSSA classification and shoot management MUST report the shooter's score as per NSSA rules and classification. Use of this system is only for that shoot, and clubs that choose to use this system MUST print it in the shoot program and also post it at the registration table. The alternate award system may be used for any of the four guns or doubles. The average based on the shooter's current classification.

Example:

| | |
|---|---|
| Upper Third | Group 1 - .9500 and over |
| Middle Third | Group 2 - .9000 to .9499 |
| Lower Third | Group 3 - Under .9000 |

Other equal breakdowns are also permissible depending on the gauge being shot and size of the field. This system is for awards purpose only, used only for that day of shooting, and will not affect any part of a shooters regular classification. The scores will be used as part of their regular reclassification.

# SECTION VI

# INTERNATIONAL SHOOTING

USA Shooting and the National Skeet Shooting Association (NSSA) have common goals concerning the support and growth of International Skeet. The major goal, after joint compliance with UIT rules and procedures, is one of congruent classification rules procedures. Unfortunately, the two organizations have not yet totally achieved that goal; Therefore, NSSA members will use the following rules for classification and record keeping in NSSA registered International Skeet events.

### A. ELIGIBLE SHOOTERS

All competitors in NSSA registered International events must have a current NSSA membership.

### B. CLASSIFICATION PROCEDURES

The classification rules and procedures for participation in NSSA registered International events are exactly the same as those set out in section V.

### C. CLASSIFICATION TABLE FOR INTERNATIONAL EVENTS

Class Averages
AA 92 and above
A 86 to 91.99
B 80 to 85.99
C 74 to 79.99
D 68 to 73.99
E 67.99 and below

### D. RECORDING SCORES

1. Only those scores shot in NSSA registered International events are to be used for determination of a shooter's NSSA International classification.
   a. These are the only scores that will be included in NSSA records and publications.
   b. These scores will NOT be included in USA Shooting records unless the tournament has also been registered with USA Shooting.
2. It is the responsibility of all shooters entering NSSA/USA Shooting registered events to determine their correct classification according to NSSA/USA Shooting rules.

### E. REPORTING SCORES

Clubs registering International events with NSSA are subject to all requirements of rule II-H, including payment of the required daily fees (in U.S. funds) for each target shot in the tournament.

### F. RECOGNITION AND AWARDS

1. Scores shot and awards won by NSSA members in USA Shooting and other UIT approved competitions will be recognized by NSSA for the purpose of All- American Team selection, if in addition, the shooter has shot the NSSA standards of 1200 NSSA registered targets, provided such scores and awards can be substantiated by official records or published reports.
2. Candidates for All-American Team selection must:
   a. Shoot at least 1200 International NSSA registered targets during the NSSA shooting year.
   b. Concurrent categories in International shooting will follow the 12 gauge NSSA standard registered targets subject to Rule II-l-1(a) page 24.

### G. MODIFIED INTERNATIONAL

See "Event 6" section VIII-E-2

# SECTION VII

# RULES OF CONDUCT

A. Each member and member club will be furnished a copy of the Official NSSA Rules, with the understanding that the member and member club will read and understand each rule. All members and member clubs are responsible to know these rules and abide by them, for their own benefit and safety as well as that of other shooters.

B. By paying the membership fee, entering a competition or holding a competition, every member and member club agrees to abide by these rules and to accept all official decisions of the NSSA interpreting and/or applying these rules.

C. It shall be a violation of these rules to:
   1. Exhibit unsportsmanlike conduct of any kind, including but not limited to: falsifying scores or classification, cheating, verbal abuse, physical abuse of any shooter, scorer, field judge, shoot official or protest committee.
   2. Disobey the order of any scorer, field judge or shoot official.
   3. Violate any safety rules as set forth in section III or engage in any activity that is considered unsafe by the NSSA Executive Committee.
   4. Shoot at any place other than the designated station.
   5. Interfere with the shoot management's procedures in conducting the shoot.
   6. Violate any rule or regulation of a club or range.
   7. Exhibit any conduct that is deemed by the Executive Committee to be harmful to the NSSA, its membership, or the sport as a whole.
   8. Failure of shoot management to submit a written report to NSSA of written complaints received along with a report of action taken.
   9. Violate any other rule or regulation of the NSSA as set forth in any other section or paragraph of the NSSA's rules and regulations.
   10. Tipping: Tipping of individual referees is not permitted.

D. Suspensions, Expulsions and Reinstatement
   1. The Executive Committee may at any time at its discretion suspend or expel any member or member club or discipline any member or member club for the violation of any NSSA rule or regulation.
   2. The procedure for suspension, expulsion or other disciplinary action is as follows:
      a. Any member, shooter, scorer, field judge, shoot official or owner or member of management of a club or range who witnesses a violation of any NSSA rule shall if warranted submit to the NSSA Director or Executive Director a written complaint within thirty (30) days of the alleged violation which shall include:
         1) he name of the alleged violator;
         2) the date and location of the alleged violation;
         3) a reasonably detailed description of the alleged violation;
         4) the names and addresses, if known, of any witnesses; and
         5) the name, address, phone number and signature of the complainant(s).
      b. Upon receipt, the NSSA Director or Executive Director shall assign each complaint a complaint number consisting of the year of receipt and consecutive number of receipt, i.e. 07-01, 07-02, etc.
      c. The NSSA Director or Executive Director shall review the complaint within ten (10) days of receipt and determine if it meets the requirements set forth above. The NSSA Director or Executive Director has the discretion to consider and investigate or dismiss any complaint that does not meet the foregoing requirements. Any complaint may be resubmitted to the Executive Committee within ten (10) days of receipt of rejection.
      d. Within ten (10) days of receipt of a complaint the NSSA Director or Executive Director, or anyone acting pursuant to direction from the Director or Executive Director, shall serve written notice of the complaint and a copy of the complaint on the alleged violator, by certified mail, return receipt requested. The written notice shall instruct the alleged violator of his right to submit a written statement, which must be signed and should include the names, addresses and phone numbers of any witnesses not named in the complaint. Such written statement must be received by the NSSA Director or Executive Director within ten (10) days of the alleged violator's receipt of the notice and complaint. All statements received after such date shall not be considered.
      e. The NSSA Director or Executive Director, or someone acting pursuant to direction from the Director or Executive Director, shall thoroughly investigate the allegations of the complaint by attempting to obtain written statements from all known witnesses. All witness statements must be in writing and signed by the witness.
      f. After time for the alleged violator to respond expires, the NSSA Director or Executive Director shall review the complaint, the statement of the alleged violator, witness statements and any other relevant evidence. Upon such review, the NSSA Director or Executive Director shall recommend to the NSSA Executive Committee a specific disciplinary action. The recommendation shall include:
         1) all evidence that was considered, including the names of any witnesses who submitted statements;
         2) a determination of whether the alleged violation occurred; and
         3) the disciplinary action, if any, the NSSA Director or Executive Director recommends that the NSSA Executive Committee impose.
      g. The NSSA Director or Executive Director shall provide each member of the NSSA Executive Committee with a copy of the complaint, the statement of the alleged violator, copies of any witness statements and a copy of the recommendation.
      h. The NSSA Director or Executive Director shall schedule a conference call between the members of the NSSA Executive Committee wherein the NSSA Executive Committee shall review all information provided by the NSSA Director or Executive Director and issue a ruling on the matter by majority vote. The NSSA Executive Committee's ruling shall include:
         1) the date of issuance;
         2) all evidence that was considered, including the names of any witnesses who submitted statements;
         3) a determination of whether the alleged violation occurred; and
         4) the disciplinary action, if any, imposed by the NSSA Executive Committee.

E. The NSSA Executive Committee shall have the discretion to suspend or expel a member or or to impose any other disciplinary action it deems appropriate. Upon issuance of a ruling, the NSSA Director or Executive Director shall serve the ruling on the violator by certified mail, return receipt requested. The ruling shall become effective on the date of issuance and continue until a hearing, if any, is held.

F. The violator shall have the right to appeal the NSSA Executive Committee's ruling by notifying the NSSA Executive Committee. Such notification of appeal must be in writing and must be post-marked no later than thirty (30) days from the date the ruling was issued.
   1. Upon receipt of the notification of appeal the NSSA Executive Committee shall hold a hearing on the matter, which will take place at the next regularly scheduled quarterly meeting of the NSSA Executive Committee.
   2. At the hearing, the violator shall have the right to be present, the right to bring counsel, the right to testify and the right to present any evidence he so chooses. No record or transcript of the hearing will be made or allowed.
   3. The NSSA Executive Committee shall review the complaint, the written statement of the violator, and any other evidence it deems appropriate. The NSSA Executive Committee may allow any and all witnesses to testify by telephone or in person. The Executive Committee may make inquiries of the witnesses but no other persons may do so.
   4. At the conclusion of such hearing, the NSSA Executive Committee shall have the authority to affirm, reverse or modify the disciplinary action imposed previously by majority vote.

G. By paying the membership fee, entering a competition or holding a competition, every member and member club agrees to abide by any decision of the NSSA Executive Committee and further agrees and recognizes that as a voluntary amateur association, the NSSA has the right to impose, interpret and enforce its rules and regulations and that all decision by the NSSA Executive Committee following a hearing are final.

# SECTION VIII

# EVENT 6

In an effort to promote and introduce shooters to skeet shooting without causing additional expense to gun clubs "Event 6" can be used to host a variety of different skeet shooting matches. These matches can be tailored to members and non-members wants and desires. Event 6 is designed to put the fun back in local skeet shoots. Anyone can shoot and be eligible for all awards. You don't have to be a member of the NSSA to shoot, and the awards are based on a class system similar to Lewis Class, so anyone can win. Awards are provided to clubs by NSSA on a cost basis. The targets are registered for NSSA members and count towards lifetime targets only and are not to be recorded on the classification card. Results of Event 6 shoots will be published in the Skeet Shooting Review.

### A. RULES

1. Any gun or gauge may be used.

2. Pulling/scoring/refereeing and following NSSA rules can be the responsibility of the squad.
3. All targets will be registered separately and will only be counted towards lifetime-registered targets.
4. Anyone and everyone can shoot and be eligible for all awards.
5. All NSSA Safety Rules apply.
6. It is permissible to squad Event 6 registered with regular registered shooters.

## B. SHOOT APPLICATIONS

1. Handle the same as in Rule II-A-7a through b2. Designate shoot as an Event 6 shoot. This will provide for standardization and effective management of shoot and financial reports.
2. When application is received and a shoot number is assigned applicable shoot, financial report forms and award order forms will be forwarded to clubs.

## C. FEES

Standard NSSA and state fees apply for both NSSA members and non-members. Fees for non-members go for daily membership to be eligible for prizes.

## D. SHOOT REPORT

1. Report all NSSA member scores by name and NSSA member number this will insure targets are added to lifetime target totals.
2. Report winners list. This list includes NSSA members and non-members as applicable. This list will be published in the Skeet Shooting Review.

## E. TYPES OF "EVENT – 6" MATCHES

1. Regular Skeet and Doubles: It is permissible to squad Event 6 registered with regular registered shooters.
2. NSSA Modified International: The same format used by the UIT, USA Shooting and NSSA will apply with the following exceptions:
   a. Targets can be thrown at standard NSSA distances requiring no modification of equipment.
   b. Ammunition used is of standard NSSA specifications and any gauge can be used.
   c. No automatic timers are required. The puller can control target release time.
   d. Target requirements can be standard NSSA specified. International targets are not required.
3. NSSA Vintage Skeet: The same format used in standard NSSA skeet with the following possible exceptions:
   a. Only pump/slide action or side-by-side guns are to be used.
   b. After mounting the gun the stock can be dropped slightly before calling for the target.

## F. DETERMINING AWARDS

Both NSSA and Daily Members are eligible to win.

1. Your program (or poster) has promised 1 award every 6 entries. You have 22 entries divided by 6 = 3.66 or 4 awards.
2. Example of scores:
   98 Winner
   97
   95
   95
   94*
   94* *Tied for Winner

   94*
   93
   92
   92
   92
   91** **Tied for Winner

   91*
   91*
   90
   90
   89
   88*** ***Tied for Winner

   88***
   88***
   88***
   82

Score below line is winner; however, if more than one score exists either above or below the line there is a tie. Ties may be divided by shoot-off or combined total of either long runs (forward and backward) or coin flip/draw card or any other method you may choose.

Club must decide how to determine winners when ties exist and post this information before shoot starts!

# SECTION IX
# GUIDELINES FOR PROTESTS

In order that protests may be more uniformly and fairly handled, the protesting shooter and the protest committee* should observe the following guidelines.

A. Record the exact time that:
   1. The incident occurred.
   2. A verbal protest was made to the field referee (if at all).
   3. A verbal protest was made to the chief referee (if at all).
   4. The chief referee ruled on the protest (if at all).
   5. The protest committee's decision was made known to the protesting shooter.

B. Determine and record:
   1. If there was a chief referee, was the complaint brought to his/her attention by the protesting shooter?
   2. Was the written protest tendered to shoot management within 12 hours of the protested incident?
   3. Is the shooter not protesting a referee's decision of fact?
   4. Is the shooter protesting: Improper application of the NSSA rules, or the conditions under which another shooter has been allowed to shoot or an error in scorekeeping?

C. If B-1 through B-4 above can all be answered yes, the Protest Committee should then decide whether to grant or deny the protest. If the answer to any of the questions B-1 through B-4 above is no the protest is invalid.

D. Any appeal to the NSSA of the Protest Committee's decision should include:
   1. The facts outlined above.
   2. A copy of the written protest.
   3. A copy of the Protest Committee's decision.

E. Shoot management should be prepared to provide the information in D-1 through D-3 above to the NSSA upon request.

   * "Protest Committee" shall be defined as: shoot management or a judge appointed by shoot management or a panel of judges appointed by shoot management.

National Skeet Shooting Association
5931 Roft Road • San Antonio, TX 78253
(210) 688-3371

# OFFICIAL RULES & REGULATIONS

# CLAYS RULES

(Revised 2009)

## ORGANIZATION OF THE NATIONAL SPORTING CLAYS ASSOCIATION

The National Sporting Clays Association (NSCA) was formed in April of 1989, as a division of the National Skeet Shooting Association (NSSA), to promote sporting clays in the United States and other countries. The following is an informative summary of the organization of the NSCA, important official policies and rules that govern the NSCA, the shooting of registered targets, the conduct of shooters and the duties of shoot management. The NSCA has the responsibility for the formulation, regulation and enforcement of these rules. For any rules or policies not contained in this book, or in the official minutes of the NSCA Advisory Council meetings, refer to the bylaws of the NSSA. The NSCA reserves the right to make alterations in, or amendments to, these rules and policies at any time, when it deems it to be in the best interest of the National Sporting Clays Association and it's members.

## I. GENERAL INFORMATION

### A. PURPOSE OF NSCA

The purpose of the National Sporting Clays Association is to promote and govern the sport of sporting clays throughout the United States and other countries, in a way which is beneficial to all who enjoy and participate in the game. The NSCA is dedicated to the development of the sport at all levels of participation. NSCA vows to create an atmosphere of healthy and safe competition and meaningful fellowship within its membership.

### B. MEMBERSHIP

1. Individual

a. Annual membership dues for an adult individual are $40 and include monthly issues of Sporting Clays magazine, beginning with the first issue available for mailing after dues received at headquarters.

b. An Associate membership is available to other adults of a household when at least one regular annual membership exists for $30, but does not include the magazine.

c. A Junior membership is available for $20 per year and includes the monthly magazine. The Junior membership is available only to individuals under the age of 21.

d. An International Shooting membership is available for $20 per year to all foreign shooters who wish to compete in NSCA sanctioned events within the US. Sporting Clays magazine is not included.

e. Six-year membership dues for an individual are $200 and include a copy of the official magazine, Sporting Clays magazine, beginning with the first issue available for mailing after dues are received at headquarters. A Six-year Associate Membership is available to dependents of members for $150, but does not include the magazine.

f. Life membership for an individual is $500 and a Husband and Wife Life membership is $750.

g. Senior Life membership for an individual 65 years of age or older is $250 and a Senior Husband and Wife Life membership is $375.

h. The membership and shooting year begins on January 1 and ends on December 31 of the same year.

i. Annual membership may be applied for by filling out an application provided at an NSCA club/ range or by contacting NSCA Headquarters for an application. Also available on NSCA website mynsca. com.

2. Clubs and Ranges

a. Annual membership dues for a club or range are $100 a year.

b. The membership and shooting year begins on January 1 and ends December 31 of the same year.

c. Annual Club/Range membership may be applied for by filling out an application provided by the NSCA. Also available on NSCA website mynsca.com.

3. Rules of Conduct

a. Each member and club will be furnished a copy of the Official NSCA rules, also available on NSCA website mynsca.com, with the understanding that the member/ member club will read and understand each rule. All members and member clubs are responsible to know these rules and abide by them, for their own benefit and safety as well as that of other shooters.

b. By paying the membership fee, entering a competition or holding a competition, every member and member club agrees to abide by these rules and to accept all official decisions of the NSCA in interpreting and/or applying these rules.

c. It shall be a violation of these rules to:

1. Exhibit unsportsmanlike conduct of any kind, including but not limited to, falsifying scores or classification, cheating, swearing, verbal or physical abuse of any shooter, scorer, field judge, shoot official or protest committee.

2. Disobey the order of any scorer, field judge or shoot official.

3. Violate any safety rules as set forth in Section II of these rules and regulations, or engage in any activity that is considered unsafe by the NSCA Executive Council.

4. Shoot at any place other than the designated station.

5. Interfere with the shoot management's procedures in conducting the shoot.

6. Violate any rule or regulation of a club or range.

7. Exhibit any conduct that is harmful to the NSCA, its membership, or the sport as a whole. Exhibit behavior that shows discrimination towards race, religion, or sex - including sexual harassment.

8. Failure to submit a written complaint to shoot management after witnessing the violation of one of the NSCA's rules or regulations.

9. Failure of shoot management to submit a written report to NSCA of written complaints received along with a report of action taken.

10. Violate any other rule or regulation of the NSCA as set forth in any other section or paragraph of the NSCA's rules and regulations.

4. Suspensions, Expulsions and Reinstatement

a. The Executive Council may, at any time at its discretion, suspend, expel or discipline any member or member club for the violation of any NSCA rule or regulation.

b. The procedure for suspension, expulsion or other disciplinary action is as follows:

1. Any member, shooter, scorer, field judge, shoot official, owner or member of management of a club or range who witnesses a violation of any NSCA rule shall submit to the NSCA Director or Executive Director a written complaint within thirty (30) days of the alleged violation. The action of being disqualified from a shoot does not start disciplinary action. The complaint must be in writing to start disciplinary action. The written complaint shall include:

i. the name of the alleged violator
ii. the date and location of the alleged violation
iii. a reasonably detailed description of the alleged violation and a request for action to be taken on the situation
iv. the names and addresses, if known, of all witnesses
v. the name, address, phone number and signature of the complainant(s).

2. Upon receipt, the NSCA Director or Executive Director shall assign each complaint a complaint number consisting of the year of the receipt and consecutive number of receipt, i.e. 07-01, 07-02, etc.

3. The NSCA Director or Executive Director shall review the complaint and determine if it meets the requirements set forth above. Any complaint may be resubmitted so long as it is received within the described requisite time period noted above. The NSCA Director or Executive Director has the discretion to consider and investigate or dismiss any complaint that does not meet the foregoing requirements.

4. Within ten (10) days of receipt of a complaint the NSCA Director or Executive Director, or anyone acting pursuant to direction from the Director or Executive Director, shall serve written notice of the complaint and a copy of the complaint on the alleged violator by Certified Mail, return receipt requested. The written notice shall instruct the alleged violator of his right to submit a written statement, which must be signed and should include the names, addresses and phone numbers of any witnesses not named in the complaint. Such written statement must be received by the NSCA Director or Executive Director within ten (10) days of the alleged violator's receipt of the notice and complaint. All statements received after such date shall not be considered.

5. The NSCA Director or Executive Director, or someone acting pursuant to direction from the Director or Executive Director, shall thoroughly investigate the allegations of the complaint by attempting to obtain written statements from all known witnesses. All witness statements must be in writing and signed by the witness.

6. After time for the alleged violator to respond expires, the NSCA Director or Executive Director shall review the complaint, the statement of the alleged violator, witness statements and any other relevant evidence. Upon such review, the NSCA Director or Executive Director shall recommend to the NSCA Executive Council a specific disciplinary action. The recommendation shall include:

i. all evidence that was considered, including the names of any witnesses who submitted statements;
ii. a determination of whether the alleged violation occurred; and
iii. the disciplinary action, if any, the NSCA Director or Executive Director recommends that the NSCA Executive Council impose.

7. The NSCA Director or Executive Director shall provide each member of the NSCA Executive Council with a copy of the complaint, the statement of the alleged violator, copies of any witness statements and a copy of the recommendation.

8. The NSCA Director or Executive Director shall schedule a conference call between the members of the NSCA Executive Council wherein the NSCA Executive Council shall review all information provided by the NSCA Director or Executive Director and issue a ruling on the matter by majority vote. The NSCA Executive Council's ruling shall include:

i. the date of issuance
ii. all evidence that was considered, including the names of any witnesses who submitted statements
iii. a determination of whether the alleged violation occurred and
iv. the disciplinary action, if any, imposed by the NSCA Executive Council.

The NSCA Executive Council shall have the discretion to suspend or expel a member or to impose any other disciplinary action it deems appropriate.

9. Upon issuance of a ruling, the NSCA Director or Executive Director shall serve the ruling on the violator by certified mail, return receipt requested. The ruling shall become effective on the date of issuance and continue until a hearing, if any, is held.

c. The violator has the right to appeal the NSCA Executive Council's ruling by notifying the NSCA Executive Council. Such notification of appeal must be in writing and must be post-marked no later than twenty (20) days from the date the ruling was issued.

1. Upon receipt of the notification of appeal, the NSCA Executive Council shall hold a hearing on the matter, which will take place at the next regularly scheduled quarterly meeting of the NSCA Executive Council.

2. At the hearing, the violator has the right to be present, the right to bring counsel, the right to testify and the right to present any evidence he so chooses. The violator does not have the right to cross-examine witnesses. The violator does not have the right to make a record and no transcript of the hearing will be made or allowed.

3. The NSCA Executive Council shall review the complaint, the written statement of the violator and any other evidence it deems appropriate. The NSCA Executive Council may allow any and all witnesses to testify by telephone or in person.

4. At the conclusion of such hearing, the NSCA Executive Council shall have the authority to affirm, reverse or modify the disciplinary action imposed previously by majority vote.

By paying the membership fee, entering a competition or holding a competition, every member and member club agrees to abide by any decision of the NSCA Executive Council and further agrees and recognizes that as a voluntary amateur association, the NSCA has the right to impose, interpret and enforce its rules and regulations and that all decisions by the NSCA Executive Council following a hearing are final.

## C. GOVERNANCE STRUCTURE

### 1. National Delegate:

National Delegates shall consist of members in good standing to hold office as follows: National Delegates shall be bona fide residents of, and elected from, the various states of the United States and from the provinces, territories, or geographic subdivisions recognized by the Association. The ratio of one National Delegate for a member population of 25 to 150, two National Delegates for a member population of 151 to 300, three National Delegates for a member population of 301 to 500, four National Delegates for a member population of 501 to 750, and five National Delegates for a member population of over 750. This ratio of National Delegates to member population may be revised by a majority vote of the seated National Delegates in years ending in zero and five.

a. Nominations. Nominations for the position of National Delegate shall be opened in July of odd numbered years for a period of no less than 21 calendar days. A member in good standing may self nominate, may be nominated by another member in good standing, or be a write in candidate. A nominated candidate must be endorsed in writing by five (5) current NSCA members in the state where he or she is a bona fide resident. The election of National Delegates shall be held in August of odd numbered years.

b. Votes Needed for Election. A candidate for the position of National Delegate must receive the votes of five (5) NSCA members from the current state membership in order for the election to be valid.

c. Term of Office. The term of office for all National Delegates shall be two (2) years. It shall begin on the first day of the target year following their election and shall end on the last day of the second target year after their election or until a successor has been elected in a valid election.

d. Vacancies. Any National Delegate vacancies occurring among the various states or provinces, territories, or geographic subdivisions recognized by the association, shall be filled for the balance of the unexpired term. A person from the same geographic subdivision receiving the next highest number of votes, in the same election as the vacant Delegate, will be eligible, as long as that number of votes is equal to five (5) members of the current state membership. If that person signifies that he or she does not choose to serve, the position shall be declared vacant and an election shall be held within 45 days to fill the vacancy.

e. Meetings. National Delegates shall meet annually during the National Championship. Notice of the time and place of the annual meeting shall be announced electronically and by mail at least 15 days prior to such meeting.

f. Powers of National Delegates. All changes made in rules, regulations, and governance shall be decided by the National Delegates. All voting for changes in rules, regulations, and governance shall be by mail ballot. Where no state association exists, the National Delegates of that state shall also approve NSCA shoot dates and the location of the state shoot.

g. Registered Targets. Candidates for the position of National Delegate are required to shoot a minimum of 500 registered targets, in the year of election and each year while serving or lose their position.

### 2. Advisory Council:

The Advisory Council is composed of NSCA members exhibiting the highest devotion to the sport, the members, and the Association. There are 45 available positions, divided equally between representatives of Industry, Range Owners, and Shooters. The primary function of the Advisory Council is to promote and guide the Association.

a. Elections. Advisory Council Members will be elected by the National Delegates.

b. Nominations. Nominations for positions on the Advisory Council shall be open in November of odd numbered years for a period of no less than 21 calendar days. Advisory Council candidates must be endorsed by five (5) current NSCA Members. Election of Advisory Council members shall be held in December of the odd numbered years.

c. Votes needed for election. A candidate for the position of Advisory Council must receive a minimum of five (5) National Delegates votes.

d. Term of Office. The term of office for all Advisory Council Members shall be two (2) years and shall begin on the first day of the target year following their election and end on the last day of the second target year after their election.

e. Meetings. All Advisory Council members must attend the annual meeting (date determined by Executive Council) each year, and in addition, either the U.S. Open or the National Championship meeting, or lose his/her position on the Advisory Council.

f. Registered Targets. Advisory Council members are required to shoot a minimum of 500 registered targets each year. Range owners are required to shoot their registered targets at ranges other then their own. The Industry category is intended primarily for major manufacturers within the clay target sports to assist with the growth and promotion of our association. Every effort should be made to continue this practice when filling Industry positions. Any NSCA member who is a fulltime employee, Promotion or Sales Representative, consultant or owner of a firm, company or corporation engaged in the manufacture of shotguns, ammunition and/or components, or any accessories/equipment used in the clay target sports is eligible for Industry category. Additionally, any NSCA member who derives the majority of their income by providing products or services to the clay target sports except for Range Owners/Mangers are also eligible. A fulltime employee who represents an organization within our Industry is also eligible.

g. Committees. The members of the Advisory Council, National Delegates, and possibly one member at large will be assigned by the Executive Council to the following committees:

1. Rules and Classification and Safety
2. Competition (Nationals, Open, Zones, State)
3. Outreach (Internet, Youth and Women's Programs)
4. Instructor Program
5. Membership and Clubs
6. State Associations
7. Awards and Recognition (Includes Hall of Fame and Museum)
8. All-American, All-Zone and Team USA
9. International

A minimum of two members of the Executive Council shall serve on each of the above committees. Chairman will report to the NSCA Director each month.

h. Attendance. Attendance at the annual meeting is mandatory. An absence from the mandatory meeting for illness or for good cause may be approved in advance of the meeting by the Chairman of the Executive Council. A member's seat on the Advisory Council shall automatically be vacated when the attendance requirement set forth in this section is not met. An appointment will be made by the Executive Council within 30 calendar days. The nominee with the next highest number of votes (with a minimum of five (5) National Delegates votes) will be eligible for the appointment.

i. Vacancies. Any Advisory Council vacancies occurring among the various categories, shall be filled for the balance of the unexpired term. A person from the same category receiving the next highest number of votes, in the same election as the vacant member, will be eligible, as long as that number is a minimum of five (5) National Delegate votes. If that person signifies that he or she does not choose to serve, the position shall be declared vacant and an election shall be held within 45 days to fill the vacancy.

### 3. Executive Council:

a. Number of Executive Council Members. The Executive Council is elected from members of the Advisory Council, composed of six (6) members: two represent industry, two represent range owners, two represent shooters, and the immediate past chairman of the Executive Council shall also serve as a member of the Executive Council. The immediate past chairman may cast a vote in matters before the Executive Council only in case of a tie. (The first two (2) year term of the Executive Council elected under the plan, the chairman of the Executive Council at the time this plan is approved by the National Delegates shall occupy the seat of the immediate past Chairman.)

b. Elections. The Executive Council election will always be at the end of the annual meeting of the Advisory Council on even numbered years. The Executive Council will elect annually a Chairman and Vice Chairman to serve on the Executive Council. The Executive Council in place at the time this plan is approved by the National Delegates will preside at the first annual meeting of the Advisory Council.

c. Term of Office. Term of office of the Executive Council is two (2) years, to begin at the end of the annual Advisory Council meeting. Members of the Executive Council may not serve more than three (3) consecutive terms.

d. Vacancies. Any vacancy occurring on the Executive Council shall be filled by an Advisory Council Member. An interim election will be conducted by the Director of the NSCA, for the balance of the unexpired term. Declaration of candidacy and balloting shall be conducted within 60 calendar days of the date the vacancy occurs.

e. Meetings. The Executive Council shall meet quarterly. Meetings shall be held during the U.S. Open Championship, The National Sporting Clays Championship, the annual Advisory Council (date to be determined by the Executive Council), and at one additional site and time as may be selected by the Executive Council.

f. Attendance. Attendance at the annual meeting and at least two of the remaining quarterly meetings will be mandatory. An absence from the mandatory annual meeting for illness or for good cause may be approved in advance of the meeting by the chairman of the Executive Council. A member's seat on the Executive Council shall automatically be vacated when the attendance requirement set forth in this section is not met. An election will be held to fill the vacancy.

g. Quorum. For purposes of conducting business of the association at any meeting, a quorum of the Executive Council shall consist of a majority of the elected members.

h. Powers. The Executive Council shall be responsible for establishing and implementing policy for the operation of the Association, including the National Championship. The Executive Council shall review the needs of the Association and prepare and submit a budget for the operation of the Association to the Executive Committee of the National Skeet Shooting Association. The Executive Council shall determine all rules, regulations, and ballot items to be submitted to the National Delegates for their votes.

### 4. State Associations:

An Association recognized by the NSCA, comprised of NSCA members and member clubs within each individual state. The primary function of the State Association is to work with the National Delegate (s) and member clubs to enhance and grow the sport.

a. By-laws. Each state association shall adopt by-laws in accordance with that state's laws of associations and shall submit the by-laws to the NSCA for approval. State bylaws must be in compliance, and are subordinate to any rule, regulation, or by-law of the National Sporting Clay Association. Any changes in by-laws must be submitted to NSCA for approval and to be kept on file.

b. State Fees. State associations may elect to assess residents and non-residents of that state a per target fee, not to be greater then the per target fee assessed by NSCA. A state resident, who is a NSCA member in good standing, shall be considered a member of the state association. Funds accrued from per target fees may be used to enhance and grow the sport in that state through grants for range development, youth program developments, or assisting in promoting state and zone championship events or such other programs approved by the state association. State funds may not be used for payment of personal services, an honorarium, or personal expenses of any member of the state association.

c. Approval of Shoot Dates. Recognized State Associations will be responsible for the approval of the shoot dates for clubs in their state.

### 5. Zone/Zone Delegates:

Zones are groups of states in a particular geographical area. One Zone Delegate is elected from each of the seven zones by vote of the National Delegates in that zone. Candidates for Zone Delegate must be currently elected National Delegates.

a. Nominations. Nominations for the positions of Zone Delegates shall be open in September of the odd numbered years, for a period of no less than 21 calendar days. A National Delegate in good standing may self nominate or be nominated by another delegate in good standing in that zone. Election of the Zone Delegates shall be held in October of odd numbered years.

b. Votes Needed for Election. A candidate for the position for Zone Delegate must receive the majority of votes, but no less than, five (5) from the current zone National Delegates in order for the election to be valid.

c. Term of Office. The term of office for all Zone Delegates shall be two (2) years. The term shall begin on the first day of the target year following their election, and shall end on the last target day of the second target year after their election or until a successor has been elected in a valid election.

d. Vacancies. An election shall be held within 45 days to fill any Zone Delegate vacancies that may occur among the various zones.

e. Duties and Responsibilities. The Zone Delegates' duties and responsibilities are set forth in the NSCA Delegates Manual. The primary responsibility of the Zone Delegate is to organize and coordinate the selection of the Zone Shoot host range, and to insure that all appropriate events and awards are offered.

### 6. Amendments:

This Governance Structure may be amended at any regular or special meeting of the National Delegates by a majority vote of the entire delegate membership. They may be amended without a meeting by written approval, upon mail ballots, signed by a majority of the entire membership of the delegates.

## II. SAFETY

### A. SAFETY IS EVERYONE'S RESPONSIBILITY

1. It is everyone's responsibility to report any unsafe shooting condition or action immediately to Shoot Officials.

2. Mandatory Eye and Ear Protection—All persons, spectators, shooters, field judges and trap personnel, must wear eye and ear protection on the course at a tournament sanctioned by NSCA.

3. The use of horizontal gun racks or horizontal gun cases are not permitted. Horizontal gun racks may not be used on any manner of conveyance or on a course where any part of the body of a shooter or guest may pass in front of a firearm's muzzle, whether the firearm is loaded or not. Failure to enforce this rule may subject the club to disciplinary action under Rule I-B-4.

4. Trap Personnel Protection—All trap personnel in front of the line of fire must be out of sight with screen protection able to withstand the charge of shot at the given distance.

5. All shooting stations must require the shooter (except wheelchair shooters) to engage all targets from the standing position.

6. Shooters must have the permission of a Field Judge to test fire any gun. Guns will be discharged only in attempt at competition targets.

7. The first person on every squad shall be allowed to view a good presentation of targets from within the shoot station. The referee may allow additional targets to be viewed as he/she deems necessary. This person is the only person permitted to mount their unloaded gun and track the targets being viewed.

8. It is the sole responsibility of the shooter to begin any event, station and/or field with sufficient equipment, including safety equipment and ammunition. Failure to do so, which, in the opinion of the Field Judge will delay the shoot, will result in the loss of all targets as required to keep the shoot moving. Make-up targets will be provided only at the discretion of the Shoot Officials.

9. The shooting stations must be positioned in such a way that all shooters, trappers, and spectators are protected from shot/target fall. Additionally, the shooting stations must be designed to restrict dangerous gun hold/movement.

10. Target Drop Zones must be clear of ALL shooters and spectators.

11. Course Design Safety is the sole responsibility of the Range Owner/Shoot Officials.

12. The shooter must fire with his/her gun shouldered for all targets.

13. The use of any drug, legal or illegal, including alcohol, prior to or during an NSCA event by a registered competitor is prohibited with the exception of prescription medicine, which does not impair a shooters ability to perform safely. Alcohol may not be in any area where shooting activities are taking place.

14. Failure to comply with the NSCA Safety Rules may subject the Range Owner/Shoot Officials/ Competitor to possible suspension.

15. Shotgun shooting safety is everyone's responsibility.

## III. CLASSIFICATION

### *A. CLASSIFICATION SYSTEM*

A shooter's classification carries over from one shooting year to the next. All new shooters will be assigned a class. During the current year, a shooter is subject to reclassify UPWARDS ONLY (with the exception of appeals). A classification card will be provided to all shooters. This card must be shown at registration every time a shooter registers for an event. To maintain the integrity of the classification system, all NSCA members shooting on the course where a NSCA Registered Event is taking place must register their targets.

#### 1. Determining Class

a. There are seven (7) classes a shooter can classify into: Master-AA-A-B-C-D-E. All registered events using the NSCA Classification system will offer all classes (including Master).

b. Non-Classified and New Members

1. A shooter who has never shot any registered clay targets will be assigned Class "D".

2. A first time NSCA member who has shot registered targets with any clay target organization other than a Sporting Clays Association (i.e. NSSA, ATA, NRA, International skeet or trap) and has been classified in "A", "AA" or "AAA" class will be assigned a NSCA class that is one class lower than his/her highest class attained in that clay target association. If the first-time member has not shot a sufficient number of targets in any other clay target association to be assigned a class, or if their class is "B" or below, they will be placed in NSCA "D" class.

3. A shooter from another sporting clays organization, (i.e., USSCA/SCA, CPSA, F.I.T.A.S.C., Non-Registered Sporting Clay Events) will shoot their earned class or higher.

4. A person who purchases an International Shooting membership or a regular foreign membership will be placed one class higher than the highest registered class in sporting or parcours de chasse; whichever is higher in their country's association. If a new International Shooter or regular foreign member does not belong to CPSA, another recognized sporting clays organization or if there is no sporting clays organization in that country then the new member will be placed in the following classes:

i. AA Class or higher, if known ability applies, for those who qualify for NSCA concurrence.

ii. Master Class for all others.

5. A shooter may be classified based on his/her "known ability". (See rule III-A-3)

#### 2. Moving up in Class

a. Shooters earn their way out of class by shooting the high score(s) or tying for the high score (s) in class.

1. NSCA Nationals and U.S. Open (main event only): The top five (5) scores and all ties in each class receive four (4) punches; the sixth and seventh highest scores and all ties in each class receive three (3) punches; the eighth and ninth highest scores and all ties in each class receive two (2) punches; the tenth highest score and all ties in each class receive one (1) punch.

2. In all events using the NSCA classification system, except the NSCA Nationals and U.S. Open main events, shooters will earn punches based on the number of entries in their respective class. Punches are awarded as follows:

Number of entries in class: Punches earned

0–4 No punch

5–9 One (1) punch for high score and all ties

10-14 Two (2) punches for high score and all ties: One (1) punch for the second highest score and all ties

15-29 Four (4) punches for high score and all ties. Two (2) punches for second highest score and all ties. One (1) punch for third highest score and all ties.

30-44 Four (4) punches for high score and all ties. Four (4) punches for second highest score and ties. Two (2) punches for third highest score and ties. One (1) punch for fourth highest score and all ties.

45+ Four (4) punches to first, second and third highest scores and all ties. Three (3) punches for fourth highest score and all ties. Two (2) punches for fifth highest score and all ties. One (1) punch for sixth highest score and all ties.

b. It is the shooter's responsibility to determine these punches and move up one class after reaching the following number of punches:

E Class to D Class 4 punches
D Class to C Class 4 punches
C Class to B Class 6 punches
B Class to A Class 8 punches
A Class to AA Class 10 punches
AA Class to Master Class 16 punches

Note: Punches must be earned in Shooter's current class in order for them to be used in moving up in class. A person earning more than the necessary punches to move up in class enters the new class with no punches.

c. In events of 100+ entries, it is the responsibility of shoot management to notify all shooters of their move up in class or punches received. The shooter is also equally responsible to shoot in his/her proper class and to inquire and inform shoot management of any move up at the next tournament entered.

d. Upon entering a shoot with multiple events, a person will remain in the class he/she started in for all events held, and any punches he/she earns will be awarded at the conclusion of all of the events at that shoot. A shooter cannot be moved up more than one class at the conclusion of the registered events based on punches; however, a shooter can be moved up more than one class based on KNOWN ABILITY.

e. All punches earned in a shooter's current class in 2007 will carry over into 2008. Carry over punches are for the target year just ended and the current year. Punches from prior target years (2006 and before) will not carry over.

f. Registered Lewis Class events—All NSCA members must register their targets. Punches will be awarded, based on NSCA classification system at all NSCA registered events of 50 targets or more (except for NSCA leagues), no matter what the prize and/or award structure.

g. All registered events of 50 targets or more are subject to receive punches based on the number of shooters in class if the NSCA classification system is used. Note: This will include sub-gauge events where the NSCA classification system is used. (See rule III-A-2)

h. The NSCA National Championship, NSCA Junior National Championship, U.S. Open, Zone Shoots and State Shoots must use the NSCA Classification system. NSCA strongly suggests that major shoots utilize the NSCA Classification system. (See rule IV-B-4)

#### 3. Reclassification/Known Ability

a. A shooter may be reclassified based on their KNOWN ABILITY. Known ability defined as:

i. Known - past participle of know

ii. Know

1. To have clear and certain perception; to have knowledge

2. To be informed, sure or aware

3. To take cognizance, to examine

b. An NSCA club, State Association, National Delegate, member (shooter) or member of the Advisory Council has the right to request a known ability review of a shooter's record if it appears that he/she is competing in a class other than his/her true level of ability. This request must be in writing. Upon review by the appropriate NSCA Committee, the shooter may be assigned a different class.

c. A shooter reclassified by NSCA will receive a new class card with the notice of the change from NSCA. The different class will become effective when it shows on the NSCA website, www.mynsca.com. Should the shooter wish to appeal this different class they must do so in writing within 30 days from receipt of the NSCA written notice. (See III-A-6)

d. A shooter may voluntarily declare into a class higher than assigned; however, the shooter must stay in that higher class for the entire year, unless the shooter subsequently punches out of the self-declared class. This applies to all classes except for Master, which must be earned and not declared. When the shooter so elects, they must (at a registered shoot) have their classification card marked before competing in the event in the class for which they are declaring. Their card shall be marked with the new classification by self-declaration in the class where they declared, and be entered on the Official Entry Form with notation self-declared.

e. A shooter may also be reclassified to a higher class by Shoot Officials based on their known ability. This reclassification will be for that event only and shooter will return to his/her original class, with one exception. If the shooter is awarded a punch or punches in the higher class in which they have been placed based on known ability, they will remain in that higher class for the remainder of the shooter year. Example: If the shooter was originally in class E and the newly assigned higher class, based on known ability, is D class and if the shooter subsequently wins sufficient punches in the event, he will advance to class C.

f. Any person who has experienced a permanent medical impairment may request a review on their classification during the shooting year. The request must be made in writing and must be accompanied by a doctor's statement.

#### 4. Classification Review

a. A shooter's classification may be reviewed after each 1,000 registered targets. Shooters must request such a review in writing. The 1,000 target review may be used to move a shooter down in class. An annual review will be done on each NSCA member with a minimum of 300 registered competition targets shot in their current class in the current shooting year.

b. A shooter who is assigned to a lower class may reject the class if the shooter wishes to remain in a higher class. To reject the assigned class, the shooter must sign the refusal form, which will be at the bottom of the classification card and return it to NSCA Headquarters by the designated time.

#### 5. Shooter's Responsibility

a. The shooter is responsible for presenting his/her classification card and/or additional documentation upon entry at any registered shoot and entering into the proper class. The classification card is intended for the purpose of providing Shoot Officials with up-to-date information regarding classification of each shooter entering a registered event.

b. The shooter is responsible for entering their scores with the date and score shot on the back of their classification card or, if more space is needed, on a supplemental record form, and to make certain that all placements and punches are properly recorded on their classification card at the conclusion of each NSCA registered tournament. Failure to accurately record scores and punches may lead to suspension from the NSCA.

c. A shooter who enters or allows themselves to be entered into a class lower than the one in which their record places them, unless the error is corrected prior to a specific time posted by shoot management, a time announced in the shoot program, completion of shoot-offs and/or the awarding of trophies and/or monies, shall be disqualified from the event and subject to the following:

1. Forfeit all rights to all winnings he/she would have earned shooting in his/her proper class.

2. For the first offense, be disqualified, entered as a re-entry for targets only, and forfeit all winnings earned while shooting in the wrong class. (see IV-S-3) Any punches earned in the lower class do not count. Their shoot history will not be corrected as the correction will affect other shooters shoot histories in a negative manner.

3. The shooter must return all winnings within 15 days after notification by the host club, National Delegates, State Association or NSCA Headquarters requesting the winnings be returned. Failure to return the winnings within the 15 day period shall subject the shooter to suspension and being PERMANENTLY barred from registered competition.

4. In the case of a second or subsequent offense of shooting in a lower class, the shooter will forfeit all winnings and also be barred from registered competition for a minimum of one (1) year and/or suspended from NSCA.

#### 6. Appeals

a. The shooter's appeal must be in writing and state specific reasons why they think they should not be moved up in class. Pending a determination of the appeal all shoots entered by the shooter must be entered at the new higher class.

b. The NSCA Classification Committee has 30 days from the receipt of the appeal to respond. At the Committee's option, additional information may be requested from the Zone Delegate, National Delegate(s) and/or State Association (if one exists) for additional input.

## IV. RULES & REGULATIONS FOR REGISTERED TOURNAMENTS

### *A. PARTICIPATION*

#### 1. Club

a. Eligibility and Responsibility

1. Only clubs affiliated with NSCA with current fees paid and in good standing with NSCA as well as their State Association (if one exists) shall be eligible to conduct registered shoots. A State Association has the authority to charge member clubs in their state an annual fee to belong to that State Association, no greater than that club's annual fees to the NSCA. Evidence of club's status in this regard must be displayed in the form of an official NSCA membership certificate for the appropriate year.

2. In applying for and holding a registered shoot, it is the responsibility of club owners, management and Shoot Officials to ensure that the shoot is conducted within NSCA official rules and safety regulations.

3. The club sponsoring a registered shoot shall check the NSCA membership card and classification card of each shooter before accepting his/her entry, and shall be responsible for the annual dues if they allow a participant to shoot when said participant's membership in NSCA has expired.

4. Shoot management may be billed by NSCA in all cases where expired members are allowed to shoot. Management may seek reimbursement from said shooters, but must first abide by IV-A-1-a-3 above.

5. Any club sponsoring a registered shoot accepts the responsibility for any clerical errors made throughout the shoot and shall correct those errors. Any error found and corrected after the shoot report has been sent to NSCA must be submitted to NSCA in writing for the corrections to be made.

b. Applying for a Registered Shoot Date

1. The club should complete an NSCA registered shoot application and forward to the State Association (if one exists) or the National Delegate (s) for signature of approval at the state level.

2. The signed application should be forwarded immediately to the NSCA office for final approval. Shoot applications must be postmarked or received by NSCA at least ten (10) days prior to the shoot date.

3. A notice of the approval will be forwarded by NSCA to the club at the address on file.

4. Shoot dates may not be altered without prior approval at the state level and notification to headquarters.

#### 2. Individual

a. Only members who have paid their annual dues and are in good standing with NSCA as well as their State Association (if one exists) may participate in registered NSCA shoots. It is the shooter's responsibility to provide their current year classification card to Shoot Officials when entering a registered shoot. This ensures that name, address, and membership number are properly recorded so that errors in records and scores can be prevented.

b. It shall be the sole responsibility of the shooter, upon entering the shoot, to see that they are entered into all the events desired on the official NSCA cashier sheet/entry form. Once entered, clerical errors are the responsibility of shoot management.

c. Residency Requirements:

1. An individual must be a bona fide resident (permanent abode) of a state to be eligible for State Championships or to shoot as a state team member, and must be a bona fide resident of a state within the zone to be eligible for Zone Championships or to shoot as a zone team member:

i. Persons with residence in more than one state must declare their eligibility by writing their home state on the face of the current year membership card. Servicemen, by the same act, may choose their home state or place in which they are permanently assigned for duty, and declare the state on the current year membership card.

ii. Persons who change their official abode shall become immediately eligible to shoot as an individual in the state or zone shoot of their new permanent address. They should contact NSCA for a new membership card reflecting change of address and present same before entering shoot.

iii. No person shall be eligible for more than one closed state or zone competition during the NSCA shooting year.

iv. A person that is a non-US citizen who holds a Resident Alien status from the Department of Homeland Security U.S. Citizenship and Immigration Services (as evidenced by a "Green/Blue Card") and is a bona fide resident of a particular state is eligible to win the Main Event Open, Concurrent and /or Class Champion awards at their home state shoot, home Zone shoot and the US Open.

v. Only bona fide US Citizens are eligible to win the Main Event Open, Concurrent and/or Class Champion awards at the NSCA National Championship and Junior National Championship. A US Citizen is defined as anyone who is eligible for a US Passport.

### *B. TYPES OF TOURNAMENTS*

Registered Shoot—A SHOOT WHERE TARGETS SHOT BY NSCA MEMBERS MUST BE REGISTERED. Nonmembers may participate, but in a separate category. Any non-member participating in a registered event in a separate category (Hunter Class) shall not be eligible for any NSCA awards or monies. If offered by shoot management, the separate category (Hunter Class) may have its own separate awards and/or monies. Shoot date(s) must be submitted to the appropriate State Association (if one exists) or the National Delegate for signature of approval at state level, who will then submit to NSCA Headquarters for final approval.

Charity/Fundraising Events - A range owner/shoot promoter hosting a charity/fundraising event (i.e., DU, QU, NWTF etc.) may award prizes in addition to NSCA awards at his/her discretion, combining scores with non-NSCA members for additional prizes.

1. Registered Small Gauge Events—Small Gauge Events may be registered, punches will be awarded and combined with punches earned in 12 gauge events for classification purposes. Small Gauges are .410, 28 and 20. The member's 12 Gauge classification will be used for all Small Gauge Event classes.

2. Major Shoot—A registered shoot, where by projection or past experience, 100 or more shooters are expected to attend. NSCA strongly suggests that these shoots utilize the NSCA Classification system.

3. State Shoot—An annual shoot held within each state, the location and dates of which are decided by the following process: Interested clubs (within the state) who are in good standing with the NSCA and the State Association (if one exists) should contact the State Association (if one exists), or the National Delegate (s). In the selection of the club for a State Shoot, the State Association (if one exists) may apply their own process for that selection. The process must be in the State Association's By-Laws and those By-Laws must be approved by the NSCA. If a process does not exist, then Rule IV-B-3-a must be followed.

a. The State Association and/or National Delegate(s) should then take a vote of (1) State Association members (if one exists) or (2) All NSCA clubs in good standing for a decision.

b. If the second method is used and the vote results in a tie, the National Delegate(s) shall cast a vote for the club they think should be awarded the tournament. This vote should break the tie; however, if there is still a tie, the Zone Delegate will be contacted. The Zone Delegate will in turn consult with the National Delegates Committee Chairman and, after discussing the situation; the Zone Delegate will cast a tie-breaking vote for the club they feel should host the state tournament.

c. All State Shoots must utilize the NSCA Classification system.

d. A person who is a legal Resident Alien and is a bona fide resident of a particular state is eligible to win the Main Event Open, Concurrent and/or Class Champion awards at their home state shoot. (See rule IV-A-2-c-iv)

e. To be eligible for class prizes, monies and/or awards at State Shoots, a shooter must have shot a minimum of 300 registered targets in the current year, prior to the shoot. The Preliminary Events do not count towards minimum targets unless they are held under a separate shoot number. Example: If a shooter does not have a minimum of 300 targets, he/she shall shoot every event at the shoot and win prizes, monies and/or awards in a penalty class, one class above his/her current class. No State Shoot shall require more or less than the 300 target minimum.

f. Following the State Shoot all shooters who were placed in a penalty class as a result of their failure to meet the 300 registered target requirement, will return to their original class, with the following exceptions: If the shooter earns a punch or punches in the penalty class they will remain in that penalty class for the remainder of the shoot year. If the shooter was originally in class E and the newly assigned higher class, based on penalty class, is class D, and if the shooter subsequently wins sufficient punches in the event, he will advance to class C.

4. Zone Shoot—One annual shoot held within each zone, the location and dates of which are decided as follows: NSCA clubs in good standing send a bid to either their State Association (if one exits) or National Delegate who will then submit the bid to the Zone Delegate. A Zone Delegate may require a proposal or bid form to be submitted by the prospective club to be considered by the National Delegates for the Zone Shoot. Zone Delegates then send a ballot to all National Delegates within the zone for a vote.

a. Zone Shoots must be conducted utilizing the NSCA Classification system. The date and location for each Zone Championship is to be established before the end of the preceding Zone Championship.

b. A person who is a legal Resident Alien and is a bona fide resident of a particular state within a particular zone is eligible to win the Main Event Open, Concurrent and/or Class Champion awards at their home zone shoot. (See rule IV-A-2-c-iv)

c. To be eligible for class prizes, monies and/or awards at Zone Shoots, a shooter must have shot a minimum of 300 registered targets in the current year, prior to the shoot. The Preliminary Events do not count towards minimum targets unless they are held under a separate shoot number. If a shooter does not have a minimum of 300 targets, he/she shall shoot every event at the shoot and win prizes, monies and/or awards in a penalty class, one class above his/her current class.

d. Following the Zone Shoot all shooters who were placed in a penalty class as a result of their failure to meet the 300 registered target requirement, will return to their original class, with the following exceptions: If the shooter earns a punch or punches in the penalty class they will remain in that penalty class for the remainder of the shoot year. Example: If the shooter was originally in class E and the newly assigned higher class, based on penalty class, is class D, and if the shooter subsequently wins sufficient punches in the event, he will advance to class C.

5. U .S. Open—An annual shoot awarded by the NSCA Advisory Council according to the criteria set for the upcoming year.

a. A person who is a legal Resident Alien and is a bona fide resident of a particular state is eligible to win the Main Event Open, Concurrent and/or Class Champion awards at the US Open. (See rule IV-A-2-c-iv)

b. To be eligible for class prizes, monies and/or awards a shooter must have shot a minimum of 500 registered targets in the current shoot year prior to the U.S. Open. The Preliminary Events do not count towards minimum targets unless they are held under a separate shoot number. If a shooter does not have a minimum of 500 targets, he/she shall shoot every event at the shoot and may win prizes, monies, and/or awards in a penalty class, one class above his/her current class.

c. Following the U.S. Open all shooters who were placed in a penalty class as a result of their failure to meet the 500 registered target requirement, will return to their original class, with the following exceptions: If the shooter earns a punch or punches in the penalty class they will remain in that penalty class for the remainder of the shoot year.

Example: If the shooter was originally in class E and the newly assigned higher class, based on penalty class, is class D, and if the shooter subsequently wins sufficient punches in the event, he will advance to class C.

6. National Championship and Junior National Championship—An annual shoot held by the National Sporting Clays Association on its Home Grounds.

a. Only bona fide US Citizens are eligible to win the Main Event Open, Concurrent and/or Class Champion awards at the NSCA Nationals and Junior Nationals. (See rule IV-A-2-c-iv) A US citizen is defined as anyone who is eligible for a US Passport.

b. To be eligible for open and/or concurrent prizes, monies and/or awards at the National Championship, a shooter must have shot a minimum of 500 registered targets in the current year, prior to the shoot. The Preliminary Events do not count towards minimum targets unless they are held under a separate shoot number. If a shooter does not have a minimum of 500 targets, he/she shall shoot every event at the shoot and may win prizes, monies and/or awards in a penalty class, one class above his/her current class.

c. Following the National Championship, all shooters who were placed in a penalty class as a result of their failure to meet the 500 registered target requirement, will return to their original class, with the following exceptions: If the shooter earns a punch or punches in the penalty class, they will remain in that penalty class for the remainder of the shoot year. Example: If the shooter was originally in class E and the newly assigned higher class, based on penalty class, is class D, and if the shooter subsequently wins sufficient punches in the event, he will advance to class C.

d. A program will be published each year giving all details of the current year's tournament.

7. League - A sporting clays, NSCA 5-Stand or Compak league may be approved as a registered event for NSCA members. Non-members may also participate in the league. A registered league's dates must be submitted by a club for approval by the appropriate State Association or National Delegate (where no State Association currently exists). A league will be conducted over a minimum 10 week period and is open to individuals or teams and may be conducted at one or more clubs concurrently. The final results of the league may be submitted as a registered event. No punches will be awarded for leagues.

8. Monthly Targets - A sporting clays, NSCA 5-Stand or Compak event beginning on the first day of a given month and ending on the last day of the same month where shooters are able to shoot any number of targets between the set days of the given month. Monthly targets may be approved as a registered event for NSCA members. Monthly target dates must be submitted by a club for approval by the appropriate State Association or National Delegate (where no State Association currently exists). Monthly targets will be held at one club, and final results may be submitted as registered targets only. No punches will be awarded for monthly targets.

9. Any NSCA registered target may be used to meet target minimums including league and monthly targets as long as the league and monthly targets have been completed prior to the start of the shoot requiring minimum targets.

### *C. GAUGE SPECIFICATIONS*

1. Twelve gauge events shall be open to all shotguns of 12 gauge or smaller, using shot loads not exceeding one and one-eighth (1 1/8) ounces.

2. Twenty gauge events shall be open to all shotguns of 20 gauge or smaller, using shot loads not exceeding seven-eights (7/8) of an ounce.

3. Twenty-eight gauge events shall be open to all shotguns of 28 gauge or smaller, using shot loads not exceeding three-quarters (3/4) of an ounce.

4. Four-ten events shall be open to all shotguns of .410 bore, using shot loads not exceeding one-half (1/2) of an ounce.

### *D. CONCURRENT EVENTS*

These are events which are offered in concurrence with the seven (7) classes of shooters (Master, AA, A, B, C, D, E) that allow the participating shooters to compete and receive prizes or awards in these separate events in addition to their class. These events are based on age (Sub-Junior, Junior, Veteran, Super Veteran and Senior Super Veteran) or gender (Lady). Where shoot programs offer special concurrent events based upon age, a shooter entering such special events must be allowed to shoot in the one for which they are qualified for by age along with any other concurrent class for which they are eligible if such a concurrent class is available (i.e. Lady could also be a Veteran, Super Veteran, Senior Super Veteran, Junior or Sub-Junior).

1. A shooter's eligibility for concurrent events which are based on age is determined by the age of the shooter on the 1st day of the target year and shall determine their eligibility for the entire upcoming shooting year. No contestant shall be eligible for more than one individual concurrent event based on age.

Sub-Junior—Any member who has not reached their 16th birthday by Jan. 1 of the target year.

Junior—Any member who has not reached their 21st birthday by Jan. 1 of the target year.

Veteran—Any person 55 years of age and over who has not yet reached their 65th birthday by Jan. 1 of the target year.

Super Veteran—Any person 65 years of age and over who has not yet reached their 75th birthday by Jan. 1 of the target year.

Senior Super Veteran—Any person 75 years of age and over by Jan. 1 of the target year.

For concurrent eligibility for F.I.T.A.S.C. (See Section VIII-D.)

Lady—A female shooter of any age.

2. NSCA Nationals, NSCA Junior Nationals, U.S. Open, Zone, State and Major shoots must offer all applicable Concurrent Events and provide some type of award.

3. Shooters are eligible to compete for both concurrent and class awards. Shoot Official (s) may specify in the tournament program that a reduced fee is offered for concurrent events. At time of entry the shooter has the option to pay the full entry fee and compete for both concurrent and class (open) titles, or pay a reduced fee and compete for concurrent titles only. If the shooter elects to pay a reduced fee and compete for concurrent titles only, they are still subject to earning punches according to Rule III-A-2.

4. No Junior or Sub-Junior shall be required to pay any part of entry fee that is to be returned to the shooter in the form of money.

5. Youth Teams—This is a concurrent category that can be offered at the host club's discretion. If offered, this team event will be shot simultaneously with an already established tournament event.

a. Teams will consist of four or five members and are required to shoot as a group.

b. All team members must be in the Junior or Sub-Junior age group.

c. Each team must have a designated coach nearby.

d. For team competition, the lowest individual score will be dropped from a five-member team score even though there may be no four-member teams participating.

e. Even though the scores of all team members may not count toward the team's event score, all team members will be counted as participants in the shoot, and in their respective classes, and all individual scores will be registered.

### *E. EQUIPMENT*

1. Targets—Targets thrown in any event may include any or all of the following:

a. Regulation SKEET or TRAP targets as specified by ATA, NSSA or NSCA.

b. Specialty targets—Mini, midi, battue, rocket or rabbit targets as specified by NSCA.

c. Any sporting clays target approved by NSCA.

d. Poison Bird—Not Allowed.

e. Pairs

1. Report Pair—Two sequential targets where the second target is launched at the sound of the gun firing at the first target. Targets may be launched from one or more traps.

2. Following Pair—Two sequential targets where the second target is launched at the official's discretion after the first target. Targets may be launched from one or more traps.

3. Simultaneous Pair—Two targets launched simultaneously. Targets may be launched from one or more traps.

f. Target number, selection and order of presentation for any competition shall be at the discretion of the Shoot Officials, but must be the same for all shooters. It is recommended that 30 percent to 40 percent of targets for tournaments be specialty targets.

g. No less than 80 percent of all targets in a shoot shall be presented with a reasonably consistent trajectory, distance and velocity to all shooters (See IV-E-2-d).

2. Traps

a. Targets will be propelled by, and launched from, any of a number of commercially produced, modified, or handmade devices which will propel an approved target in a manner to approach the characteristics (in the opinion of the Shoot Officials) of a game bird or animal typically taken by a sporting shotgun.

b. Launching devices which provide for targets traveling at varying angles and distances to the competitors (i.e. wobble or oscillating traps) may not be used in registered tournaments.

c. Devices which provide for propelling multiple targets are permitted.

d. Devices propelling targets of more than one type, and devices capable of providing targets at varying angles and distances, shall be employed only as the varying aspects of these devices will be the same for all shooters and will be free of all human element of selection.

3. Shotguns

a. Shotguns of 12 gauge or smaller, in safe working order, and capable of firing two shots are to be used in attempting all targets. No more than two (2) shells may be loaded in the gun at one time.

b. Shotguns fitted for multiple barrels (of various chokes and/or lengths) are permitted. The shooter is allowed to change barrels only between stations. Failure to comply will result in all targets on that station attempted after the infraction being scored as LOST or MISSED.

c. Shotguns with interchangeable or adjustable chokes are permitted at the shooter's discretion. The first shooter on a station may view target, then change chokes prior to shooting any targets. Only then chokes may be changed or adjusted between stations. Failure to comply will result in all targets on that station attempted after the infraction being scored as LOST or MISSED.

d. Competitors may enter a shoot with various guns and attempt targets at various stations with different guns, or the gun of another competitor. Guns may be changed only between stations except in the case of a malfunction (IV-L-1-b). Failure to comply will result in all targets on that station attempted after the infraction being scored as LOST or MISSED.

e. Guns with release type triggers are allowed and must be clearly marked and Shoot Officials notified of their presence. Safety stickers designating release trigger, with instructions on placement, are available at no charge from NSCA Headquarters. Please send your request in writing.

f. At no time may two different gauges be used in the same shotgun at the same time. (i.e., Use of a tube set with a 20 ga. in the top barrel and a 28 ga. in the bottom barrel).

4. Ammunition

a. All shot shell ammunition including reloads may be used. Shoot Officials may limit the ammunition to commercially manufactured shot shells. The National Sporting Clays Association assumes no responsibility in connection with the use of reloads or commercially manufactured ammunition.

b. Maximum loads for any gauge event may not exceed:

| Gauge Ounce | Lead |
|---|---|
| 12 | 1 1/8 |
| 20 | 7/8 |
| 28 | 3 /4 |

.410 (2 1/2" Maximum) 1 /2

c. No shot, other than steel, smaller than U.S. No. 9 (diameter 0.08) or larger than U.S. No. 7-1/2 (diameter 0.095) shall be used in any load. No steel shot smaller than U.S. No. 9 (a nominal diameter 0.080") or larger than U.S. No. 6 (a nominal diameter 0.110") shall be used in any load.

d. Shot shall be normal production spherical shot. Plated shot is permitted.

### *F. COURSE SETUP AND REQUIREMENTS*

1. Station—A shooting position from which one or more targets are attempted.

2. Field—A station or group of stations from which targets are attempted sequentially. Once a squad or individual checks onto a field, all stations and/or all targets on the field are attempted before moving to another field. NSCA 5-STAND is a group of stations considered to be one (1) field. The Shoot Officials will provide direction for execution of shooting at each field.

3. Registered events are required to throw a minimum of 25 targets. The course will provide for a predetermined number of shooting fields from which each competitor will attempt various targets.

4. The number of stations and the number and characteristics of targets from each station, on each field, will be determined by the Shoot Officials, and will be the same for all shooters. Changes in target trajectory, distance, and/or velocity due to wind, rain, time of day or any other natural cause does not constitute a violation of this rule.

5. Registered and non-registered events may not be held on the same course/field (i.e., 3-gun shoot on the same course as prelim).

6. All sub-gauge events may be held on the same course (except for Nationals and US Open). A Prelim 12 ga. event must be on a separate course. If a club has only one course, it may be used for multiple events (sub ga., 12 ga., prelim and/or main event) if the traps and/or stations are changed to create a completely different presentation at all stations. Merely changing the angle, speed, course of fire (report one event, then true pair or visa versa the next event) does not meet the intent of this rule.

### *G. SHOOT OFFICIALS AND PERSONNEL*

1. Shoot Promoter—Individual (s) or entity which provides for the facilities and organization of the competition. Shoot Promoters may also act as Shoot Officials.

2. S hoot Official—Individual(s) appointed by the Shoot Promoter and responsible for course layout, target selection and appointment of Field Judges. Shoot Officials shall be responsible for both layout and testing of the course for safety. Shoot Officials are responsible for ensuring that competitors are not allowed to shoot the course prior to the competition.

a. Anyone who shoots the course prior to the competition is ineligible to compete in the tournament. They may shoot for registered targets only, but will not be eligible for awards or punches. Their scores will be inputted as a re-entry score and will not be included in their class when determining punches.

b. Any person who sets or designs a course shall be allowed to shoot that course for registered targets only, but will not be eligible for awards or punches. Their scores will be inputted as a re-entry score and will not be included in their class when determining punches. If a person who set targets at a State or Zone Shoot earned enough points in other tournaments to make a State or Zone Team, as long as they shot the Main Event of their State or Zone Shoot for targets only.

3. Field Judge (Referee)—An individual, who has integrity and a knowledge of NSCA Rules, assigned by the Shoot Officials to enforce the rules and score targets at any NSCA event. This individual can be the Chief Referee, a certified referee or any individual appointed by the Shoot Official (s).

a. Field Judges will be required at each station, in sufficient number, to competently enforce all rules for the shooter, as well as to score the attempts accurately.

b. Numbers and positions for Field Judges shall be determined by the Shoot Officials.

4. Chief Referee—A person may be appointed by shoot management who is responsible for the general supervision over all other referees at a tournament, and who shall be present throughout the shooting.

5. Certified Referee—A person who has completed and passed an NSCA Certified Referee Examination. Examination forms may be requested from NSCA Headquarters by recognized State Associations, National Delegate (s) and NSCA club owners/managers: all of whom may administer the test to an applicant in their presence. The completed examination should then be forwarded to NSCA Headquarters, with a fee of $20 for processing. Certification will be for a period of three (3) years, ending December 31 of the 3rd year. The applicant may refer to the NSCA Rule Book to complete the examination; however, ALL questions on the examination must be answered correctly in order to pass. NSCA will issue Certified Referee credentials (patch and card) to applicants who pass the examination. This is a voluntary program. Level I and Level II Certified Instructor courses will automatically include this examination.

### *H. SHOOTING ORDER/ROTATIONS*

1. Format—Contestants shall proceed through the course and competition in one of the following formats:

a. European Rotation—Individual competitors or groups of two (2) through six (6) competitors will proceed to the various stations at random. Groups may shoot in any order of rotation selected by the shooters and may change the rotation from field-to-field. In European Rotation, a shoot start and shoot end time will be established. It will be the responsibility of each shooter to complete the entire event between these times.

b. Squadding—At the discretion of the Shoot Officials, groups of three (3) to six (6) shooters will be formed to proceed from field-to-field in a fixed sequence. Unless specified by Shoot Officials, squads may shoot in any order of rotation selected by the shooters and may change the rotation from field to field.

1. In squadding sequence, squads will be assigned a start time and it is the responsibility of each shooter to be ready on time, or within 5 minutes of that time.

2. Time—Shots not attempted by the "shoot end time" (European Rotation), or shots not attempted by the shooter joining his squad after they have begun (squadding), will

be scored as lost. The Shoot Officials shall have the right to provide for make up targets if sufficient justification can be presented. Make up targets are provided solely at the discretion of the Shoot Officials.

2. A NSCA member may not compete in a non-NSCA event on the same course until that member has shot the NSCA event. For example, if there is a 3-shot event planned on the same course as a NSCA event, a member must shoot the NSCA registered event before shooting the 3-shot event.

## I. ATTEMPTING TARGETS

1. It will be the responsibility of each shooter to be familiar with these rules. Ignorance of the rules will not be a cause to re-attempt targets lost because of rule violations.

2. It is the sole responsibility of the shooter to begin any event, station and/or field with sufficient equipment, including safety equipment and ammunition. Failure to do so, which in the opinion of the Field Judges will delay the shoot, will result in the loss of all targets as required to keep the shoot moving. Make-up targets will be provided only at the discretion of the Shoot Officials.

3. Call for Target—The target must be launched immediately or with a delay of up to three (3) seconds.

4. Shotgun Mount and Position—The shooter may start with a low gun or a pre-mounted gun when calling for the target.

## J. TARGET PRESENTATION AND SCORING

1. Targets will be presented for attempt by the shooter and scored at each station in one or more of the following formats.

   a. Single Target
   Two shots are allowed and the target will be scored dead if broken by either shot.

   b. Pairs
   Only two shots are allowed. Pairs may be presented as report, following or simultaneous.
      i. In simultaneous pairs the shooter has the right to shoot either of the targets first. If the shooter has missed the first target he may fire the second cartridge at the same target.
      ii. When shooting report or following pairs, the shooter will have the right, if missing the first target, to fire the second cartridge at the same target (the result being scored on the first target and the second target being scored as lost).

   c. Scoring Pairs
      i. Should the shooter break both targets with either the first or second shot then the result will be scored as two hits.
      ii. In the event of a no Bird on a simultaneous or following pair, nothing can be established. Two good targets must be present to record the score. This will also apply for gun/ammunition malfunctions while shooting pairs. (See IV-L)
      iii. In the event of a NO BIRD on the second target of a report pair, the first bird will be established as dead or lost and the shooter will repeat the pair to establish the result of the second target. When repeating the pair, the shooter must make a legitimate attempt at the first target.
      iv. In the event of a "shooter malfunction" on the first bird of a report pair, the first bird will be established as lost and the shooter will repeat the pair to establish the result of the second target. When repeating the pair the shooter must make a legitimate attempt at the first target. The first target has already been established as lost and the result of the second target will be recorded. (See IV-L-2)

   d. Multiple Targets
   Only two (2) shots are allowed; two (2) hits or dead birds maximum.

2. Timed reloads are not allowed in any NSCA competition.

3. Shooters Viewing Targets
The first person on every squad shall be allowed to view a good presentation of targets from within the shooting station. This is not limited to one pair. This person is the only person permitted to mount their unloaded gun and track the targets being viewed.

## K. SCORING PROCEDURE

1. Each shooter will be assigned a score card to be presented to the Field Judges at the various stations or fields. Field Judges will score each shooter's attempts on the individuals score card. The total shall be tallied and the scores written in ink and initialed by the Field Judge.

2. Each shooter is responsible for his score card from assignment, at the start of the shoot, until the card is filed with the Shoot Officials at the end of each day's shooting.

3. Scores made on re-entry will not qualify for prizes.

4. Shooters are responsible for checking the Field Judge's totals of hits and misses at each station and/or field.

5. Field Judges may be assisted by markers to record scores on the shooter's score cards.

6. Targets shall be scored as HIT or DEAD and designated on score cards by an "X" when in the opinion of the Field Judge, a visible piece has been broken from the target. Targets not struck and broken by the shooters shot shall be called LOST or MISSED and designated on score cards by an "O".

7. The call of LOST or DEAD, HIT or MISS shall be announced by the Field Judge prior to recording the score on every target.

8. If the shooter disagrees with the Field Judge's call, he/she must protest before firing at another set of targets or before leaving that station. The Field Judge may poll the spectators and may reverse his/her original call. In all cases the final decision of the Field Judge will stand.

9. During a registered event, each shooter must verify his/her score before leaving the station. Once the shooter has left the station, his/her score is final.

## L. MALFUNCTIONS

The shooter shall be allowed a combined total of three (3) malfunctions per day, per event attributed to either the shooter's gun or ammunition. Targets not attempted on the three (3) allowed malfunctions shall be treated as NO BIRDS. Targets not attempted due to the fourth or later malfunctions shall be scored as LOST.

1. Gun Malfunctions
   a. In the case of a gun malfunction, the shooter must remain in place, the gun pointed safely down range and must not open the gun or tamper with trigger, safety or barrel selector, until the Field Judge has determined the cause and made his/her ruling.
   b. In the case of an inoperable gun, the shooter has the option to use another gun, if one is available, or he/she may drop out of competition until the gun is repaired. The shooter must; however, finish the event during the allotted scheduled shooting time.

2. Shooter Malfunctions
Targets shall be scored as LOST if the shooter is unable to fire because of the following examples which include but are not limited to:
   a. Shooter has left the safety on.
   b. Shooter has forgotten to load, loaded previously fired shells or failed to properly cock the gun.
   c. Shooter has forgotten to disengage the locking device from the magazine of a semi-automatic shotgun.

   d. Shooter has not sufficiently released the trigger of a single trigger gun having fired the first shot.
   e. Shooter not seeing the target.
   f. If the shooter fails to comply with item IV-L-1-a, the target (s) will be scored as LOST or MISSED.

3. Ammunition Malfunctions
In the case of an ammunition malfunction, the shooter must remain in place, the gun pointing safely down range and must not open the gun or tamper with the trigger, safety or barrel selector, until the Field Judge has determined the cause and made his/her ruling. Examples include but are not limited to:
   a. Failure to fire, providing firing pin indentation is clearly noticeable.
   b. One in which the primer fires, but through failure of the shell or lack of components, and consequently leaves part of or all of the charge of shot or wad in the gun. A soft load in which the shot and wad leave the barrel, is not a misfire and shall be scored as LOST or MISSED. In the event of a "soft load" on the first bird of a report pair, the first bird will be established as LOST and the shooter will repeat the pair to establish the result of the second target. When repeating the pair the shooter must make a legitimate attempt at the first target. The first target has already been established as LOST and the result of the second target will be recorded.
   c. Brass pulling off hull between shots on pairs.
   d. Separation of brass from casing when gun is fired (usually accompanied by a "whistling" sound as the plastic sleeve leaves the barrel).
   e. If the shooter fails to comply with item IV-L-3, the target (s) will be scored as LOST or MISSED.

4. Trap/Target Malfunctions
   a. A target which breaks at launching shall be called NO BIRD and shooter will be provided a new target.
   b. A target which is launched in an obviously different trajectory shall be called NO BIRD and the shooter will be provided a new target.
   c. At a station of multiple targets (two or more – simultaneously launched), at least two good targets must be presented simultaneously or NO BIRD will be called and the multiple targets will be attempted again. Multiple targets shall be shot as fair pair in the air, two new shots will be attempted and scored, no scores from previous NO BIRD attempts will stand.

## M. WEATHER/MITIGATING CIRCUMSTANCES

In the event of extreme weather conditions, power failure, trap failure or unusually early darkness, the shoot management may elect to continue the event some other time (i.e. the next morning or the following weekend) but must immediately notify NSCA, with a full explanation, who will sanction the change, provided it is deemed in the best interest of sporting clays.

## N. SHOOT-OFFS

In all registered NSCA tournaments, all ties shall be shot off unless otherwise specified by shoot management and published in the program or posted at the registration table. Procedures for shoot-offs and squads shall be posted prior to beginning of shoot. If shoot-offs are held, the shoot-offs must be held on targets or positions not previously shot by any participating competitor.

## O. PROTESTS

1. A shooter may protest, if in his/her opinion, the rules as stated herein are improperly applied.

2. Any protest concerning calls or scoring of hits or misses must be made on the shooting station prior to leaving the station. The Field Judge's final decision will stand and no further protest allowed.

3. Protests shall be made immediately upon completion of the shooting at a given field with the Field Judge and with Shoot Official (s).

4. The Shoot Official (s) shall convene a predetermined JURY of three (3) to five (5) Field Judges or competitors who are known to be representative of the shooters present and knowledgeable about these rules. The Jury will decide on the validity of the protest and the resolution of the case. They will prescribe penalties or award bonuses as they determine to be fair and in the spirit of the competition.

## P. CHECKS/PAYMENTS/OVERPAYMENTS

1. Anyone who presents a check at any shoot that is returned for insufficient funds, or other causes, must be notified by Registered Mail by the club to which it was presented and has fifteen (15) days to make full payment, plus penalty, to the club. Any club receiving such a check shall report name and address of the shooter issuing the check to the NSCA.

2. Any competitor at a registered shoot who, through error, has been overpaid on any purse, added money, optional or other prize money and who is notified of the overpayment by Registered Mail, must return the overpayment within fifteen (15) days of notification. Failure to do so shall result in disbarment from all registered shoots until repayment is made. See Section I-B-4.

## Q. OFFICIAL SCORES

1. All scores or records, to be recognized as official, must be shot under all of the official NSCA rules.

2. Only the scores shot on scheduled dates, approved by NSCA, shall be registered. Scores made in shoot-offs shall not be registered, however, all NSCA rules shall apply in shoot-offs.

3. The scores of any NSCA member shooting on a course where a registered shoot is taking place shall be considered official, and shall be registered with the NSCA even though the shooter had given notice that it was not his/her intention to have their score recorded.

4. The score of a contestant who voluntarily stops or withdraws (without just cause), or who is disqualified by shoot management from an event which the contestant has started will be reported to NSCA along with the other scores of the event. This contestant's partial score for the station in which he/she is shooting shall be entered as the score for that station even though the contestant may not have actually fired on all targets.

However, the total score for this contestant will not include targets from any station where he/she did not actually fire on at least one target.

5. Scores for contestants who withdraw because of sickness or injury shall be based on and reported only on number of targets actually fired upon.

6. In the event that a station(s) must be eliminated from the competition and results must be determined on less than the original number of targets intended for the competition shoot officials must give all competitors (whether they shot the station(s) or not) credit for all targets planned for the eliminated station(s) and must report the total number of targets shot at as originally intended (i.e. 100, 150, 200, etc.) to NSCA Headquarters.

7. Scores in shoots on which complete records are not made by shoot management will not be recorded and the National Association shall not be liable to refund fees received in such cases.

## R. REGISTERED SHOOT REPORTS

1. Reporting. Requirements—It is the duty of each club holding a registered shoot to fulfill the following obligations:
   a. Make payments of all money, purses and options to the shooters. (See Section X)

b. All money collected for optional purses must be paid out 100 percent to the eligible shooter(s).

c. Range Owners are required to fulfill all registered shoot reporting requirements within fifteen (15) days of their event or a $25 delinquent fine will be imposed for all shoot reports, financial statements and fees not received at NSCA Headquarters within that period. NSCA Headquarters will also have fifteen (15) days from the date the registered shoot report is received to have all scores input or be faced with the same $25 fine to be returned to the club hosting the tournament. (See Section X)

d. Should a NSCA club not file a Shoot Report and pay the appropriate fees within 45 days from the date of the shoot, that club will be suspended from holding registered shoots until such a time as the report and fees are received by NSCA Headquarters. Upcoming scheduled shoots will be noted "SUSPENDED" on the web site notifying members that if they shoot, the targets will not be registered.

e. Shoot reports and financial forms must be sent to NSCA on all registered shoots. Standard forms available from NSCA Headquarters or any NSCA approved spreadsheet must include all information in rules IV-R-2 and 3.

f. If an approved State Association exists, clubs within the state must submit all required documents to their State Association within fifteen (15) days.

2. Financial Report

a. Daily Fees—List number of targets shot each day of shoot and remit to NSCA the required daily registration fee (in U.S. Funds). Daily fees are $.03 per target.

b. NSCA dues collected—Remittance (in U.S. Funds) and original copies of receipts for all NSCA memberships sold at your shoot must be attached. Membership applications must be completely and legibly filled out with name and address.

3. Shoot Report—An individual entry form/cashier sheet must be submitted on every shooter unless the club is using an NSCA approved spreadsheet. For every event these reports must include:

a. NSCA membership number

b. Member's full name

c. Member's complete address

d. Number of targets shot

e. Number of targets broken

f. Class in which member was entered

g. Awards won. Except for Lewis Class events, winners must be determined and reported under NSCA Classification system. This applies even if no awards are made. Do not list winners above class champions unless such awards were made.

h. Clubs are required to retain copies of scoreboard and/or field score sheets on file for 90 days after the end of the applicable shooting year. For the shooter's reference, they should keep an accurate record of the number of entries at each and every registered event.

i. It shall be the range owner's responsibility to keep on hand throughout the shoot year, a detailed list of shooters, scores and all monies paid out to shooters. If requested in writing by any participant in any event, it shall be the range owners responsibility to provide the participants with a detailed list of all participants, their scores and all money and prizes paid out and presented to shooters no sooner than within fifteen (15) days of the shoot report due date. All requests for such information shall be in writing accompanied by a stamped, self addressed envelope. Clubs are required to retain this information on file for 90 days after the end of the applicable shooting year.

### S. DISQUALIFICATION AND EXPULSION

A member may be disqualified or expelled from an event upon presentation of proper evidence of misconduct or violation of NSCA rule. Shoot management may disqualify or expel a member when a complaint has been filed in writing and after giving both parties (the party filing the complaint and the party complained of) an opportunity to be heard prior to disqualification or expulsion. When a member is disqualified or expelled from a NSCA event, a written record of the complaint, the response and the decision shall be forwarded to the NSCA Director.

Shoot management or a jury appointed by shoot management shall upon presentation of proper evidence:

1. Disqualify any shooter for the remainder of the shoot program for willful or repeated violation of gun safety precautions which endanger the safety of shooters, field personnel and/or spectators.

2. Elect to refuse the entry or cause the withdrawal of any contestant whose conduct, in the sole opinion of shoot management, is unsportsmanlike or whose participation is in any way detrimental to the best interests of the shoot.

3. Disqualify any shooter from a shoot for misrepresentation of his/her status under the eligibility rules (SANDBAGGING).

4. Expel or disqualify any shooter physically assaulting a Field Judge or any shooter using abusive language to a Field Judge upon sufficient evidence presented.

5. The shoot management shall report to NSCA all cases of disqualification and expulsion and the reasons for the same. The circumstances under which any shooter is expelled from or disqualified from any NSCA function, event, or club will be reviewed by the Executive Director after giving the shooter involved an opportunity to be heard. The Executive Council will direct the Executive Director to notify the shooter, in writing, of his/her membership status: A) No action taken, B) Expulsion/loss of membership for a term to be determined by the Executive Council, or C) Probation for one (1) year and if any other mishaps, immediate expulsion and loss of membership for one (1) year. The Executive Council can amend the length of expulsion or probation. Members may be suspended for failing to pay for goods or services ordered from NSSA/NSCA Member Club or who give to NSSA/NSCA Member Club a check that is returned for insufficient funds or other cause. Members MAY BE reinstated upon receipt in full of the outstanding balance and any fees incurred, such as bank charges, as a result of the incident. The Executive Council can determine any penalties and/or suspensions as each case merits. (See I-B-3)

6. Any disqualified shooter or one that does not finish an event for any reason will remain as an entrant of said shoot for the purposes of awarding punches.

### V. NSCA 5-STAND SPORTING

NSCA 5-STAND Sporting events consist of targets shot in 25 bird increments from five shooting stands with each shooter rotating from station to station. The game offers several different skill levels and utilizes six or eight automatic traps to simulate game birds. Targets are released in a predetermined set sequence marked on a menu card in front of each shooting cage. Targets are registered separately under a special set of rules; however, they utilize the NSCA Classification system and all targets are included for total targets shot for the year. NSCA 5-STAND Sporting rules must be followed at all times while conducting this event.

### A. LAND

1. Minimum area 50 yards wide along shooting stand line.

2. Minimum 300 yards deep left and right of the center of shooting stand line creating an 80 degree arc for safe shot fall. (Game can be overlaid on a skeet and/or trap field.)

### B. EQUIPMENT

1. Six (6) or eight (8) automatic traps are recommended.

2. Machines should include a rabbit trap and a vertical trap (minimum 60 percent).

3. Five shooting stands not less than seven (7) feet tall and not more than 54 inches across the front opening.

4. One tower not less than twelve (12) feet in height is recommended.

5. Controller (any NSCA approved).

6. Target sequence menu cards.

7. Trap location numbers.

8. Shooting stand numbers.

9. Safety rules sign.

### C. LAYOUT

1. Shooting stands must be in a STRAIGHT LINE (for safety) not less than four (4) yards apart or more than six (6) yards apart (recommended five (5) yards) center-to-center.

2. Trap placement and target flight paths may be arranged to include the following:

    a. Left to right crossing and/or quartering away target.

    b. Right to left crossing and/or quartering away target.

    c. Vertical target (Springing Teal).

    d. Rabbit target.

    e. Tower target going away.

    f. Incoming target.

3. For safety reasons, traps must be placed in a position that prevents broken targets from hitting the competitors or causing a competitors gun to be pointed in an unsafe direction. Traps placed parallel or too close to the shooting stand line can create a serious hazard. Recommended five yard minimum for any traps placed in front of shooting stands. Tower placement must be a sufficient distance back or to the side of the shooting stand line to prevent broken targets from falling on the competitors. Traps placed to the side of the shooting stand line should be a sufficient distance forward or behind the shooting stands to prevent competitors from selecting a hold point too close to the shooting stand line when calling for the target.

### D. RULES

1. Gun must be open and empty while changing stands.

2. Shooters may not leave their station until instructed to do so by the referee or until the last shooter has fired his/her last shot.

3. May only load gun while in shooting stand in ready position.

4. Shooter's feet must be behind the front opening of the shooting stand except when changing stands. Shooters will be warned, a No-Bird will be called, continued disregard will result in losing a target or being disqualified.

5. No chokes may be changed after the round has begun. Failure to comply will result in loss of all targets attempted (in that round) after choke changed.

6. Target sequence menu cards must be posted.

NOTE: Chapters and numbers correspond with official Federation rules. The Federation may from time to time change or alter rules of Parcours de Chasse (F.I.T.A.S.C.) or Compak during a NSCA shoot year. Should a material change of rule occur please take note that the Federation rules supersede the rules contained in the Parcours de Chasse (F.I.T.A.S.C.) and Compak sections of this rule book. Any material changes will be clearly posted on www.mynsca.com website and take effect upon posting.

### VI. PARCOURS DE CHASSE
### (F.I.T.A.S.C.)

F.I.T.A.S.C. (Federation Internationale de Tir aux Armes Sportives de Chasse), headquartered in Paris, France, has recognized the National Sporting Clays Association as the sole, exclusive association to govern Parcours de Chasse Sporting and Compak Sporting in the United States. F.I.T.A.S.C. targets will be registered separately and shot under F.I.T.A.S.C. rules. The F.I.T.A.S.C. gun mount rule applies in all F.I.T.A.S.C. events. The NSCA Classification system used and all targets will be included in the shooters total targets shot for the year. In case of controversial interpretation of the present regulation, the text written in French will make faith.

### A. GENERAL (Chapter 1)

1. (1.01) Shooting Stand—Taking into considerations the terrain, a sporting course must be equipped with a sufficient amount of traps so that the competitors will shoot under conditions as close as possible to game shooting: partridges, pheasants, ducks, rabbits, etc. In front, low and high, crossing and quartering in fields or in woods, hidden or not by trees and bushes.

2. (1.02) The course must have been approved by the National Federations, for the organization of national competitions and by the International Federation for the organization of international competitions.

3. (1.03) Traps—A minimum of four (4) traps are required for each old system layout. And a minimum of three (3) traps for each new system shooting stand, that is twelve (12) traps for each layout machines may be either manual, automatic or mixed, MARKED by alphabetical letters (A, B, C, D) from left to right of the shooting stand.

4. (1.04) Clays—The clays to be used are the standard targets and rabbit clays, as well as thinner clays and clays with a smaller diameter. They may also include midi, mini, battue, bourdon, flash and zz targets. The targets must be black or orange according to the layout background.

5. (1.05) Shooting Position—The shooter will adopt the ready position, i.e. standing with both feet within the limits of the shooting stand, terial [sic] changes will be clearly posted on www.mynsca.com website and take effect upon posting. With the heel of the gun touching the body under a horizontal line marked on the shooter's jacket. This line will be indicated by a tape of contrasting color fixed to the jacket by some permanent means. The horizontal line shall be located 25 cm (9.85") below an imaginary line drawn over the top of the shoulders along their axis. The shooter will maintain this position with the gun not pre-mounted until the target (s) are in sight.

6. (1.06) In a double on report, simultaneous or rafale, the position of the gun is optional for the second target only.

7. (1.07) If the shooter is in a position that is not in accordance with (1.05, #5 above) or if he aims his gun before the target appears, he will receive an initial WARNING.

8. (1.08) After the first such occurrence on the same layout the target (s) will be declared:

    a. Zero for a single target

    b. Zero and no bird for a double on report

    c. Zero & Zero for a simultaneous double

    d. Zero & Zero for a rafale double

9. (1.09) The shooter does not have the right to refuse a target unless he has not called for it. The

referee alone shall decide on the regularity of a trajectory or on NO BIRD.

10. (1.10) The shooting stands will be marked by a one (1) meter square or by a circle of one (1) meter in diameter.

11. (1.11) The shooter must fire with his gun shouldered for all targets.

12. (1.12) Under no circumstances, once the referee has clearly declared a target NO BIRD, may it be fired at. After the first warning, the shooter will be penalized:

a. Zero for a single target

b. Zero & no bird for a double on report

c. Zero & Zero for a simultaneous double

d. Zero & Zero for a rafale double

13. (1.13) Testing Guns - Under no circumstances can a gun be tested on the shooting stand before the beginning of the round. Before taking part in a sporting event, the shooter can test his/her gun, if he/she wishes, on a designated stand specially designed and laid out for test firing.

## B. ORGANIZATION OF COMPETITION (Chapter 2)

JURY

1. (2.01) International events will be supervised by a jury consisting of a representative of each country participating with a senior's team with the representative of the organizing country as chairman.

2. (2.02) The jury shall make decisions by majority vote of members present. In the case of equal votes, the chairman's casting vote is final.

3. (2.03) The jury can only make valid decisions in the presence of its chairman or his representative accompanied by a quarter of the members of the jury.

4. (2.04) In urgent cases (i.e. the risk of cessation of shooting) two (2) members of the jury, nominated by the chairman, may make a decision with the consent of the referee, provided that this decision is endorsed by the jury.

### THE ROLE OF THE JURY IS:

5. (2.05) To verify, before the shooting begins, that the course conforms to regulations and that the preparatory arrangements are suitable and correct.

6. (2.06) To appoint a technical committee whose responsibility shall be to set, on the day before the competition, the various trajectories, the location of the shooting stands, the choice and speed of the targets which will be shot during the event.

7. (2.07) No practice will be permitted before the start of events over the layouts set by the technical committee.

8. (2.08) Before the beginning of the championships the director of shooting will publish a list of the trajectories for each of the traps. Should these trajectories, established and calculated in calm conditions, be disturbed by the wind, they will still be considered regular.

9. (2.09) To require that, during the shooting, the rules are adhered to and to check the weapons, ammunition and targets by means of technical tests.

10. (2.10) To make the necessary decisions in cases of technical defects if these are not resolved by the referee.

11. (2.11) To deal with protests.

12. (2.12) To make decisions regarding penalties to be imposed on a shooter who does not adhere to the rules or behaves in an unsporting manner.

13. (2.13) To ensure that there are always at least two members of the jury present at the shooting grounds.

### APPEAL JURY

14. (2.14) An appeal jury will be set up for each international competition.

15. (2.15) In the case of a dispute concerning the decision of the jury by the shooters or by F.I.T.A.S.C., an appeal jury may be referred to. This appeal jury will consist of: the President of F.I.T.A.S.C. or his representative, the President of the Technical Committee or his representative, and the President of the Organizing Federation. This appeal jury will be formed at the same time as the jury. If there is no Appeal Jury, the Jury's decision is definitive. All the disciplinary problems will be submitted to the F.I.T.A.S.C. Disciplinary Commission.

16. (2.16) During international competitions, representatives of the same country shall be dispersed over the various squads. The organizing committee will announce the time and arrangements for a draw for the composition of the squads. Delegates from participating nations may be present.

17. (2.17) Shooting shall take place in squads of six (6) shooters as drawn, with rotation of shooters not only at each stand but also for shooting doubles. At each stand all six (6) shooters of a squad will first fire at the single targets before any shoot at the doubles.

18. (2.18) All target trajectories will be presented at each stand to the first shooter of each group. This shooter must observe them from within the shooting stand.

19. (2.19) At the time of the presentation of the target, no shooting, aiming or pretense of firing is permitted (1.07, VI-A-7)

20. (2.20) Report pairs will not be shown, only targets of SIMULTANEOUS and RAFALE doubles will be shown to the first shooter of each group.

21. (2.21) Only targets having already been fired at as singles may be shot at as report pairs.

22. (2.22) In international competitions, shooting will be conducted in stages of 25 targets. However, exceptionally, the technical committee may change this if it is judged necessary.

23. (2.23) Shooters must take all precautions in order to be at the shooting stand on time. If a shooter is not present when his/her name is called, the referee must call the name and number of the shooter loudly three (3) times during the period of one (1) minute. If he/she has not missed his/her turn to shoot the singles on the first stand, he/she may rejoin the squad. If he/she has failed to join the squad before his turn, those targets not fired at, singles or doubles will be scored zero. If the shooter presents him/her self at one of the following stands, all the clays not shot at the previous stand will be scored ZERO. In no circumstances may the shooter shoot that layout in another squad. (See rule VI-B-24.)

24. (2.24) If the shooter feels that he/she has a valid excuse for his lateness, he/she MUST:

a. Not join his/her squad if it is in the process of shooting on that layout.

b. Put his/her case to the Jury in writing.

c. Abide by the Jury's decision.

d. Only the Jury may authorize him/her to repeat the shoot of that layout in another squad.

e. If the Jury decides that the reason put forward by the shooter is unacceptable, the latter will be scored 25 zeros corresponding to the 25 clays not shot at.

25. (2.25) In the case of malfunction of a trap during the shoot, the referee will decide if the stage should be continued or interrupted because of mechanical troubles. After the trouble has been rectified the shooter has the right to have the regular target (s) shown before continuing the shoot.

26. (2.26) During international competitions the scores will be recorded by the referee or his/her delegate who may be a shooter. The results of each stage will then be posted on a central notice board.

27. (2.27) On leaving each stand the shooter must check that his correct score is recorded on the score card. If the shooter contests the result, he/she must inform the referee immediately, but the final decision rests with the referee. However, the referee may seek information and advice before making his/her final decision. No objection will be allowed after this check.

## C. FIREARMS AND AMMUNITION (Chapter 3)

1. (3.01) All firearms, including semi-automatics, are permitted providing their caliber does not exceed 12 bore, with a barrel length of 66cm minimum.

2. (3.02) All firearms, even unloaded, must be handled with the greatest care at all times.

3. (3.03) Guns must be carried open; semi-automatic guns must be carried with the breech open, and the muzzle pointing straight upwards or downwards.

4. (3.04) Straps or slings on guns are forbidden.

5. (3.05) When the shooter is not using a gun, it must be placed vertically in a gun rack or in a similar place as designated.

6. (3.06) It is forbidden to handle another shooter's gun without his/her specific permission.

7. (3.07) It is forbidden, during a competition or official championship, for two shooters of the same squad to use the same gun.

8. (3.08) In exceptional cases, owing to a malfunction of his/her gun, a shooter may be permitted to borrow the gun of another shooter with his/her permission.

9. (3.09) Complete or partial CHANGING OF A FIREARM, MOBILE CHOKE OR BARREL is allowed during the same round, between two stands or between single or double targets. However, no delay will be permitted for any of these reasons.

10. (3.10) Once the shooter is on the shooting stand he/she will not be allowed to carry out any changes which are permitted in 3.09 above.

11. (3.11) A shooter is permitted a maximum time to ready him/her self between targets, whether singles or doubles, of 20 seconds. In a case where the shooter exceeds this time the referee may, after one warning to the shooter, apply article 1.08. (VI-A-8)

12. (3.12) In the case of a gun malfunction, verified by the referee, the shooter will twice only have the right to a new target in the course of the same round. The third and subsequent malfunction will be considered ZERO. Following the decision of the referee, the shooter will have the right to continue with his/her squad on condition that he/she obtains another weapon without delay (3.08). If this is not possible he/she must leave his/her place in the squad and shoot his/her remaining birds when there is a free place in another squad and when the Jury has given permission. If the gun is repaired before the sequence on that stand is finished by his/her squad, the shooter may retake his/her place in the squad with the referee's permission.

13. (3.13) Should both barrels fire simultaneously (double discharge) due to a gun malfunction and not the shooters error, the target, whether a single or the first of a double will be declared NO BIRD with nothing established and Rule 3.12 will apply.

14. (3.14) The cartridge shot load must not exceed 28 grams. The shot will be SPHERICAL and between 2.0 and 2.5 mm in diameter.

15. (3.15) The use of dispersers or any other unusual loading device is strictly forbidden (spreader or duplex loads are not allowed). Reloaded cartridges are not permitted.

16. (3.16) The mixing of various qualities and diameters of shots is strictly forbidden.

17. (3.17) The use of black powder and tracers is forbidden.

18. (3.18) Two cartridges may be used on each single target, but the shooter will only be allowed two (2) cartridges for each double.

19. (3.19) In a double if the two targets are broken by one shot they will be scored KILL and KILL.

20. (3.20) The referee may, at any time, remove unused cartridges from a shooter's gun for inspection.

## D. DRESS AND RULES OF CONDUCT (Chapter 4)

1. (4.01) Participants in competitions must be correctly dressed. Only knee-length shorts (Bermuda style, the hem may be no more than 5 cm above the knee.) are permitted. Shirts must have at least short sleeves, with or without a collar, but must come at least to the base of the neck. Stripping to the waist under the shooting jacket is not allowed. Sandals are not permitted for safety reasons.

The shooter's number must be worn in its entirety and the whole of the number must be visible. Any failure to comply with these rules of conduct will be penalized by A REFEREE'S FIRST WARNING which may be followed by penalties up to exclusion from the competition, following the Jury's decision.

2. (4.02) A shooter may only fire on his/her proper turn and only when a target has been thrown, except when permitted by the referee (test firing).

3. (4.03) It is forbidden to aim or shoot at another shooters' target or targets.

4. (4.04) It is also forbidden to aim or shoot intentionally at living animals or birds.

5. (4.05) No pretense of shooting is permitted on the shooting stand or outside it.

6. (4.06) If a shooter, on the shooting stand, before saying READY makes a pretense of shooting, or involuntarily fires a shot, the referee is obliged to issue a WARNING to the shooter. After one warning, any further occurrence will be scored ZERO for the next target hit.

7. (4.07) When his/her name is called, the shooter must be ready to shoot immediately and must have sufficient ammunition and equipment for that stand.

8. (4.08) In no case may a shooter move to a stand before the preceding shooter has left it and it is his/her turn to shoot.

9. (4.09) The shooter is allowed to load his/her gun only when on the stand where he/she has taken his place, the gun always pointing down the range and only when the referee has authorized him/her to start shooting.

10. (4.10) Semi-automatic guns may only be loaded with a maximum of two (2) cartridges.

11. (4.11) The shooter may not turn around or leave the shooting stand before he/she has broken his/her gun and removed the cartridges from the chambers, whether they have been fired or not.

12. (4.12) During the presentation of targets or when shooting is temporarily interrupted, the shooter must open and unload his gun. It shall only be closed when authorized by the referee.

13. (4.13) In the case of a misfire or any other malfunction of the gun or ammunition, the shooter must remain in place, the gun pointing safely down the range, not broken, and without touching the safety catch until the referee has examined the gun.

14. (4.14) Shooting must proceed without interruption, shooters are allowed to speak only the necessary words of command "READY", "PULL", "GO" or another command and to answer the referee's questions.

15. (4.15) If a member of the Jury observes anything which is not according to the rules, he/she must inform the referee. If the referee is unable to take the immediate necessary action, he/she must inform the Jury.

16. (4.16) Hearing Protection - The shooters, referees, staff and members of the public on or near a layout event must wear hearing protection.

17. (4.17) Safety Glasses - The shooters, referees and staff must wear safety glasses.

## E. REFEREE (Chapter 5)

1. (5.01) The referees must be approved by the Jury before the competition. In the case of a large number of referees not being fully qualified or experienced, they must be supervised by international referees.

2. (5.02) A referee must have a wide experience of clay shooting and must possess a valid F.I.T.A.S.C. Referee's Certificate and National Association's License. If this is not the case, the Jury must agree to accept assistant referees.

3. (5.03) The referees are to ensure order and proper conduct on the shooting stand and during shoot-offs.

4. (5.04) The referee alone shall make decisions. If a shooter disagrees with the referee, the objection

must be made immediately on the shooting stand by raising the arm and saying "PROTEST" or "APPEAL". The referee will then interrupt the shooting and pronounce his final decision.

5. (5.05) The shooter may appeal against the referee's decision. The objection must be made in writing to the jury, accompanied by a deposit of a certain sum in operation on the day of the competition and which will be returned only if the objection is upheld. If the jury finds the objection justified, it may give instructions to the referee concerning future judgments or name a new referee or, finally, alter the referee's decision. No dispute shall be concerned with whether a clay was hit or missed, nor whether the thrown clay was defective - in these cases, no appeal may be made against the referee's decision.

6. (5.06) When the competitor is ready to shoot, he/she shall say "READY" to the referee and the target must be thrown between 0 and 3 seconds after the referee has passed on the shooter's command to the pullers.

7. (5.07) The referee must pass on the shooter's command to the pullers in the shortest time possible.

8. (5.08) In exceptional circumstances, the referee may suspend the shooting if there is sudden heavy rain or a violent storm which appears to be a short duration. However, he/she must inform the jury if it looks likely that this interruption will last any length of time.

9. (5.09) Under no circumstance, is it permitted to pick up a target to verify if it has been hit or not.

### F. SINGLE BIRDS – HIT OR MISSED (Chapter 6)

THE TARGET IS DECLARED KILLED when:

1. (6.01) It has been launched and the shooter has properly fired and at least one visible piece of it is broken off or is totally or partially destroyed. This applies equally to FLASH clays.

THE TARGET IS DECLARED ZERO (missed):

2. (6.02) If it is not hit, no piece is broken off or if only dust is raised (dusted bird).

3. (6.03) If the shooter is unable to fire because he/she has left the safety catch on, has forgotten to load or cock it, the gun was not sufficiently broken or closed or the shooter has forgotten to take the necessary measures to load the cartridge into the chamber when he/she is using a semi-automatic gun.

4. (6.04) If there is a third malfunction of the gun during the same round Article 3.12 will apply.

5. (6.05) If the shooter is unable to fire his/her second shot because he/she has not loaded the second cartridge or has not canceled the locking device of the loading chamber in a semi-automatic weapon or for any other reason.

6. (6.06) If the second shot cannot be fired because the shooter, using a single trigger gun, has not released it sufficiently after firing the first shot.

7. (6.07) If the shooter, in the case of malfunction of the gun, opens it him/her self or touches the safety catch before the referee has examined the gun.

8. (6.08) If the shooter adopts a ready position which is not according to Articles 1.05, 1.07 and 1.11 and has already been warned once during the same round.

### G. SINGLE CLAYS – NO BIRD (Chapter 7)

1. (7.01) The target will be declared NO BIRD and a new target will be launched, whether the shooter has fired or not:

a. If the bird is thrown broken.

b. If the bird is thrown from the wrong trap.

c. If for a single bird two clays are launched from traps on the same shooting stand.

d. On a rabbit, if the clay breaks after being launched and missed by the first shot, but before the second shot has been fired, the rabbit will be declared NO BIRD. A new target will be launched, the shooter must miss with his first shot, and the result of the second shot scored.

2. (7.02) If the target is definitely of another color from that of the other targets used on the same trajectory of the same stand.

3. (7.03) If the target is thrown before the shooter has called "READY".

4. (7.04) If the target is thrown after a delay of more than three (3) seconds after the referee's command.

5. (7.05) If the trajectory is judged irregular by the referee.

6. (7.06) If, when a semi-automatic gun is being used, the ejection of the first cartridge impedes the loading of the second cartridge (in this case when the target is thrown again the first shot shall be directed near the target but must not hit it and the result of second shot only shall be scored).

7. (7.07) If there is a fault on the first shot as a result of failure of the cartridge or malfunction of the gun not attributable to the shooter and if the shooter does not fire the second shot. If the shooter fires the second shot, the result will be scored.

8. (7.08) The referee may also declare a target NO BIRD when the shooter has clearly been disturbed.

9. (7.09) When another competitor shoots at the same target.

10. (7.10) When the referee, for any reason, cannot decide if a target has been hit or missed.

11. (7.11) All targets not declared NO BIRD by the referee, must be shot at. However, the referee may declare NO BIRD after the target (s) have been shot at (as in the case of a fast or slow pull or irregular trajectory).

12. (7.12) In the case of a cartridge misfire or malfunction of the gun not attributable to the shooter, a target will be declared NO BIRD and a new clay will be thrown. After two misfires or two malfunctions of the weapon in the same stage (whether the shooter has changed the gun or not) further incident or incidents will be declared ZERO. (See Article 3.12)

### H. DOUBLE ON REPORT (Chapter 8)

DEFINITION OF DOUBLES "ON THE GUN" (Report Pairs)

1. (8.01) Two targets from one or two different traps, the second clay being launched within a period of 0 to 3 seconds after the first clay has been shot at.

NO BIRD SHALL BE DECLARED:

2. (8.02) If two targets are launched simultaneously.

3. (8.03) When a shooter does not fire, without legitimate reason, at his first target. The second target cannot be thrown (because there is no first shot), the double will be declared ZERO/NO BIRD and a second double will be thrown to determine the result of the second shot only.

4. (8.04) If the clay is not thrown by the correct trap.

5. (8.05) If the first target is regular and the second irregular, (however, the result of the first target shall be scored KILL or ZERO as the case may be).

6. (8.06) The double will be declared NO BIRD and the shooter will be asked to fire a second double to determine the scores of both shots:

a. Violation of article 1.05, ready position for the first target (1.07 & 1.08).

b. If during a double, the two shots are fired simultaneously due to a gun malfunction, even if the first bird was broken (3.12 & 3.13).

c. If the shooter fires his/her gun involuntarily on the shooting stand, whether while loading or because of a mishap before saying "READY".

7. (8.07) In a double when the second target is irregular a NO BIRD shall be declared and the double must be attempted again, but the result of the first target will be recorded. The shooter will not have the chance to repeat the first target if it was declared ZERO but must still shoot at it.

a. If the shooter misses the first clay, and this clay hits the second one, before the second shot.

b. If pieces from the first clay hit and break the second one before the second shot.

c. If during a double, the second shot cannot be fired because of the malfunction of gun or ammunition (3.12 & 3.13).

8. (8.08) A malfunction of the gun or cartridge prevents the shooter from shooting his first bird articles 3.12 & 3.13 will apply.

9. (8.09) If the shooter does not shoot in his proper turn he will receive a WARNING, at the second incident on the same layout, the target will be declared ZERO FOR A SINGLE CLAY or ZERO NO BIRD IF IT IS A DOUBLE ON REPORT or ZERO/ZERO IF IT IS A SIMULTANEOUS DOUBLE OR RAFALE DOUBLE.

10. (8.10) The rules of articles 6.01 to 7.12 ARE APPLICABLE TO THE FIRING OF DOUBLES ON REPORT.

### I. DOUBLE ON REPORT-DECLARED KILL (Chapter 9)

ZERO AND ZERO/KILL OR ZERO/ZERO

1. (9.01) If the shooter, without legitimate reason, does not shoot at the second target of a regular double, the result of the first target shall be recorded and the second declared ZERO.

2. (9.02) The target will be declared ZERO on the third malfunction of the gun or cartridge in the same round. (See articles 3.12 & 3.13)

3. (9.03) When a shooter in a double fires both shots at the same target. The result shall be scored, and the second target of the double be declared ZERO.

4. (9.04) The rules of articles 6.01 to 7.12 are applicable to the shooting of doubles.

### J. SIMULTANEOUS DOUBLE (Chapter 10)

1. (10.01) There are two targets thrown at the same time by one or two traps.

2. (10.02) In a simultaneous double NO SCORE shall be recorded if either target has been declared NO BIRD.

3. (10.03) May be broken by a single shot and scored KILL/KILL.

4. (10.04) The targets may be shot in any order.

5. (10.05) Without any legitimate reason, the shooter does not shoot a regular double, both clays will be ZERO (8.03, VI-H-3).

SIMULTANEOUS DOUBLE NO BIRD

6. (10.06) The double will be declared NO BIRD and the shooter will be asked to shoot a second double to determine the results of both shots:

a. If the target (s) break on being thrown.

b. If the target (s) are not thrown by the correct trap.

c. If the target (s) are of clearly a different color from those used for the same double.

d. If the target (s) are thrown before the shooter has called ready.

e. If the double is thrown more than three (3) seconds after the referee's command.

f. If one of the trajectories of the doubles is judged irregular by the referee.

g. If the shooter misses his first target and it collides with the second before the shooter has fired the second shot.

h. If the fragments of the first target breaks the second before the shooter has fired the second shot.

i. Violation of articles 1.05 & 1.06, ready position for the first target (1.07 & 1.08).

j. A malfunction of the gun or cartridge prevents the shooter from shooting his first target (s) (3.12 & 3.13).

k. If in a double, the second shot cannot be fired simultaneously due to gun malfunction, the double is NO BIRD and must be repeated (3.12 & 3.13).

l. If, during a double, the two shots are fired simultaneously due to gun malfunction, the double is NO BIRD and must be repeated (3.12 & 3.13).

m. If the shooter involuntarily fires the gun on the shooting stand, whether while loading or because of a mishap before calling "READY".

7. (10.07) The rules of articles 6.02 to 6.08 are applicable to the shooting of simultaneous doubles.

### K. RAFALE DOUBLES (Chapter 11)

DEFINITION OF A RAFALE DOUBLE (following pair)

1. (11.01) Two targets are thrown from the same trap on the same trajectory.

2. (11.02) Two cartridges may be fired at the same target.

3. (11.03) They may be fired at in any order by the shooter.

4. (11.04) In a rafale double NO SCORE IS OBTAINED in the case of a NO BIRD of one of the targets.

5. (11.05) All the rules relating to a simultaneous double are applicable to a rafale double, that is articles 10.04 to 10.06.

6. (11.06) Also rules of articles 6.02 to 6.08 ARE APPLICABLE TO THE SHOOTING OF RAFALE DOUBLES.

### L. PENALTIES (Chapter 12)

1. (12.01) All shooters are required to acquaint themselves with the current regulations which apply to shooting under PARCOURS DE CHASSE rules. By taking part in competitions, they accept the penalties and other consequences resulting from violation of the rules and referees' orders.

2. (12.02) Deliberate violation of the rules will, in the first place, incur a warning from the referee or jury. In the case of further or more serious offenses, the jury may penalize the shooter with a lost bird and, in more serious cases exclude him from the round and/or competition.

3. (12.03) In the case of a jury being aware that the competitor has intentionally delayed the shooting or has acted in a dishonorable manner, it may give him/her a warning or penalize one bird or disqualify him/her from the competition.

### M. SHOOT-OFF (Chapter 13)

1. (13.01) In the case of a shoot-off, if the time allows, a new layout may be set up by the jury.

2. (13.02) Shoot-offs for the first three places (Individual or National teams) will take place in a round of 25 targets, if a result has not been established, the shooters will shoot a second zero eliminator (sudden death) round, i.e. the first target on which scores differ, the shooter with a ZERO will be eliminated, until only the winner remains. Other shooters with the same score will show as drawn.

3. (13.03) Shooting will be carried out in accordance with the preceding rules, the empty places in the squad will not be filled.

4. (13.04) When the shoot-off is not carried out at a previously announced time, the shooters

concerned must remain in contact with the committee in order to be ready to shoot within 15 minutes after being called.

5. (13.05) Shooters not present at the start of the shoot-off will be declared withdrawn.

6. (13.06) The Jury may, in exceptional circumstances, decide that the shoot-off should be carried over to the following day. Shooters not present in this case shall be considered withdrawn.

7. (13.07) Team places are decided by count-back.

## N. SCORE SHEET (Chapter 14)

1. (14.01) The score sheet will be held by the referee or someone under his/her responsibility, selected by him/her self. Every referee will use a different color pen on the same layout or on the same shooting line.

2. (14.02) Only clays ZERO will be notified on the score sheet. Every clay ZERO will be written down in order from left to right on the score sheet. Clays will be numbered in shooting order.

Example = station n°1

Clay n°1, n°2, n°3, n°4, Double n°5 and n°6.

Example = station n°2

Clay n°1, n°2, n°3, Double n°4 and n°5, Double n°6 and n°7.

To allow a further control, the number of the clay ZERO will be written in the corresponding space of the score sheet.

[For the purposes of this publication, rules for International Compak Sporting shooting have been omitted. "Compak ® Sporting" is a protected, registered trademark with sports rules, owned by F.I.T.A.S.C.]

# VIII. AWARDS AND RECOGNITION

## A. ALL-AMERICAN

1. NSCA annually recognizes up to three All-American Teams in each of the six categories, 10 members will be assigned to each team for a total of 30 members per category:

Open Team—Minimum 1,200 registered targets. Lady, Veteran and Super Veteran Teams—Minimum 1,000 registered targets.

Junior and Sub-Junior Teams—Minimum 800 registered targets.

2. Teams will be selected solely by the All-American Point system.

3. To be eligible for the All-American Team, you must be a citizen of the United States and be eligible for a U.S. passport.

## B. NSCA ALL-ZONE TEAM

NSCA will annually select an NSCA All-Zone Team for each Zone in order to recognize more shooters for their shooting ability. Selection is based on the following criteria:

1. Persons who have been selected for an All-American Team would be ineligible in order to recognize an entire new category of shooters.

2. Mandatory participation is required at the Zone Championship for all categories. If there was not a Zone Championship, no team will be selected for that zone.

3. Team selection priority: Open, Concurrent, then Class.

4. End of year residence determines zone status. More details will be posted on www.mynsca.com.

## C. NSCA ALL-STATE TEAM

NSCA will annually select an NSCA All-State Team for each state in order to recognize more shooters for their shooting ability. Selection is based on the following criteria:

1. Team consists of 17 All-State members as follows:

Five from the Open = 5

One person from each class = 7

One person from each concurrent = 5

2. Persons who have been selected for an All-American or All-Zone Team would be ineligible in order to recognize an entire new category of shooters.

3. A minimum number of 500 registered targets must be shot annually within the home state by each individual.

4. Mandatory participation is required at the State Championship for all categories. If there was not a State Championship, no team will be selected for that state.

5. NSCA All-State Teams may be in addition to any team that may have been selected by the State Association.

6. Team selection priority: Open, concurrent, then class.

7. Selection is based on wins, state shoot score and total shoot performance.

8. Team selection for each class is based on a shooter's beginning year class.

9. To be eligible for the Open Team, shooters must have attained Master or "AA" classification by year end.

10. End of year residence determines state status.

## D. TARGET PARTICIPATION PIN

An annual target participation pin provided to recognize shooters who have shot 1,000 or more targets during the year.

## E. TEAM USA (F.I.T.A.S.C. & SPORTING)

1. F.I.T.A.S.C

Five (5) teams will be selected for Team USA (F.I.T.A.S.C.) – Senior (Open), Lady, Junior*, Veteran* and Super Veteran*. Minumum criteria for annual Team USA F.I.T.A.S.C:

a. Must be a U.S. citizen. A U.S. citizen is defined as anyone who is eligible for a U.S. passport.

b. Qualification tournaments, of which a shooter must attend four (4), will be printed in Sporting Clays Magazine in "Headlines From Headquarters" and on NSCA website, mynsca.com. It is mandatory that a shooter must shoot one of three shoots - Pan Am, National FITASC or the US Grand Prix.

c. F.I.T.A.S.C. experience and performance will be the deciding criteria.

d. Consideration will be given to international performance not captured by the NSCA system, provided that the results are submitted to NSCA Headquarters along with the appropriate daily fees.

*Concurrent Eligibility for Team USA (F.I.T.A.S.C.): The NSCA International Committee will

select individuals to Team USA (F.I.T.A.S.C.) using international concurrent rules.

Junior—a shooter who is less than 21 years of age, and who will not have their 21st birthday during the year of the competition.

Veteran—a shooter who had their 55th birthday the year before the competition and who is less than 66 years of age the year of the competition.

Super Veteran—a shooter who had their 65th birthday the year before the competition.

## 2. Sporting

Five (5) teams will be selected for Team USA (Sporting) – Open, Lady, Junior*, Veteran* and Super Veteran*. Minimum criteria for annual Team USA Sporting:

a. Must be a U.S. citizen. A U.S. citizen is defined as anyone who is eligible for a U.S. passport.

b. Qualification tournaments, of which a shooter must attend five (5), will be printed in Sporting Clays magazine in "Headlines From Headquarters" and on the NSCA website, mynsca.com. To be eligible it is mandatory that a shooter must shoot either the US Open or National Championship.

c. Sporting experience and performance will be the deciding criteria.

d. Consideration will be given to international performance not captured by the NSCA system, provided that the results are submitted to NSCA Headquarters along with the appropriate daily fees.

*Concurrent Eligibility for Team USA (Sporting):

The NSCA International Committee will select individuals to Team USA (Sporting).

Refer to Section IV-D-1 for concurrent breakdown.

## F. MASTERS PIN

A pin sent to those shooters who have earned their way into Master Class honoring their accomplishment.

# IX. CERTIFIED INSTRUCTORS PROGRAM

Members who have participated in and passed an NSCA Instructor Certification Course. There are three levels of Instructor Certification available: Level I, II and III. Levels I , II & III must be taken in sequence. Level I - teaching the beginner to novice, Level II - teaching intermediates and Level III - for advanced teachers. It takes a minimum of five (5) year and over 1,900 hours of teaching to complete the certification program.

# X. NONPAYMENT PENALTIES

## A. CLUBS

1. Failure to fulfill the reporting and payment requirements shall carry the following penalties:

a. Cancellation of all subsequent shoot dates for the offending club.

b. Denial of right to apply or reapply for any further registered shoot dates for a period of thirty (30) days in case of first offense, or ninety (90) days in case of second or subsequent offense or until obligations have been met.

c. Owners, officers and managers of any delinquent club may be barred from shooting registered targets and from all functions of the NSCA either certified, elected or appointed (for example but not limited to: Advisory Council positions, National Delegate positions, Zone Delegate, Certified Instructor) until which time as written verification is provided that all required obligations of said club are met to the shooters and NSCA.

2. Club membership may be suspended for any member club who fails to pay for goods or services ordered from NSCA or who gives to NSCA a check that is returned for insufficient funds or other cause. Membership may be reinstated upon receipt in full of the outstanding balance and any penalties incurred, such as bank charges, as a result of the incident.

3. Nothing in this section shall affect, modify or overrule the provisions in Section I-B-4 or the rights and powers of the NSCA as set forth therein.

## B. INDIVIDUALS

1. Members may be suspended for failing to pay for goods or services ordered from NSCA or who give to NSCA a check that is returned for insufficient funds or other cause. Members may be reinstated upon receipt in full of the outstanding balance and any fees incurred, such as bank charges, as a result of the incident.

2. Nothing in this section shall affect, modify or overrule the provisions in Section I-B-4 or the rights and powers of the NSCA as set forth therein.

# XI. GLOSSARY

AWARDS - awards include trophies, medallions, certificates, other material recognition or punches given as a result of a shooter's score or place in class or concurrent.

"BROKEN" OR "DEAD" TARGET - A broken or dead target is one that, upon a shot, has one or more pieces visibly missing from the target or that is partially or completely pulverized.

COURSE SETTING OR DESIGN - An individual sets or designs a course for the purposes of these rules, then they make an overall scheme of targets to be set by another person, write down or record the location, type of targets, or presentations, or to place target throwers in place. An individual may design and cause to have a course set without actually having viewed any target (s) presentation on the course.

GOOD STANDING - A member or member club in substantial compliance with NSCA and NSCA sanctioned State Association rules and regulations.

"NO TARGET"/"NO BIRD" - A NO TARGET is one that is launched with one or more pieces visibly missing or which loses one or more visible pieces prior to the shot.

"LOST TARGET" - A target is determined to be LOST when a shooter fires and fails to break the target or when only dust or paint form the target is visible.

SHOT - Corresponds to firing one cartridge.

SONOPUL - Acoustic equipment triggering the trap at the sound of a shooter's voice.

SQUAD - Group of up to six (6) shooters shooting in the same round at the same time and using same installations.

TARGET - Clay pigeon.

TRAJECTORY - Line followed in space by a target.

TRAP - Machine or equipment used to throw the targets.

NATIONAL SPORTING CLAYS ASSOCIATION
5931 Roft Road, San Antonio, Texas 78253-9261